NOVELL'S

CNA^{SM} Study Guide
IntranetWare™/NetWare® 4.11

NOVELL'S

CNA^{SM} Study Guide
IntranetWare™/NetWare® 4.11

DAVID JAMES CLARKE, IV

Novell Press, San Jose

Novell's CNA Study Guide IntranetWare/NetWare 4.11

Published by
Novell Press
2180 Fortune Drive
San Jose, CA 95131

Library of Congress Catalog Card No.: 96-079590

ISBN: 0-7645-4513-2

Printed in the United States of America

10 9 8 7 6

1P/RX/RS/ZX/IN-FC

Distributed in the United States by IDG Books Worldwide, Inc.

Distributed by Macmillan Canada for Canada; by Contemporanea de Ediciones for Venezuela; by Distribuidora Cuspide for Argentina; by CITEC for Brazil; by Ediciones ZETA S.C.R. Ltda. for Peru; by Editorial Limusa SA for Mexico; by Transworld Publishers Limited in the United Kingdom and Europe; by Academic Bookshop for Egypt; by Levant Distributors S.A.R.L. for Lebanon; by Al Jassim for Saudi Arabia; by Simron Pty. Ltd. for South Africa; by Pustak Mahal for India; by The Computer Bookshop for India; by Toppan Company Ltd. for Japan; by Addison Wesley Publishing Company for Korea; by Longman Singapore Publishers Ltd. for Singapore, Malaysia, Thailand, and Indonesia; by Unalis Corporation for Taiwan; by WS Computer Publishing Company, Inc. for the Philippines; by WoodsLane Pty. Ltd. for Australia; by WoodsLane Enterprises Ltd. for New Zealand. Authorized Sales Agent: Anthony Rudkin Associates for the Middle East and North Africa.

For general information on IDG Books Worldwide's books in the U.S., contact our Consumer Customer Service department at 800-762-2974. For reseller information, including discounts and premium sales, contact our Reseller Customer Service department at 800-434-3422.

For information on where to purchase IDG Books Worldwide's books outside the U.S., contact our International Sales department at 415-655-3078 or fax 415-655-3281.

For information on foreign language translations, contact our Foreign & Subsidiary Rights department at 415-655-3018 or fax 415-655-3281.

For sales inquiries and special prices for bulk quantities, contact our Sales department at 415-655-3200 or write to the address above.

For information on using IDG Books Worldwide's books in the classroom or for ordering examination copies, contact our Educational Sales department at 800-434-2086 or fax 817-251-8174.

For authorization to photocopy items for corporate, personal, or educational use, contact the Copyright Clearance Center, 222 Rosewood Drive, Danvers, MA 01923, or fax 508-750-4470.

For general information on Novell Press books in the U.S., including information on discounts and premiums, contact IDG Books at 800-434-3422 or 415-655-3200. For information on where to purchase Novell Press books outside the U.S., contact IDG Books International at 415-655-3021 or fax 415-655-3295.

John Kilcullen, *President & CEO, IDG Books Worldwide, Inc.*
Brenda McLaughlin, *Senior Vice President & Group Publisher, IDG Books Worldwide, Inc.*
The IDG Books Worldwide logo is a trademark under exclusive license to
IDG Books Worldwide, Inc., from International Data Group, Inc.

Rosalie Kearsley, *Publisher, Novell Press, Inc.*
Novell Press and the Novell Press logo are trademarks of Novell, Inc.

Welcome to Novell Press

Novell Press, the world's leading provider of networking books, is the premier source for the most timely and useful information in the networking industry. Novell Press books cover fundamental networking issues as they emerge-from today's Novell and third-party products, to the concepts and strategies that will guide the industry's future. The result is a broad spectrum of titles for the benefit of those involved in networking at any level: end-user, department administrator, developer, systems manager, or network architect.

Novell Press books are written by experts with the full participation of Novell's technical, managerial, and marketing staff. The books are exhaustively reviewed by Novell's own technicians and are published only on the basis of final released software, never on prereleased versions.

Novell Press at IDG is an exciting partnership between two companies at the forefront of the information and communications revolution. The Press is implementing an ambitious publishing program to develop new networking titles centered on the current version of IntranetWare, GroupWise and on Novell's ManageWise products. Select Novell Press books are translated into 14 languages and are available at bookstores around the world.

Rosalie Kearsley, Publisher, Novell Press, Inc.
Colleen Bluhm, Associate Publisher, Novell Press, Inc.

Novell Press

Publisher
Rosalie Kearsley

Associate Publisher
Colleen Bluhm

Acquisitions Editors
Anne Hamilton
Jim Sumser

Managing Editor
Terry Somerson

Development Editor
Kevin Shafer

Copy Editor
Kevin Shafer

Technical Editor
Gamal Herbon

Production Director
Andrew Walker

Supervisor of Page Layout
Craig A. Harrison

Pre-Press Coordination
Tony Augsburger
Patricia R. Reynolds
Theresa Sanchez-Baker

Media/Archive Coordination
Leslie Popplewell
Michael Wilkey

Project Coordinator
Phyllis Beaty

Graphics Coordination
Shelley Lea

Production Staff
Elizabeth Cárdenas-Nelson
Renée Dunn
Stephen Noetzel

Proofreaders
Mick Arellano
Christine C. Langin-Faris

Indexer
Rebecca Plunkett

Illustrator
David Puckett

Cartoonist
Michael Kim

Cover Design
Archer Design

Cover Photographer
Jim Kranz

I dedicate this book to the human race for never ceasing to amaze me . . .
and since you're a human, I guess in some strange way, I dedicate this book to you!

About the Author

David James Clarke, IV is the original creator of the CNE study guide phenomenon. He is the author of numerous #1 best-selling books for Novell Press, including *Novell's CNE Study Guide, Novell's CNE Study Guide for NetWare 4.1,* and the new IntranetWare Study Guide series. Clarke is the co-founder of *CyberState University*, an on-line network training institute, and developer of *The Clarke Tests v3.0*, an interactive learning system. He is also the producer of the best-selling video series *So You Wanna Be a CNE?!* Clarke is a Certified Novell Instructor (CNI), Engineer (CNE), and Administrator (CNA). He speaks at numerous national conferences and currently serves as the president and CEO of Clarke Industries, Inc. He lives and works on a white sandy beach in California.

Foreword

Novell recognized very early that networking calls for a different kind of company and a different type of approach to dealing with computer systems. We know we need partners, and we regard the CNAs as being among the most important partners of all. The CNA program creates the pervasive expertise that will be needed to be of service to pervasive computing as it develops. Intelligent networking requires trained technicians on the spot, who can deal with the myriad configurations and platforms that Novell networking seeks to seamlessly connect. That in turn fosters openness, fosters freedom of choice. None of that would be well served if Novell tried to impose a one-size-fits-all networking system. So the CNA is essential right there on the ground. CNAs can go for the best answers, including those produced by other companies. They are practical, expert, and creative in fitting the technology to particular business needs. We are proud to be their partners in this unfolding enterprise.

The opportunities for CNAs have never been greater. Networking is more and more in demand; it is the solution virtually every company is turning to. A CNA understands business issues and networking capabilities, and combines them in such a way as to create and deliver effective solutions.

From a broader perspective, networking is also becoming ever more pervasive in the activities of our daily lives. The whole thing is exploding and will continue to explode in the foreseeable future. Change is happening, and the technician's skills will also need to evolve at a rapid rate. The CNA program is very conscious of the need to keep up with real world developments and future directions. So much more innovation is in store; so much more is going to be connected to computer networks—we have only begun to imagine the possibilities! All that change spells growing opportunities for everyone who participates in moving to better, more powerful solutions for our customers. In all of this, it is the CNA who will be on the front lines of progress.

Novell's CNA Study Guide IntranetWare/NetWare 4.11 by David James Clarke, IV is a great example of the Novell partnership philosophy: human, open, precise, and expert. It is an extraordinarily welcome resource to help students join with Novell in the amazing and ever-changing future of computer networking.

Drew Major

V.P. & Chief Scientist, Operating Systems

Novell, Inc.

Acknowledgments

Wow, this was fun! Even though the pace was fast and furious, we all had a great time exploring IntranetWare, writing about the CNA program, and inventing ACME—A Cure for Mother Earth. I emphasize the word "WE." I know it sounds corny, but I couldn't have written this book without the help and support of numerous friends and family. Let me introduce them to you.

Family is everything. I gained a new respect for them while writing this book, mostly because I continued to test the envelope of sanity. Crazy hours, crazy requests, crazy trips. Mary, my wife, deserves the most credit for supporting my work and bringing a great deal of happiness into my life. She is my anchor. Then there's Leia, my daughter. Somehow she knew just when I needed to be interrupted—daughter's intuition. Most of all, they both have brought much needed perspective into my otherwise one-dimensional life. For that, I owe them everything.

I also owe a great deal to my parents for their unending support and devotion. They are the architects of my life and I couldn't have accomplished anything without their guidance and love. In addition, my sister Athena and her family (Ralph and Taylor) deserve kudos for standing by me through thick and thin. In addition, thanks to my second family for opening their hearts to me. Don and Diane have been wonderfully generous to me, Mary, and their precious granddaughter, Leia. Also, Keith and Bob have been great brothers to me, and Lisa and Pam have been great sisters to Mary. Finally, Jessica has been a creative and fun influence on Leia.

Before I close my family circle, I must thank two important "extended family" members—Dr. James Buxbaum and Virginia Zakoor. They are life-friends who have always supported my writing. Together we are works-in-progress—a screenplay with James and a novel with Virginia. Someday we'll finish . . . .

 ZEN

What no wife of a writer can ever understand is that he's working when he's staring out of the window.

Burton Rascoe

Now, let's meet the true architect of this book—my partner Cathryn Ettelson. She has been instrumental in all aspects of this book—research, the Mad Scientist's laboratory, exercises, midnight phone calls, and the list goes on. I owe a great deal to this brilliant woman, and I truly couldn't have written this book without her. This is who I'm talking about when I say "WE." Thanks Cathryn. Now you can have that week-long vacation I've been promising you for years.

Next, I would like to thank Lori Ficklin, who was responsible for bringing my words to life—literally. Also, her husband, Richard, deserves a lot of credit for making sure I didn't ramble on forever. And, of course, there's Mike Kim. He's the collective funny bone of our group. Not only is Mike a gifted cartoonist, but he comes from the other side of Cyberspace—where most of the world lives. For that, he gives this book unique perspective and readability. I've been blessed to have such wonderful friends who stick with me through good times and bad. This is our eleventh book together, and I couldn't have done it without all of them.

Behind every great book is an incredible production team. It all starts with Kevin Shafer—legendary editor. His flawless organization, quick wit, and patience were instrumental in bringing this book to life. I can say without 99 percent certainty, he is the best editor I've ever worked with. Next, David Puckett deserves a great deal of praise for creating the beautiful illustrations in this book. I've always believed a picture is worth a thousand words. But his pictures are worth a few thousand more. And, of course, Jim Sumser for keeping me up to speed on all the exciting adventures at IDG. He is our Robin Hood, our Knight in Shining Armor, our Hans Solo . . . . you get the idea.

Phyllis Beaty and Stephen Noetzel deserve a lot of the credit for finishing this book on time. They both performed above and beyond the call of duty in every aspect of production. I would also like to thank Mick Arellano, Christine C. Langin-Faris and Rebecca Plunkett, and all the typesetters, artists, and management who made this book possible, especially Andrew Walker and Terry Somerson. Finally, thanks to IDG sales, marketing, and bookstores for putting this book in your hands. After all, without them I'd be selling books out of the trunk of my car.

 ZEN

You can tell a lot about a person by the way he eats jelly beans.

Ronald Reagan

Now, let's talk about Novell Press. What an amazing organization. They are truly the future of network publishing. It all starts with Rose Kearsley. She *is* Novell Press. Rose has been a wonderful friend and supportive publisher throughout the past five years. I can only hope for greater things in the future. And the dramatic revolution of these Study Guides is due in part to her almost clairvoyant insight—not to mention her uncanny ability to convince people they need to give us stuff. Then there's Colleen Bluhm who has been a wonderful friend through thick and thin—always e-mailing, calling, or popping up just at the right time. Colleen has also been my eyes and ears to Novell Education, an invaluable resource. She's a rock at Novell Press that I always count on for quick and accurate answers. Together, these great people bring Novell Press books to life. Give them a "thanks" next time you see them.

Life is not one-dimensional. Every now and then, when I leave my cave, I appreciate the support from numerous friends and colleagues. First, I'd like to thank my partner Paul Wildrick. He has been a constant source of excitement, not to mention chaos. Together we've enjoyed CyberState University, World Wire, *The Clarke Tests v3.0*, and more. Speaking of CyberState University, I'd also like to say "Thanks" to David and Michael for doing such an amazing job. You bring "Synergy" to the Synergy Learning System®. And speaking of *The Clarke Tests v3.0*, I'd like to thank my other great friends, Lisa and Brian Smith, for keeping the ship afloat. Fulfillment and Tech Support: a match made in administrative heaven.

Next, I'd like to thank all of my NetWare Users International (NUI) friends for being there with me "on the road." You're all wonderful people and you're doing great things for NetWare users everywhere. The most thanks go to Ted Lloyd for spearheading the whole thing. He's a business genius with a great, big heart. What a rare combination these days. And thanks to all my extraordinary friends at Diablo Valley College (DVC): Leslie Leong, Dan McClellan, and Matt Anderson, for being there for me in the very beginning. And to my good friend Rich Rosdal of Clarity Technologies for always believing in me.

Finally, thanks to golf courses everywhere for giving me a reason to live; Tears for Fears for inspiration; The Tick for being a superhero role model; and Babs and Buster Bunny for teaching me everything I know about people.

 ZEN

Welcome to your life, there's no turning back!

Tears for Fears

I saved the best for last. Thanks to *YOU* for caring enough about IntranetWare and your education to buy this book. You deserve a great deal of credit for your enthusiasm and dedication. Thanks again, and I hope this education changes your life. Good luck, and welcome to your new exciting life! Enjoy the show.

Introduction

Hi! I'm baaaaack!

It seems like just yesterday we were frolicking through the life of a CNA in the original *Novell's CNA Study Guide*. Well, the world's changed and CNAship has entered a new frontier—IntranetWare! It's unlike anything you've ever seen. There are clouds, trees, gardeners, and leaf objects. It's a plethora of permaculture; a virtual cornucopia of chlorophyll. And that's not all. IntranetWare introduces a whole new dimension in networking—NDS. You're in for the ride of your life. Green thumb required.

So, do you still want to be a CNA? The "007" of cyberworld? Good. Don't worry, you still get to traverse the obstacle course of unpredictable network challenges. It's just that the course has become a little bigger and the obstacles have become a little more unpredictable. The good news is the rewards still greatly outweigh the pain. You'll be more competitive in today's job market and maybe even save the world along the way. Life as a CNA has never been more exciting! Ready, set, go.

Life as a CNA!

ZEN

"Anything I've ever done that ultimately was worthwhile . . . initially scared me to death."

Betty Bender

By picking up this book, you've just shown that you are interested in taking steps toward furthering your career. Congratulations! That puts you a notch higher than a lot of your competition. Becoming an IntranetWare Certified Novell Administrator (CNA) demonstrates that you can hold your own as a network administrator. As a CNA, you're in prime position to help your users get the most out of your network, to help management get the most out of your users, and to help yourself get the most out of your career opportunities.

SO, WHO NEEDS CNAS, ANYWAY?

The whole world does, that's who. NetWare networks are, hands-down, the most popular network in the world. According to various surveys, 70 percent of all networks in the world are running some version of NetWare networking software. All other networking companies combined (including Microsoft, IBM, Banyan, and LANTastic) only account for the other 30 percent.

By early 1997, there were an estimated 5.5 million NetWare servers in the world. If you conservatively estimate an average of 10 users per server, you're looking at 55 million users. And those numbers are growing rapidly every month. Just imagine how many users will be out there by the time you read this paragraph. That's a significant number of people who need help with their networks. Lucky thing for them that you're interested in becoming a CNA.

 ZEN

"A lot of prizes have been awarded for showing that the universe is not as simple as we might have thought!"

Stephen Hawking

HOW MUCH TROUBLE IS IT?

Achieving CNA status can be one of the best ways you'll find to enhance your position in the computer industry. To become certified, you must prove that you know the fundamentals of networking and can handle the daily needs of an IntranetWare network. To prove this knowledge, you take a single exam.

Taking a test is one thing, but how do you get ready for the test? You must learn all this stuff first, right? Of course. But it may not be nearly as difficult to learn the networking ropes as you may think.

Understanding how IntranetWare networks run consists of learning some fundamental principles and a few key tools, then building on those. Once you know the fundamentals, you can begin to see how other aspects of the network fit in, how and where problems might occur, and how to solve those problems.

To learn about IntranetWare and prepare for this test, you can take a single course, study books like this one, or go the "real world" route and learn IntranetWare on the job. Even better, you can combine these methods. Most people will tell you that nothing beats actual experience when learning new things. This is true with IntranetWare, too. You can learn a lot from books and from classes, but until you get your hands into the network yourself, some concepts will still be a little foggy.

On the other hand, the "sink-or-swim" method of real-world learning can be relatively slow and painful by itself. Using a good study guide (such as this book) or taking an IntranetWare course can give you a terrific jump start on the way to knowledge. A few days spent in class or with this book can save you several months of trial-and-error.

So, if you're like most people, the best approach is to combine as much "hands-on" experience as possible with as much "book learning"' as you can stand. This book was designed to help you out, without driving you crazy. No promises.

HOW CAN THIS BOOK HELP?

The first part of this book deals with some of the more intangible aspects of network administration. For example, you'll find information about how CNA certification can help your career, as well as examples of the types of tasks real CNAs face each day. This type of information isn't on the official CNA exam, but it's the kind of information you'll need to succeed in the real world.

The second part, which is the bulk of this book, contains the information, exercises, examples, and hints that will help you keep an IntranetWare network running smoothly. This information applies directly to the material that will be covered on the CNA exam. Not only will this information help you prepare for the exam, it can also help you avoid several months' worth of accidental discovery and network meltdowns-a bargain by most standards.

So, where do we go from here? A magic carpet ride, of course. A journey down the path to enlightenment—IntranetWare Nirvana. Don't worry. You don't have to travel alone. I'll be by your side every step of the way-your trusted CNA tour guide. And, I've brought along a few other friends to help. Heroes from our unspoiled history—before instant popcorn, talking cars, and daytime television. There's Albert Einstein, Sherlock Holmes, Gandhi, and Mother Teresa, just to name a few-the IntranetWare dream team. With friends like these, you can't do anything but succeed. Ready, set, go.

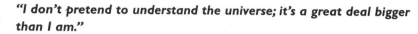

Magic Carpet Ride

ZEN

"I don't pretend to understand the universe; it's a great deal bigger than I am."

Thomas Carlyle

The journey begins with a "seed of thought." Before you know it, you'll have a huge NDS tree growing out of your head. Part I begins (oddly enough) with Chapter 1, which describes the benefits of being a CNA. It explains the reasons why certification can be useful, the benefits your management may receive, and the career opportunities that can come with certification. In addition, it talks about the pitfalls of the paper—CNA syndrome, versus real-world experience. There's even an introduction to some people who might want to help you pay for your CNA education.

Chapter 2 takes you through a typical day of CNAship, and offers some insight into normal CNA management tasks. It describes many of the routine maintenance tasks you'll be exposed to, and some practical advice for setting up and running a Help Desk for your users.

The real fun begins is Part II. Chapter 3 explores the next generation of IntranetWare, and introduces the main new feature of the book—NDS (Novell Directory Services). You'll also learn about the pseudo-fictitious organization ACME. ACME is a group of world-famous heroes from the past who have banded together to save the world. We will be using them throughout the book in examples, exercises, and case studies. In Chapter 3, we will create the team responsible for ACME's NDS tree and explore it's global MIS organization.

Then, you're in for the ride of your life. In Chapter 4, we learn that the file system represents NetWare life "within" the server. All of our focus so far has been "above" the server. Now we get a chance to work with a big, electronic filing cabinet. Chapter 5 continues this journey with a look at security. Information is now the new commodity—more valuable than money. We need to take new measures to protect our information. IntranetWare includes a five-layered security model including login/password authentication, login restrictions, NDS rights, file system access rights, and attributes. Think of it as your impenetrable network armor.

Once the LAN has been installed (born) it enters the second and third phases of its life span—configuration (childhood) and management (adulthood). In Chapter 6, the first of two related chapters, I'll walk you through the five steps of configuration using Leia as an example. Then, in Chapter 7, we're introduced to the final phase of LAN life span adulthood. Here the network gets married, has children of her own, plans for retirement, and finally retires. There are five steps in this chapter.

That leaves the last topic: printing. Printing (Chapter 8) is "the great challenge." IntranetWare printing is simple and works great until . . . you add users. It's their fault. In this chapter, we will explore some proven methods for successful IntranetWare printing installation, management, and troubleshooting. In addition, we'll get a peek at printing's future-NDPS.

That pretty much sums it up—the entire IntranetWare CNA program in one book. Wow! These chapters cover everything there is to know about IntranetWare management, life as a CNA, and saving the world. Of course, we couldn't survive our journey without six great appendices. Appendix A is an overview of Novell Education. Appendix B is a great cross-reference of CNA course objectives. It points you in the right direction—topic by topic. Appendix C has all the answers—literally. It has answers for case studies, exercises, and quizzes. Appendix D provides a plethora of CNA resources. And finally, Appendices E and F offer some additional study material for the "Intranet" part of IntranetWare (namely, the Web Server, Internet Access Server, FTP Services, and the IPX/IP Gateway). Don't worry, this information isn't testable.

Speaking of answers, I have a few life puzzles I could use answered. How about you?

► · ◄

Life Puzzles

ZEN

"Next, when you are describing,
A shape, or sound, or tint;
Don't state the matter plainly,
But put it in a hint;
And learn to look at all things,
With a sort of mental squint."

Lewis Carroll

There is a difference between puzzles and problems. Life puzzles allow you to stretch your mind and explore parts of your brain you didn't even know you had. Also, they usually have one answer—or so it seems. Life problems, on the other hand, arise through the everyday process of getting out of bed and putting on your clothes. Also, there is never a "right" answer—just shades of gray. We cover both in this book:

- ► Life Puzzles—Any fun book would be incomplete without crossword and word search puzzles. Take a crack at 11 doozies and don't blow a brain cell.

- ► Life Problems—Concepts are important, but the real test is in the doing. There are almost 30 original exercises and case studies in this book. Some are written, but most are hands-on. These labs are designed to provide you with "real-life" experience in managing local and global IntranetWare LANs. And as an extra bonus, you get to save the world in the process.

So, the moral is—read this book in bed, and enjoy the life puzzles.

In addition to life puzzles and problems, there are a myriad of other informational tidbits scattered throughout the book. These quips provide instant information in the form of Zen, Quizzes, Tips, Real World, The Brain, and SmartLinks. Check them out:

ZEN

Words of wisdom from people more enlightened than I am. Plus, they make you look really smart in front of your friends.

QUIZ

These brain puzzlers help bring much needed perspective into your difficult and absorbing journey. It's a great idea to come up for "mental air" every now and then. And these quizzes will appear at just the right time—before you mentally suffocate.

TIP

Highlights time-proven management techniques and action-oriented ideas. These tips are great ways of expanding your horizons beyond just **CNA**ship—they're your ticket to true nerdom.

▶ . . . . ◀

REAL WORLD

Welcome to the real world. I don't want you to be a two-dimensional CNA in a three-dimensional world. These icons represent the other dimension. In an attempt to bring this book to life, I've included various real-world scenarios, case studies, and situational walk-throughs.

THE BRAIN

In case yours turns to Jell-O. These are great context-sensitive references to supplemental brains. Brains-for-hire, like IntranetWare documentation, Application Notes, Albert Einstein, and so on. Enjoy them, and give yours a rest.

SMART LINK

We live in a "virtual" world: surfing the net, on-line dating, cyber children, and talking toasters. So, I thought it was only fitting to include these virtual SmartLinks in my book. All you have to do is click on the URL code with your pencil and you will be instantaneously transported to a great, cool site on the Web. You're welcome.

WHAT'S NEW

Highlights new things introduced in IntranetWare.

Are We Having Fun Yet?!

ZEN

"All the animals except man know that the principle business of life is to enjoy it."

Samuel Butler

Inevitably, at some point you're going to want to apply all this great IntranetWare knowledge to some physical structure—a WAN perhaps. One assumes you will *act* on this book's CNA concepts, theories, exercises, and examples. One assumes at some point, you'll need to scream! That's OK, I'm here for you. I care.

The main goal of this book is to take you on a magic carpet ride through the next generation of NetWare—IntranetWare. No one said it couldn't be fun! As a matter of fact, I've worked overtime to make this the most painless, and even enjoyable, IntranetWare experience of your life. I've even included a life-size poster of Lola Bunny—just kidding.

It would be irresponsible of me to abandon you at the very moment you need the most help-real life! I'm here for you—every step of the way. I'm only a cybercall away. Also, in an effort to provide you with the most complete education possible, we have developed a special *CNA Study Guide* version of *The Clarke Tests v3.0* and placed it on the CD-ROM in the back of this book. See Appendix D for complete details on the CD-ROM contents.

In addition, I spend most of the year traveling around the globe-meeting you! I speak at NetWare Users International conferences, Networld + Interop, Networks Expo, and others. But if none of that works for you, I'm always available to chat. Really! I'm sitting by the cyperphone waiting for it to cyberring. Find me:

- ▸ Internet: dciv@garnet.berkeley.edu

- ▸ The Web: http://www.cyberstateu.com/clarke.html

- ▸ CompuServe: 71700,403

- ▸ Cyber State University: 1-888-GET-EDUCATED

- ▸ World Wire: DAVID CLARKE, IV

  - ▸ Sign up at 1-510-254-1194 (on-line)

  - ▸ Phone: 1-510-254-7283

- ▸ The Clarke Tests v3.0: 1-800-684-8858

- ▸ NUI Conferences: 1-800-228-4NUI

So, get prepared for a magic carpet ride through IntranetWare administration. Fasten your seat belt, secure all loose objects, and keep your arms inside the ride at all times. There's no limit to where you can go from here!

Ready, set, go!

Contents at a Glance

Introduction   xv

Part I: Life as a CNA

Chapter 1   Why Become a CNA?   1

Chapter 2   A Day in the Life of a CNA   31

Part II: The CNA 4.1 Program

Chapter 3   Understanding IntranetWare and NDS   91

Chapter 4   IntranetWare File System   239

Chapter 5   IntranetWare Security   329

Chapter 6   IntranetWare Configuration   461

Chapter 7   IntranetWare Management   557

Chapter 8   IntranetWare Printing   677

Part III: Appendixes

Appendix A   Overview of Novell Education and the
                 CNA Program   795

Appendix B   CNA Cross-Reference to Novell Course
                 Objectives   815

Appendix C   Solutions to Quizzes, Puzzles, Exercises,
                 and Case Studies   827

Appendix D   For More Information and Help   875

Appendix E   Exploring the NetWare Web Server   **903**

Appendix F   Exploring the "Intranet" and Novell's Internet
Access Server   **929**

Index   **947**

IDG Books Worldwide, Inc. End-User License Agreement   **970**

Contents

Introduction   xv

Part I • Life as a CNA

Chapter I • Why Become a CNA?   I

The Importance of Being Certified   4
   Tangible Proof   5
   Fast Track to Knowledge   6
   Potential College Credit   7
   Fast Track to Jobs   8
     Gaining a Competitive Edge   9
     Being Multitalented Helps, Too   10
   Going After the Big Bucks   11
   Joining Professional
     Organizations   11
How Management Benefits from
   Having CNAs   12
Paper Certification Versus
     Real-World Experience   13
   Building on the CNA Foundation   15
   Gaining Credibility   16
   Getting What You Need Out of
     the CNA Program   16
Practical Education that Works   18
Paying for Your CNA Education   19
   Financial Assistance   20
     Financial Aid at School   21
     Job Training Partnership Act
       (JTPA)   22

Trade Adjustment Assistance
   (TAA)   23
Private Industry Councils
   (PICs)   23
Veterans' Administration   24
Advancing Your Career   24
   Current Outlook for the
     Networking Industry   24
   Current Outlook for Your Future   26
   A Career in Network
     Administration   26
   Upping the Ante   27
   A Stepping Stone to Other
     Careers   28

Chapter 2 • A Day in the Life of a CNA   31

Where Do CNAs Fit in the
   Organization?   33
Common Day-to-Day Activities   35
Routine Maintenance and
   Housekeeping   36
Checking Under the Hood
   (Maintaining the Hardware)   37
Refueling the Tank (Adding to
   Server Capacity)   39
Pursuing High Performance
   (Tracking How the
   Server Runs)   40

Monitoring Processor Utilization 42
Monitoring Cache Buffers 42
Monitoring Packet Receive
    Buffers 42
Accommodating Passengers
    (Managing User Accounts) 43
Testing the Anti-Theft System
    (Monitoring Security) 44
Getting Back on Track (Backing
    Up Files) 46
Adding New Accessories
    (Installing Applications) 47
Hitting the Car Wash (Cleaning
    Up the File System) 48
Listening to Those Knocks
    and Pings (Monitoring the
    Error Logs) 49
User Support 52
How Does a Help Desk Work? 53
Getting Problem Reports from
    Users 54
Prioritizing Problem Reports 55
Assigning Problem Reports to
    an Available Person 56
Tracking the Solution's
    Progress 56
Escalating the Problem 57
Resolving the Problem 57
Recording and Reporting the
    Solution 58
Tools for Help Desks 59
Help Desk Tracking Software 60
Telephony Systems 60
Help Desk Handbooks 61
Help Desk Disaster Plans 62
User Training 62

Typical Network Tasks for
    Users 64
Workstation and Application
    Skills 65
Training Tools 66
Disaster Planning and Recovery 66
So What Can a CNA Do About
    Disasters? 68
Plan Ahead 68
What Should Be in a Disaster
    Plan? 70
Keep Good Records of Your
    Network 71
Hardware and Software
    Inventory 72
Installation and Configuration
    Settings 73
Maintenance Histories 75
Volumes 77
Hot Fix Bad Block Tracking 78
Time Synchronization 81
Network Layout 81
Workstation Batch Files and
    Boot Files 81
Server SET Parameters and
    Boot Files 81
Backup Information 83
What Else Can a CNA Do? 83
Troubleshooting Tips 85
Narrow Down the List of
    Suspects 85
Check the Hardware 87
Refer to the Documentation 87
Look for Patches or Workarounds 88
Try Each Solution by Itself 88
Call for Technical Support 88
Document the Solution 89

Part II • The CNA 4.1 Program

**Chapter 3 • Understanding
IntranetWare and NDS   91**

The Foundation of
    NetWare 3.12   93
The Evolution of IntranetWare   96
What's New in IntranetWare   100
    1. Novell Directory Services   101
    2. Server Operating System   101
    3. Installation   103
    4. NetWare Licensing
       Services   104
    5. Connectivity Services   104
    6. File Services   105
    7. Application Services   105
    8. Storage Management
       Services (SMS)   106
    9. Security Services   107
    10. Print Services   107
Getting to Know NDS   112
    The "CLOUD"   115
    NDS Versus The Bindery   117
    Composition of the Tree   120
NDS Objects   123
    Understanding NDS Objects   123
    [ROOT]   125
    Container Objects   126
       Country Objects   128
       Organization Objects   129
       Organizational Unit Objects   130
    Leaf Objects   131
       User Leaf Objects   132
       Server Leaf Objects   134

Printer Leaf Objects   136
Messaging Leaf Objects   137
Network Services Leaf
    Objects   138
Informational Leaf Objects   139
Miscellaneous Leaf Objects   140
Overview of NDS Management   142
NDS Naming   144
    Context   146
       Current Context   147
       Object Context   148
       Using CX   148
    Naming Rules   150
       Distinguished Names   151
       Typeful Names   155
NDS Partitioning   161
    Understanding NDS Partitions   163
NDS Replication   167
    Replica Types   169
    Managing NDS Replicas   170
Time Synchronization   176
    Time Server Types   178
       Single-Reference Time Servers   179
       Reference Time Servers   180
       Primary Time Servers   181
       Secondary Time Servers   182
    Time Configuration   183
       Default Time Configuration   183
       Custom Time Configuration   185
Getting to Know ACME   188
    ACME Chronicles   193
       Human Rights—Gandhi in
       Sydney   193

Labs—Albert Einstein in NORAD	195
Operations—King Arthur in Camelot	197
Crime Fighting—Sherlock Holmes in Tokyo	198
Admin—George Washington in Rio	200
ACME Workflow	204
Financial	204
Distribution Centers	205
Labs and Their Inventions	205
WHI Calculations	206
Public Relations	206
Crime Fighting	207
ACME Administration	207
NetWare Administrator	208
NETADMIN	211
CX	213
Part I: NWADMIN	220
Part II: NETADMIN	227
Part III: UIMPORT	231
Part IV: SPECIAL CASES	233

Chapter 4 • IntranetWare File System 239

Understanding the IntranetWare File System	241
Understanding IntranetWare Volumes	243
System-Created Directories	248
LOGIN	250

SYSTEM	250
PUBLIC	251
MAIL	251
NLS	251
ETC	252
QUEUES	252
DELETED.SAV	252
DOC	252
DOCVIEW	252
Expanding Beyond the Default Directory Structure	253
DOS Directories	254
Application Directories	255
Configuration File Directories	255
Home Directories	255
Shared Data Directories	255
Designing Your Directory Structure	256
Managing the IntranetWare File System	258
Managing IntranetWare Volumes	260
FILER	261
NWADMIN	263
NETADMIN	266
NLIST	267
NDIR	268
Managing IntranetWare Directories	270
FILER	271
NWADMIN	274
NDIR	276
NCOPY	278
RENDIR	280

Managing IntranetWare Files	281
FILER	282
NWADMIN	284
MS Windows	286
NDIR	289
NCOPY	293
Drive Mapping	296
Network Drive Mappings	300
Search Drive Mappings	301
Directory Map Objects	304
Mapping Drives with MAP	305
MAP	306
MAP G:=WHITE-SRV1\ SYSSHARED\FINAN	306
MAP NP E:=SYSMAIL	307
MAP S3:=SYS:APPS\WP70	307
MAP INS S1:=SYS:PUBLIC	308
MAP DEL G:	309
MAP ROOT H:=SYS:ACCT\ REPORTS	309
MAP N SYS:DATA	310
MAP C I:	310
MAP S5:=.WPAPP.TOKYO. ACME	311
MAP /?	311
MAP /VER	311
Mapping Drives with MS Windows	313
Windows 95 Drive Mappings	313
NetWare User Tools for Windows Drive Mappings	314
Mapping Network Drives with Windows 95	321

Mapping Drives with NetWare User Tools for Windows	322

Chapter 5 • IntranetWare Security   329

IntranetWare Security Model	334
Layer One—Login/Password Authentication	335
Layer Two—Login Restrictions	336
Layer Three—NDS Security	336
Layer Four—File System Access Rights	338
Layer Five—Directory/File Attributes	339
Layer One—Login/Password Authentication	344
Getting In	344
Initial Authentication	347
Step One: Client Requests Authentication	348
Step Two: Server Returns Encrypted Key	349
Step Three: Client Decrypts Private Key	349
Step Four: The User Is Authenticated	349
Background Authentication	351
Layer Two—Login Restrictions	354
Account Restrictions	357
Account Disabled	358
Account Has Expiration Date	359

Limit Concurrent			Groups	392
Connections	359		Directory Map Objects	392
Last Login	359		Step Two: Filtering IRF Rights	394
Password Restrictions	359		Step Three: Calculating Effective	
Allow User to Change			Rights	397
Password	360		NDS Administration	401
Require a Password	361		Admin	401
Force Periodic Password			Distributed Administrators	402
Changes	362		Special NDS Security	405
Require Unique Passwords	362		Layer Four—File System Access	
Limit Grace Logins	363		Rights	410
Time Restrictions	364		Understanding File System	
Station Restrictions	366		Access Rights	411
Intruder Detection/Lockout	368		File System Three-Step Shuffle	416
Intruder Detection Limits	368		Step One: Assigning Trustee	
Lock Account After Detection	369		Rights	416
Layer Three—NDS Security	371		Step Two: Filtering IRF Rights	420
Understanding NDS Access			Step Three: Calculating	
Rights	373		Effective Rights	421
Object Rights	374		Layer Five—Directory/File	
Property Rights	375		Attributes	423
Default NDS Rights	378		Security Attributes	424
Initial NDS Installation	378		Feature Attributes	426
File Server Installation	379		Disk Management Attributes	427
User Creation	380		Case #1	446
Container Creation	381		Case #2	446
Step One: Assigning Trustee			Case #3	448
Rights	383		Case #1	450
Trustee Assignments	384		Case #2	451
Inheritance	388		Case #3	451
Security Equivalence	390		Case #4	452
Ancestral Inheritance (AI)	391		Case #5	453
Organizational Role (OR)	391		Case #6	454

Chapter 6 • IntranetWare Configuration 461

Step 1: Establishing Workstation
Connectivity 466
Workstation Connectivity with
Client 32 466
Understanding the Network
Connection 467
Connectivity with
Windows 95 469
Connectivity With
Windows 3.1 471
Logging In 473
Workstation Connectivity with
Client 16 475
CONFIG.SYS 476
AUTOEXEC.BAT 477
STARTNET.BAT 477
NET.CFG 479
LINK DRIVER 480
NetWare DOS Requester 482
Other NET.CFG Parameters 485
Step 2: Login Scripts 487
Login Script Types 488
Container Login Script 489
Profile Login Script 491
User Login Script 493
Default Login Script 494
Login Script Commands 495
Identifier Variables 496
A: WRITE and REMARK 499
B: Network Drive Mappings 500
C: Search Drive Mappings 502

D: COMSPEC 503
E: SET 504
F: IF...THEN...ELSE 504
G: # (DOS Executable) 505
H: NO_DEFAULT 506
I: EXIT 506
Other Login Script
Commands 507
GUI Login Script Management 508
GUI Script Page 509
GUI Variables Page 509
Step 3: Creating the Menu System 511
Organizational Commands 513
MENU 513
Item 515
Control Commands 516
EXEC 516
SHOW 517
LOAD 517
GETO 518
GETR 519
GETP 520
Menu Execution 520
Step 4: Installing Network
Applications 523
A Simple Seven-Step Model 524
Step 1: Ensuring IntranetWare
Compatibility 524
Step 2: Checking
Multiuserness 525
Step 3: Creating the
Directory Structure 525
Step 4: Managing the
Installation 525

Step 5: Assigning File
  Attributes   526
Step 6: Assigning Access
  Rights   526
Step 7: Performing
  Customization   527
IntranetWare Application
  Management   527
  Task 1—Create Application
    Objects   528
  Task 2—Configure
    Application Objects   528
  Task 3—Configure
    Workstations   529
Step 5: E-mail   531
  Understanding MHS Services   533
    Messaging Server   534
    User Mailboxes   535
    MHS Applications   535
  Managing MHS Services   536
    Message Routing Group   537
    Messaging Server   537
    Distribution List   538
    External Entity   538
    Mailbox Objects   539
  Using FirstMail   539

**Chapter 7 • IntranetWare
  Management   557**

Server Installation   560
  Before You Begin   562
    Minimum Hardware
      Requirements   564

Choosing an Installation Type 566
Stage 1: Prepare the Server
  Hard Disk   571
Stage 2: Run SERVER.EXE   575
Stage 3: Load the NetWare
  Drivers   576
Stage 4: INSTALL.NLM   577
Stage 5: Install Novell
  Directory Services (NDS)   578
Stage 6: Create Server Startup
  Files   581
Server Management   583
  Console Commands   584
    BIND   585
    BROADCAST   585
    CLEAR STATION   586
    CONFIG   587
    DOWN   588
    DSTRACE   589
    ENABLE/DISABLE LOGIN   590
    EXIT   590
    HELP   591
    LOAD/UNLOAD   591
    MODULES   591
    MOUNT   591
    REMOVE DOS   592
    RESTART SERVER   592
    TRACK ON   592
  NetWare Loadable Modules   595
    Disk Drivers   598
    LAN Drivers   598
    Name Space   599
    INSTALL.NLM   599
    MONITOR.NLM   601

SERVMAN.NLM 604
DSREPAIR 607
Server Protection 608
Physical 609
MONITOR.NLM Locking 610
Secure Console 611
REMOTE.NLM 611
Workstation Management 614
Client 32 Workstation
Architecture 616
Client 32 Installation for
Windows 95 619
Client 32 Installation Steps
for Windows 95 620
Automatic Client Upgrade
for Windows 95 621
Client 32 Installation for
Windows 3.1 622
Client 32 Installation Steps
for Windows 3.1 623
Automatic Client Upgrade
for Windows 3.1 624
Client 16 Workstation
Architecture 626
Open Datalink Interface 627
MLID 628
Link Support Layer 628
Protocol Stack 629
NetWare DOS Requester 630
Non-DOS Workstation Support 634
Storage Management Services 636
SMS Architecture 637
Device Drivers 638
SBACKUP.NLM 638

Target Service Agents 639
Using SBACKUP 640
Backup Strategies 641
Guidelines 643
Backup Steps 644
Restore Steps 646
Other SMS Considerations 647
Who Does It? 648
Workstation Backup 648
SMS Management 649
Remote Management Facility 650
RMF Architecture 651
SPX 652
Asynchronous 653
Using RCONSOLE 654
1. Prepare the Server Hard Disk 659
2. Run SERVER.EXE 663
3. Load the NetWare 4.11
Drivers 663
4. Stage 4: INSTALL.NLM 664
5. Install NOVELL Directory
Services (NDS) 665
6. Create Server Startup Files 665

Chapter 8 • IntranetWare
Printing 677

The Essence of Printing 679
Getting Started 679
Printing by Yourself 680
Printing on a Network 682
The Beginning: Capturing 685
Capturing with DOS 685
Capturing with Windows 693

Moving to the Queue	697	Managing Print Servers		
The Print Server	699	with PSC	753	
The Destination: At the Printer	701	Get Status of All Printers	753	
Local Printers	701	Mount a New Form in a		
Remote Printers	702	Printer	754	
Third-party Printing Solutions	703	Stop/Start a Printer from		
HP JetDirect Card	703	Servicing Jobs	754	
Intel NetPort	704	Show Print Server		
IntranetWare Printing Setup	704	Configuration	755	
Step 1: Create the Print Queue	706	Configuring Print Jobs with		
Step 2: Create the Printer	710	PRINTCON	755	
Step 3: Create the Print Server	713	Customizing Printing with		
Step 4: Activate the Printing		PRINTDEF	756	
System	716	Using Custom Forms	757	
Printer Status	717	Using Print Devices	762	
Print Server Information	718	The Future of Printing—NDPS	764	
Customizing IntranetWare		Making Life Easier for Users	765	
Printing	720	Bidirectional Communication	766	
Building Forms	720	Print Job Move/Copy Options	766	
Building Devices	721	Automatic Driver Download	767	
Tying It All Together	726	Job-to-Printer Matching	767	
IntranetWare Printing Management	728	Multifunction Printer and		
Managing Printing with		Device Support	767	
PCONSOLE	732	Making Life Easier for CNAs	768	
Using Quick Setup	733	Streamlined Configuration	769	
Managing Print Queues	735	Plug-and-Print	769	
Managing Printers	739	Reduced Network Traffic	770	
Managing Print Servers	744	Event Notification	770	
Using the Auditing Feature	747	Queue Creation	776	
Managing Printing with		Printer Creation	777	
NWADMIN	748	Creating the Print Server	778	
CNA Tasks	749	Finding the Printer	779	
User Tasks	751	Loading the Print Server	780	

Part III • Appendixes

Appendix A • Overview of Novell Education and the CNA Program   795

Certification Partners   796
Certification Levels   798
  CNA (Certified Novell
    Administrator)   798
  CNE   799
  Master CNE   801
  CNI (Certified Novell
    Instructor)   802
Alternatives to Taking the Novell
    Authorized Courses   802
  Video Training   803
  Computer-Based Training (CBT)   803
  Student Kits   804
  Practice Tests   804
  Independent Courses   805
Testing Your Mettle   806
  How Do You Sign Up for an
    Exam?   806
  What Is the Exam Like?   807
After the Test—Now What?   808
For More Information . . .   809

Appendix B • CNA Cross-Reference to Novell Course Objectives   815

Course 520—IntranetWare/
  NetWare 4.11 Administration   816
  Section 1: Introduction to
    NetWare 4   816

Section 2: Connecting to the
  Network and Logging In   817
Section 3: Accessing Data Files
  and Applications on the
  Network   817
Section 4: Printing to a
  Network Printer   818
Section 5: Setting Up User
  Accounts and Login
  Security   818
Section 6: Setting Up the
  Network File System   819
Section 7: Managing the File
  System   820
Section 8: Setting Up the File
  System Security   820
Section 9: Accessing and
  Protecting the NetWare
  Server Console   821
Section 10: Setting Up
  Network Printing   822
Section 11: Installing and
  Configuring Client 32 on
  Workstations   822
Section 12: Creating Login
  Scripts   823
Section 13: Configuring
  Applications for Users   823
Section 14: Managing NDS
  Security   824
Section 15: Managing Resources
  in a Multicontext
  Environment   824

Section 16: Backing Up Servers
and Workstations   825
Section 17: Performing a Simple
NetWare 4 Installation   825

**Appendix C • Solutions to
Quizzes, Puzzles, Exercises,
and Case Studies   827**

Chapter 3: Understanding
IntranetWare and NDS   828
Answers to Quizzes   828
Q3-1   828
Q3-2   828
Q3-3   828
Q3-4   828
Q3-5   829
Q3-6   829
Exercise 3-1: "Tree Walking" for
Toddlers   829
Exercise 3-2: Understanding
NDS Naming   830
Exercise 3-3: Plant a Tree in a
Cloud   832
Exercise 3-4: IntranetWare
CNA Basics   833
Chapter 4: IntranetWare File
System   834
Answers to Quizzes   834
Q4-1   834
Q4-2   834
Q4-3   834
Q4-4   834

Exercise 4-1: Mapping Drives
with MAP   834
Exercise 4-4: IntranetWare
File Cabinet of Life   836
Chapter 5: IntranetWare Security 837
Answers to Quizzes   837
Q5-1   837
Q5-2   837
Q5-3   837
Q5-4   837
Q5-5   837
Case Study: ACME Security   838
Exercise 5-1: Calculating NDS
Effective Rights   839
CASE #1   839
CASE #2   840
CASE #3   842
Exercise 5-2: Calculating File
System Effective Rights   844
CASE #1   844
CASE #2   845
CASE #3   846
CASE #4   847
CASE #5   848
CASE #6   849
Exercise 5-3: How Secure Do
You Feel?   850
Exercise 5-4: Let the Good
Guys In   851
Chapter 6: IntranetWare
Configuration   852
Answers to Quizzes   852
Q6-1   852
Q6-2   852

Q6-3	852
Q6-4	853
Q6-5	853
Q6-6	854
Q6-7	854
Exercise 6-1: Workstation Connectivity with Client 16	855
Exercise 6-3: Understanding NET.CFG	855
Case Study: Configuring ACME's Login Scripts	856
Case Study: Configuring the ACME Menu System	859
Exercise 6-4: IntranetWare Childhood	861
Chapter 7: IntranetWare Management	862
Answers to Quizzes	862
Q7-1	862
Q7-2	862
Q7-3	862
Q7-4	862
Q7-5	862
Q7-6	862
Q7-7	862
Q7-8	862
CASE STUDY: Server Management at ACME	863
Exercise 7-1: IntranetWare Adulthood	866
Chapter 8: IntranetWare Printing	867
Answers to Quizzes	867
Q8-1	867
Q8-2	867

Q8-3	867
Q8-4	867
Q8-5	867
Case Study: Building ACME's Printing System	868
Queue Creation	868
Printer Creation	868
Creating the Print Server	868
Finding the Printer	868
Loading the Print Server	869
Case Study: Using ACME's Printing System	869
Case Study: Managing ACME's Printing System	870
Exercise 8-4: The Great Challenge	872
Exercise 8-5: The Greatest Mystery of All	873

Appendix D • For More Information and Help — **875**

General Novell Product Information	877
The Novell Buyer's Guide	877
The NetWare 4.1 Manuals	878
Novell on the Internet	879
Novell Technical Support	881
Novell's Support Connection	882
DeveloperNet Novell's Developer Support	883
Novell Application Notes	884
NetWare Users International (NUI)	884

Network Professional Association
  (NPA)   886
Novell Press Books and Other
  Publications   887
World Wire   888
CyberState University   888
  The Synergy Learning System   888
  The Curriculum   889
  For More Information . . .   891
The Clarke Tests v3.0   891
  Four Study Modules to Choose
    From   892
  The Interactive Learning System   892
    The Tests   892
    The Questions   893
    Interactive Answers   893
    Tracker Scoring   894
  Installing the Clarke Tests v3.0   895
  Using the Clarke Tests v3.0   895
  Troubleshooting the Clarke
    Tests v3.0   896
    For Window 3.1 and
      Windows 95 Users   897
    For Windows 3.1 Users Only   897
    For Windows 95 Users Only   899
  For More Information . . .   901

**Appendix E • Exploring the
NetWare Web Server   903**

What Is the NetWare Web Server?   905
Installing the NetWare Web Server   907
  Locating the Web Server
    Documentation   907

Configuring TCP/IP   908
Bringing Up the NetWare Web
  Server   908
Exploring Your Web Site   910
Configuring Name Services   911
  Creating and Using a Host's File   911
  Using Domain Name Services   912
Configuration Tools for Your Web
  Site   912
  Using the NetWare Web
    Manager Utility   913
  Editing the NetWare Web
    Server Configuration Files
    Manually   914
Controlling Access to Your Web
  Site   916
  Changing Web Access Rights   916
  NetWare Rights Issues   918
Supporting Dynamic Web Pages   919
  Administering SSI Command
    Usage   920
  Supporting CGI Scripts   921
Moving the Web Server's
  Document Root Directory   922
Controlling Directory Indexing   923
Checking Site Status   925
  Viewing the NetWare Web
    Server Console   926
  Viewing and Administering
    Log Files   926
Adjusting the Web Server
  Processing Power   928
For More Information   928

**Appendix F • Exploring the
"Intranet" and Novell's
Internet Access Server   929**

Installing the Novell Internet
    Access Server Software   932
The IPX/IP Gateway   935
    Configuring the IPX/IP Gateway   936
    Adding IPX/IP Gateway Tools
        to the NetWare
        Administrator Utility   938
    Controlling Access to the
        IPX/IP Gateway   938
    Installing the IPX/IP Gateway
        Client   940
        The Windows 3.1x Client   940
        The Windows 95 Client   941
FTP Services for IntranetWare   942
    Installing FTP Services   942

Index   947

**IDG Books Worldwide, Inc.
    End-User License
    Agreement   970**

Life as a CNA

CHAPTER 1

Why Become a CNA?

All over the world, IntranetWare networks are being installed at a breathtaking pace. If you stop and think about how many thousands of users are being added to an IntranetWare network every month, it's a rather staggering concept.

Over the past ten years, network computing has completely changed how the world communicates. Where were you a decade ago? If a business associate asked for your address back then, chances are good that you gave them a street address. If you wanted to send that person a document, you probably stuffed the document in an envelope, typed the address on the envelope, and pasted a stamp in the corner.

Today, when a business associate asks your addresses, you may be inclined to give him or her your e-mail address. It's a safe bet that you haven't touched a typewriter in years (and live in dread of having to find that bottle of white-out), and that you use the Postal Service only on those rare occasions when the recipient needs an honest-to-goodness signature on something.

The rest of the time, when you want to send someone a message or letter, your fingers skip across the keyboard, lightly and quickly typing up an e-mail message. Then, with a click of a button, the message is on its way through cyberspace, arriving within minutes in your colleague's electronic mailbox—no nasty stamp-taste on your tongue, no paper cuts from the envelope, no time wasted while the letter gets carried by trucks or airplanes to its destination.

And let's talk about the information in that letter you just sent via e-mail. A decade ago, you might have spent time at the corporate library (or in the city library downtown) to find the information you needed to write that letter. You would have leafed through stacks of periodicals, research reports, or other types of documents. You would have called experts and played phone-tag while you sat cooling your heels waiting for replies. You would have trekked through buildings, gone up and down elevators, and traipsed down long hallways looking for the person who'd borrowed the manila folder containing the Johannson files. You would have spent time at a terminal, accessing the company's database that was running on an astronomically expensive mainframe.

These days, you can do most or all of that research without leaving your desk. You can access on-line libraries of information, searching for your topic through hundreds of documents in moments. To avoid the phone-tag game (and some long-distance telephone charges), you can send e-mail to colleagues, asking them for the data they have. They, in turn, can send you the Johannson files via e-mail, or you can access them yourself from the document database that your company uses. And better yet for your company's bottom line, you can get all this information from an IntranetWare network, which is much less expensive than a mainframe.

Today's business world operates at a much higher speed than it did a decade ago. The breakneck rate at which communication travels from colleague to colleague, from customer to company, and from company to company is made possible in large part by the networking infrastructure that is spreading like a huge spiderweb over the planet.

 ZEN

"The future is always beginning now."

Mark Strand, *Reasons for Moving*

Do you want to go back to where you were a decade ago? Most people don't. They may gripe about computers, and complain that they're at the mercy of those hunks of plastic and electronics taking up space on their desks. But just watch what happens when those hunks of plastic and electronics suddenly stop working. Mild-mannered accountants suddenly turn into irate bullies. Administrative assistants hide. Deals are put on hold. Transactions get stalled. Whole projects grind to a halt while everyone working on them wanders aimlessly out into the hallways to complain to each other. Frustration becomes tangible.

This is where you, the network administrator, come in.

As a network administrator, you are responsible for taking care of the IntranetWare network on a day-to-day basis. You are the front line of defense for users who have problems. You are the gatekeeper who decides who gets to use the network, and how they get to use it. You are the person who installs new workstations on the network, and who updates old applications.

As a Certified Novell Administrator (CNA), you've not only learned how to do these types of tasks, you've also proven that you can do them to Novell's satisfaction. That can mean a great deal to your manager, and it can mean even more to a prospective employer who doesn't know much at all about you.

Knowledge is the important thing, of course. You can learn all about IntranetWare and be a very competent network administrator, without having to take a test to prove it. This book is designed to help you become a competent network administrator, regardless of whether you choose to take the test. But you may find that there is value in getting officially certified, anyway.

The Importance of Being Certified

As with most fields that offer the opportunity to become certified in a particular skill, the value of that certification varies somewhat with the person who gets it. There are two different ways to look at certification. For the individual who pursues the certification, it can mean

- Tangible proof to show management you know what you're talking about

- Credibility with others in the company or industry

- A fast track to knowledge, as you take classes to prepare for the certification

- Potential college credit

- A valuable asset on your resume

- A competitive edge in the job hunt

- A valid reason to ask for a salary increase or promotion, or to ask for a high salary in a new job

- An admission ticket into user groups or professional organizations

For management, having an employee (or potential employee) with certification means

- Reassurance that the employee really knows the product and has the recommended skills to work with the product

- A way to create a career path for employees

- A clear differentiator between job applicants

> ► A way to save money and time by dividing network support into two tiers—CNAs who provide the front-line support for users with their day-to-day networking needs, and CNEs who work on more technical issues (such as design and implementation of networking strategies)

CNA certification is no different in this regard. For the person who becomes a CNA, the certification can be the ticket to career advancement, credibility, or just a marginally impressive tidbit to work into conversations at social gatherings.

For management, hiring a CNA (or sending a current employee to class to become a CNA) means that the manager can be more confident in the employee's ability to keep the IntranetWare network running smoothly.

The following sections delve a little deeper into ways you can use a CNA certification to your advantage, as well as how management benefits from having CNAs in the organization.

TANGIBLE PROOF

Managing an IntranetWare network can be a challenge. It's even more of a challenge if you don't have the background knowledge required to keep it running smoothly. If you've received your CNA certification, you've proven that you were willing and able to learn about IntranetWare.

You spent time studying how IntranetWare works. You learned the tools that make administration easier, the tricks that make each step go a little faster. You researched how your network works, and found ways to make it work more efficiently. You've made yourself available to people who have problems, and you've updated the applications that your people want to use.

Getting your CNA certification proves it. The certificate marks the fact that you've put in the hours and showed the tenacity required to learn how to run the network.

A piece of paper may not change how you do your job, but every once in a while, it's nice to be recognized for what you've accomplished. With your CNA certificate in hand, you can prove to your manager and colleagues that you know your stuff, and that you have earned the recognition of Novell.

Not to mention that it looks really cool hanging on your wall.

FAST TRACK TO KNOWLEDGE

If you've been assigned to be your network's administrator, but your knowledge of IntranetWare is fairly limited, you will eventually learn what you need to know. Either that, or you'll find another job fairly quickly.

You may learn by trial and error. You might tag along with someone else who understands the system and try to learn at that person's elbow. You can read all the manuals and try to make heads or tails of the correct processes and information that apply to your specific situation. You can experiment with the network (although, hopefully you experiment while everyone else is at home).

Regardless of the methods you use, you will eventually learn enough about the network to keep it going, at least marginally well. However, it's a good bet that it will take you several months (or more) to get to this point if you use these seat-of-the-pants methods.

If, on the other hand, you decide to really focus your attention and learn about IntranetWare as quickly as you can, choosing the CNA route can be an efficient way to speed up your learning curve.

Take a look at the course objectives (see Appendix B) of the official *IntranetWare: NetWare 4.11 Administration* course. The people who designed this Novell course believe that if you understand all the concepts and procedures described by each of the objectives, you will have a solid background of knowledge to help you run an IntranetWare network.

The content of the *IntranetWare: NetWare 4.11 Administration* test that qualifies you as an IntranetWare CNA covers this broad range of information. If you can pass the test, you should have a good grasp of all the pertinent areas of network administration on an IntranetWare network.

There will always be more to learn, of course, especially with regard to your individual network's specific characteristics. But these fundamentals will allow you to handle most situations, and will give you enough background to tackle new problems in a logical, educated approach.

How you learn these fundamentals is up to you. Armed with this book and the list of course objectives, the trial-and-error method of learning becomes much more efficient. Instead of a shotgun approach, you can plan the kinds of things you want to learn and tackle them one-by-one.

ZEN

"The only learning that's mattered is what I got on my own, doing what I want to do."

Richard Bach, *Illusions*

Taking the *IntranetWare: NetWare 4.11 Administration* course from a Novell Authorized Education Center (NAEC) or from some other source can greatly shorten the time you'll need to learn about the network. A single class can't make you an expert in a week, but it can certainly give you a head-start by giving you a broad overview of the necessary concepts. It can also give you hands-on experience on a lab network, where you don't have to worry about accidentally trashing your manager's account or deleting all the financial reports for 1997.

Whether you take an authorized course, an unauthorized course (there are plenty of people who teach similar courses, some of whom are very good, and some of whom are less so), or adopt some other method of learning, using the CNA objectives as a roadmap can help keep you in the fast lane.

POTENTIAL COLLEGE CREDIT

There are two ways you might be able to get college credit for becoming a CNA. First, you can take the authorized *IntranetWare: NetWare 4.11 Administration* course from a college or university that offers the course. Such institutions are called Novell Education Academic Partners (NEAPs). More than 100 such colleges and universities can be found in the United States, as well as some in Canada.

TIP

To receive a list of all the current NEAPs, you can call 800-233-EDUC or 801-222-7800. If you have a fax machine, you can use the Novell Education FaxBack feature. Call one of the same numbers, and follow the instructions to order the FaxBack master catalog of available documents, then order the Novell Education Academic Partner (NEAP) List. Currently, the number of this document is 1235, but document numbers are subject to change.

Second, if you have taken the *IntranetWare: NetWare 4.11 Administration* course from an NAEC, you may be able to get college credit for the course transferred from Novell to the college or university of your choice.

College credit is also offered for other authorized Novell courses, as well.

The Novell College Credit Program (NCCP) allows you to get an official transcript from Novell, showing the recommended college credit you may have earned by taking the course and passing the test.

The American Council on Education (ACE) evaluates the Novell courses and recommends the amount of college credit that should be awarded for each course.

Whether or not the college or university you're planning to attend accepts the credit is up to the college or university, however, and not up to Novell.

To apply for college credit, you must first take the full-length *IntranetWare: NetWare 4.1 Administration* course from an NAEC. Only authorized courses taught by NAECs are accepted. Next, you must successfully pass the corresponding certification exam at a Sylvan Prometric testing center. (Details on how to find NAECs in your area and how to sign up for exams at Sylvan testing centers are presented in Appendix A.)

After you've successfully passed the corresponding exam, you can obtain a college credit transcript from the NAEC and have it sent directly to the college or university in which you're interested.

To request a transcript, you must present to the NAEC an original Novell Education course certificate and an original, embossed test score report that shows a passing score. The suggested price for obtaining a transcript is $30 for the first transcript, and $5 for each additional copy made at the same time, although prices are subject to change.

After the college or university receives your transcript, they will evaluate it and decide whether they will award the college credits recommended by the ACE. (Whether the credit is awarded, and how many credits are awarded, is entirely up to the college or university, as with all transferable credits.)

FAST TRACK TO JOBS

Just about anyone you talk to these days will tell you that you must understand computers in order to compete in today's job market, regardless of the field you're in. This is largely true. Computer skills are rapidly becoming a basic requirement in many industries.

However, are general computer skills enough to guarantee you a job? No. Not having those skills may prevent you from landing a particular job, but having them just means you're in the running with everyone else. General computer skills don't differentiate you from the rest of the pack. That's where specialization and planning become important.

REAL WORLD

To make your resume stand out from the rest of the crowd, you must ensure that you have skills necessary in not just today's business world, but tomorrow's as well.

Obtaining your CNA certification can be a step in the right direction. With the range and reach of IntranetWare networks growing rapidly all over the planet, the number of people needed to manage those networks is increasing at a rapid pace, too. Thousands of people have already recognized this and have begun pursuing their CNA and CNE certifications. The competition has begun.

Gaining a Competitive Edge

Employers have started realizing that a CNA certification can be a differentiating factor in hiring. If a manager is trying to hire someone to administer an IntranetWare network, the applicant with "CNA" on his or her resume will probably move higher up the list of potential interviewees than those without. This is because the employer recognizes that less training may be required for a CNA than for a non-CNA, and training costs money.

REAL WORLD

Take a gander at the help-wanted ads in a city newspaper these days. Every week, more and more positions are being advertised for people to run a company's computer operations. Many of these ads are requesting people who have experience managing Novell NetWare and IntranetWare networks, and many even specifically ask for people with CNA or CNE certifications. Your CNA certification will be the first step toward getting an interview at these companies.

The term "CNA" on the resume also helps reassure the hiring manager that the applicant is probably being truthful about his or her knowledge of IntranetWare. Some employers have discovered too late that prospective applicants "enhanced" their resumes by claiming to understand IntranetWare when all they really knew how to do was log in and out of the network.

Being Multitalented Helps, Too

Having CNA status doesn't just help you land a job as a network administrator. Many people running IntranetWare networks are doing it as a special assignment, in addition to their "real" job. They may actually be accountants, dental hygienists, graphic artists, or account managers who showed an aptitude for computers and got the network administrator assignment as an afterthought.

 ZEN

"It takes a fast car to lead a double life."

Lawrence Ferlinghetti

With a CNA certification, you can make that special assignment a forethought rather than an afterthought. If you are applying for a job as an office manager, but you also let the employer know that you are a CNA, the employer may pick you over the competition because you can be of value in more than one area.

In this era of downsizing, more and more people are finding themselves in the sometimes uncomfortable position of having to cover more than one type of job in their company. The people who are surviving the layoffs and restructurings are often those who have more than one valuable skill. If you are capable not only of doing your regular job, but also of taking care of the network, this could possibly help you weather a layoff.

There are no guarantees, of course, but it's always a smart idea to keep yourself diversified and versatile enough that you can move easily from one position to another. Then, even if you do find yourself back out in the job market, you'll still be ahead of much of your competition because you have the marketable quality of being a CNA, in addition to whatever else you have trained for.

Chapter 2 goes into more detail about career opportunities.

GOING AFTER THE BIG BUCKS

Will getting your CNA certification translate immediately into an increase in salary? Possibly, or possibly not. Situations vary widely. It does, however, give you some real negotiating advantages.

If you're applying for a job with a new employer, you may be able to negotiate a higher salary because you are a CNA. The employer will spend less money training you and have more confidence in your abilities right from the start.

Becoming certified as a CNA may help you get a promotion at your current company. It shows a qualitative increase in your skill set, which usually translates into greater productivity for your company. Once again, it may help differentiate you from others in your company who are also vying for that promotion.

Keep in mind, however, that the value of the CNA isn't simply the certificate. It's how you apply the knowledge you received in your pursuit of the certificate. Whether or not you get that job, promotion, or salary increase will be up to you and the effort you show as a direct result of the CNA certification.

JOINING PROFESSIONAL ORGANIZATIONS

As a CNA, you can join the Network Professional Association (NPA) as an associate member. This organization of network computing professionals strives to keep its members current with the latest technology and information about the networking industry. The NPA has more than 100 local chapters that meet regularly to see presentations and hands-on demonstrations of the latest technologies.

NetWare Users International (NUI) is an organization of NetWare and IntranetWare user groups. You don't have to be a CNA to join. NUI user groups also meet regularly and try to keep their users current with the latest networking trends.

You may find that because of their experience, members of such organizations can offer advice on issues you've been wrestling with, point out tricks they've found that will save you time and money, and steer you away from decisions that could negatively affect your network (such as buying troublesome hardware, installing incompatible applications, and so on). It may also just be nice to spend time socializing with others who have had the same types of experiences.

Both of these organizations are described more fully in Appendix D.

How Management Benefits from Having CNAs

We've looked at how having CNA certification can benefit an individual. How does that CNA benefit the manager and the company? How do you convince an employer that having a CNA on board will be worth the investment?

One obvious benefit a manager gets from hiring a CNA is the reassurance that the employee has the fundamental background and recommended skills required to maintain an IntranetWare network on a daily basis. Because of the training covered by the CNA program, the new employee will know how to connect workstations to the network, how to control security and access to files on the network, and how to monitor the network's performance. In addition, the CNA will know how to back up the network data and how to take care of the most common networking needs of users.

CNA certification also provides employers with a clear differentiator between job applicants or between current employees who are working their way up the career ladder.

The biggest concerns of employers usually boil down to getting value for their investment. If your company is currently paying outside consultants to handle every support call or issue, you may be able to show how having a qualified CNA on staff could cut those expensive support calls drastically.

Alternatively, if your company doesn't use outside consultants, but does employ an expensive Information Services (IS) staff, you may be able to show them how having an entry-level CNA at the departmental level can benefit them. Such a CNA could provide on-site, personal attention to users' needs, thus improving solution turnaround time (key buzzwords here are "increased productivity in the department"), as well as off-loading many of the time-consuming (but routine) tasks from the more expensive IS employees (key buzzwords here are "efficient resource utilization").

When arguing dollars, do your homework and present an accurate picture. Try to get actual estimates of the costs of support calls, versus how much time you would realistically be able to devote to managing your network.

Also, make sure you're not comparing apples to oranges—as a CNA, you may not be qualified to accomplish everything the consultant does, so you might not be able to completely eliminate those support calls. Be practical and realistic. You don't want your eloquent arguments to backfire on you, setting up in your manager's mind some false expectations that you can't live up to.

REAL WORLD

A real-world CNA, who is also an accounting manager in Washington, says that when she was convincing her company to pay for her CNA training, "We were paying consultants $95 per hour and travel, so it made sense to have someone [a CNA] in-house. I did not have much of a fight for them to agree to pay for it all."

As an extra benefit, users' confidence in the network may increase if they know they have an on-site CNA available to help them if a problem does arise.

For larger companies, another important benefit of having a CNA aboard is that it allows the company to divide network support tasks into two levels so that support can be managed more efficiently. CNAs can handle the day-to-day administration of the network and act as the front-line support for users' needs. This frees up the more technically advanced support personnel (such as CNEs) to concentrate on more technical, company-wide networking issues (such as design and implementation of networking strategies and research into new technologies).

This division between normal administrative tasks and more advanced issues also allows companies to create a clear career path for their IS departments, from entry-level employee at the CNA level, to advanced employees at the CNE level, to senior-level employees (Master CNEs).

Paper Certification Versus Real-World Experience

Every time someone starts talking about certification, or degrees, or official credentials of any kind, someone else starts arguing about the value of those credentials versus real-world experience. It's an argument that's worth looking into for a minute.

REAL WORLD

Advice from a real-world CNA: "Use hands-on practice whenever possible. Don't try to be a paper CNA."

Official recognition (whether it's in the form of a college degree, a membership in an association, or a certificate) usually is designed to reward and recognize those people who have mastered a new skill or area of knowledge. The requirements to receive that recognition are established by experts in the field, experts who attempt to come up with a set of quantifiable or demonstrable skills or questions that indicate a certain level of proficiency.

Because there is usually no way to absolutely determine a person's full depth of knowledge about anything, the set of requirements the experts establish are more representative than comprehensive.

This unavoidable weakness in the set of requirements can sometimes lead to a certain degree of abuse by some individuals—the kid in school who cheated on exams, the college buddy who could ace any written test but didn't have the common sense promised to a doorknob, or that character at work whose resume looks stellar, but who doesn't seem to have the foggiest grasp of real business sense.

There will always be those types of people in society.

Therefore, when someone argues that a CNA or CNE is a certification that isn't worth the paper it's printed on, it probably means they've encountered one of those individuals somewhere along the line. If this is the case, they have every right to be a little skeptical.

If all someone does is learn how to regurgitate facts, but never bothers to follow up with hands-on experience, then that person really isn't qualified to carry that certification. The CNA program attempts to prevent that situation, as much as possible, but there will always be a few people who manage to get around the system. Most CNAs don't ever fall into that trap, but there will certainly be a few.

So, is it worth it to get a CNA? Or any other degree or credential, for that matter?

Yes. Definitely, yes.

But it's a mistake to think that your education begins and ends with certification.

Your CNA certification ensures that you have the foundation you need to do your job. How you build on that foundation is up to you.

REAL WORLD

Advice from a real-world CNA: "Never assume you know all the answers or that any problem will be just like the last. Often, CNEs and CNAs fall into this trap, getting complacent with problems. You need to look at problems with fresh eyes."

BUILDING ON THE CNA FOUNDATION

Once you've received your educational foundation of CNA skills, you will be able to start applying that education immediately on the job. You will quickly discover that what you do on the job will reinforce, enhance, and build upon the education you received. This is where you begin to dispel the argument that paper certification isn't worth as much as real-world experience.

As we've already discussed, pursuing a CNA through formal courses or by studying books such as this one will put you squarely on the fast track toward knowledge. You will eliminate much of the trial-and-error that comes with strictly sink-or-swim hands-on approaches. You can learn several months' worth of accidental discoveries in a few days. Then, once you have those basics down, the on-the-job learning will start at an already advanced point, and you will learn practical tricks and tips for your particular network much more quickly.

So, while the CNA certification is no substitute for hands-on experience, it gives you a definite advantage in achieving that experience rapidly.

Your response to the argument against "paper CNAs" will simply be your own experience. If you are a paper CNA (meaning you've received your CNA certification without much actual hands-on training), your response should be that your certification has prepared you for network administration by giving you the background of knowledge you need, and that you're looking forward to getting that hands-on experience that your challenger is extolling.

If you already have the real-world experience to go with your CNA certification, then your best defense against detractors is simply to show them that you really do know your stuff. That shouldn't be difficult.

GAINING CREDIBILITY

More often than encountering a skeptic, you'll probably encounter people who actually have higher expectations of you because you're a CNA.

There's something about credentials that may change many people's perceptions of you. It may not be a tremendous change, but it's one of those funny quirks of human nature that makes people raise their expectations a little higher when they know someone has a credential.

This can be good or bad, of course. If they raise their expectations of you, and you let them down, it can backfire for you. For example, if the only MBA in the office is the one who makes the most boneheaded decisions, the rest of the people in the office will probably not be impressed with other MBAs they meet in the future. This is the "paper CNA" trap just discussed.

However, what will hopefully happen to you is that they will think to themselves, "Gee, that person is a CNA. I guess all that messing around with computers was beneficial after all. Maybe he/she can help me with my printing problems." Then you take one look at their printing setup, spot the problem (the wrong print driver being used by the application), fix it, and suddenly you've reinforced their new opinion of you.

This may sound silly at first, but think about the last time your company hired an outside consultant. Chances are good that some of the recommendations the consultant made were the same ones that your fellow employees were recommending. But, by virtue of being someone with "credentials," the consultant was listened to, while the regular employees were ignored.

What's going on here? A conspiracy? Not really. It boils down to the fact that some people unknowingly have higher expectations of "officially recognized" people than they do of "home-grown" people.

Becoming a CNA is your opportunity to make this quirk of human nature work for you. If you already have the knowledge, why not make it official and raise their opinion of you a little?

GETTING WHAT YOU NEED OUT OF THE CNA PROGRAM

In the CNA program, you will learn a great deal of information about IntranetWare. Because the program is trying to cover a representative amount of knowledge that will help the most number of people adequately manage their networks, you will find that not everything in the course objectives may apply to you. However, a significant portion of it will.

REAL WORLD

What you'll have to remember is that you need to strike a balance between what the course objectives teach you, and what you'll need to learn and use on the job. Some of the information you learn in the course (or in this book) may not be of immediate use to you. Of course, you never know what the future will hold for you— the very skills you thought you could ignore in the class may be ones you need urgently in your next job.

In addition, even though you may not immediately apply some of the information you learn, the education may have a more roundabout effect on your job performance. The more exposure you have to the different features and capabilities of IntranetWare, the more easily you can adapt that knowledge to new problems, even if those specific problems were never covered by the instructor.

In addition to learning some types of information you may not need right away, you might discover that your job involves aspects of IntranetWare not covered in the CNA program. There are two reasons for this.

First, you may be encountering some of the more advanced, technical issues covered in other courses designed for the CNE program.

Second, your situation may be a less common one, which was simply not covered in either program. Again, this is probably because of the representative nature of the CNA program—the standardized courses attempt to give a broad foundation of knowledge about the most common situations that apply to the highest number of people.

Even if your particular problem isn't covered in the CNA program, the background of knowledge you learned there should help you formulate possible solutions.

Practical Education that Works

In this uncertain economy, where corporations are downsizing and layoffs are occurring with frightening frequency, it's often difficult to predict what skills and training will be in demand over the next few years.

There have been many stories of people who have trained for a skill or earned a degree that turns out to be obsolete (or at least less in demand) when they are finished with their education. This problem also has affected people who have participated in job retraining after a layoff. Too often, their job retraining has prepared them for jobs that will no longer exist when they graduate.

REAL WORLD

Because lawyers have long enjoyed a reputation for being able to charge astronomical fees, drive fancy cars, wear expensive Italian suits, and spend afternoons at the golf course, prospective law students have been flocking to law schools over the past several years without noticing that the law industry was reaching its saturation point. Now, record numbers of graduating law students are reporting that they are having a difficult time finding jobs.

In addition, there are plenty of training programs out there that are catering to fads—certifying people for unique skills that may only have a shelf life of a year or two. This type of training may land you a job for now, but leave you high-and-dry when you've decided to advance your career to the next step.

There is no surefire way to avoid these fates, but with a little planning, you can better your chances at getting training that will stay in demand for a longer period of time. With the rampant growth of computing and communications, network administration appears to be a career choice that will be growing rapidly for many years to come.

Manufacturing jobs are giving way to computerized processes. The Internet is swelling by thousands of users every month. Businesses are looking for new ways to automate their work and increase the speed of communications. All of these trends appear to be gaining in strength, and show no signs of slowing for the foreseeable future.

Because of this growth, network administration (already a strong career choice) appears to be on the upward side of the growth cycle, poised for much more growth over the coming years. Demand for skilled network administrators is increasing daily, and should continue to rise rapidly as business becomes more and more dependent on communication and computerized processes.

With this kind of predicted growth, choosing to pursue a CNA certification now should be a very good move.

Paying for Your CNA Education

How much does it cost to become a CNA? The answer depends on the route you take to "CNA-dom." If you have been working in an IntranetWare networking environment already, and you feel that this book has rounded out your knowledge sufficiently, then you may be able to simply take the exam and receive your authorization. The cost of the exam is in the neighborhood of $85.

However, if you must get more formal education, you may want to look into taking a course from an instructor—either the Novell-authorized course, or a similar course from an independent trainer. In this case, you'll incur some additional expenses.

The suggested retail price of the Novell-authorized, instructor-led *IntranetWare: NetWare 4.11 Administration* course is currently $1,195. The price may vary somewhat. It's really up to the Novell Authorized Education Center (NAEC) that is offering the course.

Courses taught by independent instructors (which are not Novell-authorized) may be a little less expensive.

For many people, paying for the course may not be a problem. If you're fortunate enough to work for a company that understands the value of having a CNA on staff, then you probably will be successful in getting the company to pay for you to attend the necessary courses. Many CNA candidates do work for such an employer. For others, the cost may seem prohibitive at first. Let's look at some of the options you might have for funding your future. Because CNA candidates come from all walks of life, you'll find that the roads they took to get here run all over the map.

FINANCIAL ASSISTANCE

If you don't have the luxury of an employer who's willing to pay for your CNA education, you will probably have to foot the bill yourself.

The good news is, the money you spend on taking the course may be tax-deductible, depending on your particular circumstance. Be sure you do some research or talk to a tax planner about this possibility.

TIP

In the United States, the IRS (Internal Revenue Service) has published a guide to claiming educational deductions on your tax return. To find out more information about this guide, call the IRS at 1-800-TAX-FORM, or write to the IRS Form Distribution Center nearest you. (You can find the address of the nearest office on the income tax package you receive every year.)

Another piece of good news is that you might be able to take advantage of some avenues for financial assistance.

If you're pursuing your CNA certification through a college or university, you may be able to get financial assistance through the school itself. If you aren't going the college route, but still need some financial assistance, you can check into the federal programs that help provide funding for education and job retraining to see if you qualify for those.

In the United States, a variety of federal programs can help provide educational money, such as the Job Training Partnership Act (JTPA) and Trade Adjustment Assistance (TAA). These programs are administered at the state level, and are managed by local employment, job service, and rehabilitation agencies. Because these programs are administered locally, the services they offer may vary from state to state. You can contact any of these agencies in your local area to find out if you qualify for possible financial aid, as well as to find out about any employment opportunities.

TIP

Your local NAEC or NEAP may also be able to point you to some possible sources for financial aid.

If you don't qualify for federal programs, you might try contacting your local banks and credit unions to see if they offer loans (possibly even low-interest student loans) that you can apply toward your educational expenses.

The following sections look at some of the options available in the United States. If you're not in the United States, contact your local government agencies, colleges, and universities for information about similar types of programs in your area.

ZEN

"Education, training and skills [are needed] to seize the opportunities of tomorrow."

President Bill Clinton, 1994 "State of the Union Address"

Financial Aid at School

If you are considering taking the *IntranetWare: NetWare 4.11 Administration* course through a college or university that is an NEAP, be sure you check with the school's financial aid office. You may discover that you are qualified to apply for a possible scholarship, low-interest loan, work-study program, or grant to help you pay for your education.

TIP

For more information about possible sources of financial aid at school, you can get a copy of *The Student Guide* by contacting the Federal Student Aid Information Line at 1-800-433-3243.

In addition, some states have private institutions that may help provide financial assistance to students in matriculated schools. These institutions sometimes offer a variety of scholarships, grants, and fellowships based on religious, sports, or heritage affiliations. To find out if such a program exists in your state, talk to your local job service agency, or look for "College Academic Services" in the white pages of your telephone book.

Job Training Partnership Act (JTPA)

Job Training Partnership Act (JTPA) agencies are designed to help people get the education they need to find employment opportunities. These agencies assist the following types of people:

- Dislocated workers

- Veterans

- Youths and adults who are financially disadvantaged

- Youths and adults whose gross household income is less than government-established poverty levels

If you fall into one of these categories, contact your local job services agency (you can find them listed in the white pages) for information about JTPA programs and eligibility requirements in your area.

JTPA agencies offer financial assistance for education that is designed to land you a full-time career. In addition, they can help you find employment after you've completed your education. Some of the services they provide include:

- On-the-job training

- Classroom and customized training

- Internships

- Resume-writing assistance

- Financial assistance for education

- Help locating educational and professional resources

- Referrals for employment or educational institutions

Trade Adjustment Assistance (TAA)

If you and your co-workers have been displaced by foreign-import competition, you may qualify for additional unemployment insurance, job retraining, and financial assistance for job search and relocation expenses.

The Trade Adjustment Assistance (TAA) program was designed to help workers in the United States who have lost their jobs as a direct consequence of foreign import competition.

TIP

To be considered for TAA funds, an employer, a group of employees, or an employee representative (such as a labor union) must file a petition with the Department of Labor. If the Department of Labor finds that the claim is valid, the employees (and possibly the employer) can receive TAA services.

The North American Free Trade Agreement (NAFTA) is also connected with TAA. It specifies that employees who lost their jobs because of trade with Mexico or Canada, and who meet eligibility requirements, can receive similar NAFTA benefits.

If you think that you and your co-workers or your employer could be eligible for TAA assistance, contact your local job services agency. Ask for the TAA Coordinator for your state, who will be able to help you find out if you're eligible for TAA services.

Private Industry Councils (PICs)

Private Industry Councils (PICs) are organizations that control how funding is allocated for various government programs. Each PIC is made up of both government representatives and local business representatives. These people act as a governing board that approves contracts for state-allocated money targeted toward lower-income and disadvantaged people.

Because the PIC is run by both government and business representatives, theoretically a balance is maintained for determining the most appropriate and practical funding levels for the programs.

PICs represent many types of government programs. Job services, vocational rehabilitation, and JTPA are a few examples of these programs. For more information about possible opportunities or financial assistance through these or other programs, call your local PIC (listed in the white pages under "Private Industry Council").

Veterans' Administration

If you are a veteran, you should certainly check with your local Veterans' Affairs office for information about any Veterans' programs you may be eligible for. Veterans' programs exist that can provide assistance with education, job training, and vocational rehabilitation. The services you qualify to receive may vary, depending on such factors as your length of service, type of discharge, or a service-related disability.

Advancing Your Career

As a CNA, what are your options for the future?

Immediately, of course, you can apply your knowledge toward managing an IntranetWare network for your company. The longer you experience the hands-on joys of network administration, the more you learn and the more valuable you will become as an employee.

But you may be wondering where you and the networking industry are headed in the future. Let's dust off the crystal ball and take a stab at some possibilities.

ZEN

"Never assume the obvious is true."

William Safire

CURRENT OUTLOOK FOR THE NETWORKING INDUSTRY

Today's international forecast calls for widespread growth of the networking industry, increasing demand for people who understand networking, and widely scattered areas of specialization—an enticing forecast for prospective CNAs.

Want a more specific forecast? Okay. Pick up any recent survey on job trends for the next ten years or so. Then look through the top jobs. In almost all the recent surveys that have been coming out, jobs relating directly to computing (such as programmers, analysts, and IS personnel) are appearing in the highest-growth categories. Of those jobs that don't specifically deal with computing, most of them require knowledge of computers and software to get the job done.

The world is quickly being engulfed in a tightly woven network of communication. The sheer number of people that will be required to maintain that network is staggering.

Whereas large companies once were the bastion of computer and networking professionals, now everyone from your friendly neighborhood dentist, to your local car dealer, to your small-town church's office worker wants to connect up and dial in to the networked world. All of those businesses need help.

People are already answering the call for qualified networking professionals in large numbers. The CNA program is the fastest growing certification program around. About 10,000 to 12,000 new CNAs are certified every quarter, and the numbers are still growing.

REAL WORLD

Advice from a real-world CNA, on becoming a CNA: "Go for it! We may have to hire a computer person in the future and we would be looking for someone with CNA certification. The world is becoming more and more networked and it needs people *with* that expertise to guide those without."

This isn't just a North American phenomenon, either. Approximately 30 percent of the CNAs being certified as of this book's writing are from outside of the United States and Canada. That number is expected to grow sharply. Because the CNA program was introduced first in the United States, the rest of the world is still considered an emerging market.

The number of CNAs in Asia and Australia is growing incredibly fast. The European market is a little more mature, but numbers there are still growing dramatically. The worldwide growth rate is very impressive.

Does this mean the market will be saturated soon? Probably not. As fast as the CNA numbers are growing, the number of people and devices being hooked up together via computers and communication channels is outpacing them.

CURRENT OUTLOOK FOR YOUR FUTURE

Even if the market for network administration skills is keeping pace (or outpacing) the number of CNAs available, you can't rest on your laurels if you want to stay marketable over the long haul.

Any certification has a limited shelf life, whether it is a CNA certificate or an engineering degree from the best university. These days, with the lightening speed of growth in the networking and computing industry, it's easy to feel like your entire base of knowledge and skills are obsolete in just a few years. You must take steps to ensure that this doesn't happen to you. Continuing education is vital.

ZEN

*"How we wish we were sunning ourselves
In a world of familiar views."*

Mark Strand, *Reasons for Moving*

The best way to plan out your continuing education needs is to consider your career goals over the long run. Today's goal is to become a network administrator. But then what? Where do you want to go next? Where do you want to be 10 or 20 years from now?

A Career in Network Administration

If network administration is right up your alley, and that's where you want to concentrate on building your career, then you must plan how you will stay current with networking technology over the coming years. For example, as Novell introduces future products, you will probably want to educate yourself in them and recertify on those products.

ZEN

"Even an old cow deserves a new cowbell."

Texas Bix Bender, *Laughing Stock, A Cow's Guide to Life*

Additionally, you will most likely find that a great deal of your time as a CNA isn't just devoted to managing the IntranetWare side of the network. Chances are very good that you'll exert a considerable amount of energy working with the applications that your users want to use. Staying current on those applications is vital.

Various software manufacturers offer certification programs for their specific applications.

Upping the Ante

As you begin to delve deeper into the technical workings of your network, you may decide that you want to focus more on design, strategy, and growth aspects of networking technologies. Perhaps you want to expand your depth of knowledge about IntranetWare networking and advance up the career ladder to IS professional or possibly become a consultant.

If this is the case, you may decide to pursue a CNE, or Master CNE, certification.

ZEN

"Here's the thing with decisions. I can make them. I just don't feel sure about them afterward."

Paul Reiser, *Couplehood*

CNEs are capable of handling jobs where they spend less time managing day-to-day network operations, and more time dealing with the larger, more technical issues of IntranetWare network management. For example, CNEs are often involved in network design, installation, implementation, and troubleshooting. CNEs specialize in various Novell products (such as IntranetWare or GroupWare), so that they can concentrate on developing their skills in those critical areas.

To become a CNE, you take additional classes and exams to learn (and demonstrate) advanced techniques and skills for planning and implementing IntranetWare networks in any size organization.

ZEN

"Never say you don't have enough time. You have exactly the same number of hours per day that were given to Helen Keller, Pasteur, Michelangelo, Mother Theresa, Leonardo da Vinci, Thomas Jefferson, and Albert Einstein."

H. Jackson Brown, Jr., *Life's Little Instruction Book*

The *IntranetWare: NetWare 4.11 Administration* exam, which you must pass to receive your CNA certification, is one of the required classes for an IntranetWare CNE certification. Therefore, you've already knocked one requirement off the list to becoming a CNE. Aren't you the clever one?

As a CNE, you may be able to move up in the IS hierarchy, moving into positions requiring greater technical backgrounds, and allowing you to get your hands into some of the more challenging technical aspects of networking. In addition, CNEs are often on the cutting edge of research, exploring new technologies and finding ways to keep their organizations in the fast lane.

A Master CNE has taken his or her education as a networking professional to an even higher level. Master CNEs declare a "graduate major" while they're pursuing their certification. These areas of specialization delve deeper into the integration- and solution-oriented aspects of running a network than the CNE level.

While CNEs provide support at the operating system and application levels, Master CNEs are expected to manage advanced access, management, and workgroup integration for multiple environments. Master CNEs can support complex networks that span several different platforms, and can perform upgrades, migration, and integration for various systems.

Periodically, as Novell introduces new generations of its products, Novell Education requires existing CNEs and Master CNEs to update their certification by learning about and demonstrating their proficiency in these new products. The need for such recertification is obvious. Without recertifying on new products, your skills can become dated, and your certification begins to lose its value.

A Stepping Stone to Other Careers

Of course, nothing says you must spend the rest of your life directly managing networks. Network administration may turn out to be the stepping stone that opens entirely new doors to you.

As we already mentioned, it is becoming increasingly difficult to find a good-paying job in a growing career field that isn't somehow tied into computers. Everywhere you look, knowledge of computers and how they affect your business and your life is becoming more and more important.

Being a network administrator can help you build that foundation of knowledge about business communications, tools, and resources. This background will become invaluable in nearly any aspect of the business world you pursue, whether you start your own business, hop onto a fast-growing startup company, or join a well-established organization.

Another benefit is that if you wisely apply the knowledge and skills you used to get your CNA certification, you will ideally establish a good reputation as a professional who is competent and productive. That reputation may help future employers recognize your ability to take on responsibilities in their organizations, even if the job they are offering is in a completely different area from network administration.

As with any certification, degree, or diploma, it is important to realize that what you make of that piece of paper is up to you. It will never be a free lunch ticket by itself. You must back up its validity by plunging into the real-world aspects of the field. Hard work, talent, skill, and knowledge go hand-in-hand with certification. With that combination, you will definitely have a strong edge over most of the rest of your competition.

ZEN

"Now I know a refuge never grows
From a chin in a hand in a thoughtful pose,
Got to tend the earth if you want a rose."

Indigo Girls

A Day in the Life of a CNA

If you're a prospective CNA, you might be wondering what typical CNAs do during the day. How do they spend the bulk of their time? What kinds of situations and tasks do they face on a daily basis? Just what, exactly, are you in for?

If you're already a CNA, you may wonder if you're typical. Do other CNAs do the same types of jobs? Do they have the same problems? Have they set up their work processes the same way you have?

You're probably hoping this chapter will definitively answer these questions, aren't you?

Well, you know that there's no such thing as "typical" in this industry. How you manage a network will depend on many things, such as

▸ Your network's size—Are you managing the network for a dentist's office or for a Fortune 500 company?

▸ Your experience—Are you new to this whole networking thing, or have you been running networks and troubleshooting PCs for years?

▸ Your user's needs—Do they just want to run a few applications and print on a single printer, or do they want to have access to a continuously changing and dizzying array of network resources?

▸ Your job description—Are you responsible for installing new workstations and printers, or do you just handle tasks such as helping users figure out their word processing problems?

▸ Your personality—Are you an organized, methodical person or a seat-of-your-pants adventurer?

No single approach to network administration will completely please everyone, of course. However, in this chapter, we'll look at some of the processes commonly used by CNAs.

Sometimes just seeing how other people work and solve problems will help you come up with your own plans. Even though those plans may differ, they are most likely rooted in the same principles.

ZEN

"To really succeed in a business or organization, it is sometimes helpful to know what your job is, and whether it involves any duties."

Dave Barry, *Claw Your Way to the Top*

Where Do CNAs Fit in the Organization?

CNAs tend to be the front-line of support for network users. When users have a problem, the first person they call is the CNA. The CNA can handle routine matters, such as creating new user accounts, resetting a user's password, or getting the user's application to print. When the user's problem or situation calls for more technical expertise than the CNA is able to offer, the CNA generally calls on a second line of support for help.

In small companies, the CNA may be the only network administrator on site. If a problem comes up that the CNA can't handle, the CNA may have to call outside support (such as the reseller, a consultant, or the software or hardware manufacturer).

ZEN

"I have personally, with my bare hands, changed my "WIN.INI" and "CONFIG.SYS" settings. This may not mean much to you, but trust me, it is a major data-processing accomplishment. Albert Einstein died without ever doing it. ("Wait a minute!" were his last words. "It erased my equation! It was 'E' equals something!")"

Dave Barry

In a large company, the second line of support may be someone up the hierarchy in the Information Services (IS) department. CNEs often fill these types of roles. The second line of support may handle issues such as new network designs, larger-scale network upgrades, tricky problems that are difficult to track down, and so on.

Another characteristic of CNAs that you might find in larger companies is that the CNAs may be divided up into specialty areas. Certain CNAs might deal with all the spreadsheet issues, for example. Another group of CNAs may cover all the word processing problems. This type of specialization allows users to get answers to their questions more rapidly, because the CNAs are able to focus their attention on those particular areas.

This type of organization also allows the CNAs to add another area of expertise—namely application experience—to their arsenal of networking knowledge. Figure 2.1 illustrates how one company might organize its IS group to handle user problems and manage the company's overall network.

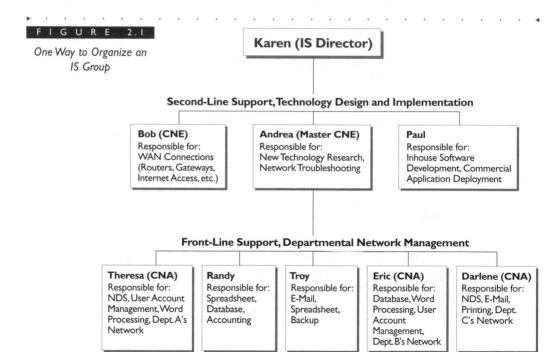

FIGURE 2.1

One Way to Organize an
IS Group

Karen (IS Director)

Second-Line Support, Technology Design and Implementation

Bob (CNE)
Responsible for:
WAN Connections
(Routers, Gateways,
Internet Access, etc.)

Andrea (Master CNE)
Responsible for:
New Technology Research,
Network Troubleshooting

Paul
Responsible for:
Inhouse Software
Development, Commercial
Application Deployment

Front-Line Support, Departmental Network Management

Theresa (CNA)
Responsible for:
NDS, User Account
Management, Word
Processing, Dept. A's
Network

Randy
Responsible for:
Spreadsheet,
Database,
Accounting

Troy
Responsible for:
E-Mail,
Spreadsheet,
Backup

Eric (CNA)
Responsible for:
Database, Word
Processing, User
Account
Management,
Dept. B's Network

Darlene (CNA)
Responsible for:
NDS, E-Mail,
Printing, Dept.
C's Network

In a smaller company, the lone CNA is generally a jack-of-all-trades, with responsibility for a variety of applications in addition to the regular IntranetWare features.

Common Day-to-Day Activities

As a network administrator, your primary job responsibility is to keep the network running smoothly so that your users can maintain a high level of productivity. If users aren't productive, management tends to get a little testy, and your job gets a little more high-profile than you might like.

ZEN

"Technology has met its promise of reducing our workload. It does this primarily by preventing us from doing any work at all."

from the "Dilbert" comic strip

In order to keep your users productive

▸ You make sure the network is set up logically so that users can easily get to the network resources they need when they need them, and so that you can easily manage those resources.

▸ After the network is set up logically, you monitor it regularly to make sure it continues to be most efficient for your users. An organization's needs can change over time (with reorganizations, new job priorities, the introduction of new technologies or applications, and so on). Your network may need to change with the organization.

▸ You prioritize and solve network problems quickly. The longer it takes for you to solve network problems, the less productive your users are.

▸ You minimize the amount of time you spend trying to teach users how to use the network.

▸ You find ways to streamline your work processes, so that you spend less of your own time trying to deal with network issues. Remember, your own productivity is important, too.

For many CNAs, these types of network-management tasks fall into two basic job responsibilities:

▸ Routine maintenance/periodic housekeeping

▸ User support

The next sections discuss some of the types of activities that fall into these two categories. Again, you may not be responsible for all of these types of tasks in your current job, but who knows where your career will take you?

Routine Maintenance and Housekeeping

If you own a car, you know that routine maintenance can be the key to extending the life of the car and avoiding costly, unnecessary repairs. You know that, on a regular basis, you must change the oil, check the transmission fluid level, refill the windshield fluid reservoir, rotate the tires, make sure there's enough water in the radiator, change the spark plugs, and so on.

REAL WORLD

It's not absolutely necessary to do routine automobile maintenance on a regular basis, of course. You could just drive the car until pieces start falling off or catching fire. However, that generally isn't the most efficient way to take care of the vehicle. It tends to be a mite expensive, too. Buying a new engine every couple of years is more expensive and more annoying than getting the oil changed every 3,000 miles.

In some ways, the same principle applies to your network. Many types of tasks, if done on a regular basis, will help you stay a few steps ahead of problems.

For example, suppose your server's disk space is gradually getting filled up with users' work. Rest assured, even if you don't do routine maintenance on your network, you'll know when the server runs out of disk space—you'll suddenly have users hysterically calling you, demanding to know why they can't open files or create new ones. You may spend several hours or days finding a new disk and getting the appropriate signatures required to pay for it, and then more time installing it when you finally get your hands on it.

On the other hand, if you make it a habit to periodically spend a few moments monitoring the amount of disk space being used on your server, you can estimate when you'll need to add a new hard disk. If you know ahead of time when to add a new disk, you can have it ordered, installed, and working long before the crisis point. Disaster will have been averted, and your users will quietly continue being productive.

REAL WORLD

Naturally, there will always be the unusual occurrences that create problems, which even the most rigid maintenance regime won't prevent. For example, rotating the tires and keeping them inflated at the correct pressure won't prevent you from driving over a nail. However, with regular maintenance, you may very well reduce the number of additional problems you do have to face—such as discovering that your spare tire is flat.

What types of routine maintenance and periodic housecleaning should you do? The following sections offer some suggestions.

CHECKING UNDER THE HOOD (MAINTAINING THE HARDWARE)

Periodically, you must "check under the hood" to see how the hardware is holding up. You may need to upgrade some pieces of hardware, replace worn items, or add new machinery to accommodate new needs.

A common hardware-related activity is to add new equipment (such as printers or workstations) to your network. As new employees join your organization, you must install new workstations for them to use. If several more employees join, your old printer may not be enough to keep up with printing demands, so you might add a new printer to meet the needs of the new users.

In addition to installing new equipment, you will likely find yourself upgrading existing equipment. Each year, new applications seem to require more memory and disk space, requiring you to add memory and larger hard disks to your current workstations.

Workers who use those workstations have bigger requirements, too—they may want to simply trade in the older computers for faster workstations. They may also start requesting better-quality printers, higher-speed modems, better plotters, and so on. Your old backup system may soon start looking like a dinosaur to you, too, and you'll find yourself hankering after a new one.

ZEN

"The only difference between men and boys is the cost of their toys."

Anonymous

Because of these ever-increasing hardware needs (okay, some are just desires), you'll want to keep up on the latest trends in computer equipment. You must make sure you know about the hardware you already have installed. Take the time to study the hardware settings and to understand what hardware requirements will satisfy the various demands of your users.

Keep records of the equipment currently installed, so that you can predict which machines may need to be upgraded soon. This will help you plan your yearly equipment budget, as well as be proactive in keeping users (and management) happy.

Another area that will bear some attention is the lowly network cabling, and its related hardware. Network cabling and network boards are notorious problem areas. Loose connections and broken wires plague the cables themselves. Network boards seem to spontaneously fizzle. Familiarize yourself with all the types of cabling hardware and network boards on your network, so that you know what types of connectors and terminators, for example, you might need when you're installing a new computer.

Another important recommendation is to keep an adequate supply of spare parts on hand. Keep extra network boards, cables, and connecting hardware handy and clearly labeled.

If you're not sure it's worth the expense to keep spare parts around, calculate the cost of the downtime for a single user, should that user's network board die. If it will take three days to order and receive a new network board, and the user can't work on the workstation for those three days, what will the three days of downtime cost? If three days of lost time costs less than the price of a network board, then you don't need to keep a spare on hand.

In most cases, however, you'll probably find that having an extra board or two available is a negligible expense for a much larger potential gain. Cables and connecting hardware are usually even less expensive, so there's really little reason not to have a ready supply.

REFUELING THE TANK (ADDING TO SERVER CAPACITY)

As your network grows (both in the number of users and in the type of usage it's getting), you'll want to monitor the server's memory and hard disk capacity.

One of the most common causes of server performance problems is a lack of adequate memory in the server. If the network seems to be operating slowly, or if you don't have enough memory to load NLMs, you may need to simply add more RAM to the server.

You should make it a habit to periodically use the Cache Utilization screen of the MONITOR NLM utility to track the percentage of Long Term Cache Hits. If Long Term Cache Hits shows less than 90 percent consistently, you should add more RAM to the server.

You can also use the MEMORY and MEMORY MAP console utilities to see how much memory the server is using.

TIP

If you can't add more RAM right away, but you still need to make more memory available to NLMs so that they can run, you can use the following temporary solution. Use SERVMAN.NLM to change the Minimum File Cache Buffers and Maximum Directory Cache Buffers parameters. By changing these parameters, you can limit the amount of memory available for file and directory caching, and give that memory to the NLMs. After you change these parameters, reboot the server to make the changes take effect. Remember, only use this as a temporary solution until you can add more RAM to the server.

TIP

If you're using an ISA bus or PCI bus in the server, remember to use the REGISTER MEMORY console utility to register any memory above 16 MB for an ISA bus, or 64 MB for a PCI bus.

Hard disk space on the server is important real estate for your users. If the disk fills up, the users won't be able to open existing files, let alone create new ones. Therefore, it's important to monitor the amount of disk space still available for each volume on your server. By tracking the available disk space, you can predict when you'll have to either clean old files off the server, or add a new hard disk.

TIP

To see how much available disk space a volume has, use the NetWare Administrator utility from a workstation. From the NetWare Administrator's Browser screen, select a volume, then choose Details from the Object menu. When the volume's Details page opens, click on the Statistics page button. The Statistics page will show you how much disk space is still free for the volume to use.

PURSUING HIGH PERFORMANCE (TRACKING HOW THE SERVER RUNS)

Obviously, you want your vehicle to be performing at the highest possible level. Your average mileage per gallon increases, mechanical parts last longer, and your engine sounds really cool at stop lights.

You can keep your server's performance tweaked so that it performs at top levels, too. It might not draw envious looks from passersby, but it will still give you a warm feeling that everything is working well.

When you monitor the server's performance, you look for key indicators that the server is functioning at an optimal level. Some of the things you should monitor include the utilization percentage of the server's processor, the number of cache buffers being regularly used, and the server's memory allocation.

Every network has different needs and usage patterns. By default, server parameters are set so that the server will perform well on most networks, but it's a good idea to monitor the server's performance periodically anyway. By doing so, you can track how your server performs under different conditions, discover potential problems, and make improvements.

TIP

Server parameters (also called SET parameters) are aspects of the server that control things such as how buffers are allocated and used, how memory is used, and so on. You can change these parameters by loading SERVMAN.NLM, or by typing the full SET command at the server's console prompt. Using SERVMAN.NLM is much easier, because you can select the SET parameters you want from menus, and SERVMAN will automatically save the command in the correct server startup file. For more information about SERVMAN, see Chapter 7.

The server will optimize itself over a period of time by leveling adjustments for low usage times with peak usage bursts. Over a day or two, the server will have allocated an optimal number of buffers for each parameter, such as packet receive buffers. If you shut down the server and reboot it, the server will automatically be reset to the default allocation for all parameters.

To speed up the optimization period, record the allocations after one or two days of server usage, then set the given parameters to the recorded values. To set these parameters, use SERVMAN.NLM to select the parameters and change them. Then, when you exit SERVMAN, it will ask you if you want to save the new settings in the STARTUP.NCF and AUTOEXEC.NCF files. Say "Yes," so that these settings will be executed by those files the next time the server is booted.

REAL WORLD

You will probably want to monitor how the server's processor is being utilized by various processes, and how cache buffers and packet receive buffers are being used.

Monitoring Processor Utilization

If one or more server processes monopolize the server's CPU, the server's performance can be degraded, or other processes may have trouble running appropriately.

To see the total percentage utilization of the processor, load MONITOR.NLM and note the percentage in the Utilization field. (This field is in the General Information screen that appears when MONITOR is first loaded.) If the utilization is high, one or more processes may be monopolizing CPU time.

Use MONITOR's Scheduling Information screen to list all server processes and to see which ones have consistently high Load values. If you want to change some of the values on the Schedules Information screen use the plus and minus keys to increase or decrease the values displayed in the Sch Delay column. Experiment with SCHDELAY times until the CPU load value is acceptable.

Put the SCHDELAY command in the server's AUTOEXEC.NCF file to keep it in effect if you reboot the server.

Monitoring Cache Buffers

If directory searches are slow, you may need to change some SET parameters to increase the allocation and use of directory cache buffers. Use SERVMAN.NLM to change the following SET parameters that relate to directory cache buffers: Directory Cache Allocation Wait Time, Maximum Directory Cache Buffers, and Minimum Directory Cache Buffers.

If disk writes are slow, use MONITOR's General Information screen to see if more than 70 percent of the cache buffers are "dirty" cache buffers. Dirty cache buffers are the file blocks in the server's memory containing information that has not yet been written to disk, but needs to be. Then use SERVMAN.NLM to increase the Maximum Concurrent Disk Cache Writes, Maximum Concurrent Directory Cache Writes, Dirty Directory Cache Delay Time, or Dirty Disk Cache Delay Time parameters.

Monitoring Packet Receive Buffers

If the server seems to be slowing down or losing workstation connections, use MONITOR's General Information screen to see how many packet receive buffers are allocated and how many are being used. If the allocated number is higher than 10, but the server doesn't respond immediately when rebooted, or if you are using EISA or microchannel bus master boards in your server and "No ECB available" error messages appear after the server boots, you may need to increase the minimum number of packet receive buffers. To do this, use SERVMAN.NLM to increase the SET parameter Minimum Packet Receive Buffers so that each board in the server can have at least five buffers.

You can also increase the Maximum Packet Receive Buffers parameter in increments of 10 until you have one buffer per workstation. (Again, if you are using EISA or microchannel bus master boards in your server increase this parameter until each board can have at least five buffers.)

After a couple of days of average network usage, use MONITOR to see how many packet receive buffers are being allocated, and compare that with the maximum number. If the two numbers are the same, increase the maximum value by 50 buffers. Continue to monitor the buffers periodically and increase the maximum value until the allocated number no longer matches the maximum.

When you've determined the optimal maximum number of packet receive buffers for your system, use SERVMAN to set both the maximum and minimum values in AUTOEXEC.NCF, so that the server can quickly optimize to these values if it is rebooted.

(See Chapter 7 for more information about SERVMAN.NLM.)

ACCOMMODATING PASSENGERS (MANAGING USER ACCOUNTS)

Occasionally, you will have to add, delete, or change user accounts. These are very common, routine types of tasks for CNAs.

When you add a new user to your network, you will need to do more than simply create a user account for that person. Some of the things you may have to set up include:

- ▶ The user's Novell Directory Services (NDS) account, which is an object for the user, with the object's related properties (information) filled in (such as the user's last name, full name, telephone number, and so on). You'll learn more about NDS in Chapter 3.

- ▶ The user's group memberships

- ▶ A home directory for the user's individual files

- ▶ A login script that maps drives to the directories and applications to which the user will need access

- ▸ NDS trustee rights (to control how the user can see and use other NDS objects in the tree)

- ▸ File system trustee rights to the files and directories with which the user needs to work (to regulate the user's access and activities in those files and directories)

- ▸ Account restrictions, if necessary, to control when the user logs in, how often the user must change passwords, and so on

- ▸ An e-mail account, if necessary

- ▸ Access to the network printers

- ▸ A menu program to prevent the user from having to use commands at the DOS prompt

When a user leaves the organization, you'll need to delete the user's account, and clean out any files the user owned. After allowing the user's manager to determine if any of the files should be transferred to another user, you'll want to delete the user's remaining directories, e-mail files, and so on.

In addition to managing user accounts, you will also manage group accounts. A *group* is simply a collection of users. You can create groups of users to allow you to quickly assign identical characteristics (such as trustee rights to a certain directory) to a large number of users at once. Every so often, you will need to update groups to add new users, delete old users, change a group's access rights to an application or directory, and so on.

Some of your most common cries for help probably will be from users who have forgotten their passwords. You can reset their passwords for them by using the NetWare Administrator utility.

All these routine tasks are described in more detail in Chapter 5, "IntranetWare Security."

TESTING THE ANTI-THEFT SYSTEM (MONITORING SECURITY)

Your network's security can be vital to your organization. Banks must ensure that all their data is completely secure from intruders. Schools must ensure that students can't get in to alter grades or records. Lawyers must protect their client-attorney privileges. Doctors must protect the privacy of their patients.

Even if you don't think you work in a high-risk organization, you should still use some forms of network security. For example, you'll probably want to make sure important files don't get deleted accidentally. And then, of course, users often succumb to that temptation to try to see those payroll files.

The five primary types of security features in IntranetWare are

- ▶ Login and password authentication, which ensures that only authorized users can log in to the network

- ▶ Login restrictions, which control how those authorized users can log in (such as restricting the times of day they can log in, specifying how often they must change their passwords, and so on)

- ▶ NDS security, which controls whether NDS objects (such as users) can see or manipulate other NDS objects and their properties

- ▶ File system access rights, which control whether users can see and work with files and directories

- ▶ Directory and file attributes, which protect individual files and directories from various types of user actions

As part of your normal CNA duties, you will probably be responsible for ensuring that the network security features are all being used wisely. When new users are added to the network, you'll make sure they have the access rights they need (and *only* the rights they need) to the appropriate files and NDS objects.

 ZEN

"My current computer, in addition to 'DOS,' has 'Windows,' which is another invention of Bill Gates, designed as a security measure to thwart those users who are somehow able to get past 'DOS.' You have to be a real stud hombre cybermuffin to handle 'Windows.'"

Dave Barry

You'll also want to take a few minutes every once in a while to go through your important files, directories, or NDS objects to verify that everyone who has rights to those items still needs those rights.

For more information about how to set up and manage network security, see Chapter 5, "IntranetWare Security."

GETTING BACK ON TRACK (BACKING UP FILES)

Suppose you're driving along the freeway, and you miss your exit. In most cases, you have three choices.

First, you can keep going and end up someplace completely different. While this might be an enticing adventure in some cases, if you were headed to Aunt Myrtle and Uncle Fred's golden wedding anniversary, you might not be real popular at the next family gathering.

Second, you could go all the way back home, and start the whole trip over again.

Third, you could return to a point just before you missed the turn-off, and then complete the trip as planned. You'll have backtracked a little, but at least you didn't have to start way back at your front door.

If you chose one of the first two options, you're probably an interesting person to know, but you may not be quite cut out for network management responsibilities.

The third option, of course, is the most efficient. You can get to where you were originally headed, with a minimum of wasted effort.

This is exactly why you make backups of your network files. If your server hard disk crashes and you must replace it, you're going to get a gold star if you can restore the network to where it was yesterday, so that only a few hours of work are lost.

We won't discuss what you get if you don't have backups, and all of the past year's work is lost irretrievably. One of your most important duties as a CNA will be to ensure that network backups are performed regularly (at a minimum, once a week).

ZEN

"When things go wrong, don't go with them."

Texas Bix Bender, Laughing Stock, A Cow's Guide to Life

Remember that backups are only useful if they can actually be restored. Therefore, you'll also want to periodically test your restoring processes during nice, calm, nonemergency situations.

For more information about using the backup software in IntranetWare, called SBACKUP, see Chapter 7, "IntranetWare Management."

ADDING NEW ACCESSORIES (INSTALLING APPLICATIONS)

Another aspect of being a CNA is application management. This is the art and science of keeping up with the latest applications that your users need. You'll be installing new applications, upgrading existing ones, and deleting old ones. Then, of course, you must also make sure they all play nicely together once you have them installed.

After a network is up and running smoothly, most of the problems users will report to you will be application-related. Printing problems are common, so you'll want to pay particular attention to how the applications use print drivers, and which print queues the applications are set up to use.

You must also be very familiar with how the applications get installed, both on the server and on individual workstations. Then, you'll need to know how to set up a workstation to access the application.

ZEN

"I have spent countless hours trying to get my computer to perform even the most basic data-processing functions, such as letting me play 'F-117A Stealth Fighter' on it."

Dave Barry

HITTING THE CAR WASH (CLEANING UP THE FILE SYSTEM)

Nothing uses up hard disk space on the server like files do. Okay, maybe that was a little too obvious. But disk space on the server can become in short supply quickly, if your users aren't scrupulous about making sure they only keep important files in their directories.

REAL WORLD

Chances of your users being scrupulous about weeding out obsolete files are about the same odds as having the Boston Red Sox win the SuperBowl. Most users simply don't play that game.

It will probably fall on your shoulders to peruse your file system on a regular basis, looking for obsolete directories or files that could be removed. Now, this doesn't mean that you should go prying through users' files. Not at all. You are the keeper of file security on the network. Don't abuse that security yourself.

All we're recommending is that you look for general areas that could be redundant or obsolete, such as application directories that contain old versions of applications that no one is using anymore. Also, make sure users who no longer work in your organization don't have old directories hanging around.

ZEN

"If you haven't used it in the last three years, throw it out!"

Your mother

If your network has directories divided up by projects, see if there are old project files that you can archive onto another medium (such as backup tapes) and remove the originals from the server's hard disk.

You can also send messages to your users, asking them to take some time to go through their own files and delete the unnecessary ones.

In IntranetWare, when files are deleted, they aren't really erased from the disk right away. The file system keeps those files in a salvageable state, so that you can restore them if you need to. IntranetWare will keep these deleted-but-not-gone files around until it begins to run out of disk space. Then it will purge these files from the disk to make more room available for new files. The deleted files are purged in chronological order, so that the ones that were deleted first are purged first.

You may not want all these files to stay on your server in a salvageable state. There may be some files you want to purge immediately whenever they are deleted, or you may want to purge files before the server gets filled to the point where it does it automatically. As part of your routine maintenance tasks, you may want to purge older files to free up disk space.

TIP

To set files or directories so that they are purged immediately when they are deleted, mark those files or directories with the Purge Immediate directory and file attributes. These attributes are explained in Chapter 5, "IntranetWare Security."

To purge files manually, use the NetWare Administrator utility (also called NWADMIN), the FILER utility (a DOS-based menu utility), or PURGE (a command line utility). These utilities are explained in Chapter 4, "IntranetWare File System."

LISTENING TO THOSE KNOCKS AND PINGS (MONITORING THE ERROR LOGS)

As the IntranetWare server goes about its merry way each day, it generously keeps log files of any error messages or event notifications that might occur. Because you are probably not sitting at the server console watching the screen 24 hours a day, reading these logs are the easiest way for you to see what you might have missed.

TIP

Not every error message that appears on the screen indicates a real problem with which you must deal. Many messages are simply normal status messages that indicate when a particular event or task occurs. The server might be keeping right on track, running the network just like it's supposed to.

Periodically, such as once a week (or more frequently if you suspect a problem), you should read these error log files to monitor how your network is doing.

You can read four different error log files:

▸ SYS$LOG.ERR logs error messages for the server. It is stored in the server's SYS:SYSTEM directory. All the messages or errors that appear on the server's console are stored in this file.

▸ VOL$LOG.ERR logs error messages for a volume. Each volume has its own log file, which is stored at the root of the volume. Any errors or messages that pertain to the volume are stored in this file.

▸ TTS$LOG.ERR logs all data that is backed out by the IntranetWare Transaction Tracking System (TTS). This file is stored in the SYS: volume. To allow this file to be created, use SERVMAN.NLM to turn the TTS Abort Dump Flag parameter to On. (For more information about using SERVMAN.NLM, see Chapter 7, "IntranetWare Management.")

▸ CONSOLE.LOG is a file that can capture all console messages during system initialization. To capture messages in this file, type the following in the AUTOEXEC.NCF file:

```
CONLOG.NLM
```

CONSOLE.LOG is stored in the SYS:ETC directory. To stop capturing messages in this file, type **UNLOAD CONLOG** at the server console.

To view any of these error log files, you can either use a text editor from a workstation, or you can use EDIT.NLM from the server. Figure 2.2 shows a portion of an example SYS$LOG.ERR file for a server.

F I G U R E   2.2

Example SYS$LOG.ERR

TIP

To use **EDIT.NLM,** type LOAD EDIT at the server console, then specify the path and name of the desired log file. See **Chapter 7, "IntranetWare Management,"** for more information about using **EDIT.NLM.**

TIP

To limit the size of the **CONSOLE.LOG** file, you can specify its maximum size in the command that loads **CONLOG.NLM.** In addition, you can specify that the previous **CONSOLE.LOG** file be saved under a different name. For example, to specify that the previous file be saved and named **LOG.SAV,** and to limit the new **CONSOLE.LOG** file to be no more than 100K in size, you would type LOAD CONLOG SAVE=LOG.SAV MAXIMUM=100.

To limit the size of the other three error log files (**SYS$LOG.ERR, VOL$LOG.ERR,** and **TTS$LOG.ERR**), use **SERVMAN.NLM** to change the approprlate **SET** parameters. Server Log File Overflow Size=*number* lets you specify the maximum size (in kilobytes) that the **SYS$LOG.ERR** file can become. Likewise, Volume Log File Overflow Size=*number* sets the maximum size for **VOL$LOG.ERR,** and Volume TTS Log File Overflow Size=*number* sets the maximum size for **TTS$LOG.ERR.**

TIP

To specify what happens to a log file when it reaches the maximum size, use **SERVMAN.NLM** to change the **Server Log File State=***number* parameter, the **Volume Log File State=***number* parameter, or the **Volume TTS Log File State=***number* parameter. With these parameters, replace *number* with **0** (leaves the log file in its current state), **1** (deletes the log file), or **2** (renames the log file and starts a new one). The default is **1**. For more information about using **SERVMAN.NLM**, see Chapter 7, "IntranetWare Management."

User Support

As a CNA, ideally you'd like to keep the network running so smoothly that your users never have a single problem or questions. However, being users, they will tend to thwart your best efforts. They insist on forgetting their passwords from time to time. They decide they want to learn a new application. They tinker with their printing setup.

Sometimes, the user's software or hardware gets into the act, as well. A workstation will develop memory problems. A newly installed application will modify a workstation file in a way that conflicts with another application. A cable will get stepped on one too many times and the wires inside it will break.

REAL WORLD

The best-laid network plans of mice and CNAs can't prevent all the problems that users will have. That's why a significant portion of your job as a CNA will most likely be spent supporting your users.

If user support is one of your tasks, you must decide how you can deal with user problems most efficiently. If you don't already belong to a formal "Help Desk" department, setting one up (even if the "Help Desk" is just you) might be beneficial in helping you stay on top of user problems and helping your users get the support they need.

If you are responsible for user training, you will most likely want to standardize how you train them.

Occasionally, Help Desks are also responsible for training, but in most cases, those are separate functions. CNAs may find themselves in either area, however.

HOW DOES A HELP DESK WORK?

If you work in a large organization, you may be part of a formal "Help Desk" department. Help Desks (which may be called by different names) usually have a set of front-line people, such as CNAs, whom users contact when they encounter a problem.

The front-line Help Desk personnel are trained to handle most common problems. They may fix problems over the phone, or they may dispatch someone to go to the user's site to resolve the issue. If the problem is more than the front-line people can handle, the problem may get escalated to a second line of support — people who have even more technical backgrounds in that area (such as CNEs).

Even if you're a one-person Help Desk, you probably have the same basic situation. Users contact you for help, then you try to solve their problem. If it's something you need help with, you call in another expert, which may be someone in another department, an outside consultant, the manufacturer, or so on.

In a nutshell, the steps used to solve a user problem go through the following sequence:

1 • The user reports the problem to the Help Desk.

2 • The Help Desk prioritizes the problem, so that the most critical problems get fixed first.

3 • The problem is assigned to a Help Desk person, if there is more than one person at the Help Desk.

4 • The Help Desk tracks the progress made toward solving the problem, to make sure the user isn't left hanging.

5 • The Help Desk escalates the problem, if necessary.

6 • The Help Desk fixes the problem.

7 • The Help Desk reports the solution to the user.

8 • The Help Desk records the solution, so that if the same problem occurs again later, the solution can be found more quickly.

Granted, if you're a single-handed Help Desk, you may be able to skip a step or two, but the basic sequence is about right.

Let's look at some of the processes Help Desks may use to make each of these steps go smoothly.

Getting Problem Reports from Users

Obviously, you can only fix a problem if someone tells you the problem exists. Right? You'd be surprised how often problems go unreported simply because the user doesn't know there is someone to call.

If you're setting up a Help Desk, or if your Help Desk is fairly new, you may want to look at how well word has spread that the Help Desk is there for users to get assistance. A considerable amount of time can be wasted by users who try to work around a problem on their own, rather than calling in the expert (you).

REAL WORLD

If you think your Help Desk is being under-utilized, look for ways to publicize it. Get an article in the company's newsletter. Get five minutes on the agenda for the next departmental staff meeting and tell everyone about your services. Send an e-mail to everyone you support. Just get the word out. (It doesn't hurt to let the "big guns" see you out and about, too, so that they know they're getting their money's worth out of you.)

If everyone knows about the Help Desk, do they know how to contact you? Most Help Desks have a preferred method for receiving problem reports from users. Some require users to send an e-mail to a particular e-mail account, describing the problem in detail, and including the user's name, location, department, phone number, and so on. Other companies prefer that users phone in their work requests. Still others use a combination, telling users to phone in high-priority problems and use e-mail for lower-priority problems. Especially in smaller departments or companies, users may simply drop by your desk and report the problem to you in person.

Choose the method that works best for you, and make sure your users know how to get their problems reported to you correctly.

Prioritizing Problem Reports

If your Help Desk receives a high number of problem reports, you have probably already devised a way to prioritize those problems. (Again, in smaller organizations, prioritization may be informal, because the requests for help may be less frequent and it's easier to take care of every problem as soon as it is reported.)

Most Help Desks tend to set up priority levels similar to the following:

- ▸ *Emergency*. This is a major problem, and needs immediate action from everyone on the Help Desk team who can help.

- ▸ *High Priority*. The user who reported the problem needs immediate help. There is no workaround for the problem, and the user cannot work until the problem is solved.

- ▸ *Medium Priority*. The problem is affecting the user's work, but there is a workaround to use until the problem is solved.

- ▸ *Low Priority*. The problem is annoying and should be fixed, but it is not time-critical.

Many Help Desks will ask the users themselves to assign a priority to their problems when they first report them. If you explain the criteria, most users will be able to recognize whether they can get along for a while without the problem being solved. By letting them specify the priority, you may make them realize that other problems may be more important than theirs, and they might be a little more patient with you.

Once you have the priorities lined up, be sure you follow the priority list when fixing the problems. Don't make a high-priority problem wait while you try to solve an annoying medium-priority issue, for example. Give the medium-priority user a good workaround solution, if necessary, then go after the high-priority problem right away.

Assigning Problem Reports to an Available Person

If you have more than one person in your Help Desk area, problem reports usually should be routed to the next available person who has the expertise to handle the issue.

In some cases, Help Desks are set up to route phone calls into the Help Desk to different personnel so that no single person receives all of the incoming problems. In other organizations, a single person may act as a clearinghouse for problems. That person determines the most logical recipient for the problem and forwards the work request to that person. If your Help Desk has specialists in different applications or IntranetWare features, someone may be responsible for routing work orders to the appropriate specialist.

Your Help Desk should use whatever method seems most efficient for your team.

Tracking the Solution's Progress

Nothing is more frustrating to a user than reporting a problem and then never hearing back from anyone to know if it got fixed, if someone's working on it, or if there's no possible solution.

Many Help Desks use a problem-tracking database to record all incoming problems. The problem is assigned a number when it is first reported. Then, whoever is assigned to the problem reports the status on the problem (such as "In Progress" or "Fixed" or "No solution"). The user can then call the Help Desk, request the status for a particular problem number, and see where it stands. Some systems can fire off an e-mail automatically to the user every time the status in the database is updated.

Not all Help Desks are this fancy, of course. Even if you are running the show by yourself, however, you should still track the problems you receive. One reason to track problems is to keep the users updated, so that they stay happy. Another is simply to remind yourself that a problem is still open.

TIP

Tracking problems allows you to keep a record of the types and frequency of problems being reported. This could help you pinpoint problem areas that may need some extra attention. It may allow you to justify new equipment purchases to management. It can also help you with your next performance evaluation by allowing you to show your manager just how you spent your last year.

It doesn't really matter how you track problems. You can keep these records in a notebook, on cocktail napkins, or in a database. What matters is that you need to be able to tell the user where the problem stands, and you may want to be able to use the records later to compile a picture of your network's problem history.

Escalating the Problem

When the problem is something you can't quite tackle by yourself, you must know who you're allowed to call in for help.

ZEN

"Who ya gonna call?"

from the movie *Ghostbusters*

If your Help Desk has an escalation team or second-line support group, there should be some guidelines for escalating the problem to them. Everyone must understand the types of problems they can escalate, and who, in particular, can be tapped for each type of request.

In addition, your Help Desk may need to establish guidelines for when it's acceptable to call a manufacturer's technical support line. (Since many companies charge fees for technical support, your organization may want to limit such phone calls strictly to higher-priority issues.)

Outside consultants are another resource for escalating problems. Since such consultants tend to be very expensive, this is another area where guidelines should be established. In addition to outlining the types of problems you can take to consultants, these guidelines also should indicate which consultants are approved for you to use.

Resolving the Problem

Resolving the problem, of course, is the most important part of the entire process. This is where you use all your training, your on-the-job experience, your intuition, and your contacts to find a solution for the user's problem.

Sometimes there is no solution. Then you must find a workaround or some other way for the users to get their work done.

ZEN

"There is no such thing as a problem without a gift for you in its hands."

Richard Bach, *Illusions*

Recording and Reporting the Solution

After you've resolved the problem, you must do two things: let the user know what the solution was, and record it so that you don't have to duplicate your efforts the next time it happens.

When telling the user how you solved the problem, decide how much the user must know. If Joe's problem is one that he is likely to encounter again because he was doing something wrong, it will probably be worth your time to carefully explain to Joe how to prevent the problem from happening again. Even if you can't find a solution to the problem, it's still important to let the user know the outcome.

TIP

If the problem wasn't related directly to any action on the user's part, you can probably skip the gory details. It will bore the user and waste time for both of you. Just let the user know that the problem was solved, that it wasn't his or her fault, and that it won't happen again (or who to contact if it does).

Documenting the solution is nearly as important as telling the user about it. In the same database or notebook where you were tracking the problem's progress, be sure to record the final resolution. This will create a history that you can use in case the same type of problem recurs later.

In larger Help Desk organizations, having problems and their solutions stored together in a database can become a kind of "shared brain." Everyone in the Help Desk group has access to the answers that others in the group have already found. Problem-solving can become more efficient throughout the group, and the turnaround time for users' problems decreases. Why go through the whole discovery process again, if someone else has already figured out how to resolve the issue once?

ZEN

"Experience is a wonderful thing; it allows you to recognize a mistake when you make it again."

Anonymous

What if the Help Desk is just you? Even for a team of one, it's still important to record problems and solutions. It will keep you from forgetting how you solved a problem that may have happened a year or two ago. It will give you a history that you can use to plan for future network improvements or hardware purchases, as explained earlier. Finally, it will make it easier for someone else to step into your shoes here when you get promoted or hired away by that great company across the street.

TIP

Some Help Desk systems automatically send an e-mail report to the user when the problem is closed in the database. With a system like this, you kill both of the proverbial birds with one stone—you document the solution and inform the user at the same time. However, the fancy software isn't necessary in a small operation, as long as you simply remember to do the follow-up somehow.

TOOLS FOR HELP DESKS

A variety of tools are available that Help Desk organizations can use to track and solve user problems. Depending on the size of your Help Desk team, you may use some of these tools already. If not, you may want to look at implementing some of them.

ZEN

"The pioneers cleared the forests from Jamestown to the Mississippi with fewer tools than are stored in the typical modern garage."

Dwayne Laws

Help Desk Tracking Software

Many software packages are available that help record and track user-reported problems. The simplest of these software solutions provide basic tracking and reporting functions. Other packages go beyond the basics, providing the ability to research problem histories, integrate with e-mail systems for forwarding assignments or reporting progress, and so on. The software products also vary in degrees of usability.

If you don't already have a tracking application in place, and are contemplating investing in one, decide what you want to accomplish with it. What type of information is important to your company? How many people will it need to support, and how many Help Desk employees will be using it? Do you need the software to be used by one centralized Help Desk, or distributed across multiple Help Desk areas? Do you want to track just the problems themselves, or do you also need to be able to research problem histories to resolve new problems?

ZEN

"The worth of a program cannot be judged by the size of its brochures or by the number of full-page ads that appear in popular computer magazines."

Geoffrey James, *The Zen of Programming*

There's no point in paying extra for features you will never use. On the other hand, there's no point in saving a few bucks on a software package, but then wasting far more than that amount in time spent manually handling problem reports. Be sure you invest in the problem-tracking product that will make your Help Desk the most efficient and productive.

Telephony Systems

Many larger organizations are beginning to use telephony systems as a way to streamline how users report problems. Different types of systems can be used to help automate a Help Desk.

With some of these telephony systems, a user can place a phone call to a single number, and the system will automatically rotate the call to the next available Help Desk person. This feature is sometimes called *automatic call distribution*.

Some systems also provide voice-response features—you know the types. These are the systems that answer with a recording that says something like, "If you need to report a hardware problem, press 1, ..." These systems can also include announcements at the beginning of the message, to report on any general news callers may need to know (such as currently downed servers, planned system upgrades, and so on).

ZEN

"More and more, the people in 'Customer Service' won't even talk to you. They prefer to let you interface with the convenient Automated Answering System until you die of old age ('. . . if your FIRST name has more than eight letters, and your LAST name begins with 'H' through 'L'—press 251 NOW. If your first name has LESS than eight letters, and your last name contains at least two E's, press 252 NOW. If your. . .')."

Dave Barry

In addition, telephony systems can be used to track the numbers of calls coming in, how many are on hold, and so on.

Help Desk Handbooks

Any Help Desk, no matter how small, should consider creating and using a Help Desk handbook. Such a handbook could be used to explain everything from Help Desk policies and procedures, to specific remedies for common user-reported problems.

A Help Desk handbook is especially useful for training new Help Desk employees. It also can serve as a record of official policies—for example, noting whose authorization is required for certain procedures.

The following types of topics could be included in a typical Help Desk handbook. You will probably think of additional topics that would be especially useful for your particular organization.

► An overview of how the Help Desk operates.

► The login procedures to get into the Help Desk problem-tracking software.

▶ An explanation of how to use the Help Desk problem-tracking software.

▶ A description of any authorization procedures. For example, if your Help Desk charges departments for Help Desk services, the handbook might list approved cost center numbers, people who are authorized to approve such services, and so on.

▶ Step-by-step procedures for fixing most common user problems, such as how to reset a user's password, how to create a new user account, how to salvage deleted files, how to set up a new workstation's desktop, and so on.

▶ Procedures for installing new equipment. This may include everything from describing which forms to fill out, to how to check for interrupt and address conflicts in network hardware.

▶ Instructions for installing or upgrading applications on the network and on workstations.

▶ A troubleshooting guide, which could include a list of common problem areas, or possibly flowcharts to help isolate the cause of problems.

Figure 2.3 shows a sample table of contents from a Help Desk handbook.

Help Desk Disaster Plans

Having a disaster plan for the Help Desk is critical. A disaster plan outlines exactly what to do in the event of a disaster. For the Help Desk team, the disaster plan should explain which servers and machines to restore immediately, how to set up the Help Desk systems quickly, and so on. Generally, the disaster plan must describe how to get the Help Desk back on-line and functional quickly.

USER TRAINING

Good training is an essential part of ensuring that users stay productive and efficient while working on the network. If you are responsible for ensuring that users know how to access and use the network, you have your work cut out for you.

FIGURE 2.3

Help Desk Handbook, Table of Contents

ACME Help Desk Handbook

I.	**Introduction to the ACME Help Desk**	
	How We're Organized	1
	The Tools We Use	3
II.	**Logging In**	
	Logging in to the Phone System	7
	Logging in to the Network	8
	Logging in to the Problem-Tracker	10
	Logging in to the Modem Pool	11
III.	**Using Problem-Tracker**	
	Main Menu	13
	Tranferring Incidents	15
	Updating Status	17
	Closing Out an Incident	18
IV.	**Authorization Procedures**	
	Which Requests Need Pre-authorization?	21
	Valid Approver List	24
	Valid Cost Center Numbers	27
V.	**Common Problems and Solutions**	
	Resetting Passwords	29
	Creating New User Accounts	31
	Salvaging Deleted Files	42
	Changing the Size of a Memory Swap File	49
	Changing an E-Mail Post Office Address	51
	Changing Print Drivers in Applications	56
VI.	**Installing New Hardware**	
	Installing a Workstation	65
	Installing a Printer	71
	Adding Memory to a Workstation	83
	Changing a Hard Disk	86
VII.	**Installing/Upgrading Applications**	
	WordPerfect	93
	Lotus Notes (Workstation License)	96
	Microsoft Project	101
	Netscape Navigator	106
VIII.	**Troubleshooting Guide**	
	Workstation Troubleshooting Flowchart	111
	Printer Troubleshooting Flowchart	115
	Server Troubleshooting Flowchart	120

ZEN

"You teach best what you most need to learn."

Richard Bach, *Illusions*

To plan a training program for users, you must evaluate several factors:

▶ How many users must you train?

▸ How often must you train new users?

▸ What network skills do you have to teach them (such as logging in, selecting print queues, and changing their passwords)?

▸ What application skills do you have to teach them? For example, do you need to train them to use the accounting software, a word processing application, or the e-mail system?

▸ How much time will you be allowed to prepare the training materials and to present the training itself?

▸ Would the users benefit by having a workbook, short manual, or other learning tool that they could refer to later, after the training?

Typical Network Tasks for Users

Some of the most typical tasks you'll need to train the user to do include basic networking activities.

 TIP

Ideally, users will not have to know much about the network. In fact, many network administrators set up their networks so that the users have to merely enter a password, then go directly into their applications.

The following list mentions some of the networking tasks you may want to tell users about.

▸ **Logging in and out of the network.** Tell them how to access and leave the network.

▸ **Passwords.** Be sure to give them guidelines for passwords. Tell them the minimum number of characters they must use, and explain that they should combine words, characters, and numbers to form words that can't be found in a dictionary.

▶ **Directory structures.** Tell them how files are organized on the network, and where they should store their own files.

▶ **Security.** In most cases, users probably do not need to know about the security features of IntranetWare. However, you will probably want to warn them about storing files on floppy disks, giving their passwords to friends, leaving their workstations without logging out, and so on.

▶ **Restrictions.** If you've set any time restrictions or disk space restrictions, you may want to tell users about them so they aren't surprised when they encounter such a boundary. It could save you some unnecessary phone calls.

▶ **On-line documentation.** If you want the users to be able to access the IntranetWare on-line documentation, you'll need to teach them how to set up the viewer on their workstations, and how to use the viewers.

Workstation and Application Skills

The bulk of your training for users may be on their workstation operating system (such as Windows 95 or Macintosh operating system) and the applications that they will be using (such as e-mail, word processing, and spreadsheet applications).

The effectiveness of workstation and application training usually is minimal if the students don't have the opportunity to actually practice the tasks first-hand. Therefore, if at all possible, try to conduct the training in a lab where the students have access to workstations and can try out things such as using the Windows File Manager, sending an e-mail, spell-checking a word-processed document, or creating a spreadsheet.

In addition, you may also want to teach the users how to set up, modify, and upgrade their IntranetWare workstation software. For example, if you want users to be able to modify their NET.CFG files or login scripts, you'll need to teach them what they can do and how to do it.

Training Tools

As you prepare for the training you'll be doing, consider what types of tools might be most helpful for your users after the training is over. Some ideas you might consider are

▸ A short reference manual

▸ A workbook, where students can fill in information or complete exercises during the class

▸ A one-sheet quick-reference page or card that users can pin up on the wall next to their workstations

▸ A video, so that new users can watch it without you having to perform a training session every time someone new is hired

If any of these tools will help train the user, as well as minimize the amount of time you must spend training or fielding questions, they may well be worth the time investment. If they aren't going to have lasting value, however, don't waste your own time creating them.

Disaster Planning and Recovery

One area of network administration that is often overlooked until it's too late is disaster planning and recovery. Often, people ignore the "planning" part of the equation, putting it off until they have more time to think about it. (Sound familiar?) Of course, that mystical force that's responsible for enforcing Murphy's Laws views this sort of procrastination as opportunity. If you're one of the unfortunate ones who never got around to planning for a disaster, and then disaster strikes, Murphy's Laws will ensure that you get to enjoy the "recovery" half of the equation in all its full glory.

On the other hand, if you're armed with an up-to-date disaster plan, good backups, and accurate records of your network, the task of reestablishing your network may not seem nearly as daunting.

In the last few years, Mother Nature has been making her presence known in very violent ways. Hurricanes, earthquakes, tornadoes, and floods have rampaged through many parts of the United States as well as the rest of the world, racking up record numbers of casualties and property destruction. The cost of insurance claims from these disasters alone has many insurance companies struggling to stay afloat themselves.

But disasters aren't always caused by nature. Where your network is concerned, disasters can come in many guises.

REAL WORLD

A disaster that affects your network could be anything from a crashed hard disk on your server, to a security breach, to a fire that destroys your building. When it comes to computers, a malfunctioning water sprinkler system can cause as much damage as a hurricane.

How long can your company function without a working network? If your server is fried by a power spike, can everyone who uses the network get by without the network for a few days (or weeks) while you order new hardware and install it?

If your building is burned to the ground, and both your network and your backup tapes are reduced to unrecognizable cinders, what happens to the company? Can it just move into the building next door and be open for business again immediately, or will it take months or years to rebuild the data that was stored on the network? In this era, many businesses are only as good as their information.

If your company depends on the network for business-critical functions, having a disaster plan for your network can be far more important than having insurance that covers the building.

SO WHAT CAN A CNA DO ABOUT DISASTERS?

As anyone who's survived a disaster can tell you, the best way to recover from a disaster is to plan for one ahead of time. It doesn't matter what type of disaster it is. If you're prepared, you can weather the storm more easily and get back to normal much faster.

As a CNA, you can help ensure that your network recovers quickly from any disasters by preparing a disaster plan. A disaster plan documents exactly what to do about the network in case a disaster strikes. Among other things, it lists key people to call, describes how to restore backed-up files to the server, and explains the priority of services provided by the network so that you can restore the critical services first.

If you are in charge of your entire network, the disaster plan will be entirely in your hands. If you are working in conjunction with a consultant (such as a CNE) or an IS (Information Services) department, you will coordinate your disaster plan with them.

For example, if you manage a departmental network, but the IS group is in charge of the company-wide network, you will need to work closely with the IS people to make sure they understand what your needs are if a problem occurs. You can provide them with such information as your key personnel, critical applications, and location of your department's printers and servers.

Then, when the disaster strikes, you will, of course, look like a hero because your department's critical functions will be up and running before the other departments have even figured out what hit them.

PLAN AHEAD

If you haven't already created a disaster plan, do it today. It doesn't need to be that difficult, and it could save you a tremendous amount of wasted time, frustrated users, lost revenue, and sleepless nights. And you know that earthquake or electrical fire isn't going to wait for a convenient time in your schedule to occur, so the sooner you plan for it, the better.

REAL WORLD

Think about it. When would you rather cook up a disaster plan—during your lunch hours this week, or while you're sitting in the middle of a water-soaked server room with your boss screaming at you because he can't log in to the network?

Assuming you're suitably convinced about the need for planning now, here are a few pointers about your disaster plan:

▶ Write it down.

▶ Make sure someone else knows how to execute the plan in case you aren't available.

▶ Get the plan approved by your management.

▶ Store multiple copies in different locations (not all in the same building).

It's important to have a documented plan because having the plan in your head only works if you happen to be around, of course. It would be just your luck to be vacationing in Tahiti when the roof over your company's headquarters in Denver collapses under the weight of a heavy snowfall.

If your disaster plan is up-to-date and easy to understand, you may be able to avoid a fast trip back home, especially if you've had the forethought to appoint someone else to be the second-in command.

Just think how smug you'll feel as you dig your toes in the sun-warmed sand on the Tahitian beach, swirl the ice in your beverage, and imagine your second-in-command calmly executing your carefully detailed disaster plan. Ah, bliss.

ZEN

"Nibblin' on sponge cake, watching the sun bake all of those tourists covered in oil . . . Wastin' away again in Margaritaville."

Jimmy Buffett

Before you go drifting off into a tropical daydream, however, there are a couple of other small details to take care of.

First, now that you've written the plan and selected a faithful sidekick, you'll want to get the plan approved by your organization's heads. This lets you make sure that the people and network services you think are the highest priorities are the same ones your management thinks are. (This is often a useful thing to verify, anyway.)

More importantly, if the CEO has approved your plan to restore the production department's network before the administration department's, you won't have to deal with politics and egos while you're trying to restring cables.

ZEN

"Never make a technical decision based upon the politics of the situation."

Geoffrey James, *The Zen of Programming*

Next, make copies of your disaster plan. Store the copies in several locations so that you'll be able to get to at least one of them should disaster strike. Make sure at least one copy is off-site in case your entire building is demolished.

What Should Be in a Disaster Plan?

What you put in your disaster plan will depend on your particular situation. If you are the only person in charge of your network, you'll need to have a thorough plan that will take you from a mass of smoldering electronics to a functioning network with happy users logging in.

If you manage one part of a network, and other people manage the entire network as a whole, you may need to merely provide those people with your department's specific information. Then the IS department can roll your information into an overall plan to restore the whole company step-by-step.

Everyone's disaster plan will be different, but there are a few key points to consider when planning yours:

> ► Plan who to call in case of an emergency. List key network personnel, such as any network administrators for various branches of the NDS tree, personnel who perform the weekly and daily backups, and so on.

You may want to include names of security personnel who should be notified in case of a potential security breach. Be sure to list home phone numbers, pager numbers, and cellular phone numbers, if you can.

▶ Plan the order in which you will restore service on your network. Who needs to be back on-line first? Should a critical department be restored before anyone else? Are there key individuals who need to be reconnected first? If you manage one department in a company, where does your department fit in the priority scheme? Do you need to be back on-line before some other department can function?

▶ Once you've identified the key people who need to be reconnected, is there an order to the files or services they'll need? Which servers need to be restored first? What applications must those users have immediately? Which files will they need right away?

▶ Document the location of your network records. Where do you keep your hardware inventory, purchase requisitions, backup logs, and so forth?

▶ Document the location of your network backup tapes or disks. Don't forget to document instructions for restoring files, or indicate the location of the backup system's documentation, in case the backup operator is unavailable. Record your backup rotation schedule so that other people can figure out how to restore files efficiently.

▶ Include a drawing of the network layout, showing the exact location of cables, servers, workstations, and other computers. Highlight the critical components, so that anyone else reading your plan will know at a glance where to find the priority servers or workstations.

KEEP GOOD RECORDS OF YOUR NETWORK

Another line in your defense against disaster is to maintain up-to-date records about your network. When something goes wrong with your network, it will be much easier to spot the problem if you have accurate documentation.

Good network documentation isn't just helpful in an emergency. Paperwork is always a distasteful task, but you'll be thankful you've done it the next time you have to add new hardware to the network, resolve an interrupt conflict, justify your hardware budget to management, get a workstation repaired under warranty, or train a new assistant.

ZEN

"One of the advantages of being disorderly is that one is constantly making exciting discoveries."

A. A. Milne

How you track your network information is up to you. You may want to keep a three-ring binder with printed information about the network, or you may prefer to keep the information on-line in databases or spreadsheets. Use whatever method works for you. The important part of your network documentation is not the format, but the content.

However you document your network, be sure to keep the information in more than one location. If a disaster occurs, you don't want to lose your only copy of the information that can help you restore the network quickly. Try to keep copies of your network information with your disaster plan, so everything can be accessed at the same time.

What types of network information should you record? Again, networks vary, as do network administrator job descriptions, so your documentation needs will vary, too. The worksheets in this chapter can help you get started. You can photocopy and use those worksheets, or design your own worksheets or databases to keep track of the information you need.

The following sections describe some of the types of information you may want to record for your network.

Hardware and Software Inventory

In any business, it's important to keep track of the company's assets. An up-to-date inventory of hardware and software purchases can help you tremendously with insurance reports and replacements, should a loss occur.

In addition, this inventory isn't just helpful in an emergency. You never know when management will ask for current capital asset information for various business reasons, and you'll avoid a fire-drill if you already have that data available.

In addition, accurate records of past purchases can assist you in predicting how your future computer purchases may grow. This will come in handy when your management asks for your budget plans for the coming year.

ZEN

"'It's a poor sort of memory that only works backwards,' the Queen remarked."

Lewis Carroll from *Alice in Wonderland*

Be sure to record each product's version number, serial number, vendor, purchase date, length of warranty, and so on.

Figure 2.4 is an example worksheet you might use to record hardware or software purchases.

Installation and Configuration Settings

Whenever you install a new piece of equipment on the network, such as a workstation, printer, or server, there's a good chance the device will have configuration settings that could conflict with some other piece of equipment on the network.

If you keep a record of configuration settings for servers, workstations, printers, and other hardware, you can quickly check existing settings to verify that the new device's settings won't cause a problem, such as interrupt conflicts. Having this information at your fingertips can save you hours of locating and resolving conflicts the hard way.

In addition, there are other types of configuration information you should record so that the data is readily available when you need it.

For example, you should record the names of all the network boards installed in a server, along with the board's LAN driver and frame type being used. In addition, you should note the amount of RAM in the server, the type of time server it is, its IPX internal address, and so on. Figure 2.5 shows an example worksheet for recording a server's installation and configuration information.

FIGURE 2.4

Worksheet: Hardware and
Software Purchases

Product: _____

Serial number: _____

Version number: _____

Vendor name: _____

       Address: _____
                     _____
       Phone: _____
       Fax: _____

Manufacturer name: _____

       Address: _____
                     _____
       Phone: _____
       Fax: _____

Purchase date: _____

Purchase order number: _____

Purchase price: _____

Warranty card sent in?   Yes ____   No ____   Not applicable ____

Length of warranty: _____

Current location of product: _____

Comments: _____
                 _____
                 _____
                 _____

For a workstation, you would document the network board installed in it, the LAN driver it uses, its location, station address, and other types of useful information. Figure 2.6 shows an example worksheet for a workstation.

Printers have configuration settings you'll want to record, too. Figure 2.7 is an example worksheet for recording printer data.

You may want to create similar worksheets for documenting other devices on your network (such as modems, tape backup drives, and so on).

F I G U R E   2.5

*Worksheet: Server
Installation and
Configuration*

Server name:_____

Make and model: _____

Current location: _____

Serial number: _____

Memory:_____

Server's internal **IPX** network number: _____

Directory tree name:_____

Type of time sync server: _____

Server's time zone: _____

Server's name context in the Directory tree: _____

Protocols

IPX/SPX (required):   TCP/IP: AppleTalk:

Yes ____ No ____   Yes ____ No ____   Yes ____ No ____

Network Board   **Network Board**

  Type: _____   Type: _____
  LAN driver:_____   LAN driver:_____
  Frame type: _____   Frame type: _____
  Node address:_____   Node address:_____
  Settings:_____   Settings:_____
  IP address (for TCP/IP only): _____   IP address (for TCP/IP only): _____
  Subnet Mask (for TCP/IP only): _____   Subnet Mask (for TCP/IP only): _____

Hard disk size: _____   **Disk Controller Board**

DOS partition size: _____   Name: _____
                                             Disk drive name: _____
Disk mirrored?   Yes ___ No ___   Settings: _____

Disk duplexed?   Yes ___ No ___
                                             Other boards
SFT III installed? Yes ___ No ___
                                             Name: _____
CD-ROM drive?   Yes ___ No ___   Settings:_____

                                             Name: _____
                                             Settings:_____

Comments: _____

           _____

Maintenance Histories

The battery in Jason's port replicator for his laptop just died. Didn't that die a few months ago, too? Who fixed it then? Is this the same problem or a new one?

If you've been keeping a maintenance or repair history on all of your computer equipment, you can quickly find the answers to these questions. A maintenance history can help you see if there's a pattern of problems emerging with a particular machine, user, or department. It can also show you if repairs done at a certain facility seem to cost more than others, or if problems recur after a particular facility has repaired a machine.

FIGURE   2.6

Worksheet: Workstation
Installation and
Configuration

Worksheet: Workstation Installation and Configuration

Workstation user and/ or location: _____

Make and model: _____

Serial number: _____

Memory: _____

Size of floppy disk drives: A: _____   B: _____

Size of hard disk: C:_____   D: _____

CD-ROM drive?   Yes: _____ No: _____

PC
   DOS version:_____
   Windows version: _____

   Windows NT version: _____
   Windows 95 version:_____

   OS/2 version:_____

MAC
   OS version (system): _____
   Filer version: _____

NetWare client software version: _____

Network Board
   Type:_____
   LAN driver:_____
   Frame type:_____
   Node address:_____
   Settings:_____

Network Board
   Type:_____
   LAN driver:_____
   Frame type:_____
   Node address:_____
   Settings:_____

Other Boards
   Name:_____
   Settings:_____
   Name:_____
   Settings:_____
   Comments: _____
   _____

When you log maintenance histories, be sure to indicate what the problem was, along with the solution. Document when the repair was made, who did the work, and how much it cost. If a warranty for the work was issued, note that as well (and its duration).

You may want to file all paperwork associated with repairs along with the worksheet that documents your original purchase of the item.

Figure 2.8 shows an example worksheet for recording maintenance histories.

F I G U R E   2 . 7

*Worksheet: Printer
Installation and
Configuration*

Worksheet: Printer Installation and Configuration

Printer object's full name: _____

Make and model: _____

Current location: _____

Serial number: _____

Directory tree name: _____

Printer number: _____

Print queues assigned: _____

_____

_____

_____

_____

Print server assigned: _____

How is the printer attached: To server ___ To workstation _____   Direct _____

Print queue operators: _____

Print server operators: _____

Printer type (parallel, serial, AppleTalk, etc.):_____

Interrupt mode (polled or specific IRQ): _____

Parallel printer configuration

   Port (LPT1, LPT2, or LPT3): _____   _____

   Poll: _____

   Interrupt (LPT1=7, LPT2=8):_____

Serial Printer Configuration:

   Port (COM1 or COM2): ____   _____

   Baud rate:_____

   Word size: _____

   Stop bits:_____

   Parity: _____

   XON/XOFF: _____

   Poll: _____

   Interrupt (COM1=4, COM2=3):_____

Comments:_____

_____

Volumes

If you have several servers and volumes on your network, it wouldn't hurt to keep a written record of the volumes installed on each server. You can document each volume's size, the server on which it is located, and even the types of files it contains. For example, you might indicate that the volume contains applications, users' daily work files, Macintosh-based drawings, or a certain department's database files.

You can also record the name spaces being used on a volume, and you can indicate whether each volume uses data migration or file compression.

Figure 2.9 shows an example worksheet for recording volume information.

FIGURE   2.8

*Worksheet: Maintenance
History*

Worksheet: Maintenance History

Product:_____

Serial number: _____

Repair date:_____

Purchase order number: _____

Repair vendor name:_____

Address:_____

Phone:_____

Fax:_____

Repair Cost: _____

    Repaired under warranty? Yes _____ No _____

    New warranty granted?   Yes _____ No _____

    Warranty expiration date:_____

Comments:_____

_____

_____

_____

_____

_____

_____

_____

_____

_____

_____

_____

_____

_____

_____

_____

_____

_____

Hot Fix Bad Block Tracking

NetWare 4.1 provides a feature called Hot Fix, which monitors the blocks that are being written to on a disk. When NetWare writes data to the server's hard disk, NetWare writes the data, then verifies that the data was written correctly by reading it again (called *read-after-write* verification).

When a bad block is encountered, the data that was being written to that block is redirected to a separate area on the disk, called the *disk redirection area*, and the bad block is listed in a *bad block table*.

FIGURE 2.9

Worksheet: Volumes

Worksheet: Volumes

Server name:_____

SYS Volume

 Size: _____

 Name spaces:_____

 File compression on?   Yes _____   No _____

 Data migration on?   Yes _____   No _____

 Block suballocation on? Yes_____   No _____

Other Volume (name): _____

 Size: _____

 Name spaces:_____

 File compression on?   Yes _____   No _____

 Data migration on?   Yes _____   No _____

 Block suballocation on? Yes_____   No _____

Other Volume (name): _____

 Size: _____

 Name spaces:_____

 File compression on?   Yes _____   No _____

 Data migration on?   Yes _____   No _____

 Block suballocation on? Yes_____   No _____

Other Volume (name): _____

 Size: _____

 Name spaces:_____

 File compression on?   Yes _____   No _____

 Data migration on?   Yes _____   No _____

 Block suballocation on? Yes_____   No

Comments: _____

_____

_____

_____

_____

TIP

Some manufacturer's hard disks maintain their own version of data redirection and do not need to use NetWare's Hot Fix feature. If your disk does use Hot Fix, the size of the redirection is set up by default when you first create a volume on the disk.

Periodically, you should monitor the NetWare Hot Fix statistics to see if a disk is showing a high number of bad blocks and is filling up the allocated redirection area. To see the number of redirection blocks being used, use MONITOR.NLM's Disk Information screen. Track the number of bad blocks being found over time, so that you can see if the disk suddenly starts to generate bad blocks at an undesirable frequency.

If more than half of the redirection space has been used for redirected data, or if the number of redirected blocks has increased significantly since the last time you checked it, the disk may be going bad. If this is the case, you may want to refer to the manufacturer's documentation to try to diagnose the disk problem.

Figure 2.10 shows an example worksheet you can use to track the number of bad blocks being found on a server.

F I G U R E   2 . 1 0

Worksheet: Hot Fix Bad Block Tracking

Worksheet: Hot Fix Bad Block Tracking

Server: _____

Disk: _____

   Total redirection area: _____

   Date:_____   Redirection blocks used: _____

   Date:_____   Redirection blocks used: _____

   Date:_____   Redirection blocks used: _____

   Date:_____   Redirection blocks used: _____

   Date:_____   Redirection blocks used: _____

   Date:_____   Redirection blocks used: _____

   Date:_____   Redirection blocks used: _____

   Date:_____   Redirection blocks used: _____

   Date:_____   Redirection blocks used: _____

   Date:_____   Redirection blocks used: _____

Comments: _____

_____

_____

_____

_____

_____

_____

_____

_____

_____

_____

_____

_____

_____

_____

_____

Time Synchronization

When an IntranetWare network is set up, each server on the network is designated as a particular type of time synchronization server. A server might be a Reference time server, a Single-Reference time server, a Primary time server, or a Secondary time server.

On larger networks, it's a good idea to keep a list of all the types of time servers on the network, so that you can determine what the effect might be on the network if you add another server or remove one from the tree.

Figure 2.11 shows an example worksheet you can use to record the types of time servers on the network.

Network Layout

Another important piece of your network documentation is a drawing of the network layout. If you store this with your disaster plan, you (and others) will be able to locate critical components quickly.

On the drawing, show how all the workstations, servers, printers, and other equipment are connected. The drawing doesn't have to be to scale, but it should show each machine in its approximate location. Label each workstation with its make and model, its location, and its user. Show the cables that connect the hardware, and show what types of cable they are.

Workstation Batch Files and Boot Files

If your idea of spending an exciting afternoon consists of re-creating AUTOEXEC.BAT, CONFIG.SYS, and NET.CFG files on workstations, then there's no need to record the existing files.

However, if you think you may have something better to do, you may want to consider printing out these files and keeping them with the worksheets that document the workstation. You may also want to store copies of the files on diskette. If the workstation must be reinstalled, you can re-create the user's environment quickly if you have these files archived.

Server SET Parameters and Boot Files

If you have modified your server's configuration settings by changing its SET parameters, you can save the settings of those parameters to a file for safe-keeping.

Worksheet: Time Synchronization Servers

NDS Directory tree: _____

Single reference server: _____

Reference server: _____

Primary servers: _____

_____

_____

_____

_____

_____

_____

_____

_____

Comments: _____

_____

_____

_____

_____

_____

_____

_____

_____

_____

_____

_____

_____

_____

_____

_____

_____

_____

   SERVMAN.NLM allows you to save a server's SET parameters to a file. If you've
changed the default SET parameters, you will probably want to print out this file
and store the printout and a diskette copy with your network records. This will
make it much easier to reinstall the server to the configuration you originally had,
should the need arise.

   It would also be a good idea to print or archive the server's boot files, including
the STARTUP.NCF and AUTOEXEC.NCF files, so that you can re-create them if
necessary, too.

TIP

SET parameters allow you to configure a wide variety of your server's performance characteristics, such as the number of cache buffers it allocates, whether the server is on Daylight Saving Time, or how close a volume can be to running out of disk space before it warns you. You can change SET parameters in several ways: by executing a SET command at the server's console, by putting a SET command in the server's AUTOEXEC.NCF or STARTUP.NCF file, or by selecting the parameter and its value in SERVMAN.NLM (which lets you select the parameters you want from menus).

Backup Information

Backups are only useful if the data on them can be restored. Sure, that's obvious, but there's more to it than just making sure your backup product works. What if you're not around? You can have the greatest backup rotation schedule in the world, but if you're the only one who knows where the backup tapes are, or in which order to restore them, the tapes are next to useless.

It is very important to record your backup rotation schedule, the location of backup tapes or disks, the names of any backup operators, the labeling system you use on your backup tapes or disks, and any other information someone may need if you're not around to restore the system.

Figure 2.12 shows an example worksheet you can use to record information about your backup schedule.

WHAT ELSE CAN A CNA DO?

In addition to writing a disaster plan, there are other ways you can plan ahead to avert (or at least diminish) disaster. Some of these preparatory measures include:

▶ Keeping a faithful schedule of backups, so that files can be restored quickly.

▶ Implementing disk mirroring (or duplexing), so that a simple hard disk failure in the server won't cause users to lose working time and files.

FIGURE 2.12

Worksheet: Backup Schedule

Server name (of server backed up): _____

Server location: _____

Backup system used (hardware and software): _____

_____

Location of backup media: _____

_____

Backup schedule: _____

  Full backup: _____

  Incremental backup: _____

  Differential backup: _____

  Custom backup: _____

If custom backups are done, describe: _____

_____

_____

Media rotation schedule: _____

_____

Media labeling instructions: _____

_____

Primary backup administrator name: _____

Phone numbers: _____

_____

Secondary backup administrator name: _____

Phone numbers: _____

_____

Comments: _____

_____

_____

_____

► Implementing SFT III (mirrored servers) on your mission-critical servers. If you can't afford to have the server go down at all, SFT III can be your best fail-safe.

► Using IntranetWare's TTS (Transaction Tracking System) if you're using database applications. TTS ensures that any transactions that are only partially completed when the server dies or the power goes out are backed out completely, so that the database isn't corrupted.

▶ Periodically reviewing your network's security, so that you can ensure that there are no potential security leaks. Investigate security measures such as NCP Packet Signature, access rights, and password security to ensure that your network is as secure as you need it to be.

TROUBLESHOOTING TIPS

Unfortunately, despite the best possible planning, something may still go wrong with your network. The majority of network problems are related to hardware issues—interrupt conflicts, faulty components, incompatible hardware, and so on. However, software creates its own set of problems, such as application incompatibility, Windows problems, and installation errors.

There are endless combinations of servers, workstations, cabling, networking hardware, operating systems, and applications. This makes it impossible to predict and document every possible problem. The closest anyone can do is approach the problem with a methodical system for isolating the problem, then fixing it.

The following troubleshooting guidelines can help you isolate the problem and find solutions.

Narrow Down the List of Suspects

First, of course, you must try to narrow your search to suspicious areas.

ZEN

"Round up the usual suspects."

From the movie *Casablanca*

▶ Were there any error messages? If so, look up their explanations in the System Messages on-line manual.

▶ How many machines did the problem affect?

▶ Can you identify a particular cabling segment or branch of the tree that is having the problem?

▶ Does the problem occur only when a user is accessing a particular application, or perhaps only when the user executes applications in a particular order?

▶ If the problem occurred when you installed a new workstation or server on the network, check their network addresses and hardware settings for conflicts with other boards or with machines that already exist on the network. Also, double-check the installation documentation to make sure you didn't misspell a command or accidentally skip a step.

▶ Are the servers and workstations using the same frame type to communicate? For example, if a server's using Ethernet 802.2 and a workstation is using Ethernet 802.3, they won't see each other.

▶ Are the servers and workstations using compatible NCP Packet Signature levels to communicate?

▶ If a user is having trouble working with files or applications, check the security features. Does the user have appropriate rights in the necessary directories? Are the files already opened by someone else? Do the files or directories have attributes assigned that are restricting the user from some actions?

▶ If some of a user's DOS path commands are gone, look in the login scripts for search drive mappings that are mapped without using the INS keyword (which inserts the mapping into the DOS path instead of overwriting existing paths).

▶ For printing problems, check that the printer, print server, and print queue are all assigned to each other correctly. You can use the IntranetWare Administrator to check on your printing setup. Select the print server from the Browser, open its Details page, then open its Print Layout page to see whether the print server, printer, and queue are all assigned together correctly. Verify that applications are using the correct print drivers for your printers. (See Chapter 8 for more information on printing.)

▶ If a volume won't mount, you may need to run VREPAIR to fix it.

Check the Hardware

Hardware problems can be relatively common in networks. Network cables are notorious for developing problems, partially because of the abuse they get being coiled up, walked on, bent around corners, and so on. A network analyzer, such as IntanetWare LANalyzer, can be a useful tool for diagnosing cable problems.

If you're suspicious that your problems may be hardware-related, try investigating the following common trouble-spots.

- ▶ Cables have an annoying tendency to work loose from their connectors, so check all connections between cables and boards first.

- ▶ Test suspicious cables by replacing them with cables you know work, and see if the problem persists.

- ▶ Make sure cables are terminated correctly, don't exceed length limits, and don't form endless loops in topologies that don't allow that.

- ▶ If the problem is with a computer or printer, try disconnecting it from the network and running it in stand-alone mode. If the problem still shows up in stand-alone mode, it's probably not a problem with the network connection. You can then eliminate the network components and concentrate on the configuration of the machine itself.

- ▶ If the problem occurred when you installed a new workstation or server, or added a board to an existing computer, check hardware settings for conflicts with other boards or with machines that already exist on the network.

Refer to the Documentation

Forget the jokes about only reading the manual as a last resort. The NetWare on-line manuals contain explanations of error messages that may occur. In addition, they include troubleshooting tips, configuration instructions, and so on.

In addition, check the manufacturer's documentation for any network hardware or applications you're using. Some applications have special instructions for installing on a network.

REAL WORLD

Contrary to popular hearsay, most of the network administrators I've known really do read the documentation before they try to install something as complex as IntranetWare. Why? Because their jobs are on the line. It's not like installing an application, where, if it doesn't work, it's easy to try again. If you mess up the company's network, it can be a really big deal, and can cost the company far more than your salary. And unfortunately, everyone immediately knows you've done something wrong. Keep this in mind the next time you're tempted to skip the documentation. There are plenty of other potential network administrators out there who would *love* to read the documentation first—and they may be your next replacement.

Look for Patches or Workarounds

When Novell engineers find a problem with IntranetWare, they usually either solve the problem with a patch (a piece of software that attaches to NetWare on your server and repairs it) or a recommended workaround.

Novell distributes these patches and workarounds on CompuServe and the Internet (at http:\www.novell.com) and in Novell's Support Connection (formerly NSEPro), so that you can easily update your server with these fixes. See Appendix D for more information about these resources.

Try Each Solution by Itself

After you've isolated the problem to a suspicious area, try implementing the solutions you've found, but implement them one at a time. The tendency is to try several possible fixes simultaneously to save time.

Start with the easiest, cheapest solution, and work up from there.

Trying solutions simultaneously may save time in the short run, but it could cost you extra money for unnecessary repairs or replacements. In addition, you won't know for sure what fixed the problem, so you'll have to start from scratch again should the problem reappear on another machine or at another time.

Call for Technical Support

There are a wide variety of places you can go to get help, advice, tips, and fixes for your NetWare problems or issues. Appendix D lists several of the resources you should know about. These resources range from Internet user groups, to classes, to publications that deal with IntranetWare support issues.

ZEN

"Help! I need somebody. Help! Not just anybody."

The Beatles

If you're looking for more formal technical support try these ideas:

▶ You can often find the technical help you need on-line, through the Internet Usenet groups that focus on NetWare, or through the Novell forums on the Internet and CompuServe. These forums are moderated by knowledgeable sysops (system operators) and populated by knowledgeable users.

▶ Try calling your reseller or consultant for help.

▶ Novell's Technical Support is available by calling 1-800-858-4000 or 801-861-4000 in the U.S. However, Novell's Technical Support is not free. You'll be charged a fee for each incident, so have your credit card handy. (An incident may involve more than one phone call, if necessary.)

▶ Before you call, be sure you've tried your other resources first— especially the documentation. It's embarrassing and expensive to have Technical Support tell you that the answer to your question is on page 25 of the Installation manual.

Document the Solution

When you find a solution, write it down and store it with your network documentation. This may prevent you or someone else from duplicating efforts and wasting time going through the same troubleshooting process to fix a similar problem later.

ZEN

"The empty page before me now, the pen is in my hand. The words don't come so easy, but I'm trying."

Kansas

The CNA 4.1 Program

▶ · · · · · · · · · · · · · · · · ◀

"We've come halfway across the galaxy to see NetWare 4!"

Understanding IntranetWare and NDS

So you think you know NetWare. Well, I have a surprise for you! Not even Bo knows IntranetWare. Novell's fifth generation of the NetWare operating system is a completely new ball game—and fortunately nobody is on strike.

Welcome to IntranetWare!

IntranetWare is the big kahuna. It represents Novell's tenth try at the NetWare network operating system. The original architects of NetWare—Drew Major and Superset—returned to the proverbial drawing board and completely redesigned the interface, communications, and functionality. The result is a powerful, flexible, and fast wide area network operating system. There's a mouthful.

IntranetWare epitomizes transparent connectivity. It unobtrusively provides the user with simultaneous access to multiple network resources from one login—whatever that means. Simply stated, users no longer belong to servers—they belong to the *network* as a whole. All resources of the wide area network (WAN) are created as objects in a hierarchical tree, much like files in a directory structure. Users, servers, printers, volumes, and groups are treated equally and given simultaneous access to each other's resources. It's been a long and winding road, but we've finally achieved IntranetWare Nirvana in true form. This is all made possible through IntranetWare's great wonder—Novell Directory Services (NDS).

NDS is an object-oriented database that organizes network resources into a *hierarchical* tree—there's that fancy word again. The global NDS tree is fully replicated and distributed throughout the network, providing efficient connectivity and network fault tolerance—which is easier said than done. NDS also features a single login and hidden security system that makes access to any server, volume, or network resource completely transparent to the user. NDS takes care of the complexities of network topology, communications, protocol translation, and authentication in the background far away from the user.

Think of NDS as a friendly cloud of joy overlooking your network! NDS is simplicity through sophistication.

TIP

NDS enables you to manage network resources (such as servers, users, and printers) and services, but it does not control the file system (directories and files). IntranetWare provides a variety of non-NDS utilities for managing the file system.

In addition to Novell Directory Services, IntranetWare offers myriad additional features and benefits. We will explore them in just a moment.

SMART LINK

For an introduction to Novell Directory Services, consult the on-line IntranetWare documentation at http://www.novell.com/manuals.

IntranetWare is not an upgrade of NetWare 3.1x—it requires a system *migration*. IntranetWare is a completely different way of approaching networking. It splits the role of networking into two halves—logical and physical. The logical half defines organizations and workgroups. The physical half defines users and servers. The beauty of this approach is that IntranetWare can be as simple or complex as you want it to be. In addition, it includes a feature called *bindery emulation* that enables a IntranetWare server to look like a NetWare 3.12 server. This is a whole new twist on backward compatibility. All in all, IntranetWare is a great solution for small-, medium-, and large-size local area networks (LANs), metropolitan area networks (MANs), and wide area networks (WANs). Also, you better get used to it, because IntranetWare is the foundation of Novell's new Enterprise approach to networking. Before you know it, NetWare 3 will be long gone and you'll be reading *Novell's CNA Study Guide for IntranetWare 2*.

TIP

NetWare 3.12 is actually more similar to IntranetWare than you might think. NetWare 3.12 was originally developed because users of NetWare 3.11 were complaining that NetWare 4.0 had all the cool features. To satisfy these users, Novell released a special version of NetWare 3.11 that included some of the new advanced NetWare 4.0 features (such as VLMs, SMS, a new menu system, on-line documentation, and better Windows support). In reality, NetWare 3.12 is a subset of IntranetWare without NDS.

THE FOUNDATION OF NETWARE 3.12

If all of this seems a little overwhelming, have no fear, Uncle David is here. IntranetWare actually isn't as alien as you might think. As a matter of fact, Novell hasn't made any dramatic changes to the fundamental architecture of the core operating system (OS). The Novell designers simply built on top of what exists in NetWare 3.12. As you can see in Figure 3.1, NetWare 3.12 consists of the core OS and some supplemental services. All the services shown in this figure are mostly unchanged in IntranetWare. These services include:

FIGURE 3.1

The Foundation of NetWare 3.12

| Inter-national | Dyna-Text | Client Services (VLMs) | Core OS | Message Handling Services (MHS) | Storage Management Services (SMS) | Menu System |

- ▸ Core OS—Of course, the core operating system has been "tweaked" a little in IntranetWare, but the fundamental 32-bit architecture remains unchanged from NetWare 3.12. IntranetWare still relies on the console prompt and NetWare Loadable Modules (NLMs).

WHAT'S NEW

I would like to interrupt this book for an emergency broadcast message from Novell. As you know, the latest release of NetWare isn't NetWare at all—it's "IntranetWare." So, what happened to NetWare? Fortunately, it's still here. As a matter of fact, the IntranetWare solution uses "NetWare 4.11" as its primary operating system. Confusing? Yes.

So, here's the bottom line: IntranetWare the network-centric WAN solution and NetWare 4.11 is the server-centric LAN OS it uses. Throughout this book, we will refer to IntranetWare as the product, and NetWare 4.11 as the core OS. Now, I will return you to your regularly scheduled programming.

- ▸ Internationalization—Both NetWare 3.12 and IntranetWare are designed to support a variety of international languages and utilities. In IntranetWare, the operating system, error message files, and documentation are available in the following languages: Chinese (simplified and traditional), French, German, Italian, Japanese, Korean, Portuguese, Russian, and Spanish.

THE BRAIN

For further information on using IntranetWare in languages other than English, refer to the "International Use of IntranetWare" section of the *Novell NetWare 4.11 Concepts* manual or surf the Web at http://www.novell.com/manuals.

▸ DynaText—The DynaText viewer included with IntranetWare offers all the functionality of the Novell DynaText viewer provided in NetWare 3.12, plus a quicker response time, enhanced graphical user interface (GUI), Macintosh and UnixWare support, and compatibility for public or private notes in on-line manuals.

▸ Client services (VLMs)—Both NetWare 3.12 and IntranetWare offer better workstation connectivity through the NetWare DOS Requester. The Requester uses Virtual Loadable Modules (VLMs) to provide enhanced workstation support for NDS, NCP packet signing, and advanced user authentication. The latest version also supports connection timeout optimization, auto-reconnect, and much better extended memory management. In addition, IntranetWare includes an optional 32-bit Client for advanced workstations.

▸ Message Handling Services (MHS)—Novell now includes a sophisticated e-mail engine with NetWare 3.12 and IntranetWare. In NetWare 3.12 this engine is implemented as Basic MHS; in IntranetWare, it is termed MHS Services for NetWare 4.11. Both versions provide a background engine for storing and forwarding IntranetWare messages. In addition, they provide a starter e-mail application called FirstMail, which includes both DOS and Windows versions. The IntranetWare version of MHS also provides full integration with NDS and IntranetWare administration utilities. It takes advantage of specific mail-oriented NDS objects and includes SFT III compatibility. Furthermore, Enterprise customers can benefit from the comprehensive messaging features of GroupWise.

▸ Storage Management Services (SMS)—Like MHS, both NetWare 3.12 and IntranetWare include a background engine for backing up and restoring server data. SMS enables data to be stored and retrieved by using a variety of front-end applications. Also, these applications can call on numerous independent storage devices attached directly to the IntranetWare server. In addition, SMS can back up a variety of file systems—including DOS, OS/2, Macintosh, MS Windows, and UNIX. Another exciting feature of SMS is workstation backup. This might seem a little backward for those of you who are used to backing up servers from the workstation—now we're backing up workstations from the server. IntranetWare's SMS adds support for NDS backup and the System Independent Data Format (SIDF).

▸ Menu System—Since NetWare 3.11, Novell has dedicated itself to providing a better integrated menu system. NetWare 3.12 and IntranetWare use the new Saber-like menu system for building a consistent user interface. It includes better memory management, a higher level of workstation security, and user input options.

 ZEN

"The guy who invented headcheese must have been really hungry."

Jerry Seinfeld

THE EVOLUTION OF INTRANETWARE

As I mentioned earlier, IntranetWare builds on the foundation of NetWare 3.12. Now, let's take a look at the evolution of IntranetWare from a server-centric OS to a network-centric OS. As you can see in Figure 3.2, there are five main features that make IntranetWare the operating system of the next generation. These features build on top of the NetWare 3.12 foundation and reach to the sky. The most pervasive of these features is NDS:

▸ Novell Directory Services (NDS)—NDS is also known as the "Cloud." It oversees all facets of network operation—from logging in to multiprotocol routing. In short, IntranetWare is NetWare 3.12 with NDS. It's that simple—or not. Life in the NDS universe is a little more complicated than you might think. The price for user transparency is your blood, sweat, and tears. NDS generates a great deal more administrative overhead than you might be used to. But all of your hard work is worth it. NDS will ultimately increase user productivity and add more value to the network. Some customers are projecting a 300 percent return on their IntranetWare investment. We'll take a much closer look at NDS in just a moment. Welcome to the X-Files.

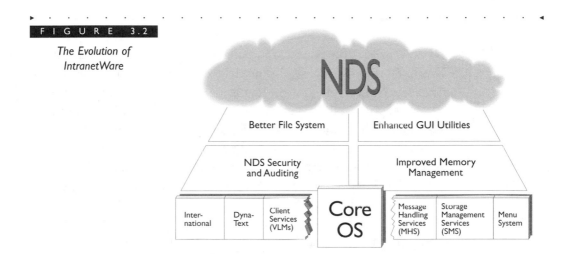

▸ Better File System—IntranetWare optimizes the server disk with three new features: file compression, data migration, and block suballocation. File compression automatically reduces the size of infrequently used files by up to 63 percent. Data migration offloads these files to near-line storage devices. Finally, block suballocation decreases storage inefficiencies by allowing multiple files to share a single disk block. More details to come.

▸ Enhanced GUI Utilities—IntranetWare has vastly improved the interface for both user and administrator utilities. At the forefront of the new utility revolution is NetWare Administrator (NWADMIN)—a fully integrated Windows-based graphical administrator tool. The NetWare Administrator centralizes all IntranetWare tasks in one graphical NDS window. IntranetWare also offers a text-based menu version of NetWare Administrator (called NETADMIN), enhanced console commands, server NLMs, and new user command line utilities (CLUs). Also, don't miss the new integrated partition management tool—NDS Manager. All in all, IntranetWare not only works better, it also looks better.

ZEN

"Image is everything."

Andre Agassi

▸ NDS Security and Auditing—IntranetWare security is controlled by a five-layer security model. This model looks very similar to the NetWare 3.12 four-layer model, except that it includes an additional layer of access security—NDS security. This layer defines security above the server by controlling movement throughout the NDS tree. NDS access rights apply at both the object and property levels. In addition to NDS security, IntranetWare includes a comprehensive and powerful auditing feature. Independent auditors can track network transactions according to a variety of strategies, including logins/logouts, trustee modifications, file access and modification, NDS activity, queue management, and object management. The beauty of IntranetWare auditing is that independent auditors can track network resources without having any other rights to the WAN. All these features allow IntranetWare to satisfy the strict requirements of C2 level security. You will learn more about IntranetWare NDS security later in Chapter 5, "IntranetWare Security."

▸ Improved Memory Management—IntranetWare manages file server RAM in a completely different way than NetWare 3.12 did. Earlier versions of NetWare allocated memory to multiple pools that served specific purposes. These pools were so inefficient that server applications could run out of RAM even if there was plenty of memory available in the main pool. IntranetWare has consolidated all server RAM into one central pool, and memory is reallocated as needed. In addition, IntranetWare includes memory protection that allows NLMs to run in a protected area of RAM. This ensures the safety of the core OS while you are testing third-party NLMs. Shields up!

As you can see from this discussion, IntranetWare represents the peak of OS evolution. It builds on the foundation of NetWare 3.12 to create a more powerful platform for the next generation of networking. For an even more detailed comparison of the NetWare 3.12 and IntranetWare features, refer to Table 3.1.

T A B L E 3.1		
IntranetWare and NetWare 3.12 Features Comparison		

FEATURE	INTRANETWARE	NETWARE 3.12
ARCHITECTURE		
Maximum number of user connections per server	1,000	250
Nondedicated server	Yes (IntranetWare for OS/2)	No
Single login to network	Yes	No
Additive licensing	Yes	No
Memory protection	Yes	No
Global directory services	Yes	No
FILE SYSTEM AND STORAGE		
File compression	Yes	No
Data migration	Yes	No
Block suballocation	Yes	No
NETWORK SECURITY		
RSA public/private key encryption	Yes	No
Restrict login to specific Macintosh addresses	Yes	No
Security auditing	Yes	No
NETWORK MANAGEMENT		
GUI utility with view of entire network	Yes	No
Remote console session security	Yes	No
Remote console modem callback	Yes	No

(continued)

TABLE 3.1	FEATURE	INTRANETWARE	NETWARE 3.12
IntranetWare and NetWare 3.12 Features Comparison (continued)	NETWORK MANAGEMENT *(continued)*		
	Maximum shared printers	256 per print server	16 per print server
	RAM used with remote printer	4.6K to 5.4K	4K to 20K
	Integrated messaging	Yes	No
	Network Link Services Protocol (NLSP)	Yes	Yes (add-on required)
	CLIENT SUPPORT AND INTEROPERABILITY		
	LPT ports on client	LPT-1 to LPT-9	LPT-1 to LPT-3
	IntranetWareMacintosh user licenses included	Matches the number of IntranetWare user licenses	5
	GUI user tools	Yes	Yes
	NetWare DOS Requester support	Yes	Yes

SMART LINK

For an quick overview of new features in IntranetWare, consult the on-line IntranetWare documentation at http://www.novell.com/manuals.

All the new features we've just discussed are included in IntranetWare and the previous version (NetWare 4.1). In addition, some new features have been introduced with IntranetWare. Let's take a moment to explore the newest features of NetWare's fifth-generation operating system.

WHAT'S NEW IN INTRANETWARE

With each release of NetWare (and now *IntranetWare*), Novell improves a number of basic and Enterprise services. With IntranetWare, ten major advancements have been made, beginning with Novell Directory Services. Let's briefly review each.

1. Novell Directory Services

The major improvement in IntranetWare NDS is a philosophical one. Novell is moving toward an OS-independent version of Directory Services. Therefore, the name is no longer NetWare Directory Services, but Novell Directory Services.

To support this enhanced Enterprise approach, the new NDS includes a variety of additional leaf objects, one of which is the User template. This object is now in a "class" by itself instead of being relegated to a type of User object. In addition, audit log files are now represented by, and managed as, Directory objects. This enables you to control access to audit log files by using Directory rights assignments. Finally, the new NDS supports a connection to multiple Directory trees. As we'll learn later, Novell has just started the creation of a new "federation." Look out Star Fleet!

In addition to these structural improvements, IntranetWare includes enhanced NDS utilities. For starters, a Windows 95 version of NetWare Administrator has been added and the interface has been improved with a configurable tool bar, a configurable status bar, and the ability to hide and sort property pages for individual Directory objects. In addition, you can manage multiple trees simultaneously within the same NWADMIN window and set property values for multiple objects with the "Details on Multiple Users Option." Finally, you can print the Directory tree from within NetWare Administrator.

In addition to improved NWADMIN and NETADMIN utilities, IntranetWare includes a new graphical hierarchical browser for partition management—called NDS Manager. NDS Manager runs as a stand-alone application or as an integrated part of NWADMIN. It provides partitioning and replication services, as well as context-sensitive help for synchronizing errors detected by the "Partition Continuity Option." NDS Manager also includes the ability to repair the Directory database from a client workstation, and an update compatibility so that any or all IntranetWare servers on a network can be updated to a newer version of the DS.NLM file. We'll be spending plenty of time with Novell Directory Services later in this chapter.

2. Server Operating System

IntranetWare is based on the same stable, secure core OS as NetWare 4.1. In addition, it has been enhanced to provide improved ABEND recovery, UPS connectivity, and CLIB.NLM support. IntranetWare Web Server and IntranetWare Symmetric MultiProcessing (SMP) features have been added, as well. Let's take a closer look.

With IntranetWare, the server operating system has improved recovery options for handling an ABnormal END (ABEND). For starters, additional information about the source of the ABEND is displayed on the server console. This information identifies the NLM or hardware problem that caused the ABEND, so an administrator can take corrective actions. Also, when an ABEND occurs, information about the ABEND is automatically written to a text file—ABEND.LOG. Finally, two new SET parameters have been added that enable the server to automatically recover in various ways—"Auto Restart After ABEND" and "Auto Restart After ABEND Delay Time."

With IntranetWare, the core operating system now supports an uninterruptible power supply (UPS) connection through a serial port. This functionality is provided by the UPS_AIO.NLM module. In addition, the IntranetWare SFT III system has been enhanced with two new SET parameters and improvements in the PROTOCOLS command. Also, the server OS includes some hardware platform-related enhancements such as server memory management routines that take advantage of the Global Page attribute in Intel's Pentium Pro microprocessor and better support for the Peripheral Component Interface (PCI) bus architecture.

With IntranetWare, the CLIB.NLM file has been modularized into several NLMs. The functionality of the previous CLIB.NLM is now available in the following modules:

- *CLIB.NLM*—ANSI-compliant run-time interface for old CLIB functions.

- *FPSM.NLM*—floating-point support library

- *THREADS.NLM*—IntranetWare standard NLM THREADS package

- *REQUESTR.NLM*—standard Requester package

- *NLMLIB.NLM*—POSIX and other basic NLM run-time support

- *NIT.NLM*—old NetWare interface tools which are being replaced by interfaces in CALN32.NLM

In addition to these core OS improvements, IntranetWare adds two new products—IntranetWare Web Server and IntranetWare Support for Symmetric MultiProcessing. The IntranetWare Web Server technology enables you to publish documents on internal corporate networks and on the World Wide Web. Because the software runs on a standard IntranetWare platform, you can establish an Internet presence without using UNIX and the expensive hardware that UNIX requires. The IntranetWare Web Server consists of a set of NLMs that are easy to install and configure. It includes support for forms, the Remote Common Gateway Interface (R-CGI) specification, access logging, BASIC and PERL script interpreters, and the ability to easily control access to the server and its file system by using standard NDS security features. In addition, you can control access to HTML documents based on IP address, username, host name, directory structure, filename, and/or group membership. (See Appendix E for more information.)

The IntranetWare Symmetric MultiProcessing (SMP) technology enables the IntranetWare operating system to run on a multiprocessor server. IntranetWare SMP enables the server to run resource-intense services (such as large databases, document management software, and multimedia applications) on a IntranetWare server. As I'm sure you can imagine, it provides increased processing power and better network performance to the Enterprise. In addition, there's support for up to 32 processors, depending on the hardware platform and Advanced Programmable Interrupt Controllers (APICs).

3. Installation

To make the installation process easier in IntranetWare, the INSTALL utility autodetects hardware devices installed in the server. In addition, Novell has partnered with Preferred Systems to develop and provide additional upgrade utilities with IntranetWare. These utilities form a logical extension of their existing DS Standard utility.

During a IntranetWare installation, the INSTALL utility automatically detects the hardware devices in a server (including hard drives, CD-ROM devices, LAN cards, and so on). It then scans for and selects applicable device drivers (.DSK and .HAM files) for the hardware.

To provide IntranetWare customers with a complete upgrade solution, Novell has partnered with Preferred Systems to develop and deliver two additional upgrade utilities in IntranetWare—DS Migrate and the IntranetWare File Migration Utility:

> ▸ *DS Migrate*—This is a new migration and modeling solution that is built into the graphical NWADMIN utility. DS Migrate enables you to upgrade

a NetWare 2.1x or NetWare 3.1x server bindery by migrating modeled bindery information to an existing IntranetWare tree. DS Migrate migrates only bindery information. Data files are migrated using either the new graphical IntranetWare File Migration utility or the DOS menu-based MIGRATE utility.

▶ *IntranetWare File Migration Utility*—This is a new utility for migrating files from NetWare 3.1x file systems to IntranetWare file systems. The IntranetWare File Migration Utility is used in conjunction with the new DS Migrate utility after NetWare 3.1x bindery migration. This facility is also incorporated into the new NWADMIN tool.

You'll get an opportunity to explore all 23 steps of the IntranetWare installation later in Chapter 7.

4. NetWare Licensing Services

With IntranetWare, Novell is introducing NetWare Licensing Services (NLS). NLS is a distributed Enterprise network service that enables administrators to monitor and control the use of licensed applications on a network. It is tightly integrated with NDS technology and is based on an Enterprise service architecture. This architecture consists of client components that support different platforms and system components that reside on IntranetWare servers. NLS also provides a basic license metering tool and libraries that export licensing service functionality to developers of other licensing systems.

5. Connectivity Services

IntranetWare is fully multiprotocol-compliant. This means IntranetWare servers can communicate over the network using the traditional IPX protocol or new integrated support for TCP/IP. NetWare/IP enables you to extend IntranetWare services and applications to nodes on an existing IP network in a manner that is transparent to users. It also allows you to interconnect TCP/IP and IPX networks, enabling users on both platforms to access IntranetWare resources on either network. You can easily manage TCP/IP addresses using the Dynamic Host Configuration Protocol (DHCP) and provide access to network printers attached to UNIX hosts using the "LPR" protocol.

To use NetWare/IP in an IP-only environment, you must use network client software that supports the TCP/IP protocol. This includes the new NetWare Client 32, the NetWare/IP version of VLMs, or the NetWare Client for Mac OS. In addition, the new IntranetWare Client for Mac OS allows Macintosh workstations to access IntranetWare servers using traditional IPX or new IP protocols. Previous connectivity required the AppleTalk protocol. For more information on IntranetWare support for TCP/IP, see Appendix F.

6. File Services

With IntranetWare, the IntranetWare file system more effectively supports extended name spaces and can hold 8 million files per volume (16 million on DOS-only volumes). In addition, IntranetWare volumes mount much faster and the file system automatically monitors volume space.

With IntranetWare, the LONG.NAM module provides extended name space to Windows 95, Windows NT, and OS/2 workstation platforms. LONG.NAM is a special type of NLM that enables non-DOS file names on a IntranetWare volume. Because extended name spaces are used more often now, LONG.NAM is loaded as part of the default server configuration.

In addition to the improvements discussed earlier, the IntranetWare file system responds more efficiently to the new 32-bit IntranetWare client architecture, delivering a higher level of performance to workstations using the new 32-bit IntranetWare client. We'll explore the IntranetWare file system in much more depth in Chapter 4.

7. Application Services

Novell has introduced two new advancements in the network application arena—the NetWare Application Manager (NAM) and NetWare Application Launcher (NAL).

The NAM utility enables you to represent applications as objects in the Directory tree. As NDS objects, you can manage applications the same way you manage other objects using NWADMIN. In addition, you can define an application directory, icon, command line parameters, and other attributes in one place; use trustee assignments to manage access to applications; and define startup scripts that establish the appropriate network environment for the application.

The NAL utility (available in both 16-bit and 32-bit versions) enables network users to launch applications represented by Application objects. When started,

NAL displays a desktop that contains Application object icons. When the network user clicks on an icon, NAL sets up the workstation and starts the associated application as defined in the Application object's properties. As a CNA, you can control to what applications the network user has access and the user's ability to adjust the NAL desktop. This is just another example of how IntranetWare and NDS are working together to integrate all Enterprise services. You'll get a chance to work with the new IntranetWare application management products in Chapter 6.

8. Storage Management Services (SMS)

In IntranetWare, the enhanced Storage Management Services (SMS) feature includes a better backup utility, more effective backup and restore capabilities for the Directory, and new Target Service Agents (TSAs). Probably the most impressive improvement involves the SBACKUP utility itself:

- ► You can create session files from tape.

- ► You can search log files for specific character strings.

- ► Backup sessions can be verified with CRC values.

- ► SBACKUP now displays a running count for up to 4.2 terabytes of data as it is backed up.

When data is restored, information about the restoration target is written to the error file.

In previous versions of NetWare 4, Directory schema extensions and the mechanisms that enable you to manage file trustee assignments from NDS were not effectively backed up. This meant key security information was lost. With IntranetWare, a server's private key, User object IDs, and file trustee assignments and replica information are effectively maintained throughout the backup-and-restore process—very good news.

In addition, IntranetWare ships with new Target Service Agents (TSAs) for Windows 95 and Macintosh workstations. The IntranetWare file system TSA has also been updated. We'll take a much closer look at SMS and all of its new IntranetWare enhancements in Chapter 7.

9. Security Services

With IntranetWare, Novell introduces NetWare Enhanced Security (NES). NetWare Enhanced Security is designed to meet the Controlled Access Implementation Class C-2 requirements. This is the minimum security specification for high-security corporate and government networks.

To facilitate NES and Class C-2 compliance, the following features are provided:

▸ The AUDITCON utility has been significantly improved to enable C2-compliant auditing.

▸ Audit log files are now represented by and managed as Directory objects. This enables you to control access to audit log files by using Directory rights assignments.

▸ A network server can be configured as an "Enhanced Security Server" by using an updated group of SET parameters.

▸ The SECURE.NCF file provides a script that configures the server as an Enhanced Security Server. You can run this script at any time from a IntranetWare server system prompt, or use the following SET parameter to enable it automatically at bootup: "Enable SECURE.NCF."

As you'll learn later in the book, we live in an Information Age. Because of this, network data has taken on a greater importance than ever before. IntranetWare and the NetWare Enhanced Security System allows you to sleep easily at night, knowing that everything is secure. Don't worry—if you don't feel fully secure yet, you will get a chance to break into IntranetWare Fort Knox in Chapter 5.

10. Print Services

In IntranetWare, traditional NetWare print services have been improved and Novell has introduced the next generation of network printing—Novell Distributed Print Services (NDPS). With the introduction of NDPS, traditional print services are frequently referred to as "queue-based printing." With IntranetWare, queue-based printing has been integrated into NWADMIN. In addition, you can use the new graphical NPRINTER Manager to enable network users to share a printer attached to a Windows 95 workstation. NPRINTER

Manager provides the same functionality that NPRINTER.EXE used to provide on a DOS or OS/2 workstation.

NDPS is Novell's next-generation printing system. It is designed for complex print management and production requirements. It is an ideal printing solution for users in diverse environments ranging from small workgroups to Enterprise WANs.

NDPS is a distributed service consisting of client, server, and connectivity components that seamlessly link and share network printers with applications. It eliminates the need to create and configure Print Queue, Printer, and Print Server objects. In fact, NDPS doesn't require you to manage print queues at all. With NDPS, a single graphical administration utility (NWADMIN) provides comprehensive management and control for all major brands and models of printers. If this all sounds too good to be true, check out Chapter 8. If it all seems too complex for you, remember that NDPS is *optional* in IntranetWare. As a matter of fact, it probably won't be available until the *next* release of IntranetWare.

Well, that completes our brief overview of the ten most exciting enhancements to IntranetWare. For a complete summary of these features, check out Table 3.2. Wow, there's so much to learn and so little time.

ZEN

Nothing in life is to be feared. It is only to be understood.

Marie Curie

TABLE 3.2

*What's New in
IntranetWare*

SERVICE	FEATURE	NETWARE 4.1	INTRANETWARE
1. Novell Directory Services	NetWare Administrator	Windows 3.1x version only	Windows 3.1x and Windows 95 versions
		Limited customization capabilities	Configurable tool bar, status bar, and property pages
		Supports connection to a single Directory tree only	Supports connection to multiple Directory trees

TABLE 3.2

What's New in
IntranetWare (continued)

SERVICE	FEATURE	NETWARE 4.1	INTRANETWARE
	Partition Management	Managed by PARTMGR and Partition Manager	Managed by the new NDS Manager utility
2. Server operating system	ABEND recovery	Limited options	Improved ABEND recovery options
	UPS connections	Limited to MAU support only	Serial port connection supported
	CLIB.NLM	A single module	Six related modules
	IntranetWare Web Server	Unavailable	Included
	IntranetWare Symmetric MultiProcessing	Available from OEM partners only	Included
3. Installation	Hardware detection	Limited	Substantially improved
	Upgrade utilities	Limited	Existing utilities improved and two additional migration utilities provided
4. NetWare Licensing Service	Integrated license management	Unavailable	Included
5. Connectivity Services	NetWare/IP	Available, but not integrated	Fully integrated
	IntranetWare Client for Mac OS	Requires AppleTalk	Can communicate using IPX or IP, doesn't require AppleTalk
6. File Services	Support for long filenames	OS2.NAM for OS/2 platform	LONG.NAM supports extended name spaces for the Windows 95, Windows NT, and OS/2 platforms
	Volume capacity	Limited to 2,000,000 directory entries	Each IntranetWare volume can handle up to 16,000,000 directory entries

(continued)

TABLE 3.2

What's New in
IntranetWare (continued)

SERVICE	FEATURE	NETWARE 4.1	INTRANETWARE
7. Application Services	NetWare Application Manager	Unavailable	Included
	NetWare Application Launcher	Unavailable	Included
8. Storage Management Services	SBACKUP	Limited backup services for NDS	Improved backup services for NDS
	Target Service Agents (TSAs)	Available for DOS, Windows 3.1x, and OS/2	Windows 95 and Mac OS TSAs included
9. Security Services	C-2 compatibility	Unavailable	Included
	AUDITCON	Limited events audited	Can audit many additional events
10. Print Services	NPRINTER Manager for Windows 95	Unavailable	Enables you to manage printers attached to Windows 95 workstations
	Quick Setup option	PCONSOLE only	NWADMIN and PCONSOLE
	Novell Distributed Print Services (NDPS)	Unavailable	Future (*optional*)

So, you bought IntranetWare and now what do you do with it? How do you design your NDS tree? Where do you put your user accounts? What steps should you take to optimize performance, transparency, and system fault tolerance? Who shot Mr. Burns? What did you get yourself into? Don't panic—these are good questions.

This book is dedicated to *YOU*. I hope to get you through IntranetWare with the least amount of pain. Who knows—you might even enjoy yourself along the way. We're going to start this first technical chapter with a detailed exploration of Novell Directory Services (NDS). Then, we'll journey through all the exciting technology that make life as an IntranetWare CNA so wonderful. Here's what's in store:

▸ Novell Directory Services (now!)

▸ IntranetWare File System (Chapter 4)

▸ IntranetWare Security (Chapter 5)

▸ IntranetWare Configuration (Chapter 6)

▸ IntranetWare Management (Chapter 7)

▸ IntranetWare Printing (Chapter 8)

In this chapter, we'll expand on the heart of IntranetWare—NDS. But this is only the beginning. Once you've been introduced to the technology, you must learn what to do with it. Imagine what could happen if this power falls into the wrong hands. Imagine what Napoleon could have done with a turbocharged water cannon! No, we must harness the power of IntranetWare by learning how to manage it. That's the true focus of *Novell's CNA Study Guide for IntranetWare*. Aah, but let's not get ahead of ourselves. It all begins with Novell Directory Services.

SMART LINK

For a quick glimpse of *Novell's CNA Study Guide for IntranetWare*, surf to http://corp.novell.com/programs/press/hot.htm.

QUIZ

I'm in a giving mood; it must be your birthday. I have three gifts for you—small, medium, and large. Each gift is wrapped with a different color paper that is red, green, or silver. In addition, I've placed a different color bow on each package, either red, green, or gold. In order to earn your gifts, describe the wrapping and bow combination for each present. Here are some clues:

▸ **The small gift has a green bow.**

▸ **The large gift is the only one that matches.**

Remember, puzzles help stretch your imagination. But whatever you do, don't pull a frontal lobe!

(Q3-1)
(See Appendix C for all quiz answers.)

Getting to Know NDS

Every cloud has a silver lining. Even Daisy-Head Mayzie had 15 minutes of fame. But she let it go to her head—literally. One sunny afternoon, sweet little Mayzie sprouted a Daisy out of her head! How odd.

After she got over the initial shock, Mayzie got a "big head." She left her family and friends to become a star in Hollywood. But all the money and fame didn't change the fact that she had a plant growing out of her cranium. And what's money worth anyway without somebody to share it with? So, Daisy-Head Mayzie realized her mistake and left the afternoon talk shows to return home. Yes, HOME. Not a SYS:USERS directory, not a base in baseball. No, this home is where everyone loves her for who she is, not what she has growing out of her head. Everyone lived happily ever after.

SMART LINK

For more Dr. Seuss fun, visit "Seussville" at http://www.seussville.com.

This could happen to you. You could become "NDS-Head Fred!" As a matter of fact, you can probably feel a slight "twinge" even as you read this. You knew that your new life as a CNA would be exciting, but no one prepared you for this. The more you learn about NDS, the faster your tree will sprout—until one day you'll be as rich and famous as Daisy-Head Mayzie. But don't make the same mistakes that she did. Don't abandon the people who got you here—your family, your friends, Novell, and Ortho Weed Killer. Keep your head out of the clouds and your two feet planted firmly *in* the ground.

ZEN

"Congratulations! Today is your day. You're off to great places! You're off and away!"

Dr. Seuss

I'm here to help you deal with this whole cranial gardening thing. As we learned in the last chapter, NDS is a virtual tree structure that helps you organize network resources. It's also referred to as the "Cloud" because it floats above physical resources—servers, printers, and users. In the next chapter, we begin our examination of the three phases of life as a CNA with a discussion of NDS design. But before we get there, you'll need an NDS tree growing out of your head to make sense of it all. That's the goal of this chapter. We hope to generate enough neurokinetic energy to stimulate cranial growth. In other words, we're going to make you think until it hurts. So, without any further ado, let's start at the beginning — with the NDS database.

NDS is your friend. It may seem a little intimidating at first, but when you get to know NDS, it's actually pretty fun. Really. NDS is a big Sta-Puff marshmallow man that keeps track of your network's resources. In more technical terms, it's a distributed object-oriented hierarchical database of physical network objects. Huh? Just think of it as a huge WAN phone book. NDS classifies all network resources into 29 different objects. These objects can be organized by function, location, size, type, or color—it doesn't matter. The point is, NDS organizes network resources independently from their physical locations. When a user logs into the network, he/she can access any object in the tree regardless of its location. This type of openness, however, does not come without a price. One obvious problem is security—which is why NDS is controlled by a complex, impenetrable armor known as *NDS access rights*.

So, what does NDS look like? From the outside, it looks like a big cloud hovering over your network. On the inside, however, it's a hierarchical tree similar to the DOS file system. As you can see in Figure 3.3, NDS organizes resources into logical groups called *containers*. This is like Tupperware gone mad. In Figure 3.3, servers are organized according to function. Then users are placed in the appropriate containers to simplify connectivity. In addition, productivity increases because users are near the resources they use. NDS also creates a global method of interconnectivity for all servers, users, groups, and other resources throughout the

WAN. The bottom line is this—users don't access physical resources anymore. Instead, they access logical objects in the NDS tree. This means they don't need to know which IntranetWare server provides a particular resource. All they need to know is where the server exists in the logical NDS world.

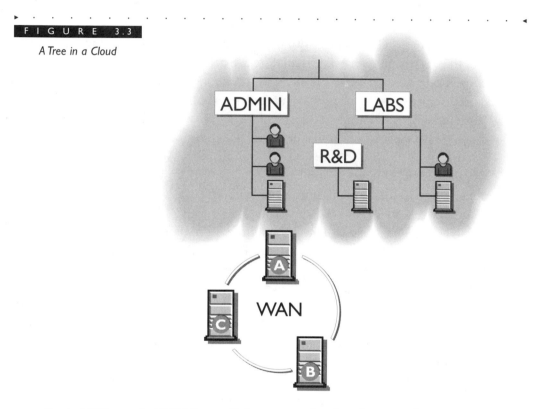

So, is NDS worth it? Well, you'll have to make that decision for yourself. But here are some of its benefits:

- ► Global database providing central access to and management of network information, resources, and services.

- ► Standard method of managing, viewing, and accessing network information, resources, and services.

- ► Logical organization of network resources that is independent of the physical characteristics or layout of the network.

▶ Dynamic mapping between an object and the physical resource to which it refers.

So, what do you think? Is NDS for you? Before you answer, let's take a moment to get to know NDS. Who knows—you might even like it.

THE "CLOUD"

NDS has many different names—the Directory, the tree, the "Cloud," the Sta-Puff marshmallow man. In reality, it's all of these things. But the most appropriate description is the "Cloud." NDS oversees physical network resources and provides users with a logical world to live in. This differs dramatically from what you're used to—NetWare 3.12. As you can see in Figure 3.4, the NetWare 3.12 bindery is *server-centric*. This means that every physical resource exists within and/or around the server. If Leia wants to access files or printers on multiple servers, she must have a login account and security access on every one. This system makes access and management both repetitive and time consuming. Also, note that nothing exists *above* the server. The server itself represents the highest level of the network organization structure. Users, volumes, files, and printers all exist within each server.

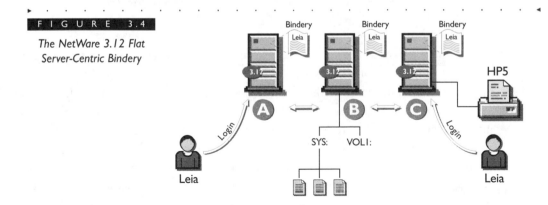

The NetWare 3.12 Flat Server-Centric Bindery

NDS, on the other hand, creates a whole new world *above* the server. As you can see in Figure 3.5, each network resource exists only once as a logical object in the "Cloud." NDS is *network-centric* in the sense that everything happens in the NDS hierarchy. Suddenly the server has gone from being at the top of the network organizational chart to being a physical object at the bottom. The beauty of this system is that Leia only logs in once and has instant access to all network resources. She doesn't log into each server—she logs into the NDS tree, and it tracks where her files and printers are. All logins, attaches, and access rights are handled in the background by NDS. This is the epitome of user transparency. The beauty is that users don't need to see inside the "Cloud"; all they need to know is that their stuff is there.

The IntranetWare Hierarchical Network-Centric NDS Cloud

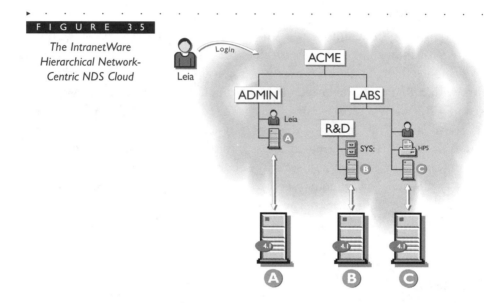

The main lesson to learn from the accompanying graphics is the direction of the arrows. In Figure 3.4, the arrows of communication are horizontal. This means that all communication exists within and between NetWare 3.12 servers. If Leia wants access to another resource, she must follow the horizontal communication path to another server by either re-logging in or attaching. In contrast, Figure 3.5 shows the communication arrows running vertically. This means that communication occurs from within and between the NDS Cloud and its physical resources. The NDS Cloud handles the problem of locating resources and transparently grabs whatever Leia wants. This vertical communication structure makes finding and using network resources much easier for the user. In addition, and this is the part you'll like, it provides a single point of central network management for CNAs.

Let's take a closer look at the differences between NDS and the NetWare 3.12 bindery.

QUIZ

Let me tell you a little story. Maybe you've heard it before. It's about this little girl named Alice, who traveled through the "looking glass." Are you with me, here? When Alice entered the Forest of Forgetfulness, she didn't forget *everything*—only certain things. She often forgot her name, and the one thing she was most likely to forget was the day of the week.

Now, the Lion and the Unicorn were frequent visitors to the forest—strange creatures. The Lion lies on Mondays, Tuesdays, and Wednesdays and tells the truth on the other days of the week. The Unicorn, on the other hand, lies on Thursdays, Fridays, and Saturdays, but tells the truth on the other days of the week. One day Alice met the Lion and the Unicorn resting under a tree. They made the following statements:

Lion: Yesterday was one of my lying days.
Unicorn: Yesterday was one of my lying days.

From these two statements, Alice (who was a very bright girl) was able to deduce the day of the week. Can you?

(Q3-2)

NDS VERSUS THE BINDERY

The bindery found in earlier versions of NetWare is a flat-file database that tracks network resources on each server. It's stored as the files NET$OBJ.SYS, NET$PROP.SYS, and NET$VAL.SYS in the SYS:SYSTEM directory. The bindery uses these three files to track network objects, properties, and values. When users need to access a server's resources, they must log in and register with its respective bindery. If the server doesn't recognize them, it disallows access. Then the administrator must create a special entry with different access security for this user. This is painstaking and dumb.

NDS, on the other hand, stores information about network resources in a global database, called the Directory. This database is distributed on all servers in the

WAN so that users can instantly get access to what they need. Suddenly, you've been escalated from a lowly bindery user to the top of the NDS food chain. As an object, you exist at the same level as the IntranetWare server. How does it feel?

Following is a brief comparison of NDS and the NetWare bindery. In each case, focus on NDS's network-centric approach.

▸ Database—The bindery is a flat-file database consisting of three files in the SYS:SYSTEM directory. Each server retains its own database. NDS, on the other hand, is an object-oriented hierarchical database, called the Directory. The Directory encompasses all objects in the WAN and is distributed across servers. It also consists of database files on the SYS: volume. These files are, however, protected in a special system-owned directory.

REAL WORLD

The Sta-Puff marshmallow man has to come down to Earth sometimes. With all this flowery talk of clouds and trees, this simple fact remains—NDS is a database stored on the SYS: volume of every IntranetWare server. More specifically, the database is made up of four protected files in the SYS:_NETWARE directory:

▸ BLOCK.NDS

▸ ENTRY.NDS

▸ PARTITIO.NDS

▸ VALUE.NDS

All these files are very hard to find. Take my word for it, they are there. If you need to see them yourself, use the Directory Scan option of RCONSOLE. See Chapter 7 ("IntranetWare Management") for more details.

▸ Server—In NetWare 3.12, the server is king of the hill. It houses the bindery and controls all network resources. In IntranetWare, however, the server's importance diminishes quite a bit. It's simply another logical object in the global NDS tree. Network resources are accessed through the "Cloud"—independently from the physical server. But don't get caught up in the logical insignificance of the IntranetWare server. In the physical realm, it's still king of the hill. After all, IntranetWare has to be installed somewhere, files have to be stored somewhere, and users have to log into something.

▸ Users—In NetWare 3.12, users are defined as objects in the server-based bindery. You must create a User object for that user on every server on which the user needs access. In NDS, however, users are logical objects in the NDS Cloud. Each user is defined only once. The system takes care of tracking the resources to which they need access. This is made possible using a concept called *context,* which we'll explain a little bit later.

▸ Login—Bindery logins are server-centric. This means that users must log in or attach to every server they use a resource from—files, printing, or applications. NDS logins are network-centric. This means that users issue one login statement for access to the entire "Cloud." Once they're in, the world is at their fingertips.

TIP

In order for NDS to identify you, you must provide your "full NDS name" at context. This includes your login name and user "context." There's that word again. A user's full name is a combination of who they are and where they live. My login name, for example, would be DAVID in CALIFORNIA in the USA. We'll talk about this later in the "NDS Naming" section of this chapter.

▸ Network Resources—In a bindery network, resources are owned by the server. Volumes and printers, for example, are tracked according to the server to which they're attached. User access to these resources requires login or attachment to the host server. NDS, on the other hand, distributes network resources independently from the server to which they're attached. It might seem strange, but volumes can be organized across the tree from their host servers. It's possible for users to have access to the IntranetWare file system without logical access to its host server. Very cool. But don't get too carried away. Physical volumes still reside inside IntranetWare servers. We haven't figured out how to separate the two yet—that's IntranetWare 2!

SMART LINK

For more information on the architecture of the NDS database, surf to the Novell Knowledgebase at http://support.novell.com/search/.

As you can see, NDS is a huge improvement over the NetWare 3.12 bindery. NDS is actually not even an improvement—it's a complete revolution. Nothing is as it appears. So if NDS isn't what you think it is, what is it? Let's take a closer look.

ZEN

"The truth is out there."

The X-Files

COMPOSITION OF THE TREE

Plant a tree in a "Cloud"—it's good for the environment.

As in nature, the NDS tree starts with the [Root] and builds from there. Next, it sprouts container objects, which are branches reaching toward the sky. Finally, leaf objects flutter in the wind and provide network functionality to users, servers, and the file system. As you can see in Figure 3.6, the tree analogy is alive and well.

FIGURE 3.6

The Figurative NDS Tree

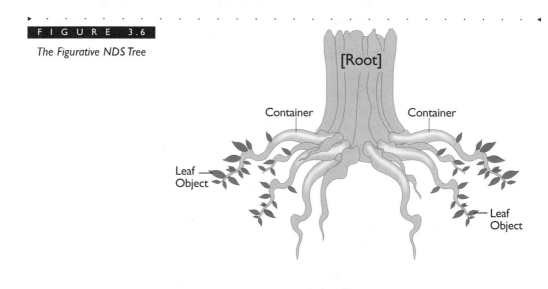

The real NDS tree is made up of special logical objects. NDS objects define logical or physical entities that provide organizational or technical function to the network. As you can see in Figure 3.7, they come in three different flavors:

- ► [Root]

- ► Container objects

- ► Leaf objects

The [Root] is the very top of the NDS tree. Because it represents the opening porthole to our NDS world, its icon is appropriately a picture of the Earth. Container objects define the organizational boundaries of the NDS tree and house other container objects and/or leaf objects. In Figure 3.7, we use container objects to define the ACME organization and its two divisions—ADMIN and LABS. Finally, leaf objects are the physical or logical network resources that provide technical services and WAN functionality. Leaf objects define the lowest level of the NDS structure. In Figure 3.7, leaf objects represent users, a printer, a server, and a group. NDS supports 24 different leaf object types. We'll discuss these types in detail in the next section.

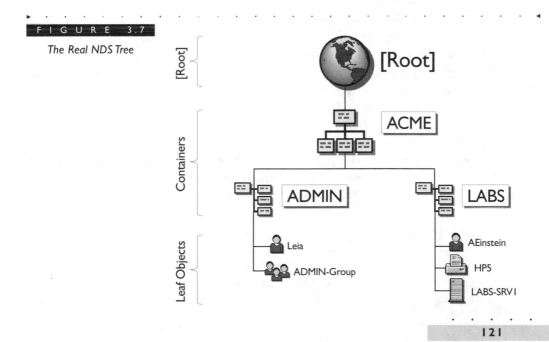

FIGURE 3.7

The Real NDS Tree

The tree can be organized any way you want, as long as it makes sense. AEinstein, for example, is placed near the resources he uses—the HP5 printer and LABS-SRV1 file server. Later in this chapter, we'll learn more about the ACME organization and what to do with their tree. For now, just focus on the conceptual framework of NDS and its tree structure.

On a more fundamental level, the NDS tree is stored in a fully replicated, globally distributed object-oriented database, called the Directory. The Directory consists of multiple hidden system files in the SYS:_NETWARE directory on each server. These files are replicated and distributed throughout the WAN to provide fault tolerance and increased connectivity. Although all IntranetWare servers use NDS, they don't have to contain their own directory database. If a server contains a portion of the database, that portion is called a *partition*. If a server doesn't have a copy of the database, then it must access it from some other server—which is less efficient. The bottom line is that a IntranetWare server can contain the entire directory database, pieces of it (partitions), or none at all.

In addition, NDS requires a temporal assurance system, called *time synchronization*. This means that everyone must agree on what time it is. Time is critical to NDS because IntranetWare uses time stamps for synchronization, auditing, and NDS security. Time synchronization is implemented by using a variety of different time server types, as you'll see later in this chapter.

Typically, a single network has only one directory. Although it's possible for a WAN to have multiple NDS trees, users can only be logged into one at a time. Also, resources cannot be shared between multiple trees. For this reason, Novell is pushing toward a single tree for the whole world. We'll see, but it sure explains the world icon for the [Root].

ZEN

"So be sure when you step, step with care and great tact. And remember that life's a great balancing act. Just never forget to be dexterous and deft. And never mix up your right foot with your left."

Dr. Seuss

Now that you understand the fundamental architecture of NDS, let's take a closer look at its different container and leaf objects. Remember, plant a tree in a Cloud—it's good for the environment.

NDS Objects

When you sprout a cranial conifer and become NDS-Head Fred, leaf objects and the [Root] will become important to you. I'd like to take this opportunity to help you out a little and explain them more. After all, even Daisy-Head Mayzie studied botany.

As we just learned, the NDS tree consists of three different types of objects— [Root], container, and leaf objects. What we didn't learn is that these objects have specific properties and values. Remember, NDS is, after all, a database. An object is similar to a record or row of information in a database table. A property is similar to a field in each database record. For example, the properties of a Sales database may be Name, Phone Number, and Last Item Purchased. Finally, values are data strings stored in each object property. These values define the information around which the database is built. Let's take a closer look.

UNDERSTANDING NDS OBJECTS

As we learned earlier, NDS objects define logical or physical entities that provide organizational or technical functionality to the network. They come in three different flavors:

- ▶ [Root]

- ▶ Container objects

- ▶ Leaf objects

As you can see, the tree analogy is alive and well. Figure 3.7 shows that objects come in many different shapes and sizes. They can be physical resources (printers and servers), NDS resources (groups), users or logical tree organizers (containers). We'll take a closer look at each of IntranetWare's 29 different object types in just a moment.

Each NDS object consists of categories of information called *properties*. Properties are similar to fields in a database record that categorize types of information. User objects, for example, have properties such as Login Name, Password, Postal Address, and Description. While the same type of object may have the same properties, the information within those properties can be different. For example, two User objects both have a Login Name property but one has a value of Leia and the other has a value of AEinstein.

In addition, a unique collection of properties define the class of an object. For example, a Printer object differs from a User object in that it has different properties. The Printer object needs to track the default queue, for example, whereas users are more interested in generational qualifiers. NDS uses two different types of properties:

▶ Required properties—The NDS object cannot be created until these properties are supplied. When creating an object, you are prompted for required values (for example, last name for users and host server/host volume for the Volume object).

▶ Multivalued properties—These properties support more than one entry. For example, the user property called Telephone Number can hold multiple numbers that apply to a single user. Other user multivalued properties include Location and Fax Number.

Finally, values are the data stored in object properties. Refer to Table 3.3 for an illustration of the relationship between NDS objects, properties, and values.

TABLE 3.3	OBJECT	PROPERTY	VALUE
NDS Objects, Properties, and Values	User	Login Name	AEinstein
		Title	Super smart scientist
		Location	NORAD
		Password	Relativity
	Printer	Common Name	HP5
		Default Queue	HP5-PQ1
		Print Server	LABS-PS1
	NCP Server	Full Name	LABS-SRV1
		Version	IntranetWare
		Operator	Admin
		Status	Running just fine

Now let's explore each of the 29 NDS objects in detail, starting with [Root]. You never know which objects you're going to have sprouting from your cerebellum.

[ROOT]

The [Root] object defines the top of the NDS organizational structure. Each Directory tree can only have one [Root], which is created during installation of the first server in that tree. The [Root] cannot be deleted, renamed, or moved. The NDS [Root] object is exceptional in that it begins the boundaries of your NDS world. It behaves very much like a container object in that it houses other container objects. The main difference is that the [Root] cannot contain leaf objects.

> **TIP**
>
> **The NDS Directory tree is sometimes confused with the [Root] object. Unlike [Root], the tree name *can* be changed.**

Each NDS object has a specific icon that depicts its purpose graphically. The [Root] object's icon is particularly interesting. Because the [Root] object represents the opening porthole to the NDS world, its icon is appropriately a picture of the Earth. As you can see in Figure 3.8, the [Root] defines the top of our tree and houses the ACME container object.

The [Root] can hold only these specific container objects:

▶ Country—An optional container object that designates the country where your network resides.

▶ Organization—A one-dimensional container that typically represents your company.

▶ Alias—A logical NDS pointer to any other object existing elsewhere in the tree. In this case, the Alias can only point to Country and Organization objects.

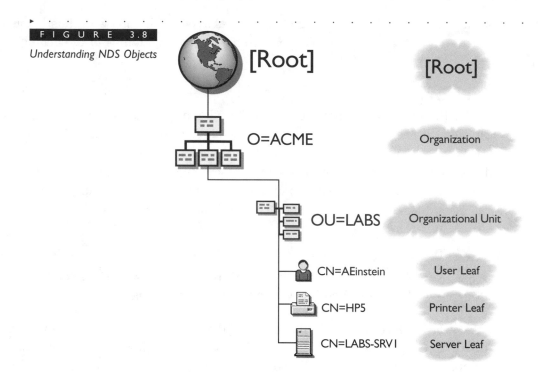

Understanding NDS Objects

The [Root] object is exceptional in one other way. It's the only NDS object without any properties. It simply exists as a placeholder for the top of the tree structure. It can have trustees, however. As we'll see in Chapter 5 ("IntranetWare Security"), any rights you assign to the [Root] are ancestrally inherited by all objects in the tree—which is a bad thing. All in all, the [Root] is a cool object, but you can't do much with it. Most of your design and management tasks will involve container and leaf objects.

CONTAINER OBJECTS

Container objects are logical organizers. They are the Tupperware bowls of our NDS kitchen. Actually the analogy works well—work with me here. The nature of Tupperware is that larger containers enclose smaller containers, which in turn house even smaller ones. Of course, the biggest Tupperware container in the world is the [Root]. Maybe in the future, when NDS takes over the world, we'll all be enclosed in a pale green, airtight, plastic bowl. Finally, Tupperware containers are used to store fruits and vegetables. In NDS, our Tupperware container objects store lettuce "leaf" objects. Sorry.

► • ◄

REAL WORLD

You might notice the square brackets ([ ]) surrounding the [Root] object. These brackets designate the object as a special NDS entity. IntranetWare supports two other such entities—[Public] and [Supervisor]. [Public] is a special trustee that applies security to all other objects in the tree. Users can inherit the rights of [Public] without having to log in. They simply need to attach. As we'll see in Chapter 5, this creates a serious NDS security loophole.

[Supervisor] is a special superuser for bindery emulation. Users from the NetWare 3.12 world can log into NDS using [Supervisor] and inherit all its special rights. [Supervisor] has other important properties that allow you to manage NetWare 3.12 and IntranetWare coexistence.

Here's a quick list of the three types of IntranetWare NDS container objects:

► Country—Designates the country where certain parts of the organization reside.

► Organization—Represents a company, university, or department. NDS only supports one layer of Organization objects, hence, the term "one-dimensional."

► Organizational Unit—Represents a division, business unit, or project team within the Organization. Organizational Units hold other Organizational Units or leaf objects. They are multidimensional.

Refer to Figure 3.8 for an illustration of the relationship between the [Root] and container objects. The ACME Organization houses other Organizational Units (including LABS), which in turn house leaf objects (like AEinstein). Let's take a closer look at these three different container objects.

ZEN

"I yelled for help. I screamed. I shrieked. I howled. I jowled. I cried, 'Oh save me from these pale green pants with nobody inside!'"

Dr. Seuss

Country Objects

The Country object is *optional*. It designates the country where your network resides and organizes other objects within the country. You can use a Country object to designate the country where your organization headquarters is or, if you have a multinational WAN, to designate each country that is part of your network. The Country object is also useful if you plan on cruising across the information superhighway. As a matter of fact, many Internet global directory providers are using the Country object as an entry point to their systems.

As I said a moment ago, the Country object is optional. It is not created as part of the default IntranetWare installation. If you want a Country object, you'll need to specifically configure it during installation of the very first server. Otherwise, adding a Country later can be a real pain. Also, this object must be a valid two-character country abbreviation. These abbreviations are defined as part of the ISO X.500 standard. Most trees don't use the Country object. Finally, Country objects can only house Organization containers and/or Organization Aliases. They cannot support leaf objects. Leafs must be stored within Organization or Organizational Unit containers.

TIP

If you don't have any compelling reasons to use the Country object, stay away from it. It only adds an unnecessary level of complexity to your WAN.

REAL WORLD

NDS supports a secret fourth container object type—Locality. The Locality object is like the Country object in that it's optional and not created as part of the default IntranetWare installation. You can use a Locality object to designate the region where your organization headquarters resides. Unlike Country objects, Locality objects can reside either under the [Root], Country, Organization, or Organizational Unit containers.

> **TIP**
>
> **IntranetWare utilities don't recognize the Locality object.**

Organization Objects

If you don't use a Country object, the next layer in the tree is typically an Organization. As you can see in Figure 3.8, ACME is represented as an "O." You can use the Organization object to designate a company, a division of a company, a university or college with various departments, and so on. Every Directory tree must contain at least one Organization object. Therefore, it is required. Many small implementations use only the Organization object and place all their resources directly underneath it. Organization objects must be placed directly below the [Root], unless a Country or Locality object is used. Finally, Organizations can contain all objects except [Root], Country, and Organization.

Earlier we defined the Organization as a one-dimensional object. This means the tree can only support one layer of Organization objects. If you look closer at the icon, you'll see a box with multiple horizontal boxes underneath. Additional vertical hierarchy is defined by Organizational Units—they are multidimensional. We'll describe them in just a moment.

Figure 3.9 illustrates the Details screen of the ACME Organization from NWADMIN. On the right side are the many page buttons, which identify categories of NDS properties. Associated with each page button is an input screen for a specific set of information. The Identification page button (shown here) allows you to define the following Organization properties:

- Name

- Other Name

- Description

- Location

- Telephone

- Fax Number

▶ · ◀

F I G U R E   3.9

Properties of an NDS Organization

Similar page buttons allow you to configure important Organization parameters, including postal information, print job configurations, trustee assignments, and so on. As far as ACME is concerned, the Organization container defines the top of the functional tree.

Organizational Unit Objects

The Organizational Unit object is a "natural group." It allows you to organize users with the leaf objects they use. You can create group login scripts, a user template for security, trustee assignments, security equivalences, and distributed administrators. All in all, Organizational Units are your friends.

Organizational Units represent a division, a business unit, or a project team. In Figure 3.8, the LABS OU represents a division within the ACME Organization. In this container, AEinstein works with his printers and servers. Organizational Units use the exact same properties as Organizations but in a slightly different way (see Figure 3.9). Organizational Units are multidimensional in that you can have many hierarchical levels of containers within containers. Remember, the Organization can only exist at one level.

Organizational Units are the most flexible Tupperware containers because they contain other OU's or leaf objects. As a matter of fact, Organizational Units can contain any NDS object type except the [Root], Country, or Organization containers (or Aliases to any of these). Now let's take a look at the real stars of our NDS world—the leafs.

LEAF OBJECTS

Leaf objects represent logical or physical network resources. Most of your CNA life will be spent designing, installing, and managing leaf objects—you'll become a vegetarian very quickly. These are the ultimate entities that IntranetWare users seek. Because leaf objects reside at the bottom of the NDS tree, they cannot hold other leafs. They represent the proverbial "end of the road." As we learned earlier, each type of leaf object has certain properties associated with it. This collection of properties differentiates the various leaf object classes. IntranetWare supports seven different categories for leaf object functionality:

▸ User leaf objects

▸ Server leaf objects

▸ Printer leaf objects

▸ Messaging leaf objects

▸ Network Services leaf objects

▸ Informational leaf objects

▸ Miscellaneous leaf objects

QUIZ

Look, there's that mischievious Alice again. She's trying to figure out when to believe the Lion. He says he'll help her escape from this crazy world. On what days of the week is it possible for the Lion to make the following two statements:

1 • **I lied yesterday.**

2 • **I will lie again tomorrow.**

Please help Alice find her way home.

(Q3-3)

In this section, we'll explore each of these seven categories and identify the key properties of all 24 NDS leaf objects. So, what's stopping you? Let's get going.

User Leaf Objects

Users are the center of your universe. After all, they are the ones that "use" the network. NDS supports five different leaf objects that help users do what they do. Let's check them out:

▶ User—Represents a person who uses the network. The user can be a beginner, a gardener, or NDS-Head Fred. The only requirement is that every person who logs into the WAN must be represented by a unique User object. When you create a User object, you can create a home directory for that user, who then has default rights to the file system. In addition, you can define default login restrictions using the special User Template object. In Figure 3.8, AEinstein is a User object in the LABS Organizational Unit. Notice the name designator—"CN." This represents Albert's login name or *common name*. As you can see in Figure 3.10, AEinstein has a plethora of user-related properties—55, to be exact. The page buttons on the right-hand side identify property categories such as Identification, Security Restrictions, Mailbox, Print Job Configurations, Login Script, and so on.

▶ User Template—A new type of object available in IntranetWare that can be used to create User objects. It's similar in function to the User Template found in earlier versions of NetWare 4, except that it's now a specific type of object rather than a User object named "User_Template," which contains particular attributes. When you define a User Template object, you can designate default values for User object creation, including NDS rights and file system rights, and a setup script for copying files to each new user's home directory. This object can only be used for setting up new users; it can't be used for modifying existing User objects.

F I G U R E   3 . 1 0

*Properties of an NDS User
Object*

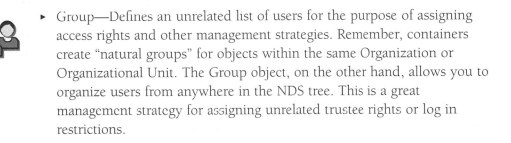

TIP

**NDS is a very powerful database with a lot of valuable user
information. Consider using it as a central company database of
employee data. If you can't find what you need in the 55 default
properties, you can always create your own. The IntranetWare SDK
(Software Developers Kit) provides interface tools for modifying and
adding NDS properties.**

▶ Group—Defines an unrelated list of users for the purpose of assigning
access rights and other management strategies. Remember, containers
create "natural groups" for objects within the same Organization or
Organizational Unit. The Group object, on the other hand, allows you to
organize users from anywhere in the NDS tree. This is a great
management strategy for assigning unrelated trustee rights or log in
restrictions.

▶ Organizational Role—Defines a position or role within the organization.
If you want to assign security to a "position" instead of an "employee,"
consider creating an Organizational Role. The occupant can change

frequently, but the responsibilities of the position will not. Whenever a user occupies the Organizational Role, they "absorb" its security. Some sample Organizational Roles include Postmaster, Chief Scientist, Administrative Assistant, and Coffee Jockey.

▶ Profile—IntranetWare's group login script. The Profile object contains a login script that can be shared by a group of unrelated users. If you have users who need to share common login script commands but are not located in the same portion of the tree, consider assigning them to a profile. As we'll see in Chapter 6, the Profile login script executes after the Container login script and before the User login script.

Server Leaf Objects

The IntranetWare server is still king of the physical hill. Even though it loses a lot of its significance in the logical realm, IntranetWare still resides on it, users still log in to it, and printers still attach to it. NDS supports three different leaf objects that apply to the logical server. Let's take a closer look:

▶ NetWare Server—Represents any server running NetWare on your network. The server can be running NetWare 2, 3, 4, or IntranetWare. The NDS Server object is created automatically during installation. The only way to insert a server object is to actually install IntranetWare on the server and place it in the tree. You can, however, create virtual servers using the Alias object. We'll take a look at this strategy a little later. If you create a bindery-based server (NetWare 2 or 3), you'll need to manually create a logical IntranetWare server object to make its file systems available. Some of the Server object properties can be seen in Figure 3.11. The page buttons provide some interesting informational categories including Identification, Error Log, Blocks Read, Blocks Written, Connect Time, and other dynamic statistics.

▶ Volume—Points to a physical volume installed somewhere on the WAN. A logical Volume object is created automatically for every physical volume installed during server creation. NWADMIN will allow you to browse the file system using an NDS Volume object. You can create other volumes as logical pointers from different parts of the tree. Otherwise, consider using the Alias object. In the Volume object's properties, you can store identification information such as the host server, volume location, and so on. You can also set restrictions for use of the volume such as disk space restrictions and attribute security. Interestingly, the NDS logical volume is stored independently from the physical server to which it's attached.

F I G U R E   3.11

*Properties of an NDS
Server Object*

▶ Directory Map—Represents a logical pointer to a physical directory in the IntranetWare file system. Directory Map objects are an excellent tool for centralizing file system management. Instead of creating drive mappings to physical directories, you can create them to logical Directory Map objects. Then when the physical location changes, you only have to change the one central object. All drive mappings will then be updated immediately. Pretty cool, huh?

ZEN

"We see them come. We see them go.
Some are fast, and some are slow.
Some are high, and some are low.
Not one of them is like another.
Don't ask us why; go ask your mother."

Dr. Seuss

Printer Leaf Objects

Like previous versions, IntranetWare printing relies on three main elements—print queue, print server, and printer. Each of these printing elements is represented in the NDS tree as a leaf object. Users print to print queues where jobs are stored until the printer is ready. Once a job gets to the top of the queue, the print server redirects it to the appropriate printer. Sounds pretty simple to me—you be the judge. Here's a quick look at these three critical NDS printer objects:

 ▶ Printer—Represents a physical printing device on the network. This logical object allows users to find the printers they need. Every printer must be represented by a corresponding NDS object and should be placed in the same container as the users who print to it. Some of the critical printer properties can be seen in Figure 3.12. These include Location, Department, Organization, Assignments, Configuration, Notification, and Features.

 ▶ Print Queue—Represents a logical print queue on the WAN. Every print queue must have a corresponding NDS object. Also, the location of the object in the tree directly impacts users' ability to print. Typically, the queues are stored in the same container as the users and printers to which they relate. IntranetWare gives you the flexibility to assign print queues on any volume, not just SYS:. It's about time.

F I G U R E   3.12

Properties of an NDS
Printer Object

Printer : HP5

Identification

Name:	HP5.LABS.NORAD.ACME
Other name:	
Description:	The H-P Laserjet Series 5 printer which services the Labs Division of ACME.
Network address:	
Location:	NORAD in Labs Bldg. C
Department:	Labs
Organization:	Labs

Identification

Assignments

Configuration

Notification

Features

See Also

OK   Cancel   Page Options...   Help

Tree: ACME_TREE   Admin.ACME   Selected: 1   Subordinates: 0

▶ Print Server—Represents a IntranetWare or third-party print server. Once again, the print server should be placed in the same container as the printers and print queues with which it is associated. Also, make sure your third-party print server software is NDS compatible. If not, you'll need to create Print Server objects manually for each of your different machines. This is especially important if your users are accessing the network through bindery emulation.

TIP

Although IntranetWare introduces a new, optional printing system (called NDPS), it's important to note that it still relies on these three critical printing objects: Printer, Print Queue, and Print Server.

Messaging Leaf Objects

IntranetWare includes an impressive messaging engine called MHS Services for NetWare 4.11. It utilizes the Message Handling Service (MHS) standard. When you install and configure MHS, a variety of messaging objects are created. These objects allow you to control communications between users throughout the WAN.

For a complete discussion of MHS Services, consult Chapter 6 ("IntranetWare Configuration"). For now, here's what they look like:

▸ Messaging Server—Represents a messaging server residing on any IntranetWare server. This object is created automatically during MHS Services installation. The messaging server sends, receives, and manages user e-mail.

▸ Message Routing Group—Represents a group of messaging servers that can transfer e-mail directly among each other. If users need to send e-mail to opposite sides of the tree, a Message Routing Group will bridge the gap.

▸ Distribution List—Represents a list of mail recipients for MHS Services. Instead of sending a message to every user individually, you can send it to the Distribution List. The MHS will then copy the message to each member individually. Using a Distribution List increases sending efficiency and cuts down on WAN traffic.

▸ External Entity—Represents a non-native NDS object that is imported for e-mail purposes. MHS Services uses this object to represent users from bindery-based directories or external e-mail. This way, other non-MHS users can participate in e-mail Distribution Lists and other NDS activities.

Network Services Leaf Objects

IntranetWare includes several exciting new object types that are designed to allow a network administrator to manage the network more easily and efficiently—saving both time and effort. In addition to the User Template object (which was discussed in the "User Leaf Objects" section earlier in this chapter), these objects include the Application object, which allows you to manage applications as objects in the NDS tree; the Auditing File object (AFO), which allows you to manage auditing file logs as objects in the tree; and the LSP (License Service Provider) object, which is used by NetWare Licensing Services to monitor and control the use of licensed applications on the network. Let's take a closer look:

▶ Application—Allows network administrators to manage applications as application objects in the NDS tree. It requires NDS, which means that you can't run an application associated with such an object if you are using a Bindery Services connection. A new IntranetWare utility that utilizes this object is the NetWare Application Launcher (NAL)—which allows users to view available applications and double-click on an icon to launch the associated application. The advantage of this object for users is that they don't have to worry about drive mappings, paths, or rights when they want to execute an application.

▶ Auditing File (AFO)—Represents an auditing log file that can be managed as an NDS object. This object is created by an auditing utility such as AUDITCON when auditing is enabled and is used to manage an auditing trail's configuration and access rights.

▶ LSP (License Service Provider)—Represents a IntranetWare server with the NLS (NetWare Licensing Services) NLM loaded. NLS is a distributed, enterprise network service that enables administrators to monitor and control the use of licensed applications on a network. An LSP object is created when you register a License Service Provider (LSP) with NDS by loading NLS.NLM with the " r" option.

Informational Leaf Objects

Most of the leaf objects so far have performed an obvious network function. Two other objects, however, exist for one purpose only—to store information. The AFP Server and Computer objects allow you to categorize information about non-critical physical resources such as AppleTalk servers and workstations. Let's take a closer look:

▶ AFP Server—Represents an AFP-based server running the AppleTalk file protocol. This service can be running on a IntranetWare server or native Macintosh machine. The point is that this object provides IntranetWare services to Apple Macintosh workstations. The AFP Server object has no effect on network operations—it only stores information about the AFP server including Description, Location, and Network Address.

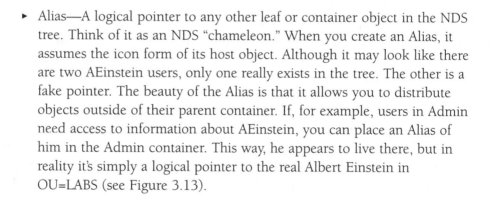

▶ Computer—Represents a non-server network computer, including workstations, routers, and notebooks. Once again, this object has no effect on network operations; it only stores information about computers. This is, however, an excellent opportunity to integrate NDS and your inventory database. A plethora of computer properties are available to you, including Description, Network Address, Serial Number, Server, Owner, and Status.

Miscellaneous Leaf Objects

No list would be complete without the final category—miscellaneous. There are four NDS leaf objects that don't fall into any other category. They're dominated by the Alias object, which points to any of the other 28 resources. In addition, there are Bindery objects, Bindery Queues, and, of course, the Unknown leaf object—whose icon, interestingly enough, is a user with a paper bag over its head. Let's check them out:

▶ Alias—A logical pointer to any other leaf or container object in the NDS tree. Think of it as an NDS "chameleon." When you create an Alias, it assumes the icon form of its host object. Although it may look like there are two AEinstein users, only one really exists in the tree. The other is a fake pointer. The beauty of the Alias is that it allows you to distribute objects outside of their parent container. If, for example, users in Admin need access to information about AEinstein, you can place an Alias of him in the Admin container. This way, he appears to live there, but in reality it's simply a logical pointer to the real Albert Einstein in OU=LABS (see Figure 3.13).

Be very careful with the Alias object. In many cases, you can't tell an Alias from the real Albert Einstein. If you delete or rename an Alias, nothing happens to the host. But if you accidentally mistake the host for the Alias and delete it, all of its Alias objects disappear into Never-Never Land. Actually, they become Unknown leaf objects.

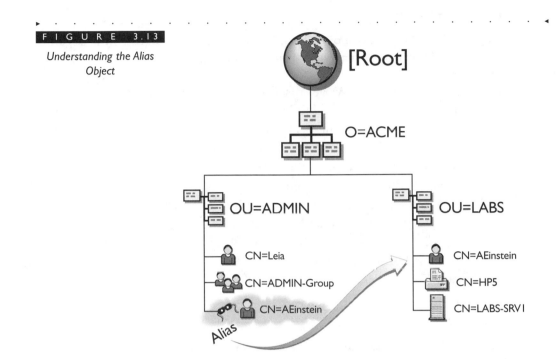

FIGURE 3.13

Understanding the Alias Object

▸ Unknown—Represents an NDS object that has been invalidated or cannot be identified as belonging to any of the other 28 classes (for example, when an Alias becomes invalidated because the user deleted the Alias's host). If you have any Unknown objects, you may want to research where they came from: It's probably a bad sign.

▸ Bindery—Represents an object placed in the NDS tree by an upgrade or migration utility. Bindery objects are used by NDS to provide backward compatibility with bindery-based utilities. This way users can access the resource from NetWare 3.12 workstations.

▸ Bindery Queue—Represents a print queue placed in the NDS tree by an upgrade or migration utility. This is a special type of Bindery object that points to older NetWare 3.12 print queues. Users accessing the tree through Bindery Services can print to bindery-based queues. Otherwise, you'll need to create a true NDS print queue object for everybody else.

SMART LINK

For a larger dose of NDS objects, surf to the Novell Knowledgebase at http://support.novell.com/search/.

That's all of them. We've discussed every NDS object supported by IntranetWare. You'll want to get to know them well because all future discussions center around how to organize, design, and manage these cute little network entities. Once you understand the relationships between NDS objects, you can start building your tree. As you've seen in this discussion, every leaf and container object is represented by an icon graphic that depicts its purpose. For example, printers are printers, servers are computers, and users are people. These icons are used throughout this book and in graphical NDS utilities. NWADMIN, for example, uses icons to provide a snapshot of the entire NDS tree in a hierarchical structure. This feature makes it easier for administrators and users to locate and use IntranetWare resources.

ZEN

"Look what we found in the park in the dark. We will take him home, we will call him Clarke. He will live at our house, he will grow and grow. Will our mother like this? We don't know."

Dr. Seuss

Overview of NDS Management

Now that you understand what the NDS tree is made of, we need to explore how it works. Three main topics dominate NDS management:

- ► NDS naming

- ► NDS partitioning

- ► Time synchronization

NDS naming defines rules for locating leaf objects. One of the most important aspects of a leaf object is its position in the NDS tree. Proper naming is required when logging in, accessing NDS utilities, printing, and for most other management tasks.

NDS partitioning deals with database performance and reliability. Since the tree houses all your network resources, it can grow large very quickly. As with any database, size can decrease performance and reliability. For this reason, IntranetWare has a built-in database distribution feature called *partitioning and replication*. Partitioning breaks the database tree into small pieces and replication places those pieces on multiple servers. This strategy increases database performance and provides distributed fault tolerance.

Time synchronization is a temporal assurance scheme that forces all IntranetWare servers to agree on what time it is. This is particularly important because all NDS background operations and security strategies rely on a time stamp. Time synchronization is accomplished through the use of four different time server types. We'll explore these types a little later in this chapter.

As you manage the NDS tree, pay particular attention to its structure. A well-designed tree will make resource access and management much easier. As a matter of fact, an efficient Directory tree provides all the following benefits:

▶ Make resource access easier for users

▶ Make administration easier for you (the CNA)

▶ Provide fault tolerance for the NDS database

▶ Decrease network traffic

The structure of the tree can be based on location, organization, or administration. In many cases, it's a combinatiion of all three. As a CNA, it is your responsibility to manage the tree, not design it. That's what CNEs are for, and you can learn all about it in *Novell's CNE Study Guide IntranetWare/NetWare 4.11*.

For now, let's focus on the three phases of NDS management: naming, partitioning, and time synchronization. Then, at the end of the chapter, we'll learn all about ACME's NDS tree design and get some hands-on experience building it.

So, without further adieu . . . let's get on with the show, starting with NDS naming.

NDS Naming

Your name identifies you as a truly unique individual. Let's take NDS-Head Fred, for example. This name says "Hi, I'm Fred, and I have an NDS tree growing out of my head!" In much the same way, an NDS object's name identifies its location in the hierarchical tree. NDS naming impacts two important IntranetWare tasks:

▸ Login—You need to identify your exact location in the NDS tree in order for IntranetWare to authenticate you during login.

▸ Resource Access—NDS naming exactly identifies the type and location of IntranetWare resources including file servers, printers, login scripts, and files.

The whole IntranetWare NDS naming scheme is much more complicated than "Hi, I'm Fred." It requires both your name and location. For example, a proper NDS name would be "Hi, I'm Fred in the ADMIN division of ACME." As you can see in Figure 3.14, Fred's NDS name identifies who he is and where he works. This naming scheme relies on a concept called *context*.

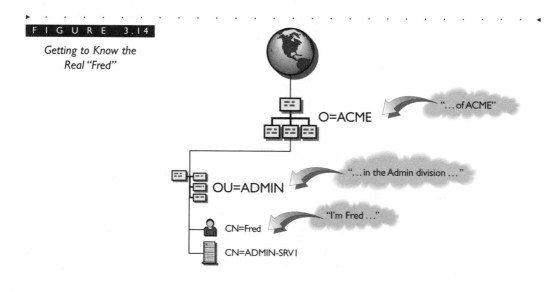

FIGURE 3.14

Getting to Know the Real "Fred"

Context defines the position of an object within the Directory tree structure. When you request a particular network resource, you must identify the object's context so that NDS can find it. IntranetWare uses very specific naming guidelines for creating an object's context, and we'll review these in just a moment. For now, let's explore why naming standards are so important.

ZEN

"Who am I? My name is Ned. I do not like my little bed. This is no good. This is not right. My feet stick out of bed all night."

Dr. Seuss

Novell recommends that before you implement NDS, you create a document that describes your naming standards. The NDS naming rules we're going to learn here only work if object names are consistent across the WAN. A naming standards document provides guidelines for naming key container and leaf objects, including users, printers, servers, volumes, print queues, and Organizational Units. In addition, it identifies standard properties and value formats. Consistency, especially in the naming scheme used for objects, provides several benefits:

▸ Consistent naming schemes provide a guideline for network administrators who will add, modify, or move objects within the Directory tree.

▸ Having the naming standards eliminates redundant planning. The standards give CNAs an efficient model to meet their needs, but leave implementation of resource objects open and flexible.

▸ Consistent naming schemes help users identify resources quickly, which maximizes users' productivity.

▸ Consistent naming allows users to identify themselves easily during login.

CONTEXT

As we learned earlier, the whole NDS naming strategy hinges on the concept of context. Context defines the position of an object within the Directory tree structure. When you request a particular network resource, you must identify the object's context so that NDS can find it.

In Figure 3.14, Fred's context is ". . . in the ADMIN division of ACME." This context identifies where Fred lives in the NDS tree structure. It identifies all container objects leading from him to the [Root]. In addition to context, Figure 3.14 identifies Fred's common name (CN). A leaf object's common name specifically identifies it within a given container. In this example, the User object's common name is "Fred."

Two objects in the same NDS tree may have the same common name—provided, however, that they have different contexts. This is why naming is so important. As you can see in Figure 3.15, our NDS tree has two "Freds," but each has a different context.

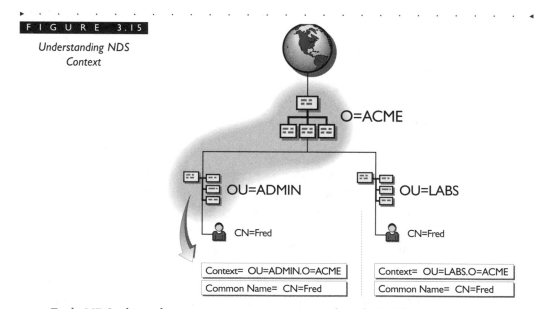

FIGURE 3.15

Understanding NDS Context

Each NDS object has a naming type associated with it. This naming type is identified with a one- or two-character abbreviation:

▸ O=Organization container

➤ OU=Organizational Unit container

➤ CN=common name of leaf object

Also notice the syntax used to create an object's context. In Figure 3.15, Fred's context is created by identifying each of his containers in reverse order leading to the [Root]. Each container is separated by a period.

There are two types of NDS context:

➤ Current context

➤ Object context

Let's take a closer look.

Current Context

Current context defines "where you are" in the NDS tree at any given time. It is *not* "where you live." This is a very important distinction. In Figure 3.15, for example, Fred "lives" in OU=ADMIN.O=ACME. But at any given time, he can hang out in O=ACME or OU=LABS.O=ACME.

This is all made possible by *tree walking*. Tree walking allows users to navigate anywhere within the NDS tree structure. Fred's current context impacts the utilities he uses and the resources he can access. In technical terms, *current context* is a logical pointer in the NetWare DOS Requester or 32-bit Client, which identifies the NDS default container for your workstation. Simply stated, it's where you are, not where you live.

A user's current context can be set in one of the following ways:

➤ During login, using the Client 32 Properties window (see Chapter 6)

➤ During login, using the NAME CONTEXT statement in NET.CFG

➤ With the CONTEXT login script command (see Chapter 6)

➤ At any time, using the CX utility (this chapter)

As we'll see in just a moment, current context also impacts how you approach object naming. As a matter of fact, it is the foundation of *distinguished naming*.

Object Context

In contrast to current context, *object context* defines "where you live." In Figure 3.15, for example, Fred's object context is OU=ADMIN.O=ACME or OU=LABS.O=ACME, depending on which Fred you're talking about. Context is identified by listing all containers starting from Fred and moving back toward the [Root]. Object context is used for two important purposes:

▶ Logging in

▶ Accessing resources

When logging in, users must provide their complete object context. In Figure 3.15, for example, Fred would type:

```
LOGIN .CN=FRED.OU=ADMIN.O=ACME
```

In addition to logging in, you'll need a resource's object context when trying to access it. This is particularly important for file servers, printers, Profile login scripts, Directory Map objects, volumes, and groups. The server in Figure 3.14, for example, has the same object context as Fred (that is, OU=ADMIN.O=ACME). Since Fred and the server have the same object context, they can refer to each other by their common names. Isn't that friendly?

You can view information about an object's context or change your own current context by using the CX command line utility. Let's take a closer look.

Using CX

CX is the key IntranetWare utility for dealing with NDS context. It allows you to perform two important tasks:

▶ Change your workstation's current context

▶ View information about any resource's object context

CX is a relatively straightforward command with a great deal of versatility. As a matter of fact, it's similar to the file system CD command in its general approach.

If you type CX by itself, the system displays your workstation's current context. This is marginally interesting, at best. CX really excels when you combine it with one or more command line switches. Here are some of the more interesting ones:

- CX—View your workstation's current context.

- CX /T—View the Directory tree structure below your current context.

- CX /A /T—View all objects in the Directory tree structure below your current context.

- CX /R /A /T—Change your current context to the [Root] and view all objects in the Directory tree.

- CX /CONT—List containers only below the current context in a vertical list with no directory structure.

- CX /C—Scroll continuously through output.

- CX .OU=ADMIN.O=ACME—Change your current context to the ADMIN container of ACME.

- CX /?—View on-line help, including various CX options.

- CX /VER—View the version number of the CX utility and the list of files it executes.

Probably the most useful CX option is

- CX /R /A /T

I'm sure there's a hidden meaning somewhere in the rodent reference. Regardless, the CX /R /A /T option displays the relative location of all objects in the NDS tree (see Figure 3.16).

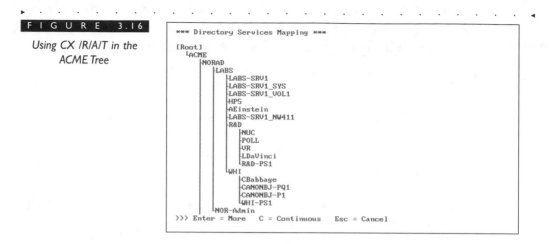

F I G U R E   3.16

Using CX /R/A/T in the
ACME Tree

ZEN

"My alphabet starts with this letter called YUZZ. It's the letter I use to spell YUZZ-A-MA-TUZZ. You'll be sort of surprised what there is to be found once you go beyond 'Z' and start poking around!"

Dr. Seuss

If you don't remember where you live, the CX utility can be your guide. You can use it before logging in to find your home context if you are in the F:\LOGIN directory. It can also be used by administrators to print out the complete NDS tree structure every Friday afternoon. Of course, this can be a valuable asset to your IntranetWare log book. All in all, CX is a very useful utility for dealing with NDS navigation and object naming.

Now that you've discovered the importance of context, it's time to review how it impacts NDS naming rules. Knowing where you live is only half of the equation. Now we have to discover exactly who you are.

NAMING RULES

Home is where the heart is. Similarly, your network productivity is defined by the container you live in—your context. To access resources efficiently, you must be in close proximity to them. Otherwise, security and naming gets more difficult. Context is the key.

Now that we understand how NDS context works, let's review the naming rules associated with it:

- ▶ Current context defines your workstation's current position in the Directory tree.

- ▶ An object's context defines its home container.

- ▶ Each object has an identifier abbreviation that defines it for naming purposes (O=Organization, OU=Organizational Unit, and CN=common name of leaf objects).

- ▶ Context is defined by listing all containers from the object to the [Root], in that order. Each object is separated by a period.

- ▶ Context is important for logging in and accessing NDS resources.

So, there you have it. That's how context works. With this in mind, it's time to explore the two main types of NDS names:

- ▶ Distinguished names

- ▶ Typeful names

Distinguished Names

An object's *distinguished name* is its complete NDS path. It is a combination of common name and object context. Each object in the NDS tree has a distinguished name that uniquely identifies it in the tree. In Figure 3.14, Fred's distinguished name would be "I'm Fred in the ADMIN division of ACME."

Notice how the distinguished name identifies Fred as an individual, as well as the context in which he lives. Similarly, in Figure 3.15, Fred's NDS distinguished name would be .CN=Fred.OU=ADMIN.O=ACME. Once again, Fred's distinguished name is a combination of his common name and his context.

Here's another example (refer to AEinstein in Figure 3.17). AEinstein's context is OU=R&D.OU=LABS.O=ACME. His common name is CN=AEinstein.

Therefore, his distinguished name is a simple mathematical addition of the two:

.CN=AEinstein.OU=R&D.OU=LABS.O=ACME.

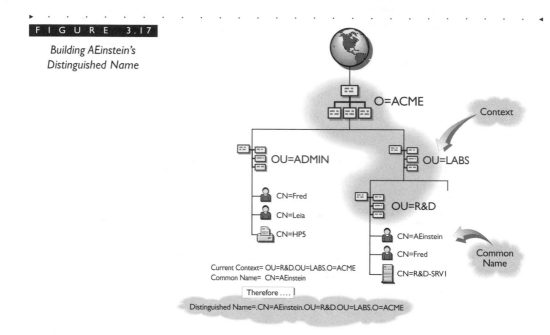

FIGURE 3.17

Building AEinstein's Distinguished Name

Elementary, my dear Einstein, elementary. There's no "new math" here; only simple addition. If you want complex calculations, refer to Chapter 5 ("IntranetWare Security").

Notice the use of periods. Neither the context nor the common name started with a period, but the distinguished name did. The leading period identifies the name as a (complete) distinguished one. Otherwise, it is assumed to be an incomplete, or *relative*, distinguished name. A relative distinguished name lists an object's path from itself up to the current context—not the [Root]. The relativity part refers to how NDS builds the distinguished name. Remember, all objects must have a unique distinguished name. The relative distinguished name is simply a shortcut.

It seems appropriate to demonstrate the relative distinguished name concept with the help of Albert Einstein.

ZEN

"The Scientific Theory I like best is that the rings of Saturn are composed entirely of lost airline luggage."

Mark Russell

Again, refer to Figure 3.17. If AEinstein's current context was the same as his object context, OU=R&D.OU=LABS.O=ACME, then his relative distinguished name would be the same as his common name, CN=AEinstein. But life is rarely this simple. What if Albert Einstein used the CX command to change his current context to OU=LABS.O=ACME? What would his relative distinguished name be now? See Figure 3.18. Correct! His relative distinguished name would become CN=AEinstein.OU=R&D. When you add this to his current context of OU=LABS.O=ACME, you get the correct distinguished name:

.CN=AEinstein.OU=R&D.OU=LABS.O=ACME

Piece of cake. Once again, notice the use of periods. The relative distinguished name does not use a leading period. This identifies it as a relative (not complete) distinguished name.

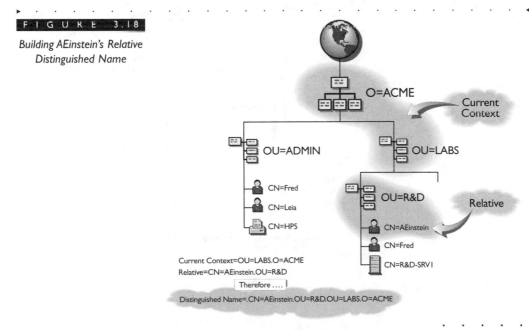

FIGURE 3.18

Building AEinstein's Relative Distinguished Name

As you can see, object and current context play a very important role in distinguished and relative distinguished naming. Whether it's fair or not, you are defined by the place you live. Of course, it can get even weirder. NDS supports trailing periods, which allow you to change the current context while using relative distinguished naming . . . as if that wasn't hard enough already. The bottom line is that each trailing period moves the current context up one container.

It seems simple at first, but it can get crazy very quickly. Let's take Leia, for example. She lives in the ADMIN container. If we were in LABS, she couldn't use a relative distinguished name to identify herself—or could she? A single trailing period would move her current context up to O=ACME. Then she could use a relative distinguished name to move down the ADMIN side of the tree (see Figure 3.19). Her current context would be OU=LABS.O=ACME, and her relative distinguished name would be

CN=Leia.OU=ADMIN.

FIGURE 3.19

Using Trailing Periods

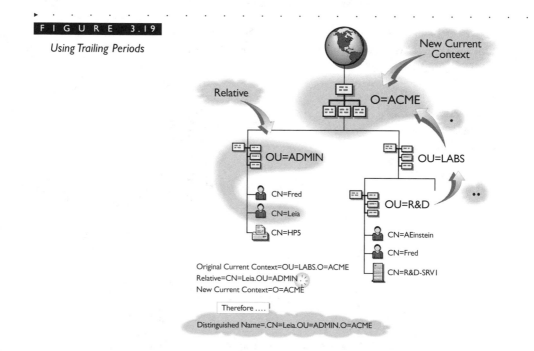

The resulting distinguished name would be Leia's relative name plus her new current context (remember, the trailing period moved the current context from OU=LABS.O=ACME up to O=ACME). That is, her distinguished name would be

.CN=Leia.OU=ADMIN.O=ACME

Piece of cake. It gets even weirder if Leia's current context is

OU=R&D.OU−LABS.O=ACME

In this case, her relative distinguished name would be

CN=Leia.OU=ADMIN..

Are we having fun yet? Just like anything in life, it's very important where you place your dots. Here's a quick summary:

▸ All objects in the NDS name are separated by dots.

▸ Distinguished names are preceded by a dot. This identifies them as complete.

▸ Relative distinguished names are *not* preceded by a dot. This identifies them as incomplete.

▸ Trailing dots can only be used in relative distinguished names, and they modify the current context. Each dot moves the context up one container.

For a complete summary of NDS distinguished naming rules, refer to Table 3.4. Now let's step back in reality for a moment and explore the other NDS naming category—typeful names.

Typeful Names

Typeful names use attribute type abbreviations to distinguish between the different container types and leaf objects in NDS names. In all the examples to this point, we've used these abbreviations to help clarify context, distinguished, and relative distinguished names. The most popular abbreviations are

▸ C: Country container

- ▶ O: Organization container

- ▶ OU: Organizational Unit container

- ▶ CN: common name of leaf objects

T A B L E 3 . 4

*Getting to Know
Distinguished Naming*

	DISTINGUISHED NAMES	RELATIVEDISTINGUISHED NAMES
What it is	Complete unique name	Incomplete name based on current context
How it works	Lists complete path from object to [Root]	Lists relative path from object to current context
Abbreviation	DN	RDN
Leading period	Leading periods required	No leading periods allowed
Trailing periods	No trailing periods allowed	Trailing periods optional

These attribute types help to avoid confusion that can occur when creating complex distinguished and relative distinguished names. I highly recommend that you use them. Of course, like most things in life—they are optional! You can imagine how crazy NDS naming gets when you choose not to use these attribute abbreviations. This insanity is known as *typeless naming*.

Typeless names operate the same as typeful names, but they don't include the object attribute type. In such cases, NDS has to "guess" what object types you're using. Take the following typeless name, for example:

```
.Admin.ACME
```

Is this the ADMIN Organizational Unit under ACME? Or is this the Admin user under ACME? In both cases, it's a valid distinguished name, except that one identifies an Organizational Unit container and the other identifies a User leaf object (see Figure 3.20). Well, here's the bottom line—which one is it? It's up to NDS.

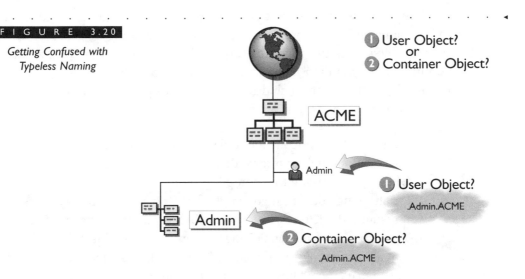

FIGURE 3.20

Getting Confused with
Typeless Naming

Fortunately, IntranetWare has some guidelines for "guessing" what the object type should be.

1 • The leftmost object is a common name (leaf object).

2 • The rightmost object is an Organization (container object).

3 • All middle objects are Organizational Units (container objects).

QUIZ

Once again, we return to the Land of Forgetfulness and find Alice in cranial combat with the Lion. She still hasn't figured him out. Here's the question on the table: When can the Lion say, "I lied yesterday and I will lie again tomorrow."? *Warning!* **The answer is** *not* **the same as that of the preceding problem!**

Hmmm
(Q3-4)

Although this works for most cases, it's only a general guideline. Many times, typeless names are more complex. Take our example in Figure 3.20, for instance. We know now that the rightmost object is an Organization, but what about "Admin?" Is it a common name or an Organizational Unit? We still don't know. Fortunately, IntranetWare includes numerous exceptions to deal with complex typeless scenarios. Here's how it works:

▶ Exception Rule 1: Container objects—Many IntranetWare utilities are intelligent enough to resolve their own typeless names depending on what they are trying to accomplish. CX, for example, is used primarily for changing context. If you apply the CX command to a typeless name, it assumes the leftmost object is an Organization or Organizational Unit. This is because you can't change context to a leaf object. Other utilities that allow you to change context include NETADMIN and NWADMIN. In summary, here's how our example from Figure 3.20 would look with the CX utility:

CX .ADMIN.ACME—.OU=ADMIN.O=ACME

▶ Exception Rule 2: Leaf objects—Similarly, resource-based utilities recognize the leftmost object of a typeless name as a leaf object. Many of these utilities are expecting to see a common name. The most prevalent are LOGIN, MAP, and CAPTURE. Here's how it works for our example in Figure 3.20:

LOGIN .Admin.ACME—.CN=Admin.O=ACME

▶ Exception Rule 3: Mixed naming schemes—It is possible to generate an NDS name that mixes both typeless and typeful naming. In this case, the typeful abbreviation is used as a reference point for resolving the typeless portion of the name. NDS simply focuses on the typeful portion and moves to the left. All subsequent typeless objects are assigned one less abbreviation. Here's an example from Figure 3.20:

.ADMIN.O=ACME—.OU=ADMIN.O=ACME

Of course, this mixed NDS name would be resolved differently if CX or LOGIN were involved. Some exception rules take precedence over others.

▶ Exception Rule 4: Using current context—If all else fails, NDS uses the current context as an example of NDS naming. If your typeless name has the same number of objects as the current context, it assigns attribute abbreviations accordingly. For example, if your current context was .OU=LABS.O=ACME, the typeless name in Figure 3.20 would become .OU=ADMIN.O=ACME.

In another example, let's assume the Country object is involved. If your current context was OU=LABS.O=ACME.C=US, then .ADMIN.ACME.US would become .OU=ADMIN.O=ACME.C=US.

If, however, the typeless name has a different number of objects as the current context, the default NDS naming rules apply. That is, rightmost is an Organization, leftmost is a common name, and all intervening objects are Organizational Units.

▶ Exception Rule 5: Country object—The Country object messes up NDS defaults in almost all cases. Naming is no exception. The Country object is a special circumstance and is assumed *not* to exist. If you introduce the Country object in either the current context or a typeful portion of the name, you'll run into trouble. In this case, NDS tries to resolve the name using any of the previous exception rules. If they don't apply, it isolates the Country object and applies the defaults to the rest of the typeless name. Pretty weird, huh?

There you have it. This completes our discussion of typeless names and NDS naming in general. As you can see, this is a very important topic because it impacts all aspects of NDS design, installation, and management. No matter what you do, you're going to have to use the correct name to log in or access NDS resources. As we've learned, an object's name is a combination of "who they are" (common name) and "where they live" (context).

SMART LINK

If NDS naming is still a great mystery to you, join us for a special course at CyberState University: http://www.cyberstateu.com.

Congratulations! You are now a professor of NDS nomenclature. And nomenclature is important. After all, where would we be without names for all of our stuff? Here are a few important ones:

▶ Biochip—A computer chip that relies on the biological function of proteins and enzymes to send signals rather than on the flow of electrons, theoretically producing faster computers, often called biocomputers or organic CPUs. Also, the foundation of IntranetWare NDS.

▶ Butterfly effect—The major impact resulting from a minor force left unchecked over a long time such as the multiplying of a draft from a butterfly's wings in Beijing to a hurricane in Rio. This is the foundation of chaos theory. And we all know that chaos theory impacts a CNA's existence more than anything.

▶ Cocktail diplomacy—Verbal persuasion and discussion rather than warfare, terrorism, or other forceful tactics of international political procedure. Also, the preferred way of dealing with IntranetWare users.

▶ Cyberphilia—The love of computers and anything to do with computers. In extreme cases, this is said to lead to "CNA widow"—a person who has lost a spouse to the fascinations of IntranetWare.

▶ Electropollution—Excessive amounts of electromagnetic waves in the environment resulting from the increasingly widespread use of electricity and the electronic equipment it powers. Many believe it will eventually lead to EMI overload and an innate propensity to feel blades of wet grass between one's toes.

▶ Faddict—A person who compulsively follows a temporary fashion. This condition has been described as *faddiction*. Of course, we know the latest fad is IntranetWareCNA-ism.

As you can see, there's a lot to NDS nomenclature. Stay tuned throughout the book for more fascinating "neo-words." For now, let's shift our focus from naming to partition management. NDS partitioning is the second of our three NDS management concepts. Don't forget your seat belt.

NDS Partitioning

As you will quickly come to appreciate, the NDS tree grows and grows and grows. Before you know it, you'll have a huge monstrosity on your hands—the size of Jupiter. Fortunately, IntranetWare includes a segmentation strategy known as NDS partitioning. *Partitioning* breaks up the NDS tree into two or more pieces that can be separated and distributed, which makes dealing with NDS objects more manageable.

Since the NDS tree is stored in a database, pieces of the database can be distributed on multiple file servers. This strategy is known as *replication*. NDS replicas provide two important benefits to the "Cloud":

- ▸ Replicas increase network performance by decreasing the size of database files and placing resources closest to the users who need them.

- ▸ Replicas increase fault tolerance because extra copies of the database are distributed on multiple servers throughout the WAN.

NDS partitions have nothing to do with the logical disk partitions you're used to on the server disk. NDS partitions are logical pieces of the "Cloud," which can be distributed on multiple servers. Hard disk partitions are physical divisions of the internal disks that separate the IntranetWare operating system from DOS. Although these two concepts are unrelated, they work together in an odd way— one is stored on top of the other. To really mess up your mind, note that logical NDS partitions are stored on internal disk partitions   brain drain!

ZEN

"Oh, the thinks you can think up if only you try!"

Dr. Seuss

As you can see in Figure 3.21, NDS partitioning simply breaks the ACME organization into two pieces:

▶ Partition A—Known as the [Root] partition because it is the only one that contains the global [Root] object.

▶ Partition B—Known as the LABS partition because OU=LABS is the highest container object in that segment. In addition, Partition B is termed a *child* of Partition A, because LABS is a subset of the ACME Organization.

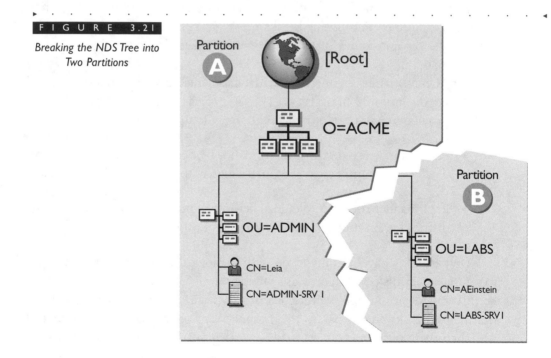

Partitioning has many advantages because it allows you to separate the tree into smaller segments. Since 90 percent of all the resources accessed by users are within their own partitions, CNAs can increase efficiency by locating users near the resources they use the most. We can also increase network fault tolerance by placing copies of other partitions on local servers. This is known as replication. IntranetWare allows you to create four different types of NDS replicas:

- ▶ Master

- ▶ Read/Write

- ▶ Read-Only

- ▶ Subordinate Reference

But I digress. Let's not get ahead of ourselves. To understand the distribution of NDS replicas, we first need to explore the concept of partitioning. More specifically, we need to understand why partitions are important and what they do for us. Granted, NDS replication is more important to you—as a CNA. But you have to start somewhere. And we're going to start with partitions.

UNDERSTANDING NDS PARTITIONS

To understand partitioning, we need to review the characteristics of our NDS Cloud:

- ▶ It is a database that replaces the bindery.

- ▶ It contains data on all objects in the Directory tree, including their names, security rights, and property values. All network information except the file system comes from the Directory.

- ▶ It is network-centric, not server-centric, like the older bindery. This allows the Directory to track *all* network resources throughout the WAN.

- ▶ NDS uses the Directory for access control to other objects in the WAN. NDS checks the Directory to make sure that you can view, manipulate, create, or delete resource objects.

- ▶ NDS uses the Directory for authentication—an important part of logging in.

▸ Except for Server and Volume objects, the Directory does *not* contain information about the file system. IntranetWare data is still restricted to internal server volumes.

Partitioning is the process of dividing the Directory into smaller, more manageable pieces. These pieces can then be distributed near the users that need them. As you can see in Figure 3.21, the ACME tree has been partitioned into two segments—the [Root] partition and the LABS partition. Notice that partitioning occurs along the boundaries of container objects. All the leaf objects in a container are included in the same partition as their parent. Also notice that a partition is named for the container closest to the [Root]. In the case of Partition B, this would be OU=LABS. The topmost container object in the partition is termed the *partition root object*. I know this is confusing, but it serves an important purpose. This partition is the parent of all other child partitions in this segment of the tree. And, as we all know, parents know best. If you get confused, remember this one simple rule: [Root] with square brackets ([Root]) describes the top of the world. There is only one [Root] partition. On the other hand, root without square brackets (root) simply describes the topmost container in a given partition. Every partition must have a partition root object; therefore, there can be many of them.

Once again, returning to Figure 3.21, Partition A is the [Root] partition and Partition B is the LABS partition, with OU=LABS as the partition root object. No sweat.

ZEN

"Did I ever tell you how lucky you are?
Thank goodness for all the things you are not!
Thank goodness you're not something someone forgot
and left all alone in some punkerish place.
Like a rusty tin coat hanger hanging in space."

Dr. Seuss

As a CNA, you have total control over NDS partitioning. You can decide how, when, and where they are created. To simplify things, NDS gives you two simple choices:

▸ Centralized

▸ Distributed

In small network environments, centralizing the Directory makes it easier to manage the information in its database. The response time for users is adequate as long as the number of users and devices in the partition remains small. In this context, the term *small* means a network with roughly 1 to 10 servers or 100 to 5,000 objects, all in the same location and not connected by WAN links. If your network meets this criteria, you probably will not partition the NDS database at all. Instead, you'll leave the tree as a single database and replicate it on each of your servers. This strategy is simple and employs the IntranetWare defaults.

On the other hand, if your network is large or has several sites with many servers, you may want to partition the Directory. Partitioning also implies distributed replication. By distributing the database, you will increase the availability of the information and provide quicker access for users. In addition, distributed replication increases fault tolerance because extra copies of the database are available throughout the WAN.

Assuming you choose the distributed approach, NDS partitioning is inevitable. Unfortunately, IntranetWare doesn't help you out at all. By default, only the [Root] partition is created during initial server installation. All subsequent servers are added to this partition. It's up to you, as a CNA, to create a new partition for each new server. In partitioning, the server is the key. Remember, partitions are replicated as portions of the database on distributed IntranetWare servers. For this reason, you want to create new partitions for each new server. Well, maybe not every new server. Here are a few guidelines to think about:

▸ At the time the first server is installed in a new container, consider creating a partition at that container level. All subsequent servers in the same container should then receive replicas of the existing partition.

▸ Every time you add a new location to the NDS WAN, consider creating a container for the new location and defining a partition around it. It's assumed that new locations will bring along their own servers.

▶ For organizational purposes, consider creating a partition for each new container object even if it doesn't have its own server. This helps segment Organization-based NDS information. Also, it allows you to plan ahead in case servers are ever added to the new container.

▶ Try to create a pyramid shape when creating NDS partitions. The top level of the tree should have fewer partitions than the lower layers. This triangular design allows you to distribute the partitions relatively close to leaf objects (particularly users). This encourages you to create small partitions and distribute them closer to the users who access resources. In addition, it also increases fault tolerance by distributing many multiple segments of the database.

Keep in mind, though, that size and number of partitions can significantly affect the synchronization and responsiveness of your network. Avoid creating partitions that are too large (greater than 5,000 objects) or with too many servers (more than 10) because they take too long to synchronize, and managing replicas becomes more complex. On the other hand, avoid partitions that are too small (fewer than 100 objects). If a partition contains only a few objects, the access and fault tolerance benefits may not be worth the time you invest in managing it.

As you can see in Figure 3.22, we've installed a new server (R&D-SRV1) in the new OU=R&D subcontainer of OU=LABS. By default, this container and all its objects (particularly the server) will be added to the existing LABS partition. According to our new philosophy, we should create an additional partition for the new container and its objects (particularly the server). Using PARTMGR, NDS Manager, or NWADMIN, we create Partition C at the OU=R&D container. This becomes the R&D partition. Now we can distribute replicas of each of the three partitions to each of the three servers in our ACME NDS tree.

Replicas are good! They allow us to increase resource access and fault tolerance by distributing copies of partitions to multiple servers throughout the WAN. Now that we've created our partitions, it's time to distribute copies (replicas) of them to strategic servers. That's NDS replication.

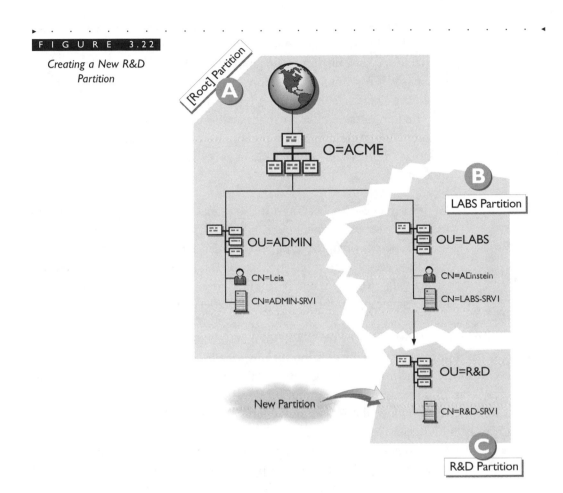

FIGURE 3.22

Creating a New R&D Partition

NDS REPLICATION

If you build the partitions . . . they will come!

Earlier we learned that NDS partitioning provides two key advantages—resource access and fault tolerance. Well, actually partitioning doesn't do anything. It only breaks up the database into little pieces. It's how we distribute these pieces to IntranetWare servers that provides the advantages. So, it's more accurate to say that NDS replication provides two key advantages:

▶ Resource access—Replication allows you to place resources closest to the users who access them. This decreases the time needed for authentication, modification, and information queries. It also increases the probability that information will be retrieved from the nearest available server. This limits the amount of traffic sent over slow and expensive WAN links. In addition, replication allows for faster *name resolution*. Name resolution is an NDS process that allows you to access information outside your current partition. Every partition stores pointers to servers containing parent and child information. An organized replication strategy allows NDS to find remote objects more quickly.

▸ Fault tolerance—Replication distributes exact copies of database segments to multiple servers throughout the WAN. If your local copy becomes unavailable or corrupted, another copy can be used for authentication or resource access. With replication, users can access the network even when their local server, router, or WAN link goes down. The goal is to never have a single point of failure in the IntranetWare Cloud.

It sounds too good to be true. Well, in many cases, it is. There's a cost associated with replication—synchronization delays. Since replicas need to be updated constantly, synchronization becomes an important issue. As you add more replicas, you create more synchronization traffic. This background overhead slows down critical data traffic—especially over WAN links. Also, replica management can be a nightmare as you continue to build up and modify the NDS tree. So, the real trick becomes, "How do I optimize replica distribution and minimize synchronization delays?" Just like any puzzle, the solution is staring you in the face. You just need to figure out where all the little pieces go. Fortunately, IntranetWare includes four different replica types for dealing with this crazy puzzle. Let's take a closer look.

 ZEN

"My shoe is off, my foot is cold.
I have a bird, I like to hold.
My hat is old, my teeth are gold.
And now my story is all told."

Dr. Seuss

Replica Types

IntranetWare includes four different replica types. Each has its own advantages and disadvantages. Some are created by default, and others apply only to specific circumstances. Before you get excited about distributing NDS replicas, let's learn what each of the four types can do. Here's a quick look:

▸ Master—A read/write copy of the original partition. Each partition has only one Master replica. When you first define a partition, the Master is created by default. If you would like to redefine a partition boundary or join it with another, you must be able to access the server that holds the Master replica of that partition. This is the key difference between the Master and other replica types. If the Master replica becomes unavailable for any reason, you can upgrade any Read/Write replica using PARTMGR, NDS Manager, or NWADMIN.

▸ Read/Write—A read/write copy of any partition. Each partition may have multiple Read/Write replica copies. When you change objects in a Read/Write replica, those changes are propagated to all other replicas of the same partition. This process, known as *replica synchronization,* creates background traffic over WAN communication lines. Both Master and Read/Write replicas generate synchronization traffic. Be careful how many of these replicas you distribute. Finally, Read/Write replicas cannot be used to redefine partition boundaries—that requires a Master.

▸ Read-Only—A read-only copy of any partition. These replicas are used for searching and viewing objects only. You cannot make any changes to a Read-Only replica. These replicas receive synchronization changes from Read/Write and Master copies. They do not generate any replica synchronization traffic.

▸ Subordinate References—A special type of replica created and maintained by NDS. A Subordinate Reference is created automatically on a server when it contains a parent replica, but not any of the children. In simpler terms, Subordinate References are created on servers "where parent is but child is not." Think of it as NDS baby-sitting. The key difference is that Subordinate References do not contain object data—they point to the replica that does. This facilitates tree connectivity. The good news is that if you eventually add a child replica to the server, the Subordinate Reference is removed automatically.

There you have it: the four NDS replica types. In general, Read/Write replicas are the most popular for CNA management. Master replicas are created automatically during partitioning, and Subordinate References flourish throughout the tree as needed. Read-Only replicas, however, can be very effective if you have many servers and few containers. Now that you understand the different replica types, it's time to distribute and manage them.

Before we learn how to manage these four different replica types, let's revisit Subordinate References. I sensed a blank stare when we came across that bullet. The bottom line is, that Subordinate References increase tree connectivity by providing bridges to partitions you don't have. In Figure 3.22, for example, each server gets a Master rpelica of its home container (provided it's the first server in the container). Now, if we place a Read/Write replica of the [Root] partition on R&D-SRV1, any user in OU=R&D could view Leia's phone number, for example. Unfortunately, NDS couldn't "walk the tree" from R&D-SRV1 to Leia unless we also had a copy of every partition along the way (namely, the LABS partition). To solve this problem, IntranetWare will automatically give R&D-SRV1 a Subordinate Reference replica of the LABS partition. The bottom line is this: Subordinate References are created on servers "where the parent is but child is not." Hopefully, you can see how Subordinate References bridge the gap by providing pointers to partitions you don't have. Without them, you'd be isolated in your own little private Idaho.

Now that we've cleared that up, let's take a closer look at managing default and new NDS replicas.

Managing NDS Replicas

As we learned earlier, partitioning itself doesn't accomplish anything productive. It simply breaks the NDS database into little pieces. Replication is where the real action is. Replication allows us to distribute these pieces among strategically placed servers. We also learned that IntranetWare doesn't partition by default. It does, however, include a simple default replication strategy: *Every partition should be replicated at least three times.*

When you install a new IntranetWare server, its host partition expands. No new partition is created. Replication of the partition depends on how many servers already exist. The first server in a partition gets the Master replica. The second and third new servers receive a Read/Write replica. All other servers in the same partition are replica-deprived. Remember, the basic premise is that every partition should be replicated at least three times.

When you merge Directory trees, source servers with [Root] replicas receive Read/Write replicas of the new [Root] Partition. They also receive Subordinate Reference replicas to the [Root]'s child partitions. Next, target servers with [Root] replicas receive Subordinate References of the top-level partition of the source tree. This allows both source and target servers to share information about one another's objects—both new and old. Finally, a NetWare 3 server upgraded to IntranetWare receives a Read/Write replica of all partitions containing the server's bindery context.

So, those are the defaults. It's a great place to start, but don't think of it as the end-all. As a matter of fact, it's only the beginning. As a CNA, you should take NDS partitions and replication very seriously. Once a new server has been installed, you should consider creating a new partition around its parent container. This strategy is illustrated in Figure 3.22 with the addition of R&D-SRV1.

Also consider placing Read/Write replicas of other partitions on the new server. In Figure 3.23, we've demonstrated a strategy known as *saturated replication*. This means that every server has either a Master or Read/Write replica of every partition in the tree.

Saturated replication works fine when you have a small number of servers. In large environments, however, it's not very practical because of synchronization delays. Replica updates take place automatically at specific intervals. Some updates, such as changing a user's password, are immediate (within 10 seconds). Other updates, such as login updates, are synchronized every five minutes. Changes made to Figure 3.23, for example, would generate 27 replica updates—that's 33. This is manageable. But consider what background traffic would look like with 50 servers and 20 different partitions—that's 9,536,743,164,062,000,000,000,000,000,000,000 updates every few minutes. Wow!

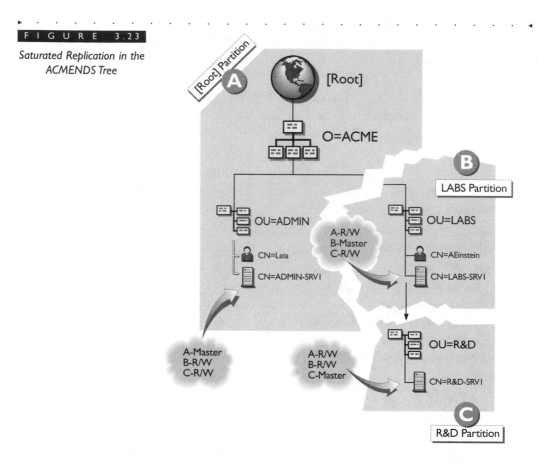

FIGURE 3.23

Saturated Replication in the ACMENDS Tree

QUIZ

Numbers can be challenging, fascinating, confusing, and frustrating, but once you have developed an interest in them, a whole new world is opened up as you discover their many characteristics and patterns. Numbers can be divided into many different categories, including amicable, abundant, deficient, perfect, and delectable numbers.

Amicable numbers **are pairs that are mutually equal to the sum of all their aliquot parts: for example, 220 and 284. The aliquot parts of 220** are 1, 2, 4, 5, 10, 11, 20, 22, 44, 55, and 110, the sum of which is 284, while the aliquot parts of 284 are 1, 2, 4, 71, and 142, the sum of which is 220. There are seven known pairs of amicable numbers, the largest of which are 9,437,056 and 7,363,584.

Abundant, deficient, and perfect numbers can be linked together because all numbers fit into these categories. An *abundant number* is one such that the sum of all its divisors (except itself) is greater than the number itself: for example, 12, because its divisors (1, 2, 3, 4, and 6) total 16. The opposite of this is a *deficient number,* where the divisors total less than the number itself: for example, 10, whose divisors (1, 2 and 5) total 8. If a number is not abundant or deficient, then it must be a *perfect number,* which means that it equals the sum of its aliquot parts: for example, 6, where its divisors (1, 2, 3) also total 6. Perfect numbers were first named in Ancient Greece by the Pythagoreans around 500 BC and to date, only 30 have been discovered. The first four perfect numbers were discovered before AD 100, and they include 6 and 496. However, the next (33,550,336) was not found until the fifteenth century. With the help of computer technology, the process of discovering new perfect numbers has been speeded up and the latest to be found has no fewer than 240 digits. One fact that has emerged is that all the perfect numbers now known are even numbers. However, no one from the time of Euclid to the present day has been able to prove that it is mathematically impossible for a perfect odd number to exist.

So, having dealt with amicable, abundant, deficient, and perfect numbers, what, may you ask, is a *delectable number*? The answer is that a nine-digit number is delectable if (a) it contains the digits 1 to 9 exactly once each (no zero) and (b) the numbers created by taking the first *n* digits (*n* runs from 1 to 9) are each divisible by *n*, so that the first digit is divisible by 1 (it always will be), the first two digits form a number divisible by 2, the first three digits form a number divisible by 3, and so on. Only one delectable number is known. Can you find out what it is?

Matching:

A) Abundant	1) 10
B) Perfect	2) 220
C) Deficient	3) 381654729
D) Amicable	4) 12
E) Delectable	5) 8128
	6) 284
	7) 386451729
	8) 28

(Q3-5)

All this synchronization magic is accomplished within a group of servers known as a *replica ring*. A replica ring is an internal system group that includes all servers containing replicas of a given partition. In Figure 3.23, the replica ring for Partition A includes:

▶ Master: CN=ADMIN-SRV1.

▶ R/W: CN=LABS-SRV1.

▶ R/W: CN=R&D-SRV1.

All synchronization takes place within the replica ring. The synchronization delay is greater when servers within a replica ring are separated by slow WAN links. Therefore, you'll want to keep track of replica rings and organize their distribution accordingly.

Let's finish off with a few general guidelines for managing NDS replicas:

▶ Fault tolerance—To meet fault tolerance needs, plan for three or more strategically placed replicas of each partition. You should also plan for possible WAN link failures whenever necessary. Don't place the entire replica ring in a single portion of the global network. This creates a single point of WAN link failure.

▶ Traffic efficiency—Generally only the information that's updated (delta) gets sent across the network. However, when you place a new replica, the entire file is copied. Each object takes up roughly 3K of space, large replicas can be in excess of 10 MB in size. Consider placing large replicas during low-traffic time periods.

▶ Workgroups—Create partitions that follow the boundaries of functional workgroups, then place replicas of each partition on the servers that are physically close to the users within that workgroup. This balances productivity and traffic efficiency.

▶ Logging in—Users need access to a Master or Read/Write replica for login authentication. In addition, NDS updates all appropriate replicas when the user logs in. For these reasons, consider distributing local Read/Write replicas closest to the servers users attach to. Let's return to Figure 3.23 as an example. Consider what happens when all ACME directors return to ADMIN headquarters for the annual meeting. AEinstein attaches to the ADMIN-SRV1 server. Since this server is part of his home partition's replica ring, he can authenticate locally. This increases login speed and decreases background synchronization traffic.

▶ [Root]—The [Root] partition is the most important segment of the entire NDS tree. Replicate it often. Consider creating a Read/Write replica of the [Root] partition on all geographically distributed servers. If you lose this partition, the entire network becomes inaccessible. There is a caveat, however. In the pyramid replica design, the [Root] partition has many children. Each server that receives replicas of the [Root] partition also receives Subordinate References for all of its child partitions. This may create more synchronization traffic than you initially intended. Be careful.

▶ Bindery Services—Be sure to follow a server's *bindery context* when distributing replicas. As we'll learn a little later, a server's bindery context lists all containers available to non-NDS users from this server. To work properly, the bindery server must have a Master or Read/Write replica of all containers in its bindery context. Don't worry—we'll revisit this topic multiple times later in the book.

▶ Moving containers—Because moving a container object directly affects partitions, it is considered a partitioning operation. You'll have to use the Partition Manager tool in NWADMIN to move a container. Before you do so, the container must be the highest object in its local partition. As you remember from our earlier discussion, this is called the partition root object. If you try to move the container without making it a partition root, an error message will appear. Once you've moved the container, give NDS a few minutes to resynchronize itself and update all objects with their new distinguished names. In addition, you may have to change the NAME CONTEXT statement in NET.CFG to reflect name changes. Finally, remind your users that they now have a new identity— since their home has moved.

Well, there you have it. That's partitioning and replication in a nutshell. Sit back, relax, and wallow in your newfound knowledge. There's time for only one more NDS management topic—time synchronization.

ZEN

"Waiting for the fish to bite or waiting for wind to fly a kite. Or waiting around for Friday night or waiting perhaps for their Uncle Jake or a pot to boil or a better break or a string of pearls or a pair of pants or a wig with curls or another chance. Everyone is just waiting."

Dr. Seuss

Time Synchronization

"Does anybody really know what time it is; does anybody really care?"

NDS does. As a matter of fact, NDS has to! Every aspect of NDS existence relies on time. Sound familiar? Time synchronization is a method of ensuring that all NDS objects report the same *time stamp*. Time stamps are important for

▶ Replica synchronization

▶ Messaging

▸ Login authentication and time-based security

▸ File and directory operations

Time stamps report time according to the Universal Time Coordinated (UTC) equivalent. This is a time system that adjusts to the local time zone and Daylight Savings Time. It is also equivalent to Greenwich Mean Time (GMT). UTC is calculated using three values for each time server:

▸ Local time

▸ +/- time zone offset from UTC

▸ - Daylight Savings Time offset

For example, in NORAD, Colorado, the time is eight hours behind GMT. Therefore, if the time in NORAD is 12:00 noon and there is no Daylight Savings Time, UTC is 19:00.

All of this fancy temporal footwork is accomplished during server installation with the Time Configuration Parameters Worksheet (see Figure 3.24). With this worksheet, you can define your new IntranetWare server as one of four different *time servers*. Time servers provide a consistent source for the time stamps that NDS and other features use. Each time you install a IntranetWare server, you must provide it with specific time configuration parameters, including time server type and the previous three UTC values.

F I G U R E   3.24

*Time Configuration
Parameters Worksheet in
INSTALL.NLM*

```
NetWare Server Installation 4.11                    NetWare Loadable Module
                    Verify/Enter Time Configuration Parameters
 Time server type:                                  Single Reference

 Standard time zone abbreviation:                   MST
 Standard time offset from UTC:                     7:00:00   BEHIND

 Does your area have daylight saving time (DST): YES
 DST time zone abbreviation:                        MDT
 DST offset from standard time:                     1:00:00   AHEAD
 DST Start: First Sunday of April at  2:00:00 am
 DST End:   Last Sunday of October at  2:00:00 am


     Standard Time Zone Abbreviation Help

     Enter the abbreviation for your time zone (standard time).  This string is
     mainly for display and formatting purposes and may be changed later in your
     AUTOEXEC.NCF configuration file.   For example, if this server is being
                      (To scroll, <F7>-up <F8>-down)
 Continue and save time parameters <F10>            Previous screen       <Esc>
 Help                               <F1>            Abort INSTALL <Alt><F10>
```

Let's explore the four different time server types and discuss the advantages and disadvantages of each.

TIME SERVER TYPES

All IntranetWare servers are *time servers* of some type. Time servers create and manage time stamps. There are two general categories of time servers: time providers and time consumers. *Time providers* provide time and are categorized as Primary, Reference or Single-Reference servers. *Time consumer servers* request their time from a provider and are categorized as Secondary servers.

Regardless, all time servers have the same fundamental responsibilities. First, they provide time to any requesting time provider, time consumer, or workstation. Second, they manage time synchronization and make sure everyone agrees what time it is. And, finally, they all adjust their internal clocks to correct discrepancies and maintain a consistent time across all IntranetWare servers.

So, which time server are you?

▸ Single-Reference—A time provider. This is the default configuration for most small WANs. It provides time to Secondary servers and cannot coexist with Primary or Reference servers.

▸ Reference—A time provider. These servers act as a central point of time control for the entire network. They get their time from an external source such as the Internet or an atomic clock.

▸ Primary—A time provider or time consumer. These servers work together with other Primary servers to "vote" on the correct time. This voting procedure determines network UTC in combination with values received from Reference servers.

▸ Secondary—A time consumer. This is part of the default configuration. These servers do not participate in voting and are told what the time is by time providers.

Let's take a closer look.

Single-Reference Time Servers

As we learned earlier, this is the default configuration for most small WANs. If used, it stands alone as the only time provider on the entire network. Therefore, it cannot coexist with Primary or Reference time providers (see Figure 3.25). All other IntranetWare servers in the same tree default to the Secondary time server type.

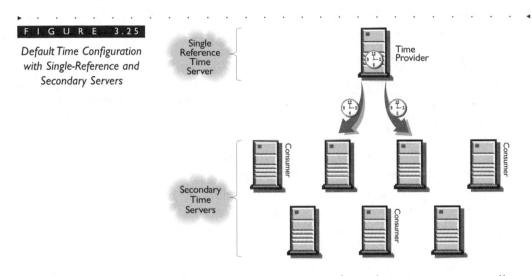

F I G U R E   3.25

Default Time Configuration with Single-Reference and Secondary Servers

It's important to note that time servers never send out their time automatically. They must be asked to report their time. This only happens when a server's *synchronization flag* has been activated. The synchronization flag occurs when the server is confident that its internal clock is within a *synchronization radius* of accepted time. The synchronization radius defaults to 2,000 milliseconds (2 seconds). You can adjust this value through SERVMAN. The key point here is that Single-Reference servers always activate their synchronization flag because they're the only ones on the network that matter.

Finally, Single-Reference time servers typically get their time from their own internal clock. You can, however, connect the server to a more reliable external time source such as the Internet, a radio clock, or atomic time provider.

> ### REAL WORLD
>
> It is possible for a Single-Reference time server to coexist with other time providers, although it's not recommended. The Single-Reference time server will not check with the other time providers when sending out NDS time stamps. As far as it's concerned, it's always right.

Reference Time Servers

Reference time servers are like Single-Reference servers in that they provide a central point of time control for the entire network. These time providers almost always get their time from an external source (such as the Internet, radio clocks, and/or atomic providers).

Reference time servers differ from Single-Reference servers in one important area—they *can* coexist with Primary servers. As you can see in Figure 3.26, Reference time servers provide time to Primary servers. Primaries then vote on what time they think it should be and eventually provide time to Secondary time consumers. Even though voting occurs with Reference time servers, it's important to note that *Reference servers always win*! No matter what time the primaries decide it is, they eventually agree with the Reference server. It's like saying, "Go ahead and argue about the time as long as your answer eventually matches mine." The Reference server is given higher priority because it's thought to be more reliable. This is because it typically uses an external time source. If you use the internal server clock, you're defeating the purpose of Reference and Primary voting.

If you have a Reference server, why bother with primaries at all? It's simple—fault tolerance. If the Reference server ever goes down, the primaries can take over and negotiate time for all the Secondary time consumers.

ZEN

"Today you don't have to be tidy or neat. If you wish, you may eat with both hands and both feet. So get in there and munch. Have a big munch-er-oo! Today is your birthday! Today you are you!"

Dr. Seuss

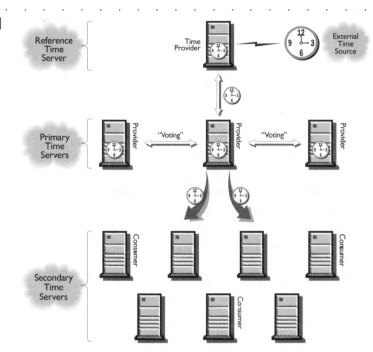

Custom Time Configuration with Reference and Primary Servers

Primary Time Servers

Primary time servers work together to vote on the correct time. This voting procedure can operate with or without the help of a Reference server. In either case, Primary servers vote every 5 minutes and adjust their internal time 50 percent of the time value discrepancy. They do not correct 100 percent because of oscillation errors. The 50 percent correction allows all the time servers to eventually converge on a single time stamp. This convergence is made easier with the presence of a Reference server, since it provides an ultimate goal. Without a Reference server, multiple primaries continue to vote until two of them agree. At this point, both synchronization flags are set and Secondary servers receive the new time stamp.

There are a few important configurations in this scenario. First, there's the *polling interval*. This is the waiting period between votes. By default, it's five minutes. Next, there's the question of who votes with whom. In one configuration method, all primaries vote with everybody, whereas in another, you can specify exactly who votes with whom. We'll explore these options a little later. Finally, there's the *offset threshold*—that is, by how much should a Primary be allowed to change its clock during voting? The default is 2 seconds. The offset threshold is also a configurable parameter.

Refer to Figure 3.26 for a review of Primary and Reference server voting. Notice that Secondary consumers ultimately get their time stamp from Primary servers. Again, this increases fault tolerance by creating redundant time providers.

Secondary Time Servers

Secondary time servers are part of the default configuration. They are the ultimate *time consumers*. They do not participate in voting and are told exactly what time it is by any of the other three types of time providers. Remember, time providers only give time stamps when they're asked for them. This puts the responsibility on the shoulders of Secondary time servers. Every 5 minutes they poll a specific time source for the correct time. If there's a discrepancy, the Secondary server changes its internal clock by 100 percent. By default, this time polling occurs every five minutes. (Of course, this is configurable.)

Probably more than 90 percent of your IntranetWare servers will be Secondary time consumers. In a generic configuration with 100 servers, you may have seven primaries, a Reference, and 92 Secondary time servers. It sure puts things in perspective.

For a summary of these four different time server types, refer to Table 3.5. Now that you're a time-server pro, let's take a closer look at the two different methods for accomplishing time synchronization—default and custom.

T A B L E   3.5

Getting to Know
IntranetWareTime Servers

FIRST SERVER TYPE	TIME PROVIDER	DESCRIPTION	GETS TIME FROM	ADJUSTS CLOCK	GIVES TIME TO
Single-Reference	Yes	Default configuration Only services Secondary time servers	Internal clock mostly	No	Secondary
Reference	Yes	Same as Single-Reference except it participates in Primary voting	External source mostly	No	Primary and Secondary

T A B L E 3.5

Getting to Know
IntranetWareTime Servers
(continued)

FIRST SERVER TYPE	TIME PROVIDER	DESCRIPTION	GETS TIME FROM	ADJUSTS CLOCK	GIVES TIME TO
Primary	Yes	Participates in voting to determine correct time stamp	Voting procedure or Reference server	Yes (50 percent correction per polling interval	Secondary
Secondary	No	Default configuration; consumes time stamp from other time providers	Single-Reference, Reference, or Primary	Yes (100 percent correction per polling interval)	Clients only

TIME CONFIGURATION

IntranetWare provides you with two methods for accomplishing time synchronization:

- Default

- Custom

The default method assumes that only two types of time servers are necessary—Single-Reference time providers and Secondary time consumers. This method is simple and efficient, but does not provide the flexibility required by large NDS implementations. The custom method, on the other hand, requires administrative planning. It uses Reference, Primary, and Secondary servers to minimize a single point of failure. In addition, the custom configuration method cuts down on network traffic by minimizing unneeded synchronization chatter. This is accomplished with the help of TIMESYNC.CFG—a custom time configuration file. Let's take a quick look at how it works.

Default Time Configuration

The default IntranetWare installation assumes only two types of time servers are necessary—Single-Reference and Secondary. This default method is simple and efficient. It also doesn't require any special time synchronization reconfiguration when new servers are added to the network. They're simply defined as Secondary time consumers.

The default method uses the Service Advertising Protocol (SAP) to advertise time from Single-Reference to Secondary servers. Although SAP is fast over a single network segment, it can overburden slow WAN links. Be careful not to set up too many time providers (no more than two) on either side of a slow link. Otherwise, the time synchronization traffic might adversely affect network performance. Also ensure that SAP filters around the network do not impede SAP traffic. Remember, NDS doesn't require SAP, and many administrators choose to turn it off. If this is the case, you'll have to use TIMESYNC.CFG and the custom method.

The default method may not be ideal for large NDS implementations with many sites connected by WAN links. If you decide to add Primary servers, the voting process could involve more network traffic than necessary. All in all, the default time configuration method is a good choice for small to medium implementations. It has the following advantages:

▸ It is easy to understand and requires no planning.

▸ It does not require a special custom configuration file. You don't have to provide any configuration information to time providers because the default method relies on SAP for time stamp advertisement.

▸ SAP is fast and dynamic. If you add or delete services from the server, the updates happen quickly.

▸ The chance of synchronization error is reduced because time consumers only talk to a specific time provider. They never negotiate with other Secondary servers.

On the other hand, the default time configuration has its shortcomings—it's not the cat's meow. Here're some disadvantages:

▸ The Single-Reference server must be contacted by every Secondary server on the network. If a WAN link goes down, Secondary time servers are left wandering in temporal space. This can cause a time/space continuum anomaly—that's bad.

▸ Using SAP means that a misconfigured server may disrupt the network. Some of the Secondary servers may synchronize to an unsynchronized time provider rather than to the authorized Single-Reference server. If NDS events occur with improper time stamps, you'll run into real trouble.

▸ One time source means a single point of failure. However, should a Single-Reference server go down, a Secondary time consumer can easily be set as the Single-Reference server using SERVMAN.

Custom Time Configuration

The custom configuration method is not difficult, but it requires some planning. It uses Reference and Primary servers as time providers to minimize a single point of failure. You'll need to know the physical layout of your network before using the custom configuration method. This helps you to distribute time providers. To use the custom configuration method, you'll need to determine which servers are time providers and where Secondary servers should go for synchronization.

For the custom configuration method to work, each server is given a special configuration file—TIMESYNC.CFG. This file provides an internal listing for time-server guidance. For Reference and Primary servers, TIMESYNC.CFG provides a voting list; for Secondary servers, TIMESYNC.CFG defines a *time provider group*.

The custom configuration method cuts down on network traffic, but requires a great deal of administration. For this reason, it is appropriate for networks with more than 30 servers in distributed geographic locations. Here are some of its advantages:

▸ As a CNA, you have complete control of the time-synchronization hierarchy. You can control who votes with whom and tell Secondary servers where to get their time.

▸ You can optimize network traffic and distribute time sources around the world.

► You can provide redundant time-synchronization paths and alternate time providers in case of network failures.

But the custom configuration method is not the cat's meow, either. There are many circumstances when its additional administrative overhead is not justified. Here are a couple of disadvantages:

► Customization requires careful planning, especially on a large network. Imagine reconfiguring numerous TIMESYNC.CFG files when the tree has changed or the company moves locations. No thanks!

► Network expansion involves too much work and reconfiguration.

It's pretty easy to see that the default configuration works well for small networks (fewer than 30 servers), and the custom configuration method works well for large networks (more than 30 servers). If you choose the custom configuration method, try to create a pyramid hierarchy structure for time providers and time consumers (see Figure 3.26). Also, keep the number of time providers as small as possible to reduce network traffic. You can further enhance network performance by making sure time consumers get their time stamp from local servers—not over WAN links.

We're all out of time! (Pun intended.)

ZEN

"Oh! The places you'll go! You'll be on your way up! You'll be seeing great sights! You'll join the high fliers who soar to high heights!"

Dr. Seuss

That's everything you need to know about the "Cloud." Well, not really, but it's a very good start. Remember, every cloud has a silver lining and this chapter has been yours. Can you feel the *twinge* in the crown of your cranium? Has your NDS tree begun to sprout? Pretty soon, you'll be NDS-Head Fred!

The goal of this chapter was to make you think until it hurt—to generate enough neurokinetic energy to stimulate cranial growth. Have we succeeded? You be the judge. It all started with an NDS getting-familiar period. Once you were comfortable with the concept of a tree in a cloud, we learned about the 29 different objects that live there—including the [Root] and leaves. We learned that NDS objects come in two different flavors: Tupperware containers and physical leaf resources. We learned about Country objects, users, Distribution Lists, and the Alias object (if that's what it's really called).

With objects come names. Names uniquely identify "who we are" and "where we live." It works much the same way in NDS. NDS naming was the first of three important management topics we covered. We learned about the common name (who) and context (where). And we learned how these two are combined to create the distinguished name.

Then we explored partitioning—the second NDS management topic. NDS partitions are small pieces of the larger IntranetWare puzzle. We can distribute these pieces on servers throughout the WAN for increased fault tolerance and better resource access. This process is known as replication. We learned about the four different NDS replica types and how and when they can be used. By now, the [Root] should have been forming around your cerebellum.

The final NDS management topic was time synchronization. NDS has to know what time it is: time stamps are required for logging in, NDS replication, and many other important network tasks. This is accomplished with the help of three different time providers (Single-Reference, Reference, and Primary) and one special time consumer server (Secondary). We not only learned about servers, we explored two different configuration methods (default and custom). That's just about when we ran out of time!

So, here we are—NDS-Head Fred! So far, we've explored the basics of IntranetWare and the intricacies of Novell Directory Services. That completes our discussion of IntranetWare CNA basics. Now you're ready to start the *real* journey:

- ▸ IntranetWare File System (Chapter 4)

- ▸ IntranetWare Security (Chapter 5)

- ▸ IntranetWare Configuration (Chapter 6)

- ▸ IntranetWare Management (Chapter 7)

- ▸ IntranetWare Printing (Chapter 8)

Don't be scared—I'll be with you every step of the way. And we'll return to these topics many times again. This is only the beginning and I can't wait for you to become a full-fledged superhero . . . .

Speaking of superheroes, let me introduce you to an organization full of them. As a matter of fact, this company's single purpose is to SAVE THE WORLD!!! Check it out!

QUIZ

If my three were a four,
And my one were a three,
What I am would be nine less
Than half what I'd be.
I'm only three digits,
Just three in a row,
So what in the world must I be?
Do you know?

Hint: Synergy.
(Q3-6)

Getting to Know ACME

The world is in a lot of trouble. If we keep abusing the Planet Earth at our current pace, there'll be nothing left in a few decades.

As a matter of fact, the Alpha Centurions have discovered this and decided to do something about it. As it turns out, they are great fans of the Planet Earth and would hate to see us destroy it. They have given us a deadline before which we must clean up our act—or else.

To save the world, we have created an organization called ACME (A Cure for Mother Earth). ACME is staffed by the greatest heroes of all time. They are the founding mothers and fathers of Earth's Golden Age.

We've traveled back in time to recruit the ACME management. Now it's your turn. You will serve as ACME's MIS department. You will build a pervasive internetwork for ACME using IntranetWare. The clock is ticking and connectivity is the key.

ZEN

"Don't Panic!"

The Hitchhiker's Guide to the Galaxy

In the social hierarchy of needs, the world is pretty screwed up. The Pyramid of Needs states that basic fundamental needs (such as food and shelter) preclude us from enjoying higher needs (such as art, education, and corn dogs). This pyramid exists at many different levels throughout the world. Almost two-thirds of our population doesn't have sufficient resources to satisfy the lowest basic needs—medicine, food, shelter, and peace—while a smaller percentage takes higher needs—like digital watches—for granted. Something needs to change.

As a matter of fact, the Alpha Centurions have discovered this and have decided to do something about it. As it turns out, they are great fans of the Planet Earth and would hate to see us destroy it. The good news is they are a benevolent and intelligent race. They understand the Pyramid of Needs and recognize that everyone should be able to enjoy digital watches. They have discovered that the top 1 percent of the Earth's population is destroying the world at an alarming pace, while the other 99 percent are just trying to survive. In an effort to save the world, they have issued an ultimatum:

Clean up your act or find another planet to exploit!

They have given us until January 1, 2000, to clean up our act—or else! It's safe to say that the fate of the human race is in your hands. To help measure our progress, the Alpha Centurions have developed a World Health Index (WHI). The WHI is a balanced calculation of seven positive and seven negative factors that determine how good or bad we're treating the Earth. They've decided that 100 is a good number to shoot for. It represents a good balance between basic and higher needs. Once the world achieves a WHI of 100, almost everyone will be able to afford a digital watch. Here's a quick list of the 14 positive and negative WHI factors:

WHI Positive	WHI Negative
Charity	Crime
Love	Pollution
Birth	Starvation
Education	Disease
Health	War
Laughing	Poverty
Sports	Corruption

Bottom line: The Alpha Centurions have given us a little more than three years to increase our WHI from its current level (-2) to 100. We have until January 1, 2000. If we don't clean up our act by then, they will mercifully eradicate all humans and let the animals and plants live peacefully on the Planet Earth.

ZEN

"This magnificent butterfly finds a little heap of dirt and sits still on it. But man will never on his heap of mud keep still."

Joseph Conrad

ACME has been designed as "A Cure for Mother Earth." It is staffed by the greatest heroes from our unspoiled history. These are the founding mothers and fathers of Earth's Golden Age—before instant popcorn, talking cars, and daytime television. It's clear that somewhere along the human timeline, progress went amuck. We need help from heroes before that time. In order to vortex back in history and grab the ACME management, we've used a prototype of the Oscillating Temporal Overthruster (OTO). We've hand-chosen only the brightest and most resourceful characters, then meticulously trained each one of them for special tasks. They're a little disoriented, but more than happy to help.

These historical heroes have been placed in an innovative organizational structure. As you can see in Figure 3.27 (see the poster bound into this book as well), ACME is organized around five main divisions. They are

- ▶ Human Rights (Gandhi)—Taking care of the world's basic needs, including medicine, food, shelter, and peace. These tasks are handled jointly by Albert Schweitzer, Mother Teresa, Florence Nightingale, and Buddha. This division's work has the most positive impact on the WHI.

▸ Labs (Albert Einstein)—Putting technology to good use. This division is the technical marvel of ACME. In addition to research and development (R&D) efforts, the Labs division is responsible for the WHI tracking center in NORAD. This division is staffed by the wizardry of Leonardo da Vinci, Sir Isaac Newton, Charles Darwin, Marie Curie, Charles Babbage, and Ada, "The Countess of Lovelace."

▸ Operations (King Arthur)—Saving the world can be a logistical nightmare. Fortunately, we have King Arthur and the Knights of the Round Table to help us out. In this division, ACME routes money from caring contributors (Charity) to those who need it most (Financial)— there's a little Robin Hood in there somewhere. Also, with the help of Merlin, we will distribute all the Human Rights and Labs material to the four corners of the globe.

▸ Crime Fighting (Sherlock Holmes and Dr. Watson)—Making the world a safer place. This division tackles the almost insurmountable task of eradicating world crime. It's a good thing we have the help of Sherlock Holmes and some of our greatest crime-fighting superheroes, including Robin Hood, Maid Marion, Wyatt Earp, and Wild Bill Hickok. These heroes deal with the single most negative factor in WHI calculations— crime. This is very important work.

▸ Admin (George Washington)—Keeping the rest of ACME running smoothly. It's just like a well-oiled machine with the help of America's Founding Fathers—George Washington, Thomas Jefferson, Abraham Lincoln, FDR, and James Madison. Their main job is public relations under the command of one of our greatest orators, Franklin Delano Roosevelt (FDR). In addition to getting the word out, Admin tracks ACME activity (auditing) and keeps the facilities operating at their best.

► · ◄

F I G U R E   3.27

ACME Organizational Chart

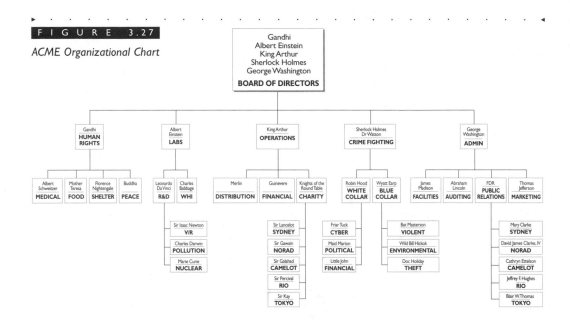

SMART LINK

If you want to meet all the great ACME heroes in cyberperson, surf the Web to http://www.cyberstateu.com/clarke/acme.htm.

Now it's your turn. You are the final piece in our globe-trotting puzzle. You are ACME's MIS department. We have recruited you as the architect of our communications strategy. As an IntranetWare CNA, you come highly recommended. Your mission—should you choose to accept it—is to build the ACME WAN. You will need courage, design experience, NDS know-how, and this book. If you succeed, you will save the world and become a CNA! All in a day's work.

ACME has a daunting task ahead of it, so we don't have any time to mess around. I'd like to begin by thanking you for choosing to accept this mission. Now you'll find some design inputs included with this book. They are *for your eyes only*. Once you have read the inputs, eat them! There's other good news—you don't have to save the world alone. The project team is here to help you. Remember, we're counting on you. Be careful not to let these facts fall into the wrong hands. Believe it or not, there are forces at work that don't share our love for the human race.

ACME CHRONICLES

A day in the life . . .

What you're about to read is for your eyes only. This is extremely confidential information. The ACME *Chronicles* is a detailed look at the life and times of ACME. This is an exceptional organization created for a singular purpose—to save the world. As you can see in Figure 3.27, ACME is organized around five main divisions:

▸ Human Rights

▸ Labs

▸ Operations

▸ Crime Fighting

▸ Admin

Let's go inside and see what makes them tick.

Human Rights—Gandhi in Sydney

This is the "heart" of ACME's purpose. Human Rights has the most profound positive effect on the WHI. Efforts here can save lives and increase our chances of surviving into the next century. The goal of Human Rights is to raise people from the bottom of the Pyramid of Needs. By satisfying their basic needs (medicine, food, shelter, and peace), we hope to give humans the strength to fight for higher needs (equality, justice, education, and digital watches). This makes the world a better place and dramatically improves the WHI.

All Human Rights materials developed here are distributed every day through ten different distribution centers around the world. This is ACME's manufacturing facility for food, shelter, and medical aid. In addition, the peacekeepers use any means necessary to thwart global wars. Let's take a closer look at the four different departments of Human Rights.

▶ Medical (Albert Schweitzer)—This department is collecting basic medical materials and training doctors and nurses for field work. Also, ACME is eagerly developing vaccines and working overtime to cure serious diseases. Finally, the medical staff is taking steps to clean up the sanitation of "dirty" countries. This is all accomplished with the help of Albert Schweitzer and his dedicated staff.

▶ Food (Mother Teresa)—With the help of her country-trained culinary heroes, Mother Teresa will determine how much Opossum Stew the whole world can eat. In addition, they are developing a series of genetically engineered organisms that will transform inedible materials into food stock. Finally, ACME's Food department has teamed up with R&D to create virtual reality (V/R) programming that teaches people how to grow food of their own. After all, if you give a person a fish, they eat for a day; but if you teach them to fish, they eat for a lifetime (and get a guest spot on ESPN's *Outdoor World*).

▶ Shelter (Florence Nightingale)—With all the new healthier and happier people in the world, our attention shifts to shelter. Fortunately, Florence Nightingale and her crack construction team have developed a cheap recyclable, geodesic dome called a Permaculture. It has central heating, air conditioning, water, plumbing, and computer-controlled maid service. The most amazing thing about the dome is that it can be constructed from any native materials—that's cacti and sand in the desert, lily pads in the marsh, and snow in the Arctic. If all else fails, they're edible.

▶ Peace (Buddha)—One of the most overlooked basic needs is peace. All the other stuff doesn't mean a hill of beans if you're living in a war zone. Buddha's job is to somehow settle the 101 wars currently plaguing our Earth. He relies on a combination of wisdom, diplomacy, military presence, and fortune cookies.

That completes our discussion of Human Rights. Check out figure 3.28. Now let's take a look at the ACME Labs division.

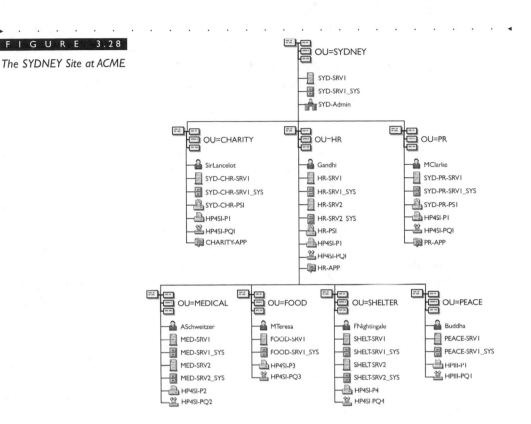

FIGURE 3.28

The SYDNEY Site at ACME

Labs—Albert Einstein in NORAD

Albert Einstein is one of the greatest minds in our history, but how far can he push technology? The U.S. Military has loaned us the NORAD facility in Colorado as a base for technical wizardry. In addition to Research & Development (R&D), this is the central point of a vast WHI data-collection network.

ACME's R&D efforts are controlled by Leonardo da Vinci and his dream team of scientists. They use technology and a little bit of magic to save the Earth. Current projects include alternative power sources, V/R programming, anti-pollutants, NDS, and a cure for bad hair days. Let's take a closer look:

> ▶ V/R (Sir Isaac Newton)—V/R programming is being developed to convince the world that a cure is necessary. The V/R devices will be sold as video games and will help ACME tap the minds of the world. This borders on mind control, but in a good way (if that's possible). There's nothing that brain power and a little bit of magic can't cure.

▸ Pollution (Charles Darwin)—This department is developing anti-pollutants and methods of transforming garbage into fuel. Also, this group is working to eradicate the world's largest scourge—ElectroPollution. Currently Leonardo da Vinci and Charles Darwin are working on airplanes powered by pencil erasure grit.

▸ Nuclear (Marie Curie)—Cybernetic soldiers (Nuclear Disarmament Squads or NDS) are being designed to infiltrate and neutralize nuclear weapons facilities. Finally, somebody's splitting atoms for good.

In addition to R&D, NORAD is the central point of a vast WHI data-collection network. This network is the pulse of ACME. Collection of world data and calculation of the WHI occur here every day. Currently, the WHI sits at -2. And, as we all know, it must climb to more than 100 by January 1, 2000. Charles Babbage and Ada diligently guard the computers and make daily adjustments to WHI calculations. Ada's sacrifice is particularly notable because she used to be the "Countess of Lovelace." But fortunately for us, she has a soft spot in her heart for mathematics and Mr. Babbage.

Distributed world data-collection centers are scattered to all four corners of the Earth. There are ten ACME WHI hubs—one in every divisional headquarters—and five more scattered to strategic points around the Earth. From each of these sites, world data is sent to NORAD and calculated on a daily basis. The results are distributed to every major newspaper so the world can chart ACME's progress. In addition to the ten WHI hubs, there are hundreds of collection clusters distributed around each hub. Each cluster sends data directly to the closest hub (via dial-up lines) and eventually back to the central site at NORAD.

ZEN

Techno-hip—comfortable with the use of the modern jargon of computers and other recent technological developments. Just think—all you have to do is memorize all the CNA nomenclature in this book and you will be a "techno-hipster." An unexpected side effect of becoming a CNA.

That completes our journey through ACME technology. Check out Figure 3.29. Now let's take a look at the Operations division.

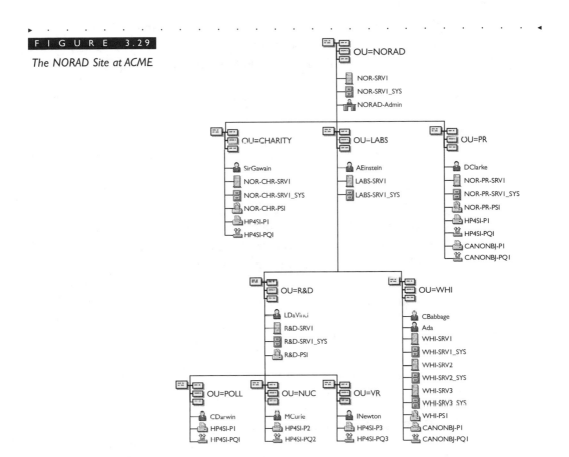

FIGURE 3.29

The NORAD Site at ACME

Operations—King Arthur in Camelot

King Arthur and his court will keep ACME financed through charity drives and financial spending. After all, "money makes the world go 'round." Never before has it been more true. In addition, the Operations division handles the arduous task of distributing ACME aid to all the people who need it. Here's how it works:

> ► Distribution (Merlin)—We're going to need all the magic we can get. This department handles the distribution of human rights materials, medical supplies, doctors, nurses, food, hardware, building supplies, and pre-fabricated geodesic domes. No guns! It also handles implementation of WHI devices from R&D, such as anti-pollutants, Nuclear Disarmament Squads (NDS), anti-hacking viruses, and V/R

programming. The latter is handled through satellite TV transmissions and video games. ACME distribution takes place through the same ten hubs as WHI. Think of it as data in (WHI) and aid out (Distribution).

▶ Financial (Guinevere)—This is the money-out department. Guinevere handles the distribution of charity contributions, including the purchase of human rights material, bailing-out of bankrupt nations, and the funding of internal ACME activities. For a more detailed discussion of Financial operations, refer to the ACME Workflow section later in this chapter.

▶ Charity (Knights of the Round Table)—This is the money-in department. The Knights collect charity from world organizations and distribute it to the Financial department for disbursement. Each of the five major Knights oversees one of five charity centers—in each of the divisional headquarters. Sir Lancelot is in Sydney, Sir Gawain is in NORAD, Sir Galahad handles Camelot, Sir Percival oversees Rio, and Sir Kay is in Tokyo. I haven't seen such dedication since the medieval ages.

Well, that's how ACME's Operations work. Check out Figure 3.30. Now let's take a look at Crime Fighting.

Crime Fighting—Sherlock Holmes in Tokyo

Crime has one of the most negative effects on the WHI. Fortunately, we have history's greatest crime-fighting mind to help us out—Sherlock Holmes. With the help of Dr. Watson, he has identified two major categories of world crime:

▶ White Collar

▶ Blue Collar

White-collar crimes include cyberhacking and political espionage. Robin Hood and his Band of Superheroes direct white-collar crime-fighting efforts from Tokyo. Here are some of the different types of crimes they're concerned with:

▶ Cyber (Friar Tuck)—With the help of the *Cyberphilia* underground, Friar Tuck attempts to thwart cyber crime. Most cyber crimes occur on The Net, so ACME must constantly monitor global communications. Tuck also has the help of an off-shoot group of guardian angels known as the Cyber Angels.

▶ Political (Maid Marion)—She can charm her way through any politically tense situation. Political crimes are especially rampant in emerging nations, so Maid Marion enlists the help of the United Nations.

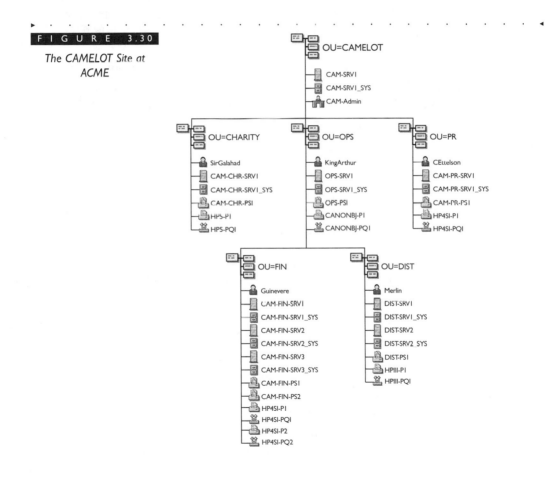

FIGURE 3.30

The CAMELOT Site at ACME

▶ Financial (Little John)—With some creative financing and the help of ex-IRS agents, Little John thwarts financial crimes throughout the world. These crimes especially hurt the middle class, so he has recruited some key Yuppies as undercover agents.

Blue-collar crimes are a little more obvious—such as violence and theft. This is familiar ground for Wyatt Earp and his band of western heroes. They're not glamorous, but they're effective. Here's a look at ACME Crime Fighting from the blue-collar point of view:

▶ Violent (Bat Masterson)—This cowboy is in his element. He thwarts violent crime by getting inside the criminal's mind—literally.

▶ Environmental (Wild Bill Hickok)—A great fan of the environment, Mr. Hickok uses his country charm to thwart environmental crimes such as excessive deforestation, toxic waste, whaling, oil spills, ElectroPollution, and forced extinction.

▶ Theft (Doc Holliday)—With his legendary sleight of hand, Doc Holliday stays one step ahead of the world's thieves.

So, that's what's happening on the crime fighting front. Check out Figure 3.31. Now let's take a close look at the final ACME division—Admin.

Admin—George Washington in Rio

Ever since the beginning of time, humans have quested for wisdom and knowledge. Now we'll need to put all of our enlightenment to good use—or else. A few centuries ago, the United States' Founding Fathers joined a growing group of men and women called Illuminoids. These people were dissatisfied with everyday life on Planet Earth and began to reach above, within, and everywhere else for a better way. The Illuminoids formed a variety of organizations dedicated to creating a New World Order including the Masons, the Trilateral Commission, the Council on Foreign Relations (CFR), and the Bilderberg Group.

Regardless of their ultimate motivation, the Illuminoids' hearts were in the right place—"let's make the world a better place." The founder of the Trilateral Commission has always claimed they are just *a group of concerned citizens interested in fostering greater understanding and cooperation among international allies.* Whether or not it's true, it sounds like a great fit for ACME. Once again, we've used the OTO to grab some of the earliest Illuminoids and solicit their help for ACME administration.

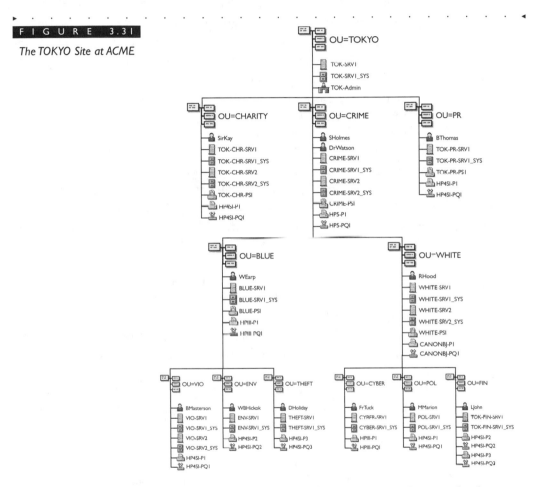

F I G U R E   3.31

The TOKYO Site at ACME

George Washington keeps the ACME ship afloat. Along with FDR, he keeps things running smoothly and makes sure the world hears about our plight. In addition, James Madison keeps the facilities running, while Abraham Lincoln makes sure ACME is held accountable for all its work. For years, the Trilateral Commission has been rumored to covertly run the world. Now they get a chance to overtly save it!

Now let's take a look at the four departments that make up ACME's administration:

▸ Public Relations (Franklin Delano Roosevelt)—This department solicits help from the rest of the world by enlisting the help of heroes from our own age—the 1990s. We're not going to be able to save the world alone. The PR department is responsible for communicating our plight to the four corners of the Earth. Department members inform everyday citizens about the Alpha Centurion ultimatum, daily WHI quotes, and requests for charity. There is a local PR office in each major location. See the organizational chart in Figure 3.27 for more details.

▸ Marketing (Thomas Jefferson)—Educating the rest of the world and soliciting help is another Marketing department responsibility. In addition to advertising, this department develops materials for distributed PR offices. Its goal is to rally all nations around ACME and our cause in order to save the Earth. They also bake really good apple pies and chocolate chip cookies.

▸ Auditing (Abraham Lincoln)—They make sure that everyone stays in line. Financial trails for all charity moneys and complete records of all changes to the WHI are tracked by the Auditing department. Although it's part of the internal ACME organization, Auditing is an independent tracking company that generates bonded reports.

▸ Facilities (James Madison)—This department keeps everyone working, happy, and fed. The Facilities department also organizes field trips and ACME parties. Imagine the doozy they're going to have when we finally succeed!

Well, there you have it. That's everything there is to know about ACME. See Figure 3.32 for a detailed look at the last ACME division. I hope these *Chronicles* have helped you and the project team to better understand what ACME is up against. This is no normal organization. If ACME goes out of business, the world is either lost or saved—it's up to you.

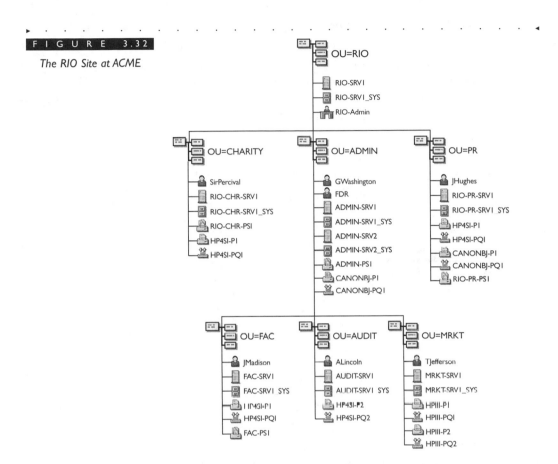

F I G U R E   3.32

The RIO Site at ACME

ZEN

Chaos theory—the systematic approach to describing very complex events in mathematics and science by rounding off numerical data to reveal very general patterns. This theory can be used to describe the irregular patterns of a dripping water faucet, fluctuations in insect populations, stock-market price changes, or the daily grind of a CNA. In all cases, chaos theory relies on the strange attractor, which is a complex and unpredictable pattern of movement—much like a user's interface with IntranetWare workstations or your understanding of ACME.

ACME WORKFLOW

Although it may look complicated, the daily grind at ACME is really pretty simple. It's a combination of workflow and dataflow. *Workflow* describes the daily operations of ACME staff and their task-oriented responsibilites. *Dataflow* describes the daily or weekly movement of data from one location to another. Although the two are not always the same, they should be compatible. This is the goal of ACME synergy.

In this section, we're going to take a detailed look at how work and data flow through the ACME organization. This data has a dramatic impact on NDS design. After all, work and data flow over the WAN infrastructure. Refer to Figure 3.33 as you follow along.

FIGURE 3.33

ACME Workflow Diagram

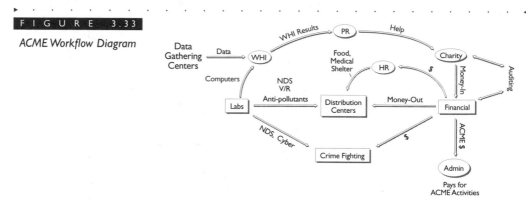

Financial

Of course, money makes the world go 'round! The Financial department has two main responsibilities:

- Money-in

- Money-out

Money-in focuses on funding ACME activities and distributing charities to needy people. With Money-out, Guinevere pays for Human Rights materials, Admin work, and Crime Fighting tools. Next, she disburses charity money through distribution centers. Money-in comes from the various Charity activities. All financial activity is audited by the internal Auditing organization.

Technically, this is accomplished from a central database at the Financial headquarters in Camelot. No money changes hands. Quarterly budgets are developed in Camelot and distributed to local banks for Human Rights, Crime Fighting, Distribution, and Admin. Each of these distributed sites sends weekly updates to the central database with the help of local servers.

Distribution Centers

The Distribution department is the hub of ACME achievements. Distribution centers disburse three kinds of aid:

▸ Human Rights materials (such as food, medicine, and shelter)

▸ Money from the Financial department

▸ Exciting inventions from Labs

Each of the ten distribution centers maintains its own distributed database. They move material to local warehouses for delivery to needy people. Weekly summary updates are sent to the central inventory management database in Camelot. The central database oversees the big picture of aid distribution.

If a center runs out of a particular resource, one of two things happens:

1 • Camelot updates the center's budget, and they purchase the resource locally.

2 • Camelot orders the movement of resources from another distribution center. This option makes sense for finite materials such as special inventions from Labs or medical supplies.

Labs and Their Inventions

This is where the brainiacs hang out. Scientists in the Labs division develop world-saving toys for:

▸ Crime Fighting—NDS and cyberviruses

▸ Distribution—V/R programming and anti-pollutants

The Labs division supports WHI and all its technical needs. New product updates are sent to Distribution and Crime Fighting for internal consumption. This is secure information.

WHI Calculations

Labs is also where the WHI (World Health Index) is calculated. Charles Babbage and Ada collect data from data-gathering centers (DGCs) throughout the world. These DGCs are housed in divisional headquarters and distribution centers throughout the ACME WAN. They are

NORAD	Seattle
Rio	Cairo
Camelot	New York
Sydney	Moscow
Tokyo	St. Andrews

Ironically, the distribution centers send aid *out* and the DGCs pull data *in*— from the same ten locations. Daily WHI summary calculations are sent to NORAD each day so the final WHI calculation can be made. Results are distributed to PR daily for inclusion in global periodicals—including the ACME *Chronicles* (an hourly interactive newsletter).

Public Relations

This is the voice of ACME. In addition to distributing daily WHI reports, Public Relations (PR) educates the world and helps solicit money for Charity. PR pulls the daily WHI results from NORAD twice a day. They're also the on-line editors of the ACME *Chronicles,* which gives them some great financial leads for Charity.

Charity—Money-In Charity is ACME's open door. It is the funnel for ACME contributions. There is a charity center in each of the five divisional headquarters. This is how the top 1 percent helps the rest of us. Their motto is:

Spread the Wealth, or the Alpha Centurions will eat you!

All money collected by Charity is sent to the Financial department for disbursement. Two of the most important uses for this money are Crime Fighting and Admin. Note that the money doesn't actually change hands. It is deposited in local divisional banks, and daily updates are sent to the central financial database in Camelot.

Crime Fighting

Remember, crime has one of the greatest negative effects on the WHI. The Crime Fighting department relies on the following sources:

- Labs' inventions (NDS and cyberviruses)

- Money from the Financial department

- The guile of Robin Hood, Wyatt Earp, and their respective heroes

ACME Administration

The ACME staff has to eat. Admin relies on money from Financial to keep things running smoothly. You can't fight bureaucracy. In addition, the Auditing department needs audit-level access to the central financial database in Camelot. They are responsible for tracking money-in from Charity and money-out from Financial.

That's all there is to it. No sweat. As you can see, ACME runs like a well-oiled machine. Someone sure put a lot of effort into designing its organizational structure—and it shows! We're in good hands with ACME.

Good luck; and by the way, thanks for saving the world!

ZEN

"Today is gone. Today was fun. Tomorrow is another one. Every day from here to there funny things are everywhere."

Dr. Seuss

SMART LINK

If you really want to get to know Dr. Seuss, check out another great site at http://www.afn.org/~afn15301/drseuss.html.

EXERCISE 3-1: "TREE WALKING" FOR TODDLERS

To complete this exercise, you will need Admin-level access to an IntranetWare NDS tree. If you don't have a tree of your own and/or you'd like to build the ACME tree, refer to the case study, "Building ACME's NDS Tree," later in this chapter. You will explore the NDS tree structure using three different utilities: NetWare Administrator (NWADMIN), NETADMIN, and CX. Before beginning this exercise, you'll need to make sure that your network administrator has set up the NetWare Administrator icon in Windows on your workstation.

NETWARE ADMINISTRATOR

The NetWare Administrator (NWADMIN) utility is undoubtedly the most versatile utility available in IntranetWare. It can be used to perform a variety of functions, including the type of network administrator tasks that are available in FILER, NETADMIN, PARTMGR, and PCONSOLE.

During IntranetWare installation, the MS Windows and OS/2 version of this utility is stored as SYS:PUBLIC\NWADMN3X, and the Windows 95 version is stored as SYS:PUBLIC\WIN95\NWADMN95. Before you run the NetWare Administrator under any of these operating systems for the first time, you'll need to create an NWADMIN icon. From then on, you can select the icon to activate the utility.

In this exercise, we are going to use NWADMIN to explore the NDS tree.

1. Exploring the browser window. Execute the NetWare Administrator (NWADMIN) utility. A Welcome to NetWare Administrator dialog box will probably be displayed and list a random tip for using this utility. Read the tip, then click on the Close button to close the dialog box. At this point, at least one NDS container object should be displayed. If not, select the NDS Browser option from the Tools menu to open a browser window. (If you do so, you'll notice that the [Root] is the default context. If you click on OK, a new browser window will be opened.)

a.   What container and its objects are displayed when you activate the NetWare Administrator utility? How can you determine what your current context is? How was your current context determined? Is it the same current context that would be displayed using the CX command at the DOS prompt?

b.   How many containers are displayed? What type of containers are represented? How many leaf objects, if any, are displayed? What type of leaf objects are represented?

2.   Changing context.

a.   Keying in a new context. Keying in the name of a new context is one of the two methods available for changing your current context. Change your context to the [Root] by selecting "Set Context..." from the View menu. A Set Context dialog box will be displayed. Type **[Root]** in the Context field and click on OK. The [Root] icon should then be displayed at the top of the screen.

b.   Walking the tree. Next, let's try the "walking the tree" method to change your current context. Select "Set Context..." from the View menu.

(1) Click on the Browser button to the right of the Context field to display the Select Object dialog box.

(2) To navigate the tree, double-click on a container in the Browse Context list box on the right side of the screen to move down one level in the tree, or double-click on the double-dot (..) to move up one level in the tree. The objects that are located the container that you select will be displayed in the Available Objects list box on the left side of the screen. Practice walking up and down the tree. When you are finished, walk all the way up the tree, so that the [Root] icon is displayed at the top of the Available Objects list box on the left side of the screen.

(3) When the container you want to select as the current context is displayed in the Available Objects list box (which in this case is the [Root] object), click on it, then click on the OK button at the bottom of the window. The container that you have selected will appear in the Context field of the Set Context dialog box. Click on the OK button at the bottom of the Set Context window to return to the main NWADMIN browser screen.

3. Opening a container object and viewing its contents. There are three methods available for opening a container and viewing its contents:

    a. Double-clicking on the container's object name or icon

    b. Clicking on the container object to select it, then selecting the Expand option from the View menu

    c. Clicking on the container object to select it, then pressing the plus key (+) on the numeric keypad portion of your computer keyboard

    Practice using all three of these methods to view the contents of various containers. Determine the type of containers that are in each container, as well as the type of leaf objects.

4. Viewing the object dialog (object details) of a container object. The object dialog lets you display and edit information relating to an object's properties. When you open an object dialog, you'll notice that there is a column of page buttons along the right side of the screen. You can click on each button, one at a time, to view the category of information indicated on the button. There are two methods available for viewing the information relating to a container object:

    a. Clicking on the container object with the left mouse button to select it, then selecting the Details option from the Object menu

    b. Clicking on the container object with the right mouse button to select it, then selecting Details from the pull-down menu that appears on the screen

Practice using both of these methods to look at the information available for various types of container objects, including the [Root], an Organization object, an Organizational Unit object, a User object, and so on.

5. Viewing the object dialog (object details) of a leaf object. There are three methods for viewing the information relating to a leaf object:

   a. Double-clicking on the leaf object

   b. Clicking on the leaf object with the left mouse button to select it, then selecting the Details option from the Object menu

   c. Clicking on the leaf object with the right mouse button to select it, then selecting the Details option from the pull-down menu that appears on the screen

   Practice using all three of these methods to look at the information available for various types of leaf objects (including Users, Groups, Print Servers, Printers, Print Queues, and so on, if they exist).

   When you are ready to exit the NetWare Administrator utility, select the Exit option from the File menu.

NETADMIN

The NETADMIN utility is a menu utility that can be used to manage NDS objects and their properties. It is much more limited in scope than the NetWare Administrator Utility.

1. Changing context. In order to change your current context for purposes of the NETADMIN utility, choose the Change Context option from the NETADMIN Options menu and press Enter. There are two methods of changing your context for the purposes of this utility. (When you exit the utility, you will return to the current context that was set before you ran the utility.) One is keying in the name of a new context in the field provided; the other is pressing the Insert key and walking the tree.

a. Press Insert. The contents of the current directory will be displayed, as well as a dot (.) representing the current directory and a double-dot (..) representing the parent directory. You will *not* need to select the dot (.) for purposes of this exercise.

b. Practice walking up and down the tree by selecting the double-dot (..) and pressing Enter to move up one level in the tree and selecting a container and pressing Enter to move down one level in the tree. You'll notice that the current context is displayed at the top-left portion of the screen. Go ahead and walk all the way up the tree by double-clicking on the double-dot (..) until the [Root] is listed as your current context, then walk down the tree by double-clicking on a container object, then double-clicking on a container object below that container object, and so on. When the current context you want is selected, press F10 to return to the NETADMIN Options menu.

2. Managing objects. In order to view and manage objects and their properties, select the Manage Objects option from the NETADMIN Options menu. You'll notice that you can walk the tree from this screen as well.

a. In order to display information about an object, select the object using the up-arrow key and down-arrow key, then press F10 to select it. You'll notice that the name and type of the object that you selected will be listed at the top of the menu that appears. Select the View or Edit Properties of this Object menu option and press Enter. A list of categories will be displayed. Select the category desired and press Enter. Review the information displayed for this category, then press Esc to return to the previous menu. Use this method to display the various properties of this object, then press Esc twice to return to the Object, Class menu. Practice using this technique to display the properties of various types of container and leaf objects.

b. When you're ready to exit the NETADMIN utility, press Esc twice when the Object, Class menu is displayed, then select Yes and press Enter when asked if you want to exit.

CX

The IntranetWare CX command line utility can be used to display or modify your context, or to view containers and leaf objects in your Directory tree. Open a DOS window in Windows 3.1x or Windows 95, or perform the following steps at the DOS prompt:

1. Change to drive F:.

   ```
   F:
   ```

2. Display your current context.

   ```
   CX
   ```

3. Display on-line help for the CX command.

   ```
   CX /?
   ```

4. Display containers in the current context.

   ```
   CX /CONT
   ```

5. Display containers and objects in the current context.

   ```
   CX /A /CONT
   ```

6. Display containers at or below the current context.

   ```
   CX /T
   ```

7. Display containers and objects at or below the current context.

   ```
   CX /A /T
   ```

8. Display all the containers and objects in the Directory tree, starting at the [Root], without changing your current context.

```
CX /R /A /T
```

9. Create and display a file that contains a visual representation of the NDS tree structure.

```
CX /R /A /T > TREE.NDS

TYPE TREE.NDS
```

10. Change your current context to the [Root].

```
CX /R
```

11. Display containers in the [Root] (because that's what your current context is).

```
CX /CONT
```

12. Move down one level in the NDS tree.

```
CX context
```

(*Context* is the name of a container that was listed in Step 11.)

13. Move up one level in the NDS tree (which, in this case, happens to be the [Root]).

```
CX .
```

14. Display all containers below the [Root] (because that's what your current context is).

```
CX /T
```

15. Move to a container several levels below the [Root].

    CX *context*

    (*Context* is a context, such as .WHITE.CRIME.TOKYO.ACME.)

16. Move up four levels in the NDS tree.

    CX ....

    (You indicate one dot for each level you want to move up in the NDS tree.)

See Appendix C for answers.

EXERCISE 3-2: UNDERSTANDING NDS NAMING

Answer the following questions using the directory structure shown in Figure 3.34.

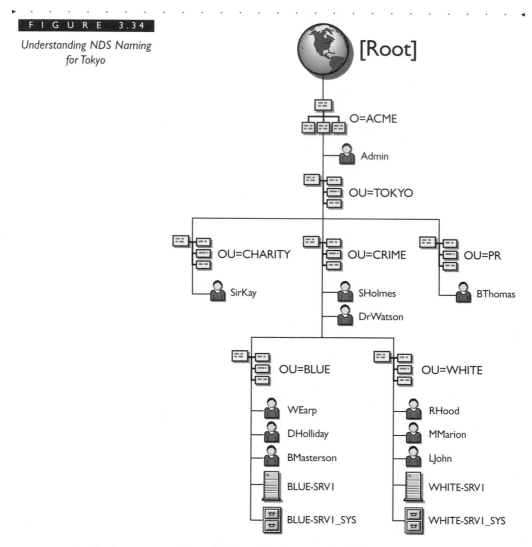

1. Indicate a typeless distinguished name for BMasterson.

2. Provide a typeful distinguished name for RHood.

3. List a typeless relative distinguished name for the CRIME Organizational Unit, assuming that your current context is the [Root].

4. Show a typeful relative distinguished name for the BLUE-SRV1 server object from the default current context.

5. If your current context is .CRIME.TOKYO.ACME, what is the shortest name that accurately references the SHolmes User object?

6. Assume your current context is .TOKYO.ACME. Indicate a typeless relative distinguished name for the LJohn User object.

7. If your current context is .PR.TOKYO.ACME, what would be a typeful relative distinguished name for SirKay?

8. Assume your current context is .WHITE.CRIME.TOKYO.ACME. Provide a typeless relative distinguished name for Admin.

9. If your current context is .BLUE.CRIME.TOKYO.ACME, what would be a typeful relative distinguished name for BThomas?

10. Assume your current context is .WHITE.CRIME.TOKYO.ACME. What is the longest possible typeful relative distinguished name for the SYS: volume on the BLUE-SRV1 server?

11. If DHolliday attaches to the BLUE-SRV1 server by default, what's his current context after login? Give two LOGIN commands for DHolliday.
    12. How would MMarion visit SirKay?

13. How can you make sure that SirKay's workstation drops him into his home context when he attaches to the "Cloud"?

14. Provide ten LOGIN commands for SHolmes from .BLUE.CRIME.TOKYO.ACME:

15. What is the easiest way to move above ACME from the .PR.TOKYO.ACME context?

See Appendix C for answers.

CASE STUDY: BUILDING ACME'S NDS TREE

Congratulations! You're ready to start building the ACME tree. The world is in very good hands with you on the job. In this exercise, we are going to build the ACME tree using three different utilities: NWADMIN (a Windows-based utility), NETADMIN (a menu utility) and UIMPORT (a batch utility). This exercise assumes that you have completed the case study, "Simple Installation," in Chapter 7.

In this exercise, you will create Organizational Unit, User, Printer, and Print Server objects in the CAMELOT, RIO, and SYDNEY branches of the tree. (You can't create Server objects because they are created automatically when you install or migrate to IntranetWare. You also can't create Print Queue objects because they require volume names for servers that haven't been installed.)

You will need the following additional information when building the tree:

▶ The Location property for each container or leaf object should always contain the city or Location (such as Camelot, Rio, or Sydney). The Department should always be the full name of the container (such as Administration, Financial, Marketing, and so on).

▶ The address, phone, and fax information for the CAMELOT Organizational Unit and its subcontainers is as follows:

> London Road
> Bracknell, Berkshire RG12 2UY
> United Kingdom
> Phone: (44 344) 724000
> Fax: (44 344) 724001

▶ The address, phone, and fax information for the RIO Organizational Unit and its subcontainers is as follows:

> Alameda Ribeirao Preto 130-12 Andar
> Sao Paulo 01331-000
> Brazil
> Phone: (55 11) 253 4866
> Fax: (55 11) 285 4847

▶ The address, phone, and fax information for the SYDNEY Organizational Unit and its subcontainers is as follows:

> 18 Level
> 201 Miller St.
> North Sydney NSW 2060
> Australia
> Phone: (61 2) 925 3000
> Fax: (61 2) 922 2113

▶ Each Organizational Unit will have the following Intruder Detection/Lockout limits:

> Incorrect Login Attempts: 5
> Intruder Attempt Reset Interval: 10 days
> Intruder Lockout Reset Interval: 20 minutes

▶ User Templates and each User object should contain the following account restrictions, unless otherwise specified:

> ▶ Each user will be limited to logging in on one workstation at a time (that is, one concurrent login).

> ▶ Each user will be required to have a *unique* password consisting of 8 characters or more, and will be required to change their password every 60 days. Each user will be allowed six grace logins.

> ▶ Each user will be restricted from logging in each day between 3:00 a.m. and 4:00 a.m. (when backups and system maintenance are done).

Now that you know the plan, let's go ahead and implement it! Ready, set, build!!

PART I: NWADMIN

1. Execute the NetWare Administrator utility.

    a. Ensure that you are logged into the network as .ADMIN.ACME.

    b. Execute the NetWare Administrator utility under Windows 3.1x or Windows 95. (If you haven't created an icon yet, you can find the NetWare Administrator utility under SYS:PUBLIC\NWADMN3X if you're using Windows 3.1x, or SYS:PUBLIC\WIN95\NWADMN32 if you're using Windows 95.)

2. Set the current context for the NetWare Administrator utility.

    a. A portion of the NDS tree should be displayed. If not, select the NDS Browser option from the Tools menu to open a browser window. Next, be sure that your current context for this utility is set to the [Root]. If the [Root] icon is displayed at the top of the screen, proceed to Step 3.

    b. If the [Root] icon is not displayed at the top of the screen, set the context to the [Root] by clicking on the Set Context option in the View menu, typing [Root] in the Context field, then clicking on the OK button.

3. Create the CAMELOT Organizational Unit.

    a. At this point, the [Root] icon and the ACME Organization icon should be displayed. If no icons are listed under the ACME Organization, you will need to expand it to display its contents using one of the following three methods: double-clicking on its icon; clicking on its icon and selecting the Expand option from the View menu; or clicking on its icon and pressing the plus sign (+) on the numeric keypad of your keyboard. The Admin User object icon should then be displayed under the ACME Organization container.

b. To create a CAMELOT Organizational Unit under the ACME Organization, be sure the ACME Organization is highlighted, then press the Insert key. (Alternately, you could select the Create option from the Object menu, or click on the ACME Organization with the right mouse button, and choose Create from the pop-up menu that appears.) A New Object dialog box appears. Choose the Organizational Unit object type by using the scroll bar on the right side of the dialog box to bring it into view, then double-clicking on it. (An alternate method would be to type the letter **O**, which happens to be the first letter in the term Organizational Unit. This would highlight the Organizational Role object class, since Organizational Role is the first object in the list that begins with the letter "O." You could then press the down-arrow key once to highlight the Organizational Unit object class, then double-click on it or click on OK.) A Create Organizational Unit dialog box will be displayed. Type **CAMELOT** in the Organizational Unit Name field, then click the Define Additional Properties check box to select it. Finally, click on the Create button to create the new Organizational Unit called CAMELOT.

c. Because you selected the Define Additional Properties check box in Step 3b, a dialog box will appear. You'll notice that, by default, the Identification page button has been selected, allowing you to key in property information for that category. Click on each Identification field in turn, keying in the following values:

> Other Name: **CAMELOT**
>
> Location: **CAMELOT**
>
> Telephone: **44 344 724000**
>
> Fax Number: **44 344 724001**

d. Next, Click on the Postal Address page button and click on each field. Fill in the following fields:

> Street: **London Road**
>
> City: **Bracknell**

State or Province: **Berkshire, United Kingdom**

Postal (Zip) Code: **RG12 2UY**

TIP

If you suddenly find yourself on the Login Script page instead of the Postal Address page, it means that you forgot to click on the first field of the Postal Address screen before you began typing. If this happens, click on the Postal Address page button, then click on the Street field before you begin typing. This is a strange idiosyncrasy of NWADMIN.

   e. Next, click on the Intruder Detection/Lockout page button and fill in the following information:

      Detect Intruders: (click on check box)

      Incorrect Login Attempts: **5**

      Intruder Attempt Reset Interval: **10 days, 0 hours, 0 minutes**

      Lock Account after Detection: (click on check box)

      Intruder Lockout Reset Interval: **0 days, 0 hours, 20 minutes**

   f. Finally, click the OK button to return to the main browser window in the NetWare Administrator utility.

  4. Create a User Template in the CAMELOT container. To create a User Template object in the CAMELOT Organizational Unit container, be sure that the CAMELOT Organizational Unit is highlighted, then press the Insert key. (Alternately, you could select the Create option from the Object menu, or click on the CAMELOT Organizational Unit with the right mouse button and choose Create from the pop-up menu that appears.) A New Object dialog box appears. Choose the Template object type by using the scroll bar on the right side of the dialog box to

bring it into view, then double-clicking on it. (An alternate method would be to type the letter **T**, which happens to be the first letter in the word Template. You could then double-click on it, or click on OK.) A Create Template dialog box will be displayed. Type **CAM-UT** in the Template Name field, then click the Define Additional Properties box to select it. Finally, click on the Create button to create the new User Template called CAM-UT.

a.   Fill in the same location, telephone, fax, and address information as you did for the CAMELOT Organizational Unit in Step 3c. (You won't be able to set any Intruder Detection parameters for this User Template, as Intruder Detection parameters are set per container, not per leaf object.) If you can't find the property page button that you're looking for, don't forget to use the scroll bar to the right of the page buttons to locate it.

b.   Next, click on the Login Restrictions page button, then click on the box in front of the Limit Concurrent Connections property. The Limit Concurrent Connections property should then list a maximum connection value of "1."

c.   To set password restrictions for this User Template, click on the Password Restrictions Page button, then do the following:

   (1) Make sure there is a checkmark in the Allow User to Change Password check box.

   (2) Click on the Require a Password check box and key in a password length of **8**.

   (3) Click on the Force Periodic Password Changes check box and key in a Days Between Forced Changes value of **60**.

   (4) Click on the Require Unique Passwords check box.

   (5) Click on the Grace Logins check box and make sure that Grace Logins Allowed field shows a value of "6."

(6) Click on the Set Password after Create check box so that you'll be prompted to indicate a password each time you create a new user using this user template.

d. Next, go ahead and restrict login privileges between 3:00 a.m. and 4:00 a.m. every day. Click on the Login Time Restrictions page button. A grid will be displayed on the screen showing days of the week along the left edge, and time of day across the top. Each cell in the grid represents a half-hour period during the week. You'll notice that when you place the mouse cursor in a cell, the day and time represented by that cell is displayed. White (blank) cells represent times during which the user is allowed to log in. Gray cells indicate times that the user is prevented from logging in. Click on the 3:00 and 3:30 cells for each day of the week. (Alternately, you can drag the cursor to select multiple cells.) When you are finished updating the User Template, click on OK to accept the changes you made.

e. Finally, click on the OK button to return to the main NetWare Administrator browser window.

5. Create the CHARITY Organizational Unit under the CAMELOT container.

a. Use the same method listed in Step 3b to create a CHARITY Organizational Unit under the CAMELOT Organizational Unit, except that you'll highlight the CAMELOT Organizational Unit instead of the ACME Organization. Next, use the method described in Steps 3c, 3d, and 3e to fill in the appropriate location, phone, fax, address, and Intruder Detection information.

b. Create a User Template for the CHARITY Organizational Unit using the method described in Step 4. This time, however, we'll save time by copying the properties from the User Template you created in the CHARITY Organizational Unit earlier rather than having to key them in again. To do this, click on the Use Template or User check box instead of the Define Additional Properties check box when you create the User Template. Next, click on the Browse button to the right of the Use Template or User field and either walk the tree or change the context so that the CAM-UT User Template object appears in the Available objects window on the left of the screen. (To walk the tree, double-click on the double dot (..) entry in the Browse Context window on the right of the screen to move up the tree one level, since the CAM-UT object is located in the CAMELOT Organizational Unit, which is one level above the current context. Alternately, you could set the context by clicking on the Change Context button, keying in CAMELOT.ACME as the context, then clicking on OK.) At this point, the CAM-UT User Template should be displayed in the Available Objects window on the left side of the screen. Click on it, then click on OK. Finally, Click on the Create button to create the new User Template.

c.   Create the SirGalahad User object by clicking on the CHARITY Organizational Unit and pressing Insert. A New Object dialog box will appear. Select the User object type by typing **U** and pressing Enter. (Alternately, you could have clicked on OK instead of pressing Enter. The Login Name and Last Name fields are required properties for a User object. Key in a login name of **SirGalahad** and a Last Name of **Galahad**, then click on the Use Template check box. Next, click on the Browse button to the right of the Use Template field. The CAM-UT User Template object should be displayed in the Available Objects window on the left side of the screen. If so, click on OK to select this User Template. (Normally, you would also create a home directory for this user, but you can't at this time because the CAM-CHR-SRV1 server has not been installed yet.) Finally, click on the Create button to create this user by using the defaults in the CHAR-UT User Template.

d.   Create the HP5-P1 Printer object by making sure the CHARITY Organizational Unit is highlighted and pressing Insert. A New Object dialog box appears. Choose the Printer object type by using the scroll bar on the right side of the dialog box to bring it into view, then double-clicking on it. A Create Printer dialog box will be displayed. Key in a Printer object name of **HP5-P1** and click on the Define Additional Properties check box, then click on the Create button. A Printer dialog box will appear. Key in **HP5-P1** in the Other Name field, **CAMELOT** in the location field, **CHARITY** in the Department field, and **ACME** in the Organization field. Then click on OK to return to the main NetWare Administrator browser screen.

e. Create the CAM-CHR-PS1 Print Server object by clicking on the CHARITY Organizational Unit and pressing Insert. A New Object dialog box appears. Choose the Print Server object type by using the scroll bar on the right side of the dialog box to bring it into view, then double-clicking on it. A Create Print Server dialog box will be displayed. Key in a print server name of **CAM-CHR-PS1**, click on the Define Additional Properties check box, then click on the Create button. A Print Server dialog box will appear. Click on the Assignments page button, then click on the Add button. A Select Object dialog box will appear. The HP5-P1 printer you created in the previous step should appear in the Available Objects list box on the left side of the screen. Double-click on the HP5-P1 printer object, then click on the OK button to return to the main NetWare Administrator browser window.

6. Create the .OPS.CAMELOT.ACME Organizational Unit using the method listed in Step 5a, then create a User Template called OPS-UT using the method described in Step 5b. Next, create the KingArthur User Object, the CANONBJ-P1 Printer object, and the OPS-PS1 Print Server object under it by using the methods covered in Steps 5c through 5e.

7. Create the .FIN.OPS.CAMELOT.ACME Organizational Unit, then create the following objects under it: the FIN-UT User Template object, the Guinevere User object, the HP4SI-P1 and HP4SI-P2 Printer objects, and the CAM-FIN-PS1 and CAM-FIN-PS2 Print Server objects.

8. Create the .DIST.OPS.CAMELOT.ACME Organizational Unit, then create the following objects under it: the DIST-UT User Template, the Merlin User object, the HPIII-P1 Printer object, and the DIST-PS1 Print Server object.

9. Create the .PR.CAMELOT.ACME Organizational Unit, then create the following objects under it: the PR-UT User Template, the CEttelson User object, the HP4SI-P1 Printer object, and the CAM-PR-PS1 Print Server object.

10. To exit the NetWare Administrator utility, chose the Exit menu option from the File menu.

PART II: NETADMIN

1. Execute the SYS:PUBLIC\NETADMIN utility.

2. Create the RIO Organizational Unit under the ACME Organization.

   a. Select the Manage Objects menu option from the NetAdmin Options menu. Walk the tree until you locate the ACME Organization. Highlight the ACME Organization using the up-arrow key and down-arrow key, press Enter to change context, then press the Insert key.

   b. A Select an Object menu will appear. Highlight the Organizational Unit object class and press Enter. A Create Object Organizational Unit dialog box appears. Key in **RIO** in the New Name field, **Y** in the Create User Template field, press Enter, then press F10 to continue. You will be informed that an Organizational Unit has been created. When asked whether to create another, select No and press Enter. The RIO Organizational Unit will be displayed in the appropriate position in the NDS tree.

c. Highlight the RIO Organizational Unit and press Enter to change context. Highlight the User Template and press F10 to select it. An "Actions for Users: User Template" menu will be displayed. Select the "View or edit properties of this object" option and press Enter. You'll see a list of property categories. Select the Identification option and press Enter. Key in the information listed below in the fields specified. (To update a field, highlight the field and press Enter to select it, then press Insert to add information. After you've finished adding information to a field, press Enter then F10 to save the information that you've added).

Other Name: **Rio de Janeiro**

Telephone: **(55 11) 253 4866**

Fax Number: **(55 11) 285 4847**

Location: **Rio**

d. When you are finished, press F10 to save the information on the Identification screen. Next, select the Postal address option from the View or edit user menu and press Enter. Key in the following information in the fields indicated:

Street: **Alameda Ribeirao Preto 130-12 Andar**

City: **Sao Paulo**

State or Province: **Brazil**

Postal (Zip) Code: **01331-000**

When you are finished, press F10 to save. Press Esc twice to return to the Object, Class window.

e. Highlight the period (.) representing the current context, then press F10 to select it. Select the View or edit properties of this object option from the Actions for Organizational Unit: Rio menu and press Enter. Select the Intruder Detection option from the Viewer, or edit Organizational Unit menu and press Enter. Fill in the following information:

Detect Intruders: **Yes**

Incorrect Login Attempts: **5**

Intruder Attempt Reset Interval: **10 days**

Lock Account After Detection: **Yes**

Intruder Lockout Reset Interval: **20 minutes**

Press F10 to save when you are finished. Press Esc three times to return to the Object, Class menu.

3. Create the ADMIN, CHARITY, and PR Organizational Units under the RIO Organizational Unit, then create the AUDIT, FAC, and MRKT Organizational Units under the .ADMIN Organizational Unit. When asked whether you want to create another Organizational Unit after creating the PR Organizational Unit, type **N** instead of Y. When creating each Organizational Unit, make sure that you create a User Template under it. You'll notice there are some disadvantages to creating a User Template using the NETADMIN utility rather than the NetWare Administrator utility. One problem is that NETADMIN creates a User object named "USER_TEMPLATE" rather than a User Template object with the name of your choice. Another problem is that NETADMIN does not allow you to copy the properties of an existing user template when creating a new one-which means you have to key in the properties for each user template manually. After you've done so, you can continue to create objects in this portion of the tree using the instructions listed below.

4. Create the GWashington User object under the ADMIN.RIO.ACME Organizational Unit object.

   a. Highlight the ADMIN Organizational Unit and press Enter, then Insert. The Select an Object Class menu appears. Type **U** to select the User Object class, then press Enter. A Create Object User dialog box will appear. Type **GWashington** in the Login Name field and **Washington** in the Last Name field. (Normally, you would create a home directory for this user, but you can't at this time, because neither the ADMIN-SRV1 nor ADMIN-SRV2 servers have been installed.) Be sure that the Copy the User Template Object field has a value of Yes, then press F10 to continue. You will then be notified that the User has been created. When asked if you'd like to create another user, select "No" and press Enter.

b. Try to create a Printer object and Print Server object in the same container. If you press Insert, the Select an Object Class menu appears. You'll notice that the Print Server, Printer, and Print Queue object classes are not listed. This is because you cannot create or manage the printing environment using the NETADMIN utility. These objects can, however, be created with the NetWare Administrator and PCONSOLE utilities.

5. Create the SirPercival User object under the CHARITY.RIO.ACME Organizational Unit.

6. Create the JHughes User object under the PR.RIO.ACME Organizational Unit.

7. Create the ALincoln User object under the AUDIT.ADMIN.RIO.ACME Organizational Unit.

8. Create the JMadison User object under the FAC.ADMIN.RIO.ACME Organizational Unit.

9. Create the TJefferson User object under the MRKT.ADMIN.RIO.ACME Organizational Unit.

10. To exit the NETADMIN utility, press the Esc key repeatedly until the "Exit?" question is displayed, then select Yes and press Enter.

PART III: UIMPORT

1. Before you can run the UIMPORT utility, you must have created two files: an ASCII control file and a comma-delimited ASCII data file. The data file is typically created by exporting user information from a database file. The control file consists of some control parameters and field definitions that define where information should be placed in the NDS. The UIMPORT utility can only be used to add users. It cannot be used to create other objects in the NDS tree. Because of this, before you run UIMPORT, you must create any Organization or Organizational Unit objects that you will need.

   a. Since you don't have a database containing the information for the users in the SYDNEY subtree, you'll need to create a data file from scratch using an ASCII text editor. Let's try a very simple test case. Let's try importing the User objects for the network administrators for HR Organizational Unit and each of its four subcontainers into the HR container. To create the data file, key in the following lines into an ASCII file you create called ACMEDATA:

      Ghandi,Ghandi,"Human Resources"

      MTeresa,Teresa,Food

      ASchweitzer,Schweitzer,Medical

      FNightingale,Nightingale,Shelter

      Buddha,Buddha,Peace

      You'll notice that Human Resources is enclosed in quotation marks. This is because it contains a space.

   b. Next, create an import control file by keying in the following lines in an ASCII file you create called ACMECTRL:

      ```
      Import Control
          Name Context=.OU=HR.OU=SYDNEY.O=ACME
      ```

```
        User Template=Y
Fields
    Name
    Last Name
    Department
```

2. Before you can import this data, you must create the NDS subtree structure using the NWADMIN or NETADMIN utilities. Use the utility of your choice (hint: NetWare Administrator is the best choice) to create the initial SYDNEY subtree structure, including:

    ▶ A SYDNEY Organizational Unit under the ACME Organization

    ▶ CHARITY, HR, and PR Organizational Units under the SYDNEY Organizational Unit.

    ▶ FOOD, MEDICAL, PEACE, and SHELTER Organizational Units under the HR Organizational Unit.

    When you create each of these containers, be sure to create a User Template object for each. Don't forget to update both the containers and the user templates with the property values listed at the beginning of this chapter.

3. After you've set up the NDS subtree structure for the SYDNEY portion of the tree, you can execute the UIMPORT utility by typing **UIMPORT ACMECTRL ACMEDATA** at the DOS prompt and pressing Enter. To see the result of using this utility, type **CX .HR.SYDNEY.ACME /A / T**.

PART IV: SPECIAL CASES

Now that you've had an opportunity to build the basic ACME tree, let's explore some of their special conditions. Following is a list of some of ACME's more challenging NDS management requirements. Please help them out.

1. ACME needs a site administrator in each location. This will be a revolving position among each of the division heads. For example, the NORAD administrator (named NORAD-Admin), will have administrative access to all divisions of NORAD and the position will alternate among AEinstein, DClarke, and SirGawain.

2. In addition, all of the site administrators will share a common login script. It will be a mechanism for global security, drive mappings, and special messaging.

3. The Human Rights Tracking application is constantly being updated. Can you think of an easier way to manage its search drive mappings?

4. Also, each of the Human Rights department administrators needs access to the Human Rights Tracking program. Security could be a problem.

5. All of the employees in the Auditing department need easy access to all the resources in the Financial container-for auditing purposes. Also, the auditors don't want to have to navigate the tree to see them.

6. In addition, the Auditing application is constantly being updated. Searching drive mapping is becoming a problem.

7. As a matter of fact, the Financial database is due for some major changes as well. A pattern is forming here. Please help us out.

8. The following traveling users need a simpler context for accessing ACME from distributed locations: AEinstein, DHoliday, and MCurie.

9. Everyone in the Crime Fighting division needs to share a common login script.

10. Finally, Leonardo DaVinci believes in empowering his scientists. After all, he's a "labrat," not a bureaucrat. To distribute the administrative load evenly, he and his scientists take turns managing the R&D department—each scientist takes the helm for three months out of the year.

EXERCISE 3-3: PLANT A TREE IN A CLOUD

Circle the 20 NDS terms hidden in this word search puzzle using the hints provided.

```
G  L  E  A  D  I  N  G  P  E  R  I  O  D  N  X  G  X  T  Q  W
Y  C  O  U  N  T  R  Y  R  F  T  I  O  V  S  I  H  R  R  I  Q
M  U  X  C  P  S  K  V  O  O  U  N  K  N  O  W  N  E  L  M  F
G  R  S  W  A  K  S  K  F  B  U  D  A  L  I  A  S  K  A  X  J
E  R  N  H  T  L  W  Y  I  N  J  P  V  M  M  U  U  A  I  I  N
R  E  G  A  J  R  I  B  L  U  Z  E  C  E  P  C  W  B  E  Q  H
Y  N  L  S  N  H  P  T  E  H  D  W  C  E  Y  X  V  Q  X  Q  O
L  T  X  P  B  F  H  R  Y  H  H  O  R  T  A  W  V  E  S  C  T
I  C  B  B  F  H  I  R  X  D  N  V  G  H  R  Q  K  E  B  Q  E
B  O  R  G  A  N  I  Z  A  T  I  O  N  A  L  R  O  L  E  T  K
V  N  Y  T  L  Y  B  X  E  S  E  R  H  F  K  F  W  G  U  Y  K
J  T  D  Y  V  R  N  X  O  T  V  G  E  E  B  T  L  Y  E  P  X
K  E  T  P  S  J  T  R  W  I  L  A  N  C  S  E  J  V  B  E  U
R  X  F  E  H  E  S  F  G  V  H  N  A  M  T  F  B  D  Y  L  L
M  T  W  F  A  S  Q  L  H  A  Q  I  D  K  R  O  D  Q  I  E  R
T  I  N  U  L  A  N  O  I  T  A  Z  I  N  A  G  R  O  W  S  Z
M  Y  D  L  H  S  W  N  C  X  D  A  U  Q  I  S  N  Y  V  S  S
O  D  B  N  L  R  C  G  T  J  O  T  O  O  Y  D  A  E  M  N  M
R  J  P  A  A  T  J  X  N  G  F  I  T  B  V  H  J  Y  F  A  B
Q  O  H  M  H  D  I  R  E  C  T  O  R  Y  S  C  A  N  P  M  P
W  U  N  E  Z  T  R  A  I  L  I  N  G  P  E  R  I  O  D  E  V
```

Hints:

1. Object that represents a logical NDS pointer to another object in the tree.
2. Container object that uses pre-determined two-character names.
3. The context that would be displayed if you issued the CX command with no options.
4. Command line utility used to view or change your current context.

5. Object that represents a logical pointer to a physical directory in the IntranetWare file system.

6. RCONSOLE menu option that can be used to display the four main files that comprise the IntranetWare NDS database.

7. An object that represents a set of users and is used for assigning rights.

8. Identifies a name as a distinguished name.

9. Similar to a Country object, except that it can exist in a Country, Organization, or Organizational Unit container.

10. Command that can be used in NET.CFG to set the current context.

11. Item that represents a resource in the NDS database.

12. Container object that is often used to represent a company, university, or association.

13. Object that represents a position or role with an organization.

14. Container object that is considered a "natural group".

15. Object that represents a login script that is used by a group of users who reside in the same or different containers.

16. Special superuser used for bindery emulation.

17. Allows you to change the current context while using relative distinguished naming.

18. Name that contains object attributes abbreviations.

19. Name that does not contain object attributes abbreviations.

20. NDS object that has been invalidated or cannot be identified as belonging to any of the other object classes.

See Appendix C for answers.

EXERCISE 3-4: INTRANETWARE CNA BASICS

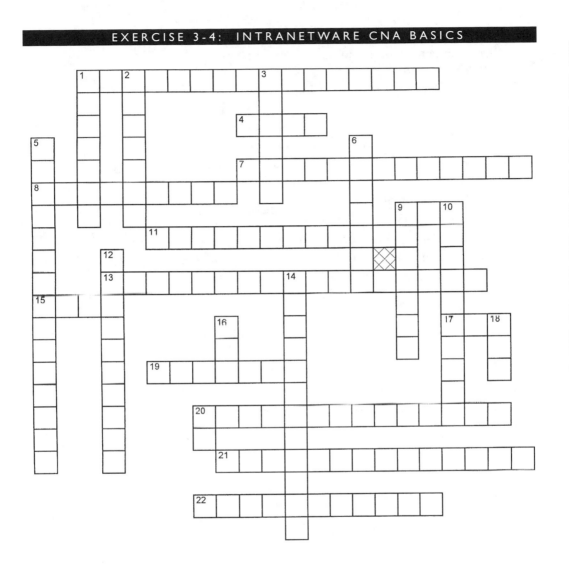

Across

1. Making NDS look old and frail, like NetWare 3
4. You, me, Albert Einstein
7. A local view of your network village
8. A piece of the "Cloud"
9. Also GMT
11. ACME in the NDS tree

13. Your name and address combined
15. Next generation printing for Novell
17. The "Cloud"
19. A copy of a piece of the "Cloud"
20. Where am I?
21. A global view of the network universe
22. They help out Friar Tuck in Cyberspace

Down

1. The old way of dealing with users in NetWare 3
2. Surfing NDS from Windows
3. The first copy of a piece of the "Cloud"
5. Great fans of the planet Earth
6. Group login script object
9. The mysterious object class
10. Who you are, not where you live
12. The new GUI tool for copying pieces of the "Cloud"
14. The NEW global approach to NetWare
16. Launching applications into space
18. Default time communications method
20. Go ahead, change your context-I dare you

See Appendix C for answers.

IntranetWare File System

Just when you think you have IntranetWare and NDS figured out, a little voice inside your head whispers, "There is another . . . ."

Another what? Listen more closely, ". . . directory structure."

Another directory structure? How could that be? You may think that there's only one IntranetWare directory structure and it's the foundation of NDS. Well, that's where you're wrong. If you look closely at Figure 4.1, you'll see *two* directory trees—one above the server and one below it.

F I G U R E   4.1

The Two IntranetWare Directory Trees

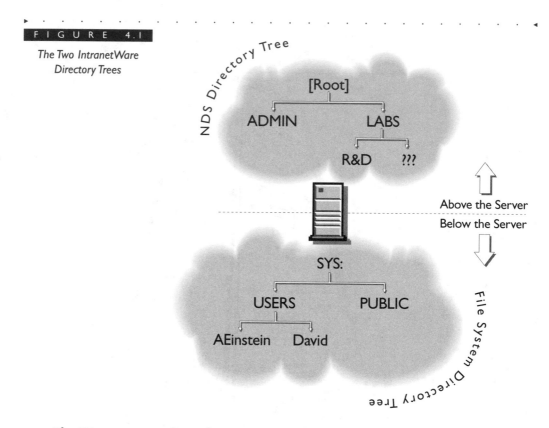

The Directory tree above the IntranetWare server is NDS. It organizes network resources into a logical WAN hierarchy. The directory tree below the server is the file system. It organizes network data files into a functional application hierarchy. Pretty simple, huh? The important thing is to separate the two in your mind. NDS handles resource data and the file system handles application data. Think of it as the "File Cabinet of Life."

ZEN

"To me, if life boils down to one significant thing—it's movement. To live is to keep moving. Unfortunately, this means that for the rest of our lives we're going to be looking for boxes!"

Jerry Seinfeld

In the past, cave-LANs relied on "sneakernet" for file sharing. First, they copied files to a diskette, then ran them down the hall to a coworker's machine. Finally, the coworker transferred the files from diskette to his or her own directory structure. Voilá!

With the advent of NetWare (and coaxial cabling), society experienced the dawning of a new age—the file server. The file server became the central repository of shared data and applications. Life was good.

Then, IntranetWare came along. Once again, society experienced the dawning of a new age—NDS. The file server suddenly became a small fish in a very large, global pond. Volumes took on a life of their own. People started treating them as independent objects; free from the servers that house them. Is this progress? I'm not so sure. It underemphasizes the importance of the file server. Let's be honest. It's still the most important resource in the WAN. And what do file servers do? They serve files. How? Through the IntranetWare file system.

Let's check it out.

SMART LINK

Go meet Jerry Seinfeld on the Web at http://www.nbc.com/entertainment/shows/seinfeld.

Understanding the IntranetWare File System

Every IntranetWare file server contains a hierarchical directory structure for storing shared data files and applications. It is called the *file system*. The file system organizes internal disks into one or more volumes. Volumes are then divided into directories that contain subdirectories or files. On the surface it looks a lot like DOS. But don't be fooled; it's a whole new world. Check out Figure 4.2!

TIP

In earlier versions of NetWare, the "file system" was referred to as the "directory structure." In IntranetWare, it is referred to as the "file system" to distinguish it from the **NDS** directory structure.

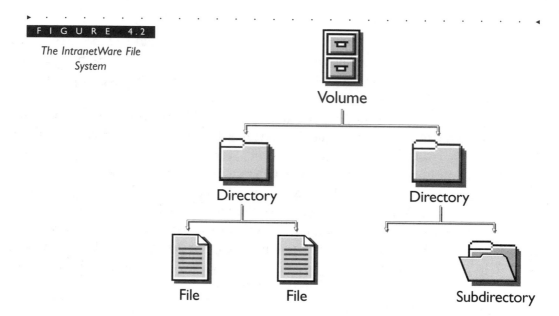

F I G U R E   4.2

The IntranetWare File System

Earlier we called the IntranetWare file system the "File Cabinet of Life." It fits. See Figure 4.3. In such an analogy, the file server is the filing cabinet and the volumes are the drawers. Also, the directories are hanging folders, the subdirectories are file folders, and the files become individual sheets of paper. Pretty nifty, huh?

With this analogy in mind, let's explore the key components of IntranetWare's exciting new file system: volumes and directories. In the first section, we will rediscover the volume, and learn about its dual personality as a logical NDS object and physical disk resource. Then, we'll focus our journey even further into the IntranetWare directory structure—starting with system-created directories, which are defined automatically on the SYS: volume during IntranetWare server installation (see Chapter 7). Next, we'll expand our horizons beyond default directories and into the realm of DOS, application, configuration, home, and shared directories. Finally, you'll get a taste of two different directory designs— shallow and deep.

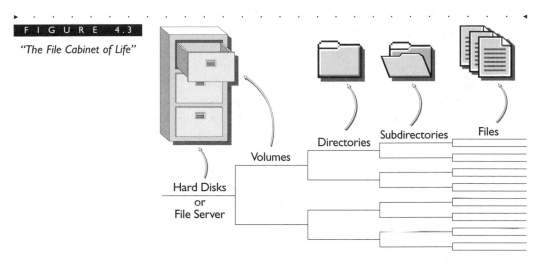

"The File Cabinet of Life"

And that's only the first section. Later in the chapter, we'll explore file system management and the land of drive mapping. Wow! So much to learn and so little time. So, without any further interruptions, let's get on with the show.

UNDERSTANDING INTRANETWARE VOLUMES

Volumes are cool— mostly because they're so unique. They can span multiple disks, or they can be subdivisions of a single disk. They are physical storage units within the file server, but also independent logical objects that stand alone. They are neither here nor there—they are everywhere!

The volume represents the highest level in the IntranetWare file system. It is the root of the server directory structure. Volumes are also leaf objects in the NDS Directory tree. Because of this unique position, they act as a bridge between NDS and the file system. The first volume on each IntranetWare server is named SYS:. It is created automatically during IntranetWare installation. In addition, an NDS volume leaf object is created in the server's home container. In our example, it is called WHITE-SRV1_SYS—a logical representation of the physical SYS: volume on server WHITE-SRV1.

None of this is set in stone, of course. You can change the context of a Volume object using NetWare Administrator (NWADMIN) or NETADMIN. You can also rename volumes. To rename a physical volume, you'll need to change its server definition with INSTALL.NLM. To rename a logical volume, on the other hand, you can use either NWADMIN or NETADMIN. Finally, you can create a special pointer to a different physical volume using the Alias object type.

ZEN

Infobit—An individual item of information, such as a recipe or a description of a place, that meets the requirements for inclusion in a databank. Also used to describe properties of NDS objects.

So, what are they? IntranetWare *volumes* are fixed units of hard disk storage that are created during server installation. They can be formed from any hard disk that contains a NetWare partition. Think of it as IntranetWare formatting. You can place 64 volumes on an IntranetWare server, and each one can span up to 32 hard disks. Do the math. That means an IntranetWare server can support 2,048 disks—wow! Also, a volume can support 32 terabytes of disk space and as many as 16 million directory entries (with only the DOS name space).

How does it work? Volumes are divided into physical volume segments. Different segments can be stored on one or more hard disks. Each volume can support up to 32 segments, and/or each hard disk can support up to 8 volume segments from one or more volumes. Because of this, a volume can

- ▸ Contain a portion of a hard disk

- ▸ Occupy an entire hard disk

- ▸ Span multiple hard disks

The simplest configuration is, of course, one hard disk per volume. The advantage of spreading a volume across multiple hard disks is performance. It allows the server to read from or write to different parts of the same volume simultaneously—thus speeding up disk input/output. The disadvantage of such a technique, however, is fault tolerance. If you span volumes across multiple disks, it increases the chances that something will go wrong. If any disk fails, the entire volume fails, and you lose all your data. Consider protecting your volumes with mirroring, duplexing, or RAID (Redundant Array of Inexpensive Disks).

TIP

RAID provides numerous performance and SFT (System Fault Tolerance) advantages. From a performance standpoint, it uses *data striping,* **which means that files are stored across multiple disks. Read and write performance is enhanced dramatically because blocks can be accessed simultaneously. In addition, RAID employs a parity algorithm that protects volumes even when a disk crashes. Cool.**

SMART LINK

For more information on RAID, surf to the Novell Knowledgebase at http://support.novell.com/search/.

IntranetWare volumes are further organized into *directories* and *files*. Directories are logical volume subdivisions that provide an administrative hierarchy to network applications and data files. They allow you to further organize your data into content-specific file folders. Directories can contain other directories (called *subdirectories*) or files.

Files are individual items of data. They represent the bottom level of the file-server food chain. Files can contain valuable user data or network applications. It doesn't matter. What does matter is their location. Files should be stored in logical subdirectories according to their purpose and security level. That's the ultimate goal of the IntranetWare file system—organize the user's data so that it's secure and easy to find.

To accomplish this goal, you must follow specific file syntax and naming rules. As with NDS object naming, filenames define the data's name and location:

```
Server\Volume:Directory\(Subdirectory)\Filename
```

Standard directory names and filenames support eight characters and an optional three-character extension. Special non-DOS filenames can extend as far as 32 characters (Macintosh) or even 255 characters (OS/2 and Windows 95). These special files require an additional volume feature called *name space* (see Chapter 7). Also, make sure to support the path conventions of standard or special filenames. IntranetWare allows 255 characters in a directory path (counting the drive letter and delimiters), whereas DOS only allows a maximum of 127 characters. Refer to Table 4.1 for more IntranetWare file system naming rules.

	PATH COMPONENT	RULES
TABLE 4.1 *IntranetWare File System Naming Rules*	File Server	Name is limited to 2 to 47 characters. First character in name cannot be a period. Name cannot contain spaces or special characters such as * + , \ / | : ; = < > [ ].
	Volume	Name length is limited to 2 to 15 characters. Physical name must end with a colon (:), which is added automatically. First volume on server must be SYS:. Two physical volumes on the same server cannot have the same name. Name cannot contain spaces or special characters such as * + , \ / | : ; = < > [ ].
	Directory	Name length is limited to a maximum of 11 characters (a directory name consisting of one to eight characters plus an optional directory name extension of up to three characters). A period (.) is used to separate the directory name from the (optional) extension. Directories should be limited to functional groups. Name cannot contain spaces or special characters such as * + , \ / | : ; = < > [ ].
	Subdirectory	Name length is limited to a maximum of 11 characters (a directory name consisting of one to eight characters plus an optional directory name extension of up to three characters). A period (.) is used to separate the directory name from the (optional) extension. Subdirectories share common functionality. The size of subdirectories is limited by disk size. Name cannot contain spaces or special characters such as * + , \ / | : ; = < > [ ].

PATH COMPONENT	RULES
T A B L E 4.1 *IntranetWare File System Naming Rules (continued)*	
Files	Name length is limited to a maximum of 11 characters (a filename consisting of 1 to 8 characters plus an optional filename extension of up to 3 characters).
	A period (.) is used to separate the directory name from the (optional) extension.
	Name cannot contain spaces or special characters such as * + , \ / | : ; = < > [ ].

Before you get too carried away with IntranetWare configuration and management, you should design the basic structure of the file system. This is just as important as designing the NDS tree. In both cases, you need to consider a number of important WAN factors, including security, administration, and accessibility. Except, this time, we're working below the server, not above it.

ZEN

Nonchaotic attractor—A pattern of movement in a system with motion that settles down to an easily describable and predictable pattern, such as a pendulum or IntranetWare volume. This can also be thought of as a normal attractor in that it is the opposite of a "strange" attractor.

Because volumes are at the top of the file system tree, they should be planned first. Here are a few things to think about:

▸ The simplest strategy is one-to-one. That is, one volume for each internal disk. In this scenario, stick with the default SYS: volume and let it occupy your entire internal disk. Then rely on directories and subdirectories for file organization and security.

▸ If the one-to-one strategy isn't for you, be sure to reserve the SYS: volume for files needed by the IntranetWare operating system. Additional volumes can be created for applications, data files, and print queues.

▸ Create a separate volume for each client operating system that allows long filenames. For instance, if you have OS/2, Windows 95, or Macintosh users in addition to DOS users, you might want to create a separate volume for the OS/2, Windows 95, or Macintosh files. This is particularly important because it enhances administration, backup procedures, and disk space usage. Also, name space adds performance overhead to ALL files on the host volume. So, minimize the files on that volume.

▸ If fault tolerance is more important than performance, create one volume per disk. If performance is more important than fault tolerance, span one IntranetWare volume over multiple hard disks (with one segment of the volume on each hard disk). If fault tolerance and performance are equally important, you can still spread volumes across multiple hard disks, but you should make sure that they are duplexed or RAIDed.

SMART LINK

For a little more input on IntranetWare volume structures, consult the on-line NetWare 4.11 documentation at http://www.novell.com/manuals.

Once the volumes are in place, it's time to shift your focus to directories. This is when it gets interesting. Fortunately, IntranetWare gives you a big head start with system-created directories and files. Let's check them out.

SYSTEM-CREATED DIRECTORIES

With the IntranetWare server installation, you get a default user (Admin) and two directory trees:

▸ The default NDS tree (server context)

▸ The default file system on SYS:

In our discussion of the IntranetWare file system, we will explore the default tree and go a few steps beyond:

▸ System-created directories

▸ DOS directories

▸ Application directories

▸ Configuration directories

▸ Home directories

▸ Shared data directories

System-created directories contain IntranetWare operating system files, NLMs, and utilities. They are divided into two main categories: Admin directories and User directories. This is a security issue. The Admin directories (SYSTEM, for example) are reserved for administrators only—they require Supervisor access rights. User directories, on the other hand, contain public utilities and are open to all users throughout the WAN (PUBLIC, for example). Next, with the system-created directories as a platform, you will spring forward into the world of file-system creativity.

DOS directories are optional. They are required only if you want users to access DOS from the server instead of from their local drives. *Application directories* contain third-party application programs such as word processing, spreadsheet, or database programs. *Configuration directories* hold user- or group-specific configuration files. These files help you manage network applications. *Home directories* hold user-specific files and create a cozy, productive network environment. Finally, *shared data directories* contain global files for groups of users throughout the WAN.

Let's start our discussion with a detailed look at the nine system-created directories. Refer to Figure 4.4. Here they are:

LOGIN	ETC
SYSTEM	QUEUES
PUBLIC	DELETED.SAV
MAIL	DOC
NLS	

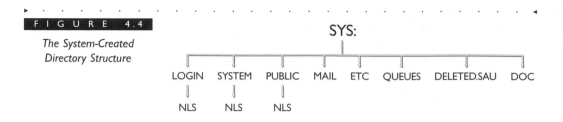

FIGURE   4.4

*The System-Created
Directory Structure*

LOGIN

LOGIN is your doormat to the WAN. From there you can knock on NetWare's door and provide the secret password for entrance. This is all accomplished with the help of LOGIN.EXE. In addition to logging in, there are other administrative tasks you (and users) can perform from the LOGIN directory—such as changing context (CX), viewing the NDS tree structure (NLIST), and mapping drives (MAP).

LOGIN is the only directory available to users prior to login. Be careful which programs you place there, because they are available to users without any security. Finally, there's an additional subdirectory under LOGIN, called OS2, which contains login programs for OS/2 clients.

Once you log in and pass through the magic NDS gates, the rest of the world opens up to you—namely the other eight system-created directories.

WHAT'S NEW

To access the LOGIN directory and log in, users must first change their network drive to D: or F:. Then they must access LOGIN.EXE and provide a valid username. This entire process is automated in the GUI environment with Client 32.

SYSTEM

SYSTEM is Admin's workroom. This directory contains special administrative tools and utilities, including OS files, NLMs, and dangerous NDS programs. For this reason, SYSTEM should be kept out of the reach of users and small children. Fortunately, it contains a "child-proof cap" in the form of Supervisor access rights. Only Admin can gain access by default.

PUBLIC

PUBLIC, on the other hand, is the user's playground. This directory contains general user commands and utilities, such as NWADMIN, NETADMIN, NWUSER, and MAP. By default, all users in the server's home container have access to PUBLIC—but only after they've logged in. In addition, a subdirectory under PUBLIC, called OS2, contains IntranetWare programs and utilities for OS/2 users.

MAIL

The MAIL directory may or may not contain subdirectories and files. It is left over from the old days when NetWare shipped with an e-mail application. Well, guess what, it does again (see Chapter 6), but it doesn't use the MAIL directory. Go figure. Instead, the MAIL subdirectory is a repository for old user-specific system configuration files, like bindery login scripts (LOGIN.) and print job configurations (PRINTCON.DAT). Of course, these files are now properties of each User object. Ah, NDS.

Oh yeah. MAIL is sometimes used by third-party e-mail applications, but not very often. It is also used by IntranetWare for bindery emulation.

NLS

NLS is IntranetWare's translator. It stands for NetWare Language Support. Each of the main system-created directories has its own NLS subdirectory. These NLS directories contain message and help files for multilingual IntranetWare utilities. If multiple languages have been installed, each language has its own subdirectory under NLS.

IntranetWare includes a great facility for multiple languages. But here's a quick preview. Each utility and message file has a general language pointer. The workstation determines which language the user wants and tells the pointer where to go for language-specific modules (that is, which NLS directory). Then, NLS displays the utility or message in the appropriate language. It is very cool.

SMART LINK

If you're interested in more information on IntranetWare's support for multiple languages, consult the "Product and Programs Quick Reference Guide" at http://www.novell.com/manuals.

ETC

ETC is aptly named. It contains a bunch of other stuff, like sample TCP/IP configuration files and, you know, other stuff.

QUEUES

QUEUES is one of the great advancements in IntranetWare. Earlier versions stored print queues on the SYS: volume only. This caused serious problems if the print job was large and SYS: ran out of space—namely, the server crashed. Now, CNAs can offload print queue storage to any volume they want. When you do, IntranetWare automatically creates a QUEUES directory off the root of the host volume.

DELETED.SAV

DELETED.SAV is file heaven. This is where files go when they die. You see, files can be brought back to life in IntranetWare—it's called *salvaging*. Normally, the files must be salvaged from their parent directory. If, in some horrible plane crash, their parent directory was also deleted, the children files can be salvaged from DELETED.SAV. This directory is only created when it's needed. Keep in mind, you can only salvage files as long as the user hasn't *purged* them.

DOC

Welcome to IntranetWare's electronic documentation—DynaText. The interesting thing about DynaText is that it becomes available *after* you need it. For example, the IntranetWare installation instructions are available once you install DynaText—*after* the server's been installed! Life has a funny way of surprising you. Remember, Murphy's law number 142: "I'm an optimist."

Anyway, IntranetWare DynaText is installed in the DOC directory using INSTALL.NLM.

DOCVIEW

The DOCVIEW directory contains the viewer files required by the DynaText utility. The DOC and DOCVIEW directories can be installed on the volume of your choice.

ZEN

"Pioneers took years to cross the country. Now people will move thousands of miles just for the summer. I don't think any pioneers did that, 'Yeah, it took us a decade to get there, and we stayed for the summer. It was nice, they had a pool, the kids loved it. And then, we left about ten years ago and we just got back. We had a great summer, it took us twenty years, and now our lives are over!'"

Jerry Seinfeld

This completes our brief pilgrimage through the IntranetWare system-created directory structure. Be sure that you do not accidentally delete, move, or rename any of these system-created directories—especially LOGIN, SYSTEM, PUBLIC, MAIL, and NLS. These directories are critical to the server and bad things will happen if they're removed.

O.K. We're cruising now. Next, let's expand our horizons beyond the default directory structure and explore the land of additional directories. You'll be amazed at what you can find there.

EXPANDING BEYOND THE DEFAULT DIRECTORY STRUCTURE

IntranetWare provides you with a big head start by building the default directory tree (see Figure 4.4). The next step is to add some productive DOS, user, application, and data directories. Think of it as a transition from Figure 4.4 to Figure 4.5. It boils down to five suggested directory components:

- ► DOS directories

- ► Application directories

- ► Configuration directories

- ► Home directories

- ► Shared data directories

Let's take a closer look.

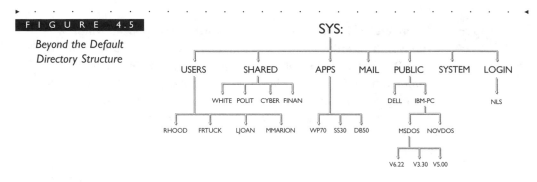

F I G U R E 4.5

*Beyond the Default
Directory Structure*

DOS Directories

DOS directories are vital because they provide support for various workstation operating systems (namely DOS and OS/2). They are, however, optional. You can choose to have users execute DOS commands and utilities from their local workstation drives or from a shared DOS directory on the server—it's up to you.

If you choose to have users run DOS from the server, you'll need to make a separate subdirectory for each version of DOS. It is preferable, of course, to have all users run the same version of DOS, but dream on—it'll never happen. Here's the trick: You'll need to somehow interrogate each workstation and point the user to the correct version of DOS. Fortunately, IntranetWare supports login script identifier variables for this very purpose. We'll explore them in more depth in Chapter 6 ("IntranetWare Configuration").

For now, you'll need to create a DOS directory structure that supports all the different types of machines and DOS versions on your WAN. As you can see in Figure 4.5, the DOS structure starts under SYS:PUBLIC because users already have access there. Next, you'll need to create a subdirectory structure for each of the following three components:

- MACHINE—IBM_PC, DELL, or other

- OS—MSDOS, NOVDOS, OS2, and so on

- OS VERSION—V7.01, V6.22, or whatever version you're using

So why should you bother? Many users simply access DOS utilities from their local drives. Well, if you're using a diskless workstation, you'll need to get DOS somewhere else—such as the server. Also, some users get better performance from the server because of file caching and a slow local disk channel. Finally, a centralized DOS structure allows you to update DOS once (on the server), instead of hundreds of times on each distributed workstation. The bottom line is that it's your choice, central DOS or local DOS—whatever you do, just DOS it!

Application Directories

A subdirectory structure should be created under SYS:APPS for each network application. For security's sake, restrict this structure to application files only—no data. Users can store their data in home directories, group areas, or SYS:SHARED—a global data directory (see the "Shared Data Directories" section).

Configuration File Directories

What about application configuration files, such as templates, interface files, and style sheets? It depends on the type of configuration file it is. Application-specific configuration files, like style sheets, should be placed in a CONFIG directory under the application. User-specific configurations, on the other hand, such as interface files, should be placed in user home directories. Let's take a closer look.

Home Directories

Each user needs a place he or she can call home. Typically, a special subdirectory is created under SYS:USERS for each user, which gives each of them a private, secure retreat for his or her own stuff. User directories serve two functions: security and organization. From a security viewpoint, they provide a secure place for private user files—a place away from coworkers' prying eyes (of course, you can look at their files because you are a CNA). From an organizational viewpoint, user directories become the parent of a complex user-specific directory structure—a place for personal games and applications.

Each user's home directory name should exactly match their login name—or at least be very close. This simplifies administration and makes them easy to find. Also, be sure to give users sufficient access rights to move around in there (see Chapter 5).

Shared Data Directories

The proper organization of network data strongly impacts user productivity. Let's be honest—the sole purpose of the IntranetWare file system is to organize data efficiently. This is accomplished in three ways:

▶ Personal data—should be stored in user home directories

▶ Group-specific data—should be stored in special group data directories under SYS:SHARED

▶ Globally shared data—should be stored in the SYS:SHARED directory off the root of SYS:

There you go. That's the IntranetWare file system. So, the only question that remains is, "What should it look like?" You have two choices: shallow or deep. Check it out.

QUIZ

I'm on this numbers kick. Numbers have an unavoidable fascination. Try this one on for size:

What is the five-digit number, no zeros, in which the first number is one-fourth of the second, the second is twice the third, the third is two-thirds of the fourth, and the fifth is half of the fourth, with the sum of all the digits being 23?

(Q4-1)
(See Appendix C for quiz answers.)

DESIGNING YOUR DIRECTORY STRUCTURE

Now that you know what the file system is made of, you need to decide what it's going to look like. You can either create a flat tree with many directories stored off the root of the volume, or you can have a deep directory structure with many levels of subdirectories (see Figure 4.6). Novell recommends that, for ease of administration, you design a directory structure that is no more than five levels deep.

A flat directory structure, such as the one in Figure 4.7, could be used for a very small company with few users. In this example, all home directories are stored in the root of the volume—not recommended, but easy to use. On the up side, this design limits file storage to a single volume, and the path names are very short. Also, the application programs are separated from data files.

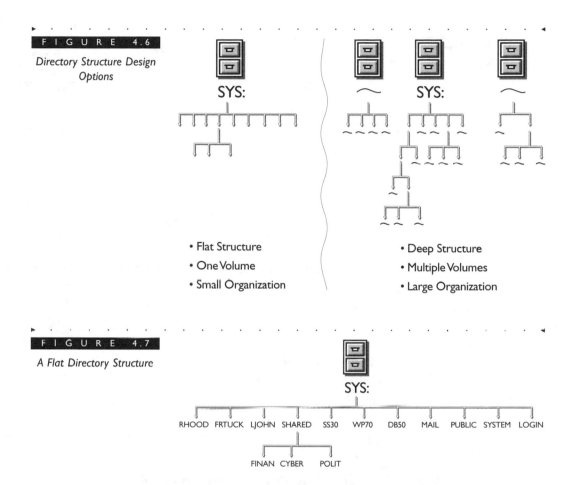

FIGURE 4.6

Directory Structure Design Options

SYS:

• Flat Structure
• One Volume
• Small Organization

SYS:

• Deep Structure
• Multiple Volumes
• Large Organization

FIGURE 4.7

A Flat Directory Structure

SYS:

RHOOD   FRTUCK   LJOHN   SHARED   SS30   WP70   DB50   MAIL   PUBLIC   SYSTEM   LOGIN

FINAN   CYBER   POLIT

On the down side, the SYS: volume shares its space with everyone else. Sometimes it just needs to be alone. Also, home directories are located in the root of the volume, and there is no shared data area.

A deeper directory structure is shown in Figure 4.8. In this design, system-created directories and applications share SYS:, while all other components have their own volumes. On the up side, the SYS: volume is more stable, because files are not added or deleted very often. Also, applications are more secure because they hang out with SYS:. Finally, you can consider using a different file system administrator for each volume.

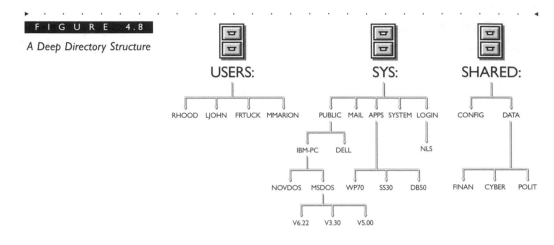

FIGURE 4.8

A Deep Directory Structure

On the down side, this design places users on different volumes, which makes security much more difficult to administer. Also, you may run out of room on a given volume, even though you have sufficient disk space on the server.

So, there you are. The "other" IntranetWare directory structure. It's not so bad. It's a lot easier than those crazy leaf objects and distinguished names. As you can see, the IntranetWare file system provides a simple, straightforward structure for sharing valuable WAN files. But what about management? How do you keep it running on a daily basis? I'm so glad you asked. That's the next topic.

Managing the IntranetWare File System

Once you've designed your file system, you'll need to develop a plan to maintain it—every day! You'll need to ask yourself the following questions:

- How much disk space is left on each volume?

- How much disk space is still available to users with volume space restrictions?

- How much room is being taken up by files that have been deleted but not yet purged?

▶ Which files have not been accessed in a long time?

▶ Are there any directories or files with no owner?

For the most part, the IntranetWare file system looks like DOS. For this reason, you can perform a lot of DOS file management tasks in IntranetWare as well. In addition, DOS tools such as DIR, COPY, and the MS Windows File Manager work just fine in the IntranetWare environment.

This is not nearly enough, however. Networking, in general, puts a great strain on file management. Fortunately, IntranetWare includes a number of file management utilities that are specifically designed to work in a network environment, such as:

▶ FILER—A text-based utility that is used to manage directories and files, display volume information, and salvage and purge deleted files.

▶ FLAG—Allows you to view or modify directory and file attributes. It can also be used to modify the owner of a directory or file and to view or modify the search mode of executable files.

▶ NCOPY—Allows you to copy network files from one location to another.

▶ NDIR—Lets you view the files once they've been copied. In addition, this utility allows you to view a plethora of information about volumes and directories—but you can't modify anything with it.

▶ NLIST—A new IntranetWare NDS utility that displays information about NDS objects and/or properties. It can be used to display information about volumes, as long as they're represented as Volume objects in NDS.

▶ NWADMIN (runs under MS Windows) and NETADMIN (runs under DOS)—NDS-based tools that can be used to perform a variety of file management tasks such as creating, deleting, renaming, copying, or moving directories and/or files. You can also use them to assign trustee rights, determine effective rights, and modify Inherited Rights Filters. In addition, they display Volume object information and, finally, allow you to purge and salvage deleted files. Wow!

TIP

Many of thse file system utilities are DOS-based command line utilities (such as FLAG, NDIR, and NLIST). If you ever need help at the command line, type the utility name followed by "/?".

It's a good thing you have so many friends to help you out. In this section, we will explore these and other IntranetWare file management tools. But we're going to approach them in a slightly unique way. Instead of talking about each utility alone, we are going to explore how they combine to help you manage three key file-system components:

▸ Volumes

▸ Directories

▸ Files

In each area, we will explore all the file management tools that apply to that component. Also, we'll provide some examples of how they can be used to simplify your life. This makes sense, because we're managing volumes, directories, and files—not utilities. So, without further ado, let's start out with IntranetWare volumes.

ZEN

"My parents live in Florida now. They moved there last year. They didn't want to move to Florida, but they're in their seventies now and that's the law!"

Jerry Seinfeld

MANAGING INTRANETWARE VOLUMES

Volumes are at the top of the file-system food chain. They also represent a bridge between physical files on server disks and logical leaf objects in the NDS tree. For your managing pleasure, IntranetWare includes five key tools for managing volumes:

▶ FILER

▶ NWADMIN

▶ NETADMIN

▶ NLIST

▶ NDIR

Let's check them out.

SMART LINK

If you want to get some real "hands-on" practice managing IntranetWare volumes, surf on over to CyberState University and World Wire: http://www.cyberstateu.com.

FILER

The DOS-based FILER menu utility can be used to display a variety of volume information, including:

▶ Volume statistics relating to space usage, directory entries, and compression

▶ Volume features such as volume type, block size, name space, and installed features (such as compression, migration, suballocation, or auditing)

▶ Date and time information, including creation date/time, owner, last modified date/time, last archived date/time, and archiver

To view information relating to the current volume, choose the "View volume information" option from the "Available options" menu, as shown in Figure 4.9. A Volume menu will appear that gives you the option of viewing volume statistics, features, or dates and times.

► · ◄

FIGURE 4.9

Available Options Menu in FILER

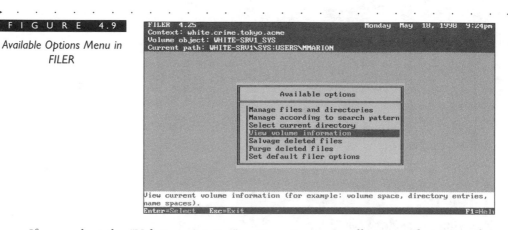

```
FILER  4.25                                Monday  May  18, 1998  9:24pm
Context: white.crime.tokyo.acme
Volume object: WHITE-SRV1_SYS
Current path: WHITE-SRV1\SYS:USERS\MMARION




                        ┌─────────────────────────────┐
                        │      Available options       │
                        ├─────────────────────────────┤
                        │Manage files and directories │
                        │Manage according to search pattern│
                        │Select current directory     │
                        │View volume information      │
                        │Salvage deleted files        │
                        │Purge deleted files          │
                        │Set default filer options    │
                        └─────────────────────────────┘



View current volume information (for example: volume space, directory entries,
name spaces).
Enter=Select   Esc=Exit                                           F1=Help
```

If you select the "Volume statistics" option, a screen will appear that is similar to the one in Figure 4.10. This screen lists statistics relating to volume space usage, maximum and available directory entries, and file-compression space usage.

► · ◄

FIGURE 4.10

Volume Statistics in FILER

```
FILER  4.25                                Monday  May  18, 1998  9:29pm
Context: white.crime.tokyo.acme
Volume object: WHITE-SRV1_SYS
Current path: WHITE-SRV1\SYS:USERS\MMARION

          ┌──────────────────────────────────────────────┐
          │                Volume statistics             │
          ├──────────────────────────────────────────────┤
          │Total space in KB(1024 bytes):  1,024,000  100.00%│
          │Active space used:                297,728   29.08%│
          │Deleted space not yet purgeable:        0    0.00%│
          │Space remaining on volume:        726,272   70.92%│
          │                                                  │
          │Maximum directory entries:         11,264         │
          │Directory entries available:        2,835   25.17%│
          │                                                  │
          │Space used if not compressed:     132,608         │
          │Total space compressed:            55,808         │
          │Space saved by compressing data:   76,800   57.92%│
          │Uncompressed space used:          260,096         │
          └──────────────────────────────────────────────┘

Esc=Escape                                                        F1=Help
```

If you select the "Volume features" option, a screen will appear that is similar to the one in Figure 4.11. This screen includes information about the volume type (that is, non-removable), the block size, the name space(s) installed, and installed features (such as compression, migration, suballocation, or auditing).

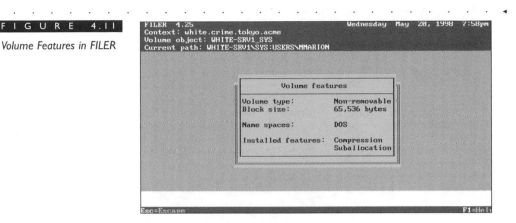

SMART LINK

Some of the most exciting IntranetWare volume features are file compression, data migration, and block suballocation. Learn them, use them, live them. Surf the Web at http://www.novell.com/manuals.

Finally, if you choose the "Dates and times" option, a Volume dates and times window will be displayed. This window displays information such as the volume creation date/time, owner, the last modified date/time, the last archived date/time, and the archiver.

FILER is the most useful non-NDS file management tool. It focuses on volumes, directories, and files as physical storage units within the IntranetWare server—no NDS nonsense to confuse you. This is appealing to many CNAs. If you want fancy NDS footwork, refer to NWADMIN.

Hey, good idea!

NWADMIN

The NetWare Administrator (NWADMIN) tool treats volumes as NDS objects. It displays roughly the same information as FILER, but from a slightly different point of view:

- ▶ Identification

- ▶ Dates and Times

> ▸ User Space Limits

> ▸ Trustee Security

> ▸ Attributes

To display volume information using NWADMIN, walk the tree until you find your desired volume—in our case it's .CN=WHITE-SRV1_SYS.OU=WHITE. OU=CRIME.OU=TOKYO.O=ACME. When you select a volume, the Identification page button activates by default. Because of this, a screen similar to the one in Figure 4.12 magically appears. It's marginally interesting, containing information on volume name, host server, IntranetWare version, host volume, and location.

F I G U R E   4.12

Identification Page for Volumes in NWADMIN

The Statistics page is the really interesting NWADMIN volume page (see Figure 4.13). It displays statistical information relating to the volume type (non-removable), deleted files, compressed files, block size, name spaces, and installed features (such as suballocation, data compression, and data migration). Colorful pie charts are also displayed, showing the percentage of disk space and directory entries used. Very cool.

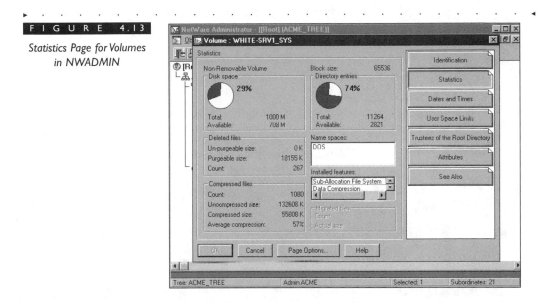

FIGURE 4.13

Statistics Page for Volumes in NWADMIN

In addition to Identification and Statistics, NWADMIN provides numerous other volume-related page buttons:

▶ Dates and Times—Displays values for the volume creation date and time, owner, last modified date, last archived date, and "user last archived by." The latter option offers valuable information for managing data backup (see Chapter 7).

▶ User Space Limits—Displays information regarding user space limits imposed on particular users (if any). This is an effective way of controlling "disk hogs."

▶ Trustees of the Root Directory—Displays security information concerning the trustees of the root directory, their effective rights, and the directory's Inherited Rights Filter. You should be careful about who gets access rights to the root directory of *any* volume—especially SYS:.

▶ Attributes—Displays directory attributes for the root directory of the given volume. This is another security option (see Chapter 5).

▸ See Also—Displays who and what is related to the Volume object. This is basically a manual information record for tracking special volume details.

NETADMIN

NETADMIN is the DOS-based version of NWADMIN for those of you who break out into hives every time you touch a mouse. It provides the same type of information as NWADMIN, but in a slightly (or greatly) less user-friendly way. This means it's very hard to use.

To view volume information with NETADMIN, you have to find the volume first. This involves a labyrinth of tree-walking through three menu choices: Manage objects, Object class, and View or edit properties of this object. Once you arrive at your destination, it looks something like Figure 4.14.

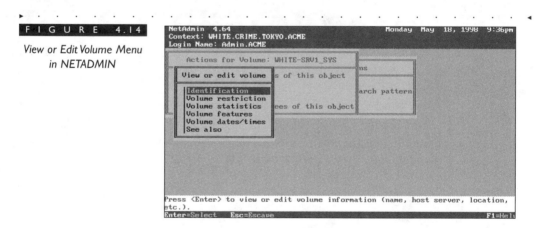

FIGURE 4.14

View or Edit Volume Menu in NETADMIN

If you select the Identification option from this menu, a screen appears showing the same type of NDS information as the NWADMIN Identification page, including volume name, host server, IntranetWare version, host volume, and location. Once again, the really interesting data is in the "Volume statistics" screen (see Figure 4.15). This screen lists numerous statistics related to volume space, maximum and available directory entries, and file-compression space. As a matter of fact, it looks a little familiar—like the Statistics screen in FILER. It's exactly the same data, just using a different DOS-based menu tool. Hmmm.

FIGURE 4.15

Volume Statistics in NETADMIN

```
NetAdmin 4.64                              Monday  May  18, 1998   9:36pm
Context: WHITE.CRIME.TOKYO.ACME
Login Name: Admin.ACME
                          Volume statistics
  Total volume space in KB (1024 bytes):        1,024,000   100.00%
  Active space used:                              276,096    26.96%
  Deleted space not yet purgeable:                      0     0.00%
  Space remaining on volume:                      747,904    73.04%

  Maximum directory entries:                       10,240
  Available directory entries:                      2,181    21.30%

  Space used if not compressed:                   132,608
  Total space compressed:                          55,808
  Space saved by compressing data:                 76,800    57.92%
  Uncompressed space used:                        220,000




This is information pertaining to the physical volume.  These fields can't be
changed.  Press <Esc> when done.
Esc=Escape                                                          F1=Help
```

In addition to Identification and Statistics, NETADMIN provides a combination of options from both NWADMIN and FILER, including:

- ► Volume restrictions

- ► Volume features

- ► Volume dates/times

- ► See also

NLIST

As we learned earlier, NLIST is a special IntranetWare NDS command line utility. It displays all related property information for any NDS object—including volumes. For our purposes, NLIST gives us access to:

- ► Object class

- ► Current context

- ► Volume name

- ► Host server name

- ► Physical volume name

▸ The number of Volume objects in the NDS tree

▸ Property values for Volume objects

NLIST can only be used to display information about NDS objects—it cannot be used to modify NDS information. Some of the most common commands used to display NDS volume information are included in Table 4.2. Check it out.

COMMAND	RESULT
NLIST VOLUME	Lists information for all volumes in the current context
NLIST VOLUME /D	Lists detailed information about a specific volume in the current context
NLIST VOLUME /N	Lists the names of the volumes in your current context

T A B L E 4.2

Partial List of NLIST Options

Output from the NLIST VOLUME /D command is shown in Figure 4.16. Notice the detailed volume-based information you can view from the command line.

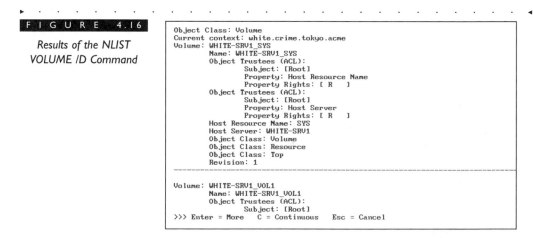

F I G U R E   4.16

Results of the NLIST VOLUME /D Command

Now let's explore the final volume management tool—NDIR. Just imagine "the forest moon of NDIR."

NDIR

NDIR, as its name implies, is mostly a directory and file utility. It does, however, offer a few statistics for IntranetWare volumes, namely:

▸ Volume space statistics

▸ Directory entry statistics

▸ Compression space statistics

Figure 4.17 shows an example of the type of information that can be displayed by typing:

```
NDIR /VOL
```

You'll notice that it lists a variety of volume information, including space used, space remaining, deleted space not yet purged, space available for use by you, maximum and available directory entries, as well as compression statistics, such as space used by compressed files, space saved by compressed files, and uncompressed space used. It's amazing that all this information can be viewed from such a small utility!

▸ · ◂

FIGURE 4.17

Results of the NDIR /VOL Command

```
U:\USERS\MMARION>NDIR /VOL

Statistics for fixed volume WHITE SRV1/SYS:
Space statistics are in KB (1024 bytes).

Total volume space:                    1,024,000  100.00%
Space used by 8,059 entries:             276,096   26.96%
Deleted space not yet purgeable:               0    0.00%
                                       ---------
Space remaining on volume:               747,904   73.04%
Space available to Admin.ACME:           747,904   73.04%

Maximum directory entries:                10,240
Available directory entries:               2,181   21.30%

Space used if files were not compressed:  132,600
Space used by compressed files:           55,808
                                       ---------
Space saved by compressing files:         76,800   57.92%

Uncompressed space used:                 220,800

U:\USERS\MMARION>
```

SMART LINK

For more information on these great IntranetWare volume management tools, check out the "Utilities Reference" at http://www.novell.com/manuals.

There you go. That's everything you wanted to know about volume management but were afraid to ask! Now that you've gotten cozy with some of IntranetWare's finest file system tools, let's see what they can do with directories and files. Who knows, you might even meet some new tools along the way.

ZEN

"If professional wrestling didn't exist, could you come up with this idea? Could you envision the popularity of huge men in tiny bathing suits pretending to fight?"

Jerry Seinfeld

MANAGING INTRANETWARE DIRECTORIES

Volumes are important, but directories win the prize. These are the true organizational containers of the IntranetWare file system. As we learned earlier, a logical directory design can save hours of security and file management. In this section, we will explore many of the same utilities as we just discussed, but from a totally different point of view:

- ▸ FILER

- ▸ NWADMIN

- ▸ NDIR

- ▸ NCOPY

- ▸ RENDIR

So, let's get started.

SMART LINK

If you want to get some real "hands-on" practice managing IntranetWare directories, surf on over to CyberState University and World Wire: http://www.cyberstateu.com.

FILER

FILER is IntranetWare's most comprehensive directory and file management tool. Earlier we learned about its volume savvy, but you ain't seen nothing yet. In its natural element, FILER can

- ▶ Create, delete, and rename directories

- ▶ Copy and move entire subdirectory structures

- ▶ View or change directory information such as owner, directory creation date/time, directory attributes, trustees, Inherited Rights Filter, and space limitations

- ▶ View your effective rights for directories

- ▶ Set up search and view filters (include and exclude options)

The first step is to select the default directory. If you look at the top of the screen, you'll notice that it lists the current path. To choose a different directory, choose the "Select current directory" option from the "Available options" menu, as shown in Figure 4.18. You can either modify the path manually or walk the tree by pressing Insert. If you walk the tree, don't forget to press Esc when you're finished selecting directories. When the correct directory is selected, press Enter to return to the "Available options" menu.

FIGURE 4.18

Available Options Menu in FILER

```
FILER 4.25                                 Monday  May  18, 1998  9:44pm
Context: white.crime.tokyo.acme
Volume object: WHITE-SRV1_SYS
Current path: WHITE-SRV1_SYS:USERS\MMARION

                        ┌─────────────────────────────────┐
                        │          Available options       │
                        ├─────────────────────────────────┤
                        │ Manage files and directories     │
                        │ Manage according to search pattern│
                        │ Select current directory         │
                        │ View volume information          │
                        │ Salvage deleted files            │
                        │ Purge deleted files              │
                        │ Set default filer options        │
                        └─────────────────────────────────┘

Select a volume object to view that volume's information or to change your
position in the tree structure.
Enter=Select   Esc=Exit                                          F1=Help
```

The next step is to determine if you want to use any search or view filters to limit the directories that are displayed. If so, select the "Manage according to search pattern" option from the "Available options" menu. As you can see in Figure 4.19, a screen appears with the directory include and exclude patterns. You can also specify Hidden and/or System directories. After you've made your selections, press F10 to return to the "Available options" menu.

F I G U R E   4.19

Set the Search Pattern and Filter Menu in FILER

Now you're ready to go exploring—inside the selected directory. Select the "Manage files and directories" choice from the "Available options" menu. You'll notice that the subdirectories and files in the current directory appear as well as a double-dot (..), representing the parent directory, and a dot (.), representing the current directory.

You can do a number of different things with this screen. For instance,

- ▶ If you want to make another directory the current directory, you can walk the tree again.

- ▶ If you want to create a new subdirectory, press Insert and type in the name.

- ▶ If you want to delete a subdirectory, press Del. If you want to delete multiple directories at once, mark them all using F5 before pressing Del.

- ▶ If you want to rename a subdirectory, highlight it and press F3, then enter the new name.

To display information about this directory, highlight the period (.) and press F10. The "Subdirectory options" menu will be displayed. Press Enter to select the "View/Set directory information" option. A directory information screen will pop up, similar to the one in Figure 4.20. This screen lists information about the directory, such as the owner, the creation date/time, the directory attributes, the inherited rights filter, the trustees of the directory, the directory space limitations, and your effective rights for this directory.

If you have the appropriate rights, you can change any parameter listed, except for effective rights, which are calculated by IntranetWare (as you'll see in painstaking detail in Chapter 5). Go ahead and press Esc twice to return to the "Directory contents" screen.

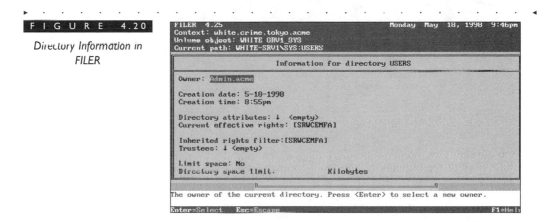

FIGURE 4.20

Directory Information in FILER

If you highlight a subdirectory and press F10, a "Subdirectory options" screen will be displayed, as shown in Figure 4.21. Two of the most interesting options allow you to move or copy an entire branch of the tree at one time. Cool.

That does it for FILER. Now, let's see what NWADMIN can do for IntranetWare directories.

QUIZ

Here's another numbers game:

Find the product of (x-a)(x-b)(x-c) . . . (x-z), where *x* is any number between 22 and 42.

(Q4-2)

FIGURE 4.21

Subdirectory Options in
FILER

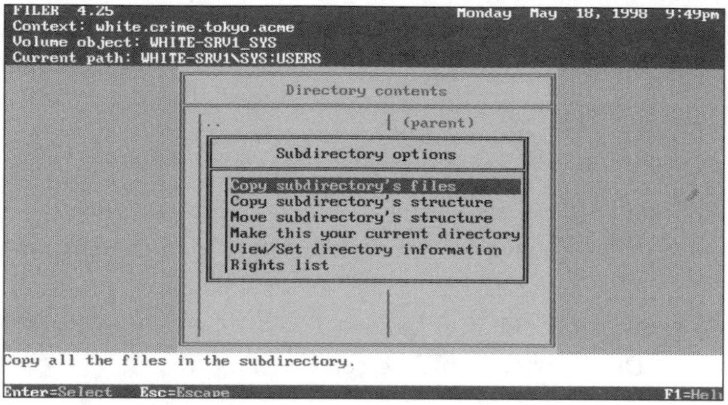

```
FILER  4.25                            Monday  May  18, 1998  9:49pm
Context: white.crime.tokyo.acme
Volume object: WHITE-SRV1_SYS
Current path: WHITE-SRV1\SYS:USERS

                        Directory contents
                   | ..  | (parent)
                   +---------------------------+
                   |   Subdirectory options    |
                   +---------------------------+
                   | Copy subdirectory's files |
                   | Copy subdirectory's structure |
                   | Move subdirectory's structure |
                   | Make this your current directory |
                   | View/Set directory information |
                   | Rights list               |
                   +---------------------------+

Copy all the files in the subdirectory.
Enter=Select    Esc=Escape                              F1=Help
```

NWADMIN

NWADMIN is primarily an NDS-management tool; however, it offers a few directory-related functions, such as:

▶ Create, move, delete, and rename directories

▶ Copy, move, and delete entire subdirectory structures

▶ View or change directory information, such as owner, attributes, trustees, Inherited Rights Filter, or space limitations

▶ Set up search and view filters (include and exclude options)

First of all, walk the tree until the directory with which you want to work is in view. Click on the directory, then click on the Object menu. If you look at the options in the Object menu, you'll notice that you can perform the following file management tasks: create a directory; delete a directory; rename, copy, and/or move a directory. You can also select the Details option to view information about your directory.

If you select Details, the Identification page button is activated by default. As you can see in Figure 4.22, this page includes two important pieces of information: the directory name and the name spaces available on the volume.

FIGURE 4.22

Identification Page for Directories in NWADMIN

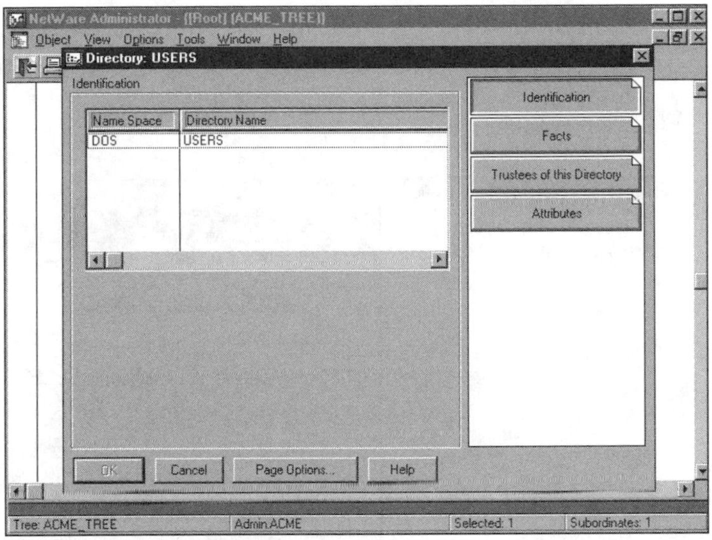

If you select the Facts page button, as shown in Figure 4.23, another screen appears with more detailed directory information, including the owner, the directory creation date/time, the last modified date/time, the last archived date/time, and the archiver. It also lists the volume space available on this directory and the space limitations (if any).

FIGURE 4.23

Facts Page in NWADMIN

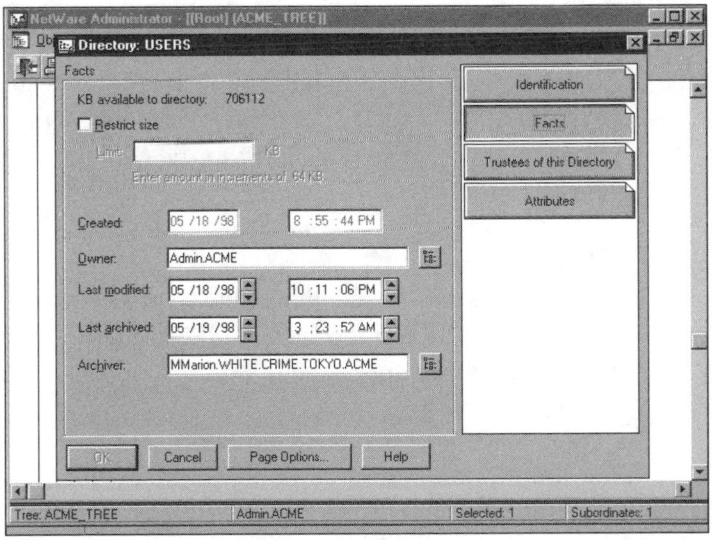

Figure 4.24 illustrates the first of two directory-specific security options in NWADMIN—the Trustees of this Directory page. This page allows you to list trustees and their effective rights as well as the inherited rights filter for this directory.

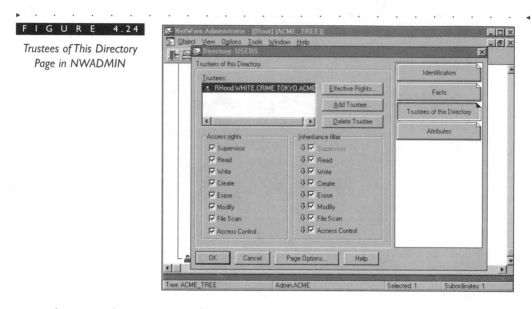

F I G U R E   4.24

Trustees of This Directory
Page in NWADMIN

The second NWADMIN file system security option deals with Attributes (see Figure 4.25). Don't worry, you'll get plenty of chances to work with security in Chapter 5.

That's enough of NWADMIN for now. As you can see, it augments the FILER functions in a prettier Windows-based user interface. Now, for something completely different. Let's go back to the command line—starting with the forest moon of NDIR.

NDIR

NDIR gives us limited functionality at the volume level—because it's not a volume utility; it's a directory/file utility. NDIR opens a new world of directory information to you, including:

▸ Owner, creation date, attributes, and archive information

▸ Subdirectories/files

▶ Inherited Rights Filter

▶ Effective rights

FIGURE 4.25

Attributes Page in
NWADMIN

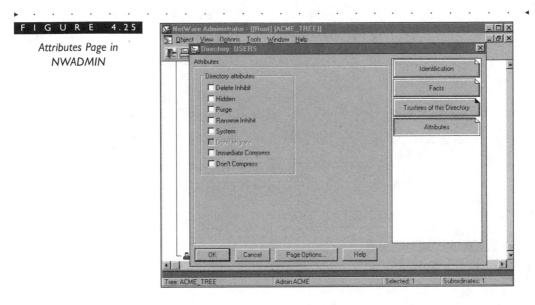

In addition, directory information can be sorted according to almost any criteria (owner, creation date, attributes, and so on). If you don't specify any formatting options, NDIR lists the following information about each directory: the directory name, Inherited Rights Filter, your effective rights, the creation date/time, and the owner.

By default, NDIR lists all subdirectories and files in the specified directory (unless otherwise noted). You can display directory information selectively by using wildcards, and/or display options. For example, use /C to scroll continuously or /SUB to include subdirectories and their files. You can also list directories that contain (or do not contain) a specific directory attribute.

The beauty of NDIR is its logic searching capabilities. NDIR also supports date options such as AFT (after), BEF (before), and EQ (equals); size options such as LE (less than), EQ (equal to), and GR (greater than); and sorting options such as /REV SORT (reverse order), /SORT CR (creation date), /SORT OW (owner), and /UN (unsorted).

Some of the more common NDIR directory commands are listed in Table 4.3.

TABLE 4.3	COMMAND	RESULT
Common NDIR Directory Commands	NDIR	Displays subdirectories and files in the current directory
	NDIR /DO	Displays directories only
	NDIR /DO /SUB	Displays directories and subdirectories only
	NDIR /SPA	Displays space limitations for this directory
	NDIR /DO /C	Displays directories only—scrolls continuously when displaying information
	NDIR /DO CR	Displays directories only—those created AFT 10/01/99 after 10/01/99
	NDIR /DO /REV	Displays directories only—sorts by SORT CR directory creation date, with newest listed first

Figure 4.26 shows an example of output from the NDIR /DO command. Use it or lose it.

FIGURE 4.26

The NDIR /DO Command

```
G:\PUBLIC>NDIR /DO
Directories      = Directories contained in this path
Filter           = Inherited Rights Filter
Rights           = Effective Rights
Created          = Date directory was created
Owner            = ID of user who created or copied the file

WHITE-SRV1/SYS:PUBLIC\*.*
Directories        Filter       Rights       Created          Owner
---------------    ---------    ---------    ----------------  ------------------
CLIENT             [SRWCEMFA]   [SRWCEMFA]   5-18-98   8:01p   WHITE-SRV1.WHITE.CRIM
IBM_PC             [SRWCEMFA]   [SRWCEMFA]   5-18-98  10:29p   Admin
NALLIB             [SRWCEMFA]   [SRWCEMFA]   5-18-98   8:00p   WHITE-SRV1.WHITE.CRIM
NLS                [SRWCEMFA]   [SRWCEMFA]   5-18-98   7:57p   WHITE-SRV1.WHITE.CRIM
OS2                [SRWCEMFA]   [SRWCEMFA]   5-18-98   7:58p   WHITE-SRV1.WHITE.CRIM
WIN95              [SRWCEMFA]   [SRWCEMFA]   5-18-98   7:58p   WHITE-SRV1.WHITE.CRIM

         6  Directories

G:\PUBLIC>
```

NCOPY

NCOPY is the IntranetWare version of COPY. Can you guess what it does? Very good—it copies stuff. NCOPY is similar in function to the DOS XCOPY command and allows the use of the same wildcards. Benefits of using NCOPY include:

▶ Directory/file attributes and name space information are automatically preserved.

▸ Read-after-write verification feature is ON by default. (You must use the /V switch to use verification if you're copying files on local drives.)

▸ IntranetWare physical or object volume names can be specified in a path.

TIP

Because NCOPY is an IntranetWare utility, it accesses the IntranetWare file allocation table (FAT) and directory entry table (DET) more efficiently than the DOS COPY or XCOPY commands. It is faster than COPY and XCOPY if the files are being copied from one directory to another on the server, because it works within server RAM rather than copying the directories and/or files to and from workstation RAM. It is also a safer method because it uses the IntranetWare read-after-write verification fault tolerance feature by default.

Some of the more common NCOPY commands are listed in Table 4.4.

T A B L E 4.4 Common NCOPY Commands	COMMAND	RESULT
	NCOPY G:REPORTS C:REPORTS	Copies the REPORTS directory from the G: drive on the server to the default directory on your workstation C: drive
	NCOPY F:DATA C:DATA /S	Copies the DATA directory from the F: drive to the C: drive, including subdirectories
	NCOPY G:1995 ..\ARCHIVE /S /E	Copies the 1995 directory on the G: drive (as well as its subdirectories and their files, including empty subdirectories) to an ARCHIVE directory under the current directory's parent directory
	NCOPY .TEMP /V	Copies the current directory to the TEMP directory and verifies that the procedure was accurate (only needed if copying files on a local drive)

RENDIR

RENDIR allows you to rename directories—what a surprise. Wildcards can be used, as well as a period (.) to represent the current directory or a colon followed by a forward slash (:/) to represent the default drive and volume. Check out Table 4.5 for some examples of the more common RENDIR commands in IntranetWare.

TABLE 4.5 Common RENDIR Commands	COMMAND	RESULT
	RENDIR REPORT REPORTS	Renames the directory called REPORT under the current directory to REPORTS
	RENDIR U:USER USERS	Renames the directory on Drive U: called USER to USERS
	RENDIR S: SAMPLES	Renames the directory to which drive S: is mapped as SAMPLES
	RENDIR . DATA	Renames the current directory to DATA
	RENDIR :/QTR1 95QTR1	Renames the directory called QTR1 on the current drive and volume to 95QTR1
	RENDIR /?	Displays on-line help for the RENDIR command

TIP

If you rename a directory, don't forget to modify any configuration files that reference it—like login scripts.

SMART LINK

For more information on these great IntranetWare directory management tools, check out the "Utilities Reference" at http://www.novell.com/manuals.

That completes our discussion of directory management. Wasn't that fun? There's only one more file system component left—and we've saved the best for last. Hold on to your hats; we're entering the file management zone.

ZEN

Sick-building syndrome—A condition found in humans, caused by a substance that pollutes the environment becoming trapped in a building, especially as a result of poor design or hazardous materials being used in construction. How are you feeling? Need some fresh air?

MANAGING INTRANETWARE FILES

Earlier, I said that directories win the prize—I lied. Files are really the most important components. After all, what's the ultimate goal of the IntranetWare file system? File sharing. What do users ask for when they log into the "Cloud"? Files. Why are we here?

Anyway, file management looks a little like directory management, and it uses most of the same tools. But that's where the similarities end. Directories are for organization; files are for productivity. And what's more important? Here's a list of the tools we'll explore in this section:

- ▶ FILER

- ▶ NWADMIN

- ▶ MS Windows

- ▶ NDIR

- ▶ NCOPY

Don't just sit there; get moving. There are only a few utilities left. Ready, set, go.

SMART LINK

If you want to get some real "hands-on" practice managing IntranetWare files, surf on over to CyberState University and World Wire: http://www.cyberstateu.com.

FILER

Let's visit our old friend FILER just one last time. Now we're focusing on real file management, including:

▶ Creating, deleting, renaming, copying, and moving files

▶ Managing files attributes

▶ Setting up search and view filters (include and exclude options)

▶ Salvaging and purging deleted files

As before, the first FILER step is to select the default directory. Refer to the directory management section for more details. Once you're there, you can alter the include and exclude filters for specific files or even check out Hidden and/or System documents. After you've made your selections, you can press F10 to return to the "Available options" menu.

In addition to the search/view filters, FILER presents Copy and Delete options when working with files. First, select the "Set default filer options" choice from the "Available options" menu. A "Filer settings" screen will appear, as shown in Figure 4.27. You can set a number of defaults for copying and deleting files, including confirmations and messaging help. When all of file management settings are correct, press Esc to return to the "Available options" menu.

FIGURE 4.27

FILER Settings Screen

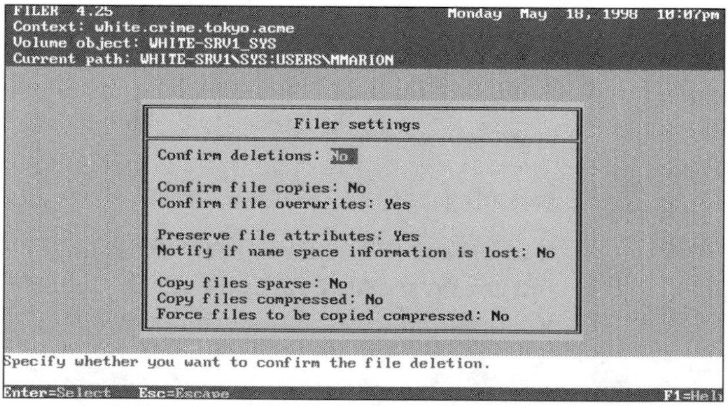

Now you're ready to display your files. Select the "Manage files and directories" option from the "Available options" menu. You'll notice a plethora of subdirectories and files in the current directory, as well as a double-dot (..) for the parent directory and a dot (.) for the current directory. Now, you're ready to get busy:

▸ Walk the tree to select another directory as the current directory.

▸ Delete a file by highlighting it and pressing Del. If you want to delete multiple files at once, mark them all with the F5 key before pressing Del.

▸ Rename a file by highlighting it and pressing F3.

Next, select a particular file to work with by highlighting it and pressing F10. The "File options" menu appears. This menu gives you the option of copying, viewing, or moving the file; displaying trustees of the file; or viewing/modifying file information. If you select the "View/Set file information" option from the "File options" menu, a file information screen pops up, similar to the one in Figure 4.28. This screen lists information about the file such as the owner; access, archive, creation, and modification dates; file attributes; the Inherited Rights Filter; the trustees of the file; the owning name space; the file size and EA size; as well as your effective rights.

FIGURE 4.28

File Information Screen in FILER

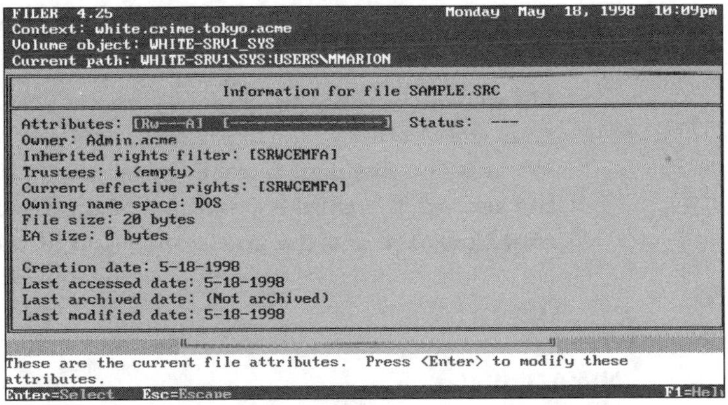

```
FILER  4.25                                    Monday  May  18, 1998   10:09pm
Context: white.crime.tokyo.acme
Volume object: WHITE-SRV1_SYS
Current path: WHITE-SRV1\SYS:USERS\MMARION
╔══════════════════════════════════════════════════════════════════════════╗
║                      Information for file SAMPLE.SRC                        ║
║                                                                            ║
║  Attributes: [Rw---A] [------------------] Status:  ---                    ║
║  Owner: Admin.acme                                                         ║
║  Inherited rights filter: [SRWCEMFA]                                       ║
║  Trustees: ↓ <empty>                                                       ║
║  Current effective rights: [SRWCEMFA]                                      ║
║  Owning name space: DOS                                                    ║
║  File size: 20 bytes                                                       ║
║  EA size: 0 bytes                                                          ║
║                                                                            ║
║  Creation date: 5-18-1998                                                  ║
║  Last accessed date: 5-18-1998                                             ║
║  Last archived date: (Not archived)                                        ║
║  Last modified date: 5-18-1998                                             ║
║                                                                            ║
║           L_____J                      ║
╚══════════════════════════════════════════════════════════════════════════╝
These are the current file attributes.  Press <Enter> to modify these
attributes.
Enter=Select    Esc=Escape                                            F1=Help
```

If you have appropriate rights, you can change most of the parameters listed, except for effective rights, owning name space, file size, and EA size. Press Esc three times to return to the "Available options" menu.

There are two more choices in the "Available options" menu that relate to files, namely "Salvage deleted files" and "Purge deleted files." Salvage allows you to recover deleted files that have not yet been purged. Purge is the process of permanently removing deleted files from the system.

If you choose "Salvage deleted files," you will be given three options:

▸ Salvage files from an existing directory

▸ Salvage files from DELETED.SAV (because the parent directory has been deleted)

▸ Set salvage options (that is, indicate whether to sort the list by filename, file size, deletion date, or deletor)

If you choose "Purge deleted files" from the "Available options" menu, you can specify the filename pattern to be used when selecting purged files. It will also allow you to choose whether to purge files in the current subdirectory only, or to purge the files in the entire subdirectory tree structure. Be very careful when purging files: You can never recover these files.

This completes our discussion of FILER all together. It's been a wonderous journey, and I hope you have learned to appreciate how helpful it can be for volume, directory, and file management. Now, let's visit NWADMIN one last time.

QUIZ

I like these number brainiacs so much, I thought I'd try another one:

What is the five-digit number in which the first digit is two-thirds of the second, the third is one-third of the second, the fourth is four times the last, and the last is one-third of the first. The digits total 28.

(Q4-3)

NWADMIN

NWADMIN is another important file management tool. It allows us to perform any of the following functions from a friendly Windows-based interface:

▸ Create, delete, and rename files

▸ Copy and move files

▸ View or change file information such as owner, attributes, trustees, and Inherited Rights Filter

▸ Set up search and view filters (include and exclude options)

▸ Salvage and purge deleted files

First of all, walk the tree until the desired file is in view. Click on the file, then click on the Object menu. If you look at the options in the Object menu, you'll notice file management options that allow you to delete the file, rename it, copy it or move it. The same options can be accessed from the Details menu as well.

If you select the Facts page button, a screen appears with the file's owner, size, file creation date/time, last modified date/time, last archived date/time, and archiver. If you have the appropriate rights, you can modify all of these parameters except for the size and creation date.

If you select the Trustees of this File page button, you will be allowed to view, add, or modify trustees and display their effective rights, as well as view or change the Inherited Rights Filter for the file. Similarly, if you select the Attributes page button, you can view the attributes that have been set for this file, and you can change them if you have the appropriate access rights (see Chapter 5).

In addition to the usual file management stuff, NWADMIN allows you to salvage or purge deleted files. Interestingly, both of these functions are handled by the same menu option: Choose Salvage from the Tools menu (see Figure 4.29).

You can select three sets of options from the Salvage menu:

▸ Include pattern using wildcards or filenames

▸ Sort options (deletion date, deletor, filename, file size, or file type)

▸ Source (current directory or deleted directories)

When all of the options are set correctly, click on the List button to list the files indicated. As with other MS Windows or Windows 95 utilities, to select the desired files, you can

▸ Select a single file by clicking on it

▶ Select sequentially listed files by clicking on the first file, holding down the Shift key, then clicking on the last file in the range

▶ Select nonsequentially listed files by holding down the Ctrl key while selecting files

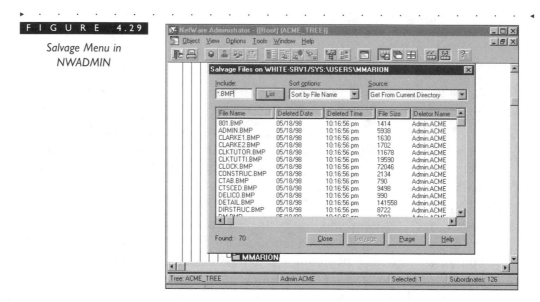

F I G U R E   4.29

Salvage Menu in NWADMIN

When you have selected all of the desired files, you can click on either the Salvage or Purge button at the bottom of the screen to salvage or purge the selected file(s). If salvaged, the IntranetWare files will be restored with their original trustee rights and extended attributes intact. Finally, when you're finished, click on the OK button to return to the NWADMIN browse screen.

MS Windows

Both the 16-bit and 32-bit versions of MS Windows provide built-in file management functions. Client 16 and Client 32 allow you to use their native Windows for managing IntranetWare volumes, directories, and files. This gives you the ability to manage the network file system just like you would your local drives.

MS Windows supports IntranetWare file management from three different platforms:

- ▸ Windows 95 Network Neighborhood

- ▸ Windows 3.1 File Manager

- ▸ NetWare User Tools for Windows

Client 32 allows you to manage the IntranetWare file system from within the Windows 95 Network Neighborhood. As you can see in Figure 4.30, it provides much of the same functions as NWADMIN. Windows 95 supports the following file management information:

- ▸ Name

- ▸ Owner

- ▸ Creation date

- ▸ Available space

- ▸ Directory entries

- ▸ File attributes

- ▸ Archive dates

- ▸ Size

- ▸ Effective rights

- ▸ Trustees

To view information about a specific IntranetWare file object in Windows 95, simply highlight a volume, directory, or file, and click the right mouse button. Then choose "Properties" from the abbreviated menu. You should get a screen similar to the one in Figure 4.30.

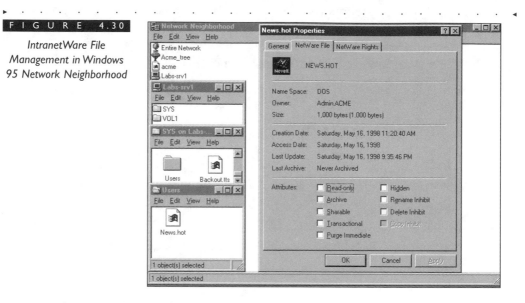

F I G U R E   4.30

IntranetWare File Management in Windows 95 Network Neighborhood

Windows 3.1 also allows limited access to directory and file information through File Manager (see Figure 4.31). This screen provides the following information:

- ▸ Name

- ▸ Owner

- ▸ Size

- ▸ Creation date

- ▸ Access date

- ▸ Last update

- ▸ Last Archive

- ▸ Attributes

To access this property page, select a file and choose Properties from the File menu. Then click the IntranetWare button to view these IntranetWare-specific properties.

FIGURE 4.31

*IntranetWare File
Management in Windows
3.1 File Manager*

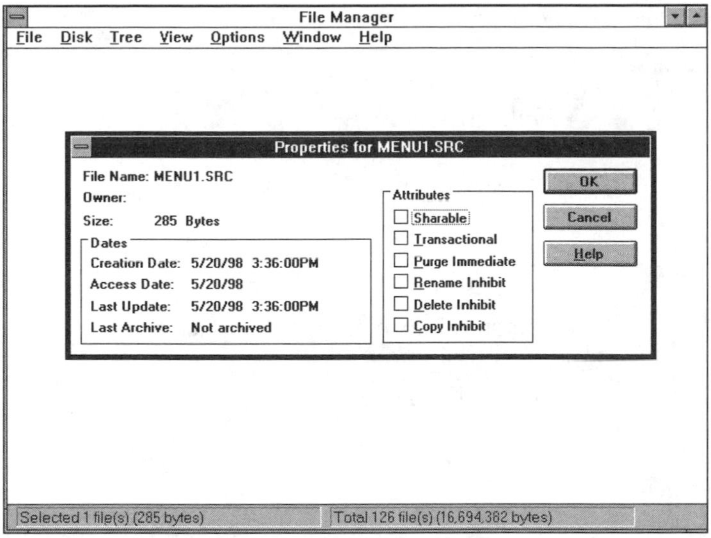

You can also use the NetWare User Tools for Windows graphical utility to view effective rights for volumes and directories. This utility can be launched from within the Windows 3.1 File Manager by selecting Network Connection from the Disk menu. As you can see in Figure 4.32, this property screen provides valuable information about your NDS tree name, server, path, username, and effective rights in a given directory.

Well, that does it for Windows. You can bid the GUI environment a fond farewell as we move to the IntranetWare command line. NDIR awaits!

NDIR

As we discussed earlier, NDIR is a very versatile command line utility that allows you to selectively list a large variety of directory and file information, sorted by a number of different parameters. From a file management standpoint, NDIR displays:

- ► Filename

- ► Owner

- ► Creation date and time

- ▸ Last modified date and time

- ▸ Size

- ▸ File attributes

- ▸ Access rights

- ▸ Macintosh files

- ▸ Version information for application files

- ▸ Extended details

▸ · ◂

FIGURE 4.32

IntranetWare File Management in NetWare User Tools for Windows

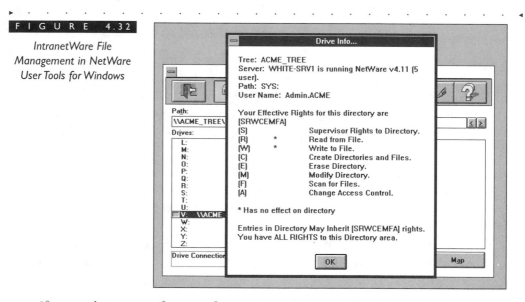

If you don't specify any formatting options, NDIR lists the following information about each file: the filename, size, last update (modified) date, and owner. You can customize the output by specifying one of the following formatting options: /COMP (compression statistics), /DA (Dates), /D (detail), /L (long names), /M (Macintosh), and /R (rights).

By default, NDIR lists all subdirectories and files in the current directory, unless otherwise noted. You can selectively list the information by specifying a particular file, using wildcards, or by indicating a display option such as /C (scroll continuously), /FI (list every occurrence within your current directory and path), /FO (list files only), /SUB (include subdirectories and their files). You can also list files that contain (or do not contain) a specific file attribute.

NDIR also lets you restrict files by specifying date options such as AFT (after), BEF (before), and EQ (equals); size options such as LE (less than), EQ (equal to), and GR (greater than); and NOT (all except).

NDIR lists files in alphabetical order by default. You can change the order files are sorted in by specifying one of the following options: /REV SORT (reverse order), /SORT AC (access date), /SORT AR (archive date), /SORT CR (creation date), /SORT UP (update date), /SORT OW (owner), /SORT SI (size), or /SORT UN (unsorted).

THE BRAIN

For further information on the options available with the NDIR command, refer to the NDIR section of the "Utilities Reference" manual, or surf the Web at http://www.novell.com/manuals.

Get to really know the NDIR command by checking out Table 4.6.

Output from the NDIR /FO command is shown in Figure 4.33. And that does it for NDIR. Now, let's explore the final IntranetWare file management tool—NCOPY.

▶ . . . . ◀

FIGURE 4.33

The NDIR /FO Command

```
G:\ETC>NDIR /FO
Files           = Files contained in this path
Size            = Number of bytes in the file
Last Update     = Date file was last updated
Owner           = ID of user who created or copied the file

WHITE-SRV1/SYS:ETC\*.*
Files                      Size Last Update      Owner
-------------------------------------------------------------------
ATTYPES.CFG                 237  9-23-93  6:56p WHITE-SRV1
BUILTINS.CFG             10,825  3-13-96  3:09p WHITE-SRV1
GATEWAYS                    500  5-24-93  4:59p WHITE-SRV1
HOSTS                       441  9-11-92  2:31p WHITE-SRV1
NETWORKS                    200  9-11-92  2:31p WHITE-SRV1
PROTOCOL                    378  9-11-92  2:31p WHITE-SRV1
SERVICES                  1,570  9-11-92  2:31p WHITE-SRV1
TRAPTARG.CFG              1,697  3-17-93  8:50a WHITE-SRV1


       15,928  bytes (17,920  bytes of disk space used)
            8  Files

G:\ETC>
```

COMMAND	RESULT
NDIR /FO	Displays files only—those in the current directory
NDIR /FO /C	Displays files only—scrolls continuously
NDIR /FO /SUB	Displays files only—those in the current directory and its subdirectories
NDIR /FO /REV SORT SI	Displays files only—sorts by size, starting with the largest file
NDIR /FO /SORT UP	Displays files only—sorts by last modified date
NDIR /FO /SORT OW	Displays files only—sorts by owner
NDIR /FO OW EQ DAVID	Displays files only—where the owner is David
NDIR R*.* /SIZE GR 500000	Displays files and directories that exceed 500K in size
NDIR *.BAT /FO	Displays files only—those in the current directory with an extension of .BAT
NDIR /FO /AC BEF 06-01-99	Displays files only—those not accessed since 06/01/99
NDIR \WHOAMI. EXE /SUB /FO	Displays files only—lists all occurrences of the WHOAMI.EXE file, starting the search at the root of the volume
NDIR Z:*.EXE /VER	Displays the version number for those files on the Z: drive with an .EXE extension
NDIR *.* /R /FO	Displays files only—lists your effective rights for each file
NDIR Z:NW ADMIN.EXE /D	Displays detailed file information for the Z:NWADMIN file
NDIR SYS: SHARED*.* /RO	Displays those files in the SYS:SHARED directory that have the Read Only attribute set
NDIR *.* /FO /NOT RO	Displays files only—those that do not have the Read Only attribute set
NDIR F:*.* /FO /REV SORT AC	Displays files only—sorts by access date, listing the file with the most recent access date first
NDIR /FO DA	Displays files only—lists access, archive, creation, and update dates

NCOPY

NCOPY can be used to copy files as well as directories. What a surprise. As we discussed earlier, NCOPY is similar in function to the DOS XCOPY command, except that directory attributes and name space information are automatically preserved. Refer to Table 4.7 for an exploration of NCOPY from a file management point of view.

THE BRAIN

For further information on the options available with the NCOPY command, refer to the NCOPY section of the "Utilities Reference" manual, or surf the Web at http://www.novell.com/manuals.

T A B L E 4 . 7 Common NCOPY Commands	COMMAND	RESULT
	NCOPY JULY.RPT F:	Copies a file in the default directory called JULY.RPT to the F: drive.
	NCOPY F:PHONE.NUM C:	Copies the PHONE.NUM file from the F: drive to the C: drive.
	NCOPY F:*.RPT A: /A	Copies files with a *.RPT extension that have the archive bit set (and thus, need to be backed up) from F: to A:.
	NCOPY DOC1.TEMP1.* /C	Copies the DOC1.WP file and WP renames the new version TEMP1.WP, without preserving extended attributes and name space information.
	NCOPY F:R*. G: /F	Copies files beginning with the letter "R" from the F: drive to the G: drive, forcing the copying of sparse files.
	NCOPY *.DOC A: /I	Copies files with a .DOC extension from the current directory to the A: drive and notifies you when extended attributes or name space information cannot be copied because the target volume doesn't support these features.

(continued)

COMMAND	RESULT
T A B L E 4.7 *Common NCOPY* *Commands (continued)*	
NCOPY F:*.DOC A: /M	Copies files with the *.DOC extension that have the archive bit set (and thus need to be backed up) from F: to A:, then turns off the archive bit of the source files. (This allows NCOPY to be used for backup purposes.)
NCOPY C:FRED.LST C:TOM.LST /V	Copies FRED.LST to TOM.LST on the C: drive using the verify option.
NCOPY /?	Displays on-line help for the NCOPY utility.

SMART LINK

For more information on these great IntranetWare file management tools, check out the "Utilities Reference" at http://www.novell.com/manuals.

Well, there you have it—the wonderful world of IntranetWare file system management. Aren't you a lucky camper? Now you are an expert in gardening NDS and non-NDS trees. In this section, we focused on the three main components of the IntranetWare file system—volumes, directories, and files. We discovered a variety of tools and learned how they help us manage each of these components. See Table 4.8 for a complete summary. The important thing is to focus on the file system, not the tool—a unique, but effective approach.

T A B L E 4.8

IntranetWare File
Management Utilities
Summary

MANAGEMENT OBJECT	MANAGEMENT TASK	MANAGEMENT UTILITY
Managing volumes	Displaying volume space usage	NetWare Administrator, NETADMIN, MS Windows, Filer, and NDIR
	Modify user space limits	NetWare Administrator and NETADMIN
	Manage file compression	NetWare Administrator, NETADMIN, Filer, and NDIR

*IntranetWare File
Management Utilities
Summary (continued)*

MANAGEMENT OBJECT	MANAGEMENT TASK	MANAGEMENT UTILITY
Managing volumes (continued)	Manage data-migration attributes	NetWare Administrator, NETADMIN, and FLAG
Managing Directories	View directory information such as creation date, last access date, owner, and attributes	NetWare Administrator, MS Windows, Filer, NDIR
	Modify directory information such as last access date, owner, and attributes	NetWare Administrator, MS Windows, Filer
	Create a directory	NetWare Administrator, MS Windows, Filer
	Rename a directory	NetWare Administrator, MS Windows, Filer, RENDIR
	Delete the contents of a directory	NetWare Administrator, MS Windows, Filer
	Remove a directory and its contents, including subdirectories	NetWare Administrator, MS Windows, Filer
	Remove multiple directories simultaneously	NetWare Administrator, MS Windows, Filer
Managing Directories	Copy a directory structure (while maintaining all IntranetWare information)	NetWare Administrator, MS Windows, Filer, NCOPY
	Move a directory structure	NetWare Administrator, MS Windows, Filer
Managing files	View file information such as creation date, last access date, owner, and attributes	NetWare Administrator, MS Windows, Filer, NDIR
	Modify file information such as creation date, last access date, owner, and attributes	NetWare Administrator, MS Windows, Filer
	Copy files	NetWare Administrator, MS Windows, Filer, NCOPY

(continued)

TABLE 4.8
IntranetWare File Management Utilities Summary (continued)

MANAGEMENT OBJECT	MANAGEMENT TASK	MANAGEMENT UTILITY
Managing files (continued)	Copy files while preserving IntranetWare attributes	NetWare Administrator, Filer, NCOPY
	Salvage deleted files	NetWare Administrator, Filer
	Purge deleted files	NetWare Administrator, Filer
	Set a file or directory to purge upon deletion	NetWare Administrator, Filer, FLAG

I guess we're done then, huh? Wrong! We haven't journeyed into the mysterious land of drive mapping yet. I'm sure you'd rather not go there, but buck up soldier, you're a CNA—you can handle it. But can your users?

 ZEN

"Fear of success is one of the newest fears that I've heard about lately. I think it's definitely a sign that we're running out of fears. A person suffering from fear of success is scraping the bottom of the fear barrel."

Jerry Seinfeld

► · ◄

Drive Mapping

Drive mapping is one of the great mysteries of life. Forget about the pyramids, alien cornfields, or quarks—drive mapping has them all beat.

It doesn't have to be this way. As a matter of fact, drive mapping is really pretty simple. The problem is that it requires you to unlearn the fundamentals of DOS. Let me explain. In the DOS world, drive letters point to *physical* devices. In Figure 4.34, the A: and B: letters point to floppy drives, C: and D: point to hard drives, and the E: drive is a CD-ROM. Pretty simple, huh? Well, it works fine on workstations, because they typically use multiple storage devices.

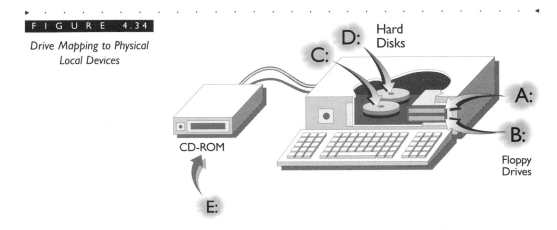

F I G U R E   4.34

Drive Mapping to Physical Local Devices

So, how does this theory apply to IntranetWare drives? If we extrapolate from the local theory, we would use 21 different drive letters (F-Z) to point to 21 physical devices—not very likely. So, Novell returned to the proverbial drawing board and came up with a slightly different approach—just different enough to confuse you, me, CNAs, and especially users. Here's how it works:

IntranetWare drive letters point to logical directories instead of physical drives.

This is also pretty simple; a little too simple (see Figure 4.35). As a matter of fact, users treat the IntranetWare drives just like local drives—*mistake*. The first time they use the CD command, all heck breaks loose. Let me tell you a little story—ironically, about Little John.

One seemingly innocent summer day in August, Little John was working on his financial files in the SYS:SHARED\FIN directory. For his convenience, you have mapped this directory to drive letter G: (see Figure 4.35). He suddenly realizes that his report templates are at home, that is, SYS:USERS\LJOHN (drive map U:). Any other time he would simply type U: and press Enter to get home, but not today. Today he confuses his network and local drives. Today is a bad day for Little John.

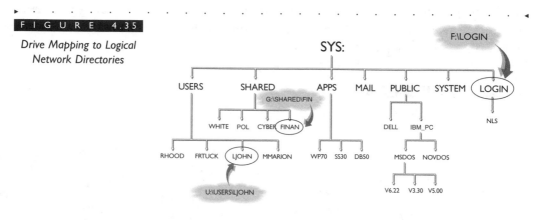

F I G U R E   4.35

Drive Mapping to Logical Network Directories

Instead of using the existing U: drive mapping, Little John types **CD\USERS\LJOHN** from the G: drive. This would work fine in the DOS world, but it's unforgivable in the IntranetWare world. What has he done? Correct. Little John has inadvertently re-mapped his G: drive to SYS:USERS\LJOHN. Remember, IntranetWare drive letters are logical pointers to IntranetWare directories, not physical devices. As you can see in Figure 4.36, Little John now has two letters mapped to his home directory. Of course, he doesn't realize this. Let's return to the story.

Oblivious to the changes in his world, Little John searches the G:\USERS\LJOHN directory for his report templates. He can't find them. "Ah," he thinks. "They're in my home directory. That's drive U:." He quickly switches over to U:\USERS\LJOHN, unaware that this is the same directory. Remember, he thinks the G: and U: drives are different hard disks. He searches in vain and doesn't find the report templates on the U: drive either—he wouldn't. This is where it gets interesting.

Disgruntled, Little John decides to return to his financial directory and continue work without the missing templates. Naturally, he types **G:** and presses Enter to return to the G:\SHARED\FIN directory—it doesn't work. "That's odd," he thinks. "It's always worked before." Much to his dismay, all of the financial files seem to have been removed from the G: drive and replaced by a duplicate copy of his home files. At least that's how it appears to Little John. Remember, he thinks the G: and U: drives are different hard disks. In actuality, Little John has re-mapped the G: drive to G:\USERS\LJOHN with the CD command. Oops.

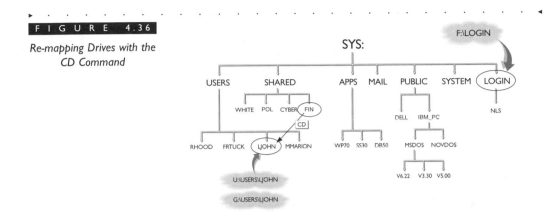

F I G U R E   4.36

Re-mapping Drives with the
CD Command

In a panic, Little John deletes the duplicate copy of his home files—hoping it will clear enough space for his financial files to return. Of course, he has inadvertently deleted *all* his home files, because they are *not* duplicates. It's simply a duplicate drive mapping. He comes rumbling down the hall to your office, screaming at the top of his lungs, "Somebody has deleted my financial files!" Incidentally, Little John is not a little man. After picking yourself off the floor, you proceed to explain to him that the IntranetWare CD command doesn't change directories as it does in DOS. Instead, it *cancels data*. Of course this is a lie, but it stops him from using the CD command in the future. Fortunately, you're a CNA and you can save the day! Use SALVAGE to undelete his files and MAP to return G: back to G:\SHARED\FIN where it belongs. Just another day in the life of a IntranetWare CNA.

ZEN

"I once had a leather jacket that got ruined in the rain. Now why does moisture ruin leather? Aren't cows outside a lot of the time?"

Jerry Seinfeld

This story has been brought to you by IntranetWare and your local neighborhood DMV (Drive Mapping Vehicle). It's a great example of what can happen when users get local and network drive mappings confused. For this reason, you have a choice to make: Do you perpetuate the myth or tell your users the truth? If you perpetuate the myth that IntranetWare drives point to physical disks, you'll need to use the MAP ROOT command to make them appear as such.

This will also nullify the effects of CD. If you decide to tell your users the truth, consider that knowledge is power. Also consider that they may not want to know the truth. Either way, IntranetWare provides you with three different approaches to drive mapping:

- ▸ Network Drive Mapping

- ▸ Search Drive Mapping

- ▸ Directory Map Objects

Network drives use a single letter to point to logical directory paths. The previous example uses network drives. *Search* drives, on the other hand, provide additional functionality by building a search list for network applications. Finally, *Directory Map objects* are centralized NDS resources that point to logical directory paths. They help ease the transition from one application version to another. Let's take a closer look.

NETWORK DRIVE MAPPINGS

Network drive mappings have a singular purpose—convenience. They provide simple directory navigation for accessing data files. As we learned earlier, IntranetWare supports 21 network drives by default: F-Z. In Figure 4.35, the F: drive points to SYS:LOGIN and the U: drive points to SYS:USERS\LJOHN. These mappings make it easy for users to find their stuff—as long as they don't use the dreaded CD command. Little John simply types **U:** followed by Enter to get home to U:\USERS\LJOHN. Without drive mappings, movement throughout the directory tree would be cumbersome and time consuming. It would involve long path names and confusing directory searches. Yuck!

TIP

On DOS and MS Windows clients, the availability of network drives is dictated by the NetWare DOS Requester configuration at the workstation. By default, the VLMs specify F: as the first network drive. You can change this by removing the FIRST NETWORK DRIVE = F statement from NET.CFG. As a matter of fact, you can use 26 network drive letters by overwriting all existing local drives. Cool!

Network drive mappings are user-specific, temporary environment variables. Each user has a different set of drive mappings within his or her workstation RAM. These mappings are created each time the user logs in. When the user logs out or turns off the machine, these mappings are lost. For this reason, you'll want to automate the creation of drive mappings in Container and Profile login scripts (see Chapter 6). Also, you can place your mappings in the Windows 95 Registry and make them permanent. This way, they'll always be available when you access the network.

Network drive mappings are created using the MAP command. We'll explore this command in depth later in this chapter. For now, consider creating any or all of the following drive mappings for your users:

▸ U:—each user's home directory (for example, SYS:USERS\LJOHN)

▸ F:—SYS.LOGIN

▸ G:—group-specific data directories (for example, SYS:SHARED\FINAN)

▸ H:—global shared directory (for example, SYS:SHARED)

Now, let's expand our understanding of IntranetWare drive mapping with search drives. They help us build an internal search list for network applications.

SEARCH DRIVE MAPPINGS

Search drive mappings extend one step beyond network mappings by helping users search for network applications. When a user executes an application, IntranetWare searches two places for the program file:

1 • The current directory.

2 • The internal IntranetWare search list. Search drive mappings build the internal search list. They are the IntranetWare equivalent of local PATH statements.

>
>
> **TIP**
>
> **Most DOS applications cannot access IntranetWare volumes by their volume name. Instead, they typically rely on network and search drive mappings.**

The beauty of the IntranetWare search list is that it allows you to prioritize application directories. IntranetWare searches for programs in the order in which they are listed. The list can be a combination of local and network directories. For example, the following search list would find Windows on the local drive first; otherwise, it would use the network version in SYS:APPS\WINDOWS:

```
S1:=SYS:PUBLIC

S2:=SYS:PUBLIC\IBM_PC\MSDOS\V6.22

S3:=C:\WINDOWS

S4:=SYS:APPS\WINDOWS

S5:=SYS:APPS\SS30
```

Because search drive mappings are primarily used to build search lists, you should be more concerned with the order of the list than with the letter assigned to each directory. As you can see from this list, IntranetWare assigns search drive mappings in search order—and each is preceded by the letter S. As a matter of convenience, IntranetWare also automatically assigns a drive letter to each search directory—in reverse order (to avoid using network drive letters). For example, the first search drive (S1:) inherits the letter Z:, the second mapping (S2:) gets the letter Y:, and so on (see Figure 4.37). This allows you to navigate through search directories if necessary, although I don't recommend it. You are limited to a total of 16 search drives that inherit network drive letters. That is, you can have more than 16 search drives, but the extra ones will have to point to already-existing drive letters—such as C:.

> **TIP**
>
> **If a search drive encounters an existing network drive letter, the drive skips the letter and inherits the next one. For this reason, you should always assign network drive mappings first.**

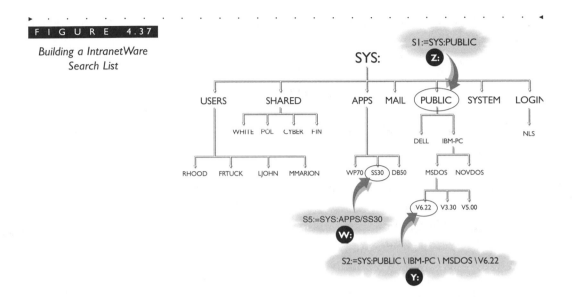

*Building a IntranetWare
Search List*

Because the IntranetWare search list and DOS PATH statements accomplish the same thing, there's a little conflict of interest. As a matter of fact, the IntranetWare search list systematically eliminates directories in the DOS path. To avoid this problem, consider incorporating your DOS path into the IntranetWare search list. This is accomplished using the MAP INSERT command (see the "Drive Mapping" section).

This completes our discussion of network and search drive mappings. Refer to Table 4.9 for a summary of how they work.

*Comparing Network and
Search Drive Mappings*

FUNCTION	NETWORK DRIVE MAPPING	SEARCH DRIVE MAPPING
Purpose	Movement	Searching
Assignment Method	As the letter	In search order
Letter Assignment	By you	By IntranetWare
First Letter	F:	Z:
Directory Types	Data	Applications

Now, let's take a moment to explore Directory Map objects before we dive into the MAP command.

DIRECTORY MAP OBJECTS

In earlier chapters, we learned about a special NDS leaf object that helped us deal with drive mapping in the IntranetWare file system—the Directory Map object. This special-purpose object allows us to map to a central logical resource instead of to the physical directory itself, mainly because physical directories change and logical objects don't have to.

This level of independence is very useful. Let's say, for example, that you have a central application server in the TOKYO container that everybody points to. On the server is an older copy of WordPerfect (WP5). You have two options for adding this application to your internal search lists:

1 • Search Drive Mapping—Use a traditional search drive mapping in each container's login script (five of them). This mapping would point to the physical directory itself—TOKYO-SRV1\SYS:APPS\WP5.

2 • Directory Map Object—Create a central Directory Map object in TOKYO called WPAPP. Then, each of the five search drive MAP commands can point to the logical object instead of the physical APPS\WP directory. Finally, here the WPAPP object points to the physical directory as TOKYO-SRV1\SYS:APPS\WP5.

Both of these scenarios accomplish the same thing: They create a search drive mapping to WordPerfect 5 for all users in the Tokyo location. But, once you upgrade WordPerfect, you'll find the second option is much more attractive. In the first scenario, you'll need to change five different search drive statements in five distributed login scripts on five different servers. This is a lot of work!

In the second scenario, however, you'll only need to change the one Directory Map object reference, and all the other MAP statements will automatically point to the right place. Amazing! In the next section, we'll explore the MAP command and learn how it can be used to reference Directory Map objects.

ZEN

"The movie ad I don't get is this one: 'If you see only one movie this year . . . . ' Why go at all? You're not going to enjoy it—there's too much pressure. You're sitting there, 'Alright, this is it for 51 more weekends, this better be good!'"

Jerry Seinfeld

MAPPING DRIVES WITH MAP

So, now that you know everything there is to know about network, search, and NDS drive mappings, the next logical question is, "How?" It's simple—the MAP command. The IntranetWare MAP command allows you to

- ▶ View drive mappings

- ▶ Create or modify network or search drive mappings

- ▶ Point to Directory Map objects

- ▶ Map drives to a fake root—to fool users or install special applications

- ▶ Change mappings from one type to another

- ▶ Integrate the network and local search lists

- ▶ All sorts of other stuff

TIP

The DOS CD command will change the MAP assignment in the DOS window, but not in the current Windows applications. Also, the MAP command is faster than CD because it has drive letters. Finally, the IntranetWare MAP command is most like the DOS SUBST command.

As I'm sure you've probably guessed, the MAP command is the heart and soul of IntranetWare drive mapping. Now, let's take a closer look at some fun and exciting MAP commands—starting with plain, old MAP. Also, there's a MAP summary table at the end of this section for your review. Ready, set, MAP!

MAP

You can use the MAP command without any options to display a list of your current drive mappings. As you can see in Figure 4.38, the local drives (A: through E:) are listed first, followed by the network drives, and finally, the search drives. Also, note the cool dashes in the middle. They separate the network drives from the search drives.

F I G U R E   4.38

The Plain Old MAP Command

```
U:\USERS\MMARION>MAP

Drives A,B,C,D,E map to a local disk.
Drive F: = WHITE-SRV1_SYS.WHITE.CRIME.TOKYO: \LOGIN
Drive G: = WHITE-SRV1_SYS.WHITE.CRIME.TOKYO: \SHARED\FIN
Drive U: = WHITE-SRV1_SYS.WHITE.CRIME.TOKYO: \USERS\MMARION
  ------      Search Drives    ------
S1: = Z:. [WHITE-SRV1_SYS.WHITE.CRIME.TOKYO: \PUBLIC]
S2: = Y:. [WHITE-SRV1_SYS.WHITE.CRIME.TOKYO: \PUBLIC\IBM_PC\MSDOS\V6.22]
S3: = C:\WINDOWS
S4: = X:. [WHITE-SRV1_SYS.WHITE.CRIME.TOKYO: \APPS\WINDOWS]
S5: = W:. [WHITE-SRV1_SYS.WHITE.CRIME.TOKYO: \APPS\SS30]

U:\USERS\MMARION>
```

TIP

IntranetWare does not track information on local drive assignments. Even though a map list will show that drives A: through E: are assigned to local drives, that doesn't necessarily mean they point to real devices. If you really want to mess with your users, map network drives to local devices. Or, even better, map local drives to network directories.

MAP G:=WHITE-SRV1\SYS:SHARED\FINAN

You can use the MAP command followed by a drive letter (A: through Z:) to create network drive mappings. In this case, the G: drive is assigned to the SYS:SHARED\FIN directory on the WHITE-SRV1 file server.

TIP

We also could have used the relative distinguished name or distinguished name for the volume instead of using the physical volume name. For instance, we could have typed

```
MAP G:=WHITE-SRV1_SYS:SHARED\FIN
```

or

```
MAP G:=.WHITE-SRV1_SYS.WHITE.CRIME.TOKYO.ACME:SHARED\FIN
```

If the G: drive already exists, it will replace the existing assignment without displaying a warning. However, if you attempt to re-map a local drive (that is, Drive A: through Drive E:), you will receive a warning that the drive is currently assigned to a local device. IntranetWare is polite and asks you if you want to assign it to a network drive anyway.

MAP NP E:=SYSMAIL

Using the NP parameter allows you to overwrite local or search drives without being prompted. It must be listed first or second. In this example, the E: drive would be re-mapped without the usual warning:

```
Warning: You are attempting to re-map a local drive.
```

MAP S3:=SYS:APPS\WP70

You can use the MAP SEARCH command followed by a search drive number (S1: through S16:) to map a directory to a specific search drive. The number in the search drive defines the pointer's place in the search list (that is, its priority).

TIP

Search drive mappings share the same environment space as the DOS path. As a result, if you assign a IntranetWare search drive number using the MAP SEARCH command, it will overwrite the corresponding pointer in the DOS path. (For instance, if you use the MAP S1: command, it will overwrite the first pointer in the DOS path.) The only way to retain existing pointers in the DOS path is to use the MAP INS or MAP S16: commands (listed later in this section), which insert new search drives into the DOS path rather than replacing existing ones.

In this example, the SYS:APPS\WP70 directory will be assigned as search drive S3:, which is the third item in the search list. It will also map the directory to the next available drive letter, starting with Z: and moving backward. Review the "Search Drive Mappings" section.

TIP

There is a way to specify which network drive letter is assigned when creating a search drive. In the previous example, if you want to assign network drive letter W: to the S3: search drive, you can use the following command:

```
MAP S3:=W:=APPS\WP70
```

REAL WORLD

A very interesting thing happens if you re-map an existing search drive number. IntranetWare assigns the new directory, as specified, without warning you that an existing search drive with the same number already exists. It does not, however, overwrite the network drive letter that was originally associated with the search drive number. Instead, it assigns a new network drive letter to the new directory and converts the old network drive letter into a full-fledged network drive mapping—thus stripping away its searching ability. Conversely, if you attempt to re-map the network drive associated with a search drive, you will receive a warning that the drive is already in use as a search drive and will be asked if you want to overwrite it. If you say "Yes," both the network drive and its associated search drive will be mapped to the new directory. Weird, huh?

MAP INS S1:=SYS:PUBLIC

The MAP INSERT command can be used to insert a new search drive into the search list, at the number specified, without overwriting an existing drive mapping. All existing search drives below the new pointer are then bumped up one level in the list and renumbered accordingly.

In this example, we are inserting a new drive as S1:. Therefore, IntranetWare bumps up and renumbers all other search drives in the list. Then, it inserts the new drive at the top of the list as search drive S1:.

The interesting thing about this scenario is that it has no effect on existing network drives. All previous drives retain their original drive letters, even though they change positions in the search list.

Earlier, we learned that both the MAP INSERT and MAP S16: commands could be used to preserve the DOS path. This way, when you log off the network, your IntranetWare search drives will be deleted, but your local PATH statements will remain intact. Remember, DOS PATH drives don't count toward your limit of 16 network search drives.

TIP

So, what happens when you mix the MAP INSERT and MAP S16: statements? You create a strange "genetic" breed. The resulting command, MAP INSERT S16: places your search drives in the IntranetWare search list but _after_ the DOS PATH directories. Weird.

QUIZ

One final numbers game: This is one of my personal favorites (see if you can figure out why). Change the position of only _one_ number to make this a palindromic sequence:
1, 4, 2, 9, 6, 1, 5, 10, 4

Hint: When in Rome . . .
(Q4-4)

MAP DEL G:

The MAP DEL command deletes an existing drive mapping. This command can be used with both network and search drive pointers. The MAP REM command performs the same function. Remember, network drive mappings and search drive mappings are deleted automatically if you log off the network or turn off your workstation.

MAP ROOT H:=SYS:ACCT\REPORTS

You can use the MAP ROOT command to create a false root. This command solves user problems like the one we had with Little John. The user sees this drive as if it were the root directory; therefore, he can't wander off too far with the dreaded CD command.

MAP ROOT can also be used for application programs that need to be installed in the root directory. For security reasons and administrative purposes, you should never install applications in the actual root, so here's a great compromise. The Install program thinks it's installing WordPerfect, for example, in the root directory, when it's actually a false root pointing to SYS:APPS.

To determine if a drive mapping is actually a false root, use the MAP command alone. As you can see in Figure 4.39, the H: drive is shown differently than are the other network drives. Instead of showing a blank space between the volume name and the directory name, it shows a blank space followed by a backslash following the directory name. This clues you in that we're dealing with a different breed—a false root.

F I G U R E   4.39

The MAP ROOT Command

```
U:\USERS\MMARION>MAP

Drives A,B,C,D,E map to a local disk.
Drive F: = WHITE-SRV1_SYS.WHITE.CRIME.TOKYO: \LOGIN
Drive G: = WHITE-SRV1_SYS.WHITE.CRIME.TOKYO: \SHARED\FIN
Drive H: = WHITE-SRV1_SYS.WHITE.CRIME.TOKYO:ACCT\REPORTS \
Drive U: = WHITE-SRV1_SYS.WHITE.CRIME.TOKYO: \USERS\MMARION
------     Search Drives     ------
S1: = Z:. [WHITE-SRV1_SYS.WHITE.CRIME.TOKYO: \PUBLIC]
S2: = Y:. [WHITE-SRV1_SYS.WHITE.CRIME.TOKYO: \PUBLIC\IBM_PC\MSDOS\V6.22]
S3: = C:\WINDOWS
S4: = X:. [WHITE-SRV1_SYS.WHITE.CRIME.TOKYO: \APPS\WINDOWS]
S5: = W:. [WHITE-SRV1_SYS.WHITE.CRIME.TOKYO: \APPS\SS30]

U:\USERS\MMARION>
```

MAP N SYS:DATA

You can use the MAP NEXT (N) command to assign the next available drive letter as a network drive mapping. It doesn't work, however, with search drive pointers.

MAP C I:

The MAP CHANGE (C) command can be used to change a regular IntranetWare drive to a search drive, or vice versa. In this example, Drive I: will still point to the same directory to which it was originally assigned, but it would also be added to the end of the IntranetWare search list. Conversely, if you use the MAP CHANGE command with a search drive, the search drive number is deleted from the search list, but the network drive letter originally associated with it is retained as a network drive mapping.

TIP

Although the MAP NEXT command doesn't work with search drives, there is another technique that you can use to achieve the same effect, namely the MAP S16: command. The MAP S16: command assigns the next available search drive number to the specified directory. Because search drives update the DOS Path, IntranetWare does not allow you to assign search drive numbers that would cause holes to exist in the DOS path. For instance, if only search drives S1: through S4: exist, IntranetWare would not let you create search drive S7:. Instead, it would just assign the next search drive number in the list (S5:, in this example).

MAP S5:=.WPAPP.TOKYO.ACME

You can also map a drive to a Directory Map object (WPAPP) instead of to the directory itself. This is especially useful if the directory name changes from time to time—such as every time you upgrade WordPerfect or Microsoft Word—and you don't want to change every MAP statement in every login script.

In this case, you only need to change the reference in the central Directory Map object. All other drive mapping commands will reflect that change instantly. It's fun at parties. But whatever you do, don't place a colon (:) at the end of the Directory Map object.

TIP

Directory Map objects appear as folders in the Windows 95 Network Neighborhood. You can activate them with the Map Network Drive option from the File menu. Also, you can access Directory Map objects on the Resource side of the NetWare User Tools for Windows.

MAP /?

The MAP /? command displays on-line help for all variations of the MAP command.

MAP /VER

The MAP /VER command lists the version of the MAP utility that you are using as well as the files the utility needs to execute. If you use the /VER option, all other parameters will be ignored.

Table 4.10 provides a quick summary of all the really amazing MAP commands you've learned today.

Getting to Know the MAP Commands

COMMAND	RESULT
MAP	Displays a list of current drive mappings.
MAP G:=WHITE-SRV1\SYS:	Maps the G: drive as a network drive that points to SHARED\FINANthe SHARED\FINAN directory on the SYS volume of the WHITE-SRV1 server (using the physical volume name).
MAP G:=.WHITE-SRV1_SYS.WHITE.	Maps the G: drive as a network drive that points to CRIME.TOKYO.ACME:SHARED\FINAN the SHARED\FINAN directory on the SYS volume of the WHITE-SRV1 server (using the Volume object name).
MAP NP E:=SYS:HR\EVAL	Maps the E: drive to the HR\EVAL directory, suppressing the warning that you are about to re-map a local drive.
MAP S3:=SYS:APPS\WP70	Maps the S3: search drive to the SYS:APSS\WP70 directory and assigns the next available drive letter in reverse alphabetical order as a network drive.
MAP S3:=W:=SYS:APPS\WP70	Maps the S3: search drive to the SYS:APPS\WP70 directory and assigns W: as the associated network drive.
MAP INS S1:=SYS:PUBLIC	Inserts a new S1: search drive at the beginning of the search list, renumbering all existing search drives accordingly. Also assigns the next available drive letter in reverse alphabetical order as a network drive.
MAP DEL G:	Deletes the G: network drive (see MAP REM command).
MAP REM G:	Deletes the G: network drive (see MAP DEL command).
MAP ROOT H:=SYS:ACCT\REPORTS	Maps the H: drive as a false root pointing to the ACCT\REPORTS directory.
MAP N SYS:DATA	Maps the next available network drive letter to the SYS:DATA directory.
MAP C I:	Changes the I: network drive to the next available search drive number.

TABLE 4.10

*Getting to Know the MAP
Commands (continued)*

COMMAND	RESULT
MAP C S4:	Changes the S4: search drive to a network drive.
MAP S5:=WPAPP	Maps the S5: search drive to a Directory Map object called WPAPP in the current container.
MAP /?	Displays on-line help information for the MAP command.
MAP /VER	Displays version information about the MAP utility, including the files it needs to execute.

MAPPING DRIVES WITH MS WINDOWS

In addition to the MAP command, IntranetWare allows you to create network and search drive mappings using MS Windows. Specifically, you can use the following two Windows environments:

▸ Windows 95

▸ NetWare User Tools for Windows

Let's take a closer look.

Windows 95 Drive Mappings

In Windows 95, you can use the Network Neighborhood to map network drives to volumes and directories. This facility does *not* allow you to create search drive mappings. To map a network drive in the Windows 95 Network Neighborhood, consult Figure 4.40 and follow these steps:

1 • Select the volume or directory you want to map.

2 • From the File menu, choose "Map Network Drive." The Map Network Drive window appears, showing the path you have selected.

3 • Choose a drive letter.

4 • Select the "Reconnect at Logon" option so that this drive will be available the next time you log in. Incidentally, these permanent settings are stored in the WIN.INI file.

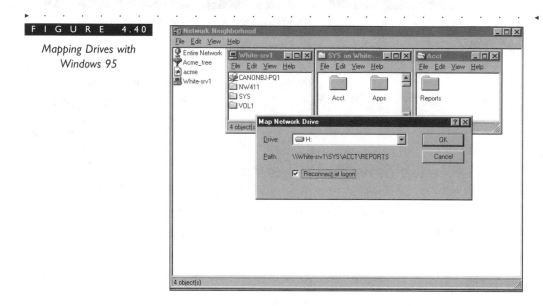

F I G U R E   4 . 40

Mapping Drives with Windows 95

It's important to note that all drive mappings are viewed globally by Client 32. Therefore, any time a drive is mapped within Windows (Windows 95 Network Neighborhood, File Manager, or at the MS-DOS prompt), the drive's accessible and visible everywhere else in Windows. In addition, whenever a drive is changed to a different directory, the directory change affects only that specific instance of the drive. For example, if the drive is changed to the SHARED directory at the MS-DOS prompt, no other MS-DOS prompt or Windows application will display this change. For this reason, you want to be sure to use the Network Neighborhood or NetWare User Tools for Windows utilities.

NetWare User Tools for Windows Drive Mappings

In Windows 3.1, you can change mappings or create new mappings with the NetWare User Tools for Windows interface. Figure 4.41 shows the split screen graphical interface. On the left side is a list of all available drives and on the right side is a list of available resources (volumes and directories).

To map a drive, drag the directory or volume object from the right size of the screen and drop it on top of the drive letter on the left side. (See Figure 4.41)

F I G U R E   4.41

Mapping Drives with NetWare User Tools for Windows

Unlike Windows 95, the NetWare User Tools for Windows utility allows you to create search drives. Follow these simple steps:

1 • Select the drive from the left side of the drive mapping window.

2 • Click the Drive Type button on the bottom of the screen.

3 • In the dialog box that appears, select Search Drive.

4 • Click OK.

This converts an already existing network drive into a IntranetWare search drive.

In addition, NetWare User Tools for Windows allows you to create permanent network or search drive mappings. Like Windows 95, these permanent settings are stored in the WIN.INI file.

In the beginning . . . there was the NDS directory tree. We discovered the [Root], leaf objects, proper naming, and Read/Write replicas. We learned how to name it, partition it, design it, install it, manage it, and groom it. Just when we thought we understood the true meaning of IntranetWare life, another tree appeared—the non-NDS directory tree.

This strange new tree is very different. Instead of a [Root], it has a root; instead of leaves, it has files; and instead of replicas, it has duplexing. But once you get past its rough exterior, you'll see that the non-NDS tree shares the same look and feel as the NDS one. And they approach life together with a similar purpose—to logically organize user resources, except this time the resources are files, not printers.

In this chapter we learned everything there is to know about our non-NDS friend. We learned how to name it, partition it, design it, install it, manage it, and groom it. All in a day's work.

ZEN

Megatrend—A far-reaching or widespread change in society such as the advent of computers and the information revolution, aerobics and physical fitness, microwave ovens and convenience food, or, most importantly, CNAs becoming florists.

So, what does the future hold? Well, now that we've learned everything about NDS and non-NDS trees, we can expand our minds to the rest of IntranetWare management. We will combine our "treeologist" skills and forge ahead into the great CNA abyss:

▶ Security

▶ Configuration

▶ Management

▶ Printing

During your journey through the rest of this book, look back to the fun times you had in gardening class. Count on your NDS and non-NDS gardening skills—because you will need them. Oh yes, you will.

Good luck, and by the way . . . thanks for saving the world.

CASE STUDY: CREATING A DIRECTORY STRUCTURE FOR ACME

You're ready to create the basic file system directory structure for the WHITE-SRV1 server. Using the scenario listed below, design the directory structure on paper first, then use the DOS MD command or the IntranetWare FILER utility to create the directory structure on the system.

As you know, initially, the Crime Fighting division, the White-Collar Crime depart-ment, and the three White-Collar Crime units (Cyber Crime, Financial Crime, and Political Crime) will all be sharing the same server (WHITE-SRV1.WHITE.CRIME.TOKYO.ACME). Although there will be some sharing of programs and data, each group will essentially function as an independent workgroup with a separate network administrator.

Because the WHITE-SRV1 server has already been installed, the system-created LOGIN, SYSTEM, PUBLIC, MAIL, and ETC directories already exist.

The USERS directory should be created in the root of the volume. It will serve as the parent directory for the home directories for each user. (The home directories will be created when you actually create the users at a later time). Each of the workgroups will have access to the SHARED directory, which will be located in the root of the volume. This directory will be used for the sharing of files between workgroups. In addition, each workgroup will have exclusive access to its own group directory under the SHARED directory (called WHITE, CYBER, FIN, and POL, respectively).

The users in the various workgroups will be running different versions of DOS. Although each user will normally run DOS off his/her local workstation, there will also be a copy of each DOS version stored on the server in case anything happens to the copy on a particular workstation. Because the DOS versions differ in manufacturer, type, and version, you will want to use the standard DOS directory structure recommended by Novell (that is, a three-level directory structure under the SYS:PUBLIC directory: the machine type on the first level, the DOS type on the second level, and the DOS version on the third). So far, you know that there will be:

- Two types of machines (DELL and IBM_PC)

- Two types of DOS (MSDOS and NOVDOS)

- Three versions of MSDOS (v3.30, v5.00, and v6.22).

The first three applications that will be installed on the server include:

▶ A word processing application (in the WP70 directory)

▶ A spreadsheet application (in the SS30 directory)

▶ A database application (in the DB50 directory)

Each of these subdirectories will be stored under the APPS directory, which will be located in the root of the volume.

The answer to this case study is located in Appendix C.

EXERCISE 4-1: MAPPING DRIVES WITH MAP

Follow the steps listed below to create sample drive mappings for the directory structure that was created in the case study titled "Creating a Directory Structure for ACME."

1. Display on-line help information for the MAP command.

2. Display your current drive mappings.

3. Map drive F: to the USERS directory. (Normally, it would point to each user's individual home directory, but they have not been created yet.)

4. Map drive G: to the POL subdirectory under the SHARED directory, using the physical name of the volume.

5. Map the J: drive to the same directory as the F: drive.

6. Map drive S: to the SHARED directory, using the Volume object name.

7. Map the S1: search drive to the SYS:PUBLIC directory without overwriting the existing pointers in the DOS path.

8. Map the S2: search drive to the V6.22 directory without overwriting the existing pointers in the DOS path.

9. Map the S3: search drive to the SS30 subdirectory.

10. Map the S4: search drive as a false root to the DB50 subdirectory.

11. Display your current drive mappings again. How does the system indicate a false root?

12. Map the S5: search drive to the WP70 subdirectory, specifying that W: be assigned as the associated network drive. Did it work?

13. To view the effect of the CD command on search drive mappings, switch to the Z: drive. Type CD .. and press Enter to switch to the root directory. Type the MAP command to list your current drive mappings. What happened? What should be done to fix the problem? Fix the problem.

14. Delete the J: drive.

15. Delete the S3: search drive using a different command than you did in Step 14. What happened to your other search drive mappings? What happened to the network drive associated with those search drives?

16. Change the S4: drive from a search drive to a network drive. What happened to the search drive itself? What happened to the network drive associated with it?

17. First volume on every IntranetWare server.

18. A directory that contains operating system files, NLMs, and administrator utilities.

19. The highest level in the IntranetWare file system.

See Appendix C for answers.

EXERCISE 4-2: MAPPING DRIVES WITH MS WINDOWS

In addition to the MAP command, IntranetWare allows you to create network and search drive mappings using MS Windows. Specifically, you can use the following two Windows environments:

▸ Windows 95

▸ NetWare User Tools for Windows

Let's run these utilities for a test drive (*pun intended*).

Mapping Network Drives with Windows 95

In Windows 95, you can use the Network Neighborhood to map network drives to volumes and directories. To map a network drive in Network Neighborhood, perform the following steps:

1. Double-click on the Network Neighborhood icon on your Windows 95 desktop. Double-click on the server icon. Double-click on the SYS: volume icon. Click on the folder corresponding to the PUBLIC directory.

2. Choose "Map Network Drive . . . " from the File menu. The Map Network Drive window appears, showing the path you have selected.

3. The next available network drive letter will be displayed. If you wish to choose a different drive letter, key it in, or click on one from the list (see Figure 4.40).

4. Click on the "Reconnect at logon" option so that this drive will be available the next time you log in. Click on OK to map the drive. Back out of this utility by clicking on the Close button in the upper-right corner of each of the open windows relating to this utility.

Mapping Drives with NetWare User Tools for Windows

In Windows 3.1, you can change mappings or create new mappings with the NetWare User Tools for Windows. Figure 4.41 shows the mappings with the graphical interface. To map a drive to a directory or volume listed on the right side of the window, you can drag the directory or volume over to the drive letter on the left side.

It's as simple as that!

In this exercise, we will use the MS Windows-based graphical NetWare Administrator utility to manage IntranetWare directories and files. First, we will create an ADMIN subdirectory under the USERS subdirectory, then we'll create subdirectories and files under the ADMIN directory. Finally, we will manipulate the files and directories we have created under the ADMIN directory using NetWare Administrator.

Follow these simple steps very carefully:

1. Run NetWare Administrator. Execute the NetWare Administrator utility. The contents of your Directory tree should be displayed.

2. Open an independent browse window for the SYS: volume. Click on the SYS volume icon. Select NDS Browser from the Tools menu and click on OK. This will set the current context for this browse window to that of the SYS: volume.

3. Create an ADMIN directory under the SYS: volume. Double-click on the SYS volume to see its contents. Click on the USERS directory using the right mouse button. Choose Create from the pull-down menu. Type **ADMIN** in the Directory name field, then click on Create to create the directory. Finally, double-click on the USERS directory to open it and see its contents.

4. Create the following three directories under the ADMIN directory: PROJECT1, PROJECT2, and PROJECT3.

   a. Create the PROJECT1 directory. Click on the ADMIN directory to select it. Press the Ins key or select Create from the Object menu. Type **PROJECT1** in the Directory name field. Click on the "Create another Directory" box, then click on Create to create the PROJECT1 directory.

b. Create the PROJECT2 directory. Enter **PROJECT2** in the Directory name field, then click on Create to create the PROJECT2 directory.

c. Create the PROJECT3 directory. Enter **PROJECT3** in the Directory name field, then click on the "Create another Directory" box to turn off the feature. Finally, click on Create to create the PROJECT3 directory.

d. Double-click on the ADMIN directory to view the directories you have just created.

5. Open a second browse window for the SYS: volume. Click on the SYS volume icon. Select NDS Browser from the Tools menu and click on OK. This will set the current context for this browse window to that of the SYS: volume. Select the Tile option under the Window menu to reshape the browse windows and view the contents of all three windows at the same time.

6. Display the contents of the ETC directory in the second browse window. Double-click on the ETC directory to open the directory and see its contents.

7. Copy each of the following files in the ETC directory to the corresponding directory you created in Step 4:

   ▸ ATTYPES.CFG to the PROJECT1 directory

   ▸ BUILTINS.CFG to the PROJECT2 directory

   ▸ TRAPTARG.CFG to the PROJECT3 directory

  a. Copy the files. Drag the ATTYPES.CFG file from the source
browser window to the PROJECT1 directory in the target
browser window. You'll notice that the Copy button is selected
by default. Click on OK to copy the file. Repeat this same
procedure for the remaining two files—making sure to drop
each one in the appropriate directory.

  b. Confirm the files were copied. Double-click on each destination
directory to confirm that the files were copied successfully.

  c. Close the source browser window. Click on the Close button in
the upper-right of the browser window that shows the contents
of the ETC directory.

8. Move the BUILTINS.CFG and TRAPTARG.CFG files from the
PROJECT2 and PROJECT3 directories to the PROJECT1 directory.
Click on the BUILTINS.CFG file. Hold down the Ctrl key and click the
TRAPTARG.CFG file. Continue to hold down the Ctrl key and drag the
files on top of the PROJECT1 directory. You'll notice that the move
button is automatically activated. Click on OK to move the files to the
PROJECT1 directory.

9. Rename the PROJECT1 directory to DONE1. Click on the PROJECT1
directory. Select Rename from the Object menu. Type **DONE1** in the
New name field, then click on OK to rename the directory.

10. Copy the DONE1 directory and its contents to the PROJECT2
directory. Drag the DONE1 directory onto the PROJECT2 directory,
then click on OK to confirm the copy.

11. Move the new DONE1 directory and its contents from the PROJECT2
directory to the PROJECT3 directory. Double-click on the PROJECT2
directory to open the directory and see its contents. Click on the
DONE1 directory under the PROJECT2 directory and hold down the
mouse button. While holding down the Ctrl key, drag the DONE1
directory from the PROJECT2 directory to the PROJECT3 directory,
then click on OK to confirm the move.

12. Set the Purge attribute for the TRAPTARG file under the PROJECT3\DONE1 directory. Double-click on the PROJECT3 directory and the DONE1 subdirectory to open them and see their contents. Double-click on the TRAPTARG.TXT file under the PROJECT3/DONE1 directory. Click on the Attributes page button. Click on the Purge Immediately attribute, then click on OK.

13. Simultaneously delete the three files in the PROJECT3/DONE1 directory. Click on the first filename listed. While holding down the Shift key, click on the last filename listed. Press the Del key, then select Yes when prompted to confirm the deletion.

14. Salvage the files you deleted in Step 13.

   a. Salvage the files. Click on the DONE1 directory under the PROJECT3 directory. Select Salvage from the Tools menu. Click on the List button at the top left of the window. You'll notice that TRAPTARG.CFG is unavailable for salvaging because you set it to "immediate purge" before deleting it. Click on the *first filename*. While holding down the Shift key, click the *second name*, then click the Salvage button. Click on the Close button to close the salvage window.

   b. Confirm the deletion. Double-click on the DONE1 directory to confirm that the two files have been salvaged.

EXERCISE 4-4: INTRANETWARE FILE CABINET

Circle the 20 IntranetWare File System terms hidden in this word search puzzle using the hints provided.

```
S  Y  S  T  E  M  C  T  E  R  R  B
Y  E  U  U  J  N  E  Q  E  K  B  U
S  N  E  A  K  E  R  N  E  T  S  R
I  W  L  L  S  J  Q  X  Y  F  Q  Z
X  A  U  C  P  P  T  V  Q  L  V  G
T  D  E  L  E  T  E  D  S  A  V  C
E  M  Z  O  V  X  V  M  W  G  P  Q
E  I  F  N  C  O  P  Y  P  L  U  N
N  N  I  G  O  L  P  R  I  B  G
R  I  D  N  L  S  D  U  A  A  L  Q
V  Q  U  E  U  E  S  I  M  M  I  K
T  A  N  B  H  K  R  W  M  E  C  D
```

Hints:

1. Directory that contains deleted files from directories that no longer exist.
2. Directory that contains IntranetWare on-line documentation files.
3. Directory that contains sample programs for use in configuring the network for TCP/IP.
4. IntranetWare file management menu utility that can be used to salvage and purge files.
5. Command line utility that can be used for assigning directory or file attributes.
6. The only directory available to users prior to login.
7. This directory may or may not contain User ID subdirectories.
8. Command line utility used for assigning network or search drive mappings.
9. Command line utility that be used for copying files from one location to another.

10. Command line utility that can be used to selectively list volume, directory, and file information.
11. Directory that contains subdirectories for different languages.
12. MS Windows-based file management utility.
13. Directory that contains IntranetWare utilities available to network users.
14. Directory that contains print queue subdirectories.
15. Another name for Redundant Array of Inexpensive Disks.
16. Maximum number of network search drives available.
17. Process used for filesharing before the advent of LANs.
18. First volume on every IntranetWare server.
19. A directory that contains operating system files, NLMs, and administrator utilities.
20. The highest level in the IntranetWare file system.

See Appendix C for answers.

IntranetWare Security

"You won't find a more secure system anywhere."

Security is an interesting thing. Everyone wants it but how much are you willing to pay? On the one extreme, you could live in a titanium vault—secure, but very uncomfortable. On the other extreme, you could live in a 1960s Woodstock fantasy—fun, but way too risky. No, I believe you live somewhere in between. Whether you know it or not, your security requirements fall in a spectrum between a titanium vault and the 1960s. The key to security is gauging the range of your boundaries.

Goal: *Let the good guys in and keep the bad guys out!*

Security in the Information Age poses an even more interesting challenge. Computers and communications have made it possible to collect volumes of data about you and me—from our last purchase at the five-and-dime to our detailed medical records. Privacy has become a commodity to be exchanged on the open market. Information is no longer the fodder of afternoon talk shows. It has become *the* unit of exchange for the 21st Century, more valuable than money.

A recent study has shown that 92 percent of the Fortune 500 companies think security is important enough to do something about. Even the government is getting involved with the "clipper chip" and other anti-theft policies. I bet you thought you left cops and robbers behind in childhood. Well, this is a variation on the game and the stakes are very high. As a CNA, it is your responsibility to design, install, and manage the IntranetWare network. But, most importantly, you must protect it. You need a brain filled with sophisticated security strategies and a utility belt full of advanced protection tools. Think of this chapter as your impenetrable network armor.

IntranetWare security is, in general, fairly good. But for many of today's WANs, it's not good enough. As a matter of fact, most of NetWare's security features need to be "turned on." It's not secure right out of the box. A truly *secure* network protects more than just user data—it protects everything! So, what is "everything"? The definition of "everything" has changed in IntranetWare. Now the world exists in a nebulous cloud full of Tupperware containers and User objects. As the IntranetWare universe becomes more open and interconnected, security becomes more and more important.

So, what is "security"? Simply stated, security is freedom from risk. Therefore, network security can be considered as any effort you take to protect your network from risk. Of course, it's difficult to protect your network from things you cannot see or understand. So, the first thing you need to do in developing a security model is to learn about risks.

So, what is "risk"? Risk is a combination of value and threat. The value you determine is the cost of your network resources should you lose them. Value extends well beyond monetary value—it encompasses data integrity, confidentiality, and the value of data to competitors. Threats are more difficult to define. They come from a variety of different sources, including people, technology, and the environment. The very nature of computer networks puts them at continual risk. In summary, sharing data makes it harder to protect data. Of course, you don't have a choice. The first step toward true network security is *risk analysis*.

The goal of risk analysis is to define your network security principles and identify the threats against them. A "threat" is a person, place, or thing that poses some danger to a network asset. Threats can be physical (file servers and workstations), topology (wire tapping), network-related (back/trapdoors, impersonation, and piggybacking), data (logic bombs and Trojan horses), and people (intentional sabotage or unintentional bumbling).

The goal of your threat-based security model is to determine how likely your network is to experience any of these threats. What are the chances, for example, that your system has a back/trapdoor in place? Is wiretapping a possibility? How about impersonation or, even worse, logic bombs? The best approach is to make a realistic judgment of each threat's probability on your WAN. This becomes the foundation of your network's risk index. You can then use this index to develop a successful system of security countermeasures.

Countermeasures are actions that create a protective barrier against network threats. In many cases, countermeasures can reduce the probability of serious threats. In addition, vulnerability decreases as countermeasures increase. There is, however, never a vulnerability level of zero because countermeasures themselves have vulnerabilities built in. The bad news is that countermeasures cost money. As a matter of fact, the more serious the threat, the higher the cost of the countermeasure. Because it's difficult to quantify the decrease in threat probability due to countermeasures, cost justification becomes a challenge. But all in all, countermeasures are necessary to keep your network running, and, therefore, money must be spent on them. After all, money makes the world go 'round.

SMART LINK

Download and Read "The Orange Book" of security from http://www.sevenlocks.com/evaluati.htm.

As a CNA, it's your job to identify network threats and implement appropriate countermeasures to eliminate them. This isn't easy. You have many factors working against you—including money, office politics, and user productivity. But there are some quick and easy countermeasures that can dramatically improve your network security:

▶ Restrict physical access to file servers. In Chapter 7, we'll learn a few strategies for physical file server protection.

▶ One of your network's most insecure entry points is through virtual links.

▶ Consider using dial-back systems with multilayered password protection. Remember, anyone with a modem and phone line can gain access to your network.

▶ Background authentication and NCP packet signing protect data packets as they travel over topology lines. In addition, data is encrypted for further protection.

▶ Many advanced routers allow you to filter SAPs, RIPs, and specific frame types. Consider filtering non-essential packets to increase performance and keep out the bad guys.

▶ Don't use the Supervisor or Admin accounts—use an equivalent instead. Also, don't delete the original Admin account once you have made yourself equivalent. There's some existentialist ramifications in there somewhere.

▶ Always create a backdoor. Consider using Alt+255 as a null character. It's hard to track. The beauty of null characters is they appear as spaces.

Intruders will see a username or password with a space and never assume it's a null character. Also, many times you can't tell how many null characters are involved—especially when they're sequentially added to the end of a username.

▸ IntranetWare includes an extensive auditing system that allows you to audit login events as well as file/directory events. Use it!

▸ Consider restricting the following file server access rights: Supervisor, Access Control, and Modify [SAM].

▸ Track rights carefully and make sure you know what you're doing before you get started. Calculating effective rights can be very tricky, especially if you use an Inherited Rights Filter (IRF). Many times users end up with rights they shouldn't have.

▸ Classify people into security levels and identify the highest security risks, then implement countermeasures against these people, including training sessions, tracking, or extensive auditing.

▸ Be careful when assigning distributed administrative responsibility. Remember, power corrupts and absolute power corrupts absolutely.

Well, there you go. Risk analysis and countermeasures. These are key factors in protecting your IntranetWare WAN. Sometimes, however, IntranetWare security isn't good enough. You need to develop appropriate countermeasures for *all* network threats, not just a few. After all, the '60s was a great decade but welcome to the '90s. This is the Information Age and your data is a valuable commodity.

Fortunately, IntranetWare has a dramatically improved security model for creating and maintaining your impenetrable network armor. This model allows us to perform risk analysis at five different levels. It also includes numerous countermeasures for dealing with "bad guys." Whatever you do, don't let this information fall into the wrong hands. Let's take a closer look.

ZEN

As you progress through this chapter, you'll find that "true security" is a mystery. What is it? How do you get it? Many times, it's not what it seems. You'll find it in the least likely places. As an example, let's rewind a few years to one of the greatest mysteries of our time—"Who shot Mr. Burns?" It all started with a simple question, from a key witness: "Who shot who in the what, now?"

Old Man

SMART LINK

Surf the Web with Homer, Marge, Bart, Lisa, and Maggie at http://www.foxinteractive.com.

IntranetWare Security Model

IntranetWare improves on earlier NetWare security models by adding supplemental front-end barriers for filtering unauthorized users. Once again, the same security goal applies:

Let the good guys in and keep the bad guys out!

As you can see in Figure 5.1, the IntranetWare security model consists of five different barriers. They are

1 • Login/Password Authentication

2 • Login Restrictions

3 • NDS Security

4 • File System Access Rights

5 • Directory/File Attributes

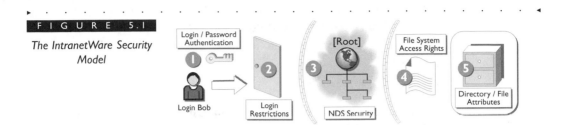

FIGURE 5.1

The IntranetWare Security Model

As you can see, each layer creates an increasingly strong barrier against user access. Each time you pass through a door, you are greeted with an even stronger barrier. This works much the same way as the opening to the TV show *Get Smart*. Maxwell would have to travel through numerous barriers until he finally reached the telephone booth. After entering the correct code, he was allowed access to Control headquarters. Users pass through similar barriers on their way to the ultimate prize—data.

Let's take a quick look.

LAYER ONE—LOGIN/PASSWORD AUTHENTICATION

As you can see from Figure 5.1, it all starts with login/password authentication. Remember, users don't log into NetWare servers anymore—they log into the "Cloud." First, the user requests access by typing **LOGIN** followed by a valid username. Once this occurs, authentication begins. There are two phases:

▶ Initialization—The server and workstation authenticate the session with an encrypted key. You are required to enter a valid password to decrypt the key.

▶ Background—IntranetWare continues to attach the key to all messages to ensure data integrity. This process is known as *background authentication*. In addition, you can enhance background security with a related feature called *NCP packet signing*. We'll explore both features later in this chapter. In addition to authentication, IntranetWare accepts passwords up to 127 characters. This is a substantial improvement over earlier versions. The limit is decreased significantly, though, for Macintosh clients. Once you have been authenticated, IntranetWare matches you against a list of global and personal login restrictions. These restrictions allow for conditional access according to a variety of criteria. That's Layer One.

WHAT'S NEW

This process occurs the same way for Client 32, except that it's a little more hidden behind GUI "windows."

LAYER TWO—LOGIN RESTRICTIONS

Once you provide a valid login name and password, you are authenticated. Congratulations! IntranetWare responds with conditional access and NDS rights take over. At this point, I stress the word *conditional* access. Permanent access is made possible by a variety of login restrictions. These login restrictions include:

▸ Account Restrictions—includes anything from "Account locked" to "Force periodic password changes"

▸ Password Restrictions—includes "Minimum password length" and "Force unique passwords"

▸ Station Restrictions—limits users to specific workstation node IDs

▸ Time Restrictions—determines when users can and cannot use the system

▸ Intruder Detection/Lockout—a global feature that detects incorrect password attempts and locks bad guys out

Each of these restrictions are configured by *you* using a variety of IntranetWare tools, including NWADMIN and NETADMIN. We'll learn all the details of how and why later in this chapter.

LAYER THREE—NDS SECURITY

Once you enter the "Cloud," your ability to access leaf and container objects is determined by a sophisticated NDS security structure. At the heart of NDS security is the Access Control List (ACL). The ACL is a property of every NDS object. It defines who can access the object (trustees) and what each trustee can do (rights). The ACL is divided into two types of rights:

- ▶ Object Rights—Defines an object's trustees and controls what the trustees can do with the object.

- ▶ Property Rights—Limits the trustees' access to only specific properties of the object.

Here's a great example (see Figure 5.2). Let's say the Group object Admin-Group has rights to the User object LEIA. Admin-Group has the Browse object right, which means that any member of the group can see LEIA and view information about her. But LEIA is shy. She wants to limit what the group can see (reasonable enough). She only wants them to see her last name, postal address, and telephone number. So, LEIA limits the group's rights by assigning the Read property right to only these three properties: Last Name, Postal Address, and Telephone Number. No sweat.

▶ · ◀

FIGURE 5.2

Understanding NDS Security

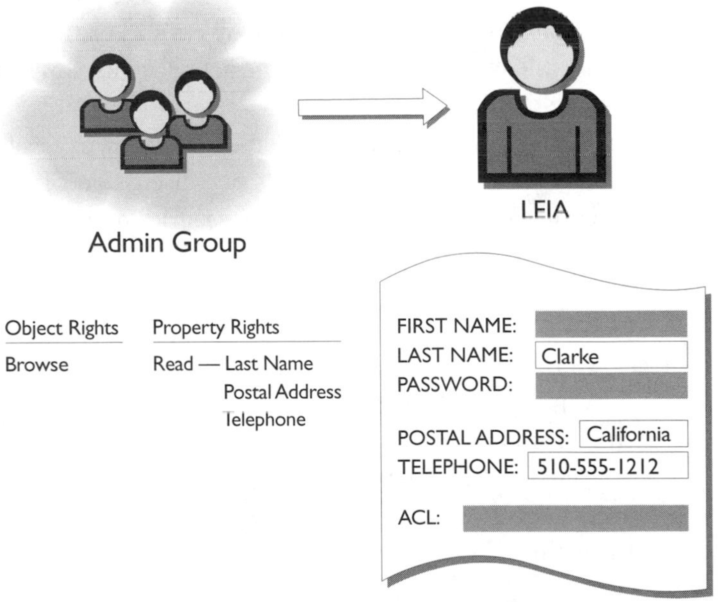

Admin Group

LEIA

Object Rights	Property Rights
Browse	Read — Last Name
	Postal Address
	Telephone

FIRST NAME:
LAST NAME: Clarke
PASSWORD:

POSTAL ADDRESS: California
TELEPHONE: 510-555-1212

ACL:

Object and property rights are designed to provide efficient access to NDS objects without making it an administrative nightmare. You be the judge. Users can acquire object rights in a variety of ways, including trustee assignment, inheritance, and security equivalence. Property rights, on the other hand, are a bit trickier. Global property rights can be inherited, but rights to specific properties must be granted through a trustee assignment.

Trustee assignments occur when an object is given explicit access to any other object or its properties. These trustee assignments are administered by adding the user to a host object's ACL property. This is accomplished using the NWADMIN or NETADMIN utilities.

Inheritance is a little simpler. If rights are granted at the container level, they are inherited by all container and leaf objects within. This means that rights assigned to the [Root] object, for example, are inherited by every object in the NDS tree. Be very careful. Fortunately, IntranetWare includes an Inherited Rights Filter (IRF), which can be used to block inherited rights.

Finally, there's *security equivalence*. This means objects can absorb rights by being associated with other objects. Sometimes the associations are obvious, but most of the time, they're not. For this reason, you should only use security equivalences for temporary assignments, or not at all. In reality, users can inherit rights ancestrally from containers, groups, organizational roles, and [Public].

Regardless of how you acquire object and property rights, the concept of *effective rights* still applies. This means the actual rights you can exercise with a given object are the combination of explicit trustee assignments, inheritance, and the IRF. The mathematical product of this mess is known as *effective NDS rights*—"modern math." And that effectively ends our discussion of NDS security and moves us on to Layer Four of the IntranetWare security model—file system access rights.

LAYER FOUR—FILE SYSTEM ACCESS RIGHTS

Well, here we are. Congratulations! You've finally made it to IntranetWare Nirvana. You've passed through three very difficult barriers of network armor and the search is over—your files await you. Ah, but not so fast! Before you can access any files on the IntranetWare server, you must have the appropriate file system access rights. Once again, another barrier pops up to bite you. Following is a list of the eight rights that control access to IntranetWare files (they almost spell a word):

▸ W—Write: Grants the right to open and change the contents of files.

▸ (O)—Doesn't exist but is needed to spell a word.

▸ R—Read: Grants the right to open files in the directory and read their contents (or run applications).

▸ M—Modify: Grants the right to change the attributes or name of a file or directory.

▸ F—File Scan: Grants the right to see files and directories.

▸ A—Access Control: Grants the right to change trustee assignments and IRFs.

▸ C Create: Grants the right to create new files and subdirectories.

▸ E—Erase: Grants the right to delete a directory, its files, and subdirectories.

▸ S—Supervisor: Grants all rights to a directory and the files and subdirectories below. This right cannot be blocked by the IRF.

Holy anatomical nematodes, Batman! That spells "WoRMFACES." It's not a pretty sight but certainly a name you will not forget. IntranetWare file system access rights are administered in much the same way as NDS object rights. They are granted with the help of trustee assignments, inheritance, and ancestral inheritance. In addition, file system rights are subject to the same rules as NDS effective rights. All in all, NDS and file server security parallel one another—one operating in the clouds (NDS) and one with its feet firmly planted on the ground (file system).

Well, that completes the majority of the IntranetWare security model. There's only one layer left, and it is seldom used—directory/file attributes. Let's take a closer look.

LAYER FIVE—DIRECTORY/FILE ATTRIBUTES

Directory and file attributes provide the final and most sophisticated layer of the IntranetWare security model. These attributes are rarely used, but provide a powerful tool for specific security solutions. If all else fails, you can always turn to attribute security to save the day.

IntranetWare supports three different types of attributes:

▶ Security Attributes—The main attribute category. Some attributes apply to both directories and files.

▶ Feature Attributes—Applies to three key features: backup, purging, and the Transactional Tracking System (TTS).

▶ Disk Management Attributes—For file compression, data migration, and block suballocation.

QUIZ

There's a hidden message in everything. The following coiled sentence contains a profound truth. Start at the correct letter, move to any touching letter, and you will find a mystery unfold.

V	E	O	E	T
E	U	Y	L	P
R	Y	S	L	A
H	T	R	O	M
I	N	A	A	D
G	E	X	R	T
E	C	O	E	I
P	O	T	F	D
T	H	W	O	L

(Q5-1)

(See Appendix C for all quiz answers.)

SMART LINK

You can learn even more about "IntranetWare Security" on the Web. Check it out in "NetWare 4 Product Information" at http://www.netware.com.

Well, there you have it. That's a brief snapshot of IntranetWare's five-layered security model. Now we'll take a much closer look at each of these layers and learn how they can be used to create your impenetrable network armor. Of course, if somebody should get lucky enough and break through your network armor, it would be nice to know what they're doing there. That's where IntranetWare auditing comes in. And, yes, we'll discuss it, too. But not yet. Now it's time to attack the first layer of IntranetWare security—login/password authentication.

REAL WORLD

In October 1967, a task force was assembled by the Department of Defense (DOD) to address computer security safeguards that would protect classified information and computer networks. The task force was formed primarily because networks were just beginning to make an impact on all the world's computers. Of course, they had no idea what they were in for the next 30 years. The DOD now explores security alternatives through the National Computer Security Center (NCSC). In December 1985, the DOD published a document affectionately known as "the Orange Book." Yes, I've seen it—it is orange. The document was entitled *The Department of Defense Trusted Computer System Evaluation Criteria* (TCSEC). The Orange Book was designed to provide security guidelines for both developers and administrators. The major goal of the document is "to encourage the computer industry to develop trusted computer systems and products making them widely available in the commercial marketplace." The book basically consists of a spectrum of evaluation criteria for differing levels of security. It lists basic requirements for very low and very high levels of security.

In order to be truly secure, your system must satisfy six fundamental requirements:

1 • It must have a clear and well-defined security policy enforced.

2 • All system elements must be associated with access control labels.

3 • All individuals accessing the system must be identified.

(continued)

(continued)

4 • Audit information must be selectively kept and protected so that all security actions can be traced.

5 • The computer system must contain hardware/software mechanisms that can be independently evaluated.

6 • The countermeasures that enforce these basic requirements must be continuously protected against tampering and/or unauthorized changes.

So, there you have it. Is your system truly secure? Well, in addition to these six requirements, the Orange Book includes evaluation criteria for four different divisions of security—A through D. Just like in school, A is good and D is bad. Working your way from the bottom, Division D is simply the bottom of the totem pole. This classification is reserved for those systems that have been evaluated, but have failed to meet the requirements for a higher evaluation class.

Division C, on the other hand, provides security on a "need to know" basis. Division C security includes auditing and accountability. The Orange Book further classifies Division C into two classes—C-1 and C-2. Most of today's network operating systems, including IntranetWare and NT, vow to meet C-2 requirements at the very minimum (the Government requires it). Class C-2 is entitled "Controlled Access Protection." Systems in this class enforce a more finely grained discretionary control than C-1 systems. C-2 users are individually accountable for their actions through login procedures, auditing of security-related events, and resource isolation. The idea here is to permit or refuse access to any single file.

The bottom line is that IntranetWare satisfies Class C-2 security through an integrated trust suite called NetWare Enhanced Security (NES). NetWare Enhanced Security is a distributed network operating system made up of three types of network components: servers, workstations, and network media.

The server component of NES contains a Network Trusted Computing Base (NTCB) partition, which is used to enforce the security policies and protect data stored on the server. The Trusted Network Interpretation (TNI) describes a Network Trusted Computing Base (NTCB) as, "the totality of protection mechanisms within a network system—including hardware, firmware, and software—the combination of which is responsible for enforcing a security policy."

For NetWare Enhanced Security, the NTCB is distributed among multiple heterogeneous server and workstation NTCB partitions. The server NTCB partition contains the trusted hardware, firmware, and software that implement the security policies enforced by the server component. Because untrusted software is not permitted on the server, the entire server is included in the server NTCB partition.

Now that you understand the importance of NTCB, let's review the requirements for each of the three NES components:

▸ Servers—The server is evaluated as a Class C-2 IAD component, which means that it provides Identification and Authentication (I), Audit (A) and Discretionary Access Control (D) functions within the enhanced security architecture. The architecture allows you to connect an arbitrary number of servers within your network. These servers must be evaluated as Class C-2 or higher security with respect to architecture, and may provide one or more of the IAD security functions. The architecture does not permit use of unevaluated servers such as NetWare 3.11 or NetWare 4.01.

▸ Workstations—The architecture permits an arbitrary number of single-user client workstations, potentially from different vendors. These products must be evaluated as Class C-2 or higher security with respect to architecture, and may provide none, some, or all of the IAD security functions. In particular, a diskless workstation might be evaluated as a Class C-2 "nil" component. This means that the workstation does not provide local enforcement of Identification and Authentication, Direct Access Control, or Auditing, but is capable of being securely used within the enhanced security network.

▸ NetWork media—Network media components are usually "nil" components, such as passive cabling.

You can compose a trusted Class C-2 network system by interconnecting an arbitrary number of IntranetWare servers, other servers, client workstations, and passive network cabling. To determine the ratings of server and client workstation components, ask the vendor for the Evaluated Products List (EPL) entry for the product.

SMART LINK

To learn more about IntranetWare security and Class C-2, check out the "NetWare Enhanced Security Administration" manual at http://www.novell.com/manuals.

Layer One—Login/Password Authentication

When you log into a IntranetWare server, the world changes. Suddenly you have access to a plethora of resources that weren't available before—printers, files, users, and e-mail. Whatever you do, don't take the login process for granted. It's a complex series of sophisticated communication steps between your client and the server.

As you'll see in the next two chapters, logging in involves ODI drivers, VLMs, context, and STARTNET.BAT. But the real goal of logging in is security. After all, it's the only way to differentiate between real users and "bad guys." Now let's take a closer look at how hard it is to get into an IntranetWare server.

GETTING IN

The first two layers of the IntranetWare security model are concerned with gaining access to the network—that is, "getting in." Once you're in, the bottom three layers take over. They control what you can do once you get there—access to NDS resources and the file system. As you can see in Figure 5.3, there's a lot going on during the login process. Also notice that there are three ways to be denied, and only two ways to be granted access to, the IntranetWare Cloud. This is because of authentication. Let's take a closer look at the flowchart in Figure 5.3.

It all starts with the LOGIN command. IntranetWare responds with a username prompt. You'll need to provide your login name with complete NDS context. This is so that IntranetWare can match you against specific user properties in the NDS database. Once you enter a username, IntranetWare goes to the nearest Read/Write replica of your parent partition to verify that you exist. If you don't exist in the context specified, you'll be denied access and the following two error messages will be displayed:

```
LOGIN — 4.12 — 895: The user does not exist in the specified
context.

LOGIN — 4.12 — 130: Access has been denied and you have been
logged out.
```

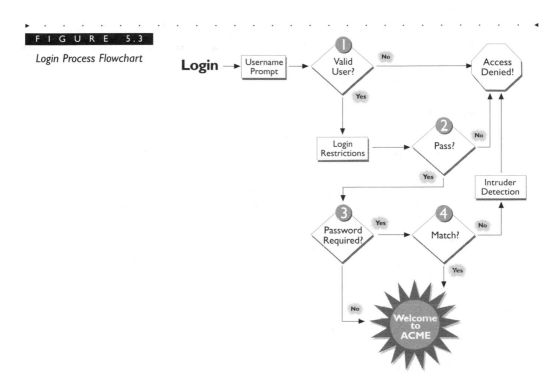

FIGURE 5.3

Login Process Flowchart

If you do provide a valid username and context, the system continues to decision two—login restrictions. Using the information provided by the Read/Write replica, IntranetWare checks all your major login restrictions including time restrictions, station restrictions, and account lockout. If you try to log in from an unauthorized workstation or during the wrong time of day, access will be denied and the following error message appears:

```
LOGIN - 4.12 -860: You have tried to log in during an
unauthorized time period.
```

If you pass login restrictions, IntranetWare moves on to the final two decisions—passwords. First, it uses your NDS information to determine whether a password is required. If a password is not required, you are authenticated automatically and access is granted. Bad idea. If a password is required, you are prompted for it. Good idea. That brings us to the final login decision: Does the password you provided match the one in the NDS database? If not, access is denied, Intruder Detection is incremented, and the following brief error message appears:

```
LOGIN — 4.12 — 100: Access has been denied.
```

SMART LINK

For more detail on IntranetWare login error codes, consult the on-line documentation at http://www.novell.com/manuals.

If you provide the correct password, IntranetWare uses it to decrypt the private authentication key. This completes the initialization phase of login authentication and access is granted. We'll discuss the two phases of authentication in just a moment.

In summary, the IntranetWare login process consists of four decisions:

1 • Are you using a valid username?

2 • Do you pass login restrictions?

3 • Is a password required?

4 • Does your password match?

If all of these conditions are met, access is granted. As you can see in Figure 5.3, there are three ways to be denied access—you type an invalid username, you don't pass login restrictions, or you provide the incorrect password. Now you should have a new appreciation for all the work that's involved when you type that one magic word: **LOGIN**.

WHAT'S NEW

WHAT'S NEW

This process is identical for Client 32, but the details are hidden behind GUI "windows."

ZEN

"Nancy Drew says that all you need to solve a mystery is an inquisitive temperament and two good friends."

Lisa Simpson

INITIAL AUTHENTICATION

From a security standpoint, the entire login process points to one goal—authentication. This is the only way you can gain access to a IntranetWare network. Authentication involves the username, the password, the client, NDS, and the IntranetWare server. There sure are a lot of cooks in the kitchen. Once you've been initially authenticated, IntranetWare activates a secondary authentication scheme—background authentication. Background authentication keeps the user validated throughout the current session. An additional feature, called *NCP packet signing*, validates *every* user packet as it's sent from the workstation to the server. This also applies to the active session only. We'll take a look at background authentication and NCP packet signing in just a moment.

In both cases, IntranetWare authentication guarantees the following:

▸ Only the purported sender built the message.

▸ The message came from the workstation where the authentication data was created.

▸ The message pertains to the current session.

▸ The message contains no information counterfeited from another session.

▸ The message has not been tampered with or corrupted.

▸ You are who you say you are.

▸ You're doing what you say you're doing.

IntranetWare authentication is based on the RSA (Rivest Shamir and Adleman) scheme. This is a public key encryption algorithm that is extremely difficult to break. In addition to RSA, authentication uses a independent private key algorithm as well. One key is public (which means that all users on the network can have access to it) while the other is kept private (which means only a designated user knows about it). If a message is encrypted with a private key, it can be decrypted with a public key and vice versa. As you can see in Figure 5.4, initial authentication consists of four sophisticated steps. Let's take a closer look.

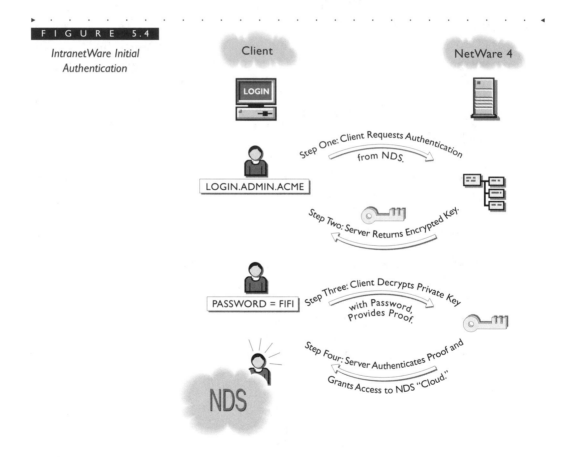

▶ • ◀

F I G U R E   5 . 4

IntranetWare Initial Authentication

Client

NetWare 4

LOGIN

LOGIN.ADMIN.ACME

Step One: Client Requests Authentication from NDS.

Step Two: Server Returns Encrypted Key.

PASSWORD = FIFI

Step Three: Client Decrypts Private Key with Password, Provides Proof.

Step Four: Server Authenticates Proof and Grants Access to NDS "Cloud."

NDS

Step One: Client Requests Authentication

IntranetWare authentication requires the NetWare DOS Requester. It uses a special VLM to control the encryption and decryption of public and private keys—RSA.VLM. In Step One, Admin logs in by providing his or her full NDS context.

The client requests authentication from the IntranetWare server. The request is then handled by a special program within the core OS—Authentication Services.

Step Two: Server Returns Encrypted Key

Once the authentication request has been accepted, IntranetWare matches the user information with an encrypted private key. This private key can only be decrypted by the user password. That's Step Three.

Step Three: Client Decrypts Private Key

In Step Three, the user provides a valid password to decrypt the private key. The password is then erased from memory to prevent a hacker from obtaining it illegally. This is where the fun begins. With the private key, the client creates an *authenticator*. This credential contains information identifying the user's complete name, the workstation's address, and a validity period (the duration of time the authenticator is valid). In addition, there are other undocumented values that make up the authenticator.

The client then creates an encryption called a *signature* using the authenticator and private key. The private key is then removed from memory while the authenticator and signature remain in workstation RAM throughout the login session. The signature is used for background authentication and validates all packets sent during this session.

Finally, the client requests authentication using a *proof*. The proof is constructed from the signature, the request for authentication, and a random-generated number. It is further encrypted by the user's private key. The proof is sent across the WAN instead of the signature to prevent anyone from illegally obtaining the valuable signature. An internal client random number generator ensures that each message sent from this workstation includes a different proof. The proof also assures IntranetWare that the message has not been modified. This is the goal of background authentication and NCP packet signing.

Step Four: The User Is Authenticated

During the final step, authentication services validates the proof as an authentic construct of the authenticator, the private key, and the message (request for authentication). Once the proof has been validated, the user is granted conditional access to the NDS Cloud. Permanent access is granted once you successfully pass Layer Two of the IntranetWare security model—login restrictions.

Table 5.1 summarizes the key concepts in initial authentication. Here's a madcap recap: Admin logs in by providing his or her complete name. The client (RSA.VLM) requests authentication from the server (authentication services). The server returns an encrypted private key. Admin enters a valid password and the private key is decrypted. The client then creates an authenticator with the private key, which includes Admin's complete name, the workstation address, a validity period, and other undocumented values. Next, the client creates a signature by encrypting the authenticator with the private key. Finally, a proof is constructed from the signature, private key, and a random number for traveling over the WAN. The proof is sent to authentication services which validate it and grant Admin access to the NDS Cloud. All of this magic occurs in less than a second. Wow!

T A B L E 5.1 *Understanding IntranetWare Authentication*	AUTHENTICATION ELEMENT	DESCRIPTION
	Client	Participates in initial authentication on behalf of the user. Controlled by special RSA VLM.
	Authentication Services	Participates in initial authentication on behalf of the server. Consists of features built into the core IntranetWare OS.
	Username	Initiates initial authentication through login request. Also is used by the server in combination with the user password to create an encrypted private key.
	Encrypted Private Key	A specific key for each user, which can be decrypted only with the valid password.
	RSA Public Key	Used by authentication services to validate user information.
	Password	Entered by the user to decrypt the private key. Once this occurs, the password is removed from workstation RAM for security purposes.
	Authenticator	A special credential created by the client with user- and session-specific information including the user's complete name, the workstation address, a validity period, and other undocumented values.

T A B L E 5.1 *Understanding IntranetWare Authentication (continued)*	AUTHENTICATION ELEMENT	DESCRIPTION
	Signature	A background authentication credential created by a combination of the authenticator and encrypted private key. The signature is used to validate all packets sent during this session. It is also the foundation of the proof.
	Proof	A temporary encryption created for traveling over the WAN. It is constructed from the signature, a message, the user's private key, and a randomly generated number. The random number generator ensures that each message contains a unique proof.

THE BRAIN

If you feel inspired to delve more deeply into the mysteries of NDS authentication, check out the AppNote entitled "Understanding the Role of Identification and Authentication in NetWare 4" in the October 1994 issue of Novell Application Notes, or surf to http://www.novell.com/manuals.

Once you have been initially authenticated, the second phase begins—background authentication. In this phase, the signature and proof are used to continually authenticate all packets during the current session. Let's take a closer look.

BACKGROUND AUTHENTICATION

Welcome to the second phase of IntranetWare incognito. Background authentication and NCP packet signing are designed to protect the WAN from experienced hackers who forge data packets or pose as unauthenticated clients. In earlier versions of IntranetWare, hackers could use protocol analyzers to capture server requests and forge their own instructions. For example, I could request something simple like log in as Guest, then capture the packet and add something harmful like, "While you're at it, please make me Supervisor Equivalent." This is a bad thing. NCP packet signing solved this problem by requiring a unique signature on all messages. The signature is represented as a *unique proof,* which is the combination of the workstation signature and a random number. If a message doesn't have the correct proof attached, it is discarded. When this occurs, an error message is sent to the error log, the affected workstation, and the server console. The alert message contains the login name and the station address of the invalid client.

NCP packet signing occurs at both the workstation and the server. IntranetWare contains a default level of packet signing—the client signs only if the server requests it and the server signs only if the client requests it. Therefore, signing doesn't occur. You can customize NCP packet signing by using the SET server console command and NET.CFG client configuration file. Here's how it works:

- ▶ At the server—Use the following SET command:

    SET NCP PACKET SIGNATURE OPTION=*n*

- ▶ At the workstation—Add the following statement to the NETWARE DOS REQUESTER section of NET.CFG:

    SIGNATURE LEVEL=*n*

In both cases, *n* represents a signature level from zero to three: 0 deactivates NCP packet signing and 3 creates the highest level of protection available. Table 5.2 shows some common client-server combinations (this is not an exhaustive list). Notice what happens when either the client or server uses packet signing levels of 0 and 3. This can cause havoc on the WAN. Consider activating minimal packet signing—client (1) and server (2).

Finally, packet signing does have a cost. This background protection scheme causes a slight decrease in server performance because of the overhead involved. Not only is the header of each packet marginally larger, but the workstations perform additional processing for each packet transmitted. The server must also perform processing to validate each signed packet. That's okay; your security is worth it.

You've been authenticated. How does it feel? Isn't it nice to know that your life has a purpose? We all need a little validation. But we're not finished yet. Remember, we just have *conditional* access to the WAN. In order to become a permanent resident of the NDS Cloud, we must successfully pass through the second layer of the IntranetWare security model—login restrictions. login restrictions offer much more administrative flexibility because you can limit users according to a large number of criteria including time of day, workstation, intruder detection, and so on. Let's get restricted.

REAL WORLD

NCP packet signing and background authentication recently became necessary because of the overzealous activities of a group of students at Lieden University in the Netherlands. These mischievous students are considered "the Netherlands hackers." This means they expose security loopholes as a means of plugging them. A few years ago, they discovered a simple piggyback intrusion mechanism for NetWare 2.2 and 3.11 servers. The NCP packet signing feature was implemented in NetWare 3.12 and all future versions as a way of slamming this backdoor. Way to go team.

TABLE 5.2 *Understanding NCP Packet Signing Options*	CLIENT LEVEL	SERVER LEVEL	DESCRIPTION
	0	3	The client does not sign packets and the server requires it; therefore, the workstation cannot log into this server.
	3	0	Packet signing is required by the workstation, but the server does not support it. Workstations with this level will not communicate with unsigning servers because they consider them to be unsecure.
	1	1	This is the default. The client signs only if the server requests it, and the server signs if the client requests it. Therefore, signing doesn't occur.
	1	2	Client signs only if the server requests it and the server does request packet signing. This is the minimal setting for activating background authentication.
	3	3	Client always signs and requires server to sign. Server always signs and requires clients to sign. Therefore, everyone signs and all is well. This is the maximum level of packet signature protection.

Layer Two—Login Restrictions

Login restrictions further scrutinize WAN access by matching the login name with a variety of NDS qualifications:

▶ Is this user authorized to log in during this time period?

▶ Is this user authorized to log in from this particular workstation?

▶ Is this user authorized to log in on this date?

▶ Will this user ever get the password right?

▶ Will this user ever change the password?

▶ Who shot Mr. Burns?

▶ What is the meaning of life?

The first layer of IntranetWare security (login authentication) restricts *invalid* users. Login restrictions, on the other hand, restrict *valid* users. At this point, IntranetWare assumes a valid username has been provided and authentication can probably be guaranteed.

As you can see in Figure 5.5, NDS supports a variety of login restriction properties. A quick scan of the right side of Figure 5.5 shows four obvious user restrictions— login, password, login time, and network address. In addition, IntranetWare supports a password tracking feature called Intruder Detection/Lockout. This security feature tracks unauthorized login attempts and automatically locks accounts when the attempts exceed a given bad login threshold count. The user account can only be unlocked by an administrator.

In summary, IntranetWare login restrictions fall into five different categories:

▶ Account restrictions

▶ Password restrictions

▶ Time restrictions

▸ Station restrictions

▸ Intruder Detection/Lockout

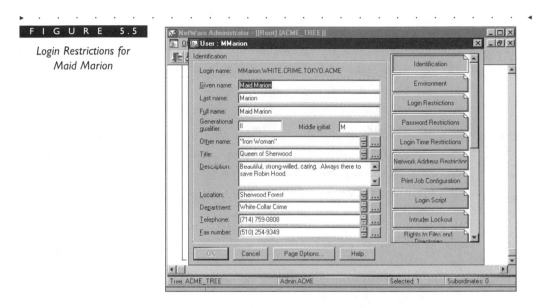

F I G U R E   5.5

Login Restrictions for
Maid Marion

Account restrictions only apply to specific users. Maid Marion, for example, can have her account expired, concurrent connections limited, or access disabled altogether. Password restrictions impact login authentication. In this screen, we can define a variety of Maid Marion's password settings, including allowing her to change her password, requiring a minimum password length, forcing periodic password changes, requiring unique passwords, and limiting grace logins. Remember, the password is used by the client to decrypt the authentication private key.

The next option is time restrictions. These limitations simply apply to when users can be connected to NDS. Time restrictions are not login restrictions per se; they are *connection restrictions*. This means users cannot log in or be connected to the tree during inactive time periods

Similarly, station restrictions do not allow users to log in or attach from unauthorized stations. NWADMIN calls this *network address restrictions* because it allows you to limit user access to a specific protocol, LAN address, or node ID.

Finally, Intruder Detection/Lockout is a global feature that is activated at the container level. All objects within the container are tracked according to a variety of parameters including Incorrect Login Attempts, Intruder Attempt Reset Interval, and Account Lockout. If, for example, Maid Marion logs in with her correct context and an incorrect password seven times within an hour, intruder lockout activates. Once her account has been locked, she has two options—wait the Intruder Lockout Reset Interval or have an administrator unlock her account. This feature allows you to sleep better at night knowing that IntranetWare is doing all it can to keep intruders out of your WAN.

SMART LINK

For more detail on IntranetWare Login Restriction parameters, consult the on-line documentation at http://www.novell.com/manuals.

All of these restrictions (except Intruder Detection/Lockout) are activated at the user level. This means you have to set them for each individual user—too much work. Fortunately, IntranetWare includes a User Template object for global configurations. If, for example, you'd like to set a minimum password length for all users in the WHITE container, you could create a User Template object with the correct settings. Then all users will dynamically inherit the properties of the User Template. This applies to all properties, not just login restrictions. Figure 5.6 shows a sample User Template configuration screen for the WHITE container. Notice all the page buttons listed on the right-hand side. I'm a big believer in the theory "Less work and more play makes life worth living." And the User Template object is right up my alley. Use it or lose it.

REAL WORLD

The User Template object maintains a link with the User object created with it. This is a dynamic link—much different from previous versions of NetWare. Also, this new wonder includes a global change button called "Details on Multiple Users." Very cool!

F I G U R E   5.6

*User Template
Saves the Day!*

NetWare Administrator - [[Root] (ACME_TREE)]

Template : WHITE-UT

Identification

Name:	WHITE-UT.WHITE.CRIME.TOKYO.ACME
Other name:	User Template
Title:	King of Templates
Description:	A rather nice template, as templates go.
Location:	Tokyo
Department:	White-Collar Crime
Telephone:	(81) (3) 5481-1141
Fax number:	(81) (3) 5481 1855

Identification

Environment

Login Restrictions

Password Restrictions

Login Time Restrictions

Network Address Restriction

Login Script

Group Membership

Security Equal To

Trustees Of New Object

OK   Cancel   Page Options...   Help

Tree: ACME_TREE   Admin.ACME   Selected: 1   Subordinates: 0

ZEN

"And when he tried to steal our sunlight, he crossed over that line between everyday villainy and cartoonish super-villainy."

Mr. Wayland Smithers

Now let's take a much closer look at each of the five IntranetWare login restrictions, starting with account restrictions.

ACCOUNT RESTRICTIONS

IntranetWare account restrictions provide a method for controlling and restricting user access to the NDS tree. Account restrictions can be found in the Login Restrictions screen of NWADMIN (see Figure 5.7). As you can see, there are four main options:

▸ Account Disabled

▸ Account Has Expiration Date

> ▸ Limit Concurrent Connections

> ▸ Last Login

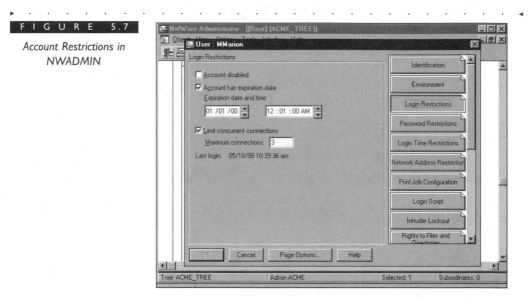

Account Restrictions in NWADMIN

Account Disabled

This option is pretty self explanatory. The account is either disabled or not. This option is not related to Intruder Detection/Lockout. It is possible for an account to be locked but not disabled. In both cases, the effect is the same—the user can't log in. In order to disable a IntranetWare account, you have two choices—manually check this box or use an expiration date.

REAL WORLD

Disabling an account will cause any connections in use by that account to be terminated within 30 minutes and will prevent future tree logins from that account. However, it does not prevent anyone who is already logged in from authenticating to another server. Therefore, the only way to force a user off the network immediately is to delete the user's NDS object. Once this change has propogated throughout the tree, the user is blocked from authenticating to *any* server!

Account Has Expiration Date

This option is a useful tool for temporary employees or students in an academic environment. It allows you to lock an account after a specific date. As you can see in Figure 5.7, the default is inactive. If you check the Account Disabled box, NOW appears as the default date and time. This means as soon as you exit NWADMIN, Maid Marion's account will be disabled. Be sure to increase the value before you leave. In Figure 5.7, Maid Marion's expiration parameters have been set to just after midnight on January 1, 2000. At this point, she will either be gone or celebrating the success of ACME.

Limit Concurrent Connections

Let's face it, users are nomadic. They like to migrate throughout the WAN and log in from multiple workstations. You can limit a user's concurrent connections by changing the inactive parameters in Figure 5.7 to something greater than zero. As you can see, an ideal setting is three concurrent connections. This means that Maid Marion can only log in from three workstations simultaneously. That's plenty. This account restriction works in conjunction with station restrictions. You can enhance a user's concurrent connection limitation by combining it with a specific physical workstation address. In this case, Maid Marion can only log in from three specific machines simultaneously.

Last Login

The Last Login parameter allows users to track activity on their login account. You should train users to periodically check this parameter for intruder logins. If, for example, Maid Marion was gone for a week, but saw that the last login was three days ago, she would have reason to believe an intruder had used her account.

That does it for login restrictions. Now let's take a closer look at password restrictions.

PASSWORD RESTRICTIONS

The next set of login restrictions properties deal with passwords. As you can see in Figure 5.8, there are five main options:

▸ Allow User to Change Password

▸ Require a Password

▶ Force Periodic Password Changes

▶ Require Unique Passwords

▶ Limit Grace Logins

FIGURE   5.8

Password Restrictions in
NWADMIN

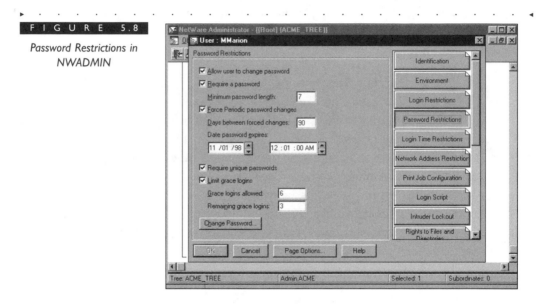

Password restrictions directly impact login authentication. As we learned in Figure 5.3, IntranetWare access can be granted in one of two ways—by providing the correct password (if one is needed) or automatically (if no password is required). Requiring a password is absolutely mandatory. Otherwise, authentication is crippled. Once you require a password, the question remains, "Who manages it?" If you place the burden of password management on the user, the other four password restriction parameters become important. Let's take a closer look

Allow User to Change Password

If you allow users to change their passwords, you're opening a can of worms. On the one hand, it shifts the burden of password management from you to them—this is a good thing. On the other hand, it allows them to mess around with an important authentication parameter—this is a bad thing. Most annoying user complaints deal with password management and printing. Well, one out of two ain't bad. If you don't allow users to change their passwords, all the work falls on you. It's your call—a balance between security and practicality.

Require a Password

By default, IntranetWare does not require a password—this is bad. This should be the very first parameter that you change when creating user accounts. If you activate Require a Password and Force Periodic Password Changes, the system will ask for a password the very first time users log in. Once you activate the Required Password parameter, it's a good idea to set a minimum password length of more than five characters (the default). There are many password hacking routines that can guess a five-character password in less than 20 minutes. On the other hand, you want a password length that doesn't intimidate fragile users. Consider that most users can't easily remember strings in excess of seven to ten characters. The last thing you want to do is force large passwords so that users have to write them down on a piece of paper and tape them to the front of their monitors. IntranetWare supports passwords up to 127 characters in length. It also supports any alphanumeric and ASCII characters. Consider creating passwords that join two unrelated words with a punctuation mark such as

- ▸ DOOR!GROUND

- ▸ SHOE;QUARK

- ▸ LATCH PURPLE

Note the last example did not use a space—it used a null character (Alt+255). Funny, it looks like a space—that's the whole point. Intruders will assume it's a space. Also, it's even trickier when used in succession at the end of a password or username. I bet you can't tell there are seven successive null characters at the end of the second example. Once you've required a password, all the other restrictions light up.

Force Periodic Password Changes

Once a password has been required and a minimum password length of seven characters has been set, you should explore using the Force Periodic Password Changes restriction. This parameter forces users to change their passwords at periodic intervals. If you activate the option, IntranetWare asks you to input the days between forced changes. The default is 40 days. This is a little short and can become a nuisance very quickly. Remember, users love to complain about password problems. A periodic password interval of 90 days seems to be optimal.

Password expiration seems to be a touchy topic for users and administrators alike. We want the interval to be short for better security, and they want the interval to be long for less interference. Either way, someone has to track it. You can train your users to check NWADMIN periodically and view the Date Password Expires property within Password Restrictions. This will tell them exactly on what date and at what time their password will expire. Once the password interval has expired, the user is required to change his or her password. This is where grace logins come in. We'll talk about them in just a second.

REAL WORLD

Many times password expiration and grace logins cause unneeded friction between CNAs and users, especially when users abuse the privilege and CNAs ultimately have to change the passwords anyway. Consider making password expiration a big "event." Use the PASSWORD_EXPIRES login script identifier variable to count down the number of days until password expiration (see Chapter 6). Then when the day arrives, throw a party, bring in balloons and cake, and have everyone change their passwords at once. Turning this event into a party makes password transition every 90 days fun and unobtrusive. It's also a great excuse to have four parties a year.

Require Unique Passwords

The Require Unique Passwords restriction works in conjunction with forcing periodic password changes. When the periodic password interval expires and the user must change his or her password, unique passwords forces him or her to enter a new *different* value. If you're going to endure the effort of forcing periodic password changes, do yourself a favor and make them unique. It doesn't make sense to have users change their passwords every 90 days if they're going to use the same one. IntranetWare only tracks the last 20 passwords. Don't let your users learn this. They will create numerical intervals such as FIFI1, FIFI2, FIFI3, and so on. Also, I've seen users change their passwords 20 times in succession so they can reuse the original ones. To solve this problem, IntranetWare requires at least 24 hours between password changes. Perpetuate the myth that IntranetWare keeps track of all passwords forever.

Limit Grace Logins

When the periodic password interval has expired, IntranetWare responds with the following statement during login:

```
Your password has expired. Would you like to change it now?
```

This provides users with an opportunity to change their passwords right away. If they do not, the system will lock their accounts. The problem with this message is the words "Would you like." It should say something like, "You better change your password now or your computer will explode." Unfortunately, this message is not configurable. So, many users see it as a choice and decide to move on using their existing passwords. This is where *grace logins* come in. Grace logins allow the users to log in without changing their passwords. This is a temporary situation because even grace logins expire. As you can see in Figure 5.8, we're giving Maid Marion six grace logins. This means she can log in six times without changing her password. But then her account will be locked. Once again, encourage your users not to rely on grace logins. There's a convenient Change Password button on the Password Restrictions screen for user access. Otherwise, they can use the SETPASS command at the IntranetWare prompt.

QUIZ

Even numbers have a certain mystery. Try to find the five-digit number, no zeros, in which the first digit is the sum of the last two digits, the second digit is twice the first digit and three times the fourth digit, and the total of all five digits is 16.

Hmmm.
(Q5-2)

SMART LINKS

SMART LINK

For more information on IntranetWare passwords, surf to the Novell Knowledgebase at http://support.novell.com/search/.

This completes our discussion of password restrictions. Aren't they fun? As you can see, there's much more to IntranetWare passwords than meets the eye. Remember, this is the foundation of our login authentication strategy. Don't underestimate the importance of passwords. Use them or suffer the consequences.

TIME RESTRICTIONS

The next two login restrictions deal with *when* and *where* you get to log in. Time restrictions determine *when*. How many of you have suffered from the curious custodial syndrome (CCS)? Let's see a show of hands. Ah, just as I thought—just about all of you. CCS is a problem that afflicts most of today's modern businesses. It's caused by the simple fact that the network stays up 24 hours a day and you don't. Since nighttime janitors have access to your equipment, they can easily hack your networks. One simple solution is time restrictions. Deactivate the network after 9:00 at night and before 6:00 in the morning. This way, no matter how curious the custodial staff is, they can't access the network after hours.

FIGURE 5.9

Time Restrictions in NWADMIN

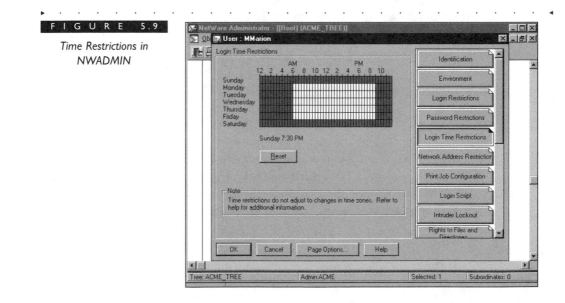

Each square in Figure 5.9 represents a 30-minute interval. The shaded area represents inactive time periods. The white area shows that users can log in any time between 6:00 a.m. and 9:00 p.m. Time restrictions go beyond login restrictions and become connection restrictions. Not only can they not log in, but they can't be connected. If Maid Marion is using the network at 8:55 p.m., she will receive a message:

```
Time expires in five minutes. Please log out.
```

She will get this message at five- and one-minute intervals. When a time restriction is encountered and the user connection is cleared, the system does not perform a proper logout. The system simply *clears* the connections without saving the file. This is a very serious problem. Clearing Maid Marion's connection could result in bindery corruption, hardware failure, or even worse, data loss. When you see a five-minute or one-minute message, be sure to pay attention and log out.

Here are some common time restriction strategies:

▶ Restrict After Hours—ACME doesn't expect employees to work between the hours of 9:00 p.m. and 6:00 a.m. They want to avoid burnout. Setting a time restriction during this period protects them from curious custodians.

▶ Restrict Weekends—Also to avoid burnout, ACME restricts anybody from accessing the network during the weekend. Remember, all work and no play . . . .

▶ Activate Backup Periods—One down side of time restrictions is that it doesn't allow a window for backup. If you're backing up the system late at night, you'll have to activate a backup time window. Test your backup to determine how long it takes and give the system a large enough window—let's say from 11:00 p.m. till 1:00 a.m.

▶ Restrict Specific Users—Remember, time restrictions are a user configuration. You can restrict everybody in a container using the User Template object or specific users individually. If temporary users, for example, only work on Tuesdays and Thursdays, consider deactivating their accounts on other days.

Don't go crazy with time restrictions. Intelligent time restrictions increase network security, but careless time restrictions can significantly hinder user productivity. You want to give users time to work but not leave the network susceptible to CCS.

STATION RESTRICTIONS

Station Restrictions are the other half of the when/where dynamic duo. They deal with *where*. Now that we've solved our CCS problem, another one will arise—Nomadic User Syndrome (NUS). NUS hinders network security for a variety of reasons. First, nomadic users take up multiple network connections and block access to other users. Secondly, NUS implies that users are logging in from workstations other than their own. And, finally, NUS impairs your ability to limit intruders from accessing physical workstations.

Station restrictions solve NUS. They allow you to virtually chain users to specific machines. Instead of restricting them with passwords, disk restrictions, or time slots, you're physically restricting the workstation from which they can log in. As you can see in Figure 5.10, IntranetWare station restrictions go a few steps farther:

- ▸ Protocol Restrictions

- ▸ Network Address Restrictions

- ▸ Node Restrictions

First you pick a protocol. IntranetWare defaults to the IPX/SPX protocol. Other options include OSI, SDLC, TCP/IP, AppleTalk, and Ethernet/Token Ring. Each protocol treats network address restrictions differently. The IPX/SPX address format consists of an 8-digit external network address and 12-digit hexadecimal node ID. The network address identifies an external LAN segment, while the node ID identifies a specific workstation. Maid Marion, for example, is restricted to any workstation (FFFFFFFFFFFF) on the 1234 LAN. We could further refine her restriction by listing one or more physical node IDs on the 1234 LAN.

F I G U R E   5.10

Getting to Know Station Restrictions

The TCP/IP address format expresses logical and physical IDs in the dotted-dash decimal notation. In this case, you can also restrict to all workstations on a logical network or a specific physical machine. Finally, the Ethernet/Token Ring address format uses a SAP (Service Access Point) address, block ID, and PU ID (physical unit). Once again, these values specify all stations on a LAN segment or a specific workstation.

Unfortunately, NWADMIN doesn't dynamically interrogate the LAN to determine addresses for you. You must use other IntranetWare or third-party utilities to gain network and node ID information. As a word of warning, don't go hogwild with station restrictions. Use it only if you suffer from NUS. Like other login restrictions, if it's abused or mishandled, station restrictions can significantly impede user productivity. What happens, for example, when Maid Marion travels to another location? Or, what if we restrict her to one workstation and the machine goes down? These are all important considerations. Although station restrictions are a useful security tool, they can also be detrimental to user relationships.

This completes our discussion of what, when, and where. Now only one question remains: "Who?"

ZEN

"If you've ever handled a penny, the government's got your DNA. Why do you think they keep them in circulation?"

Scientist Smith

INTRUDER DETECTION/LOCKOUT

Welcome to Whoville. This is not so much a restriction as it is a security tracking feature. Intruder Detection/Lockout tracks invalid login attempts by monitoring users who try to log in without correct passwords. As you recall from Figure 5.3, this feature increments every time a valid user provides an incorrect password. It also leads directly to *Access Denied!* Once Intruder Detection has reached a threshold number of attempts, the account is locked completely.

There's one very important thing you need to know about this final login restriction—it's a container-based configuration. All the previous restrictions have been user-based. As you can see in Figure 5.11, intruder detection is activated at the Organization or Organizational Unit level. Once an account has been locked, it must be reactivated at the user level. There are two main configuration elements:

- ► Intruder Detection Limits

- ► Lock Account after Detection

Once Intruder Detection/Lockout has been activated at the container level, all users in that container are tracked. Let's take a closer look.

Intruder Detection Limits

Intruder Detection is turned off by default. In order to activate it, you simply click on the Detect Intruders box. Once you activate Intruder Detection, it begins tracking incorrect login attempts. This parameter is set to seven by default. As soon as the incrementing number exceeds the threshold, account lockout occurs. Finally, the Intruder Attempt Reset Interval is a window of opportunity, so to speak. The system uses it to increment the incorrect login attempts. It is set to 30 minutes by default.

F I G U R E   5.11

Intruder Detection for WHITE

Here's how it works. Assume the Incorrect Login Attempts parameter is set to 7 and Intruder Attempt Reset Interval is set to 1 day, 12 hours (see Figure 5.11). The system will track all incorrect login activity and lock the user account if the number of incorrect login attempts exceeds 7 in the 36-hour window. Pretty simple, huh? Now let's take a look at what happens once Intruder Detection is activated.

Lock Account After Detection

This is the second half of Intruder Detection/Lockout. After all, the feature wouldn't be much good if you didn't punish the intruder for entering the wrong password. When you activate the Lock Account After Detection parameter, IntranetWare asks for an Intruder Lockout Reset Interval. By default, this value is set to 15 minutes. Doesn't make much sense, does it? This invites the hacker to come back 15 minutes later and try all over again. Typically, a value equal to or exceeding the Intruder Attempt Reset Interval is adequate. As you can see in Figure 5.11, we're locking the account for two days, giving you enough time to track down the intruder.

So, what happens to the user when the account is locked? As you can see in Figure 5.12, IntranetWare tracks account lockout at the user level. The Intruder Lockout screen provides three important pieces of information:

▶ Incorrect Login Count—A dynamic parameter that tells the user how many incorrect login attempts have been detected during this reset interval. If the account is locked, the incorrect login count should equal the lockout threshold.

▶ Account Reset Time—Informs the user how much time is remaining before the account is unlocked automatically.

▶ Last Intruder Address—Shows the network and node address of the workstation that attempted the last incorrect login. This parameter provides you with valuable information regardless of whether the account is locked. This is pretty undeniable evidence that someone tried to hack this account from a specific workstation. You don't have to worry about disputed evidence or planted gloves.

FIGURE 5.12

Intruder Lockout for MMarion

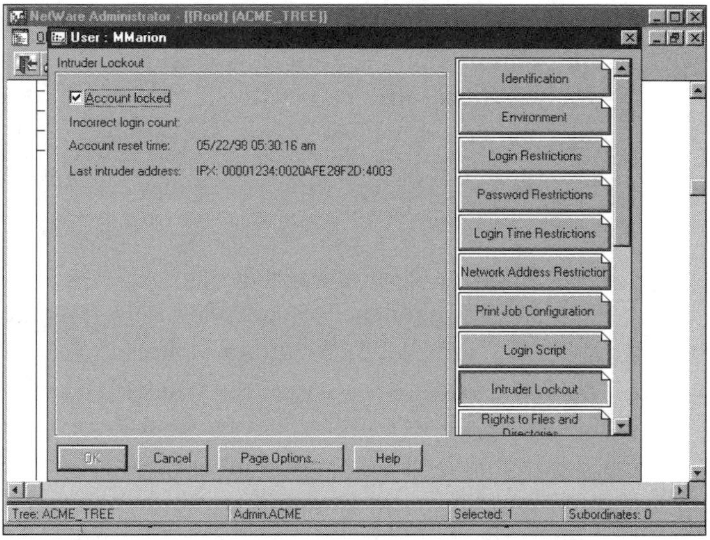

So, who's going to unlock Maid Marion's account? You! Only Admin or distributed administrators can unlock accounts that have been locked by the Intruder Detection feature. But what about Admin? After all, Admin is the most commonly hacked account—with good reason. If you don't have an Admin-equivalent user to unlock the Admin account, consider using ENABLE LOGIN at the file server console. It's always nice to have a back door.

There you have it. This completes our discussion of Intruder Detection/Lockout and login restrictions in general.

Congratulations, you are in! You've successfully navigated the first two layers of the IntranetWare security model—login/password authentication and login restrictions.

In login/password authentication, we discussed the first two phases of WAN access—initial authentication and background authentication. Initial authentication is a sophisticated four-step process that develops a user-specific, session-specific signature and proof. This signature is then used by background authentication to validate incoming workstation packets. Once you've been authenticated, IntranetWare grants you conditional access to the WAN. Permanent access relies on login restrictions.

Login restrictions are the second layer of the IntranetWare security model. They define what, when, where, and who gets access to the system. "What" is account and password restrictions, "when" is time restrictions, "where" is station restrictions, and "who" is Intruder Detection/Lockout.

IntranetWare has never been more secure. And we haven't even accessed any resources yet. The first two layers get us in, but what we do inside the "Cloud" relies on NDS and file system security. How secure do you feel now?

Layer Three—NDS Security

Welcome to the "Cloud"!

The NDS park is a great place to hang out. It has trees, swings for the kiddies, a bike trail, and external entities. Feel free to look around. Browse all day if you'd like. But don't touch anything. You haven't been secured yet.

Access to the tree is one thing; being able to do anything there is another. Until you've been granted sufficient NDS access rights, all the pretty objects are useless to you. No trees, no swings, no bike paths. Once you enter the NDS park, your ability to access leaf and container objects is determined by a sophisticated NDS security structure. At the heart of NDS security is the Access Control List (ACL).

The ACL is a property of every NDS object. It defines who can access the object (trustees) and what each trustee can do with it (access rights).

This strategy poses two important questions:

▸ What rights do I need to do stuff?

▸ How do I get these rights?

These are good questions. Fortunately, I have some simple answers. First, NDS supports two types of access rights—object and property. *Object rights* define an object's trustees and control what they can do with the object. *Property rights*, on the other hand, further refine NDS security by limiting access to only specific properties of the object. Fortunately, these rights are fairly self-explanatory. Browse, for instance, allows you to see an object. Hmmmm, no "brain drain" there.

So, that leaves us with an answer to the second question: "How do I get these rights?" It's a simple three-step process:

▸ Step One: Assigning Trustee Rights—Someone gives you specific rights to specific objects through trustee assignments, inheritance, and/or security equivalence.

▸ Step Two: Filtering IRF Rights—Someone else can filter certain rights if they want to.

▸ Step Three: Calculating Effective Rights—The result is effective rights, which define what you can actually do to the object.

As easy as A-B-C. And you thought NDS security was going to be hard—nope. It can get weird, though. As I'm sure you can imagine, the potential combination of object/property rights can be staggering—almost infinite. So, you're going to want to try to keep it under control. In this section, we'll talk about default NDS rights and how you can use the simple three-step method for limiting potential loopholes. Finally, we'll talk about NDS administration and explore Admin, distributed administrators, and "special" cases. So, without any further ado, let's get on with the show—starting with NDS access rights.

QUIZ

While establishing the credibility of Mr. Smithers' testimony, we learned a few interesting things about him. He prefers pneumonia to a cold. He likes sequoias, but not pine trees. He is facetious, but not amusing. So, the question remains, is he abstemious or sober?

(Q5-3)

UNDERSTANDING NDS ACCESS RIGHTS

Access to NDS objects is controlled by ten different NDS access rights—sounds reasonable. These ten rights are organized into two functional groups:

▸ Object rights

▸ Property rights

Let's use the famous "box analogy" to understand the difference between these two different sets of NDS access rights. Think of an NDS object as a box. Like any other three-dimensional rectangloid, the box has external characteristics. You can look at the box and describe its color, size, and shape. By describing the outside of the box, you have a good idea of the type of box it is. But you don't know anything else about it, especially what's inside the box. With object rights, you can look at the box, destroy the box, relabel the box, or create a new one. But you can't get specific information about what's inside the box—that requires property rights.

The contents of the box are similar to what's inside an NDS object—properties. In most cases, the contents of different boxes will vary. One box may contain caviar while another contains video games. In order to see what's inside the box, you need permission to open it and look inside. With the proper rights, you can compare properties in this box with properties in other boxes, you can read the packing list, or you can change the contents of the box altogether. It all depends on which property rights you have.

If you're feeling a little boxed in, that's okay. We'll try and take it slow. But before we can move on to the three-step NDS security model, we must explore each of these ten rights in depth. You'll need to have a firm understanding of default NDS rights before you start changing things around. The default rights in

IntranetWare are very sophisticated. In many cases, they're good enough. Let's start with a closer look at object and property rights.

Object Rights

Object rights control what a trustee can do with any object. As you can see in Figure 5.13, the five object rights spell a word—BCDRS. So, what do NDS object rights have to do with dinosaurs? Absolutely nothing, but it's an easy way to remember the five rights. Just visualize *Jurassic Park* and all the sick dinosaurs. What would they do without dinosaur doctors?

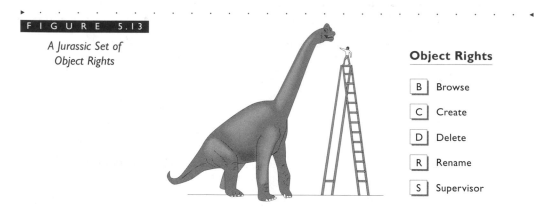

FIGURE 5.13

A Jurassic Set of Object Rights

Object Rights

B Browse

C Create

D Delete

R Rename

S Supervisor

Following is a description of the five object rights and their functions:

▸ Browse—Grants the right to see objects in the Directory tree. With this right, you can see the outside of the box.

▸ Create—Grants the right to create a new object within this container. Obviously, the Create right is only available for container objects. With this right, you can create a new box.

▸ Delete—Grants the right to delete the object from NDS. With this right, you can throw away the box.

▸ Rename—Grants the right to change the name of the object, in effect changing the naming property. This is the only object right that has any impact on properties, except Supervisor. With this right, you can relabel the box.

▸ Supervisor—Grants all access privileges. Anyone with Supervisor rights to an object has access to all its properties. The Supervisor right *can* be blocked with the Inherited Rights Filter (IRF). In effect, anyone with Supervisor rights owns the box.

Except for a few minor exceptions, object rights have no impact on properties. Remember, we're dealing with the outside of the box at this point. If you want to have control over the contents of the box, you'll need to be granted property rights.

TIP

One of the most notable object/property exceptions involves the Supervisor [S] object right. Be careful. It gives the user Supervisor [S] property rights to all properties.

Property Rights

Property rights control access to the information stored within an NDS object. They allow users to see, search for, and change the contents of the box. At the very minimal level, you must be a trustee of an object in order to be granted rights to its properties. As you can see in Figure 5.14, the property rights almost spell a word—SCRAW(L). In order to cure the dinosaur, you'll have to write a pretty big prescription. This involves that unique medical skill known as SCRAWling—wait 'til you see my signature at the end of Chapter 8.

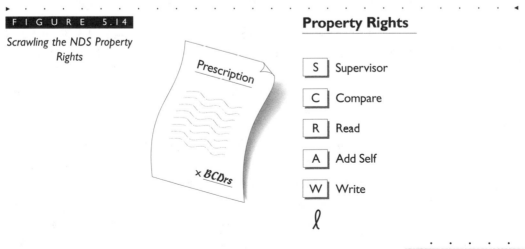

F I G U R E   5.14

Scrawling the NDS Property Rights

Property Rights

S	Supervisor
C	Compare
R	Read
A	Add Self
W	Write

Here's a description of the five IntranetWare property rights:

▶ Supervisor—Grants all rights to the property. The Supervisor right *can* be blocked by an object's Inherited Rights Filter (IRF).

▶ Compare—Allows you to compare any given value to the value within the property. This is analogous to saying, "I'm not going to tell you what my phone number is, but I'll let you guess it." With the Compare right, an operation can return True or False but will not give the value of the property. Compare is automatically granted when users have the Read property right.

▶ Read—Grants the right to read values of the property. This is better than Compare because it actually allows you to view the value.

▶ Add Self—Allows you to add or remove yourself as a value of a property. This right is only meaningful for properties that contain object names as values, such as group membership lists and mailing lists. This right is automatically granted with the Write right.

▶ Write—Grants the right to add, change, or remove any values of the property. This is better than Add Self because it allows you to change any value, not just yourself.

▶ (L)—This is not a property right but is needed to spell a word.

Property rights can be assigned in one of two ways—All Properties and/or Selected Properties. As you can see in Figure 5.15, NWADMIN provides two choices. The All Properties option assigns the rights you indicate to *all* properties of the object. A list of these properties is displayed in the Selected Properties window. The Read All Properties right selection, for example, would allow you to view the value of all the properties for a given object.

The Selected Properties option, on the other hand, allows you to fine-tune NDS security for specific properties. Simply choose the right you want to assign and highlight one or more properties from the Selected Properties window. It's important to note that the list will change for each object type. Users, for example, have 55 properties, whereas groups have only 23. Finally, granting rights to

selected properties overwrites anything granted through the All Properties option. This is very powerful because it allows you to get very specific with certain properties even though a general assignment already exists.

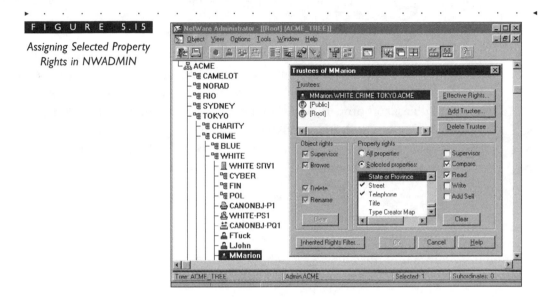

FIGURE 5.15

Assigning Selected Property Rights in NWADMIN

SMART LINK

For more information concerning NDS Object and Property rights, consult the on-line IntranetWare documentation at http://www.novell.com/manuals.

TIP

Later, in Step One of the NDS security model, we're going to learn about a concept called *inheritance*. Inheritance is based on the concept that object and property rights flow down the NDS tree from container to container to leaf objects. It's a fairly simple concept, but there's one exception you need to be aware of. Object rights and All Properties rights are inherited, but Selected Properties rights are not. This means rights you assign to selected properties apply to the specific object only—they do not flow down the tree. Keep this in the back of your mind when we get to inheritance later.

Now that you understand the ten different NDS access rights, it's time to start our three-step model. Before we do, however, let's take a detailed look at default NDS security. This discussion will help you determine when, where, and if you need to assign additional object and property rights.

Default NDS Rights

You have to start somewhere, and default NDS rights are a great place. As I said earlier, default IntranetWare security is extremely sophisticated. In many cases, it's enough. Every time a Server and/or User object is created, IntranetWare assigns a variety of object and property rights to them. Before you move on to the three-step model, you'll want to learn what these defaults are in case you can use them. There's no sense in re-inventing the wheel. Use IntranetWare's default NDS rights as a foundation and build from there.

IntranetWare assigns default NDS rights during three major events:

▶ Initial NDS installation

▶ File server installation

▶ User creation

▶ Container creation

Let's take a closer look.

Initial NDS Installation　　When NDS is installed on the very first server on a network, two key objects are created—[Root] and Admin. [Root] represents the very top of the NDS tree (the Earth) and Admin has Supervisor control over the entire network. Incidentally, Admin is placed in the Organization level of the first server's context. The following default rights are granted when NDS is first installed:

▶ Admin—Granted Supervisor [S] object rights to [Root]. This allows the first User object to administer the entire NDS tree. Distributed administrators can be created using supplemental rights. We'll take a look at this later in the chapter.

▶ [Public]—A special system-owned trustee object also created at initial installation. Every object in the NDS tree inherits the rights of [Public].

This is analogous to the EVERYONE group in NetWare 3.12. By default, [Public] is granted the Browse [B] object right to [Root]. This allows every object in the NDS tree to see every other object.

REAL WORLD

A special trustee called [Public] is created during initial NDS installation and granted the Browse [B] object right to the [Root]. This trustee establishes a global assignment for all objects. Think of it as a minimum trustee assignment. There's one problem, though—users do not have to be logged in to inherit the rights of [Public]. They simply need to be *attached*!

Therefore, any hacker with a notebook and VLMs can attach to your network and download the entire NDS tree. Consider removing [Public] as a trustee of the [Root] object and assign each Organization or Organizational Unit container Browse [B] rights to itself. This will allow users to see their portion of the NDS tree and not the entire tree. But, more importantly, users must be logged in (not just attached) to inherit these rights.

File Server Installation   When a new file server is installed in NDS, default rights are given to the creator of the Server object, the server itself, and [Public]. Remember, in order to create a Server object, you must have the Supervisor object right to that portion of the tree. By default, INSTALL.NLM asks for the Admin password. If Admin doesn't exist or has been locked out of this portion of tree, a container administrator's username and password is sufficient. In either case, this person is known as the *Creator*. Let's take a look at the default rights assigned during server installation.

- ▶ Creator—Either Admin or a container administrator. By default, this user is granted Supervisor [S] object rights to the server. This allows Admin or the container administrator to manage the Server object.

- ▶ Server—The server itself is granted Supervisor [S] object rights to itself. This allows the server to modify the parameters of its own object. Of course, in order for this to occur, the server would have to sprout arms.

▸ [Public]—Granted the Read [R] property right to a specific server property—Messaging Server. This allows any network client to identify the messaging server assigned to this file server. As you'll see in Chapter 6, this is required for MHS Services for IntranetWare. Also, [Public] gets the Read [R] property right to the Network Address property. This allows any client to identify the server.

TIP

Layers Three and Four of the IntranetWare security model are completely independent. This means rights assigned at the NDS level do *not* apply to the file system. These rights only apply to network resources like printers, users, and servers. There is, of course, one exception. If you grant anybody Supervisor [S] object rights to a Server object, they also inherit Supervisor file system rights to the [Root] of all volumes on that server. Therefore, by default, the creator of a server gets all rights to its NDS properties and file system. If you're lucky, this could be you.

User Creation   When you create a new User object in NDS, certain necessary rights are granted automatically. These rights are granted to provide the user with some degree of access to WAN resources. Remember, default NDS rights provide a very good beginning. In many cases, these rights are enough for users to be productive. In general, the User object receives enough rights to modify its own login script and print job configurations. If you don't like this idea, consider revoking these rights. Let's take a closer look:

▸ User—Each user is granted three sets of property rights by default. First, he or she is granted the Read [R] right to All Properties. This allows users to view information about themselves. Next, the user is granted the Read and Write [RW] property rights to two selected properties— Login Script and Print Job Configuration. This allows users to execute and change their own User script and/or print job configurations. As you will learn in Chapter 6, this is a moot point since User login scripts are avoided at all costs. Finally, an obvious object right assignment is missing—Browse [B] rights to yourself. While this is not explicitly granted at user creation, the right is inherited from initial NDS installation. Remember, [Public] is granted the Browse [B] right to the [Root], and, therefore, all users can see all objects, including themselves.

▶ [Root]—Granted the Read [R] property right to two specific user properties—Network Address and Group Membership. This allows anyone in the tree to identify the user's network address, location, and any groups the user belongs to.

▶ [Public]—Granted the Read [R] property right to a selected user property—Default Server. This allows anyone to determine the default server for this user. The difference between the [Public] and [Root] assignment is that [Public] rights are granted upon attaching, where [Root] rights imply a valid login authentication.

Container Creation   Any Container you create in NDS receives default rights to itself. This is to ensure that all objects in the container receive the rights they need to access their own family members (that is, resources that share a home container). Remember, the goal of NDS administration is to organize network resources (servers, printers, volumes, users, and directory maps) near the users that need them. If you accomplish this successfully, the default container rights will create an implied security equivalence for all users in the container. Very cool!

Whenever an NDS container is created it gets certain critical NDS rights to itself. First, it gets Read and Write [RW] property rights to its own Login Script property. This allows users in the container to modify the container login script. As you'll see in Chapter 6, this is not always such a good idea. Next, the container receives Read and Write [RW] property rights to its own Print Job Configuration property. This allows users in the container to modify the container's print job configurations. Also not a great idea. See Chapter 8 for more information.

This completes our discussion of the default NDS rights. Refer to Table 5.3 for a summary. Hopefully, you've gained an appreciation for the sophistication of IntranetWare default security. As you can see, users and servers are well taken care of. The only additional security you'll need to add are for special container administrators, traveling users, or groups. We'll discuss these special NDS circumstances later in the chapter.

But for now, let's put our understanding of object, property, and default rights to the test. Let's learn the simple three-step model for assigning NDS security:

▸ Step One: Assigning trustee rights

▸ Step Two: Filtering IRF Rights

▸ Step Three: Calculating effective rights

T A B L E 5.3

Default NDS Security
Summary

NDS EVENT	TRUSTEE	DEFAULT RIGHTS
Initial NDS installation	Admin	[S]—Supervisor object rights to [Root]
	[Public]	[B]—Browse object rights to [Root]
File server installation	Creator	[S]—Supervisor object rights to server
	Server	[S]—Supervisor object rights to self
	[Public]	[R]—Read right to selected server property (Messaging Server)
User creation	User	[R]—Read right to All Properties
		[RW]—Read and Write rights to selected user property (Login Script)
		[RW]—Read and Write rights to selected user property (Print Job Configuration)
	[Root]	[R]—Read right to two selected user properties (Network Address and Group Membership)
	[Public]	[R]—Read right to a selected user property (Default Server)
Container creation	Container	[RW]—Read and Write rights to Login Script property
		[RW]—Read and Write rights to Print Job Configuration property

ZEN

"When I took your father's name, I took everything that came with it—including his DNA!"

Marge Simpson

STEP ONE: ASSIGNING TRUSTEE RIGHTS

I keep talking about how simple the NDS security model is—easy as 1-2-3. Well, now I get a chance to prove it. A lot has been written about NDS security and most of it is intimidating. Granted, there are a lot of complexities involved, but if you approach it with an open mind, everything falls into place. So far, we've talked about object and property rights. Understanding these rights is a prerequisite to building an NDS security model. But it's certainly not enough. Now you have to learn how to implement these rights in the ACME NDS tree.

Step One deals with assigning these rights. In many cases, this is enough. You only need Steps Two and Three under special circumstances. NDS rights can be assigned in one of three ways:

▶ Trustee assignments

▶ Inheritance

▶ Security equivalence

Trustee assignments involve work—this is bad, of course, since our goal is to minimize the amount of work we do. But you have to start somewhere. Trustee assignments are granted using NWADMIN, NETADMIN, and/or RIGHTS. Inheritance, on the other hand, doesn't involve work—this is good. Inheritance happens automatically when you assign trustee rights at the container level. Just like water flowing down a mountain, trustee rights flow down the NDS tree—from top to bottom. The beauty of this feature is that you can assign sweeping rights for large groups of users with a single trustee assignment.

Finally, security equivalence gives us the added flexibility we need in today's modern world. There are a variety of security equivalence strategies including ancestral inheritance (AI), Organizational Roles, Groups, and Directory Map objects. You'll learn that security equivalence is a way of augmenting the other two trustee assignment strategies. Let's take a closer look at Step One, starting with trustee assignments.

Trustee Assignments

You have to start somewhere and Step One starts with work. A trustee is any NDS object with rights to any other object. Trustees are tracked through the ACL (Access Control List) property. Every object has an ACL property, and the ACL lists the trustees of that object and the rights they have. IntranetWare supports a variety of trustees, including:

▶ User—A leaf object in the NDS tree. It represents a person with access to network resources. Individual users can be assigned specific NDS rights through the User trustee type.

▶ Group—A leaf object with a membership list. The membership list includes users from anywhere in the NDS tree. When NDS rights need to be assigned to unrelated users (in different containers), the Group object is a great option. Rights granted to a Group object are passed to all members of the group.

▶ Container—All container objects are considered "natural groups" and can be used to assign NDS rights to multiple trustees. If you make any container object a trustee of any other object, all users and subcontainers inherit those same rights. The ultimate rights to all objects in the tree are granted using the [Root] object.

▶ Organizational Role—A leaf object, much like groups, except that users are identified as occupants. This object is used to specify a particular role in the organization and not a group of unrelated users. Container administrators, for example, inherit the rights from the Organizational Role they occupy.

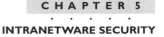

▸ [Public]—A special system-owned trustee. Rights granted to [Public] are passed to every object connected to the network. This means users do not have to be logged in in order to inherit [Public] rights. Be very careful when using the [Public] trustee.

Once you identify *who* is going to get the rights, you have to determine *what* rights you're going to give them and *where* the rights will be assigned. *What* consists of any of the ten object and property rights—simple. *Where* can be any object in the NDS tree—also simple. Take Figure 5.16, for example. As you can see, Sherlock Holmes is granted all object rights to the .OU=TOKYO.O=ACME container. In the figure, we have satisfied all three of the trustee assignment elements—who, what, and where.

▸ · ◂

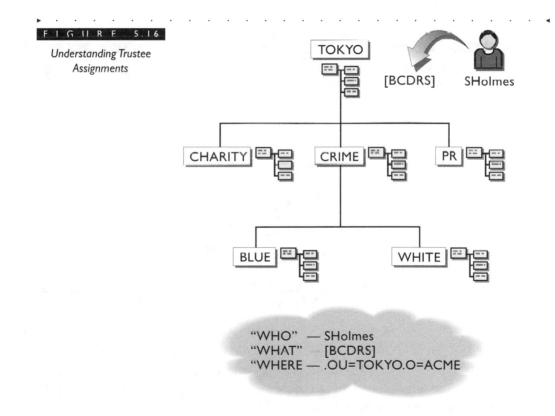

F I G U R E   5.16

Understanding Trustee Assignments

"WHO" — SHolmes
"WHAT" [BCDRS]
"WHERE — .OU=TOKYO.O=ACME

So, how is this accomplished in NWADMIN? It depends on your point of view. You have two choices:

▸ Rights to Other Objects—This is from Sherlock Holmes's point of view.

▸ Trustees of this Object—This is from OU=TOKYO's point of view.

It really doesn't matter which option you choose. You can either assign rights from the user's point of view or the object's point of view. In the first example, we assign security from Sherlock Holmes' point of view. In NWADMIN, highlight SHolmes and click on the right mouse button. An abbreviated dialogue box appears. As you can see in Figure 5.17, there are two security options. In this case, we're interested in Rights to Other Objects.

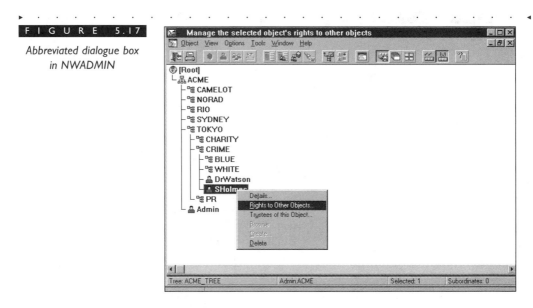

FIGURE 5.17

Abbreviated dialogue box in NWADMIN

The SHolmes menu appears. Figure 5.18 shows the security window from Sherlock Holmes' point of view. As you can see, he has been granted all object rights to the TOKYO Organizational Unit. Specifically, the Supervisor object right implies the Supervisor property rights to All Properties. This was accomplished using the Add Assignment button.

The second option allows you to assign NDS rights from TOKYO's point of view. In this case, you would select OU=TOKYO.O=ACME from the Browse window and click using the right mouse button. The same window will appear (as shown in Figure 5.17). This time, though, choose Trustees of this Object. Figure 5.19 shows the NDS security window from TOKYO's point of view. Notice the default trustees. In addition, SHolmes has been added with all object and property rights. This was accomplished using the Add Trustee button.

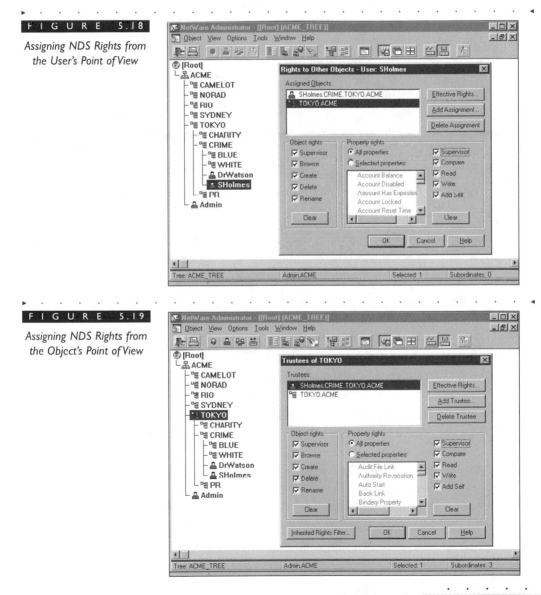

FIGURE 5.18

Assigning NDS Rights from the User's Point of View

FIGURE 5.19

Assigning NDS Rights from the Object's Point of View

SMART LINK

Get some real "hands-on" experience assigning NDS trustee rights in *IntranetWare: NetWare 4.11 Administration* at CyberState University: http://www.cyberstateu.com.

There you have it. As you can see, it doesn't matter how we assign trustee rights. Both methods accomplish the same thing—Sherlock Holmes (who) is granted [BCDRS] object rights (what) to .OU=TOKYO.O=ACME (where). I told you trustee assignments would be simple. Now that we've explored the "work" part, let's take a closer look at inheritance—the "no work" part.

▶ · ◀

REAL WORLD

All of this fancy trustee assignment footwork is accomplished using a special NDS property called the Access Control List (ACL). It controls who can access objects and what they can do with them. Some important ACL objects include Applications, printers, and users.

Inheritance

NDS rights can also be assigned through inheritance. This is an automatic side effect of trustee assignments. As you can see in Figure 5.20, Sherlock Holmes got a lot more than he bargained for. When you assigned him the [BCDRS] object rights to .OU=TOKYO.O=ACME, he actually inherited these rights for all containers and objects underneath TOKYO as well. Now he has all object rights to all containers and all objects in that portion of the tree—this might not be a good thing.

As you recall from our ACME overview in Chapter 3, Sherlock Holmes heads up the Crime Fighting division. He probably shouldn't have Supervisor object rights to Charity and PR. Fortunately, we can rectify the situation. IntranetWare provides two methods for overriding inheritance:

> ▶ New trustee assignment—Trustee assignments override inherited rights. If we assigned SHolmes Browse [B] rights to Charity and PR, he would

lose his inheritance in these containers. The new trustee assignment would become his effective rights and inheritance within these containers would reflect the changes.

▶ Inherited Rights Filter (IRF)—The IRF is much more serious. It overrides inherited rights for all objects in the tree. A [B] filter on Charity and PR wouldn't allow anybody to inherit [CDRS], including SHolmes. So, who manages these containers? What about SirKay and BThomas? Stay tuned for the answer.

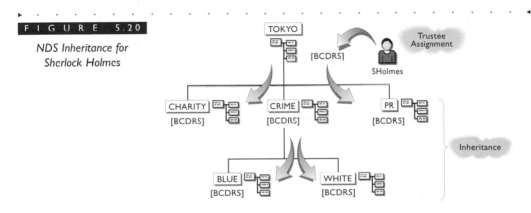

FIGURE 5.20

NDS Inheritance for Sherlock Holmes

Inheritance is a great thing. It allows you to assign sweeping NDS object rights with minimal effort. Remember, as a CNA, "work" is a bad word. As far as property rights go, only one type is inherited. Remember, there are two ways of assigning property rights—All Properties or Selected Properties. The rights assigned using the All Properties option are inherited. Rights assigned to Selected Properties are not. Combine this with what we learned about trustee assignments and we could have an effective strategy for property customization.

Here's an example. Remember, Maid Marion is shy. She's a user in the .OU=WHITE.OU=CRIME.OU=TOKYO.O=ACME container. She doesn't want Sherlock Holmes to see any of her properties except Telephone and Postal Address. This can be a problem since he inherits all rights from his [BCDRS] assignment to the TOKYO container. Fortunately, as a CNA, you have a solution. You simply assign SHolmes the Read [R] property right to Maid Marion's Selected Properties—Telephone and Postal Address. This trustee assignment overrides his inheritance through All Properties. Voilà, Maid Marion is safe. (See Figure 5.21.)

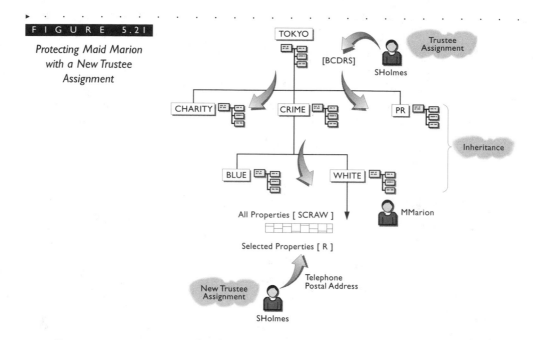

FIGURE 5.21

Protecting Maid Marion with a New Trustee Assignment

Trustee assignments and inheritance are the two main strategies of Step One. But special situations may arise when you need something more. This is where security equivalence comes in. Let's take a closer look.

Security Equivalence

If trustee assignments or inheritance aren't quite getting the job done, security equivalence may be the answer. Security equivalence simply states "one object is equivalent to another with respect to NDS rights." Users, for example, are security equivalent to their parent container. Security equivalence is different from inheritance in that it operates at the trustee assignment level. Please do not confuse the two. Security equivalence applies when an object is made equivalent to another object's explicit trustee assignments. Therefore, security equivalence overrides the IRF.

IntranetWare provides four strategies for security equivalences:

▶ Ancestral inheritance (AI)

▶ Organizational Role

▶ Groups

▶ Directory Map objects

Ancestral Inheritance (AI)   Ancestral inheritance (AI) is a very cool term. But, before you get too caught up in it, you should know a little secret   it doesn't really mean anything. AI simply implies that an object is security equivalent to its ancestor (parent container). This means any rights you assign to an NDS container are absorbed by all the objects in the container. This is not inheritance; this is security equivalence. Therefore, AI can get very strange. Earlier we learned that containers can be trustees and they're thought of as "natural groups." This is true. But, remember, any rights that you assign to a container are implicitly assigned to all objects within the container. For example, suppose we assigned OU=CRIME [BCDRS] rights to TOKYO instead of SHolmes (see Figure 5.20). Now, both users in OU=CRIME—Sherlock Holmes and Dr. Watson—gain the same trustee assignments and inheritance shown in Figure 5.20. Pretty simple.

Well, that's not all. Not only do the objects in OU=CRIME absorb its trustee assignments, but all objects underneath CRIME as well! This means Maid Marion, Robin Hood, and all their friends would get the same trustee assignments as Sherlock Holmes and Dr. Watson. Wow. This concept is also called implied security equivalence. However tempting it is, avoid AI unless you know what you're doing.

Organizational Role (OR)   Organizational Roles are another type of security equivalence. These special NDS objects are designed as task identifiers. Jobs that require multiple temporary users are excellent candidates for Organizational Roles. Postmaster, for example, is a job that can be assigned to multiple users on a rotating basis. When a user is performing the Postmaster duties, he or she will need special NDS and file system rights. Let's say the White Collar Crime Division has a Postmaster OR that changes occupants every three months. This person needs special NDS security to e-mail objects and the file system. Instead of continually moving trustee assignments around, you can define security once for the Organizational Role, then switch occupants. Let's say it's Little John's turn, for example. When you remove Maid Marion from the Postmaster OR and replace her with LJohn, he immediately absorbs the NDS security of that object. Suddenly, Little John has all the security he needs to perform Postmaster duties. An elegant solution. Later we'll explore the Organizational Role as one solution for creating distributed administrators. For now, let's move on to the next security equivalence option—Groups.

> **REAL WORLD**
>
> AI allows you to make broad trustee assignments at high levels in the tree. For example, you could place a mail server at O=ACME and grant the container rights to it. Because of AI, all objects in the ACME organization will have immediate access to the mail server. This also applies to file system rights. You could place all the CRIME files on a single server in the OU=CRIME container, then assign appropriate file system rights to OU=CRIME. Because of AI, all users in the CRIME division would have immediate access to the central server.

Groups   As we learned earlier, groups are another trustee type for assigning NDS rights. This allows us to distribute similar rights to unrelated users. That is, users not within the same area of the NDS tree. First, create a group, then assign it rights, and finally, add members. This is similar to the Organizational Role object in that it works on the security equivalence concept. Members of any group absorb (not inherit) rights assigned to the host group object. Groups also differ from AI containers in that they don't involve "implied inheritance." Rights assigned to groups only apply to specific members of the group. And, as we all know, users can be easily removed from groups.

Directory Map Objects   In very special circumstances, security equivalence can be used to facilitate Directory Map objects. As we learned in Chapter 4, these objects allow us to map directory paths to a centralized object instead of to a physical location. To accomplish this, you must first create a Directory Map object that points to a physical location in the file system, then create a logical drive pointer to the Directory Map object using the MAP command. There's one problem with this scenario: The drive mapping doesn't work until the user is assigned explicit or inherited file system rights to the physical directory. This involves a lot of planning, a lot of work, and some careful tracking. An easier solution would involve assigning the file system rights to the Directory Map object itself, then making each user a security equivalent of the NDS object. This makes security assignments much clearer.

In summary, when you create a Directory Map object, be sure to assign adequate file system rights to its physical directory. Then when you use the MAP command to create logical pointers, be sure to assign the host user security equivalence to the Directory Map object. Believe me, this will make drive mapping and security much easier to manage. Really!

REAL WORLD

Don't forget about NDS rights when dealing with Directory Map objects. If the Directory Map is outside your container, you'll need at lease Read [R] property rights to the object's PATH property.

There you have it—Step One. Don't get discouraged—this is the tricky part. Once you assign NDS rights, the rest takes care of itself. In Step One, we learned there are three different ways of assigning rights to NDS trustees—trustee assignments, inheritance, and security equivalence. We also learned there are a variety of different trustee types and to be aware of ancestral inheritance (implied security equivalence). The good news is, most of your work stops here. Only in special cases do you need to go on to Steps Two and Three. Of course, you remember Murphy's Law Number 342—special cases will appear just when you least expect them. So, in honor of Murphy and to decrease your stress level, let's take a quick look at Steps Two and Three.

ZEN

"DNA . . . . Positive ID . . . . Those won't hold up in any court. Run Dad!"

Bart Simpson

STEP TWO: FILTERING IRF RIGHTS

Earlier we learned there are two ways of blocking unwanted inherited rights:

▸ New trustee assignments

▸ Inherited Rights Filter (IRF)

Let's propose a problem with Sherlock Holmes's inheritance. Since he's been assigned [BCDRS] object rights to .OU=TOKYO.O=ACME, he becomes distributed administrator of that entire section of the tree—this is bad. Sherlock Holmes is responsible for the Crime Fighting division. He has no authority over Charity or PR. However, his inheritance model shows [BCDRS] object rights to both OU=CHARITY and OU=PR (see Figure 5.20). We're going to have to do something about this right away.

Welcome to planet IRF. IntranetWare includes an Inherited Rights Filter that blocks inherited rights at any point in the tree. Right off the bat, you'll need to understand two very important points about how the IRF works:

▸ It's an inclusive filter, which means the rights that are in the filter are the ones that are allowed to pass through.

▸ The IRF applies to everyone in the NDS tree. Once you've assigned an IRF to a container, everyone is blocked, including Admin.

TIP

The Supervisor object right can be blocked by an NDS IRF. It cannot be blocked, however, by an IRF in the file system. If you attempt to block the Supervisor [S] right with an IRF, NWADMIN will first require you to make an explicit Supervisor [S] trustee assignment to someone else (assuming, of course, that one does not already exist). This is so that access to that portion of the tree is not permanently removed. Imagine how much fun it would be if the Supervisor object right was filtered for everybody. Does the term *reinstall* mean anything to you?

The IRF can be used to block inheritance of either object rights or property rights assigned through the All Properties option. Remember, Selected Properties aren't inherited. Figure 5.22 shows how the IRF can be used to solve our Sherlock

Holmes problem. We create an inclusive IRF of [B] to block everything but the Browse right. His inheritance in OU=CRIME, however, remains unaffected.

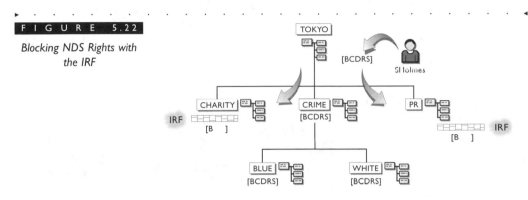

F I G U R E   5.22

Blocking NDS Rights with the IRF

So, how do we assign an IRF? Once again, NWADMIN is our friend. Earlier we learned that trustee assignments can be assigned in one of two ways—"Rights to other objects" and "Trustees of this object." IRFs are accomplished using only one of these two choices. Can you figure out which one? Correct—it's "Trustees of this object." Remember, IRFs are host-object specific. They work from the host's point of view and apply to every object in the NDS tree. Figure 5.23 shows the IRF input screen for OU=PR. Notice the downward arrows that appear next to each option box. These differentiate IRF rights from trustee assignments. Anywhere you see a downward arrow, you can assume it's an IRF filter.

REAL WORLD

Even though the IRF input window in Figure 5.23 gives you the option of choosing Selected Properties, it's not a feasible configuration. Why? Because Selected Properties are *not* inherited. Therefore, the IRF is useless. Please don't let the utility confuse you. That's my job.

If the IRF applies to all objects in the tree, who is going to administer the OU=CHARITY and OU=PR containers? As you can see in Figure 5.22, no one can have the [CDRS] object rights. Fortunately, trustee assignments override the IRF. Remember, the "I" in IRF stands for "inherited." It only works on inherited rights.

Figure 5.24 introduces two new players—SirKay (the administrator of OU=CHARITY) and BThomas (the administrator of OU=PR). We will simply assign BThomas the [BCDRS] object rights to OU=PR. Now he is the container administrator for this section of the tree and everyone else, including Sherlock Holmes and Admin, has been locked out. The same holds true for SirKay and OU=CHARITY.

F I G U R E   5.23

Filtering NDS Rights in NWADMIN

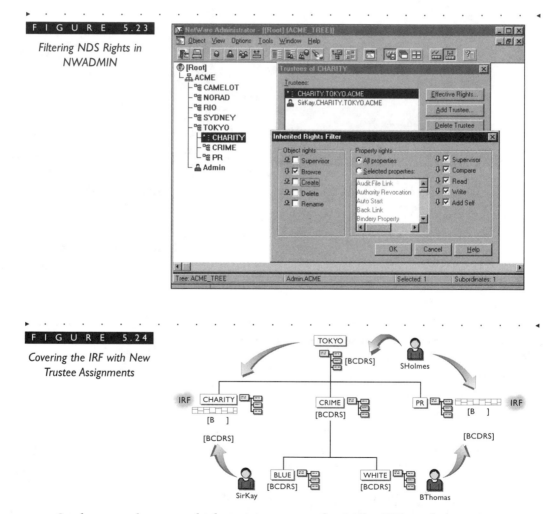

F I G U R E   5.24

Covering the IRF with New Trustee Assignments

So, let me ask you—which activity occurs first? The IRF or the new trustee assignment? Correct, the new trustee assignment. Remember, NWADMIN will *not* allow us to set an IRF for OU=PR until someone else has explicitly been granted Supervisor privileges. So, first we assign BThomas [BCDRS] privileges, then we set the IRF to [B].

Good work.

So, what's the bottom line? What can Sherlock Holmes *really* do in the TOKYO portion of the tree? "It's elementary, my dear Watson, elementary." More accurately, it's Step Three: calculating effective rights.

STEP THREE: CALCULATING EFFECTIVE RIGHTS

Effective rights are the bottom line. This is the culmination of our three-step process. In Step One, we assign the rights. In Step Two, we filter the rights. In Step Three, we calculate exactly what the rights are.

Calculating effective rights is about as simple as modern math. Any object's effective rights are the combination of NDS privileges received through any of the following:

▶ Trustee assignments made to the user

▶ Inheritance minus rights blocked by the IRF

▶ Rights granted to the special [Public] trustee

▶ Security equivalences to parent containers, groups, or Organizational Roles

I don't know if you've ever done modern math, but it's ugly. It would be easy if any of the assignments shown above canceled out the others. But, unfortunately, life isn't easy. These assignments work in combination with each other. Consider it modern math in the 7th Dimension.

Let's start with a simple example. Refer to Figure 5.25. In this first example, Sherlock Holmes is assigned [BCDRS] object rights to OU=CRIME. On the right side of the figure, we've created an effective rights calculation worksheet. This is an *effective* (pun intended) tool for helping you get through modern math. You can create one at home with paper, a pencil, and a ruler.

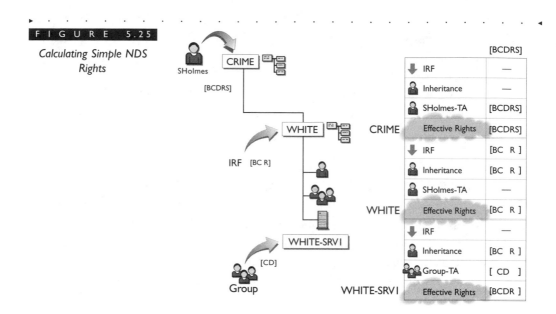

FIGURE 5.25

Calculating Simple NDS Rights

		[BCDRS]
CRIME	IRF	—
	Inheritance	—
	SHolmes-TA	[BCDRS]
	Effective Rights	[BCDRS]
	IRF	[BC R]
	Inheritance	[BC R]
	SHolmes-TA	—
WHITE	Effective Rights	[BC R]
	IRF	—
	Inheritance	[BC R]
	Group-TA	[CD]
WHITE-SRV1	Effective Rights	[BCDR]

It starts with SHolmes' trustee assignment to OU=CRIME. Since there's no inheritance or IRF involved, his effective rights in this container are the same. Those effective rights become inherited rights in all subcontainers—one of which is OU=WHITE. To further complicate things, there's an IRF of [BCR] on the WHITE container. Since the IRF blocks [DS], Sherlock Holmes's inherited rights become [BCR]. With no other trustee assignments, his effective rights in OU=WHITE are the same—[BCR].

Finally, we arrive at the WHITE-SRV1 server object. It has no IRF, so SHolmes' inherited rights are equal to the effective rights of the WHITE container—[BCR]. In addition, one of Sherlock Holmes's groups is assigned the [CD] object rights to the WHITE-SRV1 server. These rights combine with his inherited rights to create ultimate effective rights of [BCDR] for the server object. You see, that wasn't so hard. In this simple example, we had a limited number of different elements—one user trustee assignment, one group trustee assignment, and one IRF. Of course, the world is not always this simple. Now let's take a look at a more complex example.

Just when you think you understand it, they throw something like this at you. In this example (see Figure 5.26), there's one user assignment, one group trustee, an Organizational Role equivalent, AI, and three IRFs. Hold on to your hat!

TIP

One of the trickiest aspects of NDS effective rights is deciding when trustee assignment rights override inherited rights, and when they're combined. It's simple: If the trustee is the same, then TA overrides I; if trustees are different, then TA combines with I. In summary, Same = override; Different = combine!

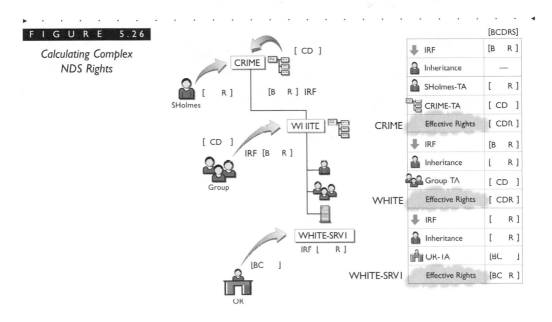

FIGURE 5.26

Calculating Complex NDS Rights

Once again, we're going to use the effective rights calculation worksheet in Figure 5.26. As before, it begins with Sherlock Holmes at the OU=CRIME container—trustee assignment of [R]. In addition, the container is granted [CD] rights to itself. Since Sherlock Holmes lives in this context, he gains an ancestral inheritance of [CD]. This, combined with his user assignment, gives the effective rights [CDR]. In this case, the IRF is useless—simple window dressing. Remember, trustee assignments override the IRF.

Sherlock Holmes's effective rights in OU=CRIME become his inherited rights in OU=WHITE. The IRF, however, blocks [CDS] so his inheritance becomes [R]. This combines with a group trustee assignment of [CD] to give the effective rights [CDR].

These effective rights pass through the [R] filter at WHITE-SRV1. These inherited rights combined with his OR equivalence give effective rights of [BCR] at the WHITE-SRV1 server object. Piece of cake.

SMART LINK

Get some more experience calculating NDS effective rights at CyberState University: http://www.cyberstateu.com.

As you can see, effective rights get very hairy very quickly—just like modern math in the 7th Dimension. This is probably because there're so many forces at work. Remember, effective rights are the combination of trustee assignments, inheritance, [Public], and security equivalence. The default NDS rights are looking better and better all the time.

There you have it. The simple three-step NDS security model:

▸ Step One: Assigning NDS Rights—through trustee assignments, inheritance, and/or security equivalence.

▸ Step Two: Filtering IRF Rights—The inclusive filter allows you to block inherited rights. Remember to avoid isolating sections of the tree by using new trustee assignments with IRFs.

▸ Step Three: Calculating Effective Rights—just like modern math in the 7th Dimension.

Now I bet you're glad you made it through the simple steps of NDS security. Fortunately, there's a sophisticated foundation of NDS default rights to start from. And Steps Two and Three are optional. Your security system doesn't need to be this complex, but in case it is, you have *Novell's CNA Study Guide for IntranetWare* to fall back on.

THE BRAIN

For more expert tips on NDS rights, see "Designing NetWare 4.x Security" in the November 1993 Novell Application Notes or surf the Web to http://www.novell.com/manuals.

Before we move on to the Fourth Layer of the IntranetWare security model (file system access rights), let's spend a few moments exploring NDS administration. These are some supplemental strategies to help you deal with the daily grind of NDS security management.

QUIZ

OK, Bart. To prove your innocence, tell me: What is the English word most often pronounced wrong?

(Q5-4)

NDS ADMINISTRATION

NDS security is a daunting task. Don't feel like you have to accomplish it all alone. The advantages of NDS are that it enables you to section off certain areas of the network and delegate network administration tasks. You can, for example, delegate portions of the tree to distributed container administrators. On the other hand, what if it's a very highly secured government installation? You may only be involved in setting up the network. The daily administration tasks may be accomplished by a high-security work group.

NDS allows you to approach administration in one of two ways:

▶ Central administration

▶ Distributed administration

Central administration means you have only one user (Admin) with Supervisor rights to the entire tree. This is the IntranetWare default. *Distributed administration*, on the other hand, allows you to designate users with Supervisor rights for branches of the Directory tree. This container administrator can either work in conjunction with Admin or replace him or her for that portion of the tree. Let's take a closer look.

Admin

The Admin user is created during installation of the first server and initially has all rights to manage NDS. As you saw in our earlier discussion, Admin is granted the [S] object right to [Root] by default. He or she consequently inherits all rights to the rest of the tree unless an IRF is applied. These rights also extend into IntranetWare file systems unless blocked by an IRF in the NDS tree.

Centralized administration is appropriate for small organizations or large implementations with a central MIS department. Some tasks that could easily be centrally administered include:

- ▶ Naming the Directory tree

- ▶ Installing the first server

- ▶ Creating the top layers of the NDS tree

- ▶ Partition management and synchronization

- ▶ Assigning container administrators

It may be difficult for one person to administer the entire tree. A central Admin may not be able to meet the daily requests of user creation, file system rights, login scripts, and so on. Therefore, you may consider assigning container administrators for busy portions of the tree.

TIP

The Admin user has few special properties beyond [S] rights to the [Root]. This user can be deleted, replaced, or generally abused. This is unlike the special Supervisor account from previous versions of NetWare, which was a "super_user" and couldn't be deleted. The moral of the story is, "Don't get delusions of grandeur if you log in as Admin." Remember, anyone can be Admin as long as he or she has Supervisor [S] rights to the [Root].

Distributed Administrators

Distributed administration means that designated users are given enough NDS rights to manage distributed branches of the NDS tree. This special type of user is often referred to as a *container administrator*. Distributed administration tends to allow you to respond to users' needs more quickly, especially in a large implementation. The following tasks can be distributed:

► Creating user accounts

► Creating and configuring print services

► Backing up and restoring data

► Assigning file system trustees

► Installing additional servers

► Creating workgroup managers

Of course, the optimum administrative strategy combines a central Admin with a few distributed administrators. As we saw in our earlier discussion, there are two ways of creating distributed administrators—IRF/new trustee assignments and Organizational Role. If only one person will administer a container, consider using the first option. Otherwise, Organizational Roles can act as a host to rotating administrators. Remember our Postmaster example.

REAL WORLD

There is a third way of creating distributed administrations—security equivalence. You can create a single container administrator and then make other users security equivalent to that object. This is not recommended, however. If you happen to delete the host administrator, all security equivalent users lose their rights. If the host was an exclusive container administrator, you've just lost all administrative control over a section of the tree. Does the term *reinstall* mean anything to you?

As we saw in an earlier example, it's possible to create an exclusive container administrator. Refer back to Figure 5.24. When the IRF was used to block all rights in the PR container, all administrators, including Admin, were locked out. But before we could block [S], we needed to make BThomas an exclusive administrator by granting him [BCDRS] object rights. Remember, NWADMIN requires you to make the trustee assignments first, then the IRF.

There are two other types of distributed administrators in addition to Admin and the container administrator:

▸ Print server operator—Responsible for managing print services. This role is often incorporated into the role of the container administrator.

▸ Print queue operator—Can assist the print server operator or container administrator in managing print jobs.

Table 5.4 summarizes the actions and requirements of central and distributed administrators. For now, suffice it to say—you don't have to do it alone. No matter who you are, there will always be some special circumstances to deal with. Let's take a look at some clever solutions for Profile login scripts, Directory Map objects, mailing list administrators, and traveling users.

T A B L E 5.4

Summary of Distributed
Administrators

ROLE	ACCOUNT INFORMATION	FUNCTIONS
Admin	Default Admin User object [S] object rights to [Root] (by default).	Name the Directory tree; install the first server; create the top levels of the NDS tree; handle partition management and synchronization; assign distributed administrators; issue initial auditor password(s); and upgrade servers, clients, and applications.
Distributed Administrator	Exclusive container administrator or Organizational Role. Requires [BCDRS] object rights to appropriate container.	Install supplemental servers; perform data backup and restoration; create and configure print services; write and maintain login scripts; monitor file server performance; track errors; monitor disk space usage, assign file system security; and upgrade respective servers, clients, and applications.

TABLE 5.4

Summary of Distributed Administrators (continued)

ROLE	ACCOUNT INFORMATION	FUNCTIONS
Print Server Operator	Print Server Operator object or Organizational Role. Must be added to "Print Server Operator" property of the respective Print Server object.	Load and shut down the print server, manage and maintain print server configurations.
Print Queue Operator	Print Queue Operator object or Organizational Role. Must be added to the "Print Queue Operator" property of the respective print queue.	Delete print jobs, change the order of print jobs, change queue status.

Special NDS Security

If you only learn one thing in this crazy chapter, I hope it's this:

Expect the unexpected.

 ZEN

"Doh!"

Homer Simpson

There are many special circumstances that require a unique approach toward NDS security. Certain objects in the tree, for example, require additional NDS rights beyond the defaults. This usually occurs when a user is defined in a different container than the resource he or she is trying to access. Also, there are special considerations for traveling users and mailing list administrators. Here are some proven solutions for dealing with special security circumstances:

▸ Profile Login Scripts—As you'll learn in Chapter 6, IntranetWare provides a facility for group login scripts—the Profile object. In order for a user to access a Profile script, he or she requires special rights. If the User and Profile objects are in the same container, no additional rights are required because he or she gets them by default. If, however, the User is in a different container, the Read [R] right to the Profile login script property is required.

▸ Directory Map—In Chapter 4, we discovered the Directory Map object as a way of reducing redundant network administration. It allows you to map logical pointers to NDS objects instead of physical volume locations. In order to access Directory Map objects, users need two sets of rights. First, NDS rights (Read [R] to the "Path" selected property of the Directory Map object) and, second, file system rights to the volume in question. If the user resides in the same container as the Directory Map object, no additional NDS rights are required. Otherwise, you'll need to make the above NDS assignment.

▸ Mailing list administrator—Postal workers are special people, too. Mailing list administrators need special NDS rights to manage certain user properties. Specifically grant him or her Read and Write [RW] properties rights to the following Selected Properties of each user in the mailing list—Telephone, Street, City, State or Province, Postal (Zip) Code and other postal office box properties. Whatever you do, don't use the All Properties option. This would give the mailing list administrator unintended power. Remember, if you grant anyone the Write [W] property right to a user's ACL property, he or she can change the user's security. This is a bad thing.

▸ Traveling user between two offices—Traveling users can cause havoc on NDS administration. These users typically bounce from location to location demanding access to distributed and centralized resources. Several of the NDS security issues you should consider when working with traveling users include access to applications, file storage in a central volume, access to distributed files, access to local and distributed printers and e-mail, login authentication, and the type of computer they're using (notebook or desktop). The user who divides his or her time between two offices needs similar resources in two different locations. The easiest way to approach this problem is create two User objects, one in each location. Give appropriate rights to any resources needed in the local location. Then give him or her the Read [R] property rights to Profile login script and Directory Map Objects (as shown above).

▶ Traveling users between various locations—Users who travel to various locations on a regular basis require a slightly different type of NDS security. In this case, you may want to create an Alias object in each location. You can also use groups or Organizational Roles, then assign the appropriate rights to the Alias for access to directories and network resources. Finally, don't forget the Profile and Directory Map objects. This strategy can also be used for traveling users who find themselves stuck in a remote location for a temporary period of time.

This completes all the "special" and not-so-special aspects of IntranetWare NDS Administration. As you can see, it's a tricky, critical piece of your life as a CNA. To help, Table 5.5 outlines all the rights necessary to create and manage daily NDS resources. Just think of it as a blueprint for NDS success. Hey that rhymes.

TABLE 5.5

*Summary of NDS Resource
Access Rights*

NDS RESOURCE	ADMINISTRATIVE ACTION	NECESSARY RIGHTS
Alias	Grant users appropriate NDS rights to the Alias Host object	Authority to grant NDS rights to objects in other containers (i.e. Write [W] privileges to the object's ACL property)
Application	1) Grant users appropriate file system rights to the application referred to by the Application object.	To perform Step 1, you must have Supervisory or Access Control file system rights to the directory or file.
	2) Associate users with Application objects.	To perform Step 2, you must have the Write [W] property right to ACL property of the Application and User objects.
Directory Map	1) Grant users appropriate file system rights to the directory referred to by the Directory Map object.	To perform Step 1, you must have Supervisory or Access Control file system rights to the directory or file.

(continued)

TABLE 5.5

*Summary of NDS Resource
Access Rights (continued)*

NDS RESOURCE	ADMINISTRATIVE ACTION	NECESSARY RIGHTS
Directory Map (continued)	2) Grant users the Read [R] property right to the Path property of the Directory Map object.	To perform Step 2, you must have the Write [W] property right to ACL property of the Directory Map object.
Group	Add users to the Group Membership list of the Group object.	Write [W] property right to the ACL property (that is, Member and Object Trustees) of the Group object.
Organizational Role	Add users to the Occupant list of the Organizational Role object.	Write [W] property right to the ACL property (that is, Occupant and Object Trustees) of the Organizational Role object.
Print Queue	Add users to the Print Queue Userslist of the Print Queue object.	Print Queue Operator status.
Printer	Add users to the Print Queue . Users list of the Print Queue object that services this printer	Print Queue Operator status.
Profile	1) Add the Profile object to each User object's Profile property. 2) Grant users the Read [R] property right to the Login Script property of the Profile object.	To perform both Steps 1 and 2, you must have the Write [W] property right to the ACL (that is, Object Trustees) property of the Profile object.
Volume/directory	Grant users the appropriate file system rights to the directory or file you want to target in the Volume object. (By default: Read and File Scan rights to SYS:PUBLIC)	Supervisory or Access Control file system rights to the directory or file you want to target in the Volume object.

SMART LINK

For more information on NDS Administration and security, surf to the Novell Knowledgebase at http://support.novell.com/search/.

Wow. That's NDS security! In this section, we've explored the simple three-step model for configuring NDS access rights. We've learned about trustee assignments, inheritance, and security equivalence. The IRF came along to help us lock inherited rights and quickly became the foundation of "modern math" in the 7th Dimension—calculating effective rights. That's all there is to it. Finally, we learned you don't have to do it alone. You can share all this fun with distributed administrators.

At the beginning of the chapter, we learned that security is "freedom from risk." At this point, you're probably thinking NDS security is freedom from sanity. Don't worry—it's not as crazy as you think. We've provided a detailed exploratorium at the end of the chapter for your enjoyment. And in the next section—file system access rights—you'll get a chance to review the three-step approach. Here's the good news. File system security is very similar to NDS security. Let's check it out.

QUIZ

So, you wanna be the next Sherlock Holmes? Let's see if you've got what it takes. Each of the following six words is the odd one out for a different reason.

ABORT

ACT

AGT

ALP

OPT

APT

Can you find all six answers? If so, you are well on your way to answering the question, "Who shot Mr. Burns?"

(Q5-5)

Layer Four—File System Access Rights

IntranetWare security exists on two functional planes:

▶ Above the server

▶ Within the server

In order to understand the two functional planes of IntranetWare security, use the server as a midpoint (see Figure 5.27). NDS security occurs above the server—the "Cloud." In this plane, the server is at the bottom of the tree. It is treated as any other leaf object, just like users, printers, and groups. NDS security applied above the server ends when it gets to a leaf object. There's no transition into the file system.

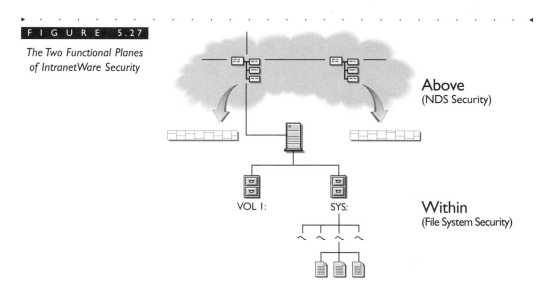

Above
(NDS Security)

VOL 1:   SYS: **Within**
(File System Security)

File system security, on the other hand, occurs within the server. In this case, the server is the top of the tree. The server contains the volumes that contain the directories that house the files. Again, file system security ends once it gets to the server. There's no transition into the NDS security structure. Understanding the server's point of view will help you understand NDS and file system security.

The good news is NDS and file system security have a lot in common. You don't have to learn a whole new model. The same simple three-step approach applies. There're trustee assignments, inheritance, and security equivalence. The file system uses an IRF and calculating effective rights is still ugly. There are, however, a few minor differences between NDS and file system security:

▶ NDS has ten access rights broken into two groups—object and property. The file system uses eight access rights.

▶ Rights do not flow from NDS into the file system except in one special instance—Supervisor [S] object right to the Server object, which grants the trustee Supervisor file rights to the [Root] of all the server's volumes.

▶ The Supervisor NDS right can be blocked by the IRF. The Supervisor file system right, on the other hand, *cannot* be blocked by the IRF.

That does it. As you can see, the file system and NDS have much more in common than you think. Let's start our discussion of security *within* the server by describing the eight file system access rights.

UNDERSTANDING FILE SYSTEM ACCESS RIGHTS

Welcome inside the server. It's kind of dark and cold in here, but very secure. Before you can access any files, though, you must have appropriate file system access rights. As you can see in Figure 5.28, they also spell a word—WoRMFACES (the "O" is implied). Holy anatomical nematodes, Batman! It's not a pretty sight, but certainly a name you will not forget. Let's check them out.

▶ W—Write: Grants the right to open and change the contents of files and directories.

▶ (O)—Doesn't exist but is needed to spell a word.

▶ R—Read: Grants the right to open files in the directory and read their contents or run applications.

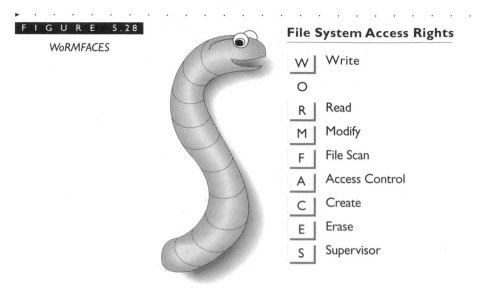

FIGURE 5.28

WoRMFACES

File System Access Rights

W	Write
O	
R	Read
M	Modify
F	File Scan
A	Access Control
C	Create
E	Erase
S	Supervisor

▸ M—Modify: Grants the right to change the attributes or name of a file or directory. As we'll learn in just a second, the Modify right has a dual personality.

▸ F—File Scan: Grants the right to see files and directories.

▸ A—Access Control: Grants the right to change trustee assignments and the IRF.

▸ C—Create: Grants the right to create new files and subdirectories.

▸ E—Erase: Grants the right to delete a directory, its files, and subdirectories.

▸ S—Supervisor: Grants all rights to a directory and its files and subdirectories. This right *cannot* be blocked by the IRF (unlike NDS security).

In this list, there are three rights you may want to steer clear of—[SAM] (and they also spell a word). The Supervisor right grants all privileges to files and directories and it cannot be filtered. Users with the Supervisor right can make trustee assignments and grant all rights to other users as well. Access Control also allows users to make trustee assignments, but they can only grant the rights they possess. In addition, these users can modify the IRF. Finally, the Modify right has a split personality—Dr. Jekyll and Mr. Hyde. As Dr. Jekyll, Modify allows users to rename files and directories. Many applications require this. As Mr. Hyde, Modify allows users to change file and directory attributes. As we'll see a little later, attributes constitute the fifth layer of the IntranetWare security model. I don't think you want users messing around with it.

REAL WORLD

The Supervisor access right is just as dangerous in the file system as it is in NDS. The tricky part is that it can leak its way into the file system without you knowing it. Any user with the Write [W] property right to a server's ACL will implicitly receive Supervisor file rights to the Root of all volumes on the server. And to make things worse, the user will not appear on any file or directory trustee list. There's a variety of ways to get the Write [W] property right to a server's ACL, including Supervisor object rights, Supervisor All Properties rights, and security equivalence. You may consider blocking these rights with a server IRF.

Recognizing the eight file system access rights is only the beginning. In order to effectively configure and manage file system security, you must understand what they do. Individually, the rights are useless. But in combination, they become valuable security tools. Table 5.6 summarizes the file system rights requirements for common network tasks. Believe me, this will be an invaluable aid when it comes time to configure application and data security. Use it or lose it.

SMART LINK

For more information on IntranetWare file system access rights and appropriate configurations, surf to the Novell Knowledgebase at http://support.novell.com/search/.

TABLE 5.6	FILE SYSTEM TASK	RIGHTS REQUIREMENTS
Rights Requirements for Common File System Tasks	Open and read a file	Read
	See a filename	File Scan
	Search a directory for files	File Scan
	Open and write to an existing file	Write, Create, Erase, and Modify
	Execute an .EXE file	Read and File Scan
	Create and write to a file	Create
	Copy files from a directory	Read and File Scan
	Copy files to a directory	Write, Create, and File Scan
	Make a new directory	Create
	Delete a file	Erase
	Salvage deleted files	Read and File Scan for the file and Create for the directory
	Change directory or file attributes	Modify (Mr. Hyde)
	Rename a file or directory	Modify (Dr. Jekyll)
	Change the IRF	Access Control
	Change trustee assignments	Access Control
	Modify a directory's disk space restrictions	Access Control

So, where do you begin? As with NDS, file system security starts with the defaults. IntranetWare provides a sophisticated set of default file system access rights. These rights should become the foundation of your application and data security strategies. They aren't, however, as comprehensive as NDS defaults. You'll need to assign security whenever you create new application and data directories. Let's take a quick look at the IntranetWare defaults:

▶ User—A unique user directory is created under SYS:USERS during User object conception. By default, the user gets all file system rights except Supervisor to the directory—[RWCEMF]. This directory will exactly match the User object name unless otherwise specified. Its location is also configurable.

▶ [Supervisor]—The Bindery Services Supervisor object is granted Supervisor [S] file rights to the [Root] of all volumes. This user performs special bindery functions using the Admin password.

▶ Creator—Whoever creates the File Server object (usually Admin) automatically gets Supervisor [S] file system rights to all volumes. This can be blocked by filtering the Supervisor [S] object right with a server IRF.

▶ Container—The server's parent container is granted Read and File Scan [RF] access rights to SYS:PUBLIC. This way all users and objects in the server's home container can access IntranetWare public utilities.

This completes our discussion of file system access rights. As you can see, there's a lot more than meets the eye. Be sure to use Table 5.6 when assigning rights to new application and data directories. Also, test these rights before you let the users loose. Many times, applications have strange unobvious requirements. Now that you know what to do, let's learn how to do it. Remember, the IntranetWare file system behaves exactly the same as NDS:

▶ Step One: Assigning Trustee Rights

▶ Step Two: Filtering IRF Rights

▶ Step Three: Calculating Effective Rights

Ready. Set. Go!

 ZEN

"I am Melvin Van Horn, and this is my associate Hershel Krustovsky. Officers, you have arrested an innocent man!"

Krusty's Sidekick

FILE SYSTEM THREE-STEP SHUFFLE

This gives us an opportunity to review the three-step NDS security model. Fortunately, file system security imitates it to the letter. Remember, IntranetWare security starts with two simple questions:

▸ What rights do I need to do stuff?

▸ How do I get these rights?

Well, so far we've learned about the eight file system access rights and what rights are needed for common network tasks. Now we get to answer the question, "How do I get these rights?" As with NDS, file system security is as easy as 1-2-3:

▸ Step One: Assigning Trustee Rights—You assign the access rights through trustee assignments, inheritance, and/or security equivalence.

▸ Step Two: Filtering IRF Rights—In special circumstances, you can filter inherited rights at the directory or file level.

▸ Step Three: Calculating Effective Rights—The result is effective rights (that is, what users can actually do to directories and files).

Once again, it's as easy as A-B-C. Except in this case, we're assigning access rights to files and directories, not NDS objects. Let's take a closer look at this simple three-step model from the file system's point of view.

Step One: Assigning Trustee Rights

You have to start somewhere, and Step One starts with work. A trustee is any NDS object with rights to directories or files. Trustees are tracked through the DET (directory table). The file system supports the same trustee types as NDS—users, groups, containers, Organizational Roles, and [Public]. Once you identify who is going to get the rights, you have to determine what rights you're going to give them and where the rights will be assigned. This is shown in Figure 5.29. MMarion is granted all rights except [SAM] to the SYS:SHARED directory. These rights are then inherited for all subdirectories underneath. As you can see, the *who* is MMarion, the *what* is [RWCEF], and the *where* is SYS:SHARED. This is an explicit trustee assignment.

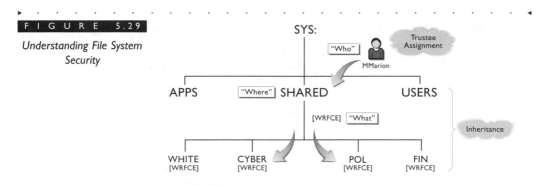

So, how is this accomplished in NWADMIN? Once again, it depends on your point of view, and you have two choices:

▶ Rights to Files and Directories—This is from Maid Marion's point of view.

▶ Trustees of this Directory—This is from SYS:SHARED's point of view.

It really doesn't matter which option you choose. You can either assign rights from the user's point of view or the directory's point of view. In the first example, we assign security from Maid Marion's point of view. In NWADMIN, double-click on Maid Marion and her User Information window appears. Choose Rights to Files and Directories from the right-hand list and voilà—Figure 5.30 appears.

Figure 5.30 shows the security window from Maid Marion's point of view. As you can see, she has been granted [RWCEF] access rights to SYS:SHARED. In addition, she's also a trustee of SYS:\USERS\POLIT\MMARION—by default. You can create trustee assignments by using the Add... button.

REAL WORLD

The Security Information window shown in Figure 5.30 only displays trustee assignments for a single volume at a time. By its very nature, NDS allows you to view information about multiple volumes throughout the WAN. In order to bring up the trustee assignments for a different volume, use the Show... button. You can also explore for other volumes by using the Find... button. In Figure 5.30, we're only looking at Maid Marion's trustee assignments for WHITE-SRV1_SYS.

FIGURE 5.30

Assigning File Rights from
the User's Point of View

The second option allows you to assign access rights from SYS:SHARED's point of view. In this case, you would double-click on WHITE-SRV1_SYS from the Browse window of NWADMIN. All of its directories should appear. Then, highlight SHARED and click the right mouse button. A pull-down menu will appear—choose Details. Once the SYS:SHARED Details window appears, choose Trustees of this Directory from the righthand list (see Figure 5.31). In this screen, NWADMIN gives you the choice of adding trustees or setting the IRF (Inherited Rights Filter). Notice that MMarion has been added with the [RWCEF] access rights. You can create other trustee assignments for SYS:SHARED using the Add Trustee... button. Also, notice the IRF allows all rights to flow through—this is the default.

There you have it. As you can see, it doesn't matter how we assign access rights. Both methods accomplish the same thing—Maid Marion (who) is granted [RWCEF] trustee rights (what) to SYS:SHARED (where).

REAL WORLD

In addition to NWADMIN, you can use FILER and RIGHTS (command line utility) to assign file system access rights.

*Assigning File Rights from
the Directory's Point of View*

Now that we've explored the "work part," let's take a closer look at inheritance—
"no work."

As we learned earlier, access rights are also assigned through inheritance. This
is an automatic side effect of trustee assignments. As you can see in Figure 5.29,
Maid Marion inherits [RWCEF] access rights in all subdirectories of SYS:SHARED.
Inheritance is a great thing. It allows you to assign sweeping file system access
rights with minimal effort. Remember, as a CNA, work is bad.

But many times, inheritance gets out of hand. Fortunately, IntranetWare allows
you to override inheritance using a new trustee assignment or an IRF. We'll explore
these topics in just a moment.

If trustee assignments or inheritance aren't quite getting the job done, security
equivalence may be the answer. Security equivalence simply states "one object is
equivalent to another with respect to file system access rights." As we learned
earlier, users, for example, are security equivalent to their parent container. We
also learned that security equivalence operates at the trustee assignment level—
this is *not* inheritance. Therefore, security equivalence overrides the IRF.

SMART LINK

Get some real "hands-on" experience assigning file system access rights in IntranetWare Administration at CyberState University: http://www.cyberstateu.com.

IntranetWare provides four strategies for security equivalence:

▸ Ancestral Inheritance (AI)—Any object is security equivalent to its ancestors (parent containers). This means any rights you assign to an NDS container are absorbed by all the objects in the container. This is not inheritance—this is security equivalence.

▸ Organizational Role—Our special NDS objects designed as task identifiers. Jobs that require multiple temporary users are excellent candidates for Organizational Roles. Simply assign file system access rights to the Role and they are absorbed by all occupants of the Role. Once again, this is not inheritance.

▸ Groups—Allows you to distribute similar rights to unrelated users. That is, users not within the same area of the NDS tree. Members of any group absorb (not inherit) rights assigned to the host Group object.

▸ Directory Map—In very special circumstances, security equivalence can be used to facilitate Directory Map objects. When you create a Directory Map object, be sure to assign adequate file system rights to its physical location. Then when you use the MAP command to create logical pointers, be sure to assign the host user security equivalence to the Directory Map object.

This completes Step One of the file system security model. Remember, this is the hard part. Step Two and Step Three are optional. Step Two allows us to filter inherited rights, and Step Three combines all rights assignments into a single mathematical formula—math in the 7th Dimension. Let's keep rolling!

Step Two: Filtering IRF Rights

Earlier we learned there are two ways of blocking unwanted inherited rights: new trustee assignments and the Inherited Rights Filter (IRF). The IRF blocks inherited rights at any point in the tree. There are, however, two very important points you must understand about how the IRF works:

▸ It's an inclusive filter, which means the rights that are in the filter are the ones that are allowed to pass through.

▸ The IRF applies to everyone in the NDS tree. Once you've assigned an IRF to a directory, everyone is blocked *except* Admin (or anyone else with the [S] file system right).

This is the only place where file system and NDS security differs. The NDS IRF blocks the Supervisor right. The file system IRF, on the other hand, *cannot* block the Supervisor right. As you can see in Figure 5.31, the IRF is assigned using the Trustees of this Directory option. Also notice that the Supervisor right has been grayed out. This means it cannot be removed. Also notice the downward arrows that appear next to each option box. These differentiate IRF rights from trustee assignments. Anywhere you see a downward arrow, you can assume it's an IRF filter.

When you assign an IRF, all sorts of crazy things happen. My word of advice is, "Avoid them at all cost." But if you can't, you'll need to deal with Step Three—calculating effective rights.

Step Three: Calculating Effective Rights

As we learned earlier, effective rights are the bottom line. This is the culmination of our three-step process. In Step One, we assign the rights. In Step Two, we filter the rights. In Step Three, we calculate exactly what the rights are. We also learned that calculating effective rights is as simple as modern math—in the 7th Dimension! Any object's effective rights are the combination of file system privileges received through any of the following:

▸ Trustee assignments made to the user

▸ Inheritance minus rights blocked by the IRF

▸ Rights granted to the special [Public] trustee

▸ Security equivalences to parent containers, groups, or Organizational Roles

As we learned earlier, calculating effective rights for NDS can be mind-boggling and fun. The file system is no different. Let's use Maid Marion as an example. Suppose we're concerned about users making changes to our political database. To protect it, we assign an [RF] filter to SYS:SHARED\POL. This will block MMarion's inherited rights of [RWCEF]. Therefore, her effective rights should be Read and File Scan [RF]. But as you can see in Figure 5.32, her effective rights in SYS:SHARED\POL are, in fact, [RWF]. How did this happen? She must be getting the [W] right from somewhere else. Ah, I remember. She's a member of the POL-Group and they've been granted Write privileges to SYS:SHARED\POL. Therefore, her effective rights become inherited rights minus the IRF *plus* group trustee assignments.

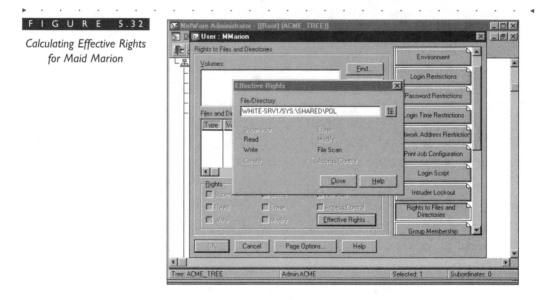

F I G U R E 5.32

Calculating Effective Rights for Maid Marion

NWADMIN provides an excellent tool for viewing effective rights—check out Figure 5.32. All you have to do is identify the user (MMarion) and the directory (SYS:SHARED\POL)—NWADMIN does all the rest.

There you have it. The simple three-step file system security model:

▶ Step One: Assigning NDS Rights—Through trustee assignments, inheritance, and/or security equivalence.

▶ Step Two: Filtering IRF Rights—The inclusive filter allows you to block inherited rights.

▸ Step Three: Calculating Effective Rights—Just like modern math in the 7th Dimension.

That was a fun review. It's fortunate for us that IntranetWare uses the same model for both NDS and file system security. Even though these two layers apply to dramatically different network elements, they approach security in a similar way. Hopefully, now you have a firm handle on access rights, default assignments, trustees, inheritance, the IRF, and effective rights. They all work together as a synergistic solution for risk management. Of course, there's always that isolated exception when four layers of security aren't quite enough. You never know when a hacker will show up with armor-piercing bullets. Fortunately, IntranetWare has one more layer for just these emergencies—file/directory attributes. Let's check it out.

ZEN

"Shot . . . by you? I'm afraid not my primitive friend. Your kind has neither the cranial capacity nor the opposable digits to operate a firearm."

Mr. Montgomery Burns

Layer Five—Directory/File Attributes

Welcome to the final layer. I bet you never thought you'd get here. Directory and file attributes provide the final and most sophisticated layer of the IntranetWare security model. These attributes are rarely used, but provide a powerful tool for specific security solutions. If all fails, you can always turn to attribute security to save the day.

Attributes are special assignments or properties that are assigned to individual directories or files. Attribute security overrides all previous trustee assignments and effective rights. Attributes can be used to prevent deleting a file, copying a file, viewing a file, and so on. Attributes also control whether files can be shared, mark files for backup purposes, or protect them from data corruption using the Transactional Tracking System (TTS).

Attributes allow you to manage what users can do with files once they have access to them. Attributes are global security elements that affect all users, regardless of their rights, and they override all previous levels of security. Let's say, for example, Maid Marion has all rights except [SAM] to the SYS:APPS\WP directory—[RWCEF]. You can still restrict her from deleting a specific file by assigning it the Read-Only attribute. Therefore, the true effective rights for Maid Marion in this directory are the combination of her effective file system rights *and* file attributes.

IntranetWare supports two types of attributes: directory and file. Directory attributes apply to directories only, whereas file attributes can be assigned to files. In both of these cases, attributes fall into one of three categories:

▶ Security attributes

▶ Feature attributes

▶ Disk management attributes

Security attributes affect users' security access—what they can do with files. Feature attributes, on the other hand, affect how the system interacts with files. That is, whether the files can be archived, purged, or transactionally tracked. Finally, disk management attributes apply to file compression, data migration, and block suballocation.

Let's take a closer look at IntranetWare attribute security, starting with security attributes.

SECURITY ATTRIBUTES

Security attributes protect information at the file and directory level by controlling two kinds of file access—file sharing and file alteration. File access security controls not so much *who* can access the files but *what kind of access* they have. Once users have been given the proper trustee assignments to a given directory, they're in the door. Security attributes tell users they what he or she can do with the files once they're there. Here's a list of IntranetWare's security attributes and a brief description. An asterisk (*) indicates any attribute that affects both directories and files.

▸ Copy Inhibit (Ci)—Only valid on Macintosh workstations. Prevents users from copying the file. Even if users have been granted the Read and File Scan [RF] rights, they still can't copy this specific file. Macintosh users can, however, remove the Ci attribute if they have been granted the Modify [M] access right.

▸ Delete Inhibit (Di)*—Prevents users from erasing the directory or file.

▸ Execute Only (X)—This is an extremely sensitive attribute and provides a very high level of IntranetWare security. Only the Supervisor, Admin, or anyone with the Supervisor [S] right can set this file attribute—and it *cannot* be cleared. The only way to remove X is to delete the file. The Execute Only attribute can only be assigned to .EXE and .COM files. These files cannot be copied or backed up—just executed or deleted. You should note that many applications don't work on files with the Execute Only attribute attached.

▸ Hidden (H)*—Valid on both DOS and OS/2 machines. Hidden is reserved for special files or directories that should not be seen, used, deleted, or copied over. However, the NDIR command will display the directory if the user has File Scan [F] access rights.

▸ Normal (N)*—No directory or file attributes have been set. This is the default. Normal files are typically flagged non-sharable, Read/Write automatically.

▸ Read-Only (Ro)—No one can write to the file. When Read Only is set or cleared, IntranetWare also sets or clears the Delete Inhibit and Rename Inhibit attributes. Consequently, a user can't write to, erase, or rename a file when Read Only is set. A user with the Modify access right can remove the Di and Ri attributes without removing Ro. In this case, the file can be deleted or renamed, but not written to.

▸ Read/Write (Rw)—Allows users to change the contents of the file. This attribute is assigned automatically using the Normal (N) attribute.

▶ Rename Inhibit (Ri)*—Prevents a user from renaming the file or directory.

▶ Sharable (Sh)—Allows the file to be accessed by more than one user at a time. This attribute is usually used in combination with Ro for application files. The default "Normal" setting is non-sharable.

▶ System (Sy)*—Applies to DOS and OS/2 workstations. The IntranetWare OS assigns this attribute to system-owned files and directories. System files are hidden and cannot be deleted, renamed, or copied. However, the IntranetWare NDIR command will display the file if the user has File Scan access rights.

That does it for security attributes. Now let's take a closer look at feature attributes.

FEATURE ATTRIBUTES

Feature attributes provide access to special IntranetWare functions or features. These features include backup, purging, and transactional tracking. As a matter of fact, there are only three feature attributes in IntranetWare, and one of them applies to both directories and files (P). Here's how they work:

▶ Archive Needed (A)—A status flag set by IntranetWare, which indicates that the file has been changed since the last time it was backed up. IntranetWare sets this attribute when a file is modified and clears it during SBACKUP full and incremental sessions. We'll learn more about this in Chapter 13.

▶ Purge (P)*—Tells IntranetWare to purge the file when it is deleted. The file then cannot be salvaged with FILER. Purge at the directory level clears all files and directories from the salvage table once they're deleted. This attribute is best used on sensitive data.

▶ Transactional (T)—Indicates that the file is protected by IntranetWare's internal Transactional Tracking System (TTS). TTS prevents data corruption by ensuring that either all changes are made or no changes are made when a file is being modified. The Transactional attribute should be assigned to TTS-tracked database and accounting files.

That does it for IntranetWare feature attributes. Now let's take a quick look at disk management.

DISK MANAGEMENT ATTRIBUTES

The remaining seven file and directory attributes apply to IntranetWare disk management—file compression, data migration, and block suballocation. File compression allows more data to be stored on a volume by compressing files that are not being used. Once you enable this disk management feature, volume capacity increases up to 63 percent. Data migration is the transfer of inactive data from an IntranetWare volume to an external optical disk storage device—called a *jukebox*. The process is transparent to the user because files appear to be stored on the volume. Data migration is made possible because of IntranetWare's internal High Capacity Storage System (HCSS). Finally, block suballocation increases disk storage efficiency by segmenting disk allocation blocks. Suballocation is also automatic, and you can turn it off using one of the following seven attributes. Here's a quick look at IntranetWare's disk management attributes:

▶ Can't Compress (Cc)—A status flag set by IntranetWare. Indicates that the file can't be compressed because of insignificant space savings. To avoid the overhead of uncompressing files that do not compress well, the system calculates the compressed size of a file before actually compressing it. If no disk space will be saved by compression, or if the size difference does not meet the value specified by the "Minimum Percentage Compression Gain" parameter, the file is not compressed. This attribute is shown on attribute lists, but cannot be set by users or CNAs.

▶ Compressed (Co)—A status flag set by IntranetWare. Indicates that the file has been compressed by the system. Once again, this attribute is shown on attribute lists but cannot be set by the user or CNAs.

▶ Don't Compress (Dc)*—Marks a file or directory so that it is never compressed. It is a way of managing file compression. This attribute is used in combination with Ic (immediate compression). We'll check this out in just a moment.

▸ Don't Migrate (Dm)*—Marks a file or directory so that it is never migrated to a secondary storage device. This is the only way you can directly manage data migration. Otherwise, all files are automatically migrated once they exceed the timeout threshold.

▸ Don't Suballocate (Ds)—Prevents an individual file from being suballocated even if suballocation is enabled on the volume. This is typically used for files that are huge or appended to frequently, such as databases. This attribute is your only tool for managing suballocation once it's been activated.

▸ Immediate Compress (Ic)*—Marks a file or directory for immediate compression. IntranetWare will compress the file as soon as it can without waiting for a specific event to initiate compression—such as a time delay. As a CNA, you can use Ic to turn on compression and Dc to turn it off. Both attributes operate at the file and directory level.

▸ Migrated (M)—A status flag set by IntranetWare. Indicates that the file has been migrated. This attribute is shown on an attribute list, but can't be set by the user or CNA.

TIP

Any of these attributes can be modified using the FLAG command line utility or NETADMIN menu utility and/or NWADMIN graphical utility. In addition to these tools, attributes can be viewed using NDIR.

These file and directory attributes, when used in combination, can create effective security tools to control who has access to do what with specialized IntranetWare files. The default attribute combination for all files is Normal—nonsharable Read/Write. There are special instances, however, when you can justify customizing these attributes, such as

▶ Stand-alone applications that are not to be shared should be flagged nonsharable Read-Only.

▶ Data files that are shared but not written to simultaneously should be flagged nonsharable Read/Write.

▶ Data files that are part of larger multiuser applications can be flagged Sharable Read/Write only if the application supports internal record locking.

▶ Application files that are accessed by simultaneous users should be flagged Sharable Read-Only.

▶ Large important database files should always be flagged with the Transactional (T) attribute, but be sure the application supports TTS.

▶ Sensitive archive files should be flagged with the attribute Hidden. These include records that are only accessed once a month.

▶ All System files owned by IntranetWare should be flagged System. This is an attribute assigned by IntranetWare, not you.

▶ Sensitive application files that cost a significant amount of money should be flagged Execute Only by the network administrator. However, be careful, because not all applications will run when flagged "X."

Congratulations! You've completed the IntranetWare's five-layered security model. Wow, what a wild ride. It all started with risk analysis and countermeasures. We learned the absolute goal of IntranetWare security:

Let the good guys in and keep the bad guys out.

We also learned that IntranetWare's five-layered security model is an increasingly more secure series of barriers against network threats—users. In Layer One, they log into the "Cloud" with initial and background authentication. Then login restrictions take over. This barrier controls the user's conditional access through five different types of restrictions—account, password, station, time, and

Intruder Detection/Lockout. Once the user passes through the first two barriers, their ability to access leaf and container objects is determined by a sophisticated NDS security structure. At the heart of NDS security is a simple three-step process—trustee assignments, IRF, and effective rights.

But what about security *within* the server? NDS security isn't enough. Now we must protect the file system. File system security operates in much the same way as NDS object rights. They're granted with the help of trustee assignments, inheritance, and security equivalence. We learned how the eight different access rights can be used to protect IntranetWare files and directories. But sometimes this isn't enough. That's where attributes come in. The final barrier allows you to override previous security with three different attribute types—security, feature, and disk management.

SMART LINK

For an in-depth review of IntranetWare's file system attributes, consult the on-line documentation at http://www.novell.com/manuals.

As a CNA, it is your responsibility to manage the IntranetWare network. But most importantly, you must protect it. Hopefully now you've gained a new appreciation for the value of an impenetrable network armor. We've filled your brain with sophisticated security strategies and given you a utility belt full of advanced protection tools—like NWADMIN and AUDITCON.

So, where do you go from here? The world is your oyster. It's amazing what a little security can do for your fragile psyche. Once all your risks are in check, there's no limit to what you can do. So far, you can manage NDS, synchronize time, map drives, and secure the WAN. I'd say you're becoming a full-fledged "IntranetWare gardener"! But what about the big picture? Now I think you're ready to journey through the life span of a LAN—starting with childhood (IntranetWare configuration) and continuing through adulthood (IntranetWare management). It all starts with a single seed.

REAL WORLD

Now you're a IntranetWare security expert—a real Sherlock Holmes of the WAN. But before you can move on to IntranetWare Configuration and Management, you should take a moment to explore a few final tips concerning NetWare Enhanced Security. Remember, information is valuable and many of today's advanced networks require Class C-2 security configurations. Here's a few "Dos" and "Don'ts".

Do List

Do read the on-line manuals before installing the server software.

Do physically restrict the console to prevent access by nonadministrative users.

Do make and securely store frequent backups of TCB configuration files. Your computer system can be replaced, but it may not be possible to replace the data stored on your system.

Do set the console parameter to disable use of audit passwords (as required for the NetWare Enhanced Security configuration).

Do configure your audit trails properly: only trusted users as Audit Administrators and Audit Viewers; only workstation TCBs as Audit Sources.

Do provide sufficient space for audit data collection.

Do archive audit files on a regular basis.

Do keep a manual record of per-user and per-file audit configuration flags, since they are not backed up by SBACKUP.

Do file reports (User Comment Forms) with Novell if you find any problems with the server programs or documentation.

Do create a separate account (for example, BBAILEY-ADM) for administrative work.

Do set up a separate administrative account for each administrator. (Don't share administrator accounts.)

Do use a strong password for your administrative accounts.

Do change the password frequently for your administrative accounts.

Do set up a separate administrative account for each dministrator (that is, do not share the ADMIN account).

(continued)

(continued)

Do configure the server to remove DOS (either UNLOAD DOS or SECURE CONSOLE) after IntranetWare has booted.

Do configure the IPX restriction on all printer objects so that print servers will accept connections only from valid printer drivers.

Do protect SYS:PUBLIC, SYS:SYSTEM, and SYS:MAIL by defining the appropriate file system rights settings.

Do set up print queues, print servers, and printers such that only trusted users are on the list of operators, only evaluated print servers are on the list of servers, and all users are on the list of users.

Do modify the "User Template" settings before creating any users: set minimum password length to at least eight characters, password required to "yes," and account disabled to "true."

Do use the user template when creating new users.

Do develop a site policy for password changes, and enforce it.

Do configure the "User Template" and all NDS User objects so that each user can change his or her own password.

Do enable password expiration.

Do configure audit trails to shut off operations when audit trails fill, to avoid audit loss.

Do physically protect the licensing diskette.

Do protect printed output and instruct users to do likewise.

Do protect removable media (such as tapes and floppy disks) and instruct users to do likewise.

Don't List

Don't allow general (nonadministrative) users to have access to the server console.

Don't type your administrative password at any time other than (a) when running INSTALL to set up the server, (b) at the server console SBACKUP prompt, or (c) to the TCB of an evaluated client component.

Don't specify the optional parameters (—s, —na, —ns) when you boot the server for normal operation. This is because the STARTUP.NCF, AUTOEXEC.NCF, and INITSYS.NCF files help initialize the server's secure state.

Don't install arbitrary untrusted NLM executables.

Don't give the [Public] object any additional rights beyond those available in the standard distribution (that is, "out of the box"). Rights given to the [Public] object are available to all users on the network.

Don't give sensitive names to what is public information (such as usernames, container names, server names, email addresses, or people's names).

Don't add unevaluated peripherals to the server hardware configuration.

Don't use workstations as queue servers or queue operators, unless the queue server is an evaluated part of a workstation component.

Don't install name space NLM programs that are not part of the NetWare Enhanced Security configuration. Consequently, only the DOS name space is supported on the server.

Don't use undocumented console operations, as they may place the server into an unevaluated configuration.

Don't load NLM programs associated with the AppleTalk Filing Protocol (AFP) or TCP/IP protocol suite.

Don't use undocumented console operations, as they violate the servicer's NetWare Enhanced Security configuration

Don't believe all telephone calls or e-mail messages you receive. For example, the Computer Emergency Response Team (CERT) has documented cases of messages telling users to temporarily change their passwords to a certain value "for debugging purposes."

CASE STUDY: ACME SECURITY

In this exercise, we are going to explore the exciting world of IntranetWare NDS and file system security. In order to complete this exercise, you will need to install a server called WHITE-SRV1 in the WHITE.CRIME.TOKYO.ACME container.

Initially, the Crime division, the White-Collar Crime department, and the three White-Collar Crime units (Cyber Crime, Financial Crime, and Political Crime) will be sharing the same server (.WHITE-SRV1.WHITE.CRIME.TOKYO.ACME)—but not the same data. The Users in the Crime division office will be located in a container called CRIME.TOKYO.ACME. The White-Collar Crime department and its three Crime units will be located in a subcontainer called WHITE.CRIME.TOKYO.ACME.

You will need to create Group objects for each of these workgroups (namely, CRIME-Group, WHITE-Group, CYBER-Group, FIN-Group, and POL-Group).

Temporarily, the managers of each workgroup will act as network administrators for their respective workgroups. Because these administrator assignments are temporary, you will need to create an Organizational Role for each (called CRIME-Admin, WHITE-Admin, CYBER-Admin, FIN-Admin, and POL-Admin, respectively).

Each workgroup will be given rights to the SYS:SHARED directory as well as to its own subdirectory under the SYS:SHARED directory (namely, SYS:SHARED\CRIME, SYS:SHARED\WHITE, SYS:SHARED\CYBER, SYS:SHARED\FIN, and SYS:SHARED\POL). The SHARED directory will contain those files that are shared by the entire division, whereas the individual subdirectories will contain those files that are shared by each workgroup. An Inherited Rights Filter (IRF) will be placed on each of the subdirectories under SHARED, so that users from one department cannot see the files from another.

Everyone in these five workgroups will have access to the word processing program (stored in SYS:APPS\WP70). In addition, the Financial Crime unit will have access to the spreadsheet program (stored in SYS:APPS\SS30) and the Cyber Crime unit will have access to the database program (stored in SYS:APPS\DB50). Each workgroup is currently generating a list of other applications that they'd like on the server.

User Template objects will be used for consistency in creating User objects and will contain the following account restrictions:

▸ Each User will be limited to one concurrent login.

▸ Each User will be required to have a *unique* password consisting of 7 characters or more and will be required to change their password every 90 days. Each User will be allowed six grace logins.

▸ Because employees in this division work long hours, there will be no time restrictions on anyone's account except between 3:00 a.m. to 4:00 a.m. daily (when system backups and network maintenance are performed).

▸ Intruder detection will be set to lock for 24 hours after 6 incorrect attempts in 24 hours. Intruder detection statistics will be kept for 30 days.

Now that you know the plan, let's go ahead and implement it!

1. Execute the NetWare Administrator utility.

    a. Make sure that you are logged into the network as .Admin.ACME.

    b. Execute the NetWare Administrator utility under Windows 3.1x or Windows 95. (If you haven't created an icon yet, you can find the NetWare Administrator utility under SYS:PUBLIC\NWADMN3X if you're using Windows 3.1x or SYS:PUBLIC\WIN95\NWADMN32 if you're using Windows 95.)

2. Set the current context for the NetWare Administrator utility.

    a. Click on the maximize button in the upper-right corner of the browser window to maximize the browser screen. A portion of the NDS tree should be displayed. If so, move on to Step 2b. If not, select the NDS Browser option from the Tools menu to open a browser window. A Set Context dialog box will be displayed. Make sure that ACME_TREE is listed in the Tree field. Type **[Root]** in the Context field, then click on OK to set the context to the [Root]. Now that you've set the context, proceed to Step 2c below.

b. Next, be sure that your current context for this utility is set to the [Root]. If the [Root] icon is displayed at the top of the screen, proceed to Step 2c. Otherwise, set the context to the [Root] by clicking on the Set Context option in the View menu. A Set Context dialog box will be displayed. Make sure that ACME_TREE is listed in the Tree field. Type **[Root]** in the Context field, then click on OK.

c. Finally, you'll want to get a visual perspective of where these containers are located in the NDS tree. If the contents of the WHITE Organizational Unit are displayed, proceed to Step 3. Otherwise, double-click on the following containers, in order: ACME , TOKYO, CRIME, and WHITE.

3. Create the basic file system directory structure. Double-click on the WHITE-SRV1_SYS Volume object in order to display the directories under it. (Use the scroll bar on the right side of the screen, if necessary, to bring it into view.)

a. Press the Insert button to display the Create Directory dialog box. To create the USERS directory, type **USERS** in the Directory Name field, then click on the Create Another Directory box, then click on the Create button.

b. Another Create Directory dialog box will be displayed. To create the SHARED directory, type **SHARED** in the Directory name field, then click on the Create Another Directory box to de-select it, then click on the Create button.

c. To create the CRIME subdirectory under the SHARED directory, click on the SHARED folder icon, then press the Insert button to display the Create Directory dialog box. Type **CRIME** in the Directory Name field, then click on the Create Another Directory box, then click on the Create button. Follow the same procedure to create the WHITE, CYBER, FIN, and POL directories under the SHARED directory.

d. Finally, use the same procedure to create a SYS:APPS directory, then create the following directories under it: DB50, SS30, and WP70.

4. Set Intruder Detection/Lockout defaults for the CRIME and WHITE containers. Click on the CRIME container with the right mouse button, then click on the Details menu option with the left mouse button. Next, click on the Intruder Detection page button. Click on the Detect Intruders box, then key in the following Intruder Detection limits:

Incorrect Login Attempts: **6**

Intruder Attempt Reset Interval: **1 days, 0 hours, 0 minutes**

Next, click on the Lock Account After Detection box and type in the following information:

Intruder Lockout Reset Interval: **30days, 0 hours, 0 minutes**

Finally, click on the OK button to save these changes, then use the same procedure to set the Intruder Detection/Lockout parameters for the WHITE container.

5. Create a User Template object for TOKYO container. As you know, changes to a User Template object affect only those users created after the changes are made. Since no users have been created yet, this will not be a problem. Make sure that the TOKYO container is highlighted, and press Insert. The New Object window will be displayed. Type **T** and press Enter to select the Template object. Type **TOKYO-UT** in the Name field, then click on the Define Additional Properties box. Finally, click on the Create button to create the User Template. You'll notice a set of page buttons along the right side of the screen. Select the page buttons listed below and make the changes indicated.

a. Identification page button. The Identification object dialog will be displayed by default. Type the following information on this screen:

Location: **Tokyo, Japan**

Telephone: **813-5481-1141**

Fax Number: **813-5481-855**

b. Environment page button. Click on the Environment page button. Walk the tree to select the following Home Directory information:

Volume: **WHITE-SRV1_SYS.WHITE.CRIME.TOKYO.ACME**

Path: **USERS**

c. Login Restrictions page button. Click on the Login Restrictions page button.

Click on the Limit Concurrent Connections box. A value of 1 will be displayed in the Maximum Connections field.

d. Password Restrictions. Click on the Password Restrictions page button, then perform the following tasks:

Make sure the Allow User to Change Password box is checked.

Click on the Require a Password box.

Indicate a Minimum Password Length of **7**.

Click on the Force Periodic Password Changes box.

e. Indicate a value of 90 for Days Between Forced Changes.

Click on the Require Unique Passwords box.

Click on the Limit Grace Logins box.

Accept the default of six Grace Logins Allowed.

Click on the Set Password after Create box so that you will be prompted to supply a login password whenever you create a User object using this User Template object.

f. Login Time Restrictions page button. Next, go ahead and restrict login privileges between 3:00 a.m. and 4:00 a.m. every day. Click on the Login Time Restrictions page button. A grid will be displayed on the screen showing days of the week along the left edge and time of day across the top. Each cell in the grid represents a half-hour period during the week. You'll notice that when you place the mouse cursor in a cell, the day and time the cell represents is displayed. White cells represent times during which the user is allowed to log in; gray cells indicate times that the user is prevented from logging in. Click on the 3:00 and 3:30 cells for each day of the week. (Alternately, you can click on the cell corresponding to 3:00 a.m. Sunday, and while holding down the mouse button, drag the mouse cursor to the rectangle representing 3:30 a.m. Saturday before releasing the mouse button.)

g. Postal Address page button. Click on the Postal Address button and fill in the following information:

Street: **Toei Mishuku Building; 1-13-1, Mishuku**

City: **Setagaya-ku, Tokyo 154**

State or Province: **Japan**

When you have finished updating the User Template, click on the OK button at the bottom of the screen to save the changes that you have made.

6. Copy the TOKYO User Template to the CRIME and WHITE containers. Click on the CRIME container and press Insert. Type **T** and press Enter to select the Template object. Type **CRIME-UT** in the Name field, then click on the Use Template or User box to copy the properties of the TOKYO-UT User template located in the TOKYO.ACME container. Follow the same procedure for copying the User Template to the WHITE container.

7. Create Group objects. Before you can create users, you will need to create the Group objects that they will be members of. Click on the CRIME container and press Insert. The New Object window will appear. Click on G and press Enter to select the Group object. Type **CRIME-Group** in the Group Name field, then click on the Define Additional Properties box, then click on the Create button. The Group Object Identification screen will be displayed. Fill in the following information:

    Location: **Tokyo, Japan**

    Department: **Crime-Fighting**

    Organization: **ACME**

    Click on the OK button when you are finished. Follow the same procedure for creating the WHITE, CYBER, FIN, and POL groups (called WHITE-Group, CYBER-Group, FIN-Group, and POL-Group respectively) in the WHITE container.

8. Create User objects. Next, you'll need to create the SHolmes and DrWatson User objects in the CRIME container and the RHood, LJohn, MMarion, and FrTuck User objects in the WHITE container.

a. Click on the CRIME container and press Insert. Type **U** and press Enter to select the User object. Type **SHolmes** in the Login Name field and **Holmes** in the Last Name field. Click on the Use Template, Create Home Directory, and Define Additional Properties boxes. Type **CRIME-UT.CRIME.TOKYO.ACME** in the Use Template field. Finally, click on the Create button. You will be asked to supply a password. Choose a password you will remember in the Password field, the same password in the Retype Password field, then click on OK.

b. The Identification screen for the SHolmes User object will be displayed. Click on the Group Membership page button to select it. (You may have to use the scrollbar along the right side of the screen to bring it into view.) Click on the Add button to display the Select Object dialog box. Double-click on the CRIME-Group object in the Available Objects box on the left side of the screen, then click on OK to add this user as a member of the CRIME-Group.

c. Follow the procedure listed above for adding the DrWatson User Object to the CRIME container and the RHood, LJohn, MMarion, and FrTuck User objects to the WHITE container (indicating the CRIME, WHITE, FIN, POL, and CYBER groups, respectively).

9. Create Organizational Role objects. Your next task will be to create an Organizational Role object for each workgroup manager. Create an Organizational Role object for SHolmes by clicking on the CRIME container, then pressing Insert. Type **O** and press Enter to select the Organizational Role object. Type **CRIME-Admin** in the Organizational Role Name field, click on the Define Additional Properties box, then click on the Create button. The CRIME-Admin Organizational Role Identification screen will be displayed. Click the browser button to the right of the Occupant field, then click on the Add ... button. Double-click on the SHolmes icon in the Available Objects list box on the left side of the screen, then click on the OK button in the Occupant Window. Finally, click on the OK button at the bottom of the screen to accept the changes you've made to this Organizational Role object.

Using this same technique, create Organizational Roles for the following users in the WHITE container: RHood (WHITE-Admin), FrTuck (CYBER-Admin), LJohn (FIN-Admin), and MMarion (POL-Admin).

10. Now that you've created the Organizational Roles for container administration, let's give them the rights they need. In this section, we will create an exclusive container administrator for CRIME (SHolmes) and WHITE (RHood). As you know, an exclusive administrator has all NDS rights to a container and blocks most rights (especially S) from everyone else.

   a. To start, assign SHolmes as the administrator for .CRIME.TOKYO.ACME. Click on the CRIME container, then press the right mouse button. Choose Trustees of this Object ... from the pull-down menu. Click on the Add Trustee ... button. Walk the tree until the SHolmes User object is listed in the Available Objects list box, then double-click on SHolmes to select it.

   b. Next, we'll need to assign SHolmes' object rights. Click on the Supervisor, Create, Delete, and Rename object rights, because the Browse box is already selected. Next, select the Supervisor, Add Self and Write property rights, because the Read and Compare property rights are already selected. With all rights in place, he's well on his way.

   c. Finally, click on the OK button at the bottom of the screen. Good work.

11. You have successfully made SHolmes an administrator of the .CRIME.TOKYO.ACME container. He currently shares this role with Admin. Now comes the "exclusive" part. We need to create an IRF of [B] for the CRIME container. This will block Admin, but not SHolmes.

a.   The CRIME container should still be highlighted in the NWADMIN Browser. Press the right mouse button, and choose Trustees of this Object.... Click on the Inherited Rights Filter.... button. Currently, the defaults are selected—that is, all five object rights [BCDRS] and all five property rights [SCRWA].

b.   To make SHolmes an exclusive administrator, click on "all rights except Browse". This will leave only the [B] object right selected. Next, click on "all five property rights" to de-select them. Finally, click on OK twice to return to the main NetWare Administrator browser window.

c.   Very good work. Now, repeat these steps (10 and 11) to make RHood the exclusive container administrator of .WHITE.CRIME.TOKYO.ACME.

12.   Assign file system rights to the file system. You are now ready to start assigning rights to the file system.

a.   Assign rights to the SHARED directory. Because all five workgroups will have the same level of access to the SHARED directory, you can grant these rights at the container level rather than at the Group level. Click on the SHARED folder (which is located under the WHITE-SRV1_SYS volume object), then select the Details option from the Object menu. Click on the Trustees of this Directory page button, then click on the Add Trustee … button. Walk the tree until the CRIME container is displayed in the Available Objects list box on the left side of the screen, then double-click on it. You'll notice that the container is automatically granted the Read and File Scan rights. Click on the Write, Create, and Erase rights, then click on the OK button to accept this trustee assignment. You will need to make the same trustee assignment to the WHITE container, because the Inherited Rights Filter (IRF) on the WHITE container will prevent these rights from flowing down from the CRIME container.

b. Assign rights to the CRIME directory under the SHARED directory. Double-click on the SHARED directory to display its contents, then click on the CRIME directory under it. Select Details from the Object menu, then click on the Trustees of this Directory page button. Next, click on the Add Trustee ... button, then walk the tree until the CRIME-Group is displayed in the Available Objects list box. Double-click on the CRIME-Group to select it.

c. As you can see, Read and File Scan rights are assigned by default when you create a trustee. Click on the Write, Create, and Erase rights to assign these rights to the CRIME-Group. Next, you'll want to change the Inherited Rights Filter for this directory so that most rights are not inherited from above. Click on each of the rights, except for the Supervisor right, in order to de-select them. The net effect will be to assign an IRF of [S]. Finally, click on OK to save your changes.

13. Assign trustee rights for the APPS subdirectories. Now that you know how to grant trustee rights for directories to containers and Group objects, use the same techniques to make the trustee assignments. If you'd really like a challenge, see if you can make these assignments from the trustee's perspective (that is, container or group) rather than the directory's perspective. (**Hint:** You can use the Rights to Other Objects ... option in the Object menu.)

a. Grant the CRIME container [RF] rights to the SYS:APPS\WP70 directory (since all five workgroups will have access to the word processing application).

b. Grant the FIN-Group [RF] rights to the SYS:APP\SS30 directory.

c. Grant the CYBER-Group [RF] rights to the SYS:APPS\DB50 subdirectory.

14. Assign trustee rights to Organizational Role objects. Grant the trustee rights listed below to the Organizational Roles indicated:

a. All five Organizational Roles should be granted all rights to the SHARED directory.

b. Each Organizational Role should be granted all rights to their corresponding workgroup's subdirectory under the SHARED directory.

c. Each Organizational Role should be granted all rights to the home directories of each user in their workgroup.

15. Verify effective rights. You can verify an object's effective rights to a directory from the object's perspective or the directory's perpective.

a. To verify an object's effective rights from the directory's perspective, you can click on the object with the right mouse button, then select the Details option from the pulldown menu that is displayed. Next, click on the Trustees of this Directory page button, then click on the Effective rights ... button. An Effective rights window will be displayed. Click on the Browser button to the right of the Trustee field. Walk the tree until the desired object is displayed in the Available Object list box on the left side of the screen. Double-click on the object to select it. The Effective rights screen will again be displayed. This time, the effective rights for this object will be displayed in black. (The rights they do not have will be displayed in gray.)

b. Practice verifying the effective rights of different objects for various directories that we worked with in this exercise from the directory's point of view.

c. Practice verifying the effective rights of different objects for various directories that we have worked with in this exercise from the object's point of view. (**Hint:** Use the Rights to Other Objects menu option.)

EXERCISE 5-1: CALCULATING NDS EFFECTIVE RIGHTS

OK, now that you're a pro with IntranetWare security, let's experiment with "modern math." Earlier in the chapter, we explored NetWare's version of calculus—calculating effective rights. We learned that both NDS and the file system have their own versions of effective rights—and they work exactly the same way:

Effective Rights = trustee assignments + inheritance - IRF (Inherited Rights Filter)

In this exercise, we'll begin Calculus 101 with NDS access rights. Then, in Exercise 11-2, you'll get an opportunity to explore file system access rights. Also, we've included some beautiful graphic worksheets to help you follow along. You can create your own at home with a pencil, some paper, and a ruler.

So, without any further ado, let's get on with CASE #1.

CASE #1

In this case, we are helping Sherlock Holmes gain administrative rights to the Crime Fighting division. Refer to Figure 5.33. It all starts at .CRIME.TOKYO.ACME, where he is granted [CD] NDS privileges. There is no IRF or inheritance in CRIME.

In the next container, WHITE, SHolmes gets [S] from his "CRIME-Group" group. Also, there's an IRF of [D]. Finally, these privileges flow down to the WHITE-SRV1 Server object and become inherited rights. But the server's IRF is set to [BR], so some of them are blocked. Also, SHolmes has an explicit trustee assignment of [D] to the WHITE-SRV1 server. Finally, Sherlock's home container, WHITE, is granted [C] privileges to the Server object.

CASE #2

After careful consideration, you decide that the above rights are inappropriate. So, let's try it one more time. But, in this case, we're going to use the WHITE-Admin Organizational Role instead of the "WHITE-Group" group. This gives us more administrative flexibility and narrows the scope of rights assignments. For this case, refer to Figure 5.34.

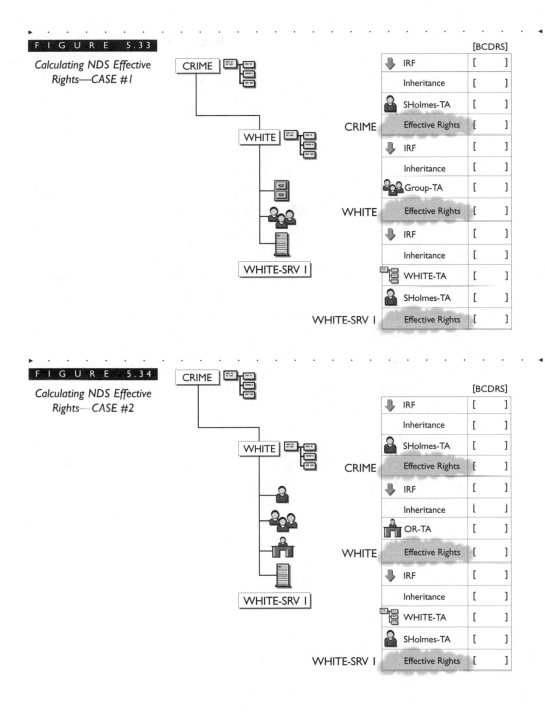

FIGURE 5.33

Calculating NDS Effective Rights—CASE #1

FIGURE 5.34

Calculating NDS Effective Rights—CASE #2

As before, it starts in the .CRIME.TOKYO.ACME container. Sherlock Holmes is granted the [BR] rights to the container. Also, there is no inheritance in CRIME, but the IRF has been set to [CD] anyway.

In the next container, WHITE, SHolmes gets [BCD] through his CRIME-Admin Organizational Role. Also, there's an IRF of [CDRS]. Finally, the container's effective rights flow down to the WHITE-SRV1 Server object and become inherited rights. But the server's IRF is set to [BR], so some of them are blocked. In addition, SHolmes has an explicit trustee assignment of [CD] to the WHITE-SRV1 server. Finally, Sherlock's home container, WHITE, is granted [B] privileges to the Server object. Now, let's see what he ends up with.

CASE #3

In this final case, let's bounce over to the .BLUE.CRIME.TOKYO.ACME container and help out Wyatt Earp—their administrator. Refer to Figure 5.35. As with most NDS trees, it actually starts much higher up—above TOKYO. Wyatt Earp inherits [BCDR] to .TOKYO.ACME through his User object. The IRF is identical, so all rights are allowed to flow through. In addition, he's granted Rename privileges as a user and Browse privileges through his home container—BLUE.

In the next container, CRIME, WEarp gets all object rights through his BLUE-Admin Organization Role. This overshadows the Browse privileges he ancestrally inherits from BLUE. Also, don't forget the CRIME IRF of [BCD]. Finally, all rights flow down to the BLUE container and become inherited. But the Organizational Unit's IRF is set to [DR], so most of them are blocked. In addition, WEarp has an explicit trustee assignment of [C] to BLUE. This assignment is enhanced by the Browse privilege he inherits from BLUE. Good luck.

Well, there you have it. Great work. Now that you're a security guru, let's dive into file system access rights. Rustle on over to Exercise 5-2.

Good luck, and by the way, thanks for saving the world!

See Appendix C for the answers.

FIGURE 5.35

*Calculating NDS Effective
Rights—CASE #3*

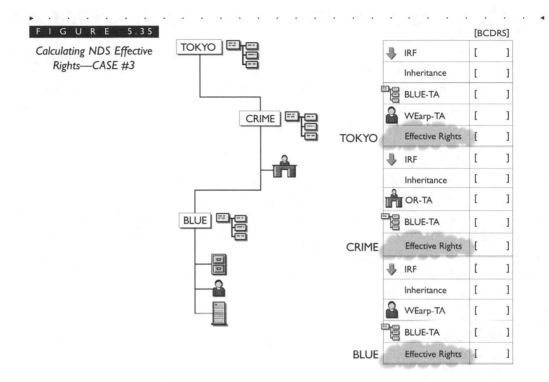

	[BCDRS]
⬇ IRF	[ ]
Inheritance	[ ]
🖧 BLUE-TA	[ ]
🧍 WEarp-TA	[ ]
TOKYO Effective Rights	[ ]
⬇ IRF	[ ]
Inheritance	[ ]
🏛 OR-TA	[ ]
🖧 BLUE-TA	[ ]
CRIME Effective Rights	[ ]
⬇ IRF	[ ]
Inheritance	[ ]
🧍 WEarp-TA	[ ]
🖧 BLUE-TA	[ ]
BLUE Effective Rights	[ ]

EXERCISE 5-2: CALCULATING FILE SYSTEM EFFECTIVE RIGHTS

Here you are. In case you're lost, here is modern math, part 2. In this exercise, we're going to explore the wonderful world of file system effective rights. Now that you've helped "administrate" Sherlock Holmes and Wyatt Earp, it's time to "liberate" the rest of the crime-fighting team, namely Robin Hood, Maid Marion, Dr. Watson, Little John, and Friar Tuck. Ah, a CNA's job is never done.

CASE #1

FrTuck has been made a trustee of the SYS:SHARED directory and granted Read, Write, Create, and File Scan rights. The IRF for the SYS:SHARED directory contains all rights; the IRF for the SYS:SHARED\CYBER directory contains Supervisor, Read, and File Scan; and the IRF for the CYBER.DOC file contains Read, Write, Create, and File Scan. Calculate FrTuck's effective rights in the SYS:SHARED directory, the SYS:SHARED\CYBER directory, and the CYBER.DOC file, using the worksheet in Figure 5.36.

▸ · · · · · · · · · · · · · · · · · · · ◂

FIGURE 5.36

Calculating File System Effective Rights—CASE #1

SYS:SHARED	S	R	C	W	E	M	F	A
Inherited Rights Filter								
Inherited Rights-User								
Inherited Rights-Group								
Trustee Assignment-User								
Trustee Assignment-Group								
Effective Rights								

SYS:SHARED\CYBER	S	R	C	W	E	M	F	A
Inherited Rights Filter								
Inherited Rights-User								
Inherited Rights-Group								
Trustee Assignment-User								
Trustee Assignment-Group								
Effective Rights								

CYBER.DOC	S	R	C	W	E	M	F	A
Inherited Rights Filter								
Inherited Rights-User								
Inherited Rights-Group								
Trustee Assignment-User								
Trustee Assignment-Group								
Effective Rights								

CASE #2

LJohn was made a trustee of the SYS:SHARED\FIN directory and granted all rights except Supervisor and Access Control. The FIN group, of which he is a member, was granted the Read, Write, Create, and File Scan rights to the SYS:SHARED directory. In addition, the FIN group was granted Read rights for the 99QTR4.RPT file. The IRF for the SYS:SHARED directory contains all rights; the IRF for the SYS:SHARED\FIN directory contains the Supervisor right; and the IRF for the 99QTR4.RPT file contains Supervisor, Read, Write, and File Scan rights. Calculate LJohn's effective rights in the SYS:SHARED directory, SYS:SHARED\FIN directory, and 99QTR4.RPT file, using the worksheet in Figure 5.37.

▶ · ◀

F I G U R E   5 . 3 7

Calculating File System Effective Rights—CASE #2

SYS:SHARED	S	R	C	W	E	M	F	A
Inherited Rights Filter								
Inherited Rights User								
Inherited Rights-Group								
Trustee Assignment-User								
Trustee Assignment-Group								
Effective Rights								

SYS:SHARED\FIN	S	R	C	W	E	M	F	A
Inherited Rights Filter								
Inherited Rights-User								
Inherited Rights-Group								
Trustee Assignment-User								
Trustee Assignment-Group								
Effective Rights								

99QTR4.RPT	S	R	C	W	E	M	F	A
Inherited Rights Filter								
Inherited Rights-User								
Inherited Rights-Group								
Trustee Assignment-User								
Trustee Assignment-Group								
Effective Rights								

CASE #3

DrWatson was granted the Read, Write, Create, and File Scan rights to the SYS:SHARED directory. The CRIME Group, of which he is a member, was granted Read, Write, Create, Erase, Modify, and File Scan rights to the SYS:CRIME directory. The CRIME Group was also granted Read and File Scan rights to the CRIME.DB file.

The IRF for the SYS:SHARED directory is all rights; the IRF for the SYS:SHARED\CRIME directory is Supervisor and Access Control; and the IRF for the CRIME.DB file is Supervisor, Read, Write, Create, and File Scan. Calculate DrWatson's effective rights in the SYS:SHARED directory, the SYS:SHARED\CRIME directory, and the CRIME.DB file, using the worksheet in Figure 5.38.

· ◄

FIGURE 5.38

Calculating File System Effective Rights—CASE #3

SYS:SHARED	S	R	C	W	E	M	F	A
Inherited Rights Filter								
Inherited Rights-User								
Inherited Rights-Group								
Trustee Assignment-User								
Trustee Assignment-Group								
Effective Rights								

SYS:SHARED\CRIME	S	R	C	W	E	M	F	A
Inherited Rights Filter								
Inherited Rights-User								
Inherited Rights-Group								
Trustee Assignment-User								
Trustee Assignment-Group								
Effective Rights								

CRIME.DB	S	R	C	W	E	M	F	A
Inherited Rights Filter								
Inherited Rights-User								
Inherited Rights-Group								
Trustee Assignment-User								
Trustee Assignment-Group								
Effective Rights								

CASE #4

MMarion was granted the Modify and Access Control rights to the SYS:SHARED\POL directory. In addition, the POL Group was granted the Read, Write, Create, Erase, and File Scan rights to both the SYS:SHARED and SYS:SHARED\POL directories. The IRF for the SYS:SHARED directory contains all rights; the IRF for the SYS:SHARED\POL directory contains the Supervisor right; and the IRF for the CRIME.RPT file contains all rights. Calculate MMarion's effective rights to the SYS:SHARED directory, the SYS:SHARED\POL directory, and the CRIMEP.RPT file, using the worksheet in Figure 5.39.

F I G U R E   5.39

Calculating File System
Effective Rights—CASE #4

SYS:SHARED	S	R	C	W	E	M	F	A
Inherited Rights Filter								
Inherited Rights-User								
Inherited Rights-Group								
Trustee Assignment-User								
Trustee Assignment-Group								
Effective Rights								

SYS:SHARED\POL	S	R	C	W	E	M	F	A
Inherited Rights Filter								
Inherited Rights-User								
Inherited Rights-Group								
Trustee Assignment-User								
Trustee Assignment-Group								
Effective Rights								

CRIME.RPT	S	R	C	W	E	M	F	A
Inherited Rights Filter								
Inherited Rights-User								
Inherited Rights-Group								
Trustee Assignment-User								
Trustee Assignment-Group								
Effective Rights								

CASE #5

SHolmes was granted all rights to the SYS:SHARED directory. The CRIME Group, of which he is a member, was granted Read, Write, Create, and File Scan rights to the SYS:SHARED\CRIME directory. The CRIME Group was also granted Read and File Scan rights to the CRIME.DB file. The IRF for the SYS:SHARED directory contains all rights; the IRF for the SYS:SHARED\CRIME directory contains the Supervisor right; and the IRF for the CRIME.DB file contains Supervisor, Read, and File Scan rights. Calculate SHolmes' effective rights to the SYS:SHARED directory, the SYS:SHARED\CRIME directory, and the CRIME.DB file, using the worksheet in Figure 5.40.

Calculating File System Effective Rights—CASE #5

SYS:SHARED	S	R	C	W	E	M	F	A
Inherited Rights Filter								
Inherited Rights-User								
Inherited Rights-Group								
Trustee Assignment-User								
Trustee Assignment-Group								
Effective Rights								

SYS:SHARED\CRIME	S	R	C	W	E	M	F	A
Inherited Rights Filter								
Inherited Rights-User								
Inherited Rights-Group								
Trustee Assignment-User								
Trustee Assignment-Group								
Effective Rights								

CRIME.DB	S	R	C	W	E	M	F	A
Inherited Rights Filter								
Inherited Rights-User								
Inherited Rights-Group								
Trustee Assignment-User								
Trustee Assignment-Group								
Effective Rights								

CASE #6

RHood was made a trustee of the SUMMARY.RPT file and granted the Read, Write, Create, Erase, and Modify rights. He was also made a trustee of the SYS:SHARED\WHITE directory and granted all rights. [PUBLIC] has been granted the Read and File Scan rights to the SYS:SHARED directory. The IRF for the SYS:SHARED directory contains the Supervisor, Read, File Scan, and Access Control rights; the IRF for the SYS:SHARED\WHITE directory contains the Supervisor, Read, and File Scan rights; and the IRF for the SUMMARY.RPT file contains the Supervisor right. Calculate RHood's effective rights for the SYS:SHARED directory, the SYS:SHARED\WHITE directory, and SUMMARY.RPT file, using the worksheet in Figure 5.41.

FIGURE 5.41

Calculating File System Effective Rights—CASE #6

SYS:SHARED	S	R	C	W	E	M	F	A
Inherited Rights Filter								
Inherited Rights-User								
Inherited Rights-Group or [Public]								
Trustee Assignment-User								
Trustee Assignment-Group or [Public]								
Effective Rights								

SYS:SHARED\WHITE	S	R	C	W	E	M	F	A
Inherited Rights Filter								
Inherited Rights-User								
Inherited Rights-Group or [Public]								
Trustee Assignment-User								
Trustee Assignment-Group or [Public]								
Effective Rights								

SUMMARY.RPT	S	R	C	W	E	M	F	A
Inherited Rights Filter								
Inherited Rights-User								
Inherited Rights-Group or [Public]								
Trustee Assignment-User								
Trustee Assignment-Group or [Public]								
Effective Rights								

The answers to all of these cases are in Appendix C.

EXERCISE 5-3: HOW SECURE DO YOU FEEL?

Circle the 20 IntranetWare Security terms hidden in this word search puzzle using the hints provided.

```
S  E  C  U  R  I  T  Y  Z  P  K  C  G  M  G  L  S  M  Y
T  J  Z  U  N  I  Q  U  E  P  A  S  S  W  O  R  D  S  Y
A  C  M  C  K  R  S  S  Z  P  Z  T  V  G  O  K  B  O  W
T  P  R  O  O  F  S  K  P  P  W  T  T  O  M  D  R  H  P
I  R  U  G  R  A  C  E  L  O  G  I  N  S  N  M  X  L  Q
O  I  O  B  J  E  C  T  R  I  G  H  T  S  J  U  T  H  S
N  V  D  Z  L  I  T  L  T  U  T  I  Y  A  B  T  Z  W  R
R  A  J  S  G  I  N  H  E  R  I  T  A  N  C  E  C  T  V
E  T  E  F  F  E  C  T  I  V  E  R  I  G  H  T  S  J  Q
S  E  C  U  R  I  T  Y  E  Q  U  I  V  A  L  E  N  C  E
T  K  R  P  R  Y  B  V  D  N  F  D  G  M  L  F  D  W  R
R  E  S  B  Q  P  G  W  P  X  G  F  W  T  W  B  H  P  J
I  Y  Y  O  B  G  V  X  L  G  O  T  B  B  M  C  A  V  M
C  L  H  F  W  T  Y  N  B  B  T  G  Y  P  T  Q  Y  E  K
T  I  M  E  R  E  S  T  R  I  C  T  I  O  N  S  U  F  P
I  N  T  R  U  D  E  R  D  E  T  E  C  T  I  O  N  X  U
O  R  U  S  T  H  G  I  R  Y  T  R  E  P  O  R  P  Q  F
N  C  P  P  A  C  K  E  T  S  I  G  N  A  T  U  R  E  F
S  N  W  P  B  Z  S  T  H  G  I  R  E  E  T  S  U  R  T
```

Hints:

1. Property of an object that lists trustees of the object.
2. The rights that an object can actually exercise for an object, directory, or file.
3. The number of times a user can log in with an expired password.
4. Flowing down of money or trustee rights.
5. Feature that tracks invalid login attempts.
6. Controls the rights that can be inherited from a parent container or directory.
7. Security feature that protects servers and workstations by preventing packet forgery.

8. Privileges assigned to an object that control its access to other objects, directories, or files.

9. An encryption scheme element that is user-specific and that can only be decrypted with a valid password.

10. A temporary encryption that is constructed from the signature, a message, the user's private key, and a randomly generated number.

11. Privileges required to view or modify the property of an object.

12. Special trustee which is similar to the EVERYONE Group found in earlier versions of NetWare.

13. Is a combination of value and threat.

14. Risk-prevention strategies.

15. Method of granting a User object the same rights as another object.

16. Login restriction that limits a user to specific workstation node IDs.

17. Login restriction that limits the hours during which a user can log in.

18. Privileges granted to an object that determine its access to another object, directory, or file.

19. System Fault Tolerance feature that protects database applications from corruption by backing out incomplete transactions.

20. Login restriction that requires a User to supply a new password that is different from previous passwords.

See Appendix C for answers.

EXERCISE 5-4: LET THE GOOD GUYS IN

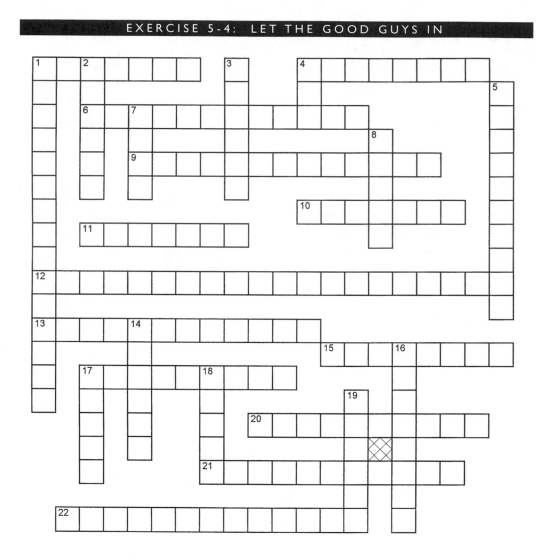

Across

1. Automatically granted with Read property right
4. Keeping the bad guys out
6. Central application control
9. Required for changing file system IRF
10. Automatically granted with Write property right
11. Graphical administrator tool

12. Object being security equivalent to parent
13. Object for global configuration
15. DOS text administrator tool
17. What is the "O" for?
20. Can be blocked by an NDS IRF
21. Third layer of NetWare 4 security
22. Property rights that can be inherited

Down

1. Preventative actions against threats
2. Required for changing file attributes
3. Required for seeing objects in the NDS tree
4. File system rights to consider restricting
5. Assigned to individual files or directories
7. Required for looking at file contents
8. Required for deleting a directory or file
14. Danger
16. Tracking important network events
17. Required for changing file contents
18. Initially is granted access to entire tree
19. For granting rights to unrelated users

See Appendix C for answers.

IntranetWare Configuration

5. E-Mail

4. Network Applications

3. Menu System

2. Login Scripts

1. Workstation
Connectivity

The birth of a LAN.

There are many different definitions of "life." The one that you choose depends entirely on your point of view. Regardless of your choice, the fundamental question remains—is your LAN alive? Judging from the following guidelines, I think so:

▶ Carbon-based organic life form—Silicon is close enough.

▶ Consumes food—Your LAN processes valuable information.

▶ Propagates—Most IntranetWare WANs include multiple servers.

▶ Self-awareness—Many times your network has a mind of its own.

There you go—your LAN must be alive. And, as a living, breathing life form, it must pass through the three phases of "life span"—birth, childhood, and adulthood. This evolution (that we all experience) can be both painful and rewarding. But there's nothing more exciting than watching it happen and being involved from Day One.

During birth, the IntranetWare server is installed. In the grand scheme of things, this event is theoretically quick and painless (although I don't know about the latter part). Decisions you make during installation may have an irrevocable impact on the server, LAN, and WAN. Birth is especially important in IntranetWare because of the importance of the NDS infrastructure.

Once the server has been installed, you are left with a simple directory structure, some workstations, and a few users—a LAN version of a cute little baby girl. Over time, this adorable little monster will learn to walk, talk, and start getting along with others. She will go to school and learn some valuable skills—ranging from how to climb the social ladder to how to deal with integral calculus. Finally, at some point, she will make an abrupt transition to adulthood—buy her first car, get her first job, and move into her first apartment.

SMART LINK

Explore your own IntranetWare Childhood at http://www.kids.com.

In IntranetWare, childhood is dominated by *IntranetWare Configuration*. During configuration, your server undergoes five important steps:

▶ Step 1: Workstation connectivity—Leia takes her first steps. In IntranetWare, workstation configuration files provide an initial attachment to the server and NDS. This is accomplished using Client 32 and Windows 95, or the 16-bit DOS solution.

▶ Step 2: Login scripts—Leia finally begins to talk (and doesn't stop for 85 years). In IntranetWare, login scripts enable you to customize user connections and establish important login settings.

▶ Step 3: Menu system—She learns how to share and begins getting along with others. In IntranetWare, the menu system provides a vital interface between users and the network. Just as Leia learns to get along with others, your users learn to get along with IntranetWare.

▶ Step 4: Network applications—Leia goes to school and learns important (and not so important) skills. In IntranetWare, applications are productivity tools that give the network value. These tools are undeniably bound to the aforementioned menu system—just like Leia is likely to make most of her friends in school.

▶ Step 5: E-mail—Leia makes a quick transition into adulthood by getting her first car, first job, and first apartment—all in the same week. In IntranetWare, e-mail provides a vital link between applications, interface, and management. Think of it as "the force that binds the network together."

ZEN

"Life is like a ten-speed bike. Most of us have gears we never use."

George Schultz

The third and final phase of "life span" is adulthood. At this point, your LAN is secure in its new purpose and the goal shifts from conception to "keeping it going." These are the golden years. During adulthood, your LAN will get married, have children of its own, plan for the future, and finally retire. Where do I sign up? This phase is controlled by *IntranetWare Management*. It goes something like this:

▶ Server management—Your LAN gets married and becomes part of a team. Remember LAN synergy—the whole is greater than the sum of its users. In IntranetWare, marriage takes the form of simple installation, server protection, console commands, and NLM parent tools.

▶ Workstation management—The family grows larger with the addition of three little "rug rats"—aka, children. Life suddenly takes on a whole new meaning. Your thoughts switch from "me" to "them"—cute little people who rely on you. In IntranetWare, these cute little people are represented by users and workstations. Workstation management relies on Client 32 or the 16-bit alternative: ODI files and the NetWare DOS Requester. You'll never truly understand the frustration and joy of running a network until you have children of your own.

▶ Storage Management Services (SMS)—With the family firmly in place and your children advancing through childhood, focus shifts to the future. You need to develop disaster recovery plans and begin saving for retirement. This is life's little backup (insurance) policy. In IntranetWare, backup management ensures job security. Remember Murphy's Law Number 107—the network WILL crash!

▶ Remote Management Facility (RMF)—Your children leave home and are off to a LAN of their own. Now it's time for you to take it easy. Through remote management, you can retire to Happy Acres and enjoy the good life. There's no reason to be involved in the daily grind anymore. In IntranetWare, RMF enables you to manage the central server from the comfort of your own office. And if you really want luxury, you can attach to the server from the comfort of your own sofa.

SMART LINK

For a more in-depth discussion of these IntranetWare management topics, refer to Chapter 7 or surf the Web to http://www.novell.com/manuals.

Wow, I bet you didn't think becoming a CNA would be such a life-changing experience! So far, the LAN has been relatively quiet—this will change. Remember, babies are cute until they learn to walk and talk and eat furniture. The daily bustle of humming workstations and crazed users will quickly take its toll on an unorganized IntranetWare LAN. That's why it's important to carefully configure it now—while things are still under control. It's imperative for you to establish workstation connections, write login scripts, and develop menu systems before the network goes into hyperactivity—configuring an active network is like tuning a moving car.

Consider this scenario: Guinevere walks into her office every morning, eager to begin a new day. She hangs up her coat, turns on the radio, and shifts her focus to the center of worklife—the computer. She gracefully reaches for the on/off switch and gives it a gentle nudge. Voilà! The day begins! During the booting process, Guinevere takes an opportunity to slip out for a quick cappuccino. When she returns, the machine displays a friendly network menu and her e-mail for the morning.

Magic! Although Guinevere doesn't pay much attention to what occurs while she's sipping her cappuccino, the LAN has undergone an entire childhood in only an instant. As a CNA, it's your responsibility to configure the system so that Guinevere doesn't have to worry about connectivity software, login scripts, VLMs, NMENU.BAT, or MHS. As a parent, it is your responsibility to make childhood as painless as possible.

Let's start our journey through the life span of a LAN with the first step— workstation connectivity.

SMART LINK

You can download the new Client 32 connectivity files for free at http://www.novell.com.

Step 1: Establishing Workstation Connectivity

Leia begins to walk.

The first step is always the most exciting. I hope you have your camcorder. While Leia's taking her first step, the network begins life anew as well. During this step, the client computer boots and activates a variety of configuration files. These configuration files establish the client environment and attach Guinevere to the network. All this magic can occur in a 32-bit or 16-bit world:

▸ Client 32—Provides 32-bit graphical access to NetWare 2.2, 3.12, and IntranetWare servers. It is the new and preferred way of networking from Windows 95, Windows 3.1, and/or DOS workstations.

▸ Client 16—Provides simple 16-bit DOS access to NetWare 2.2, 3.12, and IntranetWare servers. This is the older, stable method of accessing servers with ODI drivers, VLMs, and NET.CFG.

ZEN

In walking, just walk. In sitting, just sit. Above all, don't wobble.

Yun-Men

Once the first step of the configuration has been taken, Leia is well on her way toward childhood and Guinevere is well on her way toward LAN productivity. Let's take a closer look at these respective first steps, starting with Client 32.

WORKSTATION CONNECTIVITY WITH CLIENT 32

Client 32 is the newest and most powerful workstation connectivity software for IntranetWare. It is a 32-bit protected mode IntranetWare client that allows Windows 95, Windows 3.1, and DOS workstations to connect to NetWare 2.2, 3.12, and IntranetWare servers. In addition, it provides a graphical login utility for logging in from MS Windows. Finally, if you are running Windows 95, you can access network files and printers using the Network Neighborhood, the Windows Explorer, and various application dialog boxes.

All in all, this is a pretty powerful client system. Here's a quick checklist that will help you prepare your workstations for Client 32:

▶ An 80386 processor or better

▶ At least 6 MB of RAM for Windows 95, and at least 5 MB for Windows 3.1 and DOS

▶ 6K of conventional memory (with remaining memory allocated to extended space)

▶ A memory manager (such as HIMEM.SYS, EMM386.EXE, QEMM, or 386 MAX)

▶ Network board with the appropriate 32-bit LAN driver

▶ Physical connection to a IntranetWare WAN

▶ A supported local operating system

Before we explore the detailed steps of workstation connectivity with Client 32, let's take a moment to review the basic components of our network connection.

Understanding the Network Connection

Throughout this book, we have focused on the "network" as a distributed synergistic collection of computers. So far, we've been introduced to servers, networks, clients, and NDS. However, we haven't explored the basics of the workstation-to-server connection. This is the most fundamental platform of local and wide area networking.

In Chapter 3, we learned that the network workstation is made up of three fundamental components (see Figure 6.1):

▶ Network interface card (NIC)

▶ Workstation connectivity software

▶ Local operating system

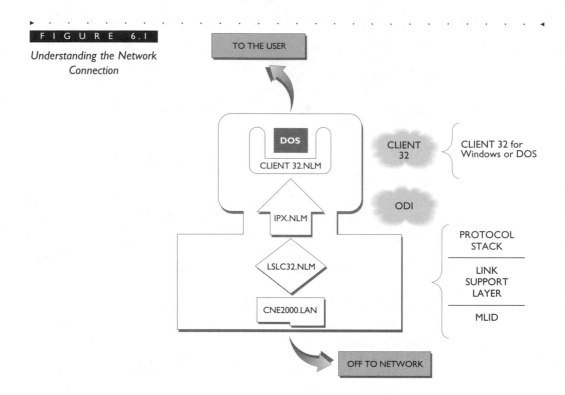

FIGURE 6.1

Understanding the Network Connection

It all starts with the NIC, which is the hardware component that provides electronic communication between the LAN cabling scheme and local operating system.

The local operating system provides a point of access for the LAN user. Without a local OS (like Windows 95 or DOS), there would be no way to tell the LAN what you need.

The vital connection between the NIC and local OS is provided by a collection of files called the "Workstation Connectivity Software." As you can see in Figure 6.1, this software consists of the following four main components:

▶ NIC driver—A driver that ontrols communications with the internal NIC. This is a hardware-specific LAN driver such as CNA2000.LAN. It's also known as the Multiple Link Interface Driver (MLID).

▸ Link Support Layer—Acts as a switchboard to route network protocol packets between the LAN driver and appropriate communications protocol. LSL is implemented at the workstation as LSLC32.NLM.

▸ Communications Protocol—A set of rules that determines the *language* used to move data across the network. The protocol guarantees that two devices using the same protocol can communicate because they speak the same language. This is accomplished at the Client 32 workstation using IPX.NLM.

▸ Client 32—A platform-independent NLM that provides 32-bit workstation access for Windows 95, Windows 3.1, and DOS operating systems. This facility is accomplished using the CLIENT32.NLM file.

Client 32 is the only client software for Windows 95 or Windows 3.1 that enables full support of NDS. Using Client 32, you can browse through network services, across multiple trees, and print from Network Neighborhood and Windows Explorer.

THE BRAIN

For more information on Client 32 architecture, refer to the "Workstation Management" section of Chapter 7.

Now that we understand the basics of workstation connectivity, let's check out Client 32 in action starting with Windows 95.

Connectivity with Windows 95

Workstation connectivity for Windows 95 and Windows 3.1 differ in one critical respect—Windows 95 is a true 32-bit native operating system environment. Windows 3.1, on the other hand, is an application that runs on top of 16-bit DOS. Because of this fact, Windows 95 benefits from all the 32-bit advantages of Client 32, including

▸ NIOS, the core Client 32 component, runs as a virtual device driver (VXD) rather than as an executable file.

▶ Client 32 does not require a STARTNET.BAT file. Windows 95 loads Client 32 at startup automatically.

▶ Client 32 does not need a NET.CFG file. Configuration settings are saved in the Windows 95 Registry allowing Client 32 parameters to be managed using the Windows 95 System Policy Editor (SPE).

▶ Client 32 for Windows 95 supports long filenames.

▶ Client 32 for Windows 95 is fully integrated into the Explorer and Network Neighborhood utilities. In addition, you can log into IntranetWare networks and run login scripts from the Windows 95 desktop environment.

▶ You're able to upgrade Windows 3.1 workstations to Windows 95 and Client 32 for Windows 95 in one installation process called the "Batch Install."

▶ Client 32 for Windows 95 supports the Windows 95 implementations of TCP/IP, WinSock, Named Pipes, and NetBIOS industry-standard protocols.

▶ Client 32 IPX protocol stack supports the Windows 95 WSOCK32.DLL.

▶ Simple Network Management Protocol (SNMP).

In addition, Windows 95 provides its own client for IntranetWare and Microsoft networks. The good news is Client 32 can coexist with the Microsoft client for Microsoft or IntranetWare networks.

Client 32 can be installed in a variety of ways using the Windows 95 Network Device Installer (NDI) and .INF script files to ensure full integration with the Windows 95 environment.

During the Client 32 installation, a directory named C:\NOVELL\CLIENT32 is created on the local hard drive. All the required files for Client 32 connectivity are placed in this directory and changes are made to the Windows 95 Registry. Refer to Table 6.1 for a list of these files and their specific load order.

	STEP	FILE	DESCRIPTION
T A B L E 6 . 1 *Client 32 Connectivity for Windows 95*	I	NIOS.VXD	The core Client 32 component. In Windows 95 it runs as a virtual device driver (VXD).
	2	LSLC32.NLM	Link Support Layer for protocol switchboarding.
	3	CNA2000.LAN	NIC driver. Remember this file is hardware-specific. Be sure to obtain the latest driver from your NIC manufacturer.
	4	CMSM.NLM	A C-based version of the Media Support Module in the ODI architecture.
	5	ETHERTSM.NLM	Client 32 uses Topology Support Modules (TSMs), which are components of the IntranetWare OS LAN Driver Architecture. ETHERTSM.NLM provides Ethernet topology support for the NIC driver.
	6	IPX.NLM	Communications protocol for the native IntranetWare IPX language.
	7	CLIENT32.NLM	The platform-independent module for all Client 32 services.

It all starts when Guinevere turns on her computer. This activates an internal 32-bit DOS system, which immediately loads the Windows 95 Registry. Once Windows 95 starts, the NIOS.VXD file activates and Table 6.1 takes over. It's as simple as 1-2-3-4-5-6-7.

Connectivity With Windows 3.1

Client 32 workstation connectivity for Windows 3.1 follows the same basic guidelines as Windows 95. The main difference is Windows 3.1 relies on a non-native, 16-bit version of DOS. For this reason, it uses the same client connectivity files as Client 16:

▸ CONFIG.SYS

▸ AUTOEXEC.BAT

▶ STARTNET.BAT

▶ NET.CFG

It all starts when Guinevere turns on her computer. At this point, DOS executes and calls CONFIG.SYS. Next AUTOEXEC.BAT activates the network-specific STARTNET.BAT batch file. Each command in STARTNET.BAT performs a specific function in creating the network connection. Check out Table 6.2.

TABLE 6.2	STEP	FILE	DESCRIPTION
Client 32 Connectivity for Windows 3.1	1	NIOS.EXE	The core Client 32 component, NIOS, runs as an executable file (.EXE) in Windows 3.1.
	2	LSLC32.NLM	Link Support Layer for protocol switchboarding.
	3	CNA2000.LAN	NIC driver. Remember this file is hardware-specific. Be sure to obtain the latest driver from your NIC manufacturer. At this point, the CMSM.NLM and ETHERTSM.NLM modules also must be loaded.
	4	IPX.NLM	Communications protocol for the native IntranetWare IPX language.
	5	CLIENT32.NLM	The platform-independent module for all Client 32 services.

Once STARTNET.BAT is completed, it returns control to AUTOEXEC.BAT. Keep in mind, it's best to eliminate STARTNET.BAT and place the specific connectivity steps from Table 6.2 directly into AUTOEXEC.BAT.

Refer to the "Workstation Connectivity with Client 16" section of this chapter for more information on client connectivity in a 16-bit environment.

Once you have connected using Client 32, you'll find that there are a few tricks for customizing its environment. The good news is Client 32 is designed to minimize the need for configuration. Most settings have default values that work well in most environments. As a matter of fact, Client 32 uses some settings as a guide, and then dynamically adjusts them for optimum performance. Therefore, you should not have to spend a lot of time configuring Client 32. However, if you have unique needs or preferences, a number of customizable configurations are available.

After you have installed Client 32, you can choose to customize the client for your workstation. To customize Client 32, select "Novell NetWare Client 32" in the Installed Components window and click Properties.

Figure 6.2 shows the Client 32 Properties page. As you can see, it allows you to change Client 32 settings at any given workstation. These properties include Preferred Server, Preferred Tree, Name Context, and First Network Drive. Incidentally, all these configurations and more can be customized in Client 16 using NET.CFG.

▶ • ◀

F I G U R E   6.2

Configuring Client 32 Properties

Logging In

Once you've connected to the network using Client 32, there's only one task left—*logging in*. As a CNA, you've already accomplished the hard part—automating the workstation connection. Now it's the user's turn. The good news is Client 32 provides a friendly GUI login utility for Windows 95 and Windows 3.1 users (see Figure 6.3).

As you can see in Figure 6.3, the GUI login utility provides simple Name and Password input boxes within the native MS Windows environment. In addition, the "Connection" page allows you to specify an NDS tree, server, and/or login context. Similarly the "Script" page allows users to override container and profile scripts with local text files. And finally, the "Variables" page provides customizable login script variables. We'll discuss these last two pages later in this chapter.

F I G U R E   6.3

GUI Login Utility for Windows 95

> **Novell NetWare Login**
>
> NetWare
>
> | Login | Connection | Script | Variables |
>
> OK
> Cancel
> Help
>
> Logging into NetWare using:
>
> WHITE-SRV1
>
> N<u>a</u>me: Admin
> <u>P</u>assword: ********

TIP

Both bindery and NDS connections are supported by the Client 32 GUI login utility.

As you can see in Figure 6.3, the GUI login page asks for two pieces of information:

▸ Name—This piece of information represents the user's login name, which is the same as the User object name. A user cannot log in until the network administrator has created a User object for that user. Once the User object has been created, the user can log in using this name.

▸ Password—After the user has entered a login name, the user should specify a password. Passwords are optional but *highly* recommended. As you can see in Figure 6.3, they do not appear on the screen when they are typed in. The letters of the password are replaced by asterisks. Refer to Chapter 5 for more information on login authentication and password restrictions.

Before a user can log in to a IntranetWare server, the user must create a network connection. This is accomplished by using the connectivity files described earlier. But that's not all. The user must also change to a valid network drive. For example, drive F: is usually the default letter used for the first network drive. However,

Client 32 can use the D: drive as well. Once the user has switched to the first default drive, the system will place the user in the SYS: login directory. By default, each user has the Read and File Scan rights to the directory, and, therefore, can run the appropriate login utility.

Speaking of the login utility, IntranetWare provides three different varieties for Windows and DOS users:

▶ LOGINW95.EXE—The GUI login utility for Windows 95 users. It is found in the C:\NOVELL\CLIENT32 subdirectory on the workstation.

▶ LOGINW31.EXE—The GUI login utility for Windows 3.1 users. It is found in the C:\NOVELL\CLIENT32 subdirectory on the workstation.

▶ LOGIN.EXE—The non-GUI login utility for DOS users. It is found in the SYS:LOGIN directory on the IntranetWare server.

Congratulations . . . you're in! That's all there is to it for workstation connectivity with Client 32. Not so bad, huh? Now let's shift gears a little bit and return to a simpler time—a time when bicycles had three wheels, a movie cost a dime, and clients connected to the network using 16-bit software.

WORKSTATION CONNECTIVITY WITH CLIENT 16

In the previous section, we learned about Leia's first step from the 32-bit point of view. Now let's explore the configuration files required for Guinevere's 16-bit DOS workstation. It all happens with the help of four simple files:

▶ CONFIG.SYS—This is the first configuration file loaded during the boot process. Because DOS and the NetWare DOS Requester share drive table information, CONFIG.SYS must include the LASTDRIVE statement.

▶ AUTOEXEC.BAT—This autoexecuting batch file is modified to activate STARTNET.BAT from the default C:\NWCLIENT subdirectory.

▶ STARTNET.BAT—This file automates the workstation connection. By default, it resides in the C:\NWCLIENT subdirectory and initializes the workstation-specific ODI and VLM drivers.

> ▸ NET.CFG—This is the final workstation configuration file that is used to customize ODI and VLM settings.

Once the first step of configuration has been taken, Leia is well on her way toward childhood and Guinevere is progressing toward LAN productivity. Let's take a closer look at these respective first steps, starting with CONFIG.SYS.

CONFIG.SYS

CONFIG.SYS is the first configuration file loaded when Guinevere turns on her computer. It is used by DOS for registering devices, managing memory, and establishing local drives. In addition, the NetWare DOS Requester uses CONFIG.SYS to identify a range of letters available for network drives. Here's how it works.

Because the NetWare DOS Requester and DOS share drive table information, we need a convention to determine where the local drives end and the network drives begin. Fortunately, the IntranetWare VLMs do this for us. They read the workstation hardware configuration and determine where the local drives end. From that point forward, they make all remaining drive letters available to the network. The key is determining exactly which drive letters are available. This is accomplished using the LASTDRIVE command.

If you place the following statement in each workstation CONFIG.SYS file, all drive letters from A through Z will be available for local and network drives:

`LASTDRIVE=Z`

Remember, you don't have to determine where the network drives begin because VLMs do it for you. For example, most standard workstations have a single floppy drive (A:), an internal hard disk (C:), and a CD-ROM (D:). This means that the first available network drive is E:. Similarly, if you have only a local floppy drive (A:—a more simple configuration), your first network drive will be B:. Undoubtedly, this sounds strange because you're used to pointing to F: as the first network drive. Fortunately, IntranetWare includes a statement in NET.CFG (by default) that ignores drives A: through E: and treats F: as the first network drive regardless of what your workstation thinks.

Once CONFIG.SYS is loaded and the LASTDRIVE statement has been activated, control shifts over to AUTOEXEC.BAT.

TIP

The **LASTDRIVE** statement works a little bit differently when used with **NETx**. In the **NETx** universe, the **LASTDRIVE** statement identifies local drives only—which means that the **LASTDRIVE=Z** command has an entirely different effect. In such a case, users are left with no network drives at all.

This is not entirely true because IntranetWare reserves certain ASCII characters for emergencies. If you use the **LASTDRIVE=Z** statement with **NETx**, the first available network is [: (a smiley-face). It really works. Try it—it's fun at parties.

AUTOEXEC.BAT

AUTOEXEC.BAT is a DOS configuration file used for activating a variety of workstation parameters, including PATH statements, the PROMPT command, SET parameters, and internal TSRs (terminate-and-stay-resident programs). By default, the IntranetWare client installation creates a file called STARTNET.BAT and places it in the C:\NWCLIENT subdirectory. It then adds the following line to the top of AUTOEXEC.BAT:

```
@CALL C:\NWCLIENT\STARTNET.BAT
```

This is a great way to automatically load workstation connectivity files while separating them from normal DOS operations. There is, however, one problem with this strategy. By placing this line at the top of AUTOEXEC.BAT, none of the other DOS statements load until STARTNET.BAT is finished—which is never. Remember, the goal of workstation connectivity is to load the drivers, automatically execute login scripts, and leave Guinevere in a menu system. This means IntranetWare will never execute the remaining statements in AUTOEXEC.BAT. A better solution is to move the @CALL C:\NWCLIENT\STARTNET statement to the end of AUTOEXEC.BAT.

Speaking of STARTNET.BAT, let's take a closer look.

STARTNET.BAT

As you recall from the previous section, IntranetWare workstation connectivity consists of two main components:

▶ Communications—ODI drivers

▶ NetWare DOS Requester—VLM files

STARTNET.BAT automates the loading of these files—isn't that special. By default, it consists of the following commands:

```
C:

cd \NWCLIENT

LSL.COM—the first ODI file

NE2000—or other MLID driver

IPXODI.COM—or other communications protocol file

VLM.EXE—loads the NetWare DOS Requester

F:—switches to the first default network drive

LOGIN Guinevere—or other username
```

By default, this file is stored in the C:\NWCLIENT subdirectory. This is also where the older NetWare 4 client installation process stores ODI drivers and VLMs. The beauty of this scenario is that it enables you to separate workstation connectivity files from other DOS programs. Also, it gives you a central point of workstation management. Once STARTNET.BAT has loaded and the workstation connectivity files are initialized, control shifts from the workstation to server login scripts.

QUIZ

Here's an easy one to warm up your gray matter. Twenty-four red socks and 24 blue socks are lying in a drawer in a dark room. What is the minimum number of socks I must take out of the drawer that will guarantee that I have at least two socks of the same color?

(Q6-1)
(See Appendix C for quiz answers.)

But not so fast. Before we move on to Step 2, you need to learn a little bit more about how these workstation connectivity files are configured. That is, you need to learn more about NET.CFG.

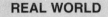

REAL WORLD

As a CNA, you'll decide how transparent the login process should be. Do you want Guinevere to input her login name and password, or have the system do it for her? While the latter is not the most secure alternative, it certainly removes the burden from Guinevere. The following line inputs Guinevere username and password automatically:

```
LOGIN GUINEVERE < C:\NWCLIENT\PASSWORD.TXT
```

This statement logs Guinevere into the network and redirects her password from a text file on the C: drive. In order for this to work, make sure to place only her password (followed by a carriage return) in the text file. Although this isn't great security, you can deter would-be hackers by placing the text file in a hidden directory or on a secure boot disk. Remember, there's always a compromise between user transparent and security.

NET.CFG

The final workstation connectivity file is NET.CFG. This file is not executed, it's simply used as a support file for customizing ODI and VLM settings for STARTNET.BAT. By default, NET.CFG must be stored in the same subdirectory as the other workstation connectivity programs. You only need to create a NET.CFG file if you plan to deviate from the established ODI/VLM defaults. You can create NET.CFG with any ASCII text editor, and it must follow these general conventions:

▸ Left-justify section headings

▸ Place options under each section heading and indent them with a tab or at least one space

▸ Use upper- or lowercase for section headings and options

▸ Precede comments with a semicolon (;) or pound sign (#) for documentation purposes

▸ End each line with a hard return

▸ Write all numbers in decimal notation except where noted

NET.CFG is your friend. Use it to customize ODI and VLM parameters as well as to automate the login process. In this section, we will explore NET.CFG as a CNA workstation management tool. You'll have a lot of parameters to think about, but keep in mind that many times the defaults are just fine. All in all, NET.CFG configurations fall into three categories:

▸ LINK DRIVER section

▸ NETWARE DOS REQUESTER section

▸ Other NET.CFG parameters

LINK DRIVER LINK DRIVER is the section heading for ODI support. You use this section to name the MLID driver and specify hardware and software settings for items such as interrupt, memory address, and frame type. Recall that ODI is a modular communications strategy that relies on NET.CFG for specific hardware settings. The IPX.COM file used in earlier versions of NetWare had these settings hardcoded into it during WSGEN configuration. This is not the case with ODI. LINK DRIVER enables you to specify nondefault MLID settings and incorporate a variety of different frame types at the NetWare and IntranetWare workstation. Following is a sample format for Guinevere LINK DRIVER heading:

```
LINK DRIVER 3C5X9
      INT 3
```

```
PORT 300
MEM D0000
FRAME Ethernet_802.2
```

Refer to Table 6.3 for a complete listing of the IntranetWare LINK DRIVER parameters.

TABLE 6.3	PARAMETER	RANGE	DESCRIPTION
LINK DRIVER Parameters for NET.CFG	INT	2 to 15	Interrupt value for the NIC (in decimal notation).
	PORT	240 to 4AFF	I/O port address for the NIC (in hexadecimal format).
	MEM	8000 to EFFF	Memory address for the NIC (in hexadecimal format).
	DMA	1 to 7	Direct memory access (DMA) channel number for the NIC.
	NODE ADDRESS	000000000000 to FFFFFFFFFFFE	Physical address for the NIC. This parameter enables you to override the physical address that is burned into each NIC at the factory. This is especially important for ARCNet.
	SLOT	1 to 8	A MicroChannel and EISA parameter that identifies the NIC slot.
	FRAME	Ethernet_802.2, Novell_RX-Net	Determines the frame type for workstation communications. By default, IntranetWare/NetWare 4/3.12 use Ethernet_802.2, whereas NetWare 3.11/2.2 use Ethernet_802.3.

NetWare DOS Requester   The majority of NET.CFG customization occurs under the NETWARE DOS REQUESTER section heading. Here you get an opportunity to specify configurations for VLM operations. Some of the activities you can control include preferred trees, preferred servers, name context, first network drive, and packet signing. In addition, you can use NET.CFG to specify which VLMs are loaded and their order of execution. Here's a sample NETWARE DOS REQUESTER section for Guinevere NET.CFG file:

```
NETWARE DOS REQUESTER
    Preferred Tree=ACME
    Name Context="OU=FIN.OU=OPS.OU=CAMELOT.O=ACME"
    First Network Drive=F
    PB Buffers=10
    Signature Level=3
```

QUIZ

What is Bullwinkle Moose's middle initial? You have a 1 in 26 chance of guessing it correctly!

(Q6-2)

SMART LINK

For a complete list of the IntranetWare NET.CFG parameters, consult the on-line IntranetWare documentation at http://www.novell.com/manuals.

Refer to Table 6.4 for a list of some of the most important NETWARE DOS REQUESTER parameters. Remember, this is the best way to customize the workstation attachment.

TABLE 6.4

*NetWare DOS Requester
Parameters*

PARAMETER	RANGE	DESCRIPTION
PREFERRED TREE	Any tree name	Forces the workstation to attach to a specified tree. By default, it will find the tree defined by the nearest available server.
PREFERRED SERVER	Any server name	Forces the workstation to attach to a specified server. By default, NET.CFG will find the nearest available server.
NAME CONTEXT	Any NDS container	Places the workstation in a specified container once a connection is established. By default, the system will use the [Root] as the workstation context.
FIRST NETWORK DRIVE	A to Z	F by default. Establishes the first available network drive provided that the command LASTDRIVE=Z appears in the workstation CONFIG.SYS file. This is used for convenience and convention.
PB BUFFERS	0 to 10	3 by default. This sets the number of buffers used by packet bursting. Larger values increase performance but occupy additional workstation RAM.
SIGNATURE LEVEL	0 to 3	1 by default. Sets the level of packet signing at the workstation. Higher values increase security, but decrease performance.
USE DEFAULTS	ON or OFF	ON by default. If set to OFF, you must specify which VLMs are loaded in what order.
VLM	Complete VLM filename	Enables you to load specific VLMs in a specific order. Be forewarned: Most VLMs are load-order dependent.
CONNECTIONS	2 to 50	8 by default. This represents the maximum number of connections available to the workstation. You may need to increase this value if your IntranetWare WAN has many active servers.
LOAD LOW CONN	ON or OFF	ON by default. When set to OFF, this parameter causes the CONN VLM to load in upper memory. This saves workstation RAM but degrades performance.
LOAD LOW IPXNCP	ON or OFF	ON by default. When set to OFF, this parameter causes IPXNCP to load in upper memory.

(continued)

TABLE 6.4

*NetWare DOS Requester
Parameters (continued)*

PARAMETER	RANGE	DESCRIPTION
MESSAGE TIMEOUT	0 to 10,000	0 by default. This controls how long the workstation waits before clearing broadcast messages. The default of 0 means users must press Ctrl+Enter to clear a broadcast message. If you want these messages to clear without user intervention, increase the value up to 6 hours—where each number equals 1/18th of a second.
NETWORK PRINTERS	0 to 9	3 by default. This sets the number of printer ports the workstation can capture. Setting the value to 0 will cause PRINT.VLM not to load and disable network printing at the workstation.
CACHE BUFFER SIZE	512 to 4,096 bytes	512 by default. This parameter sets the size of each cache buffer and can be used to increase performance. The size should be equal to (or at least an increment of) the maximum packet size.
CACHE BUFFERS	0 to 64	5 by default. This parameter sets how many cache buffers are available for sequential network files. Increasing this value speeds the movement of files across the LAN.

TIP

One important aspect of logging in is "context." In order for you to log in, the "Cloud" must be able to differentiate you from everybody else in the NDS tree. This means you have to tell the system where your home container is. In addition, most users access resources in their home container, and, therefore, should be guided there during login. You can specify a user's context during login in one of two ways. You can include the context with the login statement

```
LOGIN .CN=Guinevere.OU=FIN.OU=OPS.OU=CAMELOT.O=ACME
```

Alternatively, you can use the NAME CONTEXT parameter to specify the user's context before logging in:

```
NAME CONTEXT="OU=FIN.OU=OPS.OU=CAMELOT.O=ACME"
```

Note that the NAME CONTEXT line specifies a full distinguished name without a preceding period. This is one of those exceptions that Murphy keeps talking about.

Other NET.CFG Parameters In the past, CNAs used SHELL.CFG to define parameters for the old IPX/NETx connectivity files. Fortunately, IntranetWare supports these parameters by enabling you to include them at the top of NET.CFG. Following is a list of some of the most useful of these parameters, and remember—they must be left-justified.

- ▸ IPX RETRY COUNT—The IPX/SPX protocol uses this parameter to determine how many times to resend packets. This setting should be increased for an active network with heavy traffic and WANs that cover long distances. It works in conjunction with the SPX ABORT TIMEOUT parameter.

- ▸ SPX ABORT TIMEOUT—Adjusts the amount of time SPX waits without receiving any response from the other side. If this timeout value is exceeded, SPX aborts the connection. SPX ABORT TIMEOUT should be combined with IPX RETRY COUNT, for instance, if the workstation is using RPRINTER over routers. The default SPX ABORT TIMEOUT should be increased from 540 to about 1080 and the IPX RETRY COUNT should be doubled from 20 to 40.

- ▸ LONG MACHINE TYPE—You should use this parameter to specify the value returned by the %MACHINE login script variable. The default is IBM_PC. This parameter can be up to six characters long and should specify the type of machine being used—Altima, Compaq, Dell, NEC, and so on. This is a very important part of configuring the workstation DOS settings (as shown in Chapter 4 and the section, "Step 2: Creating Login Scripts," in this chapter).

- ▸ SHOW DOTS—Enables you to emulate the "dot" (.) and "double dot" (..) graphics in directory entries. The default is OFF, but should be set to ON for Windows support.

In addition to the above SHELL.CFG settings, NET.CFG supports one more section heading—LINK SUPPORT. This section is used for configuring receive buffers, the size of memory pools, and the number of boards and stacks for TCP/IP support. The BUFFERS option configures the number and size of receive buffers that LSL maintains. Because the IPX protocol stack does not use LSL communication buffers, this heading is rarely configured. TCP/IP, on the other hand, requires at least two link support buffers.

As a CNA, you can create NET.CFG files in one of two ways:

▸ Edit NET.CFG *after* client installation

▸ Edit INSTALL.CFG *before* client installation

After installing the NetWare DOS Requester, you will need to customize each user's NET.CFG file with additional settings. You can use any DOS text editor or the Windows WRITE application. Regardless of how you do it, each user's NET.CFG must be configured individually.

On the other hand, you can edit INSTALL.CFG before client installation and the system will automatically create a special NET.CFG for each user. During the IntranetWare server installation, INSTALL.CFG is placed in the SYS:PUBLIC\ CLIENT\DOSWIN subdirectory. You can use any DOS text editor to change the NetWare DOS Requester settings in INSTALL.CFG. The client installation program will then recognize INSTALL.CFG and create an identical NET.CFG for each user.

ZEN

"If you gaze for long into the abyss, the abyss also gazes into you."

Nietzsche

THE BRAIN

For additional information on configuring the NetWare DOS Requester and NET.CFG settings, see these *Novell Applications Notes*: "Using the DOS Requester with NetWare 4.0" (April 1993), "The Functions and Operations of the NetWare DOS Requester v1.1" (June 1994), and "Support Issues for the NetWare Requester (VLM) 1.2" (March 1995). Or, you can surf the Web at http://www.novell.com/sitemap.

This completes our discussion of NET.CFG and workstation connectivity files in general. Now the first step of configuration has been completed. Leia is well on her way to toddlership and Guinevere is well on her way to LAN productivity. At this point, the workstation computer has booted, the connectivity software has been activated, and Guinevere has been logged in. The next step is to customize Guinevere's network connection via login scripts. Let's dive in.

SMART LINK

For a more complete review of Novell's many diverse clients, surf to "NetWare Clients" at http://www.netware.com.

▶ · ◀

Step 2: Login Scripts

Chatterbox.

The next step in Leia's development is learning to talk. One day, your LAN's mindless babbling will begin to form words. Of course, we all know her first word will be "Daddy." Embrace these early days because soon she'll begin to form sentences and "Daddy" will become "Daddy, where're the car keys?" or "Daddy, I'm getting married" or, even worse, "Daddy, I want to be a CNA." Aah, the innocence of youth!

ZEN

"But the Emperor has nothing on at all!," cried the little child.

Hans Christian Andersen

Login scripts are an expression of your LAN's vocal cords. Once Guinevere has been authenticated with a valid username and password, IntranetWare greets her with login scripts. In short, login scripts are batch files for the network. They provide a simple configuration tool for user customization—drive mappings, text messages, printer redirection, and so on.

Login scripts are one of your most important configuration responsibilities. From one central location, they enable you to customize *all* users or just specific groups of users. Many of the configurations we've talked about are session-specific and disappear when users log out. Login scripts give you the ability to reestablish these settings every time Guinevere logs in. Don't underestimate the power of IntranetWare login scripts.

IntranetWare supports four types of login scripts, which are executed in systematic progression. As you can see in Figure 6.4, there's a flowchart logic to how login scripts are executed. Here's a quick look:

▶ *Container login scripts* are properties of Organization and Organizational Unit containers. They enable you to customize settings for all users within a container.

▶ *Profile login scripts* are properties of the Profile object. These scripts customize environmental parameters for groups of users. This way, users who are not directly related in the NDS tree can share a common login script.

▶ *User login scripts* are properties of each User object. They are executed after the Container and Profile scripts and provide customization to the user level.

▶ *Default login script* is executed for any user who does not have an individual User script. This script contains some basic mappings for the system and a COMSPEC command that points to the appropriate network DOS directory.

Login scripts consist of commands and identifiers just like any other program or batch file. In addition, login script syntax must follow specific rules and conventions. Let's start our discussion with a more detailed look at the four login script types and then explore the commands that make them productive.

LOGIN SCRIPT TYPES

We just saw that there are four types of IntranetWare login scripts—Container, Profile, User, and Default. All four work in concert to provide LAN customization for containers, groups, and users. As you'll quickly learn, login scripts are an integral part of your daily CNA grind. Let's start with a description of the four different login script types.

The Flow of IntranetWare Login Script Execution

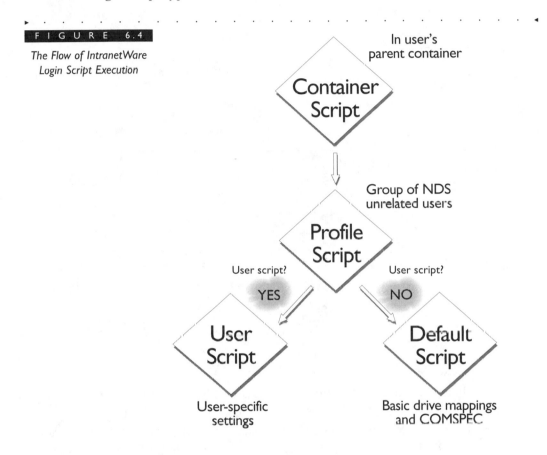

In user's parent container

Container Script

Group of NDS unrelated users

Profile Script

User script?   User script?

YES   NO

User Script

Default Script

User-specific settings

Basic drive mappings and COMSPEC

Container Login Script

Container login scripts are properties of Organization and Organizational Unit containers. In previous versions of NetWare, there was one System login script that was executed for all users. In IntranetWare, it is possible for every container to have its own login script. As you can see in Figure 6.4, the container is the first login script executed—Profile and User scripts follow.

There is one important difference between the IntranetWare Container login script and earlier System login scripts. A container script only executes for users *within* the container. As you can see in Figure 6.5, the Admin user executes the

ACME Container login script. SHolmes, on the other hand, doesn't execute any Container login script because the CRIME Organizational Unit doesn't have a script. Similarly, RHood executes the WHITE Container login script, whereas AEinstein executes none.

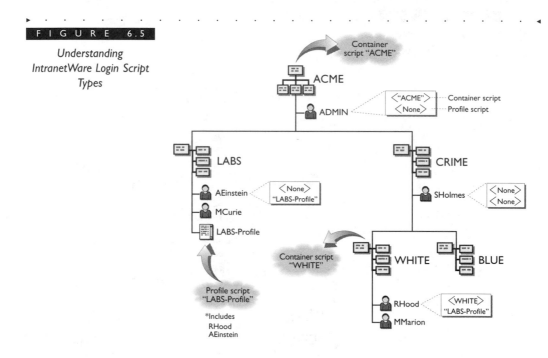

F I G U R E   6.5

Understanding IntranetWare Login Script Types

This is an important point because many CNAs assume that Container login scripts can be inherited by lower containers. This is *not* the case. If you wish to have one login script for all users to share, you have three options: (1) You can create a Profile login script and have all users point to it; (2) you can use the cut-and-paste feature within NWADMIN to copy one script to all containers; or (3) you can use an INCLUDE statement in each Container login script, which executes a text file containing these commands. Regardless, the moral of the story is IntranetWare no longer provides a single script for all users.

As you plan login scripts for your network, keep in mind that at some point you'll need to maintain them. Use Container login scripts to provide access to network resources, Profile scripts for a specific group's needs, and User login scripts only in special circumstances. Following are the types of things you might do within a Container login script:

- ▶ Send messages to users within a container

- ▶ Establish the first search drive mapping to SYS:PUBLIC

- ▶ Establish the second search drive mapping to DOS directories

- ▶ Create other search drive mappings for application directories

- ▶ Establish a network drive mapping U: to each user's home directory

- ▶ Connect users within a container to appropriate network printers

- ▶ Use IF... THEN statements for access to specific resources based on times, group memberships, and other variables

- ▶ Transfer users to an appropriate container-based menu system and/or application

Profile Login Script

The Profile login script is a property of the Profile object. This script customizes environmental parameters for groups of users. Each User object can be assigned a single Profile script—that's all. This way, users who are not directly related in the NDS tree can share a common login script. For example, Figure 6.5 shows how the AEinstein and RHood can share the LABS-Profile login script even though they live in different parts of the tree. Also note how the Profile login script executes after the Container script, and in Mr. Einstein's case, the Profile login script is the only script that executes.

Figure 6.6 shows an example of how the Profile login script is created in NWADMIN. Once the script has been defined, two things must happen so you can use it. One, each user must have the Browse right to the object and the Read property right to the Profile object's Login Script Property (assuming the user and Profile are defined in different containers). Two, the complete name of the Profile object must be defined in the user's Profile Login Script Property. See the case study at the end of this chapter.

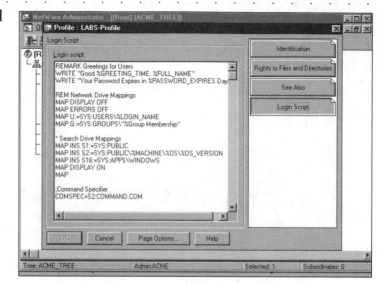

FIGURE 6.6

*Creating the LABS Profile-6
Script in NWADMIN*

TIP

**Remember, users can be assigned to only one Profile object, but
other Profile login scripts can be specified at the command line. For
example, the following line would allow RHood to execute the
"WHITE-Profile" script in addition to his default "LABS-Profile"
script:**

```
LOGIN RHOOD /P.CN=WHITE-
    Profile.OU=WHITE.OU=CRIME.OU=TOKYO.O=ACME
```

Wasn't that fun?

Profile login scripts should be used to customize specific group configurations.
Some tasks you can accomplish with Profile login scripts include

▸ Send messages to users within a group

▸ Establish network drive mappings to special data directories, report files,
  or other servers that contain critical group information

▶ Establish search drive mappings to group application directories

▶ Connect to group-specific printers such as high-resolution LaserJets, plotters, or faxes

SMART LINK

For more information about ACME's login scripts and a chance to try out NetWare Administrator on your own, surf on over to CyberState University and World Wire: http://www.cyberstateu.com.

User Login Script

The User login script is a property of each User object. The User script is executed after the Container and Profile scripts, and provides customization all the way down to the user level. Although User scripts are a nice feature, they can quickly become a maintenance nightmare—imagine hundreds and hundreds of User login scripts constantly screaming for attention. Nope, one baby is enough. A better strategy is to use Container and Profile scripts as much as possible and eliminate the User scripts altogether.

The primary purpose of the User login script is user-specific customization. This level of customization can be accomplished in the Container and Profile scripts by using IF... THEN logic commands. But, if you absolutely have to create a user-specific script, it's nice to know that it's there.

User login scripts should be created only in special circumstances. Remember, you have to *maintain* any scripts you create. Some instances when a User script might be justified include

▶ Establish network drive mappings to specific user directories, provided that these directories do not correspond with the drive mappings made in the Container script

▶ Connect to commonly used printers, in addition to the ones selected in the Container and Profile scripts

▸ Send weekly messages to remind the user about time-sensitive tasks

▸ Activate a special user-specific menu system and/or application

Default Login Script

The Default login script is executed for any user who does not have an individual User script. This poses an interesting dilemma. Earlier we said it's a good idea not to have a User script. This means the Default script will automatically execute. Oops. This is a problem because the default script typically overrides already-established drive mappings and COMSPEC settings. Fortunately, Novell has recognized this problem and provides you with the means to disable the Default login script using the following statement:

    NO_DEFAULT

This command must be placed in a Container or Profile login script.

TIP

The Default login script cannot be edited because it is included in the SYS:LOGIN\LOGIN.EXE command code. It can, however, be disabled by including the NO_DEFAULT command in a Container or Profile script.

QUIZ

So, you think you're so smart? Let's see if you can think in three dimensions. A man is 100 yards due south of a bear. He walks 100 yards due east, then faces due north, fires his gun due north, and hits the bear.

What color was the bear?

Don't underestimate this one. The answer is much more involved than you think.

(Q6-3)

This completes our discussion of the different login script types. In leaving this little discussion, consider the factors that determine how you use login scripts and which types you'll need. These factors include the needs of users, their knowledge level, the size of your network, the complexity of the WAN, the type of groups, and access requirements for different containers. Remember, login script design can go a long way toward increasing your CNA quality of life and decreasing your daily workload. This is your first shot at parenthood (system customization); don't underestimate it.

LOGIN SCRIPT COMMANDS

Login scripts consist of commands and identifiers just as any other program or batch file. In addition, login script syntax must follow specific rules and conventions. The syntax for login script programming is quite simple, but you must be sure to organize identifier variables and commands with appropriate grammar—much like learning to talk. For example, consider the following line:

```
MAP U:=SYS:USERS\%LOGIN_NAME
```

This line uses proper login script syntax—it starts with the login script command MAP and uses appropriate identifier variable grammar—%LOGIN_NAME. The cool thing about this line is that it changes for each user. For example, when Dr. Watson logs in, the system creates a U: drive for him, and it points to SYS.USERS\DRWATSON. On the other hand, when SHolmes logs in, his U: drive points to SYS:USERS\SHOLMES. Cool!

Another good example of login script vernacular is the WRITE command. Consider the following statement:

```
WRITE "Good %GREETING_TIME, %FULL_NAME!"
```

Depending on the time of day and user who logs in, this single statement will provide a custom message. For example, Guinevere gets the following message when she turns on her machine in the morning:

```
"Good Morning, Guinevere Wannamaker!"
```

This can go a long way in making users feel warm and fuzzy about the LAN. As a matter of fact, some users get the perception that IntranetWare actually *cares* about them and is personally wishing them a nice day. Regardless of the LAN's motivation, the point is that users feel good about using the network!

All this configuration magic is made possible because of two login script elements—identifier variables and commands. Let's take a closer look at how they work.

Identifier Variables

Identifier variables enable you to enter a variable (such as LAST_NAME) rather than a specific name (Wannamaker). When the login script executes, it substitutes real values for the identifier variables. This means that you can make your login scripts more efficient and more flexible. In addition, it makes the concept of a single Container script feasible. As we saw in earlier examples, identifier variables are preceded by a percent sign (%) and written in all uppercase. This is the ideal syntax for identifier variables because it allows you to use them anywhere in the script, including inside quotation marks (" "). Table 6.5 lists identifier variables available in IntranetWare. Learn them. These cute little guys can go a long way in customizing Container and Profile scripts.

TABLE 6.5	CATEGORY	IDENTIFIER VARIABLE	DESCRIPTION
Login Script Identifier Variables for IntranetWare	Date	DAY	Day number 01 through 31
		DAY_OF_WEEK	Day of week (Monday, Tuesday, and so on)
		MONTH	Month number (01 through 12)
		MONTH_NAME	Month Name (January, February, and so on)
		NDAY_OF_WEEK	Weekday number (1 through 7, where 1 equals Sunday)
		SHORT_YEAR	Last two digits of year
		YEAR	All four digits of year
	Time	AM_PM	a.m. or p.m.
		GREETING_TIME	Time of day (morning, afternoon, or evening)
		HOUR	Hour of day on a 12-hour scale

	CATEGORY	IDENTIFIER VARIABLE	DESCRIPTION
	Time	HOUR24	Hour of day on a 24-hour scale

Login Script Identifier Variables for IntranetWare (continued)

TABLE 6.5

CATEGORY	IDENTIFIER VARIABLE	DESCRIPTION
Time	HOUR24	Hour of day on a 24-hour scale
	MINUTE	Minutes (00 through 59)
	SECOND	Seconds (00 through 59)
User	CN	User's full common name as it exists in NDS
	ALIAS_CONTEXT	Y if REQUESTER_ CONTEXT is an Alias
	FULL_NAME	User's unique full name as it appears in both NDS and the bindery
	LAST_NAME	User's last name in NDS or full name in bindery-based IntranetWare
	LOGIN_CONTEXT	Context where user exists
	LOGIN_NAME	User's unique login name truncated to eight characters
	MEMBER OF "GROUP"	Group object that user is assigned to
	NOT MEMBER	Group object that the user OF "GROUP" is *not* assigned to
	PASSWORD_ EXPIRES	Number of days before password expires
	REQUESTER_ CONTEXT	Context when login started
	USER_ID	Unique hexadecimal ID assigned to each user.
Workstation	MACHINE	Type of computer (either IBM_PC or other name specified in NET.CFG)
	NETWARE_ REQUESTER	Version of Requester being used (NetWare Requester for DOS or OS/2)

(continued)

CATEGORY	IDENTIFIER VARIABLE	DESCRIPTION
Workstation	OS	Type of operating system on the workstation (MSDOS, OS/2, and so on)
	OS_VERSION	Operating system version loaded on the workstation
	P_STATION	Workstation's 12-digit hexadecimal node ID
	SHELL_TYPE	Version of the workstation's DOS shell for NetWare 2 and 3 users
	S_MACHINE	Short machine name (IBM, and so on)
	STATION	Workstation's connection number
Miscellaneous	FILE_SERVER	IntranetWare server name that workstation first attaches to
	NETWORK_ADDRESS	IPX external network number for the cabling system (8-digit hexadecimal number)
	ACCESS_SERVER	Shows whether the access server is functional (true or false)
	ERROR_LEVEL	An error number (0 equals no errors)
	%n	Replaced by parameters entered after the LOGIN command (starting with %0)

T A B L E 6.5

Login Script Identifier Variables for IntranetWare (continued)

In addition to these identifier variables, you can use any NDS property name within a IntranetWare login script. Just be sure to use the same syntax—that is, uppercase and preceded by a percent sign.

REAL WORLD

Here's a list of things to think about when creating IntranetWare login scripts. It's always a good idea to have a few guidelines in mind before you begin exploring all the possibilities:

▶ Minimum—One. All four login script types are optional. Of course, if no User script exists, the default will run. So, at the absolute minimum, you must have one User script with one command—EXIT.

▶ Case—Not case-sensitive, except for identifier variables in quotation marks. They must be uppercase and preceded by a percent sign (%). See the "WRITE" example.

▶ Characters per line—150 maximum, although 78 is recommended for readability.

▶ Commands per line—One. Also press Enter to mark the end of each line. Lines that automatically wrap are considered one command.

▶ Blank lines—Have no effect. Use them to visually separate groups of commands.

▶ Documentation—Use any variation of the REMARK command to thoroughly document what's going on.

These identifier variables have to be used with valid login script commands. As you can see in Figure 6.7, IntranetWare includes a plethora of commands that can be used in various configurations. In this discussion, we'll present the commands as part of a productive IntranetWare Container login script. In each case, refer to Figure 6.7 for appropriate syntax.

A: WRITE and REMARK

Login scripts should always start with documentation. This is accomplished using the REMARK command. Any line beginning with REMARK is ignored by IntranetWare. It does, however, provide a useful tool for documenting the many different sections of your Container and Profile scripts. Besides the word REMARK, IntranetWare supports three other variations—REM, an asterisk (*), and a semicolon (;). As you can see in Figure 6.7, all possibilities have been used. Another use of documentation is edit tracking. When multiple supervisors are maintaining the same container login script, it's a good idea to document who does what when. Finally, documentation is necessary for CNAs who follow you. After all, you do plan on winning the lottery, don't you?

ZEN

"Miami Beach is where neon goes to die."

Lenny Bruce

One of the most popular login script commands is WRITE. With it, you can display a variety of friendly messages during login script execution. One of the friendliest is shown in Figure 6.7. Other identifier variables you can use with the WRITE command include

```
Your password expires in %PASSWORD_EXPIRES days.
Today is %MONTH_NAME %DAY.
At the tone, the time is %HOUR:%MINUTE %AM_PM.
You're connected as workstation %STATION.
You're attached to %FILE_SERVER.
```

Don't underestimate the power of communication. Goodwill flourishes with a quick note to your users now and again.

B: Network Drive Mappings

The next section in Figure 6.7 establishes user-specific and group-specific drive mappings. Drive mapping is the single, most important purpose of login scripts. Mappings are essential to IntranetWare navigation and provide a facility for representing large directory paths as drive letters. The problem with mapping is that it's both session-specific (meaning drive pointers disappear when users log out) and user-specific (meaning they're unique for each user). The temporary nature of drive mappings makes them particularly annoying—because complex MAP commands must be entered each time a user logs in. Fortunately, this process can be automated using IntranetWare login scripts.

FIGURE 6.7

A Typical IntranetWare Login Script

```
A {   REMARK Greetings for users
       WRITE "Good %GREETING_TIME, %FULL_NAME!"
       WRITE "Your Password Expires in %PASSWORD_EXPIRES days"

B {   REM Network Drive Mappings
       MAP DISPLAY OFF
       MAP ERRORS OFF
       MAP U:=SYS:USERS\%LOGIN_NAME
       MAP G:=SYS:GROUPS\"%Group Membership"

C {   *Search Drive Mappings
       MAP INS S1:=SYS: PUBLIC
       MAP INS S2:=SYS: PUBLIC \%MACHINE\%OS\%OS_VERSION
       MAP INS S16:=SYS: APPS\WINDOWS
       MAP DISPLAY ON
       MAP

D {   ; Command Specifier
       COMSPEC= S2:COMMAND.COM

E {   SET PROMPT= "$P$G"
       SET TEMP= "U:\USERS\%LOGIN_NAME\TEMP"

F {   IF DAY_OF_WEEK= "Friday" THEN BEGIN
          MAP R:=.REPORTS.LABS.NORAD.ACME
          DISPLAY R:FRIDAY.TXT
          PAUSE
       END

G {   IF MEMBER OF "OPS-Group" THEN #CAPTURE P=HP4S1-P1 NT T1=10
       IF MEMBER OF "ADMIN-Group" THEN #CAPTURE P=HP5-P1 NFF NT
       IF MEMBER OF "LABS-Group" THEN #CAPTURE P=CANONBJ-P1 NB

H {   NO DEFAULT

I {   PCCOMPATIBLE
       DRIVE U:
       EXIT "Start"
```

TIP

In addition to standard MAP statements, IntranetWare login scripts support MAP NEXT and MAP %1 commands. The latter will map the first network drive to a specific directory or volume. Also, the "1" can be replaced by any number from 1 to 26.

Before you get too excited about network and search drive mappings, it's a good idea to turn off the display of drive mapping and drive mapping errors. MAP DISPLAY OFF stops complex mappings from displaying during execution, and MAP ERRORS OFF avoids confusing users with mappings to directories they don't have rights to. Don't worry, we'll turn them back on later.

The MAP command is most useful when combined with identifier variables. This way, you can accomplish user-specific and group-specific mappings with only one command. Notice the second network drive mapping in Figure 6.7. Here we're using the Group Membership property from NDS. The trick is getting the quotes in the right place.

C: Search Drive Mappings

Once the network drive mappings have been established, it's time to shift your attention to search drive mappings. By default, the first two should always be SYS:PUBLIC and the network DOS directory structure. Notice our creative use of identifier variables in search mapping 2. This single statement intelligently maps every workstation to the appropriate version of DOS. Of course, these statements must be combined with the exact DOS structure outlined in Chapter 4. The three key identifier variables are

▸ %MACHINE—Identifies the machine such as IBM_PC, Dell, NEC, and so on. These values are established using the LONG MACHINE TYPE parameter in NET.CFG.

▸ %OS—Identifies the operating system as MSDOS, OS/2, PCDOS, DRDOS, and so on.

▸ %OS_VERSION—Identifies the specific version of DOS running on the workstation (for example, v5.00, v7.01, v6.22). This value is determined by the IntranetWare client.

Next, you should create a search drive mapping for every application that users are likely to access. In these cases, you can use MAP INS S16 to systematically create mappings in order. In each case, S16 will drop to the next available search number. Finally, turn MAP DISPLAY back on and issue one final MAP command to show the user what he or she has available.

QUIZ

What is the name for the upper portion of the brain? You know, the part that really hurts right now.

(Q6-4)

TIP

Remember from **Chapter 4** that IntranetWare search mappings systematically replace the **DOS** path statement. Also, remember that using **MAP INSERT** eliminates this problem by adding the **DOS** path to the end of the IntranetWare search list. In addition, an interesting thing happens when you use "**MAP INS S16.**" The IntranetWare search drives are added *after* the DOS path. This means users will execute local applications before network ones. Sometimes, this is a good thing!

D: COMSPEC

The next step is to create a COMSPEC for the new DOS directory mapping. COMSPEC stands for "Command Specifier," and it helps IntranetWare find COMMAND.COM when it's lost. This happens all the time when TSRs and Windows applications need extra space. If COMMAND.COM cannot be found, your users will get one of these messages:

```
Invalid COMMAND.COM
COMMAND.COM cannot be found
Insert Boot Disk in Drive A
```

Interestingly, this causes the hair to stand up on the back of your neck—especially if it happens all day It must be a kinetic reaction.

COMSPEC solves the "lost DOS" problem by telling the system where to search for appropriate COMMAND.COM file. Keep in mind that each version of DOS on each of your workstations supports a different type of COMMAND.COM. You must make sure to point to the correct file. This is accomplished by using the S2: drive mapping we created earlier. Remember, it points to the correct DOS directory structure for each workstation.

TIP

Setting **COMSPEC** to a network directory for **COMMAND.COM** has its advantages. However, many **CNAs** still insist on pointing to a local drive such as **C:\DOS**. It's your choice. Here are some reasons to use the IntranetWare DOS directory structure:

- ▶ **Speed (with file caching)**
- ▶ **Central management (all workstations point to the file server)**
- ▶ **Diskless workstations (it's required)**

SMART LINK

For more information on the IntranetWare COMSPEC strategy, surf to the Novell Knowledgebase at http://support.novell.com/search/.

E: SET

The SET command enables you to configure DOS environment variables within the login script. You can use the SET command exactly the same as you would in DOS (except that you'll need to surround the values with quotation marks). Otherwise, most SET variables are configured in the user's AUTOEXEC.BAT file. In Figure 6.7, we've included two important SET variables:

```
SET PROMPT="$P$G"
```

This configures the local and network prompt to display the current directory path. We want users to feel like they're at home.

```
SET TEMP="U:\USERS\%LOGIN_NAME\TEMP"
```

This points the Windows TEMP directory to a IntranetWare drive under the user's area.

Whatever you do, don't use the SET PATH command in a Container login script; it overwrites local and network search drives.

F: IF...THEN...ELSE

The IF..THEN command enables you to use script programming logic. It checks a given condition and executes your command only if the condition is met. In addition, you can add the ELSE statement to selectively execute another command only when the condition is *not* met. For example, you can have the system display a fancy message and fire phasers whenever it is the user's birthday (using MONTH and DAY identifier variables). Otherwise, display a message pointing out that it's not his/her birthday the other 364 days of the year.

The IF..THEN command is the most versatile login script tool. Learn it, use it, be it. IF..THEN effectively enables you to execute any command based on condition, including login name, context, day of the week, or group membership. As you can see in Figure 6.7, we are executing these three commands only on Friday:

▸ MAP—Maps the R: drive to a Directory Map object.

▸ DISPLAY—Displays a text file that is stored on the R: drive.

▶ PAUSE—Temporarily stops execution of the login script to allow the user time to read the display. Just as with the DOS PAUSE command, execution resumes when the user presses any key.

Also notice the use of BEGIN and END. If you plan on including multiple commands within a nested IF . . . THEN statement, you must use BEGIN to start and END to mark the bottom of the nest. As a sidenote, IF . . . THEN statements can be nested up to 10 levels.

You can do anything with an IF . . . THEN statement. Don't be shy. Before you resign yourself to creating Profile and User login scripts, explore the use of IF . . . THEN statements in Container scripts.

G: # (DOS Executable)

The DOS executable (#) command has been included by Novell to support external programs. Because IntranetWare has a limited number of login script commands, you might run across a case where you need to run a non-login script program. The most obvious oversight that comes to mind is CAPTURE, which is a IntranetWare printing command that redirects local ports to shared network printers. This command should be included in Container and Profile scripts for user and group automation. You can do so with the following command:

```
#CAPTURE P=HP4SI-P1 NT TI=10
```

There is one problem with this scenario. While CAPTURE is running, the entire login script and LOGIN.EXE is swapped to workstation RAM. Once the # command is finished, IntranetWare reloads the login script from memory. But what if the external program is a TSR or never returns stolen RAM to the workstation? In both of these cases, you run the risk of wasting 70K to 100K of workstation RAM. This is a bad thing. By default, IntranetWare swaps login scripts and LOGIN.EXE into extended or expanded memory.

Fortunately, CAPTURE is not one of those misbehaving # commands. As you can see in Figure 6.7, we've combined the #CAPTURE program with IF... THEN statements to customize group-specific printing captures within a single Container login script. Once again, the goal is to satisfy all of your users' needs from within a single, centrally managed login script.

H: NO_DEFAULT

Here's another command that helps you avoid conflicts between a central Container script and the Default login script. As you remember from our earlier discussion, the Default login script is contained in LOGIN.EXE and cannot be edited. In addition, it conflicts with drive mappings and the COMSPEC command from Container and Profile scripts. Finally, the Default login script executes only if there is no User script, which conflicts with our goal of having one centrally managed Container login script. Fortunately, by using the IntranetWare NO_DEFAULT statement, you can skip the Default login script even without a User script. Simply place it toward the end of your Container or Profile script and everything will be fine. Sometimes life can be so easy.

I: EXIT

Congratulations, you've made it to the end of our mammoth Container login script. Don't forget Guinevere. She's counting on finding a menu system and e-mail somewhere in her future. As a CNA, it is your job to orchestrate a smooth transition from Guinevere's login script to her menu system. Fortunately, you have the EXIT command.

EXIT terminates any login script and executes a specific network program. The program can be an .EXE, .COM, or .BAT file and must reside in the default directory. When combined with the DRIVE command (as shown in Figure 6.7), EXIT can facilitate a smooth transition from a login script to a menu system. In the case of Figure 6.7, we're exiting to a START batch file residing in either SYS:PUBLIC or the user's home area. Here's what START looks like:

```
ECHO OFF
CLS
CAPTURE P=HP4SI-P1 NFF NT
TSA_SMS /SE=CAM-FIN-SRV1 /P=RUMPELSTILTSKIN /D=C /B=30
NMENU GUINEVER.DAT
```

In this scenario, the DRIVE command dumps Guinevere into her own home directory, where the menu system resides. Otherwise, she would be placed in the first available network drive (by default). In addition, the PCCOMPATIBLE line ensures that her clone workstation returns a %MACHINE value of IBM_PC.

It's important to note that the EXIT command skips all other login scripts. For this reason, you'll want to be careful where you place it. Only use EXIT in a

Container login script if you're convinced there are no Profile or User scripts, or if you'd rather not execute those scripts because they've been created by nonauthorized managers. All in all, this is a great strategy for skipping unnecessary login scripts and making a smooth transition to Guinevere's menu system.

ZEN

"When love and skill work together, expect a masterpiece."

John Ruskin

Before we move on to Step 3: Menu System, let's take a quick look at some other powerful login script commands.

Other Login Script Commands

In addition to the commands shown in Figure 6.7, IntranetWare includes a potpourri of other login script commands. For a complete listing, refer to THE BRAIN after this discussion.

- ▶ BREAK—If "BREAK ON" is included in a login script, you can press Ctrl+C or Ctrl+Break to abort the normal execution of a login script. This is not a good thing, especially in the hands of users. The default is BREAK OFF.

- ▶ CLS—Use CLS to clear the user's screen during login script execution.

- ▶ CONTEXT—This command changes the workstation's current NDS context during login script execution. It works similarly to the workstation CX utility.

- ▶ FDISPLAY—Works the same as DISPLAY, except that it filters out formatting codes before showing the file on the screen. In other words, it can be used to display the text of an ASCII file without showing all the ASCII formatting codes.

- ▶ FIRE PHASERS—Beam me up, Scotty. FIRE PHASERS can also be combined with identifier variables to indicate the number of times the phaser sound should blare. For example, FIRE PHASERS %NDAY_OF_WEEK will fire five phasers on Thursday.

- ▸ GOTO—This command enables you to execute a portion of the login script out of regular sequence. GOTO jumps to login script labels—text followed by a colon (TOP:, for example). Do not use GOTO to enter or exit a nested IF . . . THEN statement. This will cause the keyboard to explode. You can go through a lot of users that way.

- ▸ INCLUDE—As if one login script isn't enough. The INCLUDE command branches to subscripts from anywhere in the main Container script. These subscripts can be text files with valid login script syntax, or entire login scripts that belong to different objects in the NDS tree. Once the subscript has been completed, control shifts to the next line in the original script. Now we're really getting crazy. Consider using INCLUDE subscripts with IF . . . THEN statements to ultimately customize Container login scripts. Now there's no excuse for using Profile, User, or Default scripts. As a matter of fact, everyone in the WAN can share the same Container script by distributing INCLUDE statements to all Organizational Units. Think of the synergy.

- ▸ LASTLOGINTIME—As you've probably guessed, displays the last time the user logged in. This can be combined with WRITE statements to ensure that nobody is logging in as *you* while you're on vacation. When the cat's away, the mice will play.

- ▸ SWAP—As you recall from our earlier discussion, the # command swaps 100K of stuff into workstation RAM and doesn't always give it back. The SWAP command can be used to force the 100K out of workstation RAM onto the local or network disk. Simply identify a path with the SWAP command and LOGIN.EXE will bother you no more. When the # command is completed, LOGIN.EXE continues on its merry way. If this bothers you, NOSWAP will force LOGIN.EXE into conventional workstation RAM.

GUI LOGIN SCRIPT MANAGEMENT

The IntranetWare GUI login utility and Client 32 provide two important pages for login script management. They are:

▸ Script page

▸ Variables page

Let's take a closer look.

GUI Script Page

The *Script* page of the IntranetWare GUI login utility is shown in Figure 6.8. It allows users to bypass default scripts by running specified login scripts, or choosing not to run any scripts at all. As you can see in Figure 6.8, this is accomplished by entering the path and name of a text file in the login script box. This will run the file as a login script and bypass all other scripts assigned to you. Also, if you know the name of a Profile object that contains a login script you would like to run, you can enter the name in the Profile Script box.

▸ · ◂

FIGURE 6.8

GUI Login Script Page

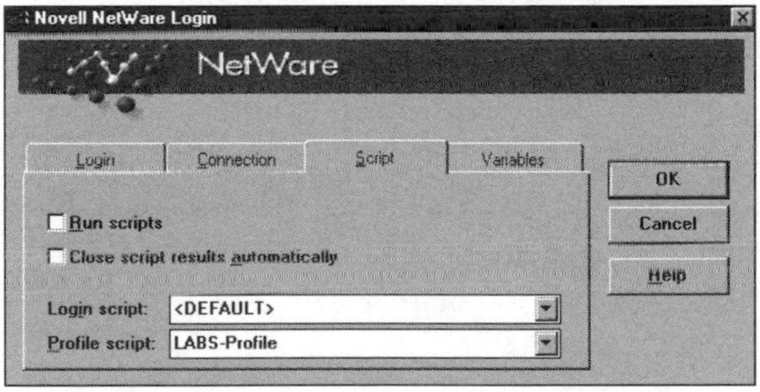

To avoid running any login scripts, deselect the Run Scripts option. By doing so, no login scripts (even those entered above) will run.

As a CNA, the GUI login utility gives you much better control over specific user login script execution. Keep in mind, however, it also places such control in the hands of the user. This power can easily be abused. Consider this fact when giving your users access to the GUI login utility.

GUI Variables Page

The *Variables* page of the IntranetWare GUI login utility can be seen in Figure 6.9. It allows you to enter different values for variables that are referenced in any login script associated with the user. As you can see in Figure 6.9, each variable is assigned to an environmental designator—%2, %3, %4, and %5.

F I G U R E   6 . 9

GUI Login Variables Page

Novell NetWare Login

NetWare

| Login | Connection | Script | Variables |

OK

Cancel

Help

Login script variables:

%2:
`USERS\RHOOD`

%3:

%4:

%5:

To use the variables, type the desired value in the corresponding field in Figure 6.9. Then reference the variables in all login scripts associated with this user.

For example, users can customize home directories by using the following MAP ROOT command and the GUI login script Variables page:

```
MAP ROOT U:=LABS-SRV1_SYS:%2
```

With this combination, users can map drive U: to different directories each time they log in. All they have to do is simply enter the desired path in the %2 variable box in Figure 6.9.

Once again, be careful when granting this login power to users. It can be used to override your login script automation strategy.

THE BRAIN

For a complete list of IntranetWare login script commands and identifier variables, refer to page 187 of the *Supervising the Network* manual. Another good reference is "Using NDS User Object Properties in NetWare 4.1 Login Script" in the May 1995 *Novell Application Notes*. Or, surf the Web at http://support.novell.com/sitemap.

That completes our discussion of IntranetWare login scripts. I hope you've gained an appreciation for how these cute little tools help you customize user and group connections. Once the Container and Profile scripts have been executed, IntranetWare automatically loads Guinevere's menu. As we saw, this is accomplished by using the EXIT login script command.

QUIZ

Now that you're warmed up, let's try something a little more interesting. Besides, Guinevere could solve it—how about you?

Alice, Brett, Catherine, and Deirdre went to school together. They became, but not necessarily respectively, an author, a biologist, a cartoonist, and a doctor. Years before, they belonged to A, B, C, and D sororities, and they came from Australia, Brazil, Canada, and Denmark. The letters of each woman's house, the initial letters of her profession, her home, and her name are all different from each other. The doctor had never been to Brazil, and the biologist had never been to Canada. Back at school, Catherine, the girl from Australia, and the biologist used to spend all their spare time together.

What was the profession, the home, and the house of each of them?

Good luck.

(Q6-5)

She can walk, she can talk; your LAN is an unstoppable bundle of joy. Now that all of the fundamentals have been accomplished, it's time to put her to the test—preschool. It's time for your LAN to learn how to get along with others.

· ·

Step 3: Creating the Menu System

Leia goes to preschool.

One of the most rewarding aspects of a child's development is watching how she gets along with others. You can't beat the thrill of discovery and the sight of two toddlers bonding. Of course, this peaceful picture hinges on the ability of children to "share"—a lesson the world hasn't quite caught onto yet. Although with Barney the dinosaur as our ambassador of sharing, I can understand why some people have resorted to violence. Not my baby! Leia's going to learn how to share without resorting to Barney-isms.

Social interaction is a valuable skill on any level. It's how the world works. Learning to get along with others is as practical a skill as tying your shoes or signing your name. As a matter of fact, you'll run into questions on your CNA job application that deal with this very topic.

SMART LINK

Preschool is a self-defining moment in LAN Childhood. Check it out at http://www.kids.com.

Social interaction is also important to our IntranetWare LAN. In order for Guinevere to get anything done, she needs a friendly menu interface for all her network applications and e-mail. A turnkey custom menu environment provides transparent access from "point A" (turning on the computer) to "point Z" (accessing her e-mail with cappuccino in hand). Fortunately, IntranetWare has a built-in menu system that provides custom IntranetWare-looking menus. This system uses a simple script format and is versatile enough to support large groups of users with a single menu file.

Menus are a good thing. They provide a comfortable, friendly interface for Guinevere and eliminate the need to learn IntranetWare command line utilities. They present information in multiple layers instead of all in one place. But let's be honest. You're probably using MS Windows. On the most fundamental level, MS Windows is a simple graphical menu. It controls what kind of information is presented and enables users to launch applications from a single place. If you're using MS Windows, you don't need this menu system. However, it does have merits as a simple network-oriented interface for small IntranetWare LANs. So, with that in mind, you're prepared to learn about it.

TIP

The IntranetWare menu system is a subset of the Saber Menu System. This software acquisition falls into the Novell category of "if you can't build it, buy it." As a partial version, IntranetWare menus have limitations. For example, you can't specify the location of menus on the screen nor avoid the default color palette—blue and gold. In addition, IntranetWare's internal menu system is limited to 11 cascading screens—1 main menu and 10 submenus. Finally, there's limited security and many missing features. So, if you're intrigued by what you learn here, consider contacting Saber and buying the full-blown version.

IntranetWare menus are built using two simple command types:

- ▸ Organizational commands—providing the menu's look and feel

- ▸ Control commands—doing the work

In addition, IntranetWare has specific rules about how menus are executed and what rights are necessary to get at them. These are the topics we're going to discuss in this section—starting with organizational commands.

ORGANIZATIONAL COMMANDS

It all starts with organizational commands. They provide the menu's look and feel. IntranetWare supports two organizational commands:

- ▸ MENU—identifies the beginning of each menu screen and provides a title

- ▸ ITEM—defines the options that appear within the menu and includes a variety of built-in "squiggly" options

As you can see in Figure 6.10, the MENU command is left-justified and followed by a number. The menu number is then followed by a comma and the title of the menu. Next, options are listed under the MENU command using the organizational tool—ITEM. Items can be specific applications or other submenus—it doesn't matter. Using Figure 6.10 as a guide, let's explore these two organizational commands.

MENU

MENU identifies the beginning of each menu screen. It is left-justified and followed by a number. A single IntranetWare menu file can support 255 different menus—1 through 255. The menu number is then followed by a comma and the title of the menu. As you can see in Figure 6.10, the first menu displays the title "Guinevere's Main Menu." Subsequent menus have systematically higher numbers (10, 15, and 20). Each menu number identifies the beginning of a new submenu for branching purposes (using the SHOW control command). Menu titles are limited to 40 characters.

F I G U R E   6.10

Guinevere's Menu System

```
MENU 01, Guinevere's Main Menu
    ITEM  ^AApplications
          SHOW 10
    ITEM  ^EE-Mail {BATCH}
          EXEC WIN WMAIL
    ITEM  ^FFun Stuff
          SHOW 15
    ITEM  ^MAdmin Menu
          LOAD G:\GROUPS\ADMIN\ADMIN.DAT
    ITEM  ^LLogout
          EXEC LOGOUT

MENU 10, Guinevere's Applications
    ITEM  ^1Windows '95 {BATCH}
          EXEC WIN
    ITEM  ^2Network Utilities
          SHOW 20
    ITEM  ^3Word Perfect {CHDIR}
          EXEC WIN WPWIN

MENU 15, Guinevere's Fun Stuff
    ITEM  Pick your Doom
          GETO ENTER THE VERSION OF DOOM (1-3):{DOOM}1,1,{}
          EXEC
    ITEM  Solitaire {BATCH}
          EXEC WIN SOL

MENU 20, Network Utilities
    ITEM  NetWare User Tools {BATCH}
          EXEC WIN NWUSER
    ITEM  Network Copy {PAUSE} {SHOW}
          GETP ENTER SOURCE FILE(S):{ }80,,{}
          GETP ENTER DESTINATION FILE(S):{ }80,,{}
          EXEC NCOPY %1 %2
```

REAL WORLD

The first menu defined in the source file is always the first menu displayed—no matter what number it uses. Subsequent submenus are referenced by their numbers. In Figure 6.10, the first menu has the number 01. This will be the first menu displayed for Guinevere—not because it's menu 01 but because it's the first menu shown in the source file. Branching to other submenus is accomplished with the SHOW command, not their numeric order. Bottom line: Menu numbers are for reference only; they don't have any systematical significance (there's a mouthful).

Item

Options are listed under each menu title using the ITEM command. Each item is automatically preceded by a letter (from A through Z) and appears in the exact order in which it is written. If you'd like to force a different letter or number for any option, simply precede the text with a caret (^) and the desired letter or number. For example, refer to menu 01 in Figure 6.10. Notice how the five items are each preceded by a caret and a letter. This forces the letter E, for example, to appear in front of "E-mail." Otherwise, it would get the letter B. Numbers can also be used as shown in Menu 10 of Figure 6.10. **Note**: If you force the letter assignment of one item, you should force the letter assignment of every item—but you don't have to. The menu program does not track forced assignments and might duplicate letters—this is a bad thing.

ITEM options can be customized using one of four built-in parameters. These are called "squiggly options" because they live inside cute "squiggly" brackets. Let's take a look:

▸ {BATCH}—shells the menu to disk and saves 32K of workstation RAM (see Figure 6.10)

▸ {CHDIR}—returns the user to the default directory upon completion of the item

▸ {PAUSE}—temporarily stops menu execution and displays the message

```
Press any key to continue.
```

ZEN

"Where's the Any key?"

Guinevere

▸ {SHOW}—displays DOS commands in the upper left-hand corner of the screen when they're executed

Once you've created the "look and feel" of your menus, it's time to move on to the real workhorses of IntranetWare menuing—control commands.

CONTROL COMMANDS

The second IntranetWare command type is control commands. These little wonders are the workhorses of the menu system. They execute menu instructions and enable branching to internal and external submenus. The IntranetWare control commands are

- EXEC—Executes any internal or external program.

- SHOW—Branches to another menu within this menu file. This is used for submenuing.

- LOAD—Branches to a completely different external menu file (with the .DAT extension).

- GETO—Supports optional user input.

- GETR—Supports required user input.

- GETP—Assigns user input to a programmable variable.

As you can see in Figure 6.10, the EXEC and SHOW control commands are the most popular. In Guinevere's main menu, for example, she has the option of branching to one of two submenus. This submenuing strategy continues throughout her complex menu file. Let's take a closer look at how these little dynamos work.

EXEC

EXEC is the most popular IntranetWare control command. It executes internal or external commands. These commands can be either an .EXE file, a .COM file, a DOS internal command, or one of four special EXEC options:

- EXEC CALL—Runs a batch file and returns to NMENU.

- EXEC DOS—Temporarily returns the user to the IntranetWare command line. Users must type **EXIT** to return to the custom menu.

- EXEC EXIT—The only way to exit a IntranetWare menu. Don't lock yourself in—use this command.

▸ EXEC LOGOUT—Exits NMENU and logs the user out. Guinevere is left at the DOS prompt without access to the network.

Be sure to include at least one of these EXEC commands toward the bottom of your main menu. As you can see in Figure 6.10, we're giving Guinevere the option of logging out. If you don't include one of these special EXEC options, the user will be trapped in the menu forever. This might not be a bad thing.

SHOW

SHOW is the second most popular IntranetWare control command. Because you can create 255 submenus within a single script file, you need a way of getting to them. SHOW branches to another menu number from within any item. This is a way of submenuing from WITHIN the same script file. Notice in Figure 6.10 how the SHOW command is used with the Applications and Fun Stuff submenus. Also, notice how Network Utilities is called as a submenu from within the Applications submenu.

TIP

Try not to confuse the SHOW control command with the SHOW squiggly option. It's unfortunate that they share the same name. The SHOW control command is used for submenuing, whereas the SHOW squiggly option displays executed DOS commands in the upper left-hand corner of your screen.

LOAD

LOAD performs exactly the same function as SHOW, but in a slightly different way. Instead of executing submenus within the same script file, LOAD branches to submenus in completely different files. Refer to Figure 6.10 for an example of how the LOAD command is used. The Admin Menu item includes a branch to ADMIN.DAT. This external menu file must be in the default directory or specified with an exact path.

There is no limit to the number of menus that you can LOAD at any one time. But remember, you can only display 11 cascading menus simultaneously.

GETO

The final three control commands allow for user input. This feature was previously not available in IntranetWare menus and is hard to find in MS Windows. GETO, GETR, and GETP are powerful tools, but their syntax is a little tricky:

`GETx prompt{PREPEND}length,prefill,{APPEND}`

▸ *x* is replaced with the type of GET command you wish to use—O for optional, R for required, and P for programmable user input.

▸ *prompt* is replaced by the message you want to send to the user. For example, in Figure 6.10, the last item asks Guinevere to "Enter source file(s):". This is the prompt.

▸ *{PREPEND}* data is attached *before* the user input. This works oppositely from *{APPEND}*. For example, in Figure 6.10, refer to the Pick your Doom item. The user is asked to enter the version of Doom he or she wish to play. The number they choose is prepended by the DOOM command, and it executes a batch file to load the appropriate game. This is a *{PREPEND}*. If no *{PREPEND}* is necessary, use the braces without any characters between them. Refer to the last item in Figure 6.10.

▸ *length* is the maximum number of characters the user can enter. Again, a length is required and the maximum is 80 characters. In the DOOM example, users can only enter a one-character answer.

▸ *prefill* displays a default response if none is given. It is separated from *length* by a comma and no spaces. Again, in the DOOM example of Figure 6.10, you're forcing a 1 to appear if no input is given. This will run the original game.

▸ *{APPEND}* defines a value that will always be appended to the user input. Once again, these braces are required, and if no data are needed, type the brackets without any characters. Refer to the last item in Figure 6.10.

TIP

Wow, what a mind-boggling collection of IntranetWare control commands. Don't GET too excited about using GETx. But if you have to, here are a few things to think about:

▸ **The GETO, GETR, and GETP commands must be entered between the ITEM line and the EXEC command associated with them.**

▸ **You can have a maximum of 100 GET commands per ITEM, although you want to limit each prompt to 1 line.**

▸ **Commands can be entered in either upper- or lowercase.**

▸ **You can enter up to 10 prompts in each dialog box. If you want a prompt to appear in its own dialog box, type a caret (^) at the beginning of the prompt text.**

▸ **During execution, the Enter key accepts input, but does not cause the command to execute. To activate the appropriate EXEC command, you must press F10.**

Now it's time to GET on with the show.

GETO allows for optional user input. As you can see in Figure 6.10, the Pick your Doom item uses an optional GET control command. If the user does not enter any input and simply presses Enter, IntranetWare executes the {PREPEND} and {prefill}, which is "DOOM1."

ZEN

"The computer is a great invention. There are just as many mistakes as ever. But now they are nobody's fault."

Anonymous

GETR

GETR requires user input. The menu will not continue until some valid information has been entered. However, the user can press Esc to return to the main menu.

GETP

GETP assigns user input to a programmable variable. If you need a variety of inputs from the user, assign each to a GETP prompt. The corresponding EXEC command can then use these prompts in combination with some valid external commands. As you can see in the final item of Figure 6.10, two GETP prompts are shown. The first input is assigned to %1 and the second to %2. The EXEC NCOPY command then uses these variables to satisfy the user's request. In addition, the {PAUSE} squiggly option enables the user to view the results as long as necessary.

Well, wasn't that fun? If you're feeling a little dizzy, now's a good time to put down the book and grab a soda . . . welcome back. Now that we've conquered the IntranetWare menu syntax, let's take a look at how these babies execute.

SMART LINK

The new and exciting Saber menu system has been integrated in a full line of network management tools. Surf over to McAfee and check them out: http://www.mcafee.com/prod/netmgt/saber.html.

MENU EXECUTION

So, how are IntranetWare menu files executed? Good question. It all starts with the source file. Menu source files are created by using any text editor, and they must have the .SRC extension. As you can see in Figure 6.11, these source files are then compiled into .DAT files using MENUMAKE.EXE. The compiled files are smaller, more flexible, and easily swapped to and from the local disk. You cannot, however, edit .DAT files. You must edit the source file and recompile it for testing.

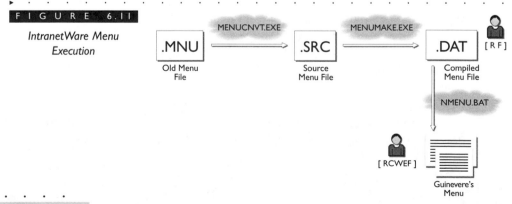

FIGURE 6.11

IntranetWare Menu Execution

The smaller, more flexible .DAT file is finally executed using NMENU.BAT. This step finally brings Guinevere's menu to life. (See Figure 6.12.)

FIGURE 6.12

Looking at Guinevere's Menu

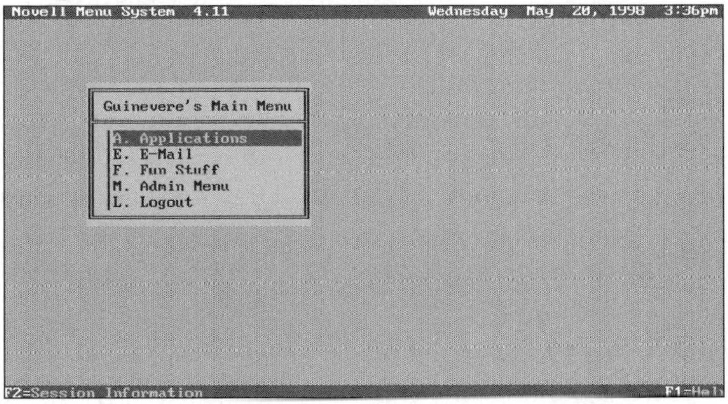

```
Novell Menu System  4.11                    Wednesday  May  20, 1998  3:36pm




              ┌─ Guinevere's Main Menu ──────┐
              │ A. Applications              │
              │ E. E-Mail                    │
              │ F. Fun Stuff                 │
              │ M. Admin Menu                │
              │ L. Logout                    │
              └──────────────────────────────┘




 F2=Session Information                                              F1=Help
```

That's not all—IntranetWare also supports older menus. NetWare 3.11 menu files (with the extension .MNU) can be converted into IntranetWare source files using MENUCNVT.EXE. These .SRC files are then compiled and displayed using MENUMAKE.EXE and NMENU.BAT. However, this is not the end of menu conversion. You must also edit some of the .SRC syntax changes, including invalid commands (such as SYSCON), preceding letters or numbers from the old menu system, and the conversion of "@1" variables into newer GETP statements.

So, what about security? The NMENU.BAT program is stored in SYS:PUBLIC so it can be accessed from anywhere by any IntranetWare user. In addition, there are access right issues concerning the location of .DAT files. Here's a summary:

▸ Users must have the Read and File Scan (RF) access rights to directories that hold the .DAT files. This is typically their home directory or a shared area such as SYS:PUBLIC.

▸ The IntranetWare menu system creates many temporary files. For this reason, users need special rights in the current default directory when executing NMENU.BAT. These rights are Read, Create, Write, Erase, and File Scan (RWCEF). Typically, this is the user's home or a temporary directory. Recall that in the previous discussion, you used EXIT to bail out of the Container login script and automatically accessed NMENU.BAT. You did this from Guinevere's home directory (with the DRIVE command) for security purposes. I knew there was a reason.

> ▸ If the menu file is going to be used by multiple users, it should be flagged as Sharable.

Once again, refer to Figure 6.11 for a summary of the access rights required at different points of menu execution.

So, what does Guinevere's menu look like? Check out Figure 6.12. As it shows, the IntranetWare menu program creates an extremely IntranetWare-looking interface. As a matter of fact, it's difficult to tell the difference between Guinevere's main menu and NETADMIN. I just hope Guinevere can tell the difference. Let's review. IntranetWare menu source files are created using any text editor. Their filenames contain the .SRC extension. These files are then compiled using MENUMAKE.EXE into a .DAT file. The smaller, more flexible .DAT file is then executed using NMENU.BAT. Piece of cake.

ZEN

"Never eat more than you can lift."

Miss Piggy

Remember, "wherever you go, there you are." With that in mind, let's take a moment to reflect on our LAN's brief, but exciting, life so far. First, she was born (installation), and then she took her first step (workstation connectivity). Once she learned to talk (login scripts), we sent her off to preschool to learn how to get along with others (menu system).

Now, it's time for our talented toddler to scurry off to kindergarten. There she'll start her long and winding journey down the road known as "SCHOOL"! During this journey, Leia will expand her body and mind to new levels—gaining valuable skills in the process. She'll make friends, buy clothes, ignore you, go to the prom, and, finally, graduate. This all leads to one inevitable climax—adulthood. Where did all the time go?

Step 4: Installing Network Applications

Leia goes to school.

Aah, school:

"The chalice of wisdom, to drink once more from thee."

I don't know what's more memorable, school or all the extracurricular activities that surround it. Regardless, this is the fire in which we forge our personalities. So many memories—my fourth grade music teacher, recess, stomach-churning school lunches, mind-boggling math homework, field trips, sports, and the junior prom. As we help Leia through this phase of her childhood, we get an opportunity to live our own school days all over again. This is probably one of the most rewarding and excruciating experiences for any parent.

In addition to life lessons, school teaches you a few academic things. With knowledge comes productivity and wisdom. Suddenly, Leia's eyes open to the wonders and possibilities of calculus, art, and prepositional phrases. And sometimes the lessons aren't so obvious. I'm sure you'll never use algebra again in your life, but consider the problem-solving skills it taught you—skills that you'll put to good use as a CNA.

SMART LINK

Speaking of school, check out Novell Education at http://education.novell.com or CyberState University at http://www.cyberstateu.com.

As your LAN learns more and more from school, your users' productivity will increase as well. After all, a network is only as useful as the users who use it (that's a triple-word score). In Step 4 of IntranetWare Configuration, you will give Guinevere all the productivity tools she needs to get her job done. That includes network applications, utilities, and a consistent user environment. Don't underestimate the value of the latter. This means if Guinevere wants to use MS Windows, her application should be in Windows. However, if she breaks out in hives every time she touches the mouse, consider giving her DOS-based applications. Please try not to mix interfaces—it gets ugly fast.

A SIMPLE SEVEN-STEP MODEL

Network applications are the productivity tools of your LAN—and IntranetWare has great support for them. This is accomplished with the help of a simple seven-step model. For the most part, these seven steps help you foster synergy between user productivity and shared application software—I learned those big words in school.

I • Make sure your applications are IntranetWare-compatible *before* you buy them.

2 • Ensure that the software is truly multiuser.

3 • Create an appropriate directory structure for the applications and all their support components.

4 • Install them.

5 • Establish file attributes for Sharable and Nonsharable network applications.

6 • In addition to file attributes, assign user access rights to network application subdirectories.

7 • Customize the workstation for specific application needs.

This is just a general discussion. Most network applications include specific instructions for making them work on a LAN. However, these guidelines are a great place to start.

Step I: Ensuring IntranetWare Compatibility

It is important to determine whether your applications are IntranetWare compatible before you buy them. Approximately 7,000 software packages are compatible and registered with Novell. This compatibility information is important, because IntranetWare makes demands on application software that can cause it to corrupt data or at least impede users' productivity. Information about IntranetWare compatibility and registration are available on NetWire or from your local Novell sales office. You should also consider contacting the software vendor directly. But, be forewarned, the company might not have the full story.

SMART LINK

For more detailed information about Novell-certified hardware and software, consult the vendor forums on NetWire, testing lab results on NSEPro, or surf to the Novell Lab's Bulletins at http://support.novell.com/sitemap.

Step 2: Checking Multiuserness

For the best results and highest level of user productivity, all applications should support multiple users simultaneously. If your application is designed to run on a stand-alone computer, don't assume it will work fine on the LAN. The good news is, most large software manufacturers routinely create multiuser versions of popular applications. Two signs of true multiuser capabilities are file sharing and multiuser access. Again, it is important to determine the level of multiuserness *before* you purchase the application. Also, be aware that almost all single-user software works in an IntranetWare environment—IntranetWare supports any DOS application. But don't expect these applications to offer data- or resource-sharing capabilities.

Step 3: Creating the Directory Structure

Before you can install the application and configure its components, you must create an intelligent directory structure for it. As you learned in Chapter 4, the application directories must support data as well as program files. Each application should have a specific subdirectory under the main SYS:APPS directory to avoid cluttering the root. This also organizes network applications for easy, efficient security implementation.

In addition, some applications create their own directory structure during the installation process. Unfortunately, these programs attack the root directory. That's fine in a local environment but doesn't work well in the IntranetWare-shared directory structure. Consider "MAP ROOTing" a network drive before installation. This way the system will think that it's installing in [Root] when in fact it's installing under the SYS:APPS directory.

Step 4: Managing the Installation

The installation process is typically left up to the application. Many install programs perform file decompression as well as application customization. This is especially true in the MS Windows environment. Be sure you do not simply copy the files from the source diskette or CD-ROM. You haven't lived until you've had to manually customize the 342 .INI files configured by Windows 95. Let the application do it—that's what you paid for.

Once the network software has been installed, three more steps help define its special configurations.

Step 5: Assigning File Attributes

Network applications must have the correct file attributes so that programs can share them without being locked out. Follow these simple guidelines:

- ▸ Shared application files—Sharable, Read-Only

- ▸ Shared data files—Sharable, Read-Write

- ▸ Nonshared data files—Nonsharable, Read/Write

Most of today's multiuser application programs provide detailed documentation about specific file attributes. I don't usually say this, but you might consider "reading the manual."

Step 6: Assigning Access Rights

In addition to file attributes, you'll need to assign user/group rights for access to network application directories. By default, users have *no* rights to the new directory structure you've created. If you install the application and walk away, users end up spinning their wheels trying to get work done. This also applies to NDS rights if you need access to other network resources, including printers and messaging objects.

As you recall from Chapter 5, most applications work fine with the Read and File Scan (RF) access rights. Also recall that these access rights can be inherited by all subdirectories under SYS:APPS. Next, you may consider assigning all rights except SAM (Supervisor, Access Control, and Modify) to data directories. Finally, consider these security guidelines:

- ▸ Application data should be stored under each application subdirectory (SYS:APPS\WP\DATA, for example).

- ▸ User-specific data should be stored in each user's home directory.

> ▸ Group-specific data should be stored in a corresponding SYS:GROUP subdirectory.

> ▸ Globally shared data should be stored in the SYS:DATA directory.

Step 7: Performing Customization

The seventh and final step in network application support is workstation customization. Many programs require special DOS configurations in order to run properly. The most notable tool is CONFIG.SYS, which customizes the DOS environment. For example, device drivers might be loaded for programs that use a mouse. Here are a few other things to think about:

> ▸ You may need to increase environment space using the SHELL command:

```
SHELL=C:\COMMAND.COM /p /e:1024
```

> ▸ You may want to load HIMEM.SYS to activate the high memory area (HMA). Then you can use the following command in CONFIG.SYS to free 60K of conventional workstation RAM:

```
DOS=HIGH
```

> ▸ Many programs require special SET parameters for environment variables and temporary directories. Consult the application's documentation.

INTRANETWARE APPLICATION MANAGEMENT

In addition to the simple seven-step model for generic network applications, IntranetWare provides a complete GUI application management system. The NetWare Application Manager (NAM) allows users to run network applications that have been configured and centralized on the server. NAM consists of application objects and a special launcher called the NetWare Application Launcher (NAL). The application's setup information is stored as an Application object in the NDS tree. This eliminates the need for users to have a drive mapping or path to an application's directory. They simply double-click on the NAL icon within Windows and the system takes care of the rest.

To configure NDS and the file system for NAM, you must complete the following three tasks:

- ▸ Task 1—Create Application objects

- ▸ Task 2—Configure Application objects

- ▸ Task 3—Configure workstations

Task 1—Create Application Objects

NAM supplies three new objects in the NDS tree, one each for Windows 95, Windows 3.1, and DOS applications.

You can create these Application objects in the same way you create any other NDS leaf. Simply select the container where the Application object will reside and choose Create from the Object menu. When creating the Application object, you must provide a name for it and a path to the application's directory. This information can be seen later in Figure 6.13.

Task 2—Configure Application Objects

Application objects contain many pages of information. However, the only data necessary is the path to the application and a list of User objects that are allowed to access it.

Figure 6.13 shows the NetWare Application object configuration screen. In the identification page, you can define an application icon title, path, and icon type. In other pages, you can associate users with the object, provide any special commands for startup, and create special scripts that define custom drive mappings when the application is launched.

As previously mentioned, Application objects can map network drives and capture printer ports when they're launched from the workstation. These drives and ports are only active as long as the application is running. When the user exits the application, the mappings and captures are deleted. This is accomplished using the Drives/Ports page.

In addition, scripts can be added to the Application object, which perform login script functions during application launching. This is accomplished using the Scripts page in Figure 6.13. Finally, you can also enter description and names of contacts for the application that is viewed by users.

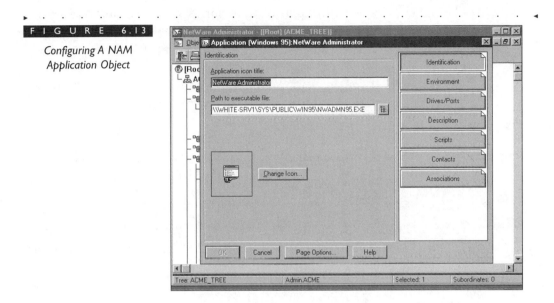

FIGURE 6.13

Configuring A NAM Application Object

One tip from the security front: Ensure that users have the appropriate NDS and file system rights to Application objects and corresponding directories before activating NAL. Speaking of NAL, that's the final task in our Application Management model.

TIP

If two or more Application objects create a drive map to the same drive letter, the first application launched from NAL will take precedence. The same is true when using Application objects to capture the same port. Be very careful when using the Drives/Ports option in NAM.

Task 3—Configure Workstations

No special configuration is needed to run NAL from a workstation. Users can run NAL from the SYS:PUBLIC directory or from a copy of NAL that is stored on the workstation's hard disk.

However, if you want to get fancy and increase network application security, you can configure NAL to replace the normal Windows interface—EXPLORER.EXE in

Windows 95 or PROGMAN.EXE in Windows 3.1. This feature automates network application access and only displays the applications to which users have rights.

To replace the Windows interface with NAL, complete the following steps:

▸ Step 1A—If you are using Windows 95 copy the following files to a directory on the local hard drive: NALW95.EXE, NALRES32.DLL,NALBMP32.DLL, and NAL.HLP.

▸ Step 1B—If you are using Windows 3.1 copy the following files to a directory on the local hard drive: NALW31.EXE, NALRES.DLL, NALBMP.DLL, and NAL.HLP.

▸ Step 2—Edit the SYS.INI file to set NAL as the SHELL. Find the line in the [boot] section that starts with "SHELL=". Here's an example of the syntax for Windows 95:

```
SHELL=EXPLORER.EXE
```

This would be replaced with the location of the NAL files on the local hard drive:

```
SHELL=C:\NALW95.EXE
```

▸ Step 3—Save the changes and restart Windows.

Once the workstation has been customized with NAL, users can launch applications by simply double-clicking the icon within Windows. When the application is launched, NAL runs any scripts associated with the Application object, checks for the path to the application, and then launches the application. Similarly, when the user exits the application, any mappings or other special commands that were set within an Application object script are reset to their original configurations.

This is a great way of further automating network applications. In addition, NAM gives you better application security and centralized control. These are all important parts of growing up in the IntranetWare universe.

SMART LINK

For more information on NetWare Application Management, surf to the Novell Knowledgebase at http://support.novell.com/search/.

Once the application software has been installed, your LAN is well on its way to enlightenment: "sipping from the chalice of knowledge." In addition, the menu interface can provide a friendly, centrally managed arena for application launching. I know this is a lot of work, but "warm and fuzzy" is a good thing. Customization increases productivity by giving users the tools they need and decreasing their LAN-phobia—not to be confused with parent-phobia!

ZEN

"Actually I'm 18. I've just lived hard."

Clint Eastwood

Speaking of phobia, Guinevere is growing up way too fast. In the blink of an eye, the prom is over and she's ready for the fifth and final step of IntranetWare childhood—moving out.

Step 5: E-mail

The time has come. Your LAN becomes a woMAN (metropolitan area network).

It's inevitable. At some point, your child grows up and becomes an adult. The transition to adulthood is a scary time for everybody. She gets her first car, her first job, and her first apartment. Suddenly, the chalice of knowledge takes on a whole new importance. Her ability to survive depends on how many business classes she slept through. Suddenly, all those nights you spent helping her with math homework equate to food on the table. Suddenly, Mom and Dad aren't so wrong anymore. It's weird how that happens—and it always does.

With adulthood comes new challenges and a new level of communication. To succeed, it's vital that you develop a high level of LAN synergy. All your users, configurations, workstations, and applications must work together as one cohesive unit. This is made possible through e-mail. The final step in IntranetWare configuration focuses on tying all of these components together.

E-mail has become one of the most critical LAN services, next to filing and printing. That's because it

▸ Improves communication—E-mail enables employees to communicate even when business meetings, travel schedules, and distributed locations prevent them from seeing each other.

▸ Increases productivity—E-mail improves the success rate for communications because unlike other forms of communication, messaging does not require conversing participants to be available at the same time. No more "telephone tag."

▸ Maximizes the use of existing resources—E-mail leverages file, printing and connectivity services by providing a way of tying them altogether, much the same way as time ties together the fabric of our universe. (Is that *esoteric* enough for you?)

QUIZ

Speaking of esoteric, here's a doozy for you. There are five men—A, B, C, D, and E—each wearing a disc on his forehead selected from a total of five white, two red, and two black. Each man can see the colors of the discs worn by the other four, but he is unable to see his own.

They are all intelligent people, and they are asked to try to deduce the color of their own disc from the colors of the other four whom they can see. In fact, they are all wearing white discs. After a pause for reflection, C, who is even more intelligent than the others, says, "I reckon I must be wearing a white disc."

Huh? How did he do that?

(Q6-6)

E-mail in IntranetWare relies on an integrated messaging platform called MHS Services for NetWare 4.11. MHS (Message Handling Service) stores, forwards, and routes user messages. These messages can be text, binary, graphics, digitized video, or audio data. MHS Services is integrated with NDS and uses many NDS objects to accomplish these magic messaging tasks.

Let's take a closer look.

REAL WORLD

MHS Servicesfor IntranetWare is *not* included in IntranetWare. It is, however, available for free from NetWire (Web or CompuServe). Incidentally, Novell would prefer that you used GroupWise as your e-mail engine. They have a good point!

SMART LINK

If you really want to use Novell's "MHS Service for NetWare 4.11," you can download it for free from http://support.novell.com/sitemap.

UNDERSTANDING MHS SERVICES

MHS Services for NetWare 4.11 is an "engine" that provides messaging capabilities. Various messaging programs can now take full advantage of this technology. In the simplest terms, this "engine" takes input from various e-mail applications and routes it to any user on the internetwork running any other type of e-mail interface. This is much like the way IntranetWare file services stores a variety of different types of files from various network applications. However, unlike file services, MHS actively deals with the communication interactions between computer users. Instead of simply storing data files, MHS moves the data from point to point and notifies the user of waiting messages.

All of this magic is accomplished with three key components:

► Messaging server

► User mailboxes

► MHS applications

Messaging Server

The *messaging server* is IntranetWare's implementation of the MHS "engine." The server accepts data from a variety of user e-mail packages and delivers it to any type of mailbox (as Figure 6.14 shows). The server can deliver messages to local user mailboxes or route them through the internetwork to other messaging engines for eventual delivery. The main point is—MHS Services supports a variety of e-mail applications and can deliver to a variety of other engine types. Also, messages can be composed of text, graphics, video, or audio data.

▶ · ◀

FIGURE 6.14

Understanding MHS Services for IntranetWare

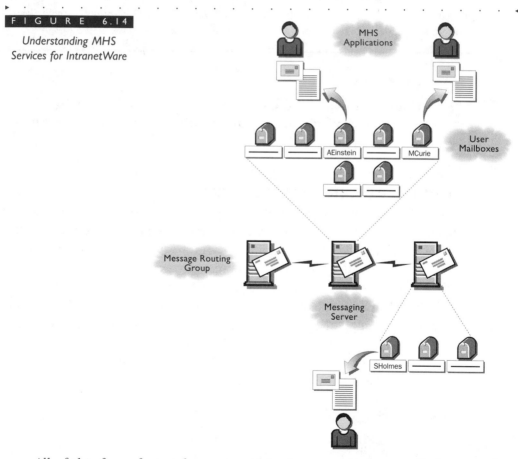

All of this fancy footwork occurs within the messaging server. Each network server that has MHS Services installed is called a *messaging server.* A *message routing group* is a group of messaging servers that communicate with each other directly—

to transfer messages. In a large WAN such as that in Figure 6.14, for example, this would be all the IntranetWare servers that share a common backbone. Each message routing group has one or more *Postmaster Generals*. This special user is automatically granted the privilege of modifying message routing groups and configuring all of the messaging servers. In addition, each of these servers has one or more *Postmasters* that configure and manage user mailboxes.

User Mailboxes

A *user mailbox* is a physical location on the messaging server where messages are delivered. You can use any MHS application to send messages to any NDS object that can be assigned a mailbox. This includes Users, Groups, Organizational Roles, and Organizational Units. Also, you can send mail to special *Distribution List* objects, which in turn copy the mail to multiple mailboxes. This reduces network traffic throughout the message routing group by creating and routing only one copy of the message and then replicating it for every mailbox on the list. Finally, user mailboxes can be configured and managed using either NWADMIN (MS Windows) or NETADMIN (DOS). Once again, refer to Figure 6.14 for an illustration of the relationship between messaging servers and user mailboxes.

MHS Applications

All this IntranetWare messaging magic is made possible through a front-end e-mail application. Without these applications, there's no way to create or read MHS messages. Just your luck, IntranetWare includes two rudimentary MHS applications—FirstMail for DOS and FirstMail for Windows. Both starter MHS applications are automatically installed in the SYS:PUBLIC subdirectory on each messaging server. The good news is, FirstMail automatically imports all user and group information from NDS. You don't need to lift a finger. This means that as soon as you install MHS Services, users can begin sending messages via FirstMail.

The bad news is, you get what you pay for. Although FirstMail for Windows has a nice interface (as shown later in Figure 6.15), it doesn't include any advanced messaging features. FirstMail is a simple starter application that can tide you over until you buy a real MHS front-end. Think of it as Guinevere's first broken-down VW or her one-room apartment under the train tracks. Even though it's not the Taj Mahal, it does represent her first shot at freedom. For this reason, you'll probably never forget FirstMail or that adorable VW Bug.

There you have it. MHS Services in a nutshell. Even though I'm sure you absorbed it all the first time, let's take a quick review—just for the heck of it. Table 6.6 is your friend.

	MHS COMPONENT	DESCRIPTION
T A B L E 6.6 *Getting to Know MHS Services for NetWare 4.11*	MHS Services for NetWare 4.11	"The Product"
	MHS engine	Implementation of "The Product"
	Messaging server	Each IntranetWare server running "The Product." Also the central communications point and storage location of user mailboxes
	Message routing group	A collection of interconnected messaging servers.
	Postmaster general	Manages the message routing group.
	Postmaster	Manages the messaging server
	User mailboxes	Physical storage location for MHS messages. They hang out on messaging servers
	MHS applications	E-mail front-ends that send and receive MHS messages
	Distribution list	A special NDS object that forwards messages to numerous user mailboxes

Now that you're a pro with MHS Services, let's explore the details of managing it. Don't have any illusions; nobody said moving out would be easy.

MANAGING MHS SERVICES

So, you've learned about Novell's MHS. Now, what do you do with it? Moving out can be such a traumatic experience. One morning you wake up and bam! It hits you that you're on your own. A thousand questions pop into your head: Who's going to make breakfast? What am I going to do with my life? Where's the laundry machine? In order to survive in this cruel and exciting world, you must have a plan and, above all, you must have friends.

Managing MHS Services is not so different. One day you'll come into work and bam! It hits you that you're using e-mail. Then a thousand questions pop into your head: Who's the Postmaster? Where's my mailbox? What's a Distribution List? Fortunately, IntranetWare provides numerous NDS objects especially for MHS Services—your friends. They are:

- ▶ Message Routing Group

- ▶ Messaging Server

- ▶ Distribution List

- ▶ External Entity

In addition to these MHS-only objects, you'll need to create and manage various mailbox owners   Users, Groups, Organizational Roles, and Organizational Units.

Now let's take a closer look at how these MHS "friends" can help you get along in the cruel and exciting world of IntranetWare messaging.

Message Routing Group

As you remember from our earlier discussions, the MHS Message Routing Group is a collection of interconnected messaging servers. As an NDS object, it represents a cluster of messaging servers that communicate directly with each other for transferring messages. A default Message Routing Group object is created during the installation of MHS Services and placed in the same container as the host IntranetWare server. Subsequent messaging servers are defaulted to this group.

Also recall that the Postmaster General manages the Message Routing Group. This is usually the Admin user but can be assigned a unique name during initial MHS Services installation.

Messaging Server

In earlier discussions, you learned that the messaging server is the central communications point and storage location of MHS Services for NetWare 4.11. As an NDS object, it identifies the host IntranetWare server and the location of the MHS directory structure (SYS:MHS). The SYS:MHS directory houses all user mailboxes assigned to this messaging server. During a standard MHS Services installation, the Messaging Server object is created automatically and placed in the same container as the Host IntranetWare server object.

In order for numerous messaging servers to communicate with one another, they must be part of the same message routing group. Once these first two MHS objects have been created, you're well on your way to e-mail paradise. With the groundwork in place, it's time to turn our attention toward the people who will be sending and receiving MHS messages. Look out, Guinevere.

Distribution List

As you recall, the Distribution List is a special NDS object that forwards messages to numerous user mailboxes. It accomplishes this in an interesting way. Only one copy of the message is delivered to the Distribution List mailbox. The message is then replicated for every mailbox in the Distribution List. This decreases network traffic between messaging servers because multiple messages are routed with only a single packet.

Group objects can also be used for messaging, but they *do* increase network traffic. Unlike Distribution List, Group objects generate a packet for every message routed between Messaging Servers. Distribution Lists also differ from Groups in that membership can be nested. In other words, a Distribution List can contain other distribution lists. This is not true for NDS group objects.

That completes our discussion of the three main MHS management objects— Message Routing Group, Messaging Server, and Distribution List. For a more practical hands-on approach toward MHS management, consult the case study at the end of this chapter. Now, let's take a quick look at the final two management objects: External Entity and Mailbox objects.

ZEN

"The only Zen you can find on the tops of mountains is the Zen you bring up there."

Robert M. Pirsig

External Entity

The *External Entity* object represents non-native NDS MHS objects. It's basically an NDS placeholder that enables you to send messages to users who are not part of the NDS tree. External Entity objects are not created during MHS Services installation; they are normally imported from special gateway software. This gateway software allows MHS to interface with other non-NDS systems.

Mailbox Objects

The discussion so far has focused on the key MHS management objects you need to deal with in order to make MHS Services work. But all of this lexicon doesn't mean a hill of beans if you don't have anyone to send the messages to. MHS Services for IntranetWare supports four types of Mailbox objects:

▸ User

▸ Group

▸ Organizational Role

▸ Organizational Unit

Each of them can send and receive MHS mail with varying degrees of sophistication. In the exercise at the end of the chapter, we will explore how to assign mailboxes to each of these objects and use them in the grand MHS scheme of things. For now, suffice it to say that you probably fall into one of these four categories—maybe more.

QUIZ

Which "Star Trek" character waited until the second season to beam aboard the Starship Enterprise?

(Q6-7)

USING FIRSTMAIL

As you learned earlier, MHS Services for NetWare 4.11 includes a rudimentary e-mail application called FirstMail, available by default in two versions (DOS and Windows), that are copied to the SYS:PUBLIC directory on each Messaging Server.

FirstMail for Windows is an intuitive messaging application with simple icons for sending, receiving, and reading e-mail. As seen in Figure 6.15, FirstMail lists all of your new messages and enables you to open, reply, forward, move, copy, or delete them. In addition, the Button Panel provides five management tasks:

▸ Send mail

- ▸ Read new mail
- ▸ Mail folders
- ▸ Address books
- ▸ Distribution Lists

FIGURE 6.15

FirstMail for Windows

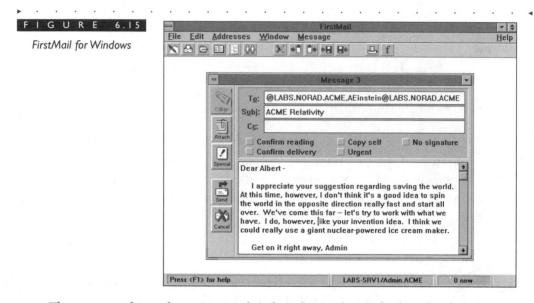

The greatest thing about FirstMail (other than it being free) is the fact that it's NDS-aware. This means you don't have to bother with user configurations; FirstMail gets everything it needs from the NDS database. Otherwise, if you're using an MHS-compatible application that's not NDS-aware, you have to register it with Directory Services and add the e-mail name to each user's list of applications. Too much work.

THE BRAIN

For more information on using MHS Services in IntranetWare, see the AppNote entitled "Integrating MHS Services with Other Novell Products" in the October 1995 issue of *Novell Application Notes,* or surf the Web at http://support.novell.com/sitemap.

Well, there you have it. That completes the final step of IntranetWare configuration. Childhood isn't so bad. Let's quickly review where we've been.

ZEN

"Ring the bells that still can ring.
Forget your perfect offering.
There is a crack in everything.
That's how the light gets in."

Leonard Cohen

It all started with Leia's first step (workstation connectivity). Once she became connected to the network, Step 2 took over—Leia learned to talk. This involved Container, Profile, and User login scripts.

Leia went to preschool. The next stage in your network's development was dominated by a friendly IntranetWare menu system. The menu system acted as a central repository for user interface, network applications, and e-mail. In Step 4, you installed and configured the network applications as Leia went to "real" school. This was the most important phase of the child's development. After all, without school (or network applications), there would be no productivity and purpose to life.

Finally, in Step 5, Leia moved out. She got her first car, her first apartment, and her first job. Although it seemed like a difficult time for everyone, moving out represented an important stage in Leia's life. She made a smooth transition from childhood to adulthood. In much the same way, your network needs a smooth transition from IntranetWare configuration to management.

In a side story, we were tracking Guinevere as she started her day with a computer and cappuccino. As a CNA, it's your responsibility to establish the configuration so that Guinevere never knows what's happening while she's sipping her cappuccino. In an ideal world, Guinevere never suspects that when she turns on her computer, it initializes workstation connectivity files, runs login scripts, establishes a menu system, and provides transparent access to network applications and e-mail—just like a child never understands what her parents go through while she's growing up. Of course, life doesn't end there; it is only the beginning. Now that you've made it through childhood in one piece, it's time to move on to the third and final phase of life—adulthood.

Get out of the way, we're coming through!

SMART LINK

Learn to find yourself in IntranetWare Adulthood at
http://www.aronson.com/ppp/birth.html.

EXERCISE 6-1: WORKSTATION CONNECTIVITY WITH CLIENT 16

1. Ensure that the 16-bit connection files are not currently loaded in workstation memory. Display the TSRs currently in workstation memory by typing: **MEM /C /P**. Ensure that LSL.COM, a LAN driver such as NE2000, IPXODI.COM, and/or VLM.EXE are not loaded. If they are, you must either unload them manually, boot off a "clean" bootable floppy, or comment out the @CALL STARTNET.BAT and related statements in your AUTOEXEC.BAT file and reboot. To manually unload these files, you must unload them in the reverse order from which they were loaded, namely by typing

   ```
   C:
   CD \NWCLIENT
   VLM /U
   IPXODI /U
   NE2000 /U (or the appropriate LAN driver)
   LSL /U
   ```

2. Load the Client 16 connection files

   a. Switch to the C:\NWCLIENT directory by typing

   ```
   C:
   CD \NWCLIENT
   ```

   b. Load the Link Support Layer software by typing

   ```
   LSL
   ```

   What happens? Can you tell from the screen what the purpose of LSL.COM is? See Figure 6.16.

Understanding the
Workstation Connection,
Part I

```
C:\NWCLIENT>LSL
Novell Link Support Layer for DOS ODI   v2.20 (960401)
(c) Copyright 1990 - 1996, by Novell, Inc. All rights reserved.

The configuration file used was "C:\NWCLIENT\NET.CFG".
Max Boards 4, Max Stacks 4


C:\NWCLIENT>3C5X9
3Com EtherLink III MLID w/ DME   v2.02 (950922)
(C) Copyright 1995 3Com Corp.   All Rights Reserved

IRQ 10, Port 320, Node Address 20AFE28F2D L
Max Frame 1514 bytes, Line Speed 10 Mbps
Board 1, Frame ETHERNET_802.2, LSB Mode

C:\NWCLIENT>IPXODI

NetWare IPX/SPX Protocol  v3.03  (960611)
(C) Copyright 1990-1995 Novell, Inc.  All Rights Reserved.

Bound to logical board 1 (3C5X9) : Protocol ID E0

C:\NWCLIENT>
```

c. Load the LAN driver by typing

NE2000 *(or appropriate LAN driver)*

d. Load the IPX communications protocol by typing

IPXODI

What happens? Does IPXODI begin workstation communications, or do you have to wait for VLM.EXE?

e. Load the NetWare DOS Requester (and display the maximum amount of related information) by typing

VLM /V4

The "/V4" parameter defines the highest level of driver verbosity. This will display all loaded VLMs and some additional troubleshooting information. Refer to Figure 6.17 for more information. What does this tell you about the relationship between IPXODI and VLM?

F I G U R E   6.17

Understanding the Workstation Connection, Part II

```
(C) Copyright 1993 - 1996 Novell, Inc.  All Rights Reserved.
Patent pending.
Patent No. 5,349,642.
NETWARE PROTOCOL NDS BIND

The VLM.EXE file is pre-initializing the VLMs.............
The VLM.EXE file is using extended memory (XMS).
CONN.VLM      - NetWare connection table manager  v1.21 (960514)
IPXNCP.VLM    - NetWare IPX transport module  v1.21 (960514)
TRAN.VLM      - NetWare transport multiplexor module  v1.21 (960514)
SECURITY.VLM  - NetWare security enhancement module  v1.21 (960514)
NDS.VLM       - NetWare directory services protocol module  v1.21 (960514)
BIND.VLM      - NetWare bindery protocol module  v1.21 (960514)
NWP.VLM       - NetWare DOS Requestor NetWare protocol module  v1.21 (960514)
FIO.VLM       - NetWare file input-output module  v1.21 (960514)
GENERAL.VLM   - NetWare general purpose function module v1.21 (960514)
FIRST NETWORK DRIVE F
REDIR.VLM     - NetWare DOS redirector module  v1.21 (960514)
FIRST NETWORK DRIVE F
PRINT.VLM     - NetWare printer redirection module  v1.21 (960514)
NETX.VLM      - NetWare workstation shell module  v4.21 (960514)
FIRST NETWORK DRIVE F
You are attached to server WHITE-SRV1

C:\NWCLIENT>
```

f.   Switch to your first network drive by typing

F:

3.   Log onto the network.

a.   Display the servers currently available on your network by typing

NLIST SERVER /B

b.   Log into the network by typing

LOGIN .ADMIN.ACME

Notice that we're logging into the NDS tree and not the server. This is a fundamental advantage of IntranetWare. Why does it still reply with a "Servername"?

c.   Display your login name and connection number by typing

WHOAMI

d.   Display users in your container that are currently logged into the network by typing

NLIST USER /A

EXERCISE 6.2: WORKSTATION CONNECTIVITY WITH CLIENT 32

In this exercise, we will walk through some very important Client 32 workstation connectivity steps: namely *Connection* and *Login*. Follow very carefully, and try this at home—if you dare!

1. On a Windows 95 workstation, click on the Start button, then select the following, in order:

    ▸ Programs

    ▸ Novell

    ▸ NetWare 4.11 Login

2. Make sure the Login tab is selected.

    a. You'll notice that this dialog box lists the network or server to which you are currently attached. You will probably find it lists ACME_TREE.

    b. Type **Admin** in the Name field. (If you wanted to log in as a different user, you could specify the common or distinguished name of that user.)

    c. Type the password for the Admin user in the Password field. You'll notice that asterisks, rather than the actual password, are displayed for security reasons.

3. Click on the Connection tab.

    a. Make sure that the radio button in front of the Tree field is selected and that ACME_TREE is displayed in this field. If not, you can either type it in, or select it from a list by clicking on the tree icon to the right of this field.

b. Type "**ACME**" (with or without quotation marks) in the Context field to indicate the location of your User object in the NDS tree. (If you had keyed in a distinguished name in Step 2b, it would override the context listed in this field.)

c. Don't type anything in the Server field. In this exercise, we are going to log into the network itself, rather than logging into a specific server. (If you wanted to specify a server, you could click on the radio button in front of the Server field, then key in the server name, or select it from a list by clicking on the server icon to the right of this field. You'll notice that it's asking for the common name of the server—not its distinguished name.) Ensure that the Bindery Connections box is *not* checked, as we want to log in as an NDS connection, not a Bindery Services connection.

d. Ensure that there is a checkmark in the Clear Current Connections box to clear any existing connections. You should always check this box if you are switching trees or servers, or logging in under a new username. If you didn't check this box, it would indicate that you wanted to make an additional tree or server connection. If you did so, you'd find that the login scripts for the new connection would overwrite any existing mappings that use the same drive letters, port numbers, and so on.

4. Click on the Script tab. Sit back and relax while you read this paragraph. We are not going to make any changes to this dialog box. It is for informational purposes only. This tab allows you to control the processing of login scripts. It allows you to override existing User and Profile login scripts assigned to this user, as well as to bypass all login scripts. For example, if you indicated a login script name in the Login Script field, it would override your existing User login script (if you had one). If you entered a login script name in the Profile Script field, it would override your existing Profile login script (if one existed). If you were to click on the Run scripts box, it would run any login scripts that had been set up for you, including any listed in this dialog

box. Because the Close script results automatically box is not checked, it will keep the Login Results window open so that you can examine the results of login script processing when you have completed the login process.

5. Click on the Variables tab. If you wanted to pass on any variables to the login script processor, you would indicate them here. (We don't want to do so, so don't make any changes to this dialog box.)

6. Click on OK to initiate the login process. A Login Results window should be displayed on the screen. You will notice that it lists information such as your current context, your User object's current context, your current tree, and the server to which you are currently attached. Review the contents of the window, then click on OK. Congratulations! You have successfully logged into the network.

EXERCISE 6-3: UNDERSTANDING NET.CFG

The ACME R&D department has special WAN requirements. Also, it's made up of the most advanced— sometimes even dangerous—users. For these reasons, they've asked you to customize their workstation NET.CFG files. Fortunately, the hardware and software have already been sufficiently standardized. Now, you need to review their accessibility requirements and build an appropriate NET.CFG.

Be forewarned, it's not as easy as it looks. Following is a list of the R&D accessibility criteria. Good luck.

▸ A comment should be inserted at the top of the file indicating that it is the standard NET.CFG file for the R&D department It should also list the author of the file (who is you) and the date it is created.

▸ Each workstation will consist of a Dell 133 MHz Pentium using ODI drivers and a 3COM C35X9 network card set to use interrupt A, I/O port 320, and Ethernet frame type 802.2.

▸ The ACME_TREE will be the only NDS tree accessed by the R&D department at this time.

▸ R&D-SRV1 will be the primary server used by the R&D department

▸ Users should have a default context of

    OU=R&D.OU=LABS.OU=NORAD.O=ACME

prior to login.

▸ The first network drive will be F:.

▸ Packet Buffers should be set to 10 to increase performance.

▸ The Signature Level for the NCP Packet Signature feature should be set to 3 for maximum security.

► The connection files should be loaded in low memory for better performance and stability.

► Users should be allowed to connect up to 10 servers simultaneously.

► Users should be allowed to capture to a maximum of five printing ports.

► Microsoft Windows will be used on the workstations.

► The LONG MACHINE TYPE variable should be set to DELL.

For hints and a complete solution, refer to Appendix C. No cheating!

CASE STUDY: CONFIGURING ACME'S LOGIN SCRIPTS

Just as the day was winding down swimmingly at ACME (at 4:50 p.m.), FDR came cruising into your office. "I'm sorry it's so late," he said, "but something's up with the Net. Can you take a quick look?" Grudgingly (because that's how you do things at 4:59 p.m.), you agree to check it out. "Oh, right," he adds, "I want all the public relations managers to share some applications and report files—any ideas?"

Of course you have ideas; after all, you are a CNA! Quickly you discover that the PR Container script has been destroyed—fortunately, you have notes from the old one in your IntranetWare Log book.

1. Here's the PR Container login script notes:

   a. Insert a comment at the top of the login script indicating the purpose of the login script, the author (who is you), and the date the file was created.

   b. Set the DOS prompt to display the drive and directory name.

   c. Display a greeting that is displayed each time a user in this container logs in, including the username, day, and date.

   d. Turn off the display of drive mappings and assign the following regular drive mappings:

      (1) Drive U: should point to the User's home directory.

      (2) Drive G: should point to the user's shared group directory.

   e. Assign the following search drive mappings, making sure not to overwrite existing drive mappings in the DOS path:

      (1) S1: pointing to SYS:PUBLIC

      (2) S2: pointing to the DOS directory on the network

      (3) S3: pointing to the SYS:APPS\WINDOWS directory

f. Insert a COMSPEC command that points to the DOS directory on the network.

g. Prevent the Default login script from executing when a user logs in that has no User login script.

h. Set up a printer capture of the HP4SI-P1 printer, specifying no tabs, no banners, and a timeout of 20 seconds.

i. On Wednesdays, fire phasers and display a reminder to members of the PR-Group that the weekly Manager meeting is at 9:00 a.m. in Conference Room 3-D.

j. Every time a user logs into the network, display a file called G:PR.NEW containing the important news of the day for the public relations department.

k. Set the default drive to U:.

l. Execute a custom menu called G:PRMAIN.DAT (which you will create in the next exercise).

m. General notes:

(1) Whenever you display a message, don't forget to insert a PAUSE statement so that the message doesn't scroll off the screen before the user has a chance to read it.

(2) Insert appropriate remarks through the login script so that someone else that looks at it can easily understand what you have done.

2. Next, you decide to create a PRMGRS-Profile login script for the public relations managers. Then you discover, astonishingly enough, that one already exists in the ACME container! Hmmmm. Must be those crazy ACME fairies again. Anyway, you might as well make FDR a member of the PRMGRS-Profile login script while you're there. (See Appendix C for hints on the basic steps involved.)

3. Log in as FDR to check things out:

```
LOGIN .FDR.ADMIN.RIO.ACME
```

Watch the screen as the Container and Profile login scripts are automatically executed. Fix any errors that occur.

CASE STUDY: CONFIGURING THE ACME MENU SYSTEM

Well, the fun never stops. It seems as though FDR has opened Pandora's box. Now, for some unexplainable reason, the ACME gremlins have hit—the PR menu system has disappeared. If you don't get home soon, you're gonna miss "Friends." You'd better hurry.

Once again, the IntranetWare Log book has saved the day. Using the criteria outlined here, create a custom menu for the Public Relations department.

1. PR Main Menu

    a. Applications (which displays an Applications submenu)

    b. E-mail (which runs the Windows version of First Mail)

    c. IntranetWare Commands (which displays a IntranetWare Commands submenu)

    d. Log off network (which exits the user from the menu and logs him or her off the network)

2. Applications Menu (submenu called by option in the Main Menu)

    a. Database (where executable file is DB)

    b. Spreadsheet (where executable file is SS)

    c. Word Processing (where executable file is WP)

3. NetWare Utilities Menu (submenu called by an option in the Main Menu)

    a. File Management

    b. NCOPY

    c. NETUSER

     d.   User Tools

     e.   WHOAMI

Next, you'll need to quickly compile and debug the new menu. Once you're finished, you can place it in the default SYS:PUBLIC subdirectory and test it. Ensure that the new login script can automatically find and execute the menu system. After all, you don't want another visit from FDR tonight.

Sweet dreams.

EXERCISE 6-4: INTRANETWARE 4 CHILDHOOD

Circle the 20 IntranetWare Configuration terms hidden in this word search puzzle using the hints provided.

```
S  D  Y  P  J  G  I  D  F  N  G  R  H  M  U  M  G  N  S
F  I  L  E  A  T  T  R  I  B  U  T  E  S  F  F  X  N  H
I  S  L  T  N  E  I  L  C  W  N  M  E  N  U  M  A  K  E
R  T  X  W  M  G  E  T  O  Y  V  E  T  X  H  M  Z  J  L
S  R  H  V  Y  I  F  X  M  J  D  W  T  S  E  A  Y  Y  L
T  I  S  R  P  Q  K  W  S  W  M  Y  S  C  Y  C  H  K  C
M  B  T  Y  I  K  Y  E  P  U  C  E  O  T  F  Q  V  O  F
A  U  S  Q  O  T  I  L  E  K  R  N  P  V  F  G  Q  S  G
I  T  H  N  W  M  W  P  C  V  T  H  U  P  J  M  Y  Y  B
L  I  D  E  N  T  I  F  I  E  R  V  A  R  I  A  B  L  E
I  O  I  X  D  B  I  C  X  G  F  S  U  M  V  W  X  G  E
N  N  G  J  D  Q  E  T  A  B  T  E  N  T  R  A  T  S  Z
K  L  S  P  O  S  T  M  A  S  T  E  R  H  O  D  T  X  P
D  I  N  L  R  L  O  M  L  D  N  M  V  E  H  G  A  N  P
R  S  Y  Y  R  O  K  V  Q  A  Q  U  T  R  R  Q  R  Z  W
I  T  C  P  O  J  F  M  D  B  E  N  T  B  P  F  C  F  S
V  D  V  S  F  A  K  I  N  S  T  A  L  L  C  F  G  S  L
E  V  I  R  D  T  S  A  L  O  G  I  N  S  C  R  I  P  T
R  M  K  M  X  C  X  J  P  E  N  J  D  B  D  F  W  E  T
```

Hints:

1. Login script command used to indicate the location of the command specifier to be used (typically COMMAND.COM).
2. Leaf object that represents a list of e-mail recipients.
3. Menu system control command used to execute a DOS or IntranetWare command.
4. Set when installing network applications through use of the FLAG or FILER utility.
5. The e-mail application that is included with IntranetWare.

6. Menu system command that requests (optional) information from the user before a menu item is executed.
7. Used in a login script instead of using literal values.
8. File that is used to create customized NET.CFG file during client installation.
9. Statement required in CONFIG.SYS for VLMs.
10. Section heading in NET.CFG.
11. File that is similar to a batch file and is executed when a user logs in.
12. Used to compile menu system source files.
13. Integrated messaging (e-mail) engine included in earlier versions of NetWare, but absent from IntranetWare.
14. NET.CFG statement used to set workstation context prior to login.
15. Workstation boot file containing network-related information used by IntranetWare.
16. Workstation directory that contains IntranetWare client files.
17. Name of the supervisor for an MHS Server object.
18. Type of login script that can contain members that reside in different containers.
19. Workstation configuration that was used in earlier versions of NetWare.
20. Batch file that is used to automate the loading of client connection files on the workstation.

See Appendix C for answers.

IntranetWare Management

"As an IntranetWare CNA, I consider myself part of the family."

Welcome to adulthood.

An interesting thing happens on the way to adulthood—we grow up. All through childhood we look forward to the days when we can drive our own car, eat junk food, and play loud music 24 hours a day—freedom!

Then it happens! What a shock. Once we grow up and become adults, we yearn for the days when life was simple. We dream of the simplicity and innocence of childhood. Wow, we need therapy. Well, you're an adult now, so deal with it. But being an adult doesn't mean you have to lose the child within. It just means the toys get bigger.

So, you have a new car, a new job, and a new apartment. Now your focus shifts from starting the "life span" (configuration) to keeping it going (management). As a CNA, you move into LAN adulthood with a new focus on IntranetWare management. Once the network is up and running, you can step back and shift your attention to the long term. Suddenly, your mind is filled with thoughts of a family (servers and workstations), a pension (SMS), and retirement (RMF). Aah, adulthood is a many-splendored thing.

IntranetWare management is the most time-consuming aspect of being a CNA. Think about it: IntranetWare configuration occurs only once, but management dominates your life forever. In IntranetWare, network management occurs through five strategies:

- ▸ Server Installation

- ▸ Server management

- ▸ Workstation management

- ▸ Storage Management Services (SMS)

- ▸ Remote Management Facility (RMF)

Server installation and management is marriage. It involves daily tasks for creating, protecting, and maintaining your relationship with the IntranetWare server. This includes server installation, console management, NetWare Loadable Modules (NLMs), and server protection. At this point, monitoring the server involves more than just walking by it once a day and making sure the green light is on.

Workstation management is like having children. It can be even more challenging than the other three strategies because you're dealing with the IntranetWare users (your children). And we all know that the user's primary purpose in life is to make CNAs miserable. In addition to battling users, our workstation management duties involve Client 32 installations, Client 16 connectivity strategies, and support for diverse client environments-DOS, Windows 95, OS/2, Macintosh, and Unix.

As the adage goes, "You never miss anything until it's gone." This holds especially true for IntranetWare data. Welcome to your pension plan. One of the most important things you can do as an IntranetWare CNA is to plan for the future by using backups. Storage Management Services (SMS) is an IntranetWare backup engine that provides data storage and retrieval from various front-end applications to numerous back-end storage devices. In this chapter, you'll learn about the fundamental architecture of SMS and explore the many features of SBACKUP.NLM.

Finally, RMF (Remote Management Facility) enables you to manage the server console from anywhere in the world-including Happy Acres. You've worked hard, and now it's time for retirement. RMF will become the cornerstone of your server maintenance schedule. Of course, it's hard to maintain the server when it's chained up and locked away in a hidden closet. Fortunately, by using RMF, you can access the server console from any distributed workstation.

 ZEN

"Every wakeful step, every mindful act is the direct path to awakening. Wherever you go, there you are."

Anonymous

Like adulthood, IntranetWare management doesn't always come naturally. You must work at it. Children have their parents to rely on, but now (as an adult) you're on your own. So, to help guide you through the mine field of CNA adulthood, I suggest these few management strategies.

First, build an IntranetWare Log book. Although few CNAs have one, it should become the foundation of your daily management life. The IntranetWare Log book is a detailed, step-by-step log of all activity from LAN conception to the present. It includes worksheets, floor plans, security restrictions, file management, pictures of LAN hardware, pictures of your mother, cabling layouts, application information, and weekly management tasks. It's vital that you take the Log book seriously, because you never know when you might need it.

Next, use the worksheets provided with IntranetWare documentation. The *Installation* manual includes various worksheets that can help you document LAN details, including file server hardware, workstation hardware, configuration files, IntranetWare directories, users and group information, default login restrictions, trustee assignments, and login scripts. Then, put these worksheets in your IntranetWare Log book for future reference. I see a pattern forming here.

Reference material is the fodder of creative minds. I don't know what that means, but it sounds good. The bottom line is, you can't know everything. Create an extensive library of reference material so that you don't have to know everything. Some of the best sources include Novell Press books, *Novell Application Notes*, the latest Novell Support Connection CD-ROM, Web pages, documentation, and, of course, this book. Don't forget your library card.

Finally, your mindset has an important impact on IntranetWare management. Psychologically, you must be committed to the network and recognize management as an important aspect of your daily life. Take time to embrace these management tasks and make sure that everyone in the organization recognizes that you need time to do them. Many times, users and management don't understand why the network must be down for VREPAIR or SMS backup. Educate them gracefully.

With these strategies in mind, let's now dive into the wild and wacky world of IntranetWare management. Remember, this is the foundation of your daily life as a CNA. NDS design happens once, installation happens once, and IntranetWare configuration happens once. On the other hand, management happens every day until you win the lottery. So, without any further adieu, let's start our jaunt through LAN adulthood, beginning with marriage.

Server Installation

Eventually you will find Mr. or Ms. Right. Your eyes will meet across a crowded dance floor, you will feel that wonderful flutter in the pit of your stomach. Your knees will buckle and then bang—you're married! Marriage changes everything. Suddenly, your focus shifts from "me, me, me" to "the family." Your spouse becomes the center of your life. It's like sharing a lifeboat with that "special someone" while careening down the whitewater rapids of love. Yuck.

Similarly, the IntranetWare server is at the center of your LAN. At some point, your focus shifts from "users, users, users" to "the server." After all, the entire WAN will crumble if your servers aren't running correctly.

IntranetWare server management consists of four components:

▶ Server installation

▶ Console commands

▶ NetWare Loadable Modules (NLMs)

▶ Server protection

It all begins with server installation. As a CNA, you must first give the server life. This is an amazing responsibility (repeat after me: "I Do"). Server installation includes SERVER.EXE, disk drivers, LAN drivers, NDS, and external network addressing. In addition, you must learn how to automate this process by using AUTOEXEC.NCF and STARTUP.NCF.

Next, your server focus shifts to the colon prompt. The colon (:) prompt is the server console. This is where you'll spend most of your server management time. The colon prompt accepts two kinds of commands—console commands and NLMs. IntranetWare includes numerous console commands for various server management and maintenance tasks, including NDS management, time synchronization, bindery services, sending messages, activating NLMs, server protection, and network optimization. This chapter explores most of the IntranetWare console commands and gives you some hints on how to use them.

All remaining server activity is accomplished by using NLMs. NLMs are modular Legos that provide supplemental functionality to the IntranetWare server. The four kinds of NLMs are disk drivers, LAN drivers, name space modules, and management utilities. In this chapter, we'll explore each of these and some key server management tools—INSTALL.NLM, MONITOR.NLM, SERVMAN.NLM, and DSREPAIR.NLM. You can think of NLMs as network management applications at the server.

Finally, we'll learn how to protect our precious IntranetWare server. This includes locking up the server, preventing access to the keyboard with MONITOR.NLM, using the SECURE CONSOLE command, and adding a password for RMF. Also, don't forget to use The Club. Server protection is a serious management task because of the vulnerability of the console—users can cause a lot of damage there. Many times, this security feature is overlooked and CNAs discover their inadequate security measures when it's too late-in the unemployment line.

ZEN

"What is the sound of one hand clapping?"

Zen Koan

As you can see, marriage takes a great deal of work. Fortunately, the rewards greatly outweigh the pain. As a CNA, you must work hard at your network marriage to keep the server running and in peak condition (and, with luck, the rewards will also outweigh the pain). In both marriage and server management, communication is the key. Let's begin with a quick "walk down the aisle" of server creation.

BEFORE YOU BEGIN

If you build it, they will come!

Welcome to IntranetWare installation. Think of this as "IntranetWare Resuscitation"—you're breathing life into an otherwise limp and lifeless LAN. Once the server is "born," you can move into the daily grind of managing it— "adulthood."

IntranetWare installation is dominated by SERVER.EXE, NLMs, and AUTOEXEC.NCF. It can be a little intimidating at first, especially if you've never installed NetWare before. But have no fear, Dr. David is here. We will traverse every installation obstacle together. We'll learn about disk partitions, IPX internal network numbers, and NDS context. In addition, there is an extensive (Simple) Installation case study (walk through) at the end of the chapter. So, sit back, relax, and enjoy the rest of your day. After all, it can only get better.

WHAT'S NEW

I would like to interrupt this book for an emergency broadcast message from Novell. As you know, the latest release of NetWare isn't NetWare at all—it's "IntranetWare". So, what happened to NetWare? Fortunately, it's still here. As a matter of fact, the IntranetWare solution uses "NetWare 4.11" as it's primary operating system. Confusing? Yes.

So, here's the bottom line: IntranetWare is the global WAN connectivity solution and NetWare 4.11 is the server-centric operating system it uses. So, when we talk about installing the server OS, we will use the term "NetWare 4.11". All other references will be to "IntranetWare." After all, that's the product. Now, I will return you to your regularly scheduled programming.

SMART LINK

If you want the "real" scoop on IntranetWare and the future of Novell, surf over to their home page at http://www.novell.com

Installing NetWare 4.11 consists of two main tasks:

▶ Installation of the NetWare 4.11 operating system on the server

▶ Installation of the client software on distributed workstations

You can also install a number of optional products on the server for added functionality. Some of these products are bundled with NetWare 4.11, including NetWare for Macintosh, MPR (Multiple Protocol Router), DynaText, Novell Internet Access Server, and Novell FTP Services. Others are available at additional cost.

Before you begin, you'll need to install various LAN hardware components, such as:

▶ Network interface cards

▶ Cabling and hubs

▶ Uninterruptible power supplies

An important concern is to make sure that no hardware conflicts exist between your LAN components and server/workstation machines. You'll also need to make sure that your "computer room" meets recommended power and operating environment requirements. You should consult your hardware documentation to determine applicable temperature, humidity, heat-dissipation, and power-consumption requirements. Novell also recommends that you use dedicated electrical lines for all hardware components (such as servers, workstations, printers, and so on). This is a good idea, especially in lightning high-risk zones.

In order to protect your network servers from power surges and voltage spikes, you'll want to connect each server to an appropriate type of uninterruptible power supply (UPS). Novell also recommends that you provide UPS protection for important network workstations and other peripherals. (If this is not feasible, you should at least protect these workstations and peripherals with surge suppressers and ferro-resonant isolation transformers.)

Minimum Hardware Requirements

The following checklist can help you prepare for the server installation:

- An IBM-compatible PC with an 80386, 80486 (SX or DX), or Pentium processor.

- 20 MB of RAM for the basic NetWare 4.11 operating system (whether it is being installed from CD-ROM or across the network).

- 115 MB of free disk space on the hard disk: 15 MB for the DOS partition and 100 MB for a NetWare partition (SYS: volume). If you copy all the optional NetWare file groups to the server, you may need a total of 140 MB or more.

- An additional 60 MB of free disk space to install the DynaText viewer and NetWare 4.11 documentation. Additional space will be necessary if you want to install the documentation in more than one language. If you are low on disk space, you can view DynaText directly from the CD-ROM, rather than storing it on the server hard disk.

- One network interface card (NIC).

▶ The appropriate network cabling (Ethernet, token ring, FDDI, ARCnet, baseband, and so on) and related components (hubs, UPS, and so on).

▶ A CD-ROM drive that can read ISO 9660-formatted CD-ROM disks (if NetWare 4.11 is being installed from CD-ROM).

REAL WORLD

The hardware requirements listed are minimums, not recommended standards. Realistically, you'll want a fast processor, more RAM, and a larger hard disk.

You'll need to add additional memory, based on the following:

▶ The RAM required for disk caching (1 to 4 MB minimum). As a general rule, the more RAM available for disk caching, the better the performance.

▶ RAM that is calculated on the basis of disk size (total disk size in megabytes multiplied by 0.008).

In terms of hard disk size, you'll need a disk that is large enough for all of your network needs, including the network operating system, optional network products, applications, documentation, and the file system. Finally, if your server contains more than 20 MB of RAM, you'll need to use 32-bit AT bus-mastering or DMA boards (unless the driver supports more than 20 MB of RAM). Contact the computer manufacturer for additional information.

THE BRAIN

For a more accurate method of calculating the amount of server RAM required, see the article titled "Server Memory-Calculating Memory Requirements for NetWare 3 and 4" in the January 1995 issue of the *Novell Application Notes*, or Appendix A of the *Novell NetWare 4.11 Installation* manual.

TIP

WARNING: If you are installing NetWare 4.11 over the network using Novell Client 32, you should set MAX CACHE SIZE less than or equal to 3 MB. If you don't, Client 32 may allocate up to 8 MB on a computer containing 20 MB of RAM—which could cause you to run out of RAM during the installation process.

There is a method to our madness. As a matter of fact, there are two methods for installing NetWare 4.11:

▸ Local CD-ROM

▸ Server-to-server (called "remote network installation area" by Novell).

The easiest way to install NetWare 4.11 is using the CD-ROM drive installed on the server. The second method, server-to-server, is typically used if your new server doesn't have a CD-ROM drive, or if you will be installing a number of servers at one time. The server-to-server method involves temporarily installing the client software on the new server, then logging into an existing NetWare server that either has a CD-ROM drive mounted as a NetWare device or a copy of the files from the Novell IntranetWare: NetWare 4.11 Operating System CD-ROM stored on a NetWare (hard disk) volume. In this chapter, we'll cover the CD-ROM method, which is the most common.

THE BRAIN

You'll find a comparison of the two types of installation methods in the "Choose an Installation Method" section in Chapter 1 of the *Novell NetWare 4.11 Installation* manual. You can find additional information regarding these two methods in the "Install from a Local CD-ROM" and "Install from a Remote Network Installation Area" sections in the same chapter of the same manual.

Choosing an Installation Type

So, you've set up your hardware and chosen your poison (CD-ROM); now it's time to get down to business. NetWare 4.11 offers two basic types of server installation:

▶ Simple installation—The faster and easier of the two methods. It makes a number of assumptions and uses default settings for most configurable parameters.

▶ Custom installation—Allows you to specify configurable parameters, such as the IPX internal network number, disk mirroring or duplexing, as well as the enabling or disabling of file compression, block suballocation, and data migration features.

Let's take a closer look.

ZEN

"When making your choice in life, do not neglect to live."

Samuel Jackson

The Simple installation approach should be used if your server meets *all* the following criteria:

▶ A DOS partition of 15+ MB exists on the server.

▶ DOS is installed on the server DOS partition.

▶ The server boots from the DOS partition rather than from boot diskettes.

▶ No disk mirroring, disk duplexing, or disk subsystem is required.

▶ All free disk space not allocated to the DOS partition is available for a NetWare partition.

▶ Each disk will contain only one NetWare volume.

▶ A randomly generated IPX number is acceptable.

▶ AUTOEXEC.BAT and CONFIG.SYS startup files can be used without modification.

▶ IPX is the only communications protocol that will be installed (although TCP/IP and/or AppleTalk can be installed manually at a later date).

▶ Novell Directory Services (NDS) will be installed using a single Organization per tree that contains all objects.

The Custom installation method should be used if your server does not meet the requirements for a Simple installation—duh! Some of the configuration options that you can specify in a Custom installation include:

▶ Boot the server from the DOS partition on the server hard disk or from boot diskettes

▶ Assign a nonrandom IPX internal network number

▶ Partition hard disks

▶ Mirror or duplex hard disks

▶ Specify volume names

▶ Span volumes across multiple drives

▶ Modify time zone parameters for NDS

▶ Edit the STARTUP.NCF and AUTOEXEC.NCF startup files

▶ Choose nonrouting TCP/IP or AppleTalk protocols in addition to IPX

▶ Install NetWare/IP

SMART LINK

For more detailed information about Novell-certified hardware and software, consult the vendor forums on NetWire, testing lab results on NSEPro, or surf to the Novell Lab's Bulletins at http://support.novell.com/sitemap.

Well, there you have it. We've installed the LAN components, inserted the Novell NetWare 4.11 CD-ROM, and chosen the Simple or Custom installation method—can we finally get started? No! It must be Monday. The last order of business is to walk down the "before you begin" checklist. It looks something like this:

❏ The name of the Directory tree. (You'll need to think of one if this is the first server in the tree.)

❏ The detailed NDS design.

❏ A password for the Admin user. (If this is the first server in the tree, you'll need to make one up.)

❏ A unique server name.

❏ A unique IPX internal network number (applicable to a Custom installation only).

❏ The type and configuration of the disk controller, as well as the appropriate driver(s), if they are not contained on the Novell NetWare 4.11 Operating System CD-ROM.

❏ The type and configuration of the network board(s), as well as the appropriate driver(s), if they are not contained on the Novell NetWare 4.11 Operating System CD-ROM.

❏ The IntranetWare/NetWare 4.11 License Diskette.

❏ One of the following IntranetWare CD-ROMs:

  ▸ Novell IntranetWare: NetWare 4.11 Operating System CD-ROM

  ▸ Novell IntranetWare: NetWare 4.11 Online Documentation (optional)

  ▸ Novell IntranetWare: Internet Access Server 4 (optional)

  ▸ Novell IntranetWare: FTP Services for IntranetWare (optional)

> ► Access to NetWare 4.11 installation files on another server. (The files can either be located on an Novell NetWare 4.11 Operating System CD-ROM mounted as an NetWare volume on that server, or the same files copied from the CD-ROM to that server's hard disk.)

Now, we're finally ready to roll.

THE BRAIN

This chapter assumes that you will be installing NetWare 4.11 on a DOS server. If you are installing NetWare 4.11 on a Windows 95 server, see the "Prepare to Install on a Windows 95 Machine" section in Chapter 1 of the *Novell NetWare 4.11 Installation* manual. If you'd like to install IntraNetWare 4.11 on an OS/2 server, refer to Chapter 4 of the same manual.

Both the Simple and Custom Installation methods consist of the same six stages. The Custom installation consists of a total of 21 steps. The Simple installation traverses the same 21 steps, but automates a few of them—leaving only 16. The six installation stages are:

Stage 1 • Prepare the server hard disk

Stage 2 • Run SERVER.EXE

Stage 3 • Load the NetWare 4.11 drivers

Stage 4 • INSTALL.NLM

Stage 5 • Install Novell Directory Services (NDS)

Stage 6 • Create server startup files

The actual process of creating the server occurs during Stages 1 and 2. When SERVER.EXE is run, the NetWare 4.11 operating system is loaded into memory and a colon prompt (:) is displayed. It's alive! At this point, the server is alive, but you can't do anything with it. It's sort of like the server being on life support. The remaining four stages add more functionality. Stage 3 adds connectivity by loading

LAN and disk drivers. Stage 4 creates a NetWare partition on the hard disk, and then defines one or more volumes. Stage 5 installs NDS. And finally, Stage 6 enables you to create/modify the STARTUP.NCF and AUTOEXEC.NCF server startup files.

QUIZ

Just to keep things simple and warm up the old noodle, here's one of my favorites: A train leaves from Boston to New York. An hour later, a train leaves from New York to Boston. The second train is traveling 15 m.p.h faster than the first, but the first has a 7.5 m.p.h. tail wind. Which train will be nearer to Boston when they meet?

(Q7-1)
(See Appendix C for quiz answers.)

I know how you feel. It's been a loooooong day already, and it's only 9:30 a.m. I feel your pain—because I care. Together we can get through this thing. Together we can conquer the NetWare 4.11 install.

We are going to take the easy way out and perform a Simple installation. Listed below is a brief description of what happens during the six phases of a Simple installation. We're just trying to get your feet wet. Fortunately, the NetWare 4.11 Simple installation is essentially a subset of the Custom installation. It's faster and easier than the Custom method, because it asks a minimum of questions and uses defaults for most configurable parameters. Detailed, step-by-step instructions for performing a Simple NetWare 4.11 installation can be found in the case study titled "Simple Installation for ACME," at the end of the chapter.

STAGE 1: PREPARE THE SERVER HARD DISK

During Stage 1, the focus is on the DOS operating system. The first step is to boot the server machine with DOS. This is because NetWare 4.11 doesn't have its own "cold boot loader," and, thus, is loaded on the server by executing the SERVER.EXE file from the DOS partition. The Simple install does not give you the option of booting the server from a diskette.

After you boot DOS, the next step is to configure the DOS partition. This consists of making at least two full backups, creating a temporary boot diskette

containing C:\DOS\FDISK.EXE and C:\DOS\FORMAT.COM, using the DOS
FDISK utility to delete existing server disk partitions and create a new DOS
partition of 15+ MB, then using the DOS FORMAT utility to format the new
partition as bootable. Wow, that was a mouthful.

Next, you'll need to configure the CD-ROM drive as a DOS device. The reason
that you'll need to do this is because IntranetWare is shipped on CD-ROM, and
you just blew away the CD-ROM drivers on the server hard disk. Oops. Be sure to
follow the CD-ROM manufacturer's instructions for this part. Next, you'll probably
have to reboot the computer to activate any changes made to the server's
AUTOEXEC.BAT and CONFIG.SYS by the CD-ROM installation program.

To begin the automated installation process, insert the Novell NetWare 4.11
Operating System CD-ROM disk in the CD-ROM drive and switch to that drive
(typically D:). Execute the INSTALL.BAT file found in the root directory of the CD-
ROM. As you can see in Figure 7.1, you will be asked to choose a language to be
used during the installation process—your choices are Deutsch, English, Español,
Français, Italiano, or Portuguese.

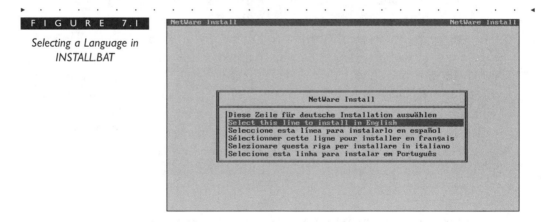

FIGURE 7.1

*Selecting a Language in
INSTALL.BAT*

After you select a language, you will be asked several questions about the type
of installation desired. Make the following menu choices, in order:

I • NetWare Server Installation (see Figure 7.2)

2 • NetWare 4.11

3 • Simple Installation of NetWare 4.11 (see Figure 7.3)

▶ . . . . ◀

FIGURE 7.2

*NetWare 4.11 Server
Installation Screen*

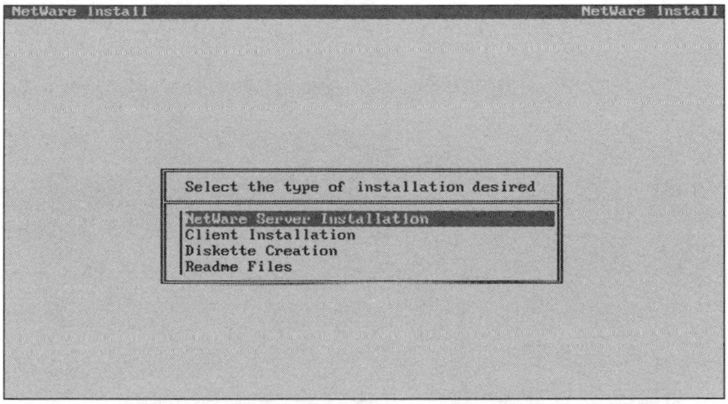

```
NetWare Install                                        NetWare Install




                  ┌─────────────────────────────────────────┐
                  │ Select the type of installation desired  │
                  ├─────────────────────────────────────────┤
                  │ NetWare Server Installation              │
                  │ Client Installation                      │
                  │ Diskette Creation                        │
                  │ Readme Files                             │
                  └─────────────────────────────────────────┘
```

▶ . . . . ◀

FIGURE 7.3

*Choosing the Installation
Method in INSTALL.BAT*

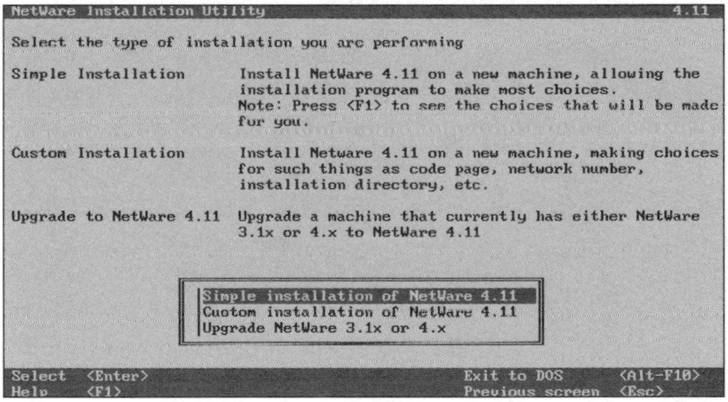

```
NetWare Installation Utility                                    4.11
Select the type of installation you are performing

Simple Installation      Install NetWare 4.11 on a new machine, allowing the
                         installation program to make most choices.
                         Note: Press <F1> to see the choices that will be made
                         for you.

Custom Installation      Install Netware 4.11 on a new machine, making choices
                         for such things as code page, network number,
                         installation directory, etc.

Upgrade to NetWare 4.11  Upgrade a machine that currently has either NetWare
                         3.1x or 4.x to NetWare 4.11


                ┌─────────────────────────────────────────┐
                │ Simple installation of NetWare 4.11      │
                │ Custom installation of NetWare 4.11      │
                │ Upgrade NetWare 3.1x or 4.x              │
                └─────────────────────────────────────────┘

Select   <Enter>                              Exit to DOS        <Alt-F10>
Help     <F1>                                 Previous screen    <Esc>
```

We're cruising now! You will then be prompted for a unique server name, as shown in Figure 7.4. You will *not* be prompted for an IPX internal network number. NetWare will automatically generate a random eight-digit hexadecimal IPX internal network number for you—without even asking (how rude). If you were performing a Custom install, you would be given the option of overriding this default (and you should).

► · ◄

FIGURE 7.4

Naming Your Server in INSTALL.BAT

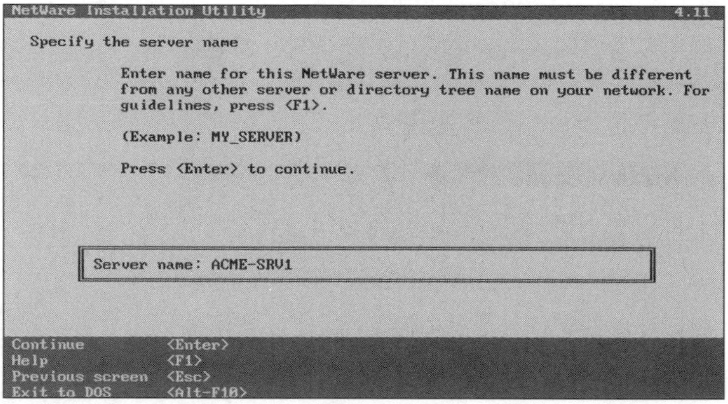

NetWare Installation Utility   4.11

Specify the server name

        Enter name for this NetWare server. This name must be different
        from any other server or directory tree name on your network. For
        guidelines, press <F1>.

        (Example: MY_SERVER)

        Press <Enter> to continue.

        ┌───┐
        │ Server name: ACME-SRV1   │
        └───┘

Continue   <Enter>
Help   <F1>
Previous screen   <Esc>
Exit to DOS   <Alt-F10>

As you can see in Figure 7.5, the system then copies a number of server boot files from the CD-ROM to the C:\NWSERVER directory on your DOS partition.

► · ◄

FIGURE 7.5

Copying Server Boot Files to the DOS Partition

NetWare Installation Utility   4.11

Copy server boot files to the DOS partition

    ┌───┐
    │ Copying File: SERVER.EXE   │
    │ ████████████████████░░░░░░░░░░░░░░░░░░░░░░░░░░░░░░░░░░░░░░░ │
    │   38%   │
    └───┘

    ┌───┐
    │ Source path: D:\PRODUCTS\NW411\INSTALL\IBM\DOS\XXX\ENGLISH │
    └───┘

    ┌───┐
    │ Destination path: C:\NWSERVER   │
    └───┘

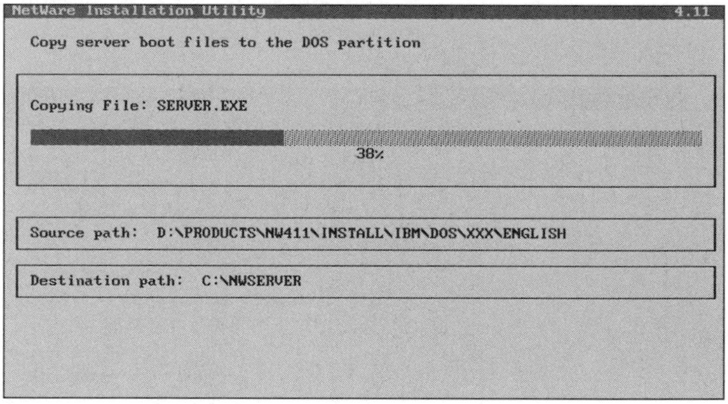

During a Simple install, the system automatically selects the locale configuration (country code, character code set, and keyboard mapping) and filename format for you. The defaults assume that you reside in the United States and want to use the DOS filename format. You would need to do a Custom install if you wanted to be able to override these defaults.

If you were performing a Custom installation, you would be given the option of customizing startup file SET parameters. Because this is a Simple install, NetWare does it for you. If your server contains a hard disk, CD-ROM, or other device that uses ASPI, the installation program automatically inserts the following line in your STARTUP.NCF file:

```
SET RESERVED BUFFERS BELOW 16 MB = 200
```

If this were a Custom install, you'd also be asked if you wanted the AUTOEXEC.BAT file to automatically execute SERVER.EXE whenever the server is booted. Since this is a Simple install, the SERVER.EXE file will *not* be added to your AUTOEXEC.BAT file.

There you have it. The DOS partition is ready to go. Next stop, SERVER.EXE.

STAGE 2: RUN SERVER.EXE

During Stage 2, the focus shifts from the DOS operating system to NetWare. The installation program automatically executes SERVER.EXE and loads NetWare 4.11 into memory. In other words, this process transfers control of the server from DOS to NetWare (see Figure 7.6). At this point, the server is up and running, but you can't do anything with it. In the next step you'll load the NetWare drivers and establish connectivity between NetWare 4.11 and the hard disk(s) and NIC(s).

▶ · ◀

F I G U R E   7.6

SERVER.EXE—From DOS to NetWare

```
System Console
SECURE.NCF file will not be executed
Novell NetWare 4.11  August 22, 1996
Processor speed: 16424
(Type SPEED at the command prompt for an explanation of the speed rating)
LCONFIG.SYS file exists, overriding default locale values
Startup file DISTRTUP.NCF will be used
Reserved Buffers Below 16 Meg set to 200
Loading module MAC.NAM
    NetWare Macintosh Name Space Support
    Version 4.11    July 29, 1996
    Copyright 1996 Novell, Inc.  All rights reserved.
Loading module INSTALL.NLM
    Netware 4.11 Installation Utility
    Version 2.24    August 12, 1996
    Copyright 1996 Novell, Inc.  All rights reserved.
```

▶ · ◀

REAL WORLD

If your server is an 80386 that was manufactured in 1987, you may find that it doesn't execute certain 32-bit instructions correctly. This could negatively affect the way NetWare 4.11 functions. If a message is displayed indicating that this problem has occurred, you may be able to solve the problem by replacing a ROM chip on the board. Contact the computer manufacturer for further details.

STAGE 3: LOAD THE NETWARE DRIVERS

During Stage 3, we jump-start our barely functioning server. We load and configure various NetWare drivers, including:

▸ Disk drivers for the internal hard disk and CD-ROM drives

▸ LAN drivers for internal NIC(s)

▸ Binding IPX to the LAN driver(s)

The good news is that, unlike earlier versions of NetWare, NetWare 4.11 has two new features called hardware autodetection and automatic selection of drivers that attempt to automatically detect the type of drivers needed for your particular hard disk(s), CD-ROM(s), and NIC(s). The INSTALL utility will display the drivers that it has selected for each, and will allow you to modify, delete, or accept the defaults, as well as to add additional drivers. Check out Figure 7.7 and Figure 7.8. Remember, when you load drivers, it's important to make sure that there are no interrupt or address conflicts with other hardware. Also, check out the "NetWare Loadable Modules" section a little later for more information concerning disk and LAN drivers.

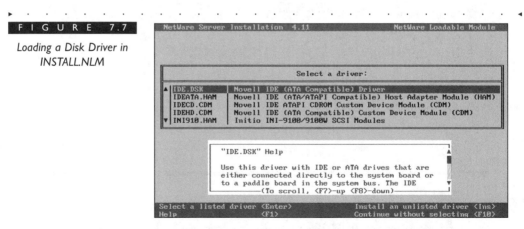

FIGURE 7.7

Loading a Disk Driver in INSTALL.NLM

So, what about additional protocols? During the Custom install, you are given the option of installing TCP/IP and/or AppleTalk in addition to IPX. But, in a Simple install, you must add them manually—afterward.

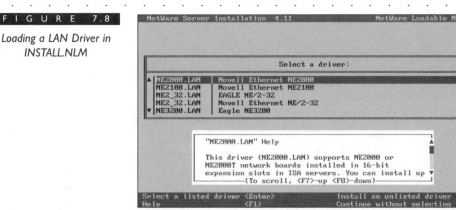

F I G U R E   7.8

Loading a LAN Driver in INSTALL.NLM

ZEN

"Though we often live unconsciously, 'on automatic pilot,' every one of us can learn to be awake. It just takes vision."

Anonymous

That's more like it. Now that the server is functioning normally, we shift our focus to INSTALL.NLM. This is where the real fun begins.

SMART LINK

Explore the latest IntranetWare drivers on the web at http://support.novell.com/sitemap

STAGE 4: INSTALL.NLM

Now that you've established connectivity, we're ready to activate the NetWare partition(s). You may be prompted with a warning saying that there is a potential conflict with the DOS CD-ROM driver. If this message is displayed, ignore the warning and select the "Continue accessing the CD-ROM via DOS" option. No worries.

Next, the installation program automatically creates a NetWare partition on the internal server disk. By default, it occupies the entire disk except for the DOS partition. Then, it creates the SYS: volume using the entire NetWare partition. Finally, NetWare 4.11 mounts the new SYS: volume.

If this were a Custom installation, you would have been given the opportunity of creating additional volumes. You would also have been able to specify a plethora of manual disk options, including specifying the size of NetWare 4.11 partitions, mirroring or duplexing, and specifying the size of the Hot Fix redirection area. You would also have been given the option of changing the default settings for file compression (default is ON), block suballocation (default is ON), and data migration (default is OFF).

If you were installing NetWare 4.11 from a network volume rather than CD-ROM, you would be given the opportunity to re-establish the server-to-server connection at this point.

Next, the system will begin automatically copying the "preliminary" (pre-installation) files to the SYSTEM and LOGIN directories on the SYS: volume. Later, in Stage 6, you'll copy the rest of the required SYSTEM and PUBLIC files to the SYS: volume. For now, let's move on to Stage 5.

STAGE 5: INSTALL NOVELL DIRECTORY SERVICES (NDS)

Once the SYSTEM and LOGIN files have been copied to the SYS: volume, it's time to begin building our tree. Don't forget your protective gloves.

At this point, NetWare searches the WAN for any existing Directory trees. Depending on the number of trees found, the installation utility will display one of four menus. Figure 7.9 shows the menu that will be displayed if no existing Directory trees were found. Depending on your particular configuration, you will need to indicate the appropriate menu choice, then either supply the name of the new tree or select an existing tree.

Once you've selected a tree, NetWare will add this server to the tree indicated and allow you to configure time synchronization for this server, as shown in Figure 7.10. For example, if we were at ACME's Admin headquarters in Camelot, you would select Great Britain.

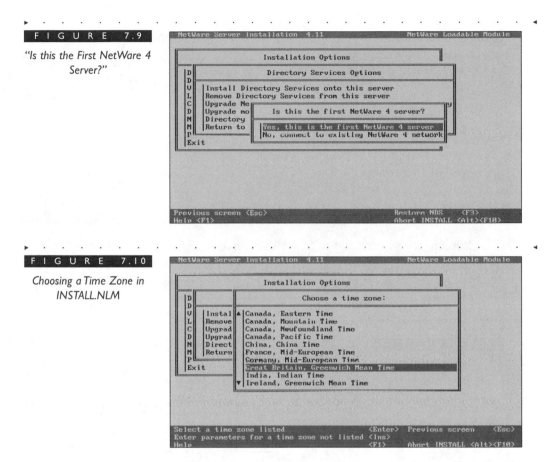

F I G U R E   7 . 9

"Is this the First NetWare 4 Server?"

F I G U R E   7 . 1 0

Choosing a Time Zone in INSTALL.NLM

Next, we move on to NDS context. Remember, we're using the Simple installation method, so the server will be placed in a single Organization container. First, you will be prompted for the name of the Organization. Second, you will be asked to supply a password for the special Admin user. If this is the first server in this tree, you'll have to make this stuff up. If you're adding this server to an existing tree, you'll have to use an established Organization name and Admin password.

After you provide the Admin password, NetWare displays a summary screen (Figure 7.11) with the following information: Directory tree name, Directory context, and Administrator name (Admin username). Be sure to write down this information, and keep it in a safe place—maybe next to the License diskette!

▶ . . . . ◀

FIGURE 7.11

Results of the ACME NDS
Installation

```
NetWare Server Installation  4.11                    NetWare Loadable Module
┌────────────────────────────────────────────────────────────────────────┐
│                          Installation Options                            │
│  ┌D┌──────────────── Directory Services Options ──────────────────┐      │
│   D│                                                               │      │
│   U│ Install Directory Services onto this server                   │      │
│   L│ Remove Directory Services from this server                    │      │
│   C│ Upgra ┌───────────────────────────────────────────────────┐  │      │
│   D│ Upgra │                                                   │  │      │
│   N│ Direc │ For your information (note these for future       │  │      │
│   M│ Retur │ reference along with the Administrator password): │  │      │
│   P│       │     Directory tree name:  ACME                    │  │      │
│  Exit       │     Directory context:    O=ACME                  │  │      │
│            │     Administrator name:   CN=Admin.O=ACME         │  │      │
│            │                                                   │  │      │
│            │ Press <Enter> to continue.                        │  │      │
│            └───────────────────────────────────────────────────┘  │      │
│                                                                    │      │
└────────────────────────────────────────────────────────────────────────┘
Use the arrow keys to highlight an option, then press <Enter>.
```

You are then prompted to insert the NetWare 4.11 License diskette, as seen in Figure 7.12. Make sure that this is a unique server disk not being used on any other server. If you attempt to use the same license on more than one server, you'll get a copyright violation warning.

▶ . . . . ◀

FIGURE 7.12

Licensing Your
NetWare 4.11 Server

```
NetWare Server Installation  4.11                    NetWare Loadable Module
┌────────────────────────────────────────────────────────────────────────┐
│                          Installation Options                            │
│  ┌Driver options     (load/unload disk and network drivers)┐            │
│   Di│                                                        │            │
│   Uo│                                                        │            │
│   Li│  Insert the disk labeled, "NetWare License", that contains the     │
│   Co│  file SERVER.MLS, into drive A.  And/or specify a different path   │
│   Di│  where the license may be found to do the license installation.   │
│   NC│                                                                    │
│   Mu│    Press <F3> to specify a different path;                         │
│   Pr│    Press <F4> to specify a remote workstation path;               │
│   Ex│    Press <Enter> to continue.                                     │
│     │                                                                    │
└────────────────────────────────────────────────────────────────────────┘
Continue                                       <Enter>
Specify a different source drive/directory     <F3>
Specify a remote source drive/directory        <F4>
Continue without installing a license          <F9>       Delete last license <F8>
Help                                           <F1>       Abort INSTALL <Alt><F10>
```

Voilà, we're finished. That wasn't so bad. Now you have a living, breathing server. But, in order to automate this process during server startup, you must create the following two configuration files: STARTUP.NCF and AUTOEXEC.NCF. That's Stage 6.

STAGE 6: CREATE SERVER STARTUP FILES

Once Novell Directory Services has been installed, the system automatically creates the STARTUP.NCF and AUTOEXEC.NCF files for you. (A sample of an AUTOEXEC.NCF screen is shown in Figure 7.13). These files help automate the server startup process. If this were a Custom install, you'd be allowed to modify these files. But, since this is a Simple install, you will have to wait until the installation process is complete in order to make any changes to these files by using INSTALL.NLM or the SERVMAN.NLM.

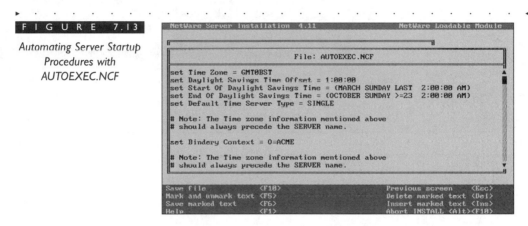

F I G U R E   7.13

*Automating Server Startup
Procedures with
AUTOEXEC.NCF*

The INSTALL utility then copies the main SYSTEM and PUBLIC to the SYS: volume. At this point, you are basically finished with the installation of the NetWare 4.11 operating system itself. Next, you'll be given an opportunity to install other installation items/products. In a Simple Install, the only choice listed is "Make diskettes."

During a Simple install, you aren't presented with the myriad of optional products to install as you are in the Custom install. Since we don't plan to make any diskettes at this time, choose Continue Installation.

Finally, a screen will be displayed like the one shown in Figure 7.14. Read the screen and press Enter to return to the system console screen. Now, you're REALLY done. Congratulations! As a safety measure, you should down the server by typing **DOWN,** and then restart it by typing **RESTART SERVER.** How exciting—your NetWare 4.11 server is alive!

F I G U R E   7.14

Congratulations! You're
Finished.

```
NetWare Server Installation  4.11                    NetWare Loadable Module

    The server installation of NetWare 4.11 is complete. It is recommended
    that you reboot the server after exiting the installation.

    Continue by installing NetWare client software, and setting up access
    to the online documentation.

    Refer to the "Installation" manual for information on installing
    client software.  Refer to "Installing and Using Novell Online
    Documentation for NetWare 4.11" for information on installing online
    documentation.  Refer to the online documentation manuals,
    "Supervising the Network" and "Utilities Reference", for information
    on administering your network, creating user accounts, etc.

    Press <Enter> to exit to the system console screen.


Continue and exit INSTALL <Enter>                  Previous screen     <Esc>
Help                         <F1>                   Abort INSTALL <Alt><F10>
```

Here's a quick review of the major stages involved in an NetWare 4.11 Simple installation:

Stage 1 • Prepare the server hard disk.

Stage 2 • Run SERVER.EXE.

Stage 3 • Load the NetWare drivers.

Stage 4 • Load INSTALL.NLM.

Stage 5 • Install NDS.

Stage 6 • Create server startup files.

SMART LINK

Learn everything there is to know about simple and custom installations in the *IntranetWare: NetWare 4.11 Installation and Configuration Workshop* at CyberState University (http://www.cyberstateu.com).

Wow, wasn't that fun? Suddenly Mondays aren't so bad anymore. The Simple installation is a breeze. But remember, it makes many assumptions for you. It's not for everyone. If you need more flexibility, or you're feeling a little more daring, you should consider tackling the Custom install. That's the true CNE obstacle course (but it's not for us).

Now, let's explore this exciting new thing known as the IntranetWare server.

ZEN

"You'll laugh. You'll cry. You'll hurl!"

Wayne's World

Server Management

"Start me up!" Consider the IntranetWare server started. It's a comforting feeling knowing the server came up smoothly—seeing the familiar "WORM" prance around the screen (assuming that MONITOR.NLM is loaded), hearing the constant hum of IntranetWare workstations, and following the IntranetWare packets as they bounce merrily along the cabling segment. A successful server startup is one of your most rewarding experiences. And so is marriage. Just like anything—if you work at it, the rewards greatly outweigh the pain.

Now that the IntranetWare server is up and running, let's shift our focus from "starting" it to "managing" it. Daily IntranetWare server management consists of three important components:

▶ Console commands—keep the server running at peak performance

▶ NetWare Loadable Modules—everything else

▶ Server protection—keep users away from the server console

Well, there you have it. Our CNA life in a nutshell. Let's get started with console commands—also known as marriage tools.

QUIZ

Here's a nice easy one to warm up with. Two U.S. coins add up to 30 cents, yet one of them is not a nickel. What coins are they? Don't spend it all in one place.

(Q7-2)

CONSOLE COMMANDS

To be successful in anything, you need the right tools. Marriage is no exception. In order to make any marriage work, both partners must bring the right tools—love, compassion, understanding, respect, flexibility, truth, and a spirit of compromise. But, more important than anything is communication. You must work together as a team and develop synergy. This strategy revolves around the single most important tool—"honey-do's." Honey-do's make the world go around. "Honey, do this," "honey, do that." As long as you pay attention to honey-do's, you'll never have to miss another Sunday football game or "mushy" movie like *On Golden Pond*. Don't forget those compromises.

IntranetWare marriage is not any different. In order to develop server management synergy, you must bring along the right tools—console commands and NLMs. *Console commands* are internal management tools that enable you to perform various server management maintenance tasks, including NDS management, time synchronization, bindery services, sending messages, activating NLMs, server protection, and network optimization. They are built into the core OS. *NLMs*, on the other hand, are modular Legos that provide supplemental functionality to the core OS. IntranetWare includes four kinds of NLMs—disk drivers, LAN drivers, name space modules, and management utilities. Let's start our discussion of IntranetWare honey-do's with a look at some important console commands.

Console commands enable CNAs to interact directly with the IntranetWare OS core. These commands are internal to SERVER.EXE and do not require any other support commands. One of the most powerful IntranetWare console commands is SET. This utility enables you to customize the OS core with more than 100 advanced parameters. These parameters are organized into 13 categories ranging from communications to file system to time synchronization. **Warning:** Don't mess around with SET unless you've been adequately trained and you're wearing protective gloves.

The syntax of console commands is relatively straightforward. The command itself is entered at the colon prompt and is followed by an Enter. Also, IntranetWare supports various command switches that customize their executions. Anybody can execute a console command as long as he or she has physical access to the file server console. This is a good reason to severely limit access to the machine and implement many of the protection schemes we discussed earlier. Also, console tools can be hazardous to the server if not handled correctly. You should ensure that they are kept out of the reach of small children and IntranetWare users. Fortunately, they have their own childproof cap (by being placed in the SYS:SYSTEM subdirectory by default).

Let's take a closer look at IntranetWare's top 15 console commands (provided here in alphabetical order). For a complete list of the console commands, refer to the *Novell NetWare 4.11 Utilities Reference Manual*.

TIP

Console commands are internal operating system tools that are similar to DOS internal commands. They are built into SERVER.EXE, just as CD or CLS is built into COMMAND.COM. You don't need to have any searching or IntranetWare directories available to access console commands.

BIND

BIND is an installation console command. As we saw earlier, it links LAN drivers to a communications protocol. Once the LAN driver is loaded, BIND must be issued to activate LAN communications. The default IntranetWare communication protocol is IPX. Here's the syntax for activating communications on the 3C5X9 NIC:

```
BIND IPX to 3C5X9
```

When you issue the BIND statement at the server console, you'll be asked for the external network number.

BROADCAST

BROADCAST is an administrative console command that enables CNAs to send brief alert messages to all attached workstations. Another related command (SEND) enables you to broadcast messages to specific users or groups of users. In both cases, the message appears at the bottom of the workstation monitor and prompts the user to press Ctrl+Enter to clear it from the screen. Only users who are currently logged in will receive these messages. BROADCAST messages can be up to 40 characters, whereas SEND supports larger messages (55 characters maximum). Here's the syntax:

BROADCAST *message*

The downside of BROADCAST and SEND is that they lock up the destination computer until Ctrl+Enter is pressed. This lockup can create harmful effects if the computer is being used for unattended backups. To avoid having messages lock up unattended machines, consider issuing SEND with the following parameters:

- ▶ /A=C—Accept messages only from the server console

- ▶ /A=N—Accept no messages (dangerous)

- ▶ /A=P—Store the last message sent until you poll to receive it

- ▶ /P—Poll the server for the last stored message

- ▶ /A=A—Accept all messages

CLEAR STATION

CLEAR STATION is an administrative console command that enables you to abruptly clear a workstation's connection. Be forewarned—this command removes all file server resources from the workstation and can cause file corruption or data loss if it is executed while the workstation is processing transactions. This command is only useful if workstations have crashed or users have turned off their machines without logging out. Here's the syntax:

CLEAR STATION *n*

The *n* specifies the connection number of the workstation you want to clear. These connection numbers can be viewed from MONITOR.NLM or with the help of NLIST. Connection numbers are incrementally allocated as workstations attach to the server and are not the same from one session to another.

CONFIG

CONFIG is a maintenance console command. It displays hardware information for all internal communication components. Figure 7.15 shows the CONFIG information for ACME's first LABS-SRV1 server, and Table 7.1 describes CONFIG parameters.

FIGURE 7.15

The CONFIG Console Command

```
LABS-SRV1:CONFIG
File server name: LABS-SRV1
IPX internal network number: 0BADCAFE
     Node address: 000000000001
     Frame type: VIRTUAL_LAN
     LAN protocol: IPX network 0BADCAFE
Server Up Time:  1 Minute 38 Seconds

3Com EtherLink III 3C5X9 Family
     Version 4.01b   October 19, 1994
     Hardware setting: I/O ports 320h to 32Fh, Interrupt Ah
     Node address: 0020AFE28F2D
     Frame type: ETHERNET_802.2
     Board name: 3C5X9_1_E82
     LAN protocol: IPX network 00001234

Tree Name: ACME_TREE
Bindery Context(s):
     LABS.NORAD.ACME

LABS-SRV1:
```

TABLE 7.1

Understanding CONFIG Parameters

PARAMETER	VALUE	DESCRIPTION
File server name	LABS-SRV1	The name of the server
IPX internal	BADCAFE	The eight-digit hexadecimal network number number used to uniquely identify this server
Node address	000000000001 0020AFE28F2D	The internal server node and unique factory address for internal 3C5X9 NIC
Frame type	VIRTUAL_LAN ETHERNET_802.2	Modular communications within the server and external communications for this NIC
LAN protocol	IPX 1234	Identifies the internal IPX address as BADCAFE and external cable segment as 1234
Board name	3C5X9_1_E82	The unique board name given to this NIC's frame type and external address

(continued)

T A B L E 7.1 *Understanding CONFIG Parameters (continued)*	PARAMETER	VALUE	DESCRIPTION
	Tree name	ACME_TREE	The name of the NDS tree in which this server participates
	Server Up Time	1 minutes 38 seconds	The amount of time the server has been active

DOWN

DOWN is a dangerous administrative console command. It completely shuts down file server activity and closes all open files. This is probably one of the most dramatic and potentially harmful IntranetWare console commands, so treat it with kid gloves. Before DOWN deactivates the server, it performs various tasks including clearing all cache buffers and writing them to disk, closing all open files, updating appropriate directory and file allocation tables, dismounting all volumes, clearing all connections, and closing the operating system. Once DOWN has been entered at the file server console, you have various options:

▶ Type **EXIT** to return to the DOS partition.

▶ Type **RESTART SERVER** to bring things back up again.

▶ Type **UP** to reactivate the server console (take a look at the following Real World section).

REAL WORLD

In many of my trials and tribulations in the NetWare world, I've seen frustrated users trying to reactivate the server by typing "UP." I've come to the conclusion that Novell missed the boat in creating a cure for the DOWN command. Because turnabout is fair play, I offer this simple solution: Create a server batch file named "UP.NCF." In it, place a single command: "RESTART SERVER." Then add the following line to the end of your AUTOEXEC.NCF file:

```
SEARCH ADD C:\NWSERVER
```

Finally, copy UP.NCF to the C:\NWSERVER directory. Now, whenever the server is brought DOWN, you can simply type UP to reactivate it. I just love it when a plan comes together.

ZEN

"Unformed people delight in the gaudy and in novelty. Cooked people delight in the ordinary."

Mao Pau Zen

DSTRACE

DSTRACE is a maintenance console command. It enables CNAs to monitor NDS replica-related activities, including advertising, synchronization, and replica-to-replica communications. As you can see in Figure 7.16, DSTRACE provides various statistics concerning ACME partitions and replicas. Here's a snapshot of some of the more interesting messages:

▸ Date and time—The date and exact second of replica synchronization is shown in parentheses.

▸ SYNC:Start sync of partition [CAMELOT.ACME]—This indicates the start of a synchronization interval. A state of [0] indicates a normal synchronization check. A value greater than [0] (such as [30]) shows replica activity such as a partition being created or a partition being merged back into its parent.

▸ SYNC:End sync of partition—This line indicates the end of the synchronization interval. The message "All processed=YES" indicates that all updates were successfully incorporated into the master replica of this partition.

THE BRAIN

For more information on using DSTRACE and its parameters, consult the SET discussion in the *Novell NetWare 4.11 Utilities Reference Manual,* **or Chapter 5 of the** *Novell NetWare 4.11 Manual Supervising the Network I.*

F I G U R E   7.16

Getting to Know DSTRACE

```
(99/12/24 03:24:06)
SYNC: Start sync of partition <RIO.ACME> state:[0] type:[1]
 SYNC: Start outbound sync with (1) [010000BC]<WHITE-SRV1.WHITE.CRIME.TOKYO.ACME
>
  SYNC: sending updates to server <CN=WHITE-SRV1>
 SYNC: update to server <CN=WHITE-SRV1> successfully completed
SYNC: End sync of partition <RIO.ACME> All processed = YES.

(99/12/24 03:24:06)
SYNC: Start sync of partition <SYDNEY.ACME> state:[0] type:[1]
 SYNC: Start outbound sync with (1) [010000BC]<WHITE-SRV1.WHITE.CRIME.TOKYO.ACME
>
  SYNC: sending updates to server <CN=WHITE-SRV1>
 SYNC: update to server <CN=WHITE-SRV1> successfully completed
SYNC: End sync of partition <SYDNEY.ACME> All processed = YES.

(99/12/24 03:24:06)
SYNC: Start sync of partition <TOKYO.ACME> state:[0] type:[1]
 SYNC: Start outbound sync with (1) [010000BC]<WHITE-SRV1.WHITE.CRIME.TOKYO.ACME
>
  SYNC: sending updates to server <CN=WHITE-SRV1>
 SYNC: update to server <CN=WHITE-SRV1> successfully completed
SYNC: End sync of partition <TOKYO.ACME> All processed = YES.
```

DSTRACE can be activated at the IntranetWare server console by issuing the SET DSTRACE=ON statement.

ENABLE/DISABLE LOGIN

ENABLE LOGIN and its counterpart are both maintenance console commands. DISABLE LOGIN enables you to prevent access to the server for troubleshooting or maintenance activities. DISABLE LOGIN is particularly useful when you are working on the NDS database, backing up files, loading software, or dismounting/repairing volumes. Keep in mind that DISABLE LOGIN does not affect users who are currently logged in. You may consider combining this command with the CLEAR STATION statement.

As I'm sure you've probably guessed, ENABLE LOGIN enables file server logins if they've been disabled. It also provides one other facility-Supervisor unlocking. If the bindery Supervisor account has been locked because of intruder detection, ENABLE LOGIN will unlock it. This only works on the bindery Supervisor or Admin accounts.

EXIT

EXIT is an administrative console command. It enables you to return to the DOS partition once the file server has been brought DOWN. You may want to EXIT the file server console to prevent any other commands from being activated, or to reissue SERVER.EXE with new parameters. In addition, EXIT can be used in conjunction with REMOVE DOS to remotely reboot the file server. Of course, this facility has already been integrated into RESTART SERVER or our new UP.NCF utility. Who needs EXIT when you've got UP?

HELP

HELP is definitely an administrative console command. Many times when you feel the CNAship is weighing you down, simply type HELP at the server console and IntranetWare will come to your rescue. You can view help about a specific console command by identifying it with the HELP command, or view a short description of all console commands by typing:

```
HELP ALL
```

Press Enter after each description to view the next command. Then press Esc to exit altogether.

LOAD/UNLOAD

LOAD is an installation console command. It is used to activate NLMs and attach them to the core OS. As you recall, the IntranetWare architecture consists of two pieces—core OS and NLMs. The LOAD console command is used to activate these NLMs and bring them to life. You can also UNLOAD NLMs when you're finished with them and free up valuable server RAM.

MODULES

MODULES is a maintenance console command. It displays a list of currently loaded NLMs and some brief information about each, including the module short name, a descriptive string for each module, and the version number if it's a disk driver, LAN driver, or management utility. MODULES can be an important part of your IntranetWare optimization strategy in that it enables you to identify which modules are occupying valuable server RAM. Also, it displays support NLMs you might not have known you're using.

MOUNT

MOUNT is an installation console command. It activates internal IntranetWare volumes. The MOUNT command makes volumes available to users and can be used on specific volumes or all of them:

```
MOUNT ALL
```

MOUNTing and DISMOUNTing volumes can be used as a security measure for volumes that are rarely accessed. You can MOUNT them during access hours and DISMOUNT them when they are not in use. No matter how clever the hacker is, no one can access a dismounted volume. Murphy's Law Number 142—never say "no one."

REMOVE DOS

REMOVE DOS is an administrative console command. As you learned earlier, REMOVE DOS eliminates COMMAND.COM from background file server RAM. This memory is then returned to IntranetWare for file caching. REMOVE DOS can also be used to increase file server security. When DOS is removed, NLMs cannot be loaded from the DOS partition—it doesn't exist any more. Also, users cannot EXIT to the DOS partition. If they try, the file server is automatically rebooted back to the NetWare partition. Recall that the SECURE CONSOLE command automatically removes DOS from file server RAM.

RESTART SERVER

RESTART SERVER is an administrative console command. It can be used to reactivate the server after it has been DOWNed. This is most useful when your troubleshooting duties require that you frequently DOWN the server. RESTART SERVER is not one of your normal daily activities. This command also has a couple of interesting parameters that improve its troubleshooting value:

- ▸ NS—Restarts the server without invoking STARTUP.NCF

- ▸ NA—Restarts the server without invoking AUTOEXEC.NCF

Remember, this console command is the foundation of our earlier server UP scheme.

TRACK ON

TRACK ON is a maintenance console command. It activates the router information protocol (RIP) tracking screen. This screen displays RIP traffic on your IntranetWare server. Keep in mind that IntranetWare NDS activities do not rely on RIP. Instead, they broadcast their own information over separate channels. In addition, it's possible to filter RIP activity using additional products, such as Novell's MultiProtocol Router. As you can see in Figure 7.17, TRACK ON fills up the server console very quickly. You can bounce between this and other screens by pressing the Alt+Esc keys simultaneously, or by using Ctrl+Esc to view a list of all active console screens.

FIGURE 7.17

Getting to Know TRACK ON

```
Router Tracking Screen
OUT   [0BADCAFE:FFFFFFFFFFFF]   3:13:49 pm    00000DAD   2/3       00001234  1/2
OUT   [00001234:FFFFFFFFFFFF]   3:13:49 pm    0BADCAFE   1/2
IN    [0BADCAFE:000000000001]   3:13:56 pm    LABS-SRV1       1
IN    [00001234:0020AFE8B8B5]   3:13:56 pm    ACME_TREE___    1     ACME_TREE___    1
        WHITE-SRV1    1    WHITE-SRV1    1     WHITE-SRV1      1
IN    [00001234:0020AFC055F3]   3:14:07 pm    Get Nearest Server
OUT   [00001234:0020AFC055F3]   3:14:07 pm    Give Nearest Server LABS-SRV1
IN    [00001234:0020AFC055F3]   3:14:07 pm    Route Request
IN    [00001234:0020AFC055F3]   3:14:07 pm    Route Request
OUT   [00001234:0020AFC055F3]   3:14:07 pm    0BADCAFE   1/2
IN    [0BADCAFE:000000000001]   3:14:16 pm    ACME_TREE___    1
OUT   [0BADCAFE:FFFFFFFFFFFF]   3:14:19 pm    ACME_TREE___    2     ACME_TREE___    2
        WHITE-SRV1    2    WHITE-SRV1    2     WHITE-SRV1      2     ACME_TREE___    1
        LABS-SRV1     1
OUT   [00001234:FFFFFFFFFFFF]   3:14:19 pm    ACME_TREE___    1     LABS-SRV1       1
        LABS-SRV1     1
OUT   [0BADCAFE:FFFFFFFFFFFF]   3:14:19 pm    LABS-SRV1       1
IN    [0BADCAFE:000000000001]   3:14:23 pm    LABS-SRV1       1
IN    [0BADCAFE:000000000001]   3:14:25 pm    LABS-SRV1       1
IN    [00001234:0020AFE8B8B5]   3:14:26 pm    00000DAD   1/2
<Use ALT-ESC or CTRL-ESC to switch screens, or any other key to pause>
```

TRACK ON information is formatted according to whether the file server is receiving the information (IN) or broadcasting the information (OUT). Figure 7.17 shows the format of TRACK ON for the ACME LAB server and provides information about the many components it tracks, including sending file server's network address, node address, name, hops from that file server to this one, network addresses known by the sending file server, and the number of ticks it takes to traverse the WAN. Refer to Table 7.2 for a more detailed discussion of these TRACK ON components. Finally, you can activate the RIP tracking screen by issuing the following command at the server colon prompt (:):

```
TRACK ON
```

TABLE 7.2

Understanding TRACK ON
Parameters

PARAMETER	VALUE	DESCRIPTION
IN	IN [network address] 3:14:07 PM	Indicates inbound information originating outside this server and the time at which it was accepted.
OUT	OUT [network address] 3:14:19 PM	Indicates outbound information originating from this server and going across the WAN.
[network address]	[0BADCAFE:000000000001]	Identifies the IPX internal network address and node address of the internal virtual LAN. This is the server's unique internal network address.

(continued)

TABLE 7.2

Understanding TRACK ON
Parameters (continued)

PARAMETER	VALUE	DESCRIPTION
[network address] (continued)	[00001234:FFFFFFFFFFFF]	The outbound network and node address for packets being sent from this server. The odd node address indicates this packet is meant to be broadcast to all workstations and servers on the 1234 external cabling segment.
	[00001234:0020AFC055F3]	Indicates a packet arriving from a specific machine—in this case, a workstation.
SAP Information	LABS-SRV1 1	Service advertising protocol (SAP) information. This includes server names and a number. The number represents how many hops the server is from this server. Each router counts as a hop. Servers displaying SAP information include file servers, print servers, and mail servers, and so on.
	WHITE-SRV1 2	SAP information showing the WHITE-SRV1 server as 2 hops from LABS-SRV1. Internal IPX routing does count as a hop.
RIP information	00001234 1/2	Routing information protocol data. The number 00001234 indicates the destination network address for this packet. The values 1/2 indicate the number of hops and ticks it will take to reach the network. A tick is 1/18th of a second and typically one more than the number of hops. If you're sending packets over a large WAN, the ticks could take much longer.
GET NEAREST SERVER		This is a broadcast from a client seeking a connection from any server. If you do not get this message, it indicates that the workstation is having trouble communicating with the server.
GIVE NEAREST SERVER		This server's response to the GET NEAREST SERVER request—LABS-SRV1.

If you haven't figured it out yet, almost every ON switch in the world has an OFF. TRACK ON is no exception. To deactivate the RIP tracking screen, simply issue the command

TRACK OFF

THE BRAIN

For more information on using TRACK ON and other server console commands, see the AppNote entitled "Using TRACK and Other Console Utilities in a Mixed NetWare Environment" in the October 1995 issue of *Novell Application Notes*.

This completes our discussion of IntranetWare marriage tools. With this knowledge, comes responsibility. Remember, wield these tools wisely. Power corrupts and absolute power corrupts absolutely. Now let's complete our journey through the world of IntranetWare server management with a final discussion of "honey-do's."

ZEN

"I know it is wet
And the sun is not sunny.
But we can have
Lots of good fun that is funny!"

Dr. Seuss

NETWARE LOADABLE MODULES

NLMs are IntranetWare honey-do's. If you ever need any help, it's nice to know NLMs are there for you. These cute little server dynamos attach to the core OS and provide additional IntranetWare functionality. As you can see in Figure 7.18, IntranetWare doesn't have much to offer without NLMs. The core operating system provides these basic network services:

▸ Novell Directory Services (NDS)

▸ File system

▸ Security

▸ Authentication

▸ Routing

FIGURE 7.18

IntranetWare Server
Architecture

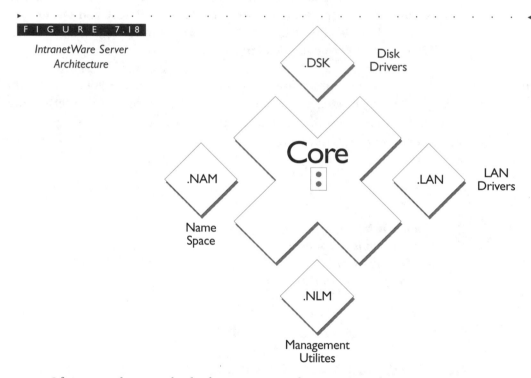

Of course, this is only the beginning. Without NLMs, the IntranetWare server would be limited to communications and file storing. Here's a list of the additional services provided by IntranetWare NLMs:

▸ Network Printing—PSERVER

▸ Storage Management Services (SMS)—SBACKUP and drivers

▶ Remote Server Console—REMOTE and RSPX/RS232

▶ Server Monitoring—MONITOR

▶ Server Customization—SERVMAN

▶ Communications—NetWare Connect (purchased separately)

▶ Network Management—Managewise (purchased separately)

▶ Messaging—Groupwise (purchased separately)

WHAT'S NEW

WHAT'S
NEW

It's important to note that server NLMs are very different from Client 32 workstation NLMs. Unfortunately, they have the same name (that is, NLMs). Server NLMs are modular utilities and drivers that interface between IntranetWare and server components. On the other hand, Client 32 workstation NLMs are connectivity programs that interface between the server and local resources (such as Windows 95 and the internal NIC). Got it? Good.

None of these facilities is available until NLMs activate internal communications and mount the file system volumes. In addition to saving the day, IntranetWare NLMs have the following advantages:

▶ NLMs free up RAM by enabling CNAs to remove inactive modules.

▶ NLMs can be loaded and unloaded without bringing down the server— hence the Lego analogy.

▶ NLMs provide an easy method for outside developers to write their own modules for IntranetWare.

From Figure 7.18, you can see that IntranetWare supports four NLM types: disk drivers, LAN drivers, name space, and management NLMs. Disk drivers are primarily responsible for the interface between IntranetWare and the internal hard disks. LAN drivers initiate communications with the internal NIC, and name space modules provide support for non-DOS naming schemes. Management NLMs are the real stars of the show. They're used for monitoring, maintenance, and configuration of the IntranetWare server environment. Let's take a closer look at each of these NLM types and explore how they can improve your quality of life— or at least your marriage.

Disk Drivers

As I just mentioned, disk drivers control communications between IntranetWare and the internal shared disk (and/or CD-ROM devices). You can load and unload disk drivers as needed. You learned earlier in this chapter that disk drivers activate the NetWare partition. They have the .DSK extension and are stored in the C:\NWSERVER directory. During the installation or startup process, your first task (after running SERVER.EXE) is to activate disk driver NLMs. This mounts the IntranetWare file system and makes all other utilities available from the SYS:SYSTEM directory. Some common .DSK drivers include ISADISK.DSK, IDE.DSK, and DCB.DSK for disk coprocessor boards. Newer disk modules written to the Novell Peripheral Architecture (NPA) standard come in pairs and have the .CDM and .HAM extensions. In summary, .HAM (Host Adapter Modules) drivers control the host bus adapter, while .CDM (Custom Device Module) drivers control the hardware devices that are attached to the host bus adapter. For more details, refer to the "Server Installation" section earlier in this chapter.

SMART LINK

For more information on the new Novell Peripheral Architecture solution, surf to the Novell Knowledgebase at http://support.novell.com/search/.

LAN Drivers

LAN drivers, on the other hand, control communication between IntranetWare and internal network interface cards (NICs). You can load and unload these drivers as needed to make communications available to all LAN users. Bear in mind that when you load the LAN driver, you must specify hardware configuration options such as interrupt, port address, memory address, and frame type.

Although disk drivers are automatically activated from STARTUP.NCF, LAN drivers are loaded from AUTOEXEC.NCF. This is because they are available from the SYS:SYSTEM directory once the NetWare partition has been activated. LAN drivers have the .LAN extension and include NE2000.LAN, TOKEN.LAN, 3C5X9.LAN, and TRXNET.LAN for ARCNet.

WHAT'S NEW

WHAT'S NEW

IntranetWare introduces an exciting new NLM loading feature: automated hardware detection. When the server is first installed, IntranetWare will automatically detect any hardware devices attached—such as disk controllers, Network Interface Cards, CD-ROMS, and so on. It will then automatically load the correct NLM drivers for each device. Wow! Things are getting easier. Imagine that.

Name Space

Name space modules enable files using non-DOS naming conventions to be stored in the IntranetWare file system. Also, native naming conventions are maintained for diverse workstations throughout the WAN. Name space is important because it allows Windows 95, Windows NT, Macintosh, Unix, and OS/2 names to be supported along with the default DOS environment. Name space modules have the .NAM extension and are stored in the SYS:SYSTEM directory with other NLMs. Some common name space modules include MAC.NAM for Macintosh users, LONG.NAM for Windows and OS/2 users, and NFS.NAM for Unix workstations. In addition to LOADing name space NLMS, you must use a console command to activate the new file system—ADD NAME SPACE.

INSTALL.NLM

This is where the fun begins. INSTALL.NLM is the first of a slew of management NLMs that help you install, manage, maintain, troubleshoot, and optimize the IntranetWare server. As you can see in Figure 7.19, INSTALL consists of ten options.

. . . . ◄

FIGURE 7.19

*Checking Out
INSTALL.NLM*

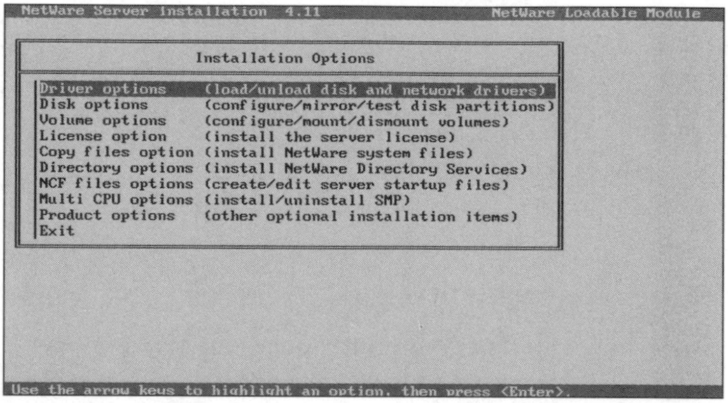

```
NetWare Server Installation  4.11                    NetWare Loadable Module

                            Installation Options
      ┌────────────────────────────────────────────────────────────┐
      │ Driver options     (load/unload disk and network drivers)   │
      │ Disk options       (configure/mirror/test disk partitions)  │
      │ Volume options     (configure/mount/dismount volumes)       │
      │ License option     (install the server license)             │
      │ Copy files option  (install NetWare system files)           │
      │ Directory options  (install NetWare Directory Services)     │
      │ NCF files options  (create/edit server startup files)       │
      │ Multi CPU options  (install/uninstall SMP)                  │
      │ Product options    (other optional installation items)      │
      │ Exit                                                         │
      └────────────────────────────────────────────────────────────┘



Use the arrow keys to highlight an option, then press <Enter>.
```

These ten INSTALL steps systematically walk you through the server install process beginning with SERVER.EXE. Once the core OS has been activated, you load the disk driver(s) and create the NetWare partition. Next, you create the default SYS: volume. Once you copy SYSTEM and PUBLIC files to the new volume, it's time to install NDS, and activate the server license. Installing NDS is the trickiest of the ten installation options. Once time synchronization and server context have been established, you can automate the whole kit and caboodle with AUTOEXEC.NCF and STARTUP.NCF files. Finally, Product Options provides support for installing other products, and Server Options gives you the choice of starting all over again. Of course, like any management NLM, if things get too hairy, you can always EXIT.

This INSTALL.NLM utility is a dramatic improvement over earlier versions. In the past, the installation process wasn't nearly as systematic or organized. Also, you can jump to any point in the journey from the main menu. Some of the tasks you might want to perform after the IntranetWare installation include:

▸ Disk duplexing

▸ Adding drives and volumes

▸ Adding incremental server licenses

▸ Redefining the hot fix redirection area

▸ Editing server configuration files

▸ Loading an upgraded IntranetWare license

▸ Installing and configuring additional products, including Web Server, NetWare/IP, additional languages, Macintosh connectivity, and Unix support

For a more detailed walkthrough of the server installation process, refer to the "Server Installation" section earlier in this chapter.

MONITOR.NLM

MONITOR.NLM has always been the "mother of all server utilities." It provides a plethora of information about key memory and communication processes. The types of resources that can be tracked using MONITOR.NLM include file connections, memory, disk information, users, file lock activity, and processor usage. Of course, with the advent of SERVMAN, there's some competition at the top of the mountain.

ZEN

"My grandfather once told me that there are two kinds of people: those who do the work and those who take the credit. He then told me to try to be in the first group, there was much less competition there."

Indira Gandhi

As you can see in Figure 7.20, MONITOR.NLM consists of two main menu screens—General Information and Available Options. Like most MONITOR windows, General Information contains dynamic statistics that change every second or so. Some of the most interesting General Information statistics include:

▸ Utilization—Reflects CPU utilization. This number is roughly the amount of time the processor is busy. For a more accurate reading of CPU utilization, use the histogram displayed from the Processor Utilization option from the main menu.

▸ Total cache buffers—The number of blocks available for file caching. This number decreases as NLMs and other server resources are loaded. Because file caching has the most dramatic impact on server file performance, you want this number to remain high. For a more accurate measure of available cache buffers, use the Resource Utilization option from the main menu.

▸ Dirty cache buffers—The number of file blocks in memory waiting to be written to disk. If this number grows large, you may have a bottleneck problem with the internal hard disk. A server crash at this point would corrupt saved data.

▸ Current service processes—The indication of the number of task handlers IntranetWare allocates to service incoming requests. This can dramatically impact server performance, because requests must wait in line when service processes are busy. Consider what happens at the grocery store around 5:00 p.m. each evening. The default maximum number of service processes is 50, with a possible range of 5 to 1,000.

▸ Current licensed connections—The number of active licensed connections the server currently recognizes. This number will always be less than the maximum number of licensed connections your server supports. If this number approaches the maximum, consider upgrading your license using INSTALL.NLM.

FIGURE 7.20

Getting to Know MONITOR.NLM

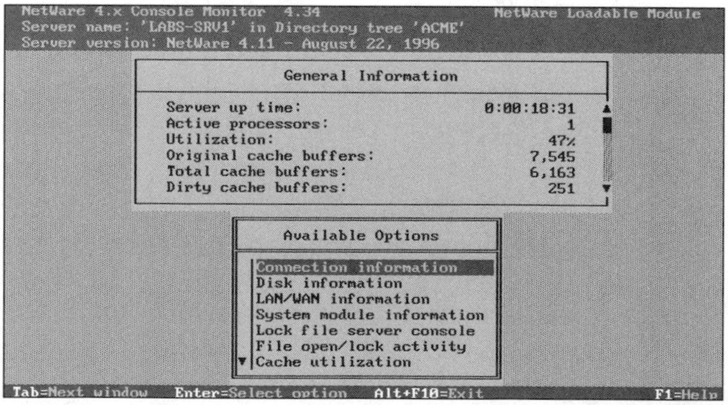

```
NetWare 4.x Console Monitor  4.34                    NetWare Loadable Module
Server name: 'LABS-SRV1' in Directory tree 'ACME'
Server version: NetWare 4.11 - August 22, 1996

                    ┌──────────── General Information ────────────┐
                    │ Server up time:              0:00:18:31    ▲ │
                    │ Active processors:                    1      │
                    │ Utilization:                        47%      │
                    │ Original cache buffers:           7,545      │
                    │ Total cache buffers:              6,163      │
                    │ Dirty cache buffers:                251    ▼ │
                    └──────────────────────────────────────────────┘

                         ┌──────── Available Options ────────┐
                         │ Connection information            │
                         │ Disk information                  │
                         │ LAN/WAN information               │
                         │ System module information         │
                         │ Lock file server console          │
                         │ File open/lock activity           │
                        ▼│ Cache utilization                 │
                         └───────────────────────────────────┘

Tab=Next window   Enter=Select option   Alt+F10=Exit            F1=Help
```

In addition to these general information statistics, MONITOR.NLM includes a plethora of Available Option submenus. Each submenu focuses on a specific subcomponent of the IntranetWare server architecture. Here's a quick look:

- Connection information—Lists all active connections and tracks their current activity. CNAs can use this option to clear specific user workstation connections.

- Disk information—Lists all available internal disks and valuable hot fix redirection statistics. CNAs can use this option to activate, deactivate, or modify internal disks.

- LAN/WAN information—Lists LAN driver configurations and statistics as well as node and network addressing.

- System module information—Lists all loaded modules by name, size, and version. In addition, you can track resource "tags" and memory usage for each module.

- Lock file server console—As you learned earlier, enables you to protect the console by specifying a password.

- File open/lock activity—Monitors files, lock activity, and status. It also enables you to view which stations have open files and general information about mounted volumes and directory structures.

- Cache utilization—View detailed caching statistics, including total cache block requests, the number of times a block request had to wait because there were no available cache blocks, long- and short-term cache hits, and dirty cache hits. This option enables you to assess the efficiency of server RAM and take corrective actions.

- Processor utilization—Provides a detailed histogram of all selected processes and their CPU usage.

▶ Resource utilization—View memory usage statistics for cache buffer pool, allocated memory, and movable and nonmovable memory pools, and code/data memory. You can also view resource tags and determine which NLMs are "hogging" valuable server RAM.

▶ Memory utilization—View detailed memory statistics such as percent of allocated memory in use, memory blocks and bytes in use, and free blocks. This option also enables you to activate garbage collection routines. You never know when you might need it.

▶ Scheduling information—View and change the priority of a process by delaying CPU execution until a later time. This options also provides a management window to IntranetWare's new SMP (Symmetric MultiProcessing) feature.

▶ EXIT—Sounds like a good time for this.

You could spend a lifetime exploring MONITOR.NLM, and you probably will once you become a CNE. But for now, settle for the MONITOR.NLM exploritorium at the end of this chapter. Stay tuned.

SERVMAN.NLM

Look out, there's a new superhero in Gotham. He is faster than a speedy microprocessor, has more storage than a CD-ROM, and is able to search huge databases in a single second. He's SERVMAN!

SERVMAN, the new SERVer MANager, is at the core of IntranetWare's new server utility strategy. It is the most exciting and versatile new server utility. SERVMAN provides a menu interface for SET parameters and displays valuable IntranetWare configurations. As you can see in Figure 7.21, SERVMAN includes two windows—Server General Information and Available Options. Each of the statistics in the Server General Information window is updated every second. Here's a quick look:

▶ Server uptime—Length of time the server has been running since it was last booted.

▶ Processor utilization—Percentage of time the server CPU is busy.

▶ Processor speed—Speed at which the processor is running based on CPU clock speed, CPU type, and the number of memory wait states. For example, the LABS-SRV1 server has a rating of 16,429. This is an average setting for a Pentium 200 MHz machine.

▶ Server processes—The number of tasks handlers currently available to handle incoming user requests.

▶ Loaded NLMs—The number of modules currently loaded on the server.

▶ Mounted volumes—The number of volumes currently active on the server.

▶ Active queues—The number of active print queues currently servicing user print jobs.

▶ Logged-in users—The number of users logged into the server.

▶ Loaded name spaces—The number of name spaces loaded on the server, and yes, DOS counts as one.

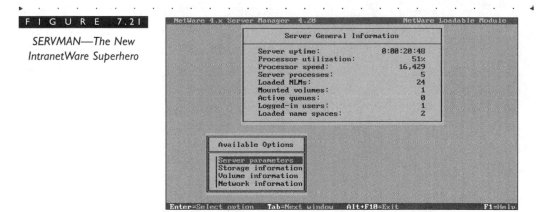

F I G U R E   7.21

SERVMAN—The New IntranetWare Superhero

As you can see, there's a little overlap between MONITOR.NLM and SERVMAN.NLM. This is not where the similarities end. Throughout SERVMAN, you'll see references back to statistics displayed in INSTALL.NLM and MONITOR.NLM. And, of course, you'll see some new configurations not available anywhere else. The idea is this: With SERVMAN, you get a single management utility for all server maintenance and customization tasks. Although it doesn't provide a facility for *all* server management tasks, SERVMAN does help you accomplish many of them. Murphy's Law Number 342—never say "all."

REAL WORLD

The processor speed rating is a measurement of the server's processing capabilities as determined by the CPU clock speed (such as 120 MHz), the CPU type (such as Pentium), and the number of memory wait states (for example, 0). For instance, a 386/33 machine should get a rating of about 320, a 486/50 should get a rating of around 1,370, a Pentium/120 should get a rating of approximately 6,576, and a Pentium/200 should get a rating around 16,429.

The Available Options menu within SERVMAN offers some valuable management capabilities, including:

▸ Server parameters—You can view and configure "almost all" IntranetWare operating system parameters. This includes SET parameters automated by AUTOEXEC.NCF and STARTUP.NCF. Changes you make in SERVMAN can optionally be reflected in the server configuration files. Cool! Plus you can view a quick description of each SET parameter and its default settings from within a menu interface.

▸ Storage information—View adapter, device, and partition information similar to INSTALL and MONITOR.

▸ Volume information—View information about volumes mounted on the file server (similar to INSTALL).

▸ Network information—View network information such as number of packets received and transmitted. This is a summary screen of the detailed LAN statistics provided by MONITOR.NLM.

All in all, SERVMAN is a great superhero. Remember, never tug on Superman's cape.

SMART LINK

For more information about IntranetWare optimization using MONITOR/SERVMAN and a chance to try out these server utilities on your own, surf over to CyberState University and World Wire: http://www.cyberstateu.com.

DSREPAIR

It's nice to know that if SERVMAN can't save the day, you can rely on DSREPAIR.NLM. This replaces the BINDFIX utility used in previous bindery-based versions of NetWare. DSREPAIR makes repairs and adjustments to the NDS database and solves inconsistencies with time and replica synchronization. Figure 7.22 shows the main menu of DSREPAIR and both synchronization options. In addition, the Advanced Options menu enables you to set advanced repair configurations such as "Log file management," "Repair local DS database," "Servers known to this database," "View remote server ID list," "Replica and Partition operations," "Check volume objects and trustees," "Check external references," "Security equivalence synchronization," "Global schema operations," and "Create a database file." If you're not sure you have a corrupted NDS database, consider the following symptoms:

▶ You cannot create, delete, or modify objects even though you have sufficient rights.

▶ You have unknown objects appearing in the tree that do not disappear after all servers are synchronized.

▶ You cannot create, merge, or modify partitions.

ZEN

"Computers come in two varieties: the 'prototype' and the 'obsolete.'"

Anonymous

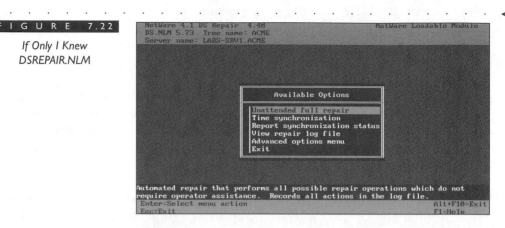

F I G U R E   7.22

*If Only I Knew
DSREPAIR.NLM*

Once DSREPAIR is completed, you can read through the DSREPAIR log as the file DSREPAIR.LOG in the SYS:SYSTEM subdirectory. Remember, DSREPAIR is your friend, but should only be used in emergency situations.

IntranetWare is a great operating system for our global electronic village. Now that we've installed, configured, activated, and maintained our server, it's time to "protect" it. In the next section, you'll learn how to create a maximum security server. If we do it right, our server will be more impenetrable than Alcatraz. Interestingly, we're trying to keep the users from breaking *in*, not *out*.

QUIZ

Speaking of time, at the next minute, it will be exactly twice as many seconds after the half-hour as it was minutes before the same half-hour last time the two hands were at right angles this afternoon. Hmmmm, help me out here—what time is it?

(Q7-3)

SERVER PROTECTION

If the server is at the heart of your IntranetWare WAN, it makes sense to take all measures you can to protect it. As we saw in Chapter 5, IntranetWare has an elaborate security system that protects NDS and data files from would-be hackers. This system does nothing, however, to protect the server console itself. Any user with mischievous intent and a little bit of knowledge can cause a lot of harm at the

IntranetWare server console. For this reason, you should take extra measure to install an impenetrable network armor at the file server console. Following are four scenarios that can go a long way in protecting your server:

▶ Physical—Lock up the physical server

▶ MONITOR.NLM locking—Use the password feature

▶ SECURE CONSOLE—Restrict access to the DOS partition

▶ REMOTE.NLM—Add a password to the built-in RMF facility

Now, let's take a closer look at how to create a "maximum security server."

Physical

No matter what security locks you put in place, someone will break them if they have physical access to the server. It's amazing how much information can be stolen from the physical server console. including SERVER.EXE, NLMs, optimization data, and company secrets. The first step in creating a maximum security server is locking up the physical machine itself. This involves three steps:

I • Lock the server into a wiring closet or other restricted room.

2 • Remove the keyboard to discourage physical access to the console.

3 • Remove the server monitor and leave the hacker "in the dark."

Although this is a great plan, you're probably wondering, "How am I supposed to manage server operations from within a locked closet and with no keyboard or monitor?" That is a good question. Fortunately, IntranetWare includes a built-in Remote Management Facility (RMF) that provides virtual access to the file server console—from a direct workstation or asynchronously remote machine. Later in this chapter, we'll explore RMF and show you how it can be used to supplement the server protection plan. For now, let's move on to the next protection scenario—MONITOR.NLM.

MONITOR.NLM Locking

If locking up the server is not an option, or if you want to increase your level of server protection, consider "locking" the console with MONITOR.NLM. This way, even if someone does get physical access to the machine, he or she can't access the console unless he or she has the MONITOR.NLM password. First, load the MONITOR.NLM utility by typing

```
LOAD MONITOR
```

at the file server console. Next, choose the Lock Server Console option from the main menu. IntranetWare will ask for a password. Enter a unique password and press Enter. All done. Now, anyone accessing the server console must first enter the MONITOR.NLM password.

By default, IntranetWare accepts the bindery supervisor's password for unlocking the server console. As you learned earlier, this is the first password assigned to the Admin user when you installed the first server in this NDS tree. Even if you delete Admin or change his or her password, the supervisor bindery password remains the same. You should specify a different password when you lock the monitor—just in case. You can also automate monitor locking by placing the following command in the server's AUTOEXEC.NCF configuration file:

```
LOAD MONITOR L
```

In this example, only the supervisor bindery password can be used to unlock the server console. Next, let's expand our server protection scheme to include the SECURE CONSOLE command.

TIP

If intruder detection/lockout disables either the bindery supervisor or Admin account, the password won't unlock MONITOR. This is a bad thing. The only way to reactivate the accounts is to issue the ENABLE LOGIN console command at the server—but we can't get there! So, as a backup measure, consider issuing a different MONITOR locking password.

SECURE CONSOLE

To further enhance server protection, you can use the SECURE CONSOLE command at the colon prompt (:) or, even better, place it in the AUTOEXEC.NCF file so it executes automatically when the server is booted. This command accomplishes four things:

► Path specifiers are disabled. Only the SYS:SYSTEM search path remains in effect. This means NLMs can only be loaded from the SYS:SYSTEM directory. SECURE CONSOLE provides protection against Trojan horse modules that are loaded from the DOS partition or diskette drives. These modules enter the core OS and access or alter valuable server information. Remember, anyone can load an NLM at the server from diskette unless he or she is physically restricted from accessing it, or the SECURE CONSOLE command has been used.

► Keyboard entry into the IntranetWare OS debugger is disabled. This stops super-nerdy hackers from altering the OS itself.

► This command prevents the server date and time from being changed by an intruder. This closes a loophole in the intruder detection/lockout feature. Without SECURE CONSOLE, users whose accounts have been disabled can simply access the server colon prompt and manually expire their lockout period. Bad user.

► COMMAND.COM is removed from server memory. This protects files on the DOS partition by preventing access to it. Remember, one of your most important IntranetWare files (SERVER.EXE) resides on the DOS partition.

I'm feeling more secure already. With the server locked up tight as a drum, there's only one more back door to close—RMF access.

REMOTE.NLM

The final server protection strategy involves restricting access to RMF—IntranetWare's built-in remote management facility. As you recall from our first protection strategy, we've already locked the server in a closet and removed the keyboard and monitor. Now, the only way to perform daily monitoring tasks is

RMF. We'll talk more about the details of RMF later in this chapter, but here's the "Cliff Notes" version.

RMF enables you to access the server console from a local or remote workstation. In either case, it relies on two key components—REMOTE.NLM at the server and RCONSOLE.EXE at the workstation. It's reasonable to assume that if *you* can access the server console from a remote workstation, so can any malevolent hacker. So, let's take measures to protect REMOTE.NLM.

When you activate REMOTE at the server console, you can specify a password using the following syntax:

```
LOAD REMOTE password
```

Replace *password* with any alphanumeric name you can remember. With the password in place, RCONSOLE prompts you for it before enabling access to the server console. Here's the catch—you'll probably want to automate this step by placing REMOTE in the AUTOEXEC.NCF file. Because AUTOEXEC.NCF is a text file in the SYS:SYSTEM subdirectory, it's reasonable to assume that any hacker worth his or her salt would be able to view the REMOTE password. Oops. But we have a solution. You can use null characters in the password or, better yet, encrypt it. Null characters appear as spaces but are actual, valid, alphanumeric characters. You can issue a null character by pressing the Alt+255 keys simultaneously. When hackers view AUTOEXEC.NCF, they'll never know the difference between a null character and a space. Or, better yet, you can encrypt the REMOTE password using LDREMOTE. For more details, see the Real World that follows.

REAL WORLD

In pre-NetWare 4.1 versions of NetWare, REMOTE.NLM accepted the supervisor's bindery password in addition to its own. This meant you could issue the LOAD REMOTE command in AUTOEXEC.NCF without having to disclose the password. In IntranetWare, the REMOTE password is required and the Supervisor bindery password no longer works. Fortunately, Novell has included an encryption scheme that enables you to encrypt what appears in AUTOEXEC.NCF. Here's how it works:

1. Load REMOTE.NLM at the server console by typing **LOAD REMOTE** and pressing Enter. IntranetWare will prompt you for an RMF password. Enter it now (for example, **Cathy**).

2. RMF is now active, but your password is not protected. Next, you can encrypt the password by typing **REMOTE ENCRYPT** at the server console and pressing Enter. Once again, IntranetWare will ask you for a password. Enter the same one from Step 1 (**Cathy**).

3. IntranetWare then responds with an encrypted LOAD statement, such as:

```
LOAD REMOTE -e 14572BFD3AFEAE4E4759
```

This is the encrypted representation of the password "Cathy."

Next, REMOTE will ask you a simple question:

```
Would you like this command written to
SYS:SYSTEM\LDREMOTE.NCF?
```

You should probably answer "Yes."

4. Now you're ready to add the REMOTE statement to AUTOEXEC.NCF without any concerns about giving away the password. Simply enter these two commands toward the end of AUTOEXEC.NCF:

```
LDREMOTE

LOAD RSPX
```

There you have it! We've increased server protection by requiring an RMF password and closed a loophole by encrypting it. In summary, use LOAD REMOTE with the password, then issue the REMOTE ENCRYPT command to encrypt the password. Provide the same password again and have IntranetWare create the LDREMOTE configuration file. Finally, automate RMF by placing LDREMOTE in the AUTOEXEC.NCF file.

Don't you feel much better now, knowing that you have a maximum security server? Just like Alcatraz, it should be almost impossible for IntranetWare criminals to "break in."

ZEN

"We could tell you what it's about. But then, of course, we'd have to kill you."

From the movie *Sneakers*

Well, there you have it—the tools of a good marriage. No matter what you do, remember: Communication is the key. If you work hard at it and develop a synergistic team, I guarantee the rewards will greatly outweigh the pain. Speaking of pain, nothing grows a marriage more strongly than nine months of pregnancy.

Workstation Management

So, you're cruising along through life, minding your own business, and wham—it hits you. Suddenly, your family is twice as big as it was a few years ago. It's an abrupt wake-up call when you finally realize *you're* not the child anymore. A strange thing happens when children have children. Even though Leia is 27 years old—firmly planted in adulthood—she's still our little baby. We were there through the rough years—login scripts, menu system, and e-mail. Now Leia's having children of her own. Suddenly her focus shifts from marriage to her baby.

Now is a good time for your focus to shift as well—from the server to your IntranetWare children (workstations). As a CNA, you will spend just as much time managing the workstations as you will managing the server—probably more. In addition, managing workstations can be even more challenging because it encompasses a much more diverse collection of users, applications, and operating systems. And we all know users can act like babies sometimes. In order to fully optimize the client connection and keep things running smoothly, you'll have to employ a stern, yet caring, workstation management strategy.

ZEN

"If my heart can become pure and simple like that of a child, I think there probably can be no greater happiness than this."

Kitaro Nishida

Of all the places you'll go in your life, few will be as interesting as the IntranetWare client. There you'll find fun, adventure, and NetWare (or Virtual) Loadable Modules (NLMs). The client is one of the most important aspects of an IntranetWare system because it's where the users meet the network. Someday, I guarantee you'll get the question, "Where's the ANY key?" In order to help you sleep at night, the interface should be as transparent as possible-avoid confusion and unnecessary support calls. In order to achieve client transparency, IntranetWare breaks the workstation into two key components (see Figure 7.23):

▸ NIC—The internal network interface card that provides communications between the local workstation operating system (WOS) and the IntranetWare server. This hardware device is managed by a series of workstation connectivity files called ODI (Open Datalink Interface). We use LAN drivers and NLMs in the Client 32 world, and simple .COM files on 16-bit workstations.

▸ Workstation operating system (WOS)—The WOS manages all local workstation services. It coordinates among local applications (word processing, spreadsheets, and databases) and local devices (file storage, screens, and printers). All these local activities must be somehow orchestrated with network services. In the Client 32 universe, this is accomplished using CLIENT32.NLM. On the other hand, Client 16 uses relies on complex suite of workstation Legos called VLMs (Virtual Loadable Modules).

▸ · ◂

FIGURE 7.23

The Two Main Components of Workstation Connectivity

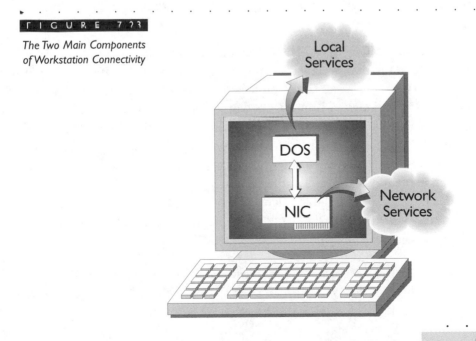

Here's a quick history lesson. Previous versions of NetWare relied on less-integrated client connectivity files. NetWare 3.11 and before used programs such as WSGEN or SHGEN to generate an IPX.COM file that implemented the IPX/SPX stack and provided the link between the workstation and internal NIC. In addition, most of the DOS Requester functionality was accomplished using one rigid file—NET.EXE.

More recent versions of NetWare (NetWare 3.12 through 4.1) relied on Client 16 connectivity files. They introduced ODI (Open Datalink Interface) drivers that provided a more flexible way of binding the IPX/SPX protocol stack. In addition, the DOS Requester functionality was expanded to include a suite of 16-bit Virtual Loadable Modules (VLMs). These VLMs together form the "NetWare DOS Requester," which provides support for DOS and MS Windows client workstations in the 16-bit environment.

Now, in IntranetWare, Novell has introduced a more integrated 32-bit client. It uses an enhanced version of ODI and 32-bit NetWare Loadable Modules at the workstation. The 32-bit solution provides graphical access to NetWare 2.2, 3.12, and 4.11 servers. It is the new and preferred way of networking from Windows 95, Windows 3.1, and/or DOS workstations.

Regardless of the way you go, you must be intimately familiar with BOTH platforms. After all, CNAs should always be prepared. So here we go.... workstation management in the 32-bit and 16-bit sandboxes.

CLIENT 32 WORKSTATION ARCHITECTURE

Client 32 is the newest and most powerful workstation connectivity software for IntranetWare. It is a 32-bit protected mode NetWare client that allows Windows 95, Windows 3.1, and DOS workstations to connect to NetWare 2.2, 3.12, and 4.11 servers. In addition, it provides a graphical login utility for logging in from MS Windows. Finally, if you are running Windows 95, you can access network files and printers using the Network Neighborhood, the Windows Explorer, and various application dialog boxes.

In Chapter 6, we learned that Client 32 uses a variety of LAN drivers and NLMs to interface with the local NIC and WOS. As you can see in Figure 7.24, this software consists of four main components:

- NIC driver—Controls communications with the internal NIC. This is a hardware-specific LAN driver such as CNE2000.LAN. It's also known as the Multiple Link Interface Driver (MLID).

▶ Link Support Layer—Acts as a switchboard to route network protocol packets between the LAN driver and appropriate communications protocol. LSL is implemented at the workstation as LSLC32.NLM.

▶ Communications Protocol—Determines (through a set of rules) the *language* used to move data across the network. The protocol guarantees that two devices using the same protocol can communicate because they speak the same language. This is accomplished at the Client 32 workstation using IPX.NLM.

▶ Client 32—Provides (through a platform-independent NLM) the workstation access for Windows 95, Windows 3.1, and DOS operating systems. This facility is accomplished using the CLIENT32.NLM file.

Client 32 is the only client software for Windows 95 or Windows 3.1 that enables full support of NDS. Using Client 32, you can browse through network services, across multiple trees, and print from Network Neighborhood and Windows Explorer.

F I G U R E   7.24

Client 32 Workstation Architecture

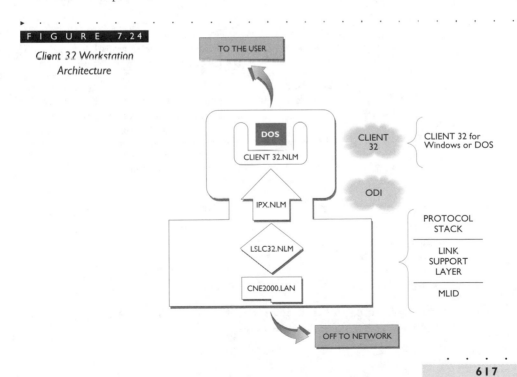

Probably the most important workstation management topic for CNAs is Client 32 installation. This is a very complex and troublesome task because the workstation is such a diverse battleground. It's where the users plot their assaults against *your* network. Also, in IntranetWare, the Client 32 installation is much more integrated with the workstation's native GUI environment than previous versions. For this reason, you must be intimately familiar with both Client 32 and MS Windows (95 and 3.1).

And that's not all. You also must understand the installation and management procedures for diverse network hardware—such as NIC boards, cabling, and related components. Also, you must make sure there are no hardware conflicts. See Table 7.3 for some client install-related action items.

TABLE 7.3 Network Board Configuration	TYPE OF BOARD	ACTION REQUIRED
	ISA Network Boards	Look at the network board to determine the settings. The documentation that came with the board should describe where each setting is located. Configurations are typically accomplished using jumpers or DIP switches.
	EISA or MCA Network Board	Run the workstation's reference or setup program. The program will list the settings for your network board.
	PCI Local Bus Network Boards	Run the workstation's reference or setup program. The program will list the settings for your network board. Configurations are stored in firmware chips on the NIC.

NOTE: If you already have a network connection established, switch to the SYS:\PUBLIC directory and type NVER and then press Enter. This will verify your configuration.

Once you're an expert in workstation hardware, it's time to move onto some even more puzzling topics: Client 32 and MS Windows (egad!). Let's start with Windows 95.

SMART LINK

You can check out and download the new Client 32 connectivity files for free at http://www.novell.com.

CLIENT 32 INSTALLATION FOR WINDOWS 95

Client 32 can be installed in four different ways using the Windows 95 Network Device Installer (NDI) and .INF script files. In addition, Novell's Client 32 installation incorporates Windows 95 property pages that were created specifically to set Client 32 configuration parameters contained in the Windows 95 registry. These pages use a graphic user interface to replace NET.CFG and other configuration files.

Here's a list of the four different Client 32 installation options for Windows 95:

▸ MSBATCH SETUP—This installation method allows you to install Client 32 files at the same time as Windows 95. It prepares the Windows 95 and Client 32 files on the server so they can be copied to the workstation simultaneously. To accomplish this, simply place the Windows 95 install image on the server and then update it to default to Client 32 instead of Microsoft's Client for NetWare Networks. Then when you run the MSBATCH SETUP, it will take care of the rest for you.

▸ NetWare 4.11 SETUP—If Windows 95 is already installed on the workstation or you're upgrading from Client 16, you can use the SETUP program on the NetWare 4.11 operating system CD-ROM. This is the typical single-user install.

▸ Custom Windows 95 Setup—The custom installation option removes the Microsoft NetWare Client and any other NetWare network component. Then it sets up files that the Microsoft NDI uses to install Client 32. A knowledgeable network user can configure network parameters (including the client parameters) manually. This is accomplished using the Windows 95 Network Control Panel and other property page features. Refer to the "Step 1: Establishing Workstation Connectivity" section of Chapter 6 for more information.

▸ Automatic Client Upgrade (ACU)—Executes an instruction placed by the CNA in a login script and then seamlessly upgrades clients during login. This method can be used to automatically upgrade NetWare Client 32 for Windows 95 or the Microsoft Client for NetWare Networks. It doesn't, however, upgrade NETx or VLM clients.

Client 32 Installation Steps for Windows 95

Once you've determined which installation method to use, it's time to get on with the show. Following are the general steps for Client 32 installation in Windows 95:

Step 1: Run SETUP.EXE from within Windows 95. On the server, it will be in the SYS:PUBLIC\CLIENT\WIN95\IBM_ENU directory. On the NetWare 4.11 operating system CD-ROM, it can be found in the D:\PRODUCTS\WIN95\IBM_ENU directory.

Step 2: The NetWare Client 32 Installation window appears once you bypass the Software License Agreement. Select Start to begin the installation.

TIP

Microsoft Networks use NDIS drivers for protocol connectivity. The NetWare Client 32 prefers ODI drivers. To upgrade NDIS drivers to ODI automatically, click the appropriate box in the Client 32 installation screen.

Step 3: Setup will automatically install and configure Client 32 with default properties. During this process, you may be asked to insert your Windows 95 CD-ROM and supply a source location for the CAB files. They can be found in the D:\WIN95 subdirectory.

Step 4: When Setup is complete, click on Customize, Novell NetWare Client 32, and finally, Properties. This allows us to personalize many Client 32 properties such as

- ▸ Preferred Server

- ▸ Preferred Tree

- ▸ Name Context

- ▸ Login Scripts

- ▸ NIC Settings

Once you're finished inputting custom configurations, Windows 95 will build a driver information database. When it's completed, restart your computer and the Network Login Dialog Box appears. Congratulations, installation complete!

Now, that wasn't so bad. As you can see, the Client 32 Installation for Windows 95 is simple, graphical, and straightforward. Unfortunately, however, it is not *Automated*. Have no fear—ACU is here!

Automatic Client Upgrade for Windows 95

You can also use the Automatic Client Upgrade (ACU) program to upgrade older Client 32 files to the newest 32-bit connectivity drivers. It also upgrades the Microsoft Client for NetWare Networks. This version doesn't, however, upgrade NETx or VLM drivers. That functionality is provided by the Client 32 for Windows 3.1 ACU program (see the section, "Client 32 Installation for Windows 3.1," later in this chapter). ACU uses fancy login scripts to automate the upgrade process. Here's how it works in the Windows 95 world:

Step 1: To use ACU, you must first place the Client 32 installation files and Windows 95 .CAB files in a directory where they can be read during client login. We recommend the SYS:LOGIN subdirectory. Remember, the user must have Read and File Scan [RF] access rights to this directory.

Step 2: Next, you must place the following statement in a Container or Profile login script:

```
#SYS:PUBLIC\CLIENT\WIN95\IBM_ENU\SETUP.EXE /ACU
```

This instruction will automatically upgrade old workstations to Client 32 during the next login. When the workstation logs in, ACU checks the client's file to see if the System files are newer. If they are, the user gets a dialog with the following message:

```
"A newer version of the Novell Client Software is
available. Click Continue to install the newer version
or Cancel to retain your existing client software."
```

Step 3: If the user chooses Continue, the upgrade starts automatically and the files are copied to the workstation.

Step 4: If the user chooses Cancel, the workstation continues to use the older client software. However, each time the user logs in with the older client, ACU will again attempt to upgrade the workstation's software.

Step 5: Finally, once the client has been upgraded, the user is prompted to reboot the workstation in order to utilize the new Client 32 software.

Well, that does it for Windows 95. Simple, huh? But, that's not the end. We can't ignore all our older 16-bit GUI users. That wouldn't be polite. Now let's take a moment to explore Client 32 installation for Windows 3.1.

QUIZ

My first is in day, but not in night.
My second, in flame, but not in light.
My third is in milk, but not in tea.
My fourth in slip, but not in plea.
My last in yellow, not in whale.
My whole for love will tell a tale.
What am I?

(Q7-4)

CLIENT 32 INSTALLATION FOR WINDOWS 3.1

DOS and Windows 3.1 workstations need a different set of Client 32 files to connect to an IntranetWare WAN. During the Client 32 installation process, several drivers and configuration files are copied to C:\WINDOWS and C:\WINDOWS\SYSTEM.

In addition, the following workstation configuration files are modified:

▶ CONFIG.SYS—Automates drive mapping settings

▶ AUTOEXEC.BAT—Automates workstation connectivity at startup

▶ NET.CFG—Establishes driver settings

Client 32 Installation Steps for Windows 3.1

Here's a brief overview of the Client 32 installation process for DOS/Windows 3.1 workstations:

Step 1: To start the Client 32 installation, run INSTALL.EXE from DOS or SETUP.EXE from Windows 3.1. Both of these applications are located on the IntranetWare Client 32 Installation diskettes. You can create these diskettes using the "Other Products" option of INSTALL.NLM (see the "Server Installation" section earlier in this chapter).

Step 2: Once the installation program begins, you will be greeted with a language selection screen, welcome message, and Software License Agreement. Click OK, Continue, and Yes, in that order.

Step 3: Next, you will be presented with the Directory Locations dialog box. You can accept the default (C:\NOVELL\CLIENT32), or choose a directory of your own. Click Next to move onto the LAN driver selection screen. Choose the correct ODI-compliat driver that matches your workstation's NIC card. Click Next to continue.

Step 4: At this point, SETUP.EXE will copy necessary drivers to your workstation and make adjustments to local configuration files. Finally, click Next to bypass the Additional Options screen and choose Restart Computer to complete the installation. Piece of cake.

Step 5: Not so fast. Now you must customize the Client 32 installation properties to automate workstation connectivity. This can be accomplished using two utilities-NET.CFG and NetWare User Tools for Windows. First, use a DOS text editor to customize NET.CFG in the C:\NOVELL\CLIENT32 directory (check out the "NET.CFG" section of Chapter 6 for more information). Second, activate NetWare User Tools for Windows and click the NetWare Settings option. Next, click Startup and Login. Make sure the following options are selected: "Display Connection Page," "Display Script Page," "Display Variables Page," and "Restore Permanent Connections." Now you're really finished. Congratulations!

Automatic Client Upgrade for Windows 3.1

You can also use the Windows 3.1 Automatic Client Upgrade (ACU) program to upgrade NETx, VLMs, or older Client 32 files to the newest 32-bit connectivity drivers. As we learned earlier in the "Client 32 Installation for Windows 95" section, ACU uses fancy login scripts to automated the upgrade process. Here's how it works in the Windows 3.1 world:

Step 1: Choose a login script—container, profile, or user. The type of script you use depends on the type of workstation you want to upgrade. Refer to Chapter 6 for more information on IntranetWare login scripts.

Step 2: Install the Client 32 for Windows 3.1 files on a shared network server. Make sure users have Read and File Scan [RF] access rights to the SYS:PUBLIC\CLIENT\DOSWIN32 directory.

Step 3: Copy the ACU utilities and files to the Client 32 directory. These files are located in the SYS:PUBLIC\CLIENT\DOSWIN32\ADMIN\ DOS_ACU directory. **Note:** Be sure to use the "NCOPY /S" command for comprehensive copying. When you're finished, create a "LOG" subdirectory under SYS:PUBLIC\CLIENT\DOSWIN32 to store status information about each client upgrade process.

Step 4: Edit INSTALL.CFG. This ACU configuration file is located in the Client 32 parent directory (that is, SYS:PUBLIC\CLIENT\DOSWIN32). Make sure the "InstallType" setting is configured as "AUTO" so ACU workstations can be upgrade without user intervention:

```
[Setup]

    InstallType=AUTO
```

Step 5: Finally, it's time to configure the ACU login script. Add the following statements to the container, profile, or user script you chose in Step 1:

```
MAP I:=ACME-SRV1/SYS:PUBLIC\CLIENT\DOSWIN32
#I:NWDETECT Novell_Client32 4.1.0
```

```
IF ERROR_LEVEL = "1" THEN
        #I:INSTALL
        IF ERROR_LEVEL = "0" THEN
                #I:NWSTAMP Novell_Client32 4.1.0
                #I:NWLOG /F I:.\LOG\UPDATE.LOG
                #I:REBOOT
        END
END
MAP DEL I:
```

So, what's going on here? Here's a detailed description of this mysterious and magical ACU login script statement:

- ▶ Line 1: First, the "I:" drive is temporarily mapped to the Client 32/ACU parent directory. In this case, it's SYS:PUBLIC\CLIENT\DOSWIN32. The drive is removed at the end of the statement (Line 11).

- ▶ Line 2: NWDETECT is executed from the ACU parent directory using the "#" login script command. NWDETECT looks in the workstation's NET.CFG file for an Install Stamp. If no Install Stamp exists or if the stamp doesn't match "Novell_Client32 4.1.0," then NWDETECT returns an error code of "1".

- ▶ Line 3: If NWDETECT returns an error code of "1", the IF/THEN statement executes.

- ▶ Line 4: The Client 32 for Windows 3.1 installation program (INSTALL.EXE) runs from the Client 32 parent directory.

- ▶ Line 5: If the INSTALL.EXE program doesn't run successfully, it returns an error code of "1" and the nested IF/THEN statement doesn't run.

- ▶ Line 6: This is the first of three nested programs, once the Client 32 for Windows 3.1 installation program upgrades the workstation. NWSTAMP updates the client's NET.CFG file with the correct Install Stamp.

- ▸ Line 7: NWLOG writes a log file called "UPDATE.LOG" to the Client 32 LOG directory. It contains the date, time, username, IPX number, node address, and optionally, any message defined by you.

- ▸ Line 8: Finally, REBOOT automatically reboots the workstation so it can benefit from the new upgrade client software.

ZEN

"If I have the belief that I can do it, I shall surely acquire the capacity to do it even if I may not have had it at the beginning."

Mahatma Gandhi

Children aren't so bad. Once you get the hang of it, I think you might even enjoy adulthood. Having servers and workstations enables you to relive a little bit of your own childhood and adds years to your life (yeah, right). Of course, all the while, you must be thinking about the future and what happens when your children get children of their own. What a disaster. But let's not get ahead of ourselves. Now, let's take a moment to return to a simpler time and play in the 16-bit sandbox.

CLIENT 16 WORKSTATION ARCHITECTURE

Welcome to 16-bit land.

Earlier we learned that 16-bit workstations attack the local NIC and WOS in a slightly less-GUI way. As with most family matters, it all starts with communications. Figure 7.25 illustrates the bottom three layers of the 16-bit workstation architecture. Together, these files are part of a solution called ODI (Open Datalink Interface). Then, further workstation management is handled by a group of VLMs called the NetWare DOS Requester. They lie between the WOS and ODI to make transparent network communications possible. This is Leia making sure her brother David doesn't get into any trouble.

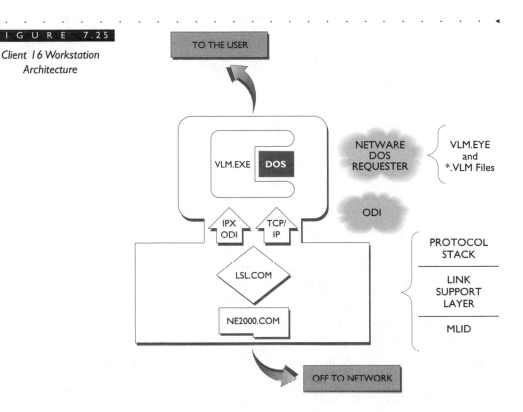

*Client 16 Workstation
Architecture*

Let's take a closer look at these two important pieces of the 16-bit workstation puzzle.

Open Datalink Interface

Interestingly, Open Datalink Interface (or ODI) is also the name of an old TV character and a cartoon dog. What does this mean? Using ODI, your network can run multiple protocols on the same cabling system. This enables devices that use different communication protocols to coexist on one WAN, thus increasing your network's functionality and flexibility. For example, both IPX and TCP/IP can run on the same workstation using the same NIC. This means that a user may concurrently access services from an IntranetWare server using IPX and a Unix host using TCP/IP. Very cool.

As you can see in Figure 7.25, the workstation ODI architecture consists of three main components:

▶ MLID (the Multiple Link Interface Driver)—This component interfaces with the internal NIC.

▶ LSL (the Link Support Layer)—Acts as a switchboard to route packets between MLID and the protocol stack.

▶ Protocol stack—One of three protocol-specific files used to translate and negotiate network communications. This is the real star of the ODI show.

Let's take a closer look.

MLID   It all starts at the bottom of the ODI picture-MLID. Each physical NIC has its own specific MLID driver. MLIDs accept any type of packet and either send them up to LSL or down to the NIC. In either case, MLIDs handle workstation communications. In IntranetWare, MLIDs come in various shapes and sizes-each matching the specific NIC. The MLID driver NE2000.COM, for example, handles communications for the Novell NE2000 NIC. Similarly, the MLID driver 3C5X9.COM handles communications for the popular 3COM 3C5X9 NIC. The beauty of the modular ODI approach is that MLID drivers can be loaded and unloaded as needed. Also, their configuration settings are handled by a single text file—NET.CFG.

Link Support Layer   The Link Support Layer (LSL) is the next point in the ODI picture. It acts as a switchboard to route packets between the MLID driver and appropriate protocol stack. LSL identifies the packet and then passes it to either IPX/SPX, TCP/IP, or AppleTalk. At the DOS workstation, LSL is implemented as LSL.COM. A IntranetWare client can use any of the three protocols because LSL directs information to the appropriate one. Think of it as your client traffic cop.

Protocol Stack   The final ODI layer contains protocol stacks such as IPX/SPX, TCP/IP, and AppleTalk. Once a packet arrives at the specific protocol stack, it either passes through and communicates with the NetWare DOS Requester, or is sent back down to another network. One of the main features of ODI is that it supports multiple protocols on the same cabling segment. This enables devices that allow different communication protocols to coexist on one network, thus increasing your WAN's functionality and flexibility. This is particularly important in IntranetWare because it is the foundation of a multiprotocol, multinational, and multilingual operating system. Protocol implementation for the default IPX/SPX LAN is handled by IPXODI.COM, whereas TCP/IP implementation works through TCPIP.EXE.

ODI loading at the workstation works a little bit differently. Although the MLID layer is the bottom and is the first point of contact for incoming packets, it is not the first ODI driver loaded—go figure. Here's how it works:

▸ LSL.COM

▸ 3C5X9.COM (or other *MLID*)

▸ IPXODI.COM (or other *protocol stack*)

As you learned in Chapter 6, customization and configuration of the ODI files is implemented using NET.CFG. So, how do you unload them? It's easy. Simply type the name followed by a /U. Make sure, however, that you unload the drivers in reverse order, because they build on top of each other. And always unload the NetWare DOS Requester before unloading ODI drivers.

ZEN

"Dishes. Relationships. Wind. This guy breaks everything!"

From the movie *Drop Dead Fred*

Once the packet finds its way up through the correct protocol stack, it's time for the WOS to take over. WOS connectivity at the IntranetWare client is handled by VLMs—the NetWare DOS Requester.

REAL WORLD

The ODI drivers have some interesting command line switches. Although these are not widely known, they can help you in special circumstances:

▶ IPXODI /C—Indicates an alternate filename for configuration information. This way, you can specify a different NET.CFG for ODI settings. The /c parameter also works with LSL and VLM.

▶ IPXODI /A—Eliminates the diagnostic responder and SPX communications. Although this reduces the memory size by 9 KB, it does eliminate support for RCONSOLE and dedicated print servers. Be careful when you use this option.

▶ IPXODI /D—eliminates the diagnostic responder only reducing memory size by 3 KB.

▶ IPXODI /F—Forcibly unloads IPXODI from memory, even if other modules are loaded above it. Use this only in extreme circumstances, because it might cause the system to hang.

▶ IPXODI /?—All the ODI and VLM drivers have detailed help screens.

NetWare DOS Requester

The NetWare DOS Requester is a connection point between your WOS and network services. A DOS workstation, for example, is typically a stand-alone computer. It uses a local operating system to provide basic local services. These services include file storage to local disks, screen display access, printer access, and communications. DOS itself and most WOSs are not capable of communicating with the network. Therefore, they need a little help.

VLMs to the rescue! As you can see in Figure 7.25, the NetWare DOS Requester is a marshmallow-looking thing that surrounds DOS and provides transparent connectivity between user applications and the network. It shares drive table information with DOS, therefore reducing memory usage. The Requester performs such tasks as file and print redirection, connection maintenance, and packet handling. This is all made possible through various modular files, VLMs. Each VLM performs a specific function, including PRINT.VLM for printer redirection, CONN.VLM for connectivity, FIO.VLM for file services, and NETX.VLM for backward compatibility to NETx. Of course, none of this could be possible without the conductor of our orchestra—VLM.EXE.

VLM.EXE manages 16-bit VLMs in an interesting load-order architecture. This model consists of three layers:

▶ Transport protocol—Maintains server connections and provides transmission and other transport-related services.

▶ Service protocol—Handles requests for specific services such as broadcast messages, file reads and writes, and print redirection. Service protocol VLMs are the heart and soul of IntranetWare client connectivity.

▶ DOS redirection—REDIR.VLM is responsible for DOS redirection services. The Requester makes an IntranetWare server look like a DOS driver to the user by having REDIR.VLM make decisions about client requests. This is analogous to the major functionality of NETX.EXE.

So, who's in charge here? The VLM manager—VLM.EXE. When you run it, it oversees the loading and sequencing of VLM files. Because VLMs are load-order dependent, you must make sure VLM.EXE activates them in the correct order. In addition, the NetWare DOS Requester supports two types of VLMs—core and optional. Core VLMs are activated automatically in a specific order when you execute VLM.EXE. There are 13 of them shown in Table 7.4—and they're listed in respective load order. Optional VLMs, on the other hand, can be activated by issuing the following commands under the NetWare DOS Requester section heading of NET.CFG:

```
NetWare DOS Requester
  VLM=C:\NWCLIENT\AUTO.VLM
  VLM=C:\NWCLIENT\RSA.VLM
  VLM=C:\NWCLIENT\NMR.VLM
```

As you can see in Table 7.4, these are the three most popular optional VLMs. In addition, you can exclude core VLMs from loading, but only if you follow these two steps: First, add the following statement to the NetWare DOS Requester section of NET.CFG:

```
USE DEFAULTS=OFF
```

Then, second, specify every VLM you do want to load in correct order. The bottom line is, you either load all 13 core VLMs, or specify the ones you want in correct order.

	LOAD ORDER	VLM	DESCRIPTION
TABLE 7.4 *Load Order for Core VLMs*	1	BIND.VLM	NetWare protocol implementation using bindery services. This is an optional core VLM for IntranetWare NDS. (Child)
	2	CONN.VLM	Connection table manager. Communicates between the three layers of VLM architecture. (Parent)
	3	FIO.VLM	File input and output services. (Parent)
	4	GENERAL.VLM	Miscellaneous functions for NETX.VLM and REDIR.VLM. (Child)
	5	IPXNCP.VLM	Transport protocol using IPX/SPX. (Child)
	6	NDS.VLM	NWP implementation using NDS support. This VLM is required for IntranetWare NDS. (Child)
	7	NETX.VLM	NetWare shell compatibility for previous versions of NetWare. (Parent)
	8	NWP.VLM	NetWare protocol multiplexer. This parent VLM overlooks key IntranetWare client services. (Parent)
	9	PNW.VLM	NWP implementation for Personal NetWare. (Child)
	10	PRINT.VLM	Printer redirector that provides CAPTURE capabilities for the DOS workstation. (Parent)
	11	REDIR.VLM	DOS redirector. This VLM performs most of the tasks of earlier NETx. (Parent)
	12	SECURITY.VLM	NetWare-enhanced security. (Parent)
	13	TRAN.VLM	The transport protocol multiplexer that oversees IPX and TCP/IP communications. (Parent)

The Requester supports DOS 3.1 and above, and works with extended, expanded, and conventional memory. VLM.EXE, by default, tries to load all VLMs in extended memory first. Expanded memory is the second choice, and, if extended or expanded memory is unavailable, conventional memory is used. VLM.EXE itself can be loaded in high memory, but this is not the default state. In addition to memory support, VLM has various switches that customize its activities.

▸ /?—Displays the help screen.

▸ /Mx—Loads VLM.EXE and associated files in conventional (C), expanded (E), or extended (X) memory.

▸ /Vx—Displays the detailed level of messaging where x runs from 0 to 4. Verbosity can display copyright messages and critical errors (0), warning messages (1), program load information (2), configuration information (3), or everything, including diagnostics (4).

▸ /PS—Specifies the preferred server during connection.

▸ /PT—Specifies the preferred tree during connection.

▸ /D—Displays file diagnostics such as status information, memory type, current ID, and VLM manager functioning.

Well, that just about does it for the NetWare DOS Requester and ODI. Both of these workstation connectivity strategies rely on workstation-specific configuration files for implementation and customization. As you learned in Chapter 6, NET.CFG enables CNAs to increase user transparency and pinpoint communication problems. In summary, here's what it does for ODI and VLMs:

▸ ODI—NET.CFG provides vital information for NIC configuration. It includes a section heading called LINK DRIVER for ODI support. CNAs can use this section to name the MLID file and specify hardware and software settings, including interrupt, I/O port, memory address, and frame type. Fortunately, you only need to use NET.CFG if you plan on deviating from the established ODI defaults.

▸ VLMs—NET.CFG can also be used to customize default VLM settings. As we saw earlier, it includes a NetWare DOS Requester section heading for defining workstation connections, the first network drive, and activating specific core and optional VLMs.

QUIZ

I was out house-hunting the other day, and this one really bothered me. There was this odd house, on which the two halves of the roof were unequally pitched. One half sloped downward at an angle of 60° (left) and the other half at an angle of 70° (right). I wondered, if a rooster layed an egg on the exact peak, where would the egg roll—left or right? Help.

(Q7-5)

Well, there you have it. Life in the 32-bit and 16-bit sandboxes. Aren't children grand. Don't they just take you back to a simpler life—no work and all play. Speaking of play, let's take a second to explore workstation management in the twilight zone—that is, Macintosh, OS/2, and Unix. I know you want to.

NON-DOS WORKSTATION SUPPORT

IntranetWare prides itself on the ability to transparently support a multitude of workstation environments. After all, IntranetWare was designed to provide centralized connectivity for diverse WANs spanning the globe. In other words, IntranetWare lets lots of different people talk to each other. So, how does it do it? As you can see in Figure 7.26, IntranetWare supports five workstation environments: three on the client side and two on the server side. If you access the network from a DOS, OS/2, or Windows 95 client, the connectivity software resides on the workstation. On the other hand, if you access the network from a Macintosh or Unix client, the connectivity software resides on the IntranetWare server. I wonder if Novell is making a subtle statement here.

Either way, the goal is to allow all of these five diverse clients to coexist on the same WAN. In addition, file and print services appear to each client using their native interface. Cool! This means DOS users operate with the C:\, and GUI users (Windows 95, Macintosh, and OS/2) hang out in folders. This may seem magic to the user, but it requires a great deal of work for you, the CNE. But wait! This isn't a CNE book. Thank goodness. Non-DOS workstation support is a CNE's job. It's not for CNAs. So, frolic in the innocence of CNAship, and now you have another great topic to look forward to when the CNE book arrives.

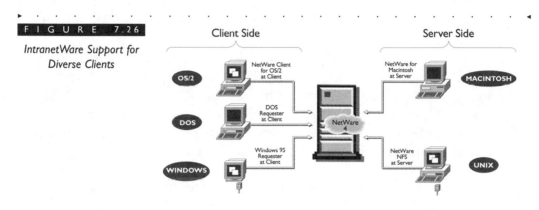

FIGURE 7.26

IntranetWare Support for Diverse Clients

ZEN

*"In dwelling, live close to the ground.
In thinking, keep to the simple.
In conflict, be fair and generous.
In governing, don't try to control.
In work, do what you enjoy.
In family life, be completely present."*

Tao Te Ching

Speaking of family, ours is growing quickly. We watched Leia go through a childhood of her own and now she's experiencing the growing pangs of parenthood. Of course, one of our most important parent responsibilities is the family. And we can learn an important lesson from the Girl Scouts of America-be prepared! Let's continue our journey through adulthood with a detailed look at the "second half" of life—pension and retirement.

Storage Management Services

Call it a pension, a "nest egg," or whatever you like, planning for the future is important business. With a family comes serious financial concerns—college education, emergency fund, and retirement. And these financial decisions aren't as simple as they used to be. You must choose among IRAs, annuities, mutual funds, pension plans, and (my old favorite) the "sock in the bedpost." Regardless of what you do, it's critical that you plan for the future.

One of the most exciting things about life is that you never know what's around the corner. To be prepared, you must have a backup plan. Also, as your network grows in complexity, the value of its services grows as well. And we all know nothing becomes more valuable until it is lost. That's Murphy's Law Number 193.

Welcome to IntranetWare backup. Backup provides both a prevention and maintenance strategy:

▸ Prevention—Backup is a proactive strategy toward disaster recovery. You don't want to be wondering what to do *after* the data is lost.

▸ Maintenance—Backup doesn't always prevent a disaster from occurring; it simply expedites recovery.

As soon as your network data is lost, file backup should be the first thing that pops into your mind. In many cases, having current backups can spell the difference between a successful and prosperous CNA career and the unemployment line. *Never* neglect your IntranetWare backup duties. Fortunately, IntranetWare includes a versatile new backup feature called Storage Management Services (SMS).

SMS is a combination of related services that enable data to be stored and retrieved. The SMS backup process involves a *host* server and a *target*. The host server is the IntranetWare machine on which the backup program resides. The target is the IntranetWare server or client that contains the data needing to be backed up. In addition, SMS uses an application on the host server to communicate with modules on target devices—SBACKUP.NLM is included for free. This discussion first explores the fundamental architecture of SMS. Then we'll take a closer look at backing up and restoring data using the default SMS application—SBACKUP.NLM. What are we waiting for? Let's go.

SMS ARCHITECTURE

As you learned earlier, SMS is a combination of related services that enable you to store and retrieve data from various targets—Target Service Agents (TSAs). SMS operates as a backup engine that is independent from the front-end application and back-end device. As you can see in Figure 7.27, SMS supports various TSA front-ends, including IntranetWare file systems, NDS, DOS and OS/2 file systems, and BTRIEVE databases. Any or all of these resources can be backed up to various back-end devices including DOS read/write disks, tape, and optical drives.

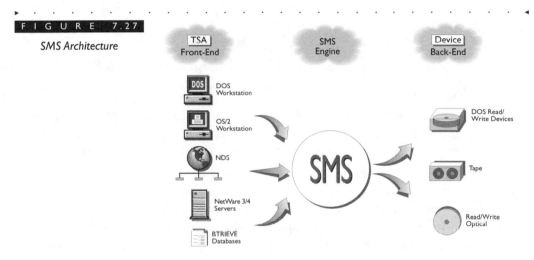

FIGURE 7.27

SMS Architecture

There are three main components to the SMS architecture model:

▸ Device drivers

▸ SBACKUP.NLM

▸ Target Service Agents

You can see the interaction among these components in Figure 7.28. The device drivers interface between SBACKUP.NLM and the internal host device. Then, SBACKUP uses Target Service Agents to activate source file systems. Let's take a closer look.

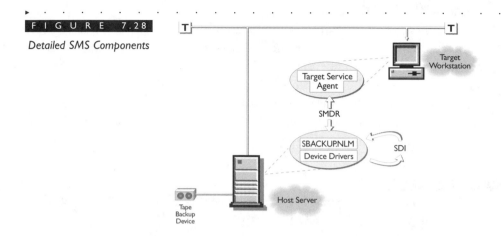

F I G U R E   7.28

Detailed SMS Components

Device Drivers

Device drivers lie at the bottom of the SMS model. They control the mechanical operation of the host storage device. In addition, they must be specifically configured for each backup device and interface with the SBACKUP.NLM application. When device drivers are loaded, SBACKUP recognizes the storage device.

Device drivers are loaded at the host server and therefore must be NLMs. The following files are included with IntranetWare: TAPEDAI.DSK (Novell's generic tape driver for most ASPI-compatible SCSI controllers); MNS*.DSK (Mountain Backup devices); PS2SCSI.DSK (for IBM PS2 SCSI controllers); and AHA*.DSK (Adaptec SCSI devices). Before SBACKUP.NLM recognizes the host device, you must register it with IntranetWare using the following command:

```
SCAN FOR NEW DEVICES
```

SBACKUP.NLM

The backup application (SBACKUP, in this case) communicates with device drivers through SDI—the Storage Device Interface. It is loaded as an NLM on the host server. Once the backup device is activated, you can enter the SMS application—SBACKUP.NLM. This utility works within the SMS architecture to route data requests from the source and to the device through SDI. Interestingly, we are now backing up clients from the server—isn't this backward? Later in this section, we'll explore the ins and outs of using SBACKUP.NLM.

Target Service Agents

The final component in the SMS architecture model is TSAs—Target Service Agents. TSAs must be loaded on target servers or workstations. SBACKUP.NLM recognizes TSAs through the Storage Management Data Requester (SMDR), which is an NLM running on the host server. IntranetWare supports various TSAs, including:

▸ IntranetWare server—TSA411

▸ NetWare 4 server—TSA410 or TSA400

▸ NetWare 3 server—TSA312 or TSA311

▸ DOS workstation—TSADOS and TSASMS

▸ OS/2 workstation—TSAPROXY and TSAOS2

▸ Macintosh workstation—TSAMAC and TSASMS

▸ NDS database—TSANDS

▸ Btrieve SQL Databases—TSASQL

Remember, if you're backing up data on the host server, you still have to load TSA410 and TSANDS. Finally, SBACKUP.NLM only recognizes targets that have loaded the appropriate TSA module.

ZEN

"Don't hurry, don't worry. You're only here for a short visit. So, be sure to stop and smell the flowers."

Walter Hagen

Now that you understand the fundamental SMS architecture, let's explore SBACKUP.NLM in more depth. Keep in mind, any third-party backup application can be used with SMS, as long as it follows this fundamental design.

USING SBACKUP

At the heart of the SMS model is the backup application. IntranetWare includes a starter program called SBACKUP.NLM. You can use any server application, as long as it's SMS-compliant. SBACKUP, for example, is an NLM that operates at the IntranetWare server and communicates directly with the host backup device. Running SBACKUP at the server has its advantages. First, it supports multiple file server connections at one time. Also, it operates faster because it doesn't cause an additional communications load on the network. Because the tape unit is connected directly to the file server, SBACKUP doesn't route packets over the LAN. Finally, SBACKUP supports a wide variety of backup devices because of their independent *.DSK device drivers.

Just like any application, you'll have to learn the SBACKUP "lingo" to use it efficiently. Following are a few terms you should be aware of:

▸ Host—The IntranetWare server running SBACKUP.NLM. Also, the backup device is attached to it.

▸ Target—Any IntranetWare server, workstation, or NDS database that has a TSA loaded. This is where the backup source material resides.

▸ Parent—A data set that may have subordinate data sets. In IntranetWare, a parent would be a directory, a subdirectory, or a container.

▸ Child—A data set that has no subordinates. In IntranetWare, for example, a child would be a file or leaf object.

Let's explore SBACKUP.NLM by first learning about its four main backup strategies. Then we'll discuss some guidelines before diving into the detailed steps of SMS backup and restore.

SMART LINK

For a more in-depth discussion of SBACKUP and backup/restore procedures, surf the Web to http://www.novell.com/manuals.

Backup Strategies

So how does it work? SBACKUP provides four strategies that can be used for backing up and restoring data. Each strategy provides a different balance of performance and efficiency. In Figure 7.29, you can see the three main strategies—full, incremental, and differential. Here's how they work.

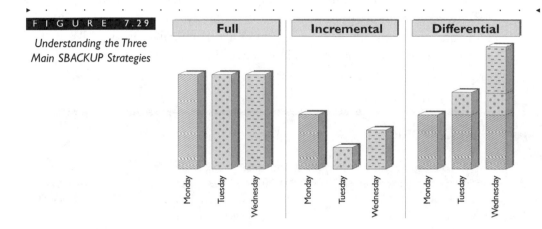

FIGURE 7.29

Understanding the Three Main SBACKUP Strategies

As you can see in Figure 7.29, the full backup option is the most thorough. It is, however, not practical. During a full backup, all data is copied, regardless of when or if it has been previously backed up. While this option is the most time-consuming, it does allow for very fast and easy restores—you only have to restore the latest full backup. During a full backup, the "Modify" bit of each file is cleared—we'll discuss why a little later. (Incidentally, the "Modify" bit is a file attribute that changes each time a file is modified. It is the same as the "Archive Needed" attribute from Chapter 5.)

The second option (incremental) backs up only the files that have changed since the last backup. Although this option offers a quick backup, restoring can be quite a nightmare. In order to restore all the data, you must restore the last full backup and every incremental backup since then, *in order.* If one is missing or doesn't work, you're up a creek. During an incremental backup, the "Modify" bit of each file is cleared, so SBACKUP skips them the next time.

The differential backup is a new and interesting strategy. It backs up all the data that has been modified since the last full backup. Differential backup is the best balance of efficiency and performance because it minimizes the number of restore sessions. You only need to restore the last full and the latest differential.

Also, the backup session is optimized because only the files that have changed are being copied.

The main improvement with the differential strategy is the state of the "Modify" bit—it is *not* cleared. This way, all the files that have changed since the last full backup are copied each time. This is why the full backup strategy clears the modify bit. Notice in Figure 7.29 how the volume of data systematically increases. One word of warning, however—since the "Modify" bit is also cleared during an incremental backup, this can mess up your differential strategy. Make sure you never perform an incremental backup between differential and full backups.

REAL WORLD

As you can see, the incremental and differential backup strategies provide many options when backing up and restoring IntranetWare data. They don't, however, allow you to back up NDS. Only the full backup strategy can backup the NDS database. This is a very important point to keep in mind when planning your backup schedule.

The fourth and final SBACKUP strategy is "custom." The custom method enables you to specify which files are backed up, and whether the "Modify" bit is cleared. This provides the ultimate level of flexibility.

Table 7.5 shows a comparison of the four SBACKUP strategies. The best combination is

▸ Every day—Differential

▸ Once a week on Friday—Full

▸ Once a month—Custom

Once you've chosen your backup strategy, you must follow some simple SBACKUP guidelines during backup and restore sessions. Let's take a look.

T A B L E 7.5	SBACKUP STRATEGY	BACKUP	RESTORE	MODIFY BIT
Understanding the Four Main SBACKUP Strategies	Full	Slow	Easy	Cleared
	Incremental	Quick	Hard	Cleared
	Differential	Quick	Easy	Not cleared
	Custom	Whatever	Your choice	Doesn't matter

Guidelines

You gotta have rules. Without rules, the world would be a very wacky place. Let me rephrase that—the world would be an even wackier place. SBACKUP is no exception. Here are a few guidelines you must follow when using this SMS application:

▸ Make sure you have enough disk space on the host server's SYS: volume for temporary files and log files (1 MB should be sufficient). Run SBACKUP.NLM from an IntranetWare server and attach the backup device to the same host server. Also, be sure to run updated support NLMs (such as STREAMS, SPXS, TLI, CLIB, and NWSNUT).

▸ Limit access to SBACKUP to maintain the security of your IntranetWare server and to ensure data integrity. Also, be aware that security can be compromised if a delayed backup session does not fit on inserted media. If you are prompted to insert another tape, the program pauses at that point and does not exit. To reduce this risk, set APPEND to NO.

▸ When you are entering a filename that has a non-DOS format, use the DOS equivalent naming scheme. SBACKUP does support OS/2 and Macintosh naming schemes, but the application interface doesn't. So, even though you're backing up long filenames (September99, for example), they appear in their DOS equivalent (September, for example). You can track this by using the SBACKUP error and backup log files. They display both the DOS equivalent and the name space version of each directory or file.

► Monitor the size of SBACKUP temporary files. SBACKUP creates temporary files on the target server as well as the host machine. These temporary files may become quite large if you have extended attributes or linked Unix files.

► Do not mount or dismount volumes or unload drivers during a backup session. You may corrupt data or abend the host server—duh!

► Know the passwords assigned to target servers and workstations.

ZEN

"Don't wait for your ship to come in; swim out to it!"

Anonymous

QUIZ

The "Puzzler" strikes again:
What will you break even if you name it?
What fastens two people yet touches only one?
What grows larger the more you take away?
What grows larger the more you contract it?

(Q7-6)

Backup Steps

Once you understand these guidelines, you're ready to perform your first SMS backup using SBACKUP.NLM. I can hardly contain my excitement. Follow the bouncing ball as we outline the seven steps of an SMS backup. For a more detailed walkthrough, try it yourself. C'mon in, the water's fine.

1 • Load the backup device driver on the host server.

2 • Load appropriate TSA drivers on all target devices. This includes the host server, if you plan on backing it up. When you load the TSAs, all support modules are activated automatically.

3 • Load SBACKUP.NLM at the host server. Once you've activated SBACKUP, certain support modules are automatically loaded, including SMDR. The SBACKUP main menu is then displayed, as shown in Figure 7.30.

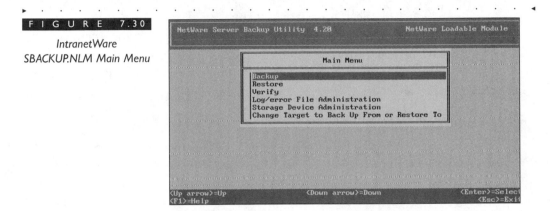

4 • Select a target to be backed up from the TSA list. **Note:** Targets will only appear if the appropriate TSAs have been loaded properly. You can get to the TSA list by choosing the "Change Target to Back Up From or Restore To" option from the main menu of SBACKUP.NLM. If you choose a remote server, you'll be asked for a valid username and password for authentication. Recall you can only back up files matching that user's access rights.

5 • Select the backup device from an Available Options list. The list should reflect all devices that are attached to the host server and have appropriate drivers loaded. If only one backup device driver is loaded, SBACKUP automatically selects this device. The list appears when you choose Storage Device Administration from the main menu of SBACKUP.NLM.

6 • Perform appropriate SBACKUP administration, including selecting a location for the log and error file, selecting the type of backup, and providing a session description. All of these tasks are accomplished using the Log/Error File Administration option within the main menu.

7 • Finally, you're ready to back up. You can either proceed "now" or "later." If you choose "later," you'll be prompted for a date and time. If you choose "now," you'll be asked to insert the backup media and enter a unique label for it.

You're finished. That wasn't so difficult. Whatever you do, don't *trust* your backup. Always test SBACKUP tapes by selectively restoring them at regular intervals. This might involve restoring random files to a secondary volume or the entire SBACKUP session. Whatever you do, don't discover SBACKUP doesn't work after you've lost your disk.

Restore Steps

This is where "Murphy" comes in. If you must restore, something bad happened. Let's hope you never have to implement the following seven steps. But, before you begin, make sure the target server or workstation has enough free disk space. It must have approximately 20 percent *more* than the amount needed to restore. The overhead space stores temporary files and additional name space information. Here's a brief outline of the SBACKUP restore steps:

1 • Load the backup device driver on the host server (same as Backup Step 1).

2 • Load the appropriate TSA software on all targets you wish to restore to. This includes the host server if you plan on restoring to it.

3 • Load SBACKUP.NLM at the host server (same as Backup Step 3).

4 • Select a target to restore to. The Available Options within SBACKUP should reflect all devices that have loaded the appropriate TSA. Once again, this is accomplished using the "Change Target to Backup From or Restore To" option from the main menu of SBACKUP. Once you choose a TSA, a list of recognized restore sessions will appear. Select one.

5 • Perform SBACKUP administration, including selecting a location for the log and error file and inserting the backup media.

6 • Select a restore device from the Available Options list. This list should match all attached devices and loaded drivers. If only one backup device driver is loaded, SBACKUP automatically selects this device.

7 • Now, we finally get to restore. First, select the type of restore from the following list of three—One File or Directory, Entire Session, or Custom Restore. Second, choose the files and objects you want to restore. Finally, select one of the following restore options—"Proceed now" or "Later."

There you have it. Let's hope you never have to perform a "real" SBACKUP restore. You should practice, though—every week.

ZEN

"Learn not to sweat the small stuff."

Dr. Kenneth Greenspan

THE BRAIN

When backing up NDS with SBACKUP, there are a number of issues to be aware of. These are covered in detail in an AppNote entitled "Backing Up and Restoring NetWare Directory Services in NetWare 4" in the August 1995 *Novell Application Notes*.

Well, that wasn't so hard, was it? That's SBACKUP.NLM in a nutshell. After you've completed the SBACKUP steps each day, you'll find a certain peace of mind knowing that you have these hot little tapes in your hands. It matches the peace of mind knowing that your children can go to college and someday you'll finally get to retire to the beaches of Tahiti. But, that time is not now, so stop daydreaming and move on to the final section of IntranetWare SMS—other SMS considerations.

OTHER SMS CONSIDERATIONS

We're not quite finished yet. In order to take full advantage of IntranetWare's SMS feature, you'll need to explore a few other considerations. They are

▶ Who does it?

▶ Workstation backup

▶ SMS management

So, who's the lucky person? Probably you. Count your blessings because you're the lucky person chosen to be the SBACKUP administrator. Remember, you wanted to be a CNA. In addition to understanding the rights needed for SMS duties, you must understand the special drivers that load at the SMS workstation. Finally, there are a few SMS management issues that can help you troubleshoot and optimize SBACKUP duties. Any questions? Good, time to move on.

Who Does It?

Being assigned SBACKUP responsibilities is a dubious distinction. Although it has its status in the IntranetWare management realm, it also has a price. You don't want to mess up here. The person you assign to back up your network must have certain qualifications and access privileges, including:

▶ The backup administrator needs Read and File Scan (RF) access rights to the files he or she plans to back up. The administrator will also need additional rights for restoring (RWCEMF).

▶ The backup administrator will need the Browse Object right and Read Property right for backing up NDS information.

▶ The backup administrator must know the password on all servers and workstations that act as hosts and targets. A standard naming scheme would be a great idea at this point.

If you're the lucky soul chosen as SBACKUP administrator, continue with the next two considerations. If not, go grab a soda.

Workstation Backup

As if by some inspiration, Novell finally allows workstation backup from the server. This long-awaited feature has been implemented in the new SMS. SMS uses SBACKUP.NLM to back up and restore information from local DOS or OS/2 workstations. You can back up certain directories or the entire workstation including floppy and hard drives.

The DOS workstation TSA is a TSR (terminate-and-stay-resident) program that you can run on any target workstation. Some DOS TSA options include /P for password, /T for no password, and /D for drive designation. Here's how the TSA works:

1 • Load TSADOS.NLM at the server for DOS workstations and TSAPROXY.NLM for OS/2.

2 • Load TSASMS.COM at the DOS workstation and TSAOS2.COM at the OS/2 workstation. This is where you specify the TSA parameters we just discussed. One additional parameter you may want to employ is /N to give the workstation a unique name. This name will appear in the TSA list of SBACKUP.NLM.

3 • Select the appropriate DOS TSA from the SBACKUP target list. The name that appears should match the name given in Step 2.

Workstation backup is a cool feature, but make sure that you use the correct parameters with the DOS TSA and that you remember to load the appropriate NLMs at the host server. And, if those are not enough to worry about, check out the next discussion.

SMS Management

A few SMS management issues can help you journey through the SBACKUP jungle. Let's start with performance. The speed of SBACKUP varies depending on the configuration and location of the data being backed up. If a file server backs up its own data, for example, it runs about four times faster than if it backs up data from a remote server. The difference is because of the communications required between the host server and the target servers. The speed of communications also depends on the availability of packet receive buffers at the host server.

Next, let's talk about SBACKUP session files. Session files are "backup logs" that contain information to help you effectively manage SMS backups. The information also facilitates the restore process and helps you to troubleshoot anything that goes wrong. The two most important session files are the backup log and error log. The backup log consists of a list of all data backed up during the session and the media ID, session date and time, session description, and location of data on the storage media.

The error file, on the other hand, is generated on the host server when a particular group of data is initially backed up. It contains the same header data as the backup log, but also provides error information (such as the names of files that were not backed up, files that were not restored, who accessed the NDS database, and error codes). As you recall from our earlier discussion, we identified the location of these session files during Step 6 of the backup process.

Now we're really finished. Congratulations! You've been made SBACKUP administrator. I hope you understand the responsibility that accompanies this honor. But, if you perform your duties admirably, everyone will treat you like a hero.

Pension planning works much the same way. Although it's a dubious honor to be responsible for the family's financial future, many times the rewards greatly outweigh the pain. I see a trend here. All I know is, retirement in Tahiti is sounding better and better all the time.

QUIZ

Here's a quick brain-stretching exercise before you tackle IntranetWare retirement:

A common English word can be made from the letters on the top row of a standard typewriter. For those of you who do not have a typewriter keyboard handy, the letters are Q, W, E, R, T, Y, U, I, O, P. Not all letters must be used and some letters may be used more than once.

(Q7-7)

Remote Management Facility

The final step in our life journey is retirement-RMF. Our life's been an exciting adventure and now it's time to kick back and put it in cruise control. Welcome to Happy Acres!

Now, no one is saying that retirement has to be boring. Quite the contrary: It provides us with an opportunity to enjoy all the adventures we never had time for in the past. You can learn to scuba dive, hang-glide, golf, and even bungee jump. And the best part is, you get to do it on your own terms. It sure sounds appealing—where do I sign up?

RMF is the final step in IntranetWare configuration and management. It enables you to manage all your IntranetWare file servers from one central location. This is particularly useful because file server security states that the machine should be locked away in a cabinet with no monitor or keyboard. Also, IntranetWare prides itself on managing multiple servers spanning wide geographic boundaries. In both cases, you'll spend more time trying to access the servers than doing the important stuff—maintaining and managing them.

Now, let's take a moment to explore the details of RMF and learn how it can help you enjoy your new IntranetWare retirement.

RMF ARCHITECTURE

So, how does it work? As you can see in Figure 7.31, RMF supports access from both the workstation and a modem. In either case, it consists of two main components: server NLMs and RCONSOLE.EXE.

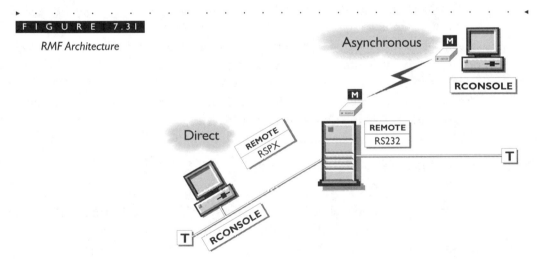

FIGURE 7.31

RMF Architecture

The RMF server NLMs are broken into two functions—REMOTE and connection services. The REMOTE.NLM module manages information exchange to and from the workstation and the server. In addition, REMOTE.NLM enables you to specify an RMF password.

Connection services are a little bit trickier. As you remember from our earlier discussion, RMF supports access from both a direct workstation or from a modem.

In either case, the connection NLM is different. When you access RMF from a direct workstation, connection services are provided by RSPX.NLM. This module provides communication support and advertises the server's availability for remote access. On the other hand, when you access RMF from an asynchronous modem, connection services are provided by RS232.NLM. This module initializes the server modem port and transfers screen and keystroke information to REMOTE.NLM.

Let's take a closer look.

ZEN

"Millions long for immortality who do not know what to do with themselves on a rainy Sunday afternoon."

Susan Ertz

SPX

The most popular RMF connection approach is direct—through SPX. Direct connection services are provided through the RSPX.NLM module. When you load RSPX, you have the option of requiring packet signatures—this ensures security. The default is ON, which means that packet signatures are required. However, packets with signatures are not compatible with NetWare 3.11. If your IntranetWare server coexists with NetWare 3.11 machines, you'll need to deactivate packet signing by using the SIGNATURES OFF switch with RSPX.

In summary, the server modules required for a direct RMF connection are

```
LOAD REMOTE
LOAD RSPX
```

Finally, a quick note about REMOTE passwords. As you learned earlier in the chapter, REMOTE.NLM includes a password facility that enables you to restrict access to the server console. As a matter of fact, in IntranetWare, a REMOTE password is required. This creates a security loophole when the command is placed in AUTOEXEC.NCF. To work around this weakness, consider using LDREMOTE and encrypted passwords. See the earlier "Server Protection" discussion for more details.

> **TIP**
>
> **If you use the IPXODI /A parameter to deactivate SPX and gain conventional workstation RAM, RCONSOLE won't work. I wouldn't want you to be surprised at a bad time.**

Asynchronous

In addition to a direct connection, RMF supports asynchronous connectivity. As you can see in Figure 7.31, the remote workstation can be attached to the server via a modem. This means that you really can manage the IntranetWare server from Tahiti. In this case, connection services are provided by the RS232.NLM module. When you load RS232.NLM, IntranetWare will ask you for some simple modem configurations, including the communications port number, baud rate, and an option for callback.

A callback list enables you to create a list of authorized modem numbers that can be used to access the server. When a connection attempt is made, the server notes the number of the modem that is calling and then terminates the connection. The server then compares the number to the numbers in the call-back list. If the number is in the list, the server calls the modem at that number and re-establishes the connection. If it is not, the server ignores the call. This is another security feature that limits "hacker" access to your server console.

In summary, the following NLM command entries must be given at the IntranetWare server to activate asynchronous RMF:

```
LOAD REMOTE
LOAD RS232 1 9600 C
```

In this example, "1" is the com port, "9600" is the modem speed, and "C" activates the call-back option. The authorized list is defined as CALLBACK.LST in the SYS:SYSTEM directory.

Table 7.6 summarizes these two RMF options.

T A B L E 7.6	DIRECT SPX	ASYNCHRONOUS MODEM
Understanding RMF	REMOTE.NLM	REMOTE.NLM
	RSPX.NLM	RS232.NLM

Whether you're accessing RMF from a direct workstation or asynchronous modem, you will need RCONSOLE.EXE.

REAL WORLD

The SPX and Asynchronous connections differ dramatically in how they affect network traffic and server utilization. The SPX method increases network traffic, but doesn't have a noticeable effect on server utilization. Conversely, the Asynchronous method generates little network traffic, but causes considerable overhead at the server. For this reason, the Asynchronous connection method shouldn't be used during peak hours.

USING RCONSOLE

RCONSOLE is the front-end for IntranetWare RMF. It provides direct access to the IntranetWare server console screen from a workstation and enables you to perform any task as if you were standing right in front of it. In addition, RCONSOLE provides an Available Options menu with supplemental tasks, including changing screens, scanning server directories, and performing a remote install. All in all, RCONSOLE is your friend because it enables you to enjoy the good life without having to run around like a chicken with your head cut off.

Like most IntranetWare utilities, RCONSOLE has both DOS and Windows versions. The DOS version is executed as RCONSOLE.EXE at any workstation DOS prompt. RCONSOLE.EXE resides in the SYS:PUBLIC subdirectory, but you may want to move it to SYS:SYSTEM to ensure it doesn't fall into the wrong hands.

Whether you access RCONSOLE from DOS or Windows, you'll get the same main screen asking the same simple question: "What connection type do you want?" The available choices are SPX (for a direct connection) or Asynchronous (for a modem connection). The SPX option brings up a list of available servers as shown in Figure 7.32. Once you choose a server, the password prompt appears. Upon entering the correct password, you'll find yourself staring at the all-too-familiar colon prompt (:). Figure 7.33 shows the Remote Server console screen from the "Tools" option in NWADMIN.

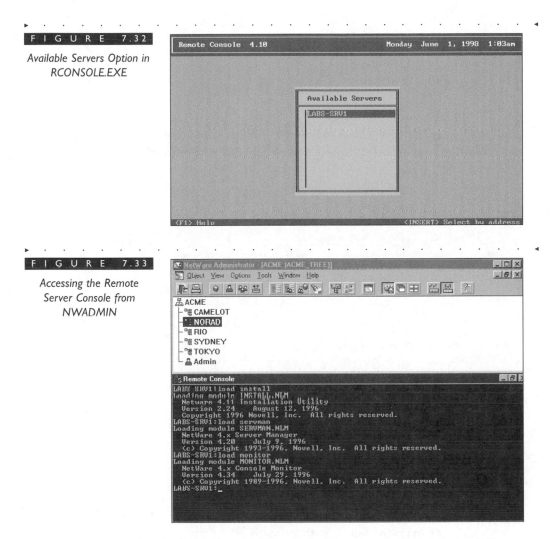

Available Servers Option in RCONSOLE.EXE

Accessing the Remote Server Console from NWADMIN

On the other hand, if you choose the asynchronous connection type, a different menu appears. The Asynchronous Options menu provides two choices: Connect to Remote Location and Configuration. From here, you can either dial a remote server or configure your local modem. Once your connection is established, a callback list will be activated and/or the password prompt will appear. Once again, after you enter the correct password, you'll find yourself staring down the barrel of the IntranetWare console (as in Figure 7.33).

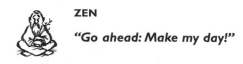

ZEN

"Go ahead: Make my day!"

Clint Eastwood

Once the RCONSOLE session is established, you can perform any available server task as if you were standing in the wiring closet yourself—closed quarters. In addition to standard console activities, you can perform various special RCONSOLE tasks, including:

- ▶ Change screens

- ▶ Scan server directories

- ▶ Transfer files to the server

- ▶ Shell to DOS

- ▶ End remote session

- ▶ Resume remote session

- ▶ View your local workstation address

- ▶ Configure keystroke buffering

SMART LINK

Access a "real" IntranetWare server using RCONSOLE. It's as easy as http://www.cyberstateu.com

All of these fun-filled activities are accomplished using the RMF Available Options menu. This menu is activated by pressing the Alt+F1 keys simultaneously and can be seen in Figure 7.34. Also, a list of RCONSOLE function keys can be found in Table 7.7.

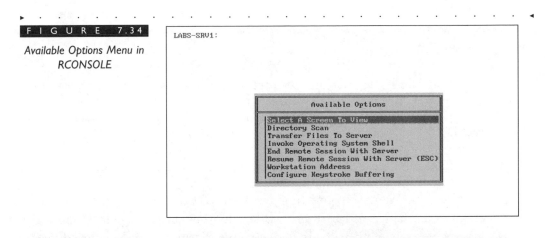

FIGURE 7.34

Available Options Menu in
RCONSOLE

TABLE 7.7	KEYS	TASK
IntranetWare RCONSOLE Function Keys	Alt+F1	View the RMF Available Options menu.
	Alt+F2	Exit RCONSOLE.
	Alt+F3	Move forward through the server console screens. Similar to Alt+Esc at the physical server console itself.
	Alt+F4	Move backward through the server console screens.
	Alt+F5	Show your workstation address.
	F1	Display remote console help from within the Available Options menu.
	Esc	Resume remote session with server.

Whenever a remote session is granted to RCONSOLE, the file server broadcasts a message to the error log and console prompt, indicating that a remote session was attempted at a particular node address and whether or not it was granted. This is useful information if you like to track who's accessing the file server colon prompt using RMF—good idea!

Well, that does it. Your life in a nutshell!

We've brought our LAN from birth through childhood and the rewards of adulthood. Through IntranetWare configuration and management, we've transformed a relatively limp and lifeless LAN into a powerful and productive business tool. How did we do it?

> ## REAL WORLD
>
> RMF is cool. RMF is so cool, in fact, that it enables you to remotely install IntranetWare. Talk about extended vacations! This means you can actually install an IntranetWare server in Camelot from Tahiti. Think of it. Sand between your toes and SERVER.EXE bouncing through your head. Just be sure to copy the PUBLIC files locally, or you're in for an unhappy phone bill!

In IntranetWare configuration, we walked Leia through the five steps of childhood. She learned to walk (workstation connectivity), talk (login scripts), and get along with others in preschool (menu system). Then she enjoyed the many splendors of school (network applications) and finally moved out (e-mail).

In IntranetWare management, Leia continued her "life span" through marriage (server installation and management) and children of her own (workstation management). Now, in her later years, Leia planned her pension (SMS) and finally retired to Tahiti (RMF).

It was a long and winding road, but certainly an adventure for all of us. No matter how much you might want to, you can't just set up the server and walk away. You're a CNA, and, as one, your life is irrevocably bound to the childhood and adulthood of IntranetWare.

SMART LINK

Explore your own IntranetWare Childhood at http://www.kids.com or Adulthood at http://www.aronson.com/ppp/birth.html.

QUIZ

This pretty much sums up IntranetWare childhood and adulthood:

"Individuals who are completely devoid of sapience in all respects indicate a propensity to cast themselves without hesitation onto those areas where beings of a heavenly nature would reflect seriously and be timorous about proceeding."

(Q7-8)

CASE STUDY: SIMPLE INSTALLATION FOR ACME

As you know, saving the world is a challenging task. Fortunately, ACME is on the job. In this simple installation exercise, we will install ACME's very first server—ACME-SRV1. Remember, a simple installation makes numerous decisions for you—such as where to put the server. In this case, it must be O=ACME. Which, of course, is in Camelot.

Have fun and enjoy ACME. After all, no one said saving the world had to be a drag.

I. PREPARE THE SERVER HARD DISK

a.   Step 1: Configure the server DOS partition.

(1) Back up existing data. Choose a computer to be used as the server and make at least two backup copies of all data. (Remember: All existing data on this computer's hard disk will be destroyed during the server installation process!)

(2) Create a boot diskette. Insert a blank diskette in drive A:. Make it bootable by typing **FORMAT A: /S**. After the disk is formatted, copy the following files to it:

(a) Required files: C:\DOS\FDISK.EXE, C:\DOS\FORMAT.COM, the appropriate CD-ROM drivers, plus any other drivers that your computer needs in order to operate properly. (Be sure that you make a printout of your AUTOEXEC.BAT and CONFIG.SYS so that you can see the proper syntax for executing each driver.)

(b) Optional files: C:\DOS\EDIT.COM and C:\DOS\MEM.EXE.

(3) Use FDISK to delete existing partitions and create a 15 MB DOS partition. (The directions listed here were designed for use with MS-DOS v6.2. The steps required for your version of DOS may differ.)

(a) Display the existing partitions. Make sure the bootable disk you made in the previous step is in drive A:. Type **A:** and press Enter to switch to the floppy drive. Type **FDISK** and press Enter to execute the FDISK command. Type **4** and press Enter to select the Display Partition Information option. Take note of the number and type of partitions that exist on your hard disk. Press Esc to return to the previous menu.

(b) Delete a non-DOS partition (if one exists). To delete a non-DOS partition, type **3** and press Enter to choose the Delete partition or Logical DOS Drive option. Type **4** and press Enter to choose the Delete Non-DOS Partition option. When you are prompted, key in the number of the non-DOS partition to be deleted and press Enter. Type **Y** and press Enter when you are asked if you wish to continue. Note the number and type of partitions remaining. Press Esc to return to the FDISK Options menu. At this point, the only partition remaining should be your DOS partition. If there are Extended, Logical, or Non-DOS partitions remaining, execute the appropriate menu choices to delete them.

(c) Delete the primary DOS partition. Type **3** and press Enter to select the Delete partition or Logical DOS Drive option. Type **1** and press Enter to select the Delete Primary DOS Partition option. When you are asked what primary DOS partition to delete, type the number of the Primary DOS partition and press Enter. When you are asked for the volume label of the Primary DOS partition, type the volume label and press Enter. (Press Enter alone if the partition has no volume label.) When you are asked whether you are sure, type **Y** and press Enter. Press Esc to return to the FDISK Options screen.

(d) Create a 15-MB DOS partition. Type **1** and press Enter to select the Create DOS partition or Logical DOS Drive option. Type **1** and press Enter to select the Create Primary DOS Partition option. Type **N** and press Enter when you are asked whether you wish to use the maximum available size for a Primary DOS Partition. Type **15** and press Enter when you are asked to enter a partition size in megabytes or percentage of disk space. (It will assume that you are entering the number in megabytes if you don't use a percent sign.)

You may notice that the installation program creates a partition that is slightly larger than 15 MB. Press Esc to return to the FDISK Options screen. Type **2** and press Enter to select the Set Active Partition option. Type **1** and press Enter when you are prompted for the number of the partition you want to make active. Press Esc to return to the FDISK Options screen. Press Esc again to exit the FDISK utility.

When you are prompted to insert a system diskette into drive A: and strike a key, just press any key. This will cause the computer to reboot. When you are prompted for the correct date, key in the correct date if an incorrect one is displayed and press Enter. (Press Enter alone to accept the default.) When you are prompted for the correct time, key in the correct time if an incorrect one is displayed and press Enter. (Press Enter alone to accept the default.) If this is your only server and the date and/or time listed is incorrect, this would be a good time to change the "hardware" date and time using the CMOS setup program built into your computer. (If you have a relatively recent version of DOS, you may find that the DATE and TIME commands do this for you.) See the manual that came with your computer for the exact procedure.

(4) Format the DOS partition and make it bootable. Type **FORMAT C: /S** and press Enter to format the DOS partition and install system files. Type **Y** and press Enter when you are asked whether to proceed with the format. Type **ACME-SRV1** and press Enter when you are asked for a volume label.

(5) Install and configure the CD-ROM drive as a DOS device. Execute the installation program included with your CD-ROM in order to configure your CD-ROM to function as a DOS device. When you are finished, don't forget to boot the computer to reflect any changes made to your AUTOEXEC.BAT and/or CONFIG.SYS files. Next, insert the Novell IntranetWare NetWare 4.11 Operating System CD-ROM in your CD-ROM drive, then type **D:** (or the appropriate drive letter) and press Enter to switch to the CD-ROM drive.

b. Step 2: Select the type of installation. Type **INSTALL** and press Enter to execute the INSTALL.BAT file in the root directory of the CD-ROM. A menu will be displayed allowing you to select the language to use during the installation process. Choose the Select This Line to Install in English option from the NetWare Install menu and press Enter if you want to display the installation instructions in English. Choose one of the other five options (Deutsch, Español, Français, Italiano, or Portuguese) and press Enter if you want the installation instructions to be displayed in another language. At this point, a Novell Terms and Conditions screen will be displayed. Read each screen of this multiscreen document carefully, pressing Enter (or any other key) after reading each screen to display the next screen. Next, choose the NetWare Server Installation option from the Select the Type of Installation Desired menu and press Enter. Then, select the NetWare 4.11 option from the Choose the Product You Want to Install menu and press Enter. Finally, select the Simple Installation of NetWare 4.11 option from the Select the Type of Installation You Are Performing menu and press Enter.

c. Step 3: Assign the server name. Type **ACME-SRV1** as the server name and press Enter.

d. Step 4: Copy the server boot files to the DOS partition. At this point, the installation program will automatically copy a number of server boot files from the CD-ROM to the C:\NWSERVER directory on the DOS partition.

2. RUN SERVER.EXE

a. Step 5: Start the server. The SERVER.EXE file will be executed
    automatically. (The system essentially does a warm boot as it flushes
    the DOS operating system from server RAM and replaces it with the
    NetWare 4.11 operating system.) The installation program will then
    load the INSTALL.NLM utility.

3. LOAD THE NETWARE 4.11 DRIVERS

a. Step 6: Load and configure the server hard disk and CD-ROM
    driver(s). The INSTALL utility will attempt to detect the hardware in
    your server and select the appropriate disk, CD-ROM, and LAN
    drivers. It will then list the ones it has selected for you on the Choose
    the Server Drivers—Summary screen. In Step 6, we are only concerned
    with hard disk and CD-ROM drivers. (We will worry about LAN
    driver(s) in Step 7.) You'll notice that the Driver Names field contains
    only the first two drivers of each type.

    (1) Use the arrow keys on your server keyboard to highlight the
        disk and CD-ROM driver(s) listed and press Enter to see a
        complete list of all disk and CD-ROM drivers selected.

    (2) First, select the Edit/View Parameters for a Selected Driver
        option from the Additional Driver Actions menu and press
        Enter. Next, select the first disk/CD-ROM driver and press Enter
        to view its parameters. If the parameters look correct, select the
        "Save Parameters and Continue" option from the "Driver...
        Parameters Actions" menu and press Enter. (If you don't have a
        clue, just keep your fingers crossed and assume they are correct
        for now.) Repeat this procedure for each driver listed.

    (3) When you are finished viewing the parameters for the selected
        disk and CD-ROM drivers, choose the Continue Installation
        option from the Additional Driver Actions menu and press Enter.

b. Step 7: Load and configure the appropriate server LAN driver(s).

(1) The LAN driver(s) that were automatically selected for this server should be highlighted. Press Enter to see a complete list of LAN drivers selected. (There may be only one.)

(2) Select the Edit/View Parameters for a Selected Driver option from the Additional Driver Actions menu and press Enter. Next, select the first LAN driver and press Enter to view its parameters. If the parameters look correct, select the "Save Parameters and Continue" option from the "Board…Driver … Actions" menu and press Enter. (If you don't have a clue, just keep your fingers crossed and assume they are correct for now.) Repeat this process for any additional drivers that may be listed.

(3) When you are finished viewing the parameters for the selected LAN drivers, choose the Continue Installation option from the Additional Driver Actions menu and press Enter. Next, select the Continue Installation option from the Driver Actions menu and press Enter.

4. STAGE 4: INSTALL.NLM

a. Step 8: Configure the CD-ROM as a DOS or NetWare device. If you are prompted with a warning that there may be a conflict with the DOS CD-ROM driver, ignore the warning, select the "Continue accessing the CD-ROM via DOS" option, and press Enter. (You will probably be able to continue normally despite the warning.)

b. Step 9: Mount the SYS: volume. At this point, the system automatically creates a NetWare partition on the hard disk, creates a SYS: volume within that partition, and mounts the SYS: volume.

c. Step 10: Re-establish the server-to-server connection. If you were installing across the network, you'd re-establish the server-to-server connection at this point. Since we're installing from CD-ROM, just ignore this step. At this point, the system will begin copying the appropriate "preliminary" (pre-installation) files from CD-ROM to the SYSTEM and LOGIN directories on the SYS: volume.

5. INSTALL NOVELL DIRECTORY SERVICES (NDS)

a. Step 11: Install NDS. If this is the first NetWare 4 server in your tree, a menu will be displayed asking if this is the first NetWare 4 server. Select "Yes, this is the first NetWare server" and press Enter. Next, select the appropriate time zone for this server which will be located in Camelot (namely "Great Britain, Greenwich Mean Time") and press Enter. When you are prompted for the Organization name, type **ACME** and press Enter. When you are prompted for the Admin password, type in a password and press Enter, then key it in again and press Enter when you are prompted to retype it for verification. (Make sure you choose a password you will remember!) At this point, NDS will be installed on the server. When the Directory tree name, Directory context, and administrator name are displayed on the screen, write them down (along with the Admin password chosen earlier) and press Enter.

b. Step 12: License the NetWare 4.11 operating system. When you are prompted, insert the IntranetWare/NetWare 4.11 License disk in drive A: and press Enter to continue.

6. CREATE SERVER STARTUP FILES

a. Step 13: Copy the SYSTEM and PUBLIC files to the SYS: volume. The system will begin copying the "main" files from the CD ROM to the SYS:SYSTEM and SYS:PUBLIC directories. Interestingly, you may find that the time bar indicates that 100 percent of the copying is complete before it actually is. If so, just wait until all of the files are copied.

b. Step 14: Perform other installation options. Ignore this step, as we are not going to install any optional products at this point. Select the Continue Installation option from the Other Installation Actions menu and press Enter to continue.

c. Step 15: Complete the installation. Read the information screen that is displayed on the screen, then press Enter to exit to the system console screen.

d. Step 16: Boot the server using the STARTUP.NCF and AUTOEXEC.NCF files. Remove the IntranetWare/NetWare 4.11 License disk from drive A: and store it in a safe place-such as on the refrigerator door in the lunchroom. Be sure to use a "certified" broccoli magnet for support (Just kidding!) After you've removed the diskette, type **DOWN** to down the server, then type **EXIT** to exit to the DOS prompt. Reboot the server. Finally, type **CD \NWSERVER** and press Enter to switch to the NWSERVER directory, then type **SERVER** and press Enter to reload the NetWare 4.11 operating system.

Congratulations—you have just installed a NetWare 4.11 server using the Simple Installation option. There you have it. ACME is now in business—thanks to you.

Now you're ready. Let's go on an "incredible journey" through one of ACME's most exciting servers—ACME-SRV1. Don't blink; you might miss something. This IntranetWare exploratorium is packed with console commands, NLMs, NDS, and pixie dust. Hold on tight!

Let's start at the beginning. As you know, before you can log into the network, you must load the 16-bit client connection files. This is accomplished using the "Client-16 Connectivity" guidelines from Chapter 6. During this process, the 16-bit connection files are automatically loaded each time you boot your workstation. Let's investigate how this is accomplished.

First, take a look at your AUTOEXEC.BAT file. You'll notice that the Client Installation program added two lines: one to call the STARTNET.BAT batch file and the other to add C:\NWCLIENT to the path. Next, review the STARTNET.BAT file. You'll see that it designates the language to be used and loads the connection files and the NetWare DOS Requester. Finally, examine the CONFIG.SYS file. You'll find that the client installation program added a LASTDRIVE statement that is used by the DOS Requester to determine what drives are available to be used as IntranetWare drives.

Now that you understand how these files are loaded, try to accomplish the following tasks:

1. First, check to see if the files are currently loaded in workstation RAM by typing

    ```
    MEM /C /P
    ```

2. Next, unload the connection files in the reverse order from which they were originally loaded, using the /U (that is, unload) switch with each command. (Look at the C:\NWCLIENT\STARTNET.BAT file if you want to see how they were originally loaded.)

    Question 1: What commands did you use to unload the connection files from workstation RAM?

3. Finally, load all four of the connection files manually, specifying "maximum verbosity" for VLM.EXE. (If you don't remember which switch to use, use the command line help method for viewing options that can be used with VLM.EXE.)

> **Question 2**: What command did you use to list the options available for use with VLM.EXE?

> **Question 3**: What command did you use to load VLM.EXE with maximum verbosity?

As soon as you execute VLM.EXE with the appropriate switch, various information will be displayed on the screen. Use the information displayed to answer the following questions:

> **Question 4**: Which version of VLM.EXE are you running?

> **Question 5**: What type of RAM is being used to load the VLMs?

> **Question 6**: Which is the first VLM loaded by VLM.EXE? Which is the last?

4. Once you have successfully loaded the connection files, log into the network by typing

```
F:
LOGIN .ADMIN.ACME
```

5. The next thing you want to do is to explore the Remote Management Facility (RMF). As you know, RMF is a wonderful feature you can use to access the file server console screen from your workstation. Because security is a concern, we will load this utility using an encrypted password.

The first thing you must do is to activate the RMF on the server by performing the following tasks at the server console, ending each entry by pressing Enter:

a. Load the REMOTE.NLM utility by typing

    `LOAD REMOTE`

    IntranetWare will prompt you for an RMF password. Enter it now:

    `CATHY`

b. RMF is now active, but your password is not protected. You can encrypt the password by typing

    `REMOTE ENCRYPT`

    Once again, IntranetWare will ask you for a password. Enter the same one:

    `CATHY`

c. IntranetWare then responds with an encrypted LOAD statement such as: LOAD REMOTE -e 14572BFD3AFEAE4E4759. (The number will be different every time you try this.) This is the encrypted representation of the password CATHY. Next, when you are asked whether you'd like for this command to be written to SYS:SYSTEM\LDREMOTE.NCF, type

    `Y`

d. Load RSPX.NLM by typing

    `LOAD RSPX`

e. Now that you've activated the RMF on the server, you must run the RCONSOLE utility on the workstation by typing

    `RCONSOLE`

    Read the message that is displayed regarding the fact that MS Windows may cause RCONSOLE to behave erratically, then press Enter. Because our workstation is connected to the server via cable rather than via modem, select SPX when you are asked to choose the connection type. Next, choose the IntranetWare file server from the Available Servers menu by selecting ACME-SRV1.

Finally, when you are asked to provide the password, type

CATHY

At this point, the same information that is displayed on the file server console screen should be displayed on your workstation screen.

Question 7: How can you tell that you are viewing the file server console screen?

Question 8: What type of warning is displayed at the bottom of the screen? Why is this important?

Because you are running the RCONSOLE utility, you can now execute console commands at your workstation rather than having to type them at the file server console.

6. Next, let's take a look at the INSTALL.NLM utility. This utility is used for various functions such as installing the NetWare operating system and additional products, creating NetWare partitions and volumes, mirroring the hard disk, copying SYSTEM and PUBLIC files to the SYS: volume, and creating/editing the AUTOEXEC.NCF and STARTUP.NCF configuration files. To load the INSTALL.NLM utility, type

LOAD INSTALL

The first thing you want to do in this utility is to add the RMF commands to the AUTOEXEC.NCF file so that it will be activated with the encrypted password every time you boot the server. Select the NCF Files options choice from the Installation Options menu and press Enter, then select the Edit AUTOEXEC.NCF file option from the Available NCF Files Options menu and press Enter. The AUTOEXEC.NCF file will then be displayed on the screen. Add the following two lines to the end of the file:

```
LDREMOTE
LOAD RSPX
```

Save the file and return to the Available NCF Files Options menu. Next, choose the appropriate options to view (edit) the AUTOEXEC.NCF and STARTUP.NCF configuration files so that you can answer the questions listed here:

Question 9: Which configuration file loads the LAN driver? Which one loads the disk driver?

Question 10: What time server type is designated for this server?

Question 11: If you have an Ethernet network board, what frame type is being used?

Next, press Esc once to return to the Installation options menu. Choose the appropriate options from this menu to answer the following questions:

Question 12: What percentage of the NetWare partition is reserved for the hot fix area?

Question 13: Is this disk mirrored?

Question 14: What volume block size is being used for SYS:, and why? On the SYS: volume are file compression, block suballocation, and data migration turned on or off?

Question 15: For how many connections is this server currently licensed?

Question 16: Which menu choice would you select to install DOS/Windows Client files?

7. Let's leave INSTALL.NLM and move onto the MONITOR.NLM utility. To load the MONITOR.NLM utility, type

   `LOAD MONITOR`

   Press the Tab key to expand the General Information window.

   Question 17: How long has your server been up and what do the four sets of numbers separated by colons represent? At what level is your CPU processor utilization? What is the total number of cache buffers currently being used? What is the number of current service processes in use? How many licensed connections are available at the moment? Press Esc to contract the General Information window.

   Question 18: What is the server's hot fix status? Have any blocks been redirected to the hot fix area?

   Question 19: What protocol(s) is/are currently supported on your server?

   Question 20: What is the load filename of the IntranetWare Directory Services Module? What is the size of this file?

   Question 21: Finally, cruise over to Processor Utilization. Which IntranetWare process occupies the most server CPU time?

8. Now let's exit MONITOR and warp ahead to SERVMAN. To load SERVMAN, type

   `LOAD SERVMAN`

   Question 22: Which general statistics overlap MONITOR functionality?

Question 23: Explore some SET parameters. What console command could be used instead of SERVMAN to change SET parameters?

Question 24: Next, switch to the server console without exiting SERVMAN. What method did you use? Next, check out the RMF Available Options menu. What method did you use to activate it?

Question 25: Which option is similar to one found in INSTALL.NLM? How is this one different?

Question 26: Press Esc to switch back to the server console. Use the appropriate console command to activate the RIP tracking screen. What command did you use? What is ACME's tree name? How about the IPX internal network number of other servers? Where else can you get this information?

Question 27: Switch to the server console and send yourself a message. What command did you use? Acknowledge receipt of the message. How did you do so? Aren't such messages annoying? How can you set your workstation so that it does not receive messages from other users?

Question 28: What name spaces are loaded on the SYS: volume?

9. Turn off the RIP tracking screen and exit the SERVMAN utility.

Question 29: What method could you use to review a quick list of IntranetWare console commands that are available?

Question 30: Use a console command to see what NLMs are currently loaded. Which console command did you use? What NLM would give you a count of the NLMs that are currently loaded?

10. Exit RCONSOLE, log off the network, and call it a day! Very good, you lived through the exploratorium without a scratch. Now, wasn't that fun?

See Appendix C for answers.

EXERCISE 7-1: INTRANETWARE ADULTHOOD

Circle the 20 IntranetWare Management terms hidden in this word search puzzle using the hints provided.

```
S  B  A  C  K  U  P  N  Z  W  W  Q  X  Q  C
E  M  O  N  I  T  O  R  N  L  M  R  C  N  O
C  N  D  D  S  R  E  P  A  I  R  N  L  M  C
U  M  L  R  I  A  O  B  H  H  K  H  O  U  Z
R  N  A  M  E  S  P  A  C  E  H  J  C  I  Y
E  R  L  F  S  E  R  V  M  A  N  M  S  U  K
C  O  N  S  O  L  E  C  O  M  M  A  N  D  S
O  E  O  T  R  A  C  K  O  N  E  S  W  J  U
N  Y  H  O  S  T  H  K  L  N  X  T  B  O  T
S  V  L  M  P  A  C  V  B  X  S  W  S  Q  R
O  M  S  S  X  Q  E  R  X  D  L  O  X  K  N
L  C  T  T  L  C  U  M  H  Q  T  T  L  Y  G
E  L  S  P  F  I  W  M  K  L  U  G  S  E  N
```

Hints:

1. Executed at the colon prompt.
2. NLM used to detect and correct problems in the NDS database.
3. Term used to refer to the server that a tape backup unit is attached to.
4. ODI layer which acts as a switchboard to route packets between MLID and the protocol stack.
5. NLM used to view server RAM activity for troubleshooting and optimization purposes.
6. Module that is used to allow the storage of non-DOS files on a NetWare 4.11 server.
7. Modular server programs.
8. Architecture which allows multiple LAN drivers and protocols to coexist on network systems.
9. Workstation command line utility used to remotely access the server console.

10. IntranetWare feature which allows remote access of the file server console.

11. NLM used to allow RCONSOLE to access a server over a direct connection.

12. Protocol used by servers to advertise their services on an IntranetWare internetwork.

13. NLM used to back up and restore data for a server, workstation, or service.

14. Console command used to increase security at the server console.

15. NLM used to view and configure system parameters. Can be used in place of the SET command.

16. Used to pass commands and information between SBACKUP and Target Service Agents.

17. IntranetWare backup/restore engine used by the SBACKUP utility.

18. Console command used to display the RIP tracking screen.

19. Program used to process data moving between a target and an SMS-compliant backup engine such as SBACKUP.

20. Modular executable program that runs on a DOS workstation and enables communication with an IntranetWare server.

See Appendix C for answers.

IntranetWare Printing

Adding users to NetWare 4 printing is like putting Godzilla in a mosh pit.

Now that you've lived through the life span of a LAN, I think you're ready to discover one of the greatest mysteries of life—printing. The meaning of life?—Nah. The Great Pyramids?—Nah. The Sphinx?—No chance. Printing has them all beat. More brain cells have been lost pondering IntranetWare printing than any other philosophical question.

Why? It's not that printing itself is so puzzling. As a matter of fact, the concept of printing is fairly easy to comprehend—you click a button on the workstation, and a piece of paper comes out of the printer down the hall. No rocket science here. It's true. The fundamental architecture of IntranetWare printing is solid-rock solid. So, why is it such a mystery? One word—users! It's the users' fault. They introduce so much complexity to printing, it's a wonder the paper finds its way anywhere, let alone to the correct printer. And to make matters worse, users expect too much:

▶ They want the page to be formatted correctly every time.

▶ They want their print jobs to arrive at the "correct" printer (when they don't even know what that means).

▶ They always want their jobs to come out first.

So, how do you possibly satisfy the lofty expectations of your users while maintaining a rock-solid IntranetWare printing architecture? That's the greatest mystery of them all. Fortunately, Novell is on your side, and they've come up with some answers. The IntranetWare printing system has been improved dramatically in several ways—easier setup, better management, more flexibility. They certainly haven't solved your mystery entirely, but they've given you some great tools to help you crack the case—and we're gonna learn all about them.

In this chapter, we're going to explore this great printing mystery and discover some startling answers. You're going to learn about the four steps of printing setup, all the great tools available for printing management, and the future of IntranetWare printing through NDPS. But first, we need to spend a few moments meditating on the true essence of printing. You must become one with the printer. It works. Trust me.

The Essence of Printing

Now, repeat after me—I *am* a printer, I *am* a printer. The best way to handle IntranetWare printing is to *be* IntranetWare printing. This is the essence of printing.

Actually, the essence of printing is a little more technical than that. It is a wondrous journey from the user's workstation to the network printer down the hall. Here's how it works:

▶ Capturing—The job moves from the local workstation to the IntranetWare server.

▶ Moving to the queue—It waits in line (first come; first served).

▶ The print server—The brains behind the process.

▶ At the printer—Finally, the print job arrives at the printer and prints correctly (fingers crossed).

This is the Printing Journey. But before we take a closer look at the Journey, let's take a history lesson in network printing. Get out your notebooks.

ZEN

"School, thank God for school. I need those seven hours of personal time. I mean, how can I continue to be the bright, vivacious Nanny everyone knows and loves if I have to spend all day with the kids?"

Nanny Fine

GETTING STARTED

We already know what a great job IntranetWare does with its file services, but printing is just as important to users. Initially, all users need access to file storage and shared print services to get the most out of IntranetWare.

Setting up and using printing services under IntranetWare can be a challenging part of setting up the network. But printing isn't as difficult as it seems—especially if you understand the system's essence. This chapter provides some insight into the overall architecture of network printing, and, in the process, should make print services setup a whole lot easier.

Printing by Yourself

Most people are familiar with printing from a local workstation. In this scenario, a PC or other station has a stand-alone printer (a LaserJet, dot matrix, or other type of printer) that is dedicated to that station. With a dedicated printer, you have much less to worry about when it comes to printing documents. Issues such as *print drivers* or notification when the print job is complete do not apply. You can see the printer on your desk (or nearby, at least), and hopefully the correct print driver (with the proper version) has already been set up. When the document is printed, you need only reach over and grab it from the printer.

To better understand network printing, it helps to have a solid foundation of how local printing works. Starting from the beginning, the workstation has one or more local ports. Most PCs have at least one *parallel* port, labeled LPT1, LPT2, and so on. Many PCs also have a *serial* port as well. Serial ports typically are used as communication ports (that is, for modems), because they work faster than do parallel ports.

When you begin printing (if a printer is attached), the default output for printing is LPT1. LPT1 outputs to parallel port one, LPT2 outputs to parallel port two, and so on. Serial output is not enabled by default. If you print something, the software program you are using will usually default to LPT1. Otherwise, it may ask you which port you prefer (LPT1–LPT*n*).

Once you have hit the magic button to print something, the machine takes over. If you are running strictly DOS (no Windows in sight), then the machine may halt while printing. This is because DOS is set up to do only one thing at a time. But there are ways to trick DOS into not halting your machine, such as by using the PRINT command. This command will take the print data and store it locally on the hard disk while it feeds the data to the printer in the background. This will allow you to do other things while the system is printing (for more information on the PRINT command, see your DOS reference manual). If you don't trick the computer, you'll have to wait for the document (or other print job) to finish printing before the machine will return control back to you (just like the old *Outer Limits* program, huh!).

If you are printing to a serial port under DOS, you'll need to do a bit of preparation. First, you must *redirect* the LPT output from the parallel port to a serial port. This is done by using another DOS command called MODE. The MODE command works similarly to how network printing works in general. MODE simply takes LPT1 output and redirects it to the serial port. The program *thinks* it's sending to the LPT port. DOS takes the output, however, and streams it to the serial device (see Figure 8.1).

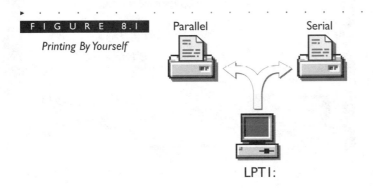

FIGURE 8.1

Printing By Yourself

Parallel

Serial

LPT1:

If you are using Windows (3.x or Windows 95), a neat little program called Print Manager can be used to manage local printing from Windows. Print Manager also provides the same capabilities as the DOS PRINT program—such as the ability to spool the print data locally and feed it to the printer. Print Manager has a few more features than PRINT. For example, it will allow you to view the current printing job, delete it, or postpone it.

Typically, when you are printing to the network, those features are already provided by IntranetWare utilities, thereby making Print Manager functions unnecessary. Many users will disable Print Manager when using IntranetWare for this reason. Print Manager can actually slow network printing because the print job will be spooled once locally, and then again to the network queue.

Instead of disabling Print Manager, you can select the Print Net Jobs Direct option (select Options and then Network Settings from the Print Manager). This will enable any network print jobs to spool directly to a IntranetWare queue and bypass local hard disk spooling. Check out the screen in Figure 8.2.

FIGURE 8.2

Network Printing in
Microsoft Windows

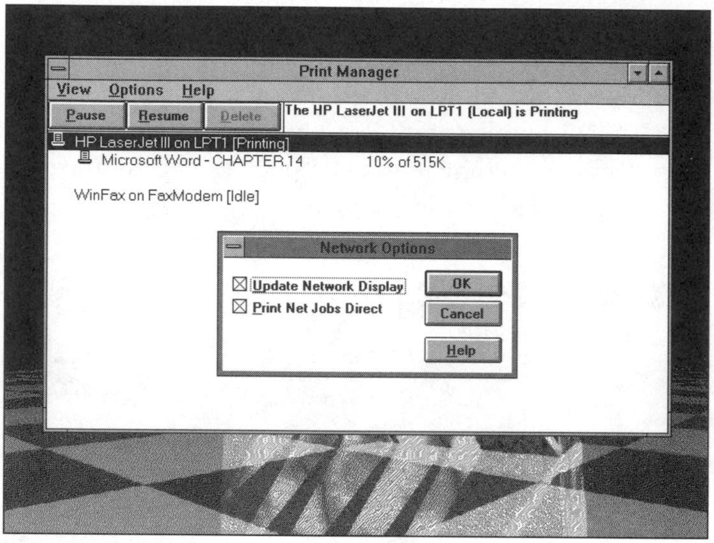

Once you attach a workstation to a network, the rules change a little. Some considerations are

1 • Does the workstation have the proper driver for the network printer?

2 • How will you know when the document has completed printing?

3 • How does the server know when you have stopped sending print data?

4 • What if the printer runs out of paper? How will you or the administrator be notified?

Printing on a Network

The flow for network printing works something like this. The user has enabled printing to a network device from the workstation, or the administrator has automatically enabled it via a batch file (AUTOEXEC.BAT) or a login script (Container, System, Personal, and so on). This is similar to using the MODE command under DOS, except that when an application prints, the output gets redirected to a queue on a server somewhere. The workstation command line utility to enable printing is called CAPTURE.

When CAPTURE is executed, the local LPT port that is being redirected to the network is specified. By default, this is usually LPT1. With this approach, the application may send output via LPT2 and the IntranetWare shell knows to capture data coming from the LPT2 port and redirect it to the appropriate queue. As a default, the CAPTURE command automatically assumes that data will be sent via LPT1. Most applications also assume that this is the default port on which to send data. Remember, the LPT port is merely a channel, port, or stream as far as the application knows. It may *point* at a parallel port, a serial port, a file, or the network queue. This concept is shown in Figure 8.3.

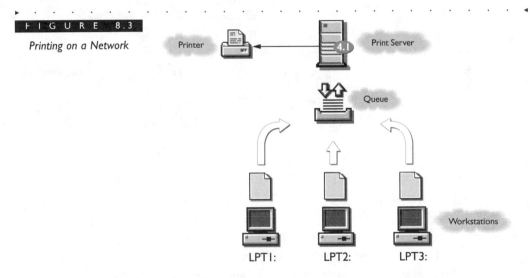

FIGURE 8.3

Printing on a Network

Printer · Print Server

Queue

Workstations

LPT1:   LPT2:   LPT3:

Understanding Print Queues   Now that capturing is on, the user starts to print via the application, DOS, or Windows. The output can be an existing file (such as DATA.TXT) or raw data from a word processing program (such as WordPerfect). The data being printed will be sent to an area on a specified server called a *queue*. Queues are nothing more than a subdirectory with a *.QDR extension. The data will be spooled into an automatically created file. When the user signals that he or she is finished sending data, the file is closed and prepared for printing.

Understanding Print Servers   Now that the data file is closed and ready, it can be serviced from the QUEUE directory. A *print server* is a device that is assigned to watch a particular queue or queues. When it sees a job waiting to be serviced, it opens the job (file) and starts to read from it. The print server then prints the data in the file to a printer attached to the print server. *Which* printer it sends the file to depends on the setup of the print server (see the "IntranetWare Printing Setup" section). See Figure 8.4 for a quick preview. Incidentally, the IntranetWare native print server must by loaded on the server as PSERVER.NLM.

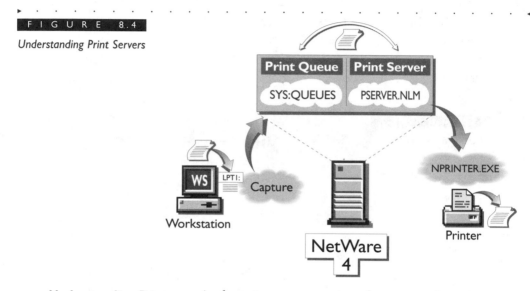

F I G U R E   8.4

Understanding Print Servers

Understanding Printers   As the print server services the request, it attempts to print the data to a locally attached printer (physically attached to the print server) or a remotely attached printer (perhaps a printer attached to a workstation, but remotely attached via software to the print server). If the printer is a remote printer, the print server *thinks* it is attached locally, when, in fact, the data is being sent across the network to where the remote printer physically resides.

Once the contents of the data file have been printed, the data file residing in the queue will be deleted to recover the disk space. In addition, if it has been set up to do so, a notification will be sent to the user (and possibly others) that the job has been successfully printed and is ready to be picked up.

QUIZ

Let's begin our IntranetWare "sleuthing" with a simple one. Here goes .... At a college reunion, a group of men and women were discussing their lives after they had received their undergraduate degrees. It turned out that everyone in the group had gone on to receive an advanced degree, so each of them had two degrees. Each degree holder had both a B.A. and an M.S., an M.A., an M.B.A., or an M.F.A. Half of them had an M.S., one-quarter had an M.A., one-sixth had an M.B.A., and just one had an M.F.A. How many were there in total?

(Q8-1)
(See Appendix C for all quiz answers.)

THE BEGINNING: CAPTURING

This is the beginning of your printing journey. Hold on to your hat. As we learned earlier, IntranetWare printing is a wondrous journey from the user's workstation to the network printer down the hall. Here's how it works:

▸ The Beginning: Capturing—The job moves from the local workstation to the IntranetWare server.

▸ Moving to the queue—It waits in line (first come; first served).

▸ The print server—The brains behind the process.

▸ The Destination: At the printer—Finally, the print job arrives at the printer and prints correctly (fingers crossed).

In this first stop, we will explore the details of IntranetWare printing from the PC workstation's perspective. Two areas will be covered: printing from DOS and printing from Windows. This discussion assumes that you have some knowledge of DOS and Windows in order to understand the elements of network printing.

This section also assumes that a printing system has already been set up (print server, print queue, and remote/local printer) and that the user has been granted access. If not, you can jump ahead to the section "IntranetWare Printing Setup" and then return to this section.

Capturing with DOS

To enable network printing, you must first tell the network client (for example, Client 32, VLM, or NETx) that you want to print to the network. You can do this by using the IntranetWare command-line utility CAPTURE, or the IntranetWare menu utility NETUSER (see Figure 8.5).

▶ · ◀

F I G U R E   8.5

Capturing a Local Port

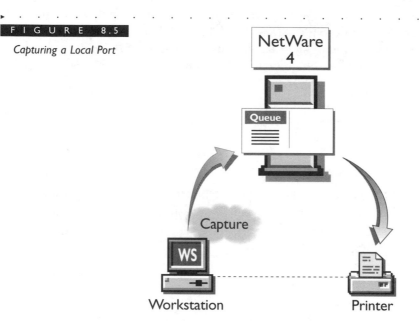

WHAT'S NEW

The printer redirection information stored in Client 32 is temporary and is lost when you log out or disconnect from the network. For this reason, you should automate Capturing with the help of login scripts or batch files.

The CAPTURE command is included with IntranetWare, and allows you to start and end network printing. It can be used in a DOS-only environment, or it can be executed *before* starting Windows 3.x to allow capturing under Windows. In Windows 95 environments, you can use the Win95 Print Manager or NWUSER (a Windows 3.1 IntranetWare tool). We'll explore these options in a little while.

CAPTURE has several command line options that allow you to customize how the network capture will work. These options include:

▶ /?—This option will show help for the CAPTURE command if you need it. You can also use CAPTURE /? ALL to show every possible option and explanation for CAPTURE.

▸ **/SH (Show)**—This is a very useful command to see how you are currently captured to the network. CAPTURE /SH will show all LPT ports currently enabled for network printing, as well as other flags (such as banners, copies, and so on). The Show parameter will *not* initiate a print capture. It is for informational purposes only.

▸ **/S (Server)**—This option allows you to specify the server to which you want to print. In IntranetWare environments, this is usually unnecessary because the user is oblivious to servers per se. When capturing, the user can just specify the printer name using a distinguished name (for example, HP5-P1.CRIME.TOKYO.ACME), and the server will automatically be found and attached. In a NetWare 3 environment, however, /S can be used to point to a server with a particular printer/queue that you want to use. If you are not logged in/attached to that particular server, then the CAPTURE command will attempt to log in as GUEST. If the GUEST account does not exist, printing on that server will be denied to the user. This is a good reason (in an open environment) to keep the GUEST account around on a public NetWare 3 server.

▸ **/Q (Queue)**—This command line option allows the user to specify the queue to which data should be sent. In a NetWare 3 environment, it can be combined with the /S option to specify a server name and queue name that the user desires. In a IntranetWare network, the queue name can be a relative distinguished name (for example, HP5-PQ1) or a distinguished name (for example, HP5-PQ1.CRIME.TOKYO.ACME). If a distinguished name is used, there is much less of a chance of ambiguity between printer and queue names. For example, if the user is in context CYBER.WHITE.CRIME.TOKYO.ACME, and he or she wants to print to a queue in BLUE.CRIME.TOKYO.ACME, there is a chance that the relative distinguished name HPIII-PQ1 may exist in both locations (and it does). In such a case, if a user types in the command **CAPTURE /Q=HPIII-PQ1**, the printer captured will be the one in CYBER.WHITE.CRIME.TOKYO.ACME.

► /AU (AutoEndCap)—This option allows the application to decide if the user is finished sending capture data. For example, when a user sends data, how does the network shell know when the application/user is finished sending data? There are three ways:

1 • The user stops sending capture data (via the CAPTURE command—discussed later).

2 • The application sends a IntranetWare-specific command to signal the end of capture data (this is the case with network-aware applications such as WordPerfect).

3 • The shell assumes you are finished via AutoEndCap or timeouts. When AutoEndCap is enabled, the shell assumes you are finished sending data if you leave the application that began sending capture data. Consider a user who enables capture (via the CAPTURE command), sends a print job via the application (such as WordPerfect), and then exits the application. The shell can safely assume that since the user exited, he or she was finished sending data. If AutoEndCap were *not* enabled, the user would still have to terminate CAPTURE to signal the end of capture data.

► /TI (TimeOut)—This option is similar to the AutoEndCap command, except that the user does not need to exit the application. Instead, a timeout is specified when capture was started (such as CAPTURE TI=8). This means the network shell will assume that once capture data has been sent, if no more data has been sent after 8 seconds, the job will automatically be completed and scheduled for printing. The only problem with this command is what happens when an application pauses between spurts of data. For example, if a database program were sending data and then paused 10 seconds before sending page totals, the first data would be sent as one print job and the page totals would be sent as a second, thereby violating the integrity of the job.

▶ /K (Keep/No Keep)—This option tells the shell what to do if something interrupts the flow of data from the workstation to the queue on the server. For example, if a print job were started and then interrupted when the workstation lost power, all data sent to the queue up to that point would be lost if Keep were not enabled. If Keep is enabled, any data sent up to that point will be printed.

▶ /T (Tabs)—The Tabs option was included from the earlier versions of NetWare when printing documents was not always done through the application. As a result, when a document was printed, the proper spaces were not inserted for a tab character. Therefore, the IntranetWare shell was enabled to observe a tab character during the print process, remove it, and send the proper amount of spaces to the printer. This option was enabled in versions of NetWare 3.11 and below. The default amount of spaces per tab character was eight. Current versions no longer support this as a default. This is because most applications now format their own printing and convert tabs to the proper spaces. This option, if enabled, can cause printing problems, since some graphics programs or other raw text may have characters that signify a tab. If T is enabled, the shell will strip the tab, send the spaces, and you'll end up with garbled print output. NT (No Tabs) is the default.

▶ /C (Copies)—This option specifies the number of copies you want of the printout. The default is 1.

▶ /B (Banner)—This option (enabled by default) will send a print banner at the beginning of the print job. You can specify the name of the person who submitted the document, as well as the name of the job itself (B=<*user name*> and N=<*job name*>). If nothing is specified, then the document will either be the name of the file being printed (if an existing file is being printed) or PRN: if the print job is output from an application. The name will be the username of the person who submitted it.

▶ /NB (No Banner)—This option disables the Banner option. It is usually used when a small office is involved or with a local workgroup.

▶ /NFF (NoFormFeed)—This option prevents an additional page from being sent at the end of the print job. This may be necessary with some applications that do not send a form feed after a print job has been submitted.

▶ /FF (FormFeed)—This option sends a form feed after the job has been completed (default). This is necessary when the application doesn't do this automatically, since the last page of the document may not be ejected by the printer (especially when using a LaserJet printer). NFF (No Form Feed) turns off form feed.

▶ /L=n (Local Port Number)—DOS provides several channels for print output. The first and primary channel is LPT1. There can be more than one, however. Many applications today can output print data on LPT2–LPTn. Most default to LPT1. If your application is outputting on LPT2, you must use this command to tell IntranetWare which LPT port is being used. For example, you might have a local printer attached to LPT1 and you want network printing to go out via LPT2. The CAPTURE command would look like this: **CAPTURE /L=2**. That way, through the application, you can print to LPT1 and the output will go to the local printer. If you print out to LPT2, however, the output will go to the network. Keep in mind, you can print to "logical" parallel ports even if a physical one doesn't exist.

▶ /F (Form)—Forms allow network users to share the same printer for a variety of functions. When (and if) forms are defined, a user can submit a job of a particular form type and the print server will ensure that the printer being used is ready to accept a print job of that form type. For example, this option would allow one user to submit a purchase requisition (that requires a preprinted form), while another user could submit an invoice (also requiring a preprinted form). When the job is submitted, a form name or number is used to specify which form is to be used when printing the job. Form names and numbers are defined using the PRINTDEF utility.

▶ /CR (Create)—This option allows the user to send output to a file instead of to a print queue. When this option is specified, the user must also specify the filename to which output should be directed. If the file does not exist, it will be created automatically. After the first print job output has completed, subsequent print jobs will be sent to a normal queue. For example, if we typed **CAPTURE /CR=SYS:TEST.TXT /Q=.HP5-PQ1.CRIME.TOKYO.ACME**, the data will be captured to the printer HP5-P1, but the initial output will go to file TEST.TXT. We then submit data for print (through the application or an existing file). The data will go into the file TEST.TXT instead of being printed! If we print again, the data will be spooled to HP5-P1 and printed on the physical printer. This parameter is useful when you need to encapsulate an entire print job (printer escape codes and all) into a file. Another user could merely submit the entire file for printing (without the source application being available), and the data will print successfully.

▶ /NOTI (Notify)—With this option, provided the print server has been created to support it, a message will be sent to the user *after* the job has been printed successfully. In addition, the print server can be created to notify the user or other responsible parties (such as Admin or the print server administrator) if any problems arose (for example, if the printer ran out of paper or if it went off-line). NNOTI disables notification.

▶ /EC (EndCapture)—This option is used to return LPT output to the local port (usually the local parallel port). Since the CAPTURE command could have been started for LPT2, LPT3, and so on, ENDCAP can be used with the L=*n* switch to turn off CAPTURE on a specific port.

A sample CAPTURE command might look like this:

```
CAPTURE /NB /L=2 /K /Q=HP5-PQ1.CRIME.TOKYO.ACME /TI=10
```

For this print job:

▶ No banner will be prefixed to the print job.

▶ Output will be via LPT2.

► Data will be kept and printed *if* the capture is not formally closed.

► The queue to be used is HP5-PQ1.CRIME.TOKYO.ACME.

► A timeout of 10 seconds will be used.

SMART LINK

For a complete list of the IntranetWare CAPTURE parameters, consult the on-line IntranetWare documentation at http://www.novell.com/manuals.

In the menu world, NETUSER provides a simpler capturing interface for users. The NETUSER (also known as NetWare User Tools for DOS) main menu is shown in Figure 8.6. As you can see, it's a full-service user utility. From a printing point of view, it allows users to capture local ports and manage their current print jobs.

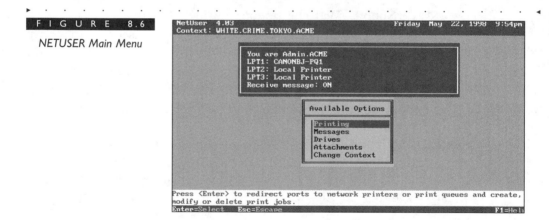

F I G U R E   8.6

NETUSER Main Menu

Just like with the other DOS utilities, it's important to note the context at the very top of the NETUSER screen. Anything done in NETUSER from this point will be from the .WHITE.CRIME.TOKYO.ACME context.

You should also notice the box above the "Available options" menu, indicating current user and capturing information. In Figure 8.6, we are currently logged in as Admin and LPT1 is captured to the queue servicing the Canon Bubble Jet. To capture a printer port with NETUSER, under the Printers option, select the port you want to capture and choose Change Printers. You are then presented with a list of printers and print queues in your current context. Use the arrow keys to highlight the printer you want (or the print queue assigned to it) and press Enter. Any capturing done through NETUSER will remain active during the current login session only. One disadvantage this utility has in comparison with its Windows (NWADMIN) counterpart is that there is no way to make the capturing permanent.

In addition to capturing, NETUSER allows users to manage their current print jobs. When you select Printing from the "Available options" menu, you are shown a list of the available LPT ports. If you select an LPT port, you are given two options: Print Jobs and Change Printers. Since we have already captured LPT1 to the CANONBJ-PQ1 queue, we can select the queue by pressing Enter and view a list of print jobs currently in the queue. If you select a print job, you are presented with the Printing Management menu. This is the same screen we'll use later to manage printing in PCONSOLE. Be patient.

Now let's explore the GUI world, and see what capturing is like with Windows.

Capturing with Windows

There are three ways to CAPTURE a local port under Windows:

▶ Use the CAPTURE command, and then start Windows.

▶ Use the Windows 95 Print Manager.

▶ Use the Windows 3.1 NWUSER utility.

Since we have already covered CAPTURE, let's start our GUI journey with a closer look at the Windows 95 Print Manager.

You can redirect print jobs in Windows 95 using the Printer Properties screen shown in Figure 8.7. Here's how you get there. Click Start, Settings, and then Control Panel. Finally, click Printers and you'll get a list of available printers. Highlight your printer, click the right mouse button, and choose Properties. You will be greeted with the input screen shown in Figure 8.7.

FIGURE 8.7

Windows 95 Print Manager

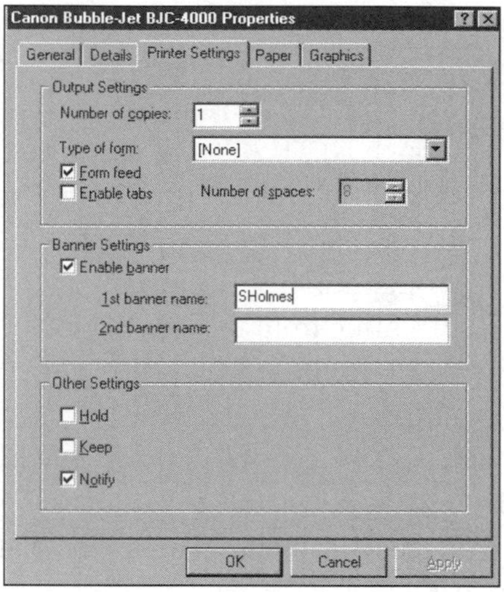

As you can see, there's a plethora of great printing functionality available in this screen. You can

▸ Redirect print jobs to a printer or queue.

▸ Configure print job redirection using options such as Enable Banner. This is the equivalent to the switch settings in CAPTURE.

▸ Make redirection permanent (unlike CAPTURE or NETUSER).

▸ Select the correct parallel port and print driver.

Windows 95 provides a native configuration screen for printer redirection (as seen in Figure 8.7). Windows 3.1, however, relies on a special IntranetWare utility for capturing. It's called NetWare User Tools for Windows (or NWUSER). To start NWUSER, find the icon under the NetWare Tools Program Group. This is installed as part of the NetWare Requester or Client 32 connectivity software. NWUSER is simply a launcher for the Novell Driver for Windows. Another option is to launch File Manager and choose Disk/Network Connections. This will also launch the NetWare Tools utility.

TIP

If you have a sound card, choose the IntranetWare Settings option from the button bar (the one that has a key) and click once over the Novell icon in the upper left-hand corner—surprise!

Once the tool is running, choose the printer icon (third icon from the left on the button bar). This will display all the printers available to you in the browser window to the right. You can also walk the tree to find other printers and queues in your network. You will also see any queues available for any NetWare 3.12 or 2.2 servers that you are logged into.

To capture to a printer, select the printer/queue you want and then choose Capture (or merely drag and drop the chosen printer from the right window to the desired LPT port on the left). Once completed, you can double-click on the newly captured printer and select Printing Options. These options correspond to the flags used under CAPTURE at the DOS prompt (see Figure 8.8).

FIGURE 8.8

Capture Settings in NetWare User Tools for Windows

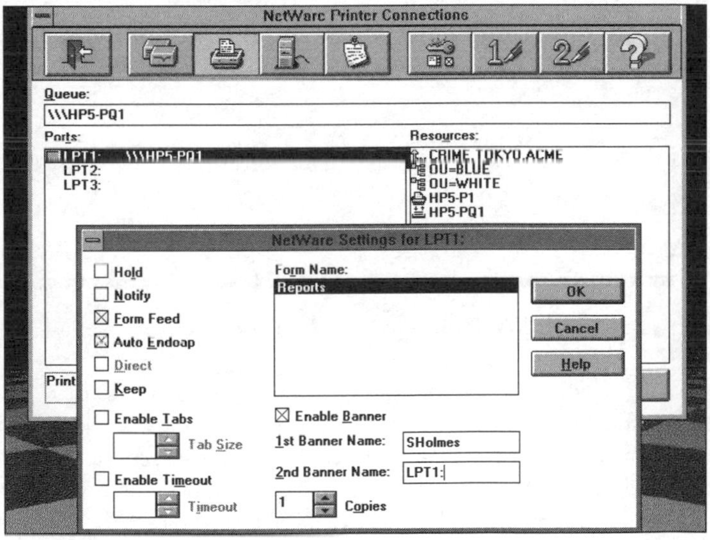

Like Windows 95, NWUSER allows you to select the Permanent option after capturing a printer. This will automatically recapture the printer every time you start Windows. If it is a NetWare 3.12 or 2.2 printer/queue, you may be required to log into the server again before capturing is complete.

To end CAPTURE under Windows, drag the printer mapping from the left window to the right. You can also select the desired printer/queue and choose End Capture from the lower button bar.

REAL WORLD

Printers and queues are referred to in the same way, since they are so closely related. More will be explained later, but for clarification's sake, a print job always must be submitted to a queue before it can be serviced by a printer via a print server. To minimize complexity, Novell allows you to choose a printer by name, and you will be captured automatically to the queue that services that printer. This way, you don't need to know which queue services which printer.

ZEN

"Don't underestimate the power of these adenoids. I had next-door neighbors move closer to the airport."

Nanny Fine

REAL WORLD

If you don't want to capture your local ports for whatever reason, you still have another option. You can print your job to a file and then send the file to an IntranetWare queue. Most applications can send a print job to a file on disk. Simply provide a filename (such as C:\TEMP\PRINT) instead of a local port name (like LTP1). Next, use NRPRINT or PCONSOLE to redirect the file to an IntranetWare queue. It's pretty easy and very flexible.

MOVING TO THE QUEUE

Once capturing has begun, the print data is sent to the print queue from an application via the local port. Before the data is sent, however, some very interesting things occur. If you analyze the anatomy of a print stream (see Figure 8.9), you'll see there are three parts: the print header, the print body (data sent), and the print tail. The purpose of these other components becomes important when drivers are involved.

▶ · ◀

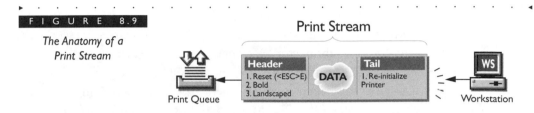

FIGURE 8.9

The Anatomy of a Print Stream

Print Stream

Header
1. Reset (<ESC>E)
2. Bold
3. Landscaped

DATA

Tail
1. Re-initialize Printer

Print Queue

Workstation

IntranetWare allows the user to specify escape codes that can be sent before the print data reaches the printer (a *print header*). And, at the end of the print data, a *print tail* sends the proper escape codes to reset the printer to a default state. This leaves the printer ready for the next user. To use this feature, two things must have been created:

▶ PRINTDEF database—includes escape code information for printers and modes of operation (collections of escape codes)

▶ Print Job Definition—specifies details about how the capture should be handled

Remember the options for CAPTURE? Well, these can be incorporated into a file stored in NDS that is read and utilized when the user begins a CAPTURE session. Any command line options used when executing the CAPTURE command will override the Print Job Definition options.

The print server's job is to control the flow of the print job from its beginning until it is finally printed on a printer *somewhere*. That somewhere is dictated by the queue typically.

Several server elements are involved in printing: the queue (which always resides on a server volume somewhere), the print server (which may reside on a file server, IntranetWare router, any other NLM platform, or even inside the printer itself), and finally, the printer (which prints the data and notifies the print server of completion and any problems that may arise).

IntranetWare queue services are designed to provide more than just support for printing. Other applications can take advantage of the queue API under IntranetWare to service jobs based on a queuing mechanism. As a result, not all queue characteristics look related to printing.

A queue is basically comprised of a subdirectory stored on a volume of a server somewhere. Since the queue is there to hold files waiting to be printed, it must be on a storage area (volume) on a file server. Where the subdirectory exists is up to the person who created it. In NetWare 3 and below, the directories always existed under the SYS:SYSTEM subdirectory. IntranetWare, on the other hand, allows you to create them anywhere—under the subdirectory QUEUES on any volume.

Once a print job has begun from the client, the queue servicing the request (selected by the user via CAPTURE, Print Job Settings, or NWUSER) will create a temporary file inside the queue's subdirectory. This file is used to keep track of the job as it flows through the system. One of the data items kept in the file is the *Job Entry Record,* which contains information such as

- ► When the job was submitted

- ► Who submitted the job

- ► Size of the data

- ► Whether the job can be printed immediately

- ► How many copies to print

And more. This information can be called up via NWADMIN or PCONSOLE. See Figure 8.10 for an example of the Print Job Detail screen in NWADMIN.

The queue also has security assigned to it. During setup, we can designate users, groups, or containers that may submit jobs to the queue. We can also restrict which print servers may service jobs from our queue. Finally, there is a security designation called Queue Manager. This entity, when designated, may delete jobs submitted by other users. In this manner, print queue administration may be delegated to other users.

FIGURE 8.10

The Print Job Detail Screen
in NWADMIN

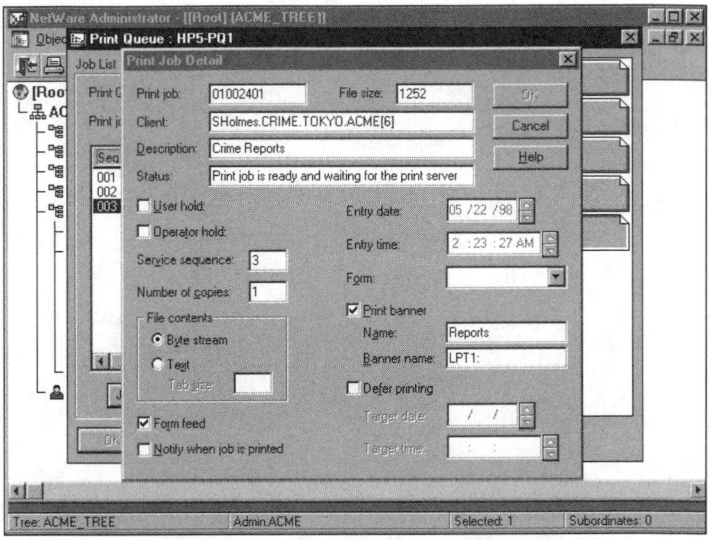

There are some utilities available that allow users and administrators to manage and view the flow of printing, including PCONSOLE (under DOS) and NWADMIN (under Windows). We'll explore printing management later in the chapter.

THE PRINT SERVER

Once the print server is loaded and functioning, it must then log into the servers it is servicing. This allows it to poll the queues it has been assigned. It is a very good idea to password-protect all the print servers in the network to minimize security problems.

Once the server is fully initialized, it will begin polling the queues it has been assigned and service print jobs within those queues. Some factors may affect which queues get serviced first. They include:

> Queue priorities—When a queue is assigned to a print server, a priority can be assigned. This priority tells the print server that if any jobs are waiting in the highest priority queue, it must service them once the currently serviced job has completed. This can be set up as part of

security, allowing certain users to have better access to a printer than others. This would be the case if two queues were servicing the same physical printer. Users having access to the higher priority queue will have their jobs completed before the users that submitted jobs to a lesser priority queue.

▸ Forms servicing—This topic will be covered later in the chapter, but the Print Server Manager can designate how forms are serviced. As such, a print server may be required to service all forms of a particular type within a queue before it can move to the next queue. Or, it may have to print all jobs that have a certain designated Form Type across all queues to which it is assigned, before servicing jobs with a different form type.

REAL WORLD

Here's an example of how "Forms Servicing" works. Suppose print server Alpha were supporting Q1 and Q2. And further assume that it must service all jobs using a particular form before moving to the next form. If User1 submits a job of form type 0 into Q1, and User2 submits a job with form type 5 thereafter, User2 will have to wait if User3 submits a job of form type 0 into Q2, even if User3 submitted it *after* User2. Once User3's job is complete, the print server can begin to service jobs using form type 5.

Much like a print queue, print servers have security:

▸ Print server users—These are users, groups, and containers that can view current jobs being serviced. Print server users can also abort their jobs if they wish.

▸ Print server operators—These are users, groups, and containers that can abort anyone's job currently being serviced. They can also view the status of any currently printing job.

Other things that can be controlled on print servers include how often the print server polls the assigned queues looking for jobs. As mentioned earlier, you can modify the queue priority and how forms get serviced using Admin utilities described later in this chapter. When setting up print services, you should know the options available. The relationship of queues and print servers to printers can be:

▸ One to many

▸ One to one

▸ Many to many

▸ Many to one

Print servers usually reside at the file server, although they may reside as NLMs elsewhere, such as in a special third-party printer or IntranetWare router. Print servers, when created, are assigned the queues they are to service and which printers they will support. Unlike queues, print servers do not require disk storage; therefore, they can reside just about anywhere.

THE DESTINATION: AT THE PRINTER

Once a print server has been initialized, it will first attempt to find any printers it is supposed to support. Print servers support two types of printers: local and remote. The print server software, in NLM form, is called PSERVER.NLM, which, by itself, does not know how to talk to a printer. Therefore, a separate printer support module must be provided. Let's take a closer look.

Local Printers

If the printer is local (as defined during print server creation), then the PSERVER.NLM automatically loads a local NLM called NPRINTER.NLM. NPRINTER.NLM has a bidirectional communication with the print server, as well as a communication to the local port it is servicing. The local port is usually either a parallel or serial port. These printers are known as "Auto-Load" because NPRINTER is automatically loaded at the server.

This design has several advantages, including:

▸ PSERVER can theoretically talk to devices other than serial and parallel ports.

▸ By design, IntranetWare SFTIII has two parts: one that talks to hardware (IOEngine) and one that is common to both servers. Using this method, the PSERVER resides in the shared engine and NPRINTER resides in the IOEngine.

Remote Printers

If the designated printer is a remote printer, PSERVER.NLM attempts to contact it using SPX as the communications method. This necessitates loading the NPRINTER.EXE module on a workstation that has the desired remote printer attached to it. Once NPRINTER.EXE has been loaded, a communication will be established and remote printing can be supported. This printer is known as "Manual Load" because NPRINTER is loaded manually at the workstation.

REAL WORLD

You can automate the loading of NPRINTER.EXE by placing it in the workstation's AUTOEXEC.BAT file. It is not necessary to log in, but you must load IPX/SPX with IPXODI.COM (or IPX.NLM with Client 32). Also, make sure the following three files are available on the local disk: NPRINTER.EXE, NPRINTER.HLP, and NPRINTER.MSG. You can find them on the Install CD-ROM or in the SYS:PUBLIC directory. Finally, use the "/U" switch to unload NPRINTER.

ZEN

"Some people say Yoga is a great way to keep your energy up. For me, it's a Snickers and a Diet Coke."

Nanny Fine

That finishes our discussion of IntranetWare printing fundamentals. But, hold on, we're not done yet. Just when you think you're at the end of your journey, the tour guide throws in a few side stops. Don't you just hate that? In our case, it's time to explore a few third-party printing solutions, before we move on to setup and management.

THIRD-PARTY PRINTING SOLUTIONS

Several good add-ons are available for the IntranetWare printing system. These usually can augment the services already provided within the printing infrastructure.

For example, in a generic IntranetWare environment using remote printers, the job must go from the user to the queue, to the print server, and finally to the remote printer. Using a device that encapsulates these functions into one subsystem can greatly reduce the network traffic required to print. Two of these devices are the HP JetDirect Card and Intel's NetPort.

HP JetDirect Card

This device resides in a printer (such as an HP LaserJet4M or 4SI) and acts as a peer device on the network. It can be configured either as a print server or as a remote printer.

Ideally, the JetDirect card should be configured as a print server. This reduces the flow of network printing since the print job only has to go from the user to the queue, and then to the JetDirect card in the printer. The challenge is when you are running a system that the JetDirect card can't log into (for example, with an older JetDirect card and IntranetWare).

The other option is to set up the JetDirect as a remote printer. In this scenario, the JetDirect will have a name assigned to it when configured. This name must correspond to the name given to the remote printer when it was defined under IntranetWare. This way, the print server knows how to communicate with the JetDirect card. The down side is that you still have the same traffic, but you do not need a machine dedicated to support the remote printer. Finally, HP has developed a wonderful Windows-based printing management system called JetAdmin. It helps you set up and manage HP JetDirect cards.

SMART LINK

Explore Hewlett Packard's home page for more information on the HP JetDirect printing solution: http://www.hp.com.

Intel NetPort

Intel's solution is similar to HP's, except an Intel NetPort can only be configured as a peer device on the network. It plugs into an Ethernet cable just like another node on the network. It can then have a standard parallel cable attached to it, enabling it to communicate with a standard printer (unlike the HP JetDirect card, which only plugs into HP printers). The other options typically apply to the NetPort. Both modes can be supported, either as a remote printer or a print server.

Now, we're really at the end of our journey. They say, "A well-traveled person is an enlightened person." Do you feel well traveled? Do you feel enlightened? You should feel *something* right about now.

So, that's the essence of printing. It's not so bad. I think IntranetWare printing gets a bad rap. It's not very mysterious—you click a button on the workstation and your document comes out of the printer down the hall, assuming, of course, that you set it up correctly. Now would be a good time to explore that aspect of IntranetWare printing.

SMART LINK

Explore Intel's home page for more information on the Intel NetPort printing solution at http://www.intel.com.

IntranetWare Printing Setup

Welcome to IntranetWare printing setup. Now that you understand the essence of printing, it's time to do something about it. This is where the mystery begins to unfold. This is where the clues appear. This is "Sherlock Holmes 101."

SMART LINK

Visit Sherlock Holmes at http://www.citsoft.com/holmes.html.

Creating print services for a IntranetWare network requires a little bit of planning. In a simple environment, IntranetWare allows you to create a basic printing system by using the DOS utility PCONSOLE.

Under Windows, you must create the items separately and associate them. This is a relatively simple process—once you understand how printing works under IntranetWare. If you have read the previous section, this should appear relatively obvious.

As you recall, there are three elements to the printing system that must be present in order to print. They are

▸ The Queue—used to store the print jobs on the way to the printer

▸ The Print Server—polls the queue for jobs and prints them on assigned printers

▸ The Printer—defines whether the printer is local to the file server or remotely attached

You can use NWADMIN to create the IntranetWare printing system. NWADMIN is a Windows-based graphical utility that integrates several aspects of managing IntranetWare (including rights assignments and user creation) into one easy-to-use application.

The order in which you create the print system items (queue, print server, and printer) really makes no difference. The most efficient way is to start with the queue, since it is central to the printing system. Here's how I like to do it:

▸ Step 1: Create the print queue

▸ Step 2: Create the printer

▸ Step 3: Create the print server

▸ Step 4: Activate the printing system

There you have it. Four simple steps. No mystery here. Let's take a closer look, and don't forget your IntranetWare magnifying glass.

ZEN

"I've often wondered how the British know what everyone's feeling. They all must wear mood rings."

Nanny Fine

STEP 1: CREATE THE PRINT QUEUE

It is important to remember that when you create a queue, it should be central to the users who are going to use it. When using NDS, you usually want to keep the queues and print servers proximal to each other.

TIP

IntranetWare Printing Setup is closely related to NDS and partitioning. It is more efficient to have the area where the jobs get stored (Queue Volume) as close to the users as possible. If you reside in Camelot, it makes no sense to print something to a queue in Tokyo (unless you *want* the print job to print in Tokyo). See Chapter 3 for more information on replica distribution.

The first step is to choose the context where you create the queue. This is usually in the container where the users reside who will be using the queue the most.

To create the queue under NWADMIN, select Object/Create or select the container and press Insert. You'll be presented with a dialog box asking for the type of object you wish to create. Choose Print Queue and press Enter (see Figure 8.11). The items you need to define next are shown in Table 8.1 and Figure 8.11.

REAL WORLD

In previous versions of NetWare, the queue was *always* stored under SYS:SYSTEM in the volume SYS:. In IntranetWare, the NWADMIN utility will create a subdirectory off of the root of the volume chosen (which can be other than SYS: now!) and call it QUEUES. This is where the data will be stored for the queue.

Step 1: Create the Print Queue

T A B L E 8.1	PROPERTY	DESCRIPTION
Important Print Queue Properties	Directory Queue vs. Bindery Queue	If you are creating a regular queue (and we are), choose Directory Services Queue. A Bindery Reference Queue can service jobs out of a queue that resides on a 2.x or 3.x server. This can be useful if you have a mixed environment and must support queues from a single location.
		In addition, you can submit a job to Bindery Reference Queue and it will be sent automatically to the reference queue on the 3.x server.
	Print Queue Name	Usually you want to name a queue descriptively. It is easier to find a queue named CANONBJ-PQ1 than just Bubble Printer.
	Print Queue Volume	This is the physical space where the job will be stored as it is spooled and when it is serviced. Therefore, this property must reference a volume somewhere in the IntranetWare tree.
		In addition, the container in which the queue is created must have rights to that volume in order to create print jobs there.

At this point, you can choose to define other queue properties (which will be brought up in a dialog box), or let IntranetWare create the queue and allow you to create another. For our example, let's click the Define Additional Properties check box, then click on Create.

Data added to the Print Queue Identification page (such as Other Name and Location) can be useful when searching for queues under NWADMIN. This allows the user to find a queue based on unique information entered here, but the additional data is purely optional (see Figure 8.12 and Table 8.2).

F I G U R E   8.12

The Print Queue
Identification Page in
NWADMIN

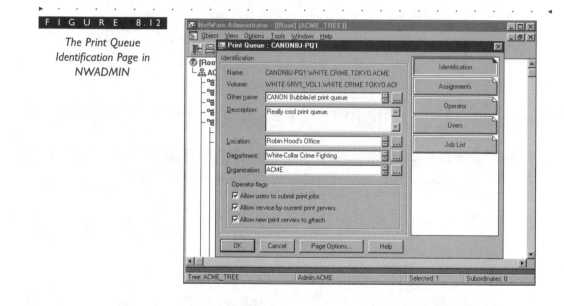

T A B L E 8.2

Additional Print Queue
Pages

PRINT QUEUE PAGE	DESCRIPTION
Assignments	The Assignments page is a view-only screen used to show which printer(s) the queue is servicing and which print server is servicing this queue.
Operator	The Operator page contains some of the most important information for the queue. Print queue operators can do several valuable management items, such as: Create new jobs in the queue Delete jobs submitted by other users Affect the availability of the queue

T A B L E 8.2	PRINT QUEUE PAGE	DESCRIPTION
Additional Print Queue Pages (continued)	Operator	Place holds on their own submitted jobs Place holds on jobs submitted by other users Grant access to other users to use the queue By default, the user that created the queue is the queue operator. You can add other users, if necessary.
	Users	The Print Queue Users page is the most important item for the queue because it is where you designate who may use the queue (that is, who may submit jobs via CAPTURE or through Windows). By default, anyone in the container where the queue was created as well as any containers below this container may submit print jobs to this queue. To limit this, you can assign other objects such as Groups, Organizational Roles, or specific users the ability to submit print jobs to the queue.
	Job List	Job List is a management function available to users and operators alike. It allows a user to view the current jobs in the queue as well as change details about the job. If you are a print queue operator, you can change aspects of jobs submitted by other users in addition to your own. To do this, highlight the job you want to change and click on Job Details. If the job is not actively being serviced, you can change aspects of the job such as number of copies, form feed after print, and so on. A print queue operator can change the priority of a job by changing its sequence number. For example, changing a job from sequence 3 to sequence 1 bumps the first job to sequence 2, 3 to 4, and so on. More of this function will be covered in the section "IntranetWare Printing Management."

STEP 2: CREATE THE PRINTER

The next step is to create a printer that will be serviced by the queue. Creating the printer is similar to creating the queue. Choose the container where the printer will be stored by selecting it with your mouse and pressing Insert (or choosing Create from the Object option on the toolbar). Choose Printer and give it a descriptive name. Click on Define Additional Properties and choose Create.

> **TIP**
>
> **You don't have to create the printer, print server, and queue in the same container. You can locate them in three different areas and then associate them. For our example, it is easier to create them all in the same container.**

You can use the Printer Identification page to provide information that NDS can use for searches, as well as to provide more descriptive information for users and other administrators. Check out Figure 8.13 and Table 8.3.

T A B L E 8.3	PRINTER PAGE	DESCRIPTION
Additional Printer Pages	Assignments	This page is where you tell the printer which queue(s) it will be servicing. You may have one printer that services multiple queues, or multiple printers servicing one queue. If you have more than one queue per printer, you can assign a priority, the highest being 1. Any jobs submitted to a higher-priority queue will get serviced before any waiting jobs in a lower-priority queue (see Figure 8.14).
		The default queue is used when a user chooses to capture to the network by using a printer name instead of a queue name. When you choose a printer name, the job will be sent to the default queue.
		For this option, choose the queue that you just created.
	Configuration	This option determines whether the printer is physically attached to the print server or remotely attached to a workstation.
		The first option, Printer Type, determines what kind of printer this is. Typically, it is either serial or parallel. The other options (such as AppleTalk and XNP) are configured and used with additional software.
		The Communication option specifies the local port that will be used. If the printer is polled, it will be sent printer output in a polled fashion instead of using interrupts to control print flow. Manual Load indicates that the remote printer software (NPRINTER.EXE) will be loaded instead of the local NPRINTER.NLM. If you choose Auto Load, the print server will know to load the NPRINTER.NLM at the server to service a locally attached printer.
		Another security feature of remote printers is the ability to limit the network address that the remote printer can use. This way, only the allowed address can load NPRINTER.EXE and support the print server as a remotely defined printer.

(continued)

T A B L E 8.3	PRINTER PAGE	DESCRIPTION
Additional Printer Pages (continued)	Notification	The Notification page is where you determine who will be notified in the event the printer has a problem. This is different than notifying the user when the print job submitted is complete.
		The default user is whoever submitted the print job. In a small office, this setting works just fine, but in a larger network, this setting is usually deleted and an IS group or person is added instead. This makes servicing the printer (for example, when it is out of paper) the job of such a person.
		You can also specify how often (in minutes) the person gets notified. First indicates how long before the first message is sent, and Next is the interval at which subsequent messages will be sent.
	Features	This page allows more descriptive data to be placed in NDS, which allows for better searching. For example, a user/administrator could search for printers supporting PCL with 4 MB memory and a fax card. This search could occur network-wide, or could be limited to a subarea of the directory tree.

▶ · ◀

F I G U R E 8.14

The Printer Assignments Page in NWADMIN

REAL WORLD

The Printer Configuration page in NWADMIN is where you configure options for third-party printer support such as HP JetDirect cards or Intel's Netport. These devices can act either as a remote printer or as a print server to an IntranetWare server. Older versions of these products may only be used as remote printers and not as print servers in a IntranetWare environment.

STEP 3: CREATE THE PRINT SERVER

To create a print server, use the NWADMIN utility. Select the container that will store the print server and press Insert while the container is highlighted. Choose Print Server off of the list, and then choose OK.

First, you need to give the print server a name. Once again, descriptive names work best (such as WHITE-PS1). This will help you search for print servers later.

After entering the name, click on the Define Additional Properties check box and choose Create. The Print Server Identification page will appear (see Figure 8.15). Table 8.4 lists the basic information you will need to provide to complete print server creation.

FIGURE 8.15

The Print Server Identification Page in NWADMIN

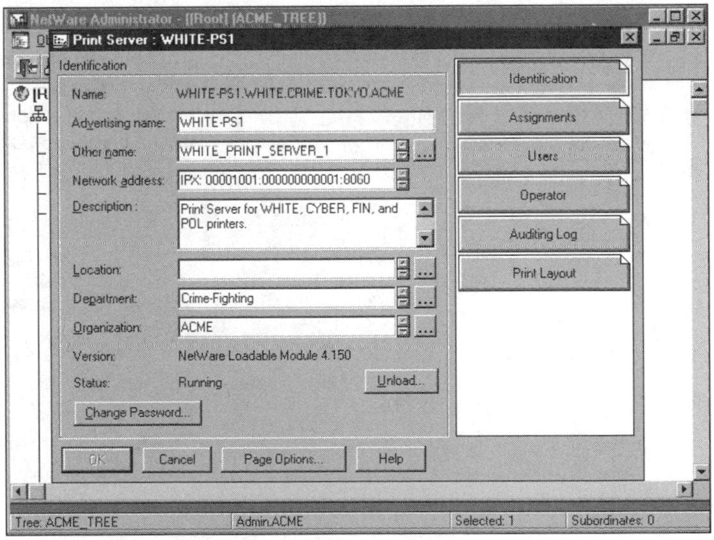

	PRINTER	DESCRIPTION
T A B L E 8.4 *Additional Print Server Pages*	Assignments	This page allows you to tell the print server which printers it will be servicing. Note that it may support several (up to 256) for one print server. Naturally, not all the printers can be attached physically to the print server (only 5). The rest would be attached remotely. Select the printer you just created by choosing Add (see Figure 8.16). The printer will be added with a Printer Number. Usually this number will not be referenced on a day-to-day basis. One or two IntranetWare utilities still require it, such as Print Server Control (PSC), which is covered in the "IntranetWare Printing Management" section.
	Users	Users information is not necessary for a user to print, even if this print server is servicing jobs in queues where the user has submitted a print job. This page is provided so that users can check the status of a print server using the management utilities (such as PSC or NWADMIN). If the user never needs to do this (for example, if printer management is handled by IS), then the user doesn't need the print server user status. By default, all users in the container where the print server was created are given the print server user status.
	Operator	Print server operators are similar to queue operators in that they can manage the print server. For example, print server operators may take printers off-line remotely, shut down the print server, and abort jobs in process.
	Auditing Log	This page allows you to enable an auditing function for the print server. You can limit the size of the audit file, as well as how many jobs it will keep in its auditing log. The file can be printed or it can be viewed under NWADMIN.
	Print Layout	This is a very handy function in that you can graphically see the printing layout in one screen. This function works for all printers and queues associated with this print server.

T A B L E 8.4	PRINTER	DESCRIPTION
Additional Print Server Pages (continued)	Print Layout (continued)	An additional function called Status allows the print server operator to view the status of all elements in the printing hierarchy. Simply select one of the printing components and click on Status. Figure 8.17 shows an example of the Print Server Status screen.

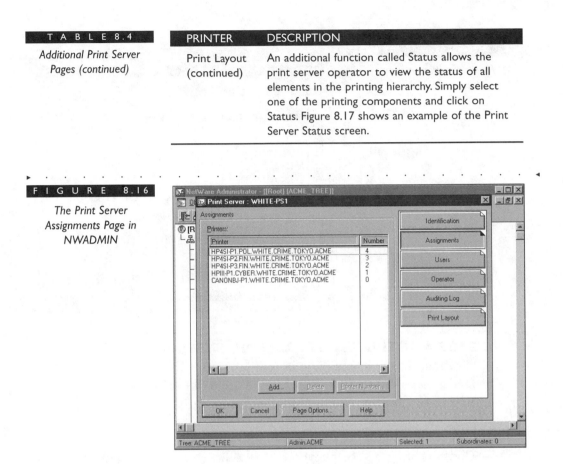

F I G U R E   8.16

The Print Server
Assignments Page in
NWADMIN

When you create a print server, you should set a password for the print server for security reasons. You can set a password under the Print Server Creation screen by pressing the Change Password button. You will be asked for the password at server load time.

ZEN

"Danny bought me some lingerie for my birthday. It was so inappropriate. It's a good thing my mother's birthday was two days later or I'd still be stuck with the thing."

Nanny Fine

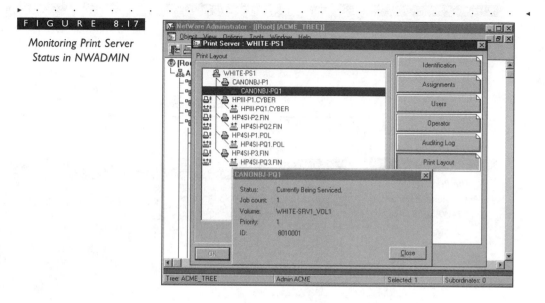

FIGURE 8.17

*Monitoring Print Server
Status in NWADMIN*

STEP 4: ACTIVATE THE PRINTING SYSTEM

Now that the configuration is set, the last step is to start the print server. This is done either at the server, or remotely by using RCONSOLE.

To start the print server, load PSERVER.NLM at the console by typing

LOAD PSERVER

This will bring up the menu for PSERVER. It will show the context that the server is in within the directory tree. If you need to change where the print server is, you can either type in the new context or browse by pressing Enter. Selecting ".." moves up in the tree or you can select another container by choosing a container name and hitting enter. Once you have found the print server, load it by highlighting it and pressing Enter.

Three things will happen:

1 • The print server will load. Any printers that are locally defined for this print server will be supported by NPRINTER.NLM, which is loaded automatically if it is needed by local printers. The local printers will have a status of "Waiting for Jobs" once this is complete.

2 • Remote printers defined for this server will attempt to find a remote printer. If they cannot, they will wait for remote printer software to contact them (either IntranetWare's NPRINTER.EXE, or a third-party solution such as HP's JetDirect card or Intel's Netport).

3 • The print server will ask for a password before loading. Passwords are desirable especially in larger networks. If you need to add or change a print server password, use NWADMIN and select the print server. PCONSOLE also allows you to change passwords as well.

TIP

When the IntranetWare print server loads, it looks to the corresponding NDS Print Server object for three vital pieces of information: password for access to printing console, available printers serviced by this print server, and the user/operator list. If you change any of these values in NDS, they will not take effect until the print server is brought down and back up again.

The print server Main Menu provides you with two options: Printer Status and Print Server Information.

Printer Status

This option allows you to view status of all printers defined for this print server (see Figure 8.18). You can also execute some printer management functions, such as:

► Abort currently printing jobs

► Stop printer output

► Start printer output

► Eject a page (form feed)

In addition, you can change how forms (discussed later) get serviced on the selected printer. All of these functions can also be done via NWADMIN and PSC (a DOS utility).

F I G U R E   8.18

The Print Server Status Window

```
NetWare Print Server  4.15                    NetWare Loadable Module
Print server: WHITE-PS1.WHITE.CRIME.TOKYO.ACME
                           Status: Running

Printer:      CANONBJ-P1.WHITE.CRIME.TOKYO.ACME
Type:         Manual Load (Remote), LPT1
Address:      00001234:00A024563DEE:403B                  Printer control

Current status:   Waiting for job

Queues serviced:  (See list)                      Abort print job
Service mode:     Minimize form changes within print qu   Form feed
Mounted form:     0                                       Mark top of form
                                                          Pause printer
NetWare server:                                           Private / Shared
Print queue:                                              Start printer
Print job ID:                                             Stop printer
Description:
Print job form:

Copies requested:                        Finished:
Size of 1 copy:                          Finished:
Percent complete:
```

Print Server Information

The Print Server Information screen has two functions:

▸ Allows you to view print server information such as version and name

▸ Allows the print server to be shut down gracefully

Ideally, the print server should be shut down either remotely (via NWADMIN or PCONSOLE), or at the server using this option.

To shut down the print server, choose Current Status and press Enter. You can then shut down the print server in one of two ways:

1 • Immediately—With this option, any currently running jobs are suspended. They will continue when the print server is restarted.

2 • Unload after active print jobs—This allows any printing jobs to complete before the print server terminates.

In either case, the print server will advertise that it is no longer available and then terminate. Let's take a look at how changes to print servers take effect.

When you make the following changes, the print server must be unloaded and reloaded at the file server/router where the print server is running. This way, IntranetWare can read the new information and effect the changes.

Changes made directly to a print server:

▸ Assigned printers

▸ Passwords

Changes made to printers and queues assigned to a print server:

▸ Queue assignments

▸ Printer definition (parallel, serial, remote, or local)

▸ Forms servicing

▸ Notification of service alerts

Changes to the following take place immediately:

▸ Queue users

▸ Print server users

▸ Queue operators

▸ Print server operators

Understanding that some changes take place immediately and others take place after loading/reloading will help you avoid frustration when the print server appears to accept changes, but does not effect them immediately.

SMART LINK

If IntranetWare printing setup is still a great mystery to you, join us for a special printing course at CyberState University at http://www.cyberstateu.com

This completes our discussion of the fundamentals of IntranetWare printing setup. But before we dive into the depths of printing management, let's take a moment to explore some extracurricular setup options—namely, setup customization with forms and devices.

CUSTOMIZING INTRANETWARE PRINTING

Forms and devices add another dimension to the IntranetWare printing system. You should be able to determine now if forms or device definitions are needed in your network.

The first step is to determine where in the tree the devices need to exist. If forms or devices do not exist in a particular context, the printing system will look into the next higher context until it finds a definition. This would allow an administrator to create forms and devices at the Organization level of the tree, and all users in the entire organization would benefit.

Users will always use the forms and devices in their own contexts if they exist. If they do exist within the context, then the users cannot see any others above their own context.

Creating forms and definitions can be done either under NWADMIN (graphically under Windows) or using the DOS menu command PRINTDEF. Once they have been created, you can assign forms or devices to users with either NWADMIN (under Windows) or PRINTCON (under DOS). This is accomplished by creating a print job configuration for the user or container.

Building Forms

1 • Choose the context where you wish the form or forms to exists. This could be at the root or deep within the directory.

2 • Select the Organizational Unit (container) and click the right mouse button.

3 • Choose Details.

4 • Choose Printer Forms.

5 • Choose Create.

6 • Give the new form a descriptive name. Typically form 0 is the first form. Therefore, it should be the most commonly used form. This might be labeled BLANK or WORDPROC.

7 • The form number is used from the command line under CAPTURE, although CAPTURE can now use form names as well. Usually the form is referenced by name not by number.

8 • Choose OK.

This will create the form desired within the selected context. The next step is to assign it to a user. This can be done two ways:

▶ Set up a *print job configuration*. This is a collection of printing attributes that the user can select by a given name. One of the attributes can be the form name used when submitting jobs.

▶ Select a form name when capturing a printer under NWUSER (Windows 3.1). This is usually chosen by the user before printing, as opposed to using a preset configuration such as print job configurations.

Creating print job configurations will be covered later (see the section "Tying It All Together").

Building Devices

Creating devices requires two steps:

▶ Step 1: Creating functions—These are printing-specific. They would include codes for things such as Reset, Landscape, Portrait, Letter-size, Graphics mode, and so on. To get these codes, you must refer to the manual that came with your printer.

▶ Step 2: Creating modes—These are made of up one or more functions. They allow you to send a series of functions to the printer before your job prints.. For example, you can

    ▶ Reset the printer

    ▶ Change to landscape

    ▶ Change to A4 format

Together, functions and modes constitute a *device* definition. The idea is that when you start to print to the network printer, IntranetWare will send these codes to the desired printer and properly initialize it for you.

TIP

As stated before, it is much more desirable to allow the application (such as WordPerfect) to send its own codes. If that is not possible, then IntranetWare can send them for you via this interface.

To create functions and modes, you must decide where you want them to be available. As with forms, you can create them once at the root of the tree and make them globally available, or deeper in the directory tree. Also as with forms, when looking for devices, IntranetWare looks in the current container, and, if none is found, it continues to looks into superior containers until one is found. If none is found, no devices will be available.

REAL WORLD

NWUSER allows you to choose a form when capturing under Windows. However, NWUSER doesn't look into superior containers for other forms if none exists in the current context. Therefore, you may need to create a form in the users' context anyway, or change contexts.

To create a device, first choose the container where the device will be stored. As noted previously this will have an impact on who will be able to see and use the device. Then create the device as follows:

1 • Click the right mouse button on the desired container.

2 • Choose Details.

3 • Choose Print Devices.

4 • Choose Create.

5 • Next, we must create a device name (such as HP4SI). To do this, put in a name under Name and press Enter.

6 • Next, we must create functions, since modes are created from one or more functions. As a sample, we'll create a reset function. Choose Modify.

7 • Choose Create Function (see Figure 8.19).

8 • First you must give the function a name. This should be descriptive of the function. As described previously, you can obtain the function codes from your printer manual. There are some codes that you cannot type in (such as ESCAPE). These codes are typed in within delimiters to tell IntranetWare that a special character is needed. For example, you can indicate ESCAPE in other ways, such as <ESC> or <ESCAPE>. To represent reset string of Escape E, you would represent it as <ESCAPE>E.

9 • Once you have created one or more functions, you can now create a mode. To create a mode, choose Create Mode. There is a default mode called *reinitialize* that is automatically created. This mode can be populated with the reset function (created earlier) for the print device you are defining. To add the reset function we just created, choose Add Above or Add Below.

TIP

Above and *Below* will make a difference in how the mode works. Naturally, you would want to send a reset function before you send the function for Landscape. It the functions were reversed, it wouldn't do you any good (setting Landscape, then reset!). Adding Above and Add Below allows you to place functions where they need to be in the mode list.

10 • Be sure to give the mode a name. This should be descriptive of what the mode needs to do. In our case, the mode name Reset is perfect. You may also want to add the reset function to the predefined mode reinitialize.

F I G U R E   8.19

Creating a New Function in NWADMIN

Importing Devices   A nice capability is importing into the system predefined devices defined by someone else. This does not include device drivers from application manufacturers. Only IntranetWare-defined devices can be imported (and exported).

An example might be where another administrator already went through the pain of creating a print driver for a new device. They can export that device (see the "Exporting Devices" section) into a file that can then be imported into your system.

To do this, follow these steps:

1 • Choose the container where you wish to import the device.

2 • Click the right mouse button and choose Details.

3 • Choose Print Devices.

4 • Choose Import.

5 • Under filename, type **Z:\PUBLIC** and press Enter (this step is shown in Figure 8.20).

> **TIP**
>
> **Novell includes many predefined devices as examples for real applications. They are stored in SYS:PUBLIC during install.**

6 • Choose a device name, such as HPLJ4.PDF. (PDF stands for Printer Definition File.) Then choose OK.

7 • The file will now be imported into NDS as a new device. To verify, check the modes and functions defined for this device.

▶ • ◀

F I G U R E   8.20

Importing Devices in NWADMIN

Remember that to utilize these forms and devices, you must create a print job configuration for a user and either make it a default for the user or allow the user to activate the configuration via a batch file or command line.

Exporting Devices   This option is similar to import. The steps are as follows:

1 • Choose the container where the device exists.

2 • Open Details on the container.

3 • Choose Print Devices.

4 • Choose Export.

5 • Choose a filename and directory where you want to store the exported device in the form of a file.

6 • Choose OK.

NWADMIN will then export all functions and modes for the device and store them in a file. At that point, you may copy it to a diskette, e-mail it, or otherwise make it available for other administrators.

QUIZ

Let's test your mystery-solving abilities. What English word can have four of its five letters removed and still retain the same pronunciation?

(Q8-2)

Tying It All Together

You now know how to create forms and devices, but how do you assign them to users? That is the next step. IntranetWare has a method for integrating together a series of printing options into a named grouping of items. This is called a *print job configuration*. Print job configurations can be used in several ways:

► They can be created for a particular user.

► They can be created for a container. Then all users/objects in the container can use it.

► You can use a print job configuration defined for another user and assign it to another user in lieu of creating a duplicate configuration.

► You can make a print job configuration *default*. This means that if the user issues a CAPTURE command (under a Login Script or command line), then the items defined in the job will take effect.

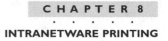
To create a print job (either for a user or a container):

1 • Choose the item in NWADMIN and select Details.

2 • Choose Print Job Configuration.

3 • Choose New.

4 • Give the job a name.

5 • You must choose a print queue for this job. Other options (for example, banners, copies, and form feed) are at the discretion of the creator. You can also assign a device, mode, and form (if they are created and within the scope of the configuration being created (see Figure 8.21).

6 • Choose OK.

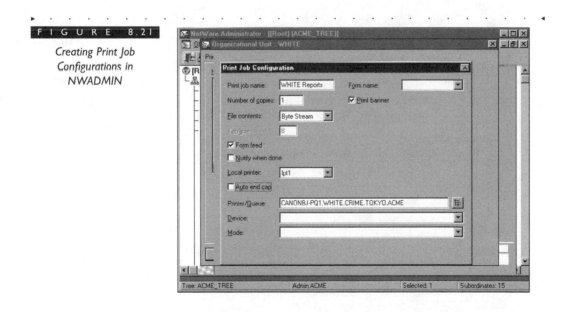

FIGURE 8.21

Creating Print Job Configurations in NWADMIN

After creating the print job configuration, you can now optionally make it a default. For obvious reasons, there can be only one default. You can make other configurations the default if you wish. To select the default, highlight the desired configuration and click on Default. You should see a small printer icon next to the chosen configuration.

To use a configuration other than the default, use the /J option with the CAPTURE command on the command line (or when using CAPTURE in a Login Script).

Congratulations! You've passed the first test. You successfully set up IntranetWare printing. Now comes the fun part—keeping it running. This is the *real* mystery of life.

IntranetWare Printing Management

IntranetWare printing setup was a breeze. And now the system is working flawlessly. You've tested a few documents, and they printed fine. You're probably getting a little overconfident right about now. Be careful, it happens to the best of us.

Now for the real test—letting the users loose on your new, clean, "working" printing system. You know it can print in a vacuum, but what about in a war zone? Welcome to IntranetWare printing management. In this section, we will explore five key management responsibilities, and learn about five key printing management tools. They are

▶ Managing printing with PCONSOLE

▶ Managing printing with NWADMIN

▶ Managing print servers with PSC

▶ Configuring print jobs with PRINTCON

▶ Customizing printing with PRINTDEF

With the release of IntranetWare, many of the DOS-based administration utilities that have been around since the beginning of NetWare were replaced by new utilities that support NDS. Even though the new NDS utilities have the same C-worthy look and feel, most of them have changed entirely—much to the dismay of some of us old NetWare junkies! Fortunately, for those who prefer to work under DOS, the DOS-based printing utilities under IntranetWare survived the cut with a few minor changes.

This section describes how IntranetWare print services can be managed in a distributed environment. We'll also cover some common printing issues and how to resolve them.

SMART LINK

For a comprehensive discussion of IntranetWare's numerous printing utilities, check out "NetWare Printing and Utilities" at http://support.novell.com/sitemap.

The main areas that can be managed are shown in Table 8.5. Take a look.

T A B L E 8.5	COMPONENT	HOW YOU CAN MANAGE THIS COMPONENT
IntranetWare Printing Management Components	Print Servers	If you are a print server operator, you can Unload the print server View auditing records
	Queues	For queue operators and users, the queue allows for great flexibility in what can be seen and changed remotely (under NWADMIN and PCONSOLE). For example, you can: Delete a job (NWADMIN and PCONSOLE) Create a job (PCONSOLE) Suspend a queue from receiving new jobs (NWADMIN and PCONSOLE) Suspend servicing of jobs (NWADMIN and PCONSOLE) Place an operator hold on a job (NWADMIN and PCONSOLE) Place a user hold on a job (NWADMIN and PCONSOLE)

(continued)

TABLE 8.5	COMPONENT	HOW YOU CAN MANAGE THIS COMPONENT
IntranetWare Printing Management Components (continued)	Printers	For printers, you can: View how much of a job has been completed (NWADMIN and PCONSOLE) Mount a new form (NWADMIN and PCONSOLE) Pause and restart a printer (NWADMIN and PCONSOLE) Abort a currently printing job

Some of the same general-purpose utilities that you use to create print services are the same ones that you use for management. Some special-purpose utilities (such as PSC) are only used for management. Table 8.6 summarizes these utilities.

TABLE 8.6	TOOL	FUNCTION
IntranetWare Printing Management Tools	NWADMIN	Used to do most print system component management. This includes: Deleting jobs Changing mounted forms Stopping and starting printers Checking the status of jobs in the queue Placing holds on jobs Aborting currently printing jobs
	PCONSOLE	This is a DOS/MENU utility and encompasses most of the queue and print server creation and management functions. These include: Deleting jobs from a queue Submitting a new job (not possible under NWADMIN) Placing holds on a job Stopping and starting printers Aborting currently printing jobs
	PSC	This is a command line utility that can be used to manage print servers from a command line. This includes: Mounting new forms Stopping and starting printers Aborting currently printing jobs

For the most part, users are more interested in getting information about print jobs than they are in completing particular tasks. Most of the time, users need to know when a job will complete, or if the printer is available. They might need to delete a submitted job, but otherwise, they probably don't need to be able to do too many things to a printer or print job. The double-X's in Table 8.7 show the minimum rights needed to complete certain tasks.

T A B L E 8.7

*IntranetWare Printing
Management Administrators*

FUNCTION	QUEUE OPERATOR	QUEUE USER	PRINT SERVER OPERATOR	PRINT SERVER USER
View any submitted job		XX		
Delete a submitted job (personal)		XX		
Delete another user's jobs	XX			
Create a new job		XX		
Prevent users from submitting jobs to a queue	XX			
Suspend servicing of print jobs	XX			
Abort a printing job on a printer			XX	
Stop a printer			XX	
Restart a printer			XX	
Mount a new form for a printer		XX		
Check printer status			XX	
Place a user hold on a job (personal)		XX		
Place an operator hold on a job	XX			
Check printer status				XX
Check percentage of the job printed				XX

Now that you've got your battle plan, let's arm you with some powerful printing management weapons, starting with the strongest of them all—PCONSOLE.

ZEN

"Men can't be rushed. They're like children. You cook them too fast, they get tough. Whereas, you take your time, let them simmer for a while, they fall apart in your hands."

Nanny Fine

MANAGING PRINTING WITH PCONSOLE

PCONSOLE is the general of printing utilities. IntranetWare's print console allows for the configuration and administration of NDS printing objects. Let's take a look at the PCONSOLE main menu (see Figure 8.22).

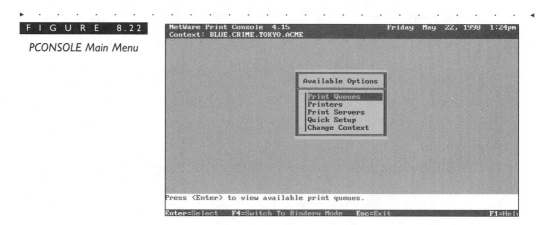

F I G U R E   8.22

PCONSOLE Main Menu

Before we begin exploring the PCONSOLE menu options, you should be aware of a few important things about PCONSOLE. First, notice the top of the screen. In addition to the version of PCONSOLE that is running and the date and time, you will see your current context. This is very important, because any menu option we choose at this point will affect this context only. For example, if we were to choose Print Queues, we would see the print queues configured in the current context only. A common mistake when using PCONSOLE is to be in the wrong context, select one of the menu items, and then find yourself wondering, "What happened to all of my printing objects?" So, before beginning your printing administration, be sure that you are in the proper context.

The default PCONSOLE context will be whatever context you were in when you ran PCONSOLE.EXE. Generally, this will be the context you were placed in at login. If your current context isn't correct, you can use the Change Context option to move to the proper context. Let's do that now. When you select Change Context, you are prompted to either type the context you desire, or to use the Insert key to browse for the desired context. Using the Insert key is the easiest, most foolproof method since it eliminates any guessing. When you press Insert, you will be presented with the Container object below your current context.

By selecting the Organizational Unit, you can move deeper in the tree. Just like in a DOS file system directory structure, the two dots indicate "parent," so, if you press Enter at the two dots, you'll move up the tree to the parent container. When you have finished browsing for the desired context, press F10 or Esc to save the new context.

The second important item to notice on the PCONSOLE main menu is the menu bar at the bottom of the screen. Most of the options are self-explanatory: Enter to select, F10 or Esc to exit, F1 for help, but the one you should pay close attention to is F4=Switch To Bindery Mode. This option is a toggle switch. By pressing F4, PCONSOLE will change the display from NDS objects to Bindery objects. This option is normally used when you are logged into a bindery-based NetWare server (that is, NetWare 3 or NetWare 2). It can also be used if you are logged in as a user who is in the bindery context of the server to which you are authenticated. If you are not, when you press F4, you will receive a bindery context error message.

This option is useful in a mixed NetWare 3 and IntranetWare environment because it allows you to toggle back and forth between NDS and bindery, and easily manage network printing in both environments.

Using Quick Setup

Before we get into the details of PCONSOLE, let's take a look at the best part of the utility—Quick Setup. One of the most frustrating parts of configuring network printing is trying to remember the next step in the process. Administrators frequently create all of the necessary printing objects correctly, but miss one step in the process of linking print queues to printers and printers to print servers. The result: hours of trying to figure out why jobs go to the print queue but never print.

Quick Setup allows you to set up a print server, printer, and print queue very quickly (hence the name), making all of the necessary assignments for you. This option is great for the administrator who doesn't like to hop back and forth between menus, trying to remember the next step in the print setup process.

If you choose Quick Setup from a context that does not have print services configured, the system will present you with default print object names, as shown in Figure 8.23.

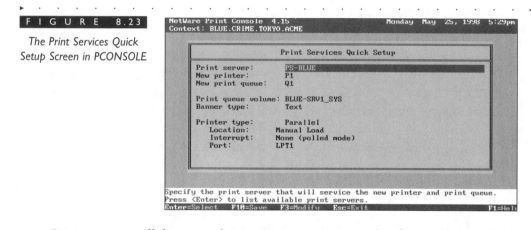

F I G U R E   8.23

The Print Services Quick
Setup Screen in PCONSOLE

Print servers will be named PS-<Container_Name>, the first printer will be named P1, and the first print queue will be named Q1. These defaults can be changed as necessary to match the naming standards of your organization.

Default assumptions will also be made about the print queue volume, banner type, and printer configuration. These defaults can also be changed as necessary.

To change the printer configuration, arrow down to Printer type and press Enter. Select the appropriate printer type—Parallel, Serial, or other printer type—and press Enter. You will also need to specify whether this printer is an Auto Load printer (directly attached to the print server) or a Manual Load (workstation or network attached).

Generally, the Interrupt field can be left at the default of None (polled mode). If you choose to use an interrupt method, this field can be configured to indicate the interrupt of the port hardware. This field must match the port hardware if an interrupt is used. The Port field must match the port to which this printer is physically attached—LPT1, LPT2, and so on.

Quick Setup is the foolproof method for configuring IntranetWare printing. Unfortunately, this option is only available in PCONSOLE, not NWADMIN. So, for those of you who are die-hard GUI administrators, if you find yourself caught in a DOS utility, this is the easiest way to set up IntranetWare printing.

Quick Setup is not the only way to create printing objects in PCONSOLE—it's just the easiest! The objects can also be created using the individual Print Queues, Printers, and Print Servers options from the PCONSOLE main menu as described in the following sections.

Managing Print Queues

By selecting the Print Queues option from the PCONSOLE main menu, you are shown a list of print queues currently configured in the current context. By pressing Insert, a new print queue can be created. When creating a new print queue, you will be asked for two pieces of information: print queue name and print queue volume.

The name assigned to a print queue can be any hexadecimal name from 1 to 64 characters, including spaces and underscores. Even though this provides tremendous flexibility, it is recommended that you keep your print queue names short and descriptive. For example, a print queue that is serviced by an HPIII LaserJet printer might be named HPIII-PQ1.

The second piece of information that will be required when creating a new print queue is the print queue volume. This is the volume where the print jobs sent to this queue will be spooled. Since the volume name entered here must be the full NDS name of the volume, use the Insert key to browse the tree to find the appropriate volume. When you have found the volume on which you want to create this queue, press Enter or F10 to accept your selection.

Remember, before any new print queue created can be used, all of the proper printing assignments must be made, including assigning a print server to service this queue and attaching a printer. This process is described in the following discussion.

By selecting Print Queues from the PCONSOLE Available Options menu you can also manage existing NDS print queues. The left side of Figure 8.24 shows the print queues configured in the context .BLUE.CRIME.TOKYO.ACME.

▶ · ◀

F I G U R E   8.24

The Print Queue
Information Screen in
PCONSOLE

```
NetWare Print Console  4.15                    Monday  May   25, 1998  5:32pm
Context: BLUE.CRIME.TOKYO.ACME


        ┌─────── Print Queues ───────┐
        │ HPIII-PQ1          │vailable Optio│ Print Queue Information │
        │                    │Print Queues  │ Print Jobs              │
        │                    │Printers      │ Status                  │
        │                    │Print Servers │ Attached Print Servers  │
        │                    │Quick Setup   │ Information              │
        │                    │Change Context│ Users                   │
        │                    │              │ Operators               │
        │                    │              │ Print Servers           │
        │                    │              │                         │
        └────────────────────┘

 Press <Enter> to view a list of print jobs in the print queue.
 Enter=Select   Esc=Exit                                              F1=Help
```

When you select an available print queue, you will see the available information about this print queue displayed on the right side of the screen (see Figure 8.24). Table 8.8 summarizes the information found in each menu option listed.

T A B L E 8.8

Print Queue Information
Parameters

MENU OPTION	PURPOSE
Print Jobs	Allows you to view the current print jobs in this queue. Also allows a print queue operator to delete jobs from the queue, reorder jobs in the queue, and put an operator hold on the jobs in the queue. Regular users (non-operators) can only modify jobs that they have submitted.
Status	Allows you to view the status of this print queue, including number of jobs, number of print servers servicing this queue and operator flags.
Attached Print Servers	Shows a list of active print servers servicing this print queue. The print server must be loaded in order to be active.
Information	Allows you to view the print queue identification number, and the server and volume in which this queue is created on. The print queue ID number is the subdirectory name of this print queue plus a .QDR extension. This subdirectory will be in the QUEUES directory of the indicated volume.

TABLE 8.8	MENU OPTION	PURPOSE
Print Queue Information Parameters (continued)	Users	Shows a list of users and groups who are authorized to submit jobs to this queue. Also allows you to add new users.
	Operators	Shows a list of users and groups who are authorized to manage this queue. Also allows you to add new operators.
	Print Servers	Allows you to view the print servers authorized to service this queue. Also allows you to authorize additional print servers to service this queue.

Viewing Jobs in a Print Queue   By selecting Print Jobs from the Print Queue Information menu, you can see all of the print jobs in this queue that are waiting to be serviced. Print queue operators will be shown all jobs in the queue. Regular users, or non-operators of the queue, will only be shown the jobs that they submitted. By selecting a specific print job, you will see information about that job, as shown in Figure 8.25.

FIGURE 8.25

The Print Job Information Screen in PCONSOLE

```
NetWare Print Console  4.15                  Monday  May  25, 1998  5:54pm
Context: BLUE.CRIME.TOKYO.ACME
                           Print Job Information
 Print job:        0193E001              File size:        5522
 Client:           WEarp[7]
 Description:      J:USERS\WEARP\BLUCRIME.RPT
 Status:           Print job is ready and waiting for the print server.

 User hold:        No                    Entry date:       5-25-1998
 Operator hold:    No                    Entry time:       5:52:39 pm
 Service sequence: 1
                                         Form:             Reports
 Number of copies: 1                     Print banner:     Yes
                                         Name:             WEarp
 File contents:    Byte stream          Banner name:      LPT1
 Tab size:
                                         Defer printing:   No
 Form feed:        Yes                   Target date:
 Notify when done: No                    Target time:

 Enter up to 49 characters to describe the print job.

Esc=Exit                                                         F1=Help
```

This screen shows the print job ID number, who submitted the job, the filename, and the status of the job. This screen also allow a user or operator hold to be placed on the job. If the job is placed on hold, it will stay in the queue until the hold is removed.

The "Service sequence" field allows you to reorder jobs in the queue. In our example, there is only one job currently in the queue, so the service sequence is

1—indicating that this job is next in line to be serviced by the print server. If there were jobs in the queue ahead of this one, we could change the service sequence number, thereby moving it up in the queue. Only print queue operators can place one user's job ahead of another's. Users can only reorder their own jobs.

If you look closely at the remaining options, you'll notice that these are all of the parameters used with CAPTURE. So, if you send a print job with CAPTURE parameters and would like to change the parameters after the job is sent, you can do that here.

The last option on this screen is "Defer printing." If this option is set to Yes, you will be able to specify the date and time for which you would like this job to print. This option is useful if you are printing large jobs that you would like to defer until a later, less busy, time.

Putting Print Queues on Hold   Using the Status option of the Print Queue Information menu, a print queue operator can put the select print queue on hold. There are three hold options in this menu:

- ▸ Allow users to submit print jobs—When set to No, this option prevents users from placing additional jobs in the queue. Any jobs already in the queue will continue to be serviced by the print server. This is useful when you are planning to do maintenance on a printer, or if you are planning to change print queue definitions.

- ▸ Allow service by current print servers—This option, when set to No, will allow users to continue to place jobs in the queue, but those jobs will not be printed until this flag is removed. Again, this option is useful when doing printer or print server maintenance.

- ▸ Allow new print servers to attach—This option prevents new print servers from attaching to this queue.

Assigning Print Queue Users and Operators   The Users option of the PCONSOLE Print Queue Information menu allows you to authorize users and groups to place jobs in this queue. When you select this option, you are presented with a list of current print queue users. Use the Insert key to browse the tree and then authorize new users, groups, or containers as users of this print queue by highlighting an object and pressing F10. Multiple objects can be selected by using the F5 key to mark them and F10 to select. To remove print queue users, highlight the object in the user list and press Delete.

Assigning print queue operators is done is a similar fashion. Select the Operators menu option and use the Insert key to browse and F10 to select.

Attaching Print Servers to a Queue To assign a print server to service a queue, select the Print Servers option from the Print Queue Information menu. You will be shown a list of the print servers currently assigned to service this queue. Use the Insert key to browse the NDS tree to find the print server you would like to service this queue. To add a print server to the list, highlight the server name and press F10 or Esc. Before the print server will actively service this queue, it must be loaded at a file server.

ZEN

"Big hair makes your hips look smaller."

Nanny Fine

Managing Printers

When you select the Printer option from the PCONSOLE main menu, you will be shown a list of print queues configured in the current context. Use the Insert key to create a new printer. When you create a printer in PCONSOLE, the only information you are asked for at this point is the printer name. This can be a little deceiving because additional steps are required to complete the printer setup.

Once the printer is created, you will need to select the printer by pressing Enter and configure it from the resulting Printer Configuration screen (shown in the background of the screen in Figure 8.26).

This default configuration assumes that you are configuring a parallel printer attached to LPT1 of a remote workstation. So, in order to complete the configuration, you must provide the following information if the default configuration is not correct:

▶ Printer type—Whether this printer is a parallel, serial, or other type of printer.

▸ Configuration—To which port this printer is attached (LPT1, LPT2, and so on), and the location of this printer; that is, locally (directly) attached or remotely (workstation) attached.

▸ Interrupt—IntranetWare defaults to a polled mode when checking a print queue for new print jobs. If you choose to use an interrupt mode instead, this field can be configured to indicate the interrupt of the port hardware. This field must match the port hardware if an interrupt is used.

▸ Address restriction—This optional field allows you to restrict this printer to being loaded on the specified workstation or network.

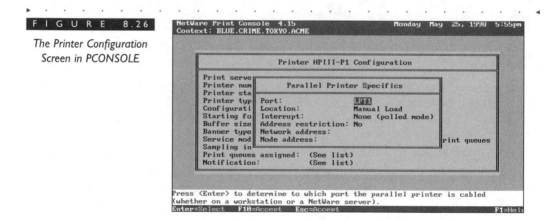

FIGURE 8.26

The Printer Configuration Screen in PCONSOLE

To complete the printer configuration, you must assign a print queue for this printer to service and link a print server.

To manage NDS printing objects with PCONSOLE, select the Printers option from the PCONSOLE main menu. This allows you to manage NDS printer objects in the current context. By selecting an available printer, you can see the current configuration of this printer (see Figure 8.27).

Table 8.9 summarizes the information found in Figure 8.27.

F I G U R E   8.27

Printer Configuration Screen for an HPIII LaserJet Printer

```
NetWare Print Console  4.15                    Monday  May  25, 1998  6:00pm
Context: BLUE.CRIME.TOKYO.ACME

              ┌─────────────────────────────────────────────┐
              │         Printer HPIII-P1 Configuration        │
              ├─────────────────────────────────────────────┤
              │ Print server:          BLUE-PS1               │
              │ Printer number:        0                      │
              │ Printer status:        (See form)             │
              │ Printer type:          Parallel               │
              │ Configuration:         (See form)             │
              │ Starting form:         0                      │
              │ Buffer size in KB:     3                      │
              │ Banner type:           Text                   │
              │ Service mode for forms: Minimize form changes within print queues │
              │ Sampling interval:     5                      │
              │ Print queues assigned: (See list)             │
              │ Notification:          (See list)             │
              └─────────────────────────────────────────────┘

Press <Enter> to view the status of this active printer.
Enter=Select   F10=Save   F8=Port Driver Name   Esc=Exit                F1=Help
```

T A B L E 8.9

Printer Configuration Parameters

PARAMETER	FUNCTION
Print server	Specifies the active print server currently servicing this printer.
Printer number	Displays the logical printer number assigned to this printer.
Printer status	Displays the status of this printer and the active print job. Also allows a print server operator to change the queue service mode, change the currently mounted form, and issue printer control commands.
Printer type	Displays the configured printer type. Available printer types include parallel, serial, UNIX printer, AppleTalk printer, Other/Unknown, XNP, and AIO.
Configuration	Displays the configuration information about this printer, including port, location, and interrupt. For serial printers this field also includes COM port configuration information, such as baud rate, stop bits, data bits, and parity.
Starting form	Indicates the PRINTDEF form that the print server will assume is mounted on the printer when the print server starts.

(continued)

	PARAMETER	FUNCTION
TABLE 8.9 *Printer Configuration Parameters (continued)*	Buffer size in KB	Indicates the size of the print server's internal buffer for this printer. Increasing this number may improve printer performance if the printer stops and restarts in the middle of a print job.
	Banner type	Specifies the default banner type for this printer. Options are Text or Postscript.
	Service mode for forms	Specifies how the print server will service jobs in the queue when forms are used.
	Sampling interval	When the printer is idle, this number specifies how often (in seconds) that the print server will poll the queue assigned to this printer for new print jobs. When the printer is active, the print server will automatically service the next job in the queue.
	Print queues assigned	Allows you to view the print queues this printer is assigned to service. Also allows you to add new print queues to be serviced.
	Notification	Displays the users and groups assigned to be notified if there is a problem with this printer. Also allows you to add users or groups to the notification list.

Assigning a Print Queue   Assigning a print queue to a printer can be done through the Printer Configuration screen as well. To do so, select the Print queues assigned option and press Enter. You can then use the Insert key to browse the directory tree for the print queue to which you would like to assign this printer. Once you have located the desired print queue, press Enter or F10 to select it.

When you assign a print queue to a printer, you can also set the priority level and default status of the queue. After you select the print queue, a Priority Configuration screen appears. The priority of this queue can be set to any number between 1 and 10. Priority 1 is the highest; 10 is the lowest.

If this printer is servicing multiple queues, you can use the "Make this the default queue" option to define the default queue for this printer. When network users capture to this printer instead of a queue assigned to it, print jobs will be spooled to the default queue assigned here.

In the background, you will see to what priority this queue is set and the state. As shown at the bottom of this screen, a printer's state can be one of the following:

▶ [A]: Active

▶ [C]: Configured

▶ [AC]: Active and configured

▶ [D]: Default

Using Forms   If you have defined print forms using NWADMIN or PRINTDEF, the Printers option under PCONSOLE will also allow you to configure how those forms are used. Referring back to the Printer Configuration screen (Figure 8.27), there are a number of areas that affect forms.

Under the "Printer status" option, there are two forms options. The first is "Service mode." This option determines how the printer will service the print queue when forms are being used. The next option is "Mounted form." This is the form that is currently mounted at this printer. You would use this option to change the currently mounted form through PCONSOLE. The currently mounted form can also be change through NWADMIN, PSC, and at the print server console.

The next option that affects forms from the Printer Configuration menu is "Starting form." This option defines the default starting form to be used when the printer starts up. This form number should represent the most commonly used form on this printer.

Finally, there is the "Service mode for forms" option. When you select this option, you are presented with the screen in Figure 8.28. Take a quick peek.

The first option, "Change forms as needed," requires you to mount a new form at this printer each time a print job with a different form number is submitted to the queue. The print jobs in the queue will be serviced based on priority (on a first-in, first-out basis). So, if many different form types are used, this option may require you to change forms often.

To minimize the number of times form changes occur, you may consider leaving the default ("Minimize form changes within print queues") enabled. With this option enabled, all of the print jobs with the same priority submitted to the queue with the currently mounted form requested will be serviced first. Lower-priority jobs with a different form requested will require a form change before being serviced.

> **F I G U R E   8.28**
>
> *Service Modes for Custom Forms in PCONSOLE*

```
NetWare Print Console 4.15                  Monday  May  25, 1998  6:00pm
Context: BLUE.CRIME.TOKYO.ACME

                      Printer HPIII-P1 Configuration

      Print server:             BLUE-PS1
      Printer nu┌─────────────────────────────────────────┐
      Printer st│               Service Modes              │
      Printer ty│                                          │
      Configurat│ Change forms as needed                   │
      Starting f│ Minimize form changes within print queues│
      Buffer siz│ Service only currently mounted form      │
      Banner typ│ Minimize form changes across print queues│
      Service mo└─────────────────────────────────────┘int queues
      Sampling interval:        5
      Print queues assigned:    (See list)
      Notification:             (See list)



Press <Enter> to have the printers service batches of print jobs according to
their form in each print queue.
Enter=Select   F10=Save   F8=Port Driver Name   Esc=Exit          F1=Help
```

The next option, "Service currently mounted form," will only service jobs submitted with the mounted form type. If this option is enabled, the print server will not prompt for a form change if a job with a different form type is submitted to the queue. These jobs will never be printed unless this option is changed to one of the other options.

The final option on this menu, "Minimize form changes across print queues," is similar to the default option, except, in this case, all jobs with the currently mounted form will be serviced first, regardless of priority.

ZEN

"If it ain't half off, it ain't on sale."

Nanny Fine

Managing Print Servers

When you select the Print Servers option from the PCONSOLE main menu, you are shown a list of print servers configured in the current context. When you press Insert, a prompt appears, at which you enter the print server name.

The print server can be any hexadecimal name from 1 to 64 characters, including spaces and underscores. Even though this gives you tremendous flexibility, you should keep your print server names short and descriptive. For example, the second print server created to service printers in the BLUE division might be named BLUE-PS2. When you press Enter to create the print server, a message appears on the screen indicating that it may take up to 60 seconds for the print server to be created. Though it rarely takes 60 seconds to create a new print server, this message is just to reassure you that the system is still working.

Once the print server is created, to complete the configuration you will need to assign this print server to service printers and print queues.

To manage NDS print servers with PCONSOLE, select the Print Servers option from the PCONSOLE main menu. By selecting Print Servers you can create new NDS print server objects or view existing print servers in the current context. The left side of Figure 8.29 shows the print servers configured in the current context.

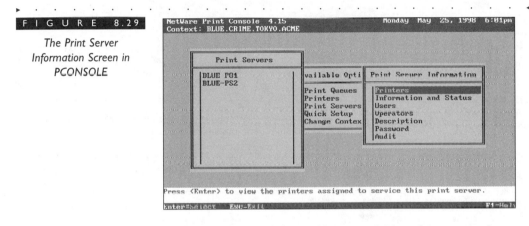

F I G U R E   8.29

The Print Server Information Screen in PCONSOLE

After you select an available print server, all of the available information about that server will be displayed on the right side of the screen, as seen in Figure 8.29. Table 8.10 summarizes the information found in each menu option.

Assigning Printers to be Serviced   To assign printers to this print server, select Printers from the Print Server Information menu. A list of the printers currently being serviced by this print server will be displayed. Pressing Insert will allow you to browse the directory tree for the desired printer.

The Printers option will also show you the state of the attached printers. A printer's state can be one of the following:

- ► [A]: Active

- ► [C]: Configured

- ► [AC]: Active and configured

T A B L E 8.10	MENU OPTION	PURPOSE
Print Server Information Parameters	Printers	Displays the printers assigned to be serviced by this print server and their state. Also allows printers to be assigned or removed from this print server.
	Information and status	Displays print server type, status, version, number of printers serviced, and advertising name. If the print server is running, this option also allows it to be taken down.
	Users	Displays users and groups who are authorized to view the print server's status and active configuration. Allows print server users to be added or removed.
	Operators	Displays users and groups who are authorized to manage the print server's status and active configuration. Allows print server operators to be added or removed.
	Description	Allows an optional text description to be entered for this print server.
	Password	Allows a print server password to be entered. This prevents unauthorized users from loading the print server.
	Audit	Allows you to view or modify this print server's auditing information.

Selecting a configured printer from this screen will take you to the same Printer Configuration screen we saw when we were creating and configuring printers (see Figure 8.27). This is a nice shortcut when you are setting up printing services with this utility.

Assigning Print Server Users and Operators Print server users are network users who have the ability to view the information and status of a print server. Print server operators have the ability to actually change that information. Selecting the Users option from the PCONSOLE Print Server Information menu allows you to authorize users and groups as print server users. You do not have to be a print server user to have print jobs routed by a particular print server, but you do to view its configuration and status. When you select the Users option, you will be presented with a list of current print server users. Use the Insert key to browse the tree for users, groups, or containers to be authorized as print server users. To select an object, highlight the object and press F10. Multiple objects can be selected by using the F5 key to mark them, and then using F10 to select. To remove print server users, highlight the object in the user list and press Delete.

Assigning print server operators is done in a similar fashion. Select the Operators menu option and use the Insert key to browse and F10 to select. To remove a print server operator, use the Delete key.

Using the Auditing Feature

To keep track of printing transactions, print server auditing can be enabled. When auditing is enabled, information about each completed print job will be logged in an audit file called PSERVER.LOG. This log file can be viewed using PCONSOLE or NWADMIN. Also, because PSERVER.LOG is a text file, it can be viewed with any text editor.

To enable auditing, or to view or delete the audit file for a particular print server, choose Audit from the Print Server Information menu. Figure 8.30 shows the resulting screen.

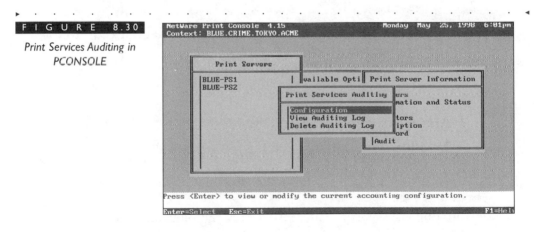

FIGURE 8.30

Print Services Auditing in PCONSOLE

To enable auditing, choose Configuration and set the "Enable auditing field" to Yes. When you enable auditing, you are given the option of limiting the size of the audit file. If you do not limit this file's size, it could grow to the maximum of the available disk space. To prevent the file from getting out of hand, you may want to limit its size. When the file size is limited, the print server will log entries until the maximum size is reached, and then it will stop until the file is deleted or this field is changed.

Any time a change is made in the Auditing Information screen, the print server must be shut down and restarted before the changes will take place.

QUIZ

To be a crack sleuth, you have to know your codes. Decode the following:

C V C   C V C   V ! C   V C   V C V C V C V C   V C   C V C V C V C .
18 2   99 3 4   11 2   10 2   1515 1   5 2   15 2 22 5   15154   5   9920   3 2   2 4   3 2 3

(Q8-3)

That completes our in-depth exploration of PCONSOLE. As you can see, it provides a lot of printing management punch. But for those of you who still prefer a GUI world, NWADMIN provides some printing management capabilities as well, albeit, not as many as PCONSOLE. Let's check it out.

SMART LINK

For more detail on the PCONSOLE printing utility, surf to the "IntranetWare Utilities Reference" at http://www.novell.com/manuals.

MANAGING PRINTING WITH NWADMIN

Management under Windows is one of the easiest ways to track jobs and the status of print servers. NWADMIN and NWUSER are the main tools for doing this. Even though NWADMIN is primarily an administrator's tool, users can benefit from it as well.

Printing management under NWADMIN is broken into two sets of tasks:

- ▶ CNA tasks

- ▶ User tasks

Let's take a closer look.

CNA Tasks

As a manager of printers and queues, you will need to do several things:

▸ Mount new printer forms

▸ Stop/start printers

▸ Unload the print server

▸ Place a hold on a job

▸ Delete a job

Remember, you must be an operator (printer or queue) to carry out these management functions. Table 8.11 shows the steps required to accomplish these functions. This assumes you are already in NWADMIN and at the context where the objects reside.

TABLE 8.11 CNA Printing Tasks in NWADMIN	TASK	STEPS INVOLVED
	Mount new printer forms	1 • Choose the printer (highlight and double-click).
		2 • Select Printer Status.
		3 • Select Mount Form.
		4 • Choose the form name (or number).
	Stop/start printers (see Figure 8.31)	1 • Choose the printer.
		2 • Select Printer Status.
		3 • Select Pause to stop or Start to resume printer output.
	Unload the print server	1 • Choose the print server.
		2 • At the lower middle of the screen, choose Unload.
		3 • Choose Immediately or After Jobs based on whether you wish current jobs to complete before the print server terminates.

(continued)

	T A B L E 8.11	TASK	STEPS INVOLVED
	CNA Printing Tasks in NWADMIN (continued)	Place a hold on a job (see Figure 8.32)	1 • Select the queue that is servicing the job.
			2 • Select Job List.
			3 • Select Hold Job.
		Release a job hold	1 • Select the queue that is servicing the job.
			2 • Select Job List.
			3 • Select Resume.
		Delete a job	1 • Select the queue that is servicing the job.
			2 • Select Job List.
			3 • Highlight the specific job.
			4 • Select Delete.

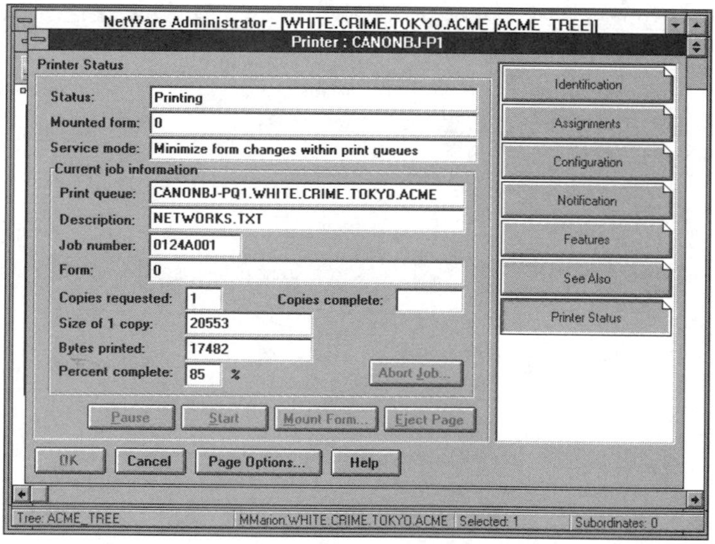

▶ F I G U R E 8.31

The Printer Status Screen in NWADMIN

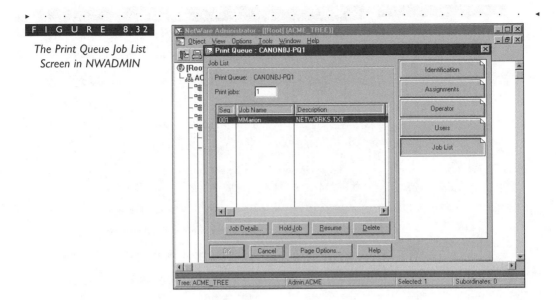

User Tasks

Some user management functions are similar to operator functions. Typically, they are basic view functions to check on the status of a job. These functions include:

- ▸ Viewing status of a job in a queue

- ▸ Viewing amount of job printed on a printer

- ▸ Deleting a job submitted

- ▸ Placing/releasing a user hold on the job

These functions require that you have at least user access on the print server or queue in question. Refer to Table 8.12 for a quick review.

TASK	STEPS INVOLVED
View job status	1 • Select the queue that is servicing the job.
	2 • Select Job List.
	3 • Locate the job in question.
	4 • Scroll right to view status (Active, Held, Ready).

(continued)

TABLE 8.12	TASK	STEPS INVOLVED
User Printing Tasks in NWADMIN (continued)	View percent completed	1 • Select printer that is printing the job.
		2 • Select Printer Status.
	Delete a job	1 • Select the queue that is servicing the job.
		2 • Select Job List.
		3 • Highlight the chosen job.
		4 • Select Delete.
	Place/release a user (see 8.33)	1 • Select the queue that is servicing the hold Figure job.
		2 • Select Job List.
		3 • Select the job to hold/release.
		4 • Select Hold Job to hold and Resume to release.

FIGURE 8.33

The Print Job Detail Window in NWADMIN

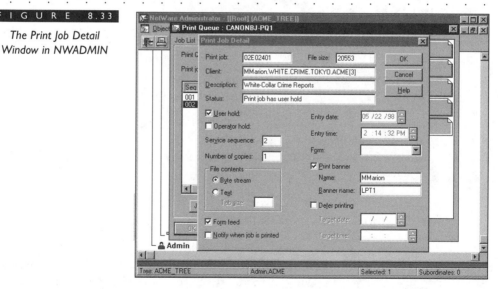

That completes our discussion of general printing management with PCONSOLE and NWADMIN. These two tools are the cornerstone of your arsenal. But you never know when you might need a special utility. So, the next three topics deal with less common printing management components—such as print servers, print job configurations, and print forms customization. Ready, set, explore.

SMART LINK

For more detail on NWADMIN as a printing utility, surf to the "IntranetWare Utilities Reference" at http://www.novell.com/manuals.

MANAGING PRINT SERVERS WITH PSC

Print Server Control (PSC) is the first of the printing specialty tools. To use PSC, you need the following information:

1 • The print server name—This could be either the name of the print server on a bindery server (NetWare 2.2 or 3.12) or an NDS Print Server object name (such as WHITE-PS1.WHITE.CRIME.TOKYO.ACME).

2 • The name of the printer to manage—This could be P1, HP4SI-P1, and so on. The names were defined under PCONSOLE or NWADMIN.

3 • The command desired (for example, STATUS, MOUNT, DISMOUNT)

One of the more helpful options is the /? option, which will show all the options available for the PSC command. The next section covers some of the fun things that you can do with PSC.

Get Status of All Printers

This option shows all printers for the print server and their status (see Figure 8.34). Following is the syntax:

```
PSC PS=WHITE-PS1.WHITE.CRIME.TOKYO.ACME P=ALL STAT
```

F I G U R E   8.34

Getting Printer Status
with PSC

```
Z:\PUBLIC>PSC PS=.WHITE-PS1.WHITE.CRIME.TOKYO.ACME P=ALL STAT
Printer CANONBJ-P1 (printer number 0)
      Status:Not connected

Printer HPIII-P1 (printer number 1)
      Status:Not connected

Printer HP4SI-P3 (printer number 2)
      Status:Not connected

Printer HP4SI-P2 (printer number 3)
      Status:Not connected

Printer HP4SI-P1 (printer number 4)
      Status:Printing job
      Off-line
      Print job name: LPT1
      Print job ID: 212001
      Complete: 93%


Z:\PUBLIC>
```

Mount a New Form in a Printer

This option will make the desired form number the currently mounted form. Here's the syntax:

```
PSC PS=WHITE-PS1.WHITE.CRIME.TOKYO.ACME P=CANONBJ-P1
Mount Form=Reports
```

You may also indicate the printer and/or form by number:

```
PSC PS=WHITE-PS1.WHITE.CRIME.TOKYO.ACME P=0 Mount Form=1
```

Stop/Start a Printer from Servicing Jobs

This option will tell the printer to stop printing once it's local buffer is empty. This would be useful if it's necessary to change paper or fix a problem without deleting jobs in the queue.

In this example, we'll assume that we're already in the context WHITE.CRIME. TOKYO.ACME. Therefore, we only need to specify the name of the print server.

```
PSC PS=WHITE-PS1 P=CANONBJ-P1 STOP
```

To restart the printer, type:

```
PSC PS=WHITE-PS1 P=CANONBJ-P1 START
```

Show Print Server Configuration

This option will show you the printer layout for the specified print server. This includes all printers and queues assigned to the print server. The syntax for this option is:

```
PSC PS=WHITE-PS1 List
```

This option helps you to find the name of the printers attached to the print server so that you can use the above options to get more specific details (see Figure 8.35).

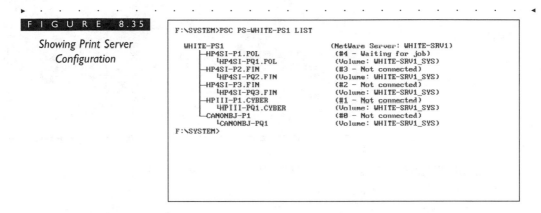

FIGURE 8.35

Showing Print Server Configuration

```
F:\SYSTEM>PSC PS=WHITE-PS1 LIST

    WHITE-PS1                                (NetWare Server: WHITE-SRV1)
        ├─HP4SI-P1.POL                       (#4 - Waiting for job)
        │   └HP4SI-PQ1.POL                   (Volume: WHITE-SRV1_SYS)
        ├─HP4SI-P2.FIN                       (#3 - Not connected)
        │   └HP4SI-PQ2.FIN                   (Volume: WHITE-SRV1_SYS)
        ├─HP4SI-P3.FIN                       (#2 - Not connected)
        │   └HP4SI-PQ3.FIN                   (Volume: WHITE-SRV1_SYS)
        ├─HPIII-P1.CYBER                     (#1 - Not connected)
        │   └HPIII-PQ1.CYBER                 (Volume: WHITE-SRV1_SYS)
        └─CANONBJ-P1                         (#0 - Not connected)
            └CANONBJ-PQ1                     (Volume: WHITE-SRV1_SYS)
    F:\SYSTEM>
```

That's it for PSC. The next specialty printing tool is PRINTCON.

SMART LINK

For more detail on the PSC printing utility, surf to the "Utilities Reference" at http://www.novell.com/manuals.

CONFIGURING PRINT JOBS WITH PRINTCON

Back in the days before NetWare supported Windows, the only way to capture printers was with the CAPTURE command, either through a login script or a batch file. To make this process easier, PRINTCON was used to create print job configurations that consisted of common user CAPTURE statements. Then, rather than having to enter long and cryptic CAPTURE statements, the CAPTURE command was simply

```
CAPTURE J=<job_configuration>
```

Today, with the NWUSER Windows utility, we have an easier option: Just drag and drop to capture a printer once and select the Permanent option. But, even with this easier option, PRINTCON is still around for those who would like to use it. Figure 8.36 shows the PRINTCON main menu.

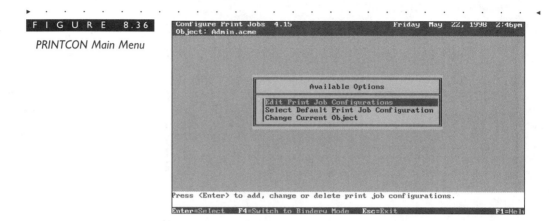

FIGURE 8.36

PRINTCON Main Menu

CUSTOMIZING PRINTING WITH PRINTDEF

Now that everything is set up and running smoothly, we need to shift our printing focus to customization. These are the advanced tasks that separate CNAs from pretenders. PRINTDEF is our friend. This DOS-based printing utility allows us to customize two important printing components:

▶ Print forms

▶ Print devices

Multiple print forms can be supported by attaching special instructions to specific print jobs. In addition, customized formatting is allowed with special print devices. All of this is accomplished using PRINTDEF.

The PRINTDEF utility is used to define and store printer definitions or command strings and printer form definitions. It's probably the least frequently used of all of the IntranetWare printing utilities, but it comes in handy when you have multiple paper types used on a single printer or you wish to exploit printer functionality that your application doesn't support. Let's take a look at the PRINTDEF main menu (see Figure 8.37).

F I G U R E   8 . 3 7

PRINTDEF Main Menu

```
Printer Definition 4.15                    Friday  May  22, 1998  2:48pm
Context: WHITE.CRIME.TOKYO.ACME




                        ┌──────────────────────────────┐
                        │      Available Options        │
                        ├──────────────────────────────┤
                        │ Print Devices                 │
                        │ Printer Forms                 │
                        │ Change Current Context         │
                        └──────────────────────────────┘




Press <Enter> to add, change or delete print devices.
Enter=Select    F4=Switch To Bindery Mode    Esc=Exit              F1=Help
```

As with the other DOS-based print utilities, it's important to notice the context at the top of the screen before creating or modifying devices or forms. When creating or modifying devices or forms, the context shown at the top of the screen is where they will be created. Any user under the context where the forms or devices are defined will have access to them.

Devices and forms will flow down through the NDS tree until another definition is defined at a lower level. For example, if a print form is defined in ACME, all users in all Organizational Units below ACME will have access to that form. If forms are then defined in the .WHITE.CRIME.TOKYO.ACME container, users in that container will get only those forms and not the ones defined in ACME.

ZEN

"My Aunt Miriam always says, 'The more the merrier, unless you're talking about chins.'"

Nanny Fine

Using Custom Forms

In certain cases, a printing environment may require the use of preprinted forms for print jobs such as invoices, paychecks, return forms, and purchase orders. If this is the case, the administrator and the network must ensure that submitted print jobs get printed on the proper forms. Imagine if a paycheck were printed on an invoice form. The person on the receiving end of the paycheck wouldn't be too happy.

One way around this is to have a dedicated printer for every type of possible print job that requires the form. In fact, in companies that require high-volume print services, this is usually the case. This means the printers seldom have to be reset except to add new forms when they run out.

In environments where the volume is lower, preprinted forms may be required, but multiple form types may need to be consolidated to a single printer. This is where forms are used (see Figure 8.38).

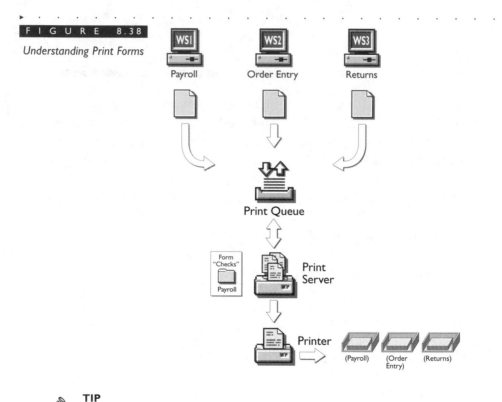

F I G U R E   8.38

Understanding Print Forms

TIP

In the situation where you have dedicated forms printers, you can ignore forms altogether. Configuring forms where not needed just adds another layer of complexity.

A good example would be where the company ACME needs to print invoices and purchase requisitions on the same printer. ACME needs to have two forms defined plus a potential third if normal draft printing is also done on the same printer. In our example, we have defined three forms:

- ▸ INVOICE (0)

- ▸ PURCHASE (1)

- ▸ DRAFT (2)

Notice that each form also has a number. When referencing forms, you can use either a form name or a reference number—IntranetWare doesn't care which.

To specify the form to use, when the workstation is initially captured you can use the /F option under the CAPTURE command, or a form may be specified under a user's print job configuration. The administrator may also have more than one print job configuration per user specifically for that reason. That way the workstation will default to the standard print configuration for the user (perhaps using a draft form—standard blank paper, for instance), but the user can still choose a print job that specifies a particular form.

Ideally, form selection could be set via a batch file, login script, or Windows PIF file. This would eliminate the burden on the user of choosing the right print job configuration.

Servicing Print Forms   Once a user has submitted a print job with a specific form, the form number (and the name) will be kept as part of the Job Entry Record. If you recall, a Job Entry Record is kept for every print job submitted to the IntranetWare print system.

When the print server first comes up, it defaults to form type 0 even though form 0 may be undefined. Typically, most administrators make form 0 the most used form in a multiple-forms environment.

REAL WORLD

IntranetWare needs only the form number and not necessarily the form name. Therefore, when any print server initializes, it will default to form 0 for all printers serviced by that print server.

Once the print server has found a job in the queue to service, it will look to see what form type the job requires. It then decides whether to service the job immediately or to hold it temporarily for efficiency reasons. We'll assume for now that the print server will service jobs on a first come, first served basis.

The print server then opens the data file associated with the print job and checks the form type currently being used for the printer. Remember that the print server usually initializes the printer with form 0 (the default can be set when the printer is defined with IntranetWare). If the print server notes that the job submitted requires a different form that the currently mounted type, then the server halts the printer and sends a message to the designated persons that a new form needs to be mounted.

The printing administrator or whoever is designated to manage the print server can then take several steps to continue printing:

▸ Remove the current paper type in the printer

▸ Feed in the required form type

▸ Use a server set command to indicate that the proper form is now in the printer

▸ Restart the printer

If the next print job requires a different form type, the process must be repeated.

Changing Print Forms   As you can see, changing forms can become quite tiresome if many different types of jobs are passing through, all with different form types. To minimize the number of form changes, IntranetWare allows you to optimize how forms get serviced.

By default, a print server services form types on a first come, first served basis. But if you're in a multi-form environment, you may want to change this default. When the print server is configured, you can specify how to handle forms when the print server encounters them. Options include:

▸ Minimize form changes within queues—This option will ask you to change form types only when all of the currently mounted forms have been serviced within the queue. If there were one form 0, three form 3, and five form 4 print jobs, here's what would happen: Assume that form

0 is currently mounted. First, the form 0 job would be printed, then the three form 3 jobs, followed by the five form 4 jobs, regardless of their submission order. When all jobs were completed, if there were another queue being serviced by the printer, the print server would rotate to the next queue and do the same.

▸ Minimize form changes across queues—This option is similar to the previous, except the print server will do all the form 0 print jobs across all queues being serviced by the one printer, then move on to the next form and so on, until all print jobs had been serviced. This is used only when more than one queue services a single printer.

▸ Service only the currently mounted form—This option allows the print server operator to control when jobs with forms get printed. The currently mounted form type will be the only type serviced until the operator changes the printer's mounted form. Then the print server will only service that form. This is useful in an environment where the main form (invoices, for example) are being printed all day long, and the other form(s) only need to be batch printed at intervals (like at the end of the day).

Remember, in an ideal situation, each preprinted form should have its own dedicated printer, in which case, no forms definition is necessary. If forms are necessary (more than one form printed per printer), then there are two ways to configure forms: CAPTURE (discussed earlier) and NWADMIN (discussed below).

Under NWADMIN, you may define forms under a container to service the objects (users, for example) of that container. To do this:

1 • Start NWADMIN and locate the container where the desired print server resides.

2 • Place the pointer over the container icon and click the right mouse button once.

3 • Choose Details.

4 • Choose Forms.

In most cases, applications send all the formatting information needed by a plotter or a printer via their own native print drivers. In addition, Windows has support for every major printer available today.

In certain cases, IntranetWare may need to send printer formatting functions along with the actual print data. This is accomplished through the printer definition database (PRINTDEF), which can be defined by the administrator.

To review, every print job has three parts in the actual data stream; a print header, the print data, and the print tail. When you are using the PRINTDEF database, you are telling IntranetWare what to put in the print header. The header information reaches the printer first and will format it properly before the data starts to print. The print tail is used normally to reset the printer to its initial state so that it's ready for the next print job.

Once you have assigned a user either a form or a device (or both) using PRINTCON or NWADMIN, when the user prints, the device information will get appended to the print job data. For example, if you have chosen HPLaserJet4 and Landscape as a function, the proper escape codes will be part of the print header. In addition, if the function for printer reset (under the reinitialize mode) has been set, IntranetWare will automatically send the reset string after the job data has been sent. This way, IntranetWare can ensure that the printer is left in a reset state after a function has been used.

Using Print Devices

To define a new print device, select Print Devices from the PRINTDEF main menu. Print devices can be created manually by using the Insert key and entering each escape sequence that represents your printer's command strings. The easiest way to define a new printer definition is to take advantage of the 57 predefined print devices that come with IntranetWare. Those print devices are stored in the SYS:PUBLIC directory of each IntranetWare file server. These print devices can be imported into your current context by selecting Import Print Devices from the Print Device Options menu.

If the printer you are using is not on the list, check your printer manual because your printer may emulate a printer that is on the list.

PRINTDEF print devices consist of two parts: print devices and print modes. *Print devices* are the various printer command strings that you often find in the back of printer manuals. *Print modes* are made up of one or more print functions and represent the various modes a printer supports. For example, the reinitialize mode will reset the printer after each print job. Another example of a common printer mode is landscape mode.

QUIZ

Try this one on for size. A man is walking his dog on a leash towards home at a steady 3 mph. When they are 7 miles from home, the man lets his dog off the leash. The dog immediately runs off towards home at 8 mph. When the dog reaches the house, it turns round and runs back to the man at the same speed. When it reaches the man it turns back for the house. This is repeated until the man gets home and lets the dog in. How many miles does the dog cover from being let off the leash to being let into the house?

(Q8-4)

That pretty much finishes our journey through printing management LANd-otherwise know as the IntranetWare "war zone."

SMART LINK

For more detail on the PRINTDEF printing utility, surf to the "Utilities Reference" at http://www.novell.com/manuals.

That completes our discussion of IntranetWare's printing management tools. Wow, there's a lot to work with. We learned about PCONSOLE, NWADMIN, PSC, PRINTCON, and PRINTDEF. With all of these tools, it should be easy to keep IntranetWare printing running smoothly. It is . . . until somebody tries to print something! That's when it gets a little out of hand.

I hope you've enjoyed this in-depth exploration of IntranetWare printing as it is today. But what about tomorrow? The good news is—the future's so bright you've got to wear shades. And it's all because of a little four-letter acronym called NDPS. Check it out.

ZEN

"I just can't tame this darn charisma. Can I help it if I effervesce?"

Nanny Fine

The Future of Printing—NDPS

Ask any network administrator what the most frustrating part of managing their network is and nine times out of ten the answer will be printing. In an average networking environment, 80 percent of all support calls are printer related.

IntranetWare today provides the best network printing services available on the market. But, even with the robustness and flexibility of IntranetWare's print services, a number of challenges still exist for network users and administrators when it comes to network printing.

Users often can't find the printer they want to print to, and when they do, chances are likely they won't have the necessary driver for it. So, they just do the best they can at guessing. The result is generally pages and pages of wasted paper with a bunch of printer error codes.

Network administrators face complex configuration and management with network printing today. Earlier in the chapter we looked at how to set up network printing, and for the first-time IntranetWare user, it's not a simple task. Just to add a new printer to the network, there are many steps involved. After the new printer hardware is installed and configured, the administrator must create a print queue and a print server to service that printer. Then, after the printer is set up, each user may need to have the correct driver installed on his/her desktop. The whole process of installing a new printer is quite time-consuming.

These reasons alone were enough for Novell to stop and take a good hard look at IntranetWare's printing services. Recognizing these issues and others, Novell partnered with Xerox and Hewlett-Packard to develop an entirely new printing architecture called Novell Distributed Print Services (NDPS). NDPS will be delivered with the next release of IntranetWare and, at the time of this writing, is still largely in development.

The goal of NDPS is to take the guesswork out of managing and using network printing. NDPS will provide simple plug-and-print configuration of network printers, eliminating the need to spend hours configuring network printing. NDPS will also take advantage of the intelligence built in to many of today's printers, giving users more information about network printers and more control over their print jobs than ever before.

SMART LINK

For a more in-depth discussion of NDPS, surf to "Novell Directory Print Services" at http://www.netware.com.

NDPS will provide many benefits to users and to CNAs. Those benefits are described below. Ready, set, print.

ZEN

"My hair. The outer shell is hair spray. Inside, there's gel, mousse, volumizer—a whole infrastructure. The only difference between me and the Kingdome is Astroturf!"

Nanny Fine

MAKING LIFE EASIER FOR USERS

Did you ever notice that just about every time you send a print job to the network something unexpected happens? Unfortunately, that unexpected something is usually bad. You accidentally sent a PCL print job to a postscript printer, or somebody else did something weird and your print job is stuck behind about 15 others, so you go to lunch and come back an hour later to find that your job still hasn't printed! And, through all of this, the network never once gave you any indication that there was a problem.

NDPS solves these network printing problems by providing the following capabilities:

- Bidirectional communication

- Print job move/copy options

- Automatic driver download

- Job-to-printer matching

- Multifunction printer and device support

Bidirectional Communication

NDPS takes advantage of the intelligence built in to today's network printing by providing bidirectional information exchange between network users and printers. This exchange provides feedback so that users always know the state of their print jobs. When something is wrong with the printer that a user has selected, the user can be notified of the problem and how to fix it. For example, if the selected printer is out of paper, the user can be notified and given the option of either adding paper and resuming the job or rerouting the job to another printer. Administrators can also be notified of critical printer problems such as low toner or printer failure. This notification can be in the form of an on-screen pop-up message, an e-mail message, a telephone call, or a pager beep.

Print Job Move/Copy Options

Users have complete flexibility when it comes to rerouting print jobs after they have been submitted to the network for printing. With the current IntranetWare printing services, once a print job has been submitted to the queue, there is not a whole lot a user can do with it except delete it or put it on hold. NDPS will provide users with the option to move or copy print jobs to other printers after they have been submitted to the network for printing.

As mentioned above, the bidirectional communication functionality allows for printers to notify users of the state of their print jobs. Users can then take action based on that information. For example, let's say you have 20 minutes to get to a meeting that's all the way on the other side of town. And, of course, you need to print a document to take to that meeting. So, you think, "20 minutes . . . no sweat, it'll take 5 minutes to print the job and I'll be on the road in 10." (Yeah, right.) So you submit the job to the network for printing.

Now, in today's printing environment, when your job doesn't print right away, you run around like a chicken with its head cut off trying to figure out where the problem is. With NDPS, you'll get a nice little message right at your desktop that says something like, "The printer you selected is not available. Would you like to reroute the job?" Of course you would, so the job is routed to another printer that meets the requirements of your job (for example, postscript printing), and you're on your way as planned. Sounds like a dream, huh?

Automatic Driver Download

Another big area of frustration for users is never having the right driver for the printer they'd like to use. With NDPS, if a user selects a printer that he/she does not have a driver for, the system will automatically download that driver to their desktop. Also, when installing new printers on the network, the administrator can specify an automatic driver download for the users who will be using that printer. This saves a tremendous amount of time since the administrator no longer has to go to each workstation to physically install the driver.

Job-to-Printer Matching

With NDPS, the user is presented with a "best fit" printer that meets the requirements for the print job he/she is sending, whether the requirements are locality, resolution, color, or speed. Also, if the user sends a print job to the incorrect type of printer, such as a PCL job to a postscript printer, NDPS will notify the user of the problem and provide him/her with a list of printers he/she is authorized to use and that match the job requirements. And if the user doesn't have a driver for the selected printer, the driver will be downloaded to his/her workstation automatically. Users also are able to filter the available printers based on which ones are most important to them.

Multifunction Printer and Device Support

The current IntranetWare printing architecture isolates applications from network printers. When a user sends a print job from within an application, that job is directed to a local LPT port. IntranetWare then captures that print job and redirects it to a print queue at the file server. The print server then routes the print job to the appropriate network printer. Since applications can't access network printers directly, they cannot take advantage of new network printer functionality that is emerging today, such as gluing, stapling, or duplex options.

NDPS provides an open integration platform for both hardware vendors and software developers. The architecture is fully extensible, increasing user and application awareness of printer capabilities. Hardware vendors can expose their printer capabilities to users through standard NDPS APIs. Through the NDS and NDPS APIs, software developers can create desktop applications that let users select printer capabilities from within applications.

This extensible design will also accommodate add-on printer functionality, such as gluing and stapling, that can be provided through third-party drivers and extensions or through embedding of NDPS functionality into a variety of print devices and products.

The NDPS architecture also supports fax, scan, and multifunction devices. As nontraditional types of devices such as these become integrated into the network, the NDPS functionality will extend to support them.

ZEN

"Fourteen is a very vulnerable age. I remember once my mother picked me up from school in a halter top and pedal pushers. I'm still looking for the right support group."

Nanny Fine

That's great for the users, but what about us?! Fortunately, NDPS includes a myriad of great features for CNAs as well. Check them out.

SMART LINK

Visit Nanny Fine at http://www.cbs.com/primetime/nanny.html.

MAKING LIFE EASIER FOR CNAS

The usability features of NDPS alone make administrators eager for the next release of IntranetWare. But it gets better. NDPS also provides a number of administration features that make creating and administering IntranetWare printing quick and easy. These features include:

- ▸ Streamlined configuration

- ▸ Plug-and-print

- ▸ Reduced network traffic

- ▸ Event notification

Streamlined Configuration

NDPS streamlines printing configuration by eliminating print servers and print queues found in previous versions of IntranetWare. NDPS contains a logical print management agent that acts as an intelligent, simplified print server, spooler, and print queue all in one. This agent maintains information about specific physical printers and accepts operations from print clients. These agents appear as NDS objects and take advantage of IntranetWare services such as management and security. These agents can be physically embedded on NDPS enabled printers or can be run as an NLM at a IntranetWare file server. This allows for support of both NDPS-enabled and legacy printers.

NDPS also allows all printers to be managed remotely from within NWADMIN. Printer manufacturers can write NWADMIN snap-ins that provide printer management from within the utility. The administrator can then control a printer remotely without ever leaving his/her desk. For example, if the administrator would like to issue a form feed on an NDPS printer, he/she simply clicks on the NDS object that represents the printer and is presented with a graphical representation of the device. The administrator then checks the status, issues a form feed or performs any other function that would normally be done at the printer.

Plug-and-Print

Adding new printers to a Novell network has never been easy. Not only do you have to set up and configure the hardware, but you also have to deal with the IntranetWare printing setup, which we've just spent an entire chapter trying to teach you. NDPS's plug-and-print feature will eliminate the time and frustration of adding printers to the network. When a new NDPS-enabled printer is added to the network, you will be able to plug it in and begin printing.

Plug-and-print is where Novell's partnership with HP and Xerox comes in. In addition to teaming up with Novell to develop the NDPS architecture, these printer vendors will be delivering NDPS-enabled printers with the logical NDPS management agent embedded in them. This eliminates the need for the administrator to set up printers, queues, and print servers in NDS. When the printer is plugged into the network, it will automatically register with NDS as an available printer and no other configuration will be required.

HP and Xerox will be the first printer manufacturers to provide NDPS-enabled printers. After the initial release of NDPS, other printer manufactures will begin providing NDPS-enabled printers.

Reduced Network Traffic

Currently, when network attached printers are used, they immediately begin advertising their availability to IntranetWare users as soon as they are plugged in. This advertising is done through IntranetWare's Service Advertising Protocol (SAP). These devices will send a SAP broadcast out on the network every 60 seconds, which results in increased network traffic. With NDPS, when a network-attached printer is added to the network, it will register once with NDS, and NDS will take care of the rest. This will greatly reduce network traffic because network-attached printers will no longer be required to advertise their availability.

Event Notification

NDPS not only provides event notification for users, but also for administrators. An administrator can be notified of important events such as emergency breakdowns or other out-of-service conditions. They can also receive advance notice of when service will be required, such as a low-toner situation. This notification can be received in a number of different ways: as an on-screen pop-up message, an e-mail message, a fax, or even a pager beep. With Novell's promise of workflow management within IntranetWare, NDPS could send an e-mail to the administrator to indicate that the toner is low on a specific printer and at the same time place an order for a new toner cartridge. Other information can be kept and communicated on demand, such as printer utilization statistics and accounting information.

NDPS is scalable from the smallest network to the largest enterprise. With features like plug-and-print, organizations won't require printing experts to install and maintain printers. This benefits small and large organizations alike. For enterprise environments where centralized security and control are required, NDPS provides the distributed management capabilities and security necessary. And for the small company, anyone can add a new printer to the network without having to be a IntranetWare guru.

QUIZ

Here's the ultimate numbers mystery. Let's see if you're up to the task. Fill the grid below with the numbers 1 to 16 to form a magic square so that each vertical and horizontal line, each corner to corner diagonal line, the four corner numbers, each block of four corner squares and the middle four block of numbers each add up to 34. The number 7 has been filled in for good luck. Ready, set, calculate.

7			

(Q8-5)

Congratulations! Mystery solved. The answer to the question of life is a four letter acronym—NDPS. And it doesn't stand for "Never Darn Purple Socks" or "Neanderthal's Don't Purchase Spaghetti." NDPS is Novell's answer for the current state of IntranetWare printing. But you can't have it yet, sorry. Patience is a virtue—and whoever said that never had to deal with IntranetWare users.

I enjoy a good mystery, how about you? IntranetWare printing is a great place to start. We discovered a lot of interesting things about it today, and I think you're definitely ready to attack it on your own. But if you're still feeling a little skittish, here's a quick review:

It all started with the essence of printing. In the old days, we used to print by ourselves. Now, we get to share this honor with hundreds of strangers. Network printing is has probably had a major impact on the social fabric of humanity—we just don't notice it. We went on a little journey through the life of a print job—starting with CAPTURE, then to the queue, print server, and ultimately the printer. Wasn't that fun?

Then, we learned all the steps involved in printing setup. It's not so bad. There are only four steps and they're not very hard. First, you create the print queue, then the printer, and finally the print server. Then, to top it all off, you activate the print server. No sweat. We also discovered a few secrets about customizing IntranetWare printing with print forms and devices.

Once it's up an running, the fun part starts-keeping it running. IntranetWare printing management focused on five CNA and user tools, namely PCONSOLE, NWADMIN, PSC, PRINTCON, and PRINTDEF. We learned how to configure, manage, and customize the IntranetWare printing system. I bet you didn't realize how much help there is out there! Don't worry—you're not alone.

Finally, we took a peak at IntranetWare's printing future—NDPS. I'm excited, how about you. It's great to know there's help around the corner—if you need it. NDPS provides a myriad of benefits for both using (users) and managing (CNAs) IntranetWare printing. Look for it soon at a printing store near you.

ZEN

"I was thinking about the Pilgrims. How'd they know what to pack? I mean, you're going to a new world. Is it hot, . . . cold, . . . rainy? There are no brochures! So they all wear the same thing and what a mistake. Very few people look good in a bit hat, a big collar, AND a big buckle. What were they thinking?"

Nanny Fine

So, how do you feel now? A little better? Did all that wisdom from Nanny Fine soothe your brain? Well, if you're still a little worried about going out on your own, I have a surprise for you—exercises! You want practice, I've got practice. A bunch of hands-on exercises are just the cure for printing cold feet. Once you've cruised through the following seven exercises, you'll be a printing pro. You'll be ready for anything . . . except a shopping spree with Nanny Fine—ouch!

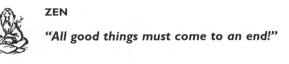

ZEN

"All good things must come to an end!"

Q

Congratulations! You made it. Welcome to the next generation of networking—IntranetWare! And more importantly, welcome to the end of this book. It's been a long and winding road, but we struggled through it together. We learned about NDS, the file system, security, the life span of a LAN, and printing. All in a day's work. Oh yeah . . . and we saved the world too!

Oh, my goodness! Would you look at the time—where has it all gone? I've just been rambling away here . . . sorry, if you missed your train or something. I guess I'm done. There's not much more that can be said about life as an IntranetWare CNA. Are you interested in golf? We could talk about that for awhile. Nah, I better save that for another book.

Before you leave, let's take a quick moment to review your journey. It's been quite a wild ride, and you should be very proud of yourself for surviving it in one piece—or so it seems. Do you still want to be a CNA? An IntranetWare superhero? Good. Because the world needs a few good CNAs, and you're a great place to start. Speaking of starting . . . .

The journey began in Part I with a brief peek at "life as a CNA"! In this section, we learned about the reasons for becoming a CNA and acquired an appreciation for the tasks tackled each day by CNAs all over the world.

The journey really got rolling in Part II—"IntranetWare Administration". It all started with a brief introduction of IntranetWare and a detailed exploration of Novell Directory Services (Chapter 3). In addition, we were introduced to ACME (A Cure for Mother Earth) and learned about their plight—aka, saving the world! There's a lot more to being an IntranetWare CNA than meets the eye.

SMART LINK

Visit ACME in cyberperson, surf the Web to http://www.cyberstateu.com/clarke/acme.htm.

In Chapter 4, we learned that the file system represents IntranetWare life *within* the server. All of our focus shifted to IntranetWare's big, electronic filing cabinet. Chapter 5 continued this journey with a look at security. Information is now the new commodity—more valuable than money. We need to take new measures to protect our information. We discovered IntranetWare's five-layered security model—login/password authentication, login restrictions, NDS rights, file system access rights, and attributes. Think of it as your impenetrable network armor.

Once the LAN has been installed (born), it enters the second and third phases of its lifespan—configuration (childhood) and management (adulthood). In Chapter 6, the first of two related chapters, we walked through the five steps of configuration using Leia as an example. Then in Chapter 7, we discovered the final phase of LAN lifespan—adulthood. Here your network got married, had children, planned for retirement, and finally retired. How about you?

In the final chapter, we ended the journey with IntranetWare printing (Chapter 8). We learned that IntranetWare printing is simple, and works great until . . . . You add users. In this final chapter, we learned some tme-proven methods for successful printing installation, management, and troubleshooting. We even explored printing's future—NDPS.

SMART LINK

It was a pleasure saving the world with you. Come say "Hi!" at http://www.cyberstateu.com/clarke.htm.

Well, that does it! The End . . . Finito . . . Kaput. Everything you wanted to know about IntranetWare (and life as a CNA), but were afraid to ask. I hope you've had as much fun reading this book as I've had writing it. It's been a long and winding road—a life changer. Thanks for spending the last 800 pages with me, and I bid you a fond farewell in the only way I know how:

> *"See ya' later, alligator!"*
>
> *"After a while, crocodile!"*
>
> *"Hasta la vista, baby!"*
>
> *"Live long and prosper!"*
>
> *"So long and thanks for all the fish!"*
>
> *"May the force be with you . . . ."*

GOOD LUCK, AND BY THE WAY....
THANKS FOR SAVING THE WORLD!!

CASE STUDY: BUILDING ACME'S PRINTING SYSTEM

This exercise will walk you though the creation and loading of a basic print system using the NWADMIN (Windows) graphical interface. This assumes you have already created ACME's NDS tree. We'll be working in the Crime Fighting department today. Seems appropriate, since we're trying to solve a mystery. Where's Sherlock Holmes when you need him?

For the exercise, we will assume the following names:

▶ *Print server:* WHITE-PS1

▶ *Print queue:* CANONBJ-PQ1

▶ *Printer:* CANONBJ-P1

First we will create the queue.

QUEUE CREATION

1. Log into the network as .Admin.ACME, then execute the NetWare Administrator utility under Windows 3.1 or Windows 95.

2. Click on the WHITE.CRIME.TOKYO.ACME container, then press Insert or choose Object/Create from the menu bar. A New Object dialog box will be displayed. Select Print Queue as the type of object to be created, then click on OK.

3. A Create Print Queue dialog box will be displayed. Type **CANONBJ-PQ1** in the Print Queue Name field, then click on the browser button to the right of the Print Queue Volume field. Walk the tree until WHITE-SRV1_SYS volume is shown in the Available Objects list box. Click on WHITE-SRV1_SYS volume, then click on OK to select it. The Create Print Queue dialog box will be displayed again at this point. Click on the Define Additional Properties box, then click on the Create button.

4. The CANONBJ-PQ1 Print Queue Identification page will be displayed by default. Type **MainQ** in the Other Name field and **Downtown** in the Location field.

5. Click on the Users page button. Who is/are assigned as queue users? Why?

6. Temporarily switch to a DOS prompt. Type **F:** (or the appropriate network drive letter) and press Enter. Type **DIR \Q*.*** and notice what you see.

7. Use the DOS CD command to switch to the directory found. Count how many subdirectories exist with a QDR extension.

8. Return to the NWADMIN utility. Click on OK to save your changes to the CANONBJ-PQ1 print queue.

Next, we need to create the printer.

PRINTER CREATION

1. Select the WHITE.CRIME.TOKYO.ACME container again. Press Insert (or Object/Create), and choose a printer as the type of object to be created.

2. Name the printer **CANONBJ-P1**. Click on Define Additional Properties and then on Create.

3. Type **Booking Printer** in the Other Name field.

4. Click on the Assignments page button and add the print queue just created.

5. Click on the Configuration button, then the "Communication…" button, then click on Auto Load (local to Print Server), then click on OK.

6. Click on the Notification page button. Click on Notify Print Job Owner to deselect the option. Note what happens.

7. Click on Notify Print Job Owner again to re-select, and note what happens.

8. Click on Features. Type **Fingerprint** in the Supported Cartridges field, then click on OK.

Finally, it's time to build the print server.

CREATING THE PRINT SERVER

1. Select the WHITE.CRIME.TOKYO.ACME container again.

2. Press Insert (or Object/Create), and select Print Server as the type of object to create.

3. Name the print server WHITE-PS1, then click on the Define Additional Properties box and click on CREATE.

4. Click on "Change Password...." Enter the password **Secret** and reconfirm, then click on OK.

5. Click on the Assignments page button. Add the **CANONBJ-P1** printer click on OK.

6. Click on the Users page button. Who is the current print server user? Why?

7. Delete the current print server user and add yourself.

8. Click on the Operator page button. Who is the operator and why?

9. Click on the Auditing Log page button, then click on the Enable Auditing button. Finally, click on OK to save your changes to this print server.

10. Double-click on the WHITE-PS1 print server, then click on the Print Layout page button. Note the exclamation point next to the print server. What do you think this means?

11. Click on the print server to select it, then click on Status. Note what you see.

12. Click on Close, then click on Cancel to return to the main NetWare Administrator browser screen.

Congratulations! You've built ACME's printing system. Now all you have to do is find the right printer and load the print server. Ready, set, print.

FINDING THE PRINTER

1. Click on the [Root] of the tree. Choose Object/Search from the menu bar. A Search dialog box will be displayed.

2. You'll notice that [Root] is listed in the Search From field.

3. Click on the Search Entire Subtree box.

4. Type **Printer** in the Search For field, then type **Cartridge** in the Property field.

6. Type **Fingerprint** in the blank entry box to the right of Equal To field, then click on OK to start the search.

8. A message will be displayed advising you that searching the entire tree could take a long time and asking if you want to continue. Click on Yes.

9. Note the results from the search.

10. Double-click on the printer to verify that it's correct.

LOADING THE PRINT SERVER

1. At the server console, ensure that you are at the colon prompt.

2. Type **LOAD PSERVER** and press Enter.

3. Enter **WHITE-PS1.WHITE.CRIME.TOKYO.ACME** as the name of the print server and press Enter.

4. What happens next?

5. Take steps to allow loading to continue.

6. Select Printer Status from the Available Options menu and press Enter. The CANONBJ-P1.WHITE.CRIME.TOKYO.ACME printer should be highlighted. Press Enter to select it.

7. Note the status of the printer.

8. Press Esc twice to return to the Available Options screen.

9. Choose Print Server Information from the Available Options screen.

10. Choose Current Status.

11. Select Running and press Enter, then select Unload and press Enter. What happens?

12. Reload the print server again.

See Appendix C for answers.

CASE STUDY: USING ACME'S PRINTING SYSTEM

This section assumes that you have two users set up in the WHITE.CRIME.TOKYO.ACME container. This will allow us to test capturing data and enabling print job configurations. You should have already completed the previous exercise. You will log in as two different users in this exercise:

- ▶ Robin Hood (RHood)

- ▶ Maid Marion (MMarion)

1. Make sure you are logged into the network as .Admin.ACME

2. Go to a DOS box under Windows.

3. Type **CAPTURE SH** and note the results.

4. Type **CAPTURE** and note what happens.

5. Change to the context where the CANONBJ-PQ1 exists. How do you do this?

6. CAPTURE to the CANONBJ-PQ1 using the Q option. What does the command look like?

7. End the capture using CAPTURE. How do you do this?

8. Return to Windows.

9. Run the NWUSER utility. (This utility is only available under Windows 3.1x. If you are running Windows 95, skip to Step 15.)

10. Click on the printer icon.

11. Walk the tree in the Resources list box on the right side of the screen to locate the WHITE.CRIME.TOKYO.ACME context.

12. Drag either the CANONBJ-P1 printer or the CANONBJ-PQ1 print queue onto LPT1: in the Ports list box.

13. Double-click on the new printer mapping. Note the default settings for the capture.

14. Leave the NWUSER utility.

15. Log out as the .Admin.ACME user, then log in as RHood. Before you do this, ensure that he has at least Read and File Scan rights, and a search drive mapping to the SYS:PUBLIC directory.

16. From a DOS box, change to the WHITE.CRIME.TOKYO.ACME container using the CX command.

17. Attempt to CAPTURE to the CANONBJ-PQ1 queue. What happens and why?

18. Re-login as yourself again. How would you grant access to the user RHood?

19. Change to the context WHITE.CRIME.TOKYO.ACME and re-enable capture to the network queue CANONBJ-PQ1. How can you do this?

20. Start the NetWare Administrator utility.

21. Choose Object/Print from the NWADMIN menu bar and print the current NetWare Administrator screen.

22. Ensure that the capture is working. Where can you look in NWADMIN to verify this?

23. Return to a DOS box and ensure that CAPTURE is working. What is the command to do this?

24. Print a DOS text file to the network. How can you do this while CAPTURE is activated?

25. End the capture and return to Windows.

26. Create a print job configuration for the container WHITE.CRIME.TOKYO.ACME and call it Main. Where would this be done?

27. Grant the container WHITE.CRIME.TOKYO.ACME access to the print queue CANONBJ-PQ1. How would you do this?

28. Log in as RHood.

29. Under DOS, type **CAPTURE** and note what happens.

30. Log in as .Admin.ACME to modify the queue.

31. Return to the NetWare Administrator utility. Right mouse click on the WHITE.CRIME.TOKYO.ACME container and select Details from the pull-down menu that is displayed. Click on the Print Job Configuration page button and make sure the Main print job configuration is highlighted. Click on the Default button to make this the default print job configuration for this container. Note the printer icon that now appears next to the configuration. Also note the options for the configuration (copies, queue, notification). Finally, click on OK to save this change.

32. Log in as RHood again.

33. Return to a DOS box and execute CAPTURE. What happens now?

34. Type **CAPTURE SH**. What do you note about the settings?

See Appendix C for answers.

CASE STUDY: MANAGING ACME'S PRINTING SYSTEM

This case study assumes the following: that the WHITE-PS1 print server is running on the .WHITE.CRIME.TOKYO.ACME server; that a printer is attached to the server and is ready to print (that is, on-line, with paper); and that you are using a Windows 3.1x workstation. (This case study will not work with a Windows 95 workstation.)

1. Log in as .Admin.ACME on a Windows 3.1x workstation and execute the NetWare Administrator utility.

2. Select the CANONBJ-P1 printer by double-clicking on it.

3. Click on the Printer Status page button, then click on the Pause button. What changes with the printer?

4. Send two jobs to the queue CANONBJ-PQ1.

5. Double-click on CANONBJ-PQ1, then click on the Job List page button. What do you see?

6. Select the first print job and click on the "Details..." button.

7. Click on the User Hold box. What status is displayed?

8. Return to the main NetWare Administrator browser screen. Click on the CANONBJ-P1, then click on Printer Status.

9. Click on the Resume button to re-enable the printer. What happens?

10. Place the printer off-line after the job has completed printing. (Use the printer's on-line/off-line button for this.)

11. View the CANONBJ-P1's status under NetWare Administrator. Note the status of the printer.

12. With the printer status up (viewing percentage and such), place the printer back on-line and watch what happens.

13. Once the job has completed printing, click on the CANCEL button, then double-click on WHITE-PS1.

14. Click on the Print Layout page button. Select each item, one at a time, then click on the Status button to check its status. What do you see?

15. Click on the Identification page button, then click on the UNLOAD button. Select Unload Print Server Immediately, then click on OK. Monitor the file server console screen, if possible. What happens?

16. Click on the Cancel button to leave the Print Server Identification screen. Double-click on WHITE-PS1, then click on the Print Layout page button. What do you notice that's different? What do you think it means?

17. Click on WHITE-PS1, then click on the Status button. Does this verify your assumption?

18. Submit another job to CANONBJ-PQ1.

19. Double-click on CANONBJ-PQ1, then select Job List. Select any job other than the first (Seq 1) and click on Job Details. Locate the Service Sequence field on the middle left-hand side. Change the Service Sequence to 1, then click on OK.

20. What looks different?

See Appendix C for answers.

EXERCISE 8-1: USING QUICK SETUP IN PCONSOLE

The following exercise will walk you through the process of creating IntranetWare printing objects using the Quick Setup option of PCONSOLE. Before beginning this exercise, be sure that you are in the context that you want to create new printing objects in, and that you are logged in as a user with sufficient rights to create objects.

1. From the DOS command line, run the PCONSOLE utility by typing **PCONSOLE** and pressing Enter.

2. Use the arrow keys to select Quick Setup and press Enter.

3. From the Print Services Configuration menu, modify the print server, printer, and print queue name to match the naming standards of your organization.

4. Verify the volume you want this print queue to be created on. If necessary, select the existing volume and press Enter, then press the Insert key to browse the tree and select the appropriate volume.

5. Specify the banner type. This should be based on the type of printer you are using. PCL printers use text banners.

6. Specify the printer type (parallel, serial, and so on), location (manual load-workstation or network attached; or auto load-locally attached to the print server).

7. Specify the interrupt or polled mode (recommended). If interrupt is chosen, it must match the configuration of the physical printer port.

8. Specify the port to which this printer is attached.

9. When configuration is complete, press Esc and Yes to save, then Esc and Yes to exit the PCONSOLE utility.

EXERCISE 8-2: MANUAL PRINTING SETUP IN PCONSOLE

The following exercise will walk you through the process of creating IntranetWare printing objects using the individual print queues, printers, and print server options of PCONSOLE. Before beginning this exercise, be sure that you are in the context that you want to create new printing objects in, and that you are logged in as a user with sufficient rights to create objects.

1. From the DOS command line, run the PCONSOLE utility by typing **PCONSOLE** and then pressing Enter.

2. Choose the Print Queues option from the Available Options menu.

3. Use the Insert key to create a new print queue.

4. Enter a print queue name that matches the naming standards of your organization and press Enter.

5. Enter the print queue's volume. Press the Insert key and browse the NDS tree to choose the appropriate volume and press Enter to select.

6. Press Esc to return to the Available Options menu.

7. Choose the Printers option from the Available Options menu.

8. Press the Insert key to create a new printer.

9. Enter a printer name that matches the naming standards of your organization and press Enter.

10. Select the printer by pressing Enter.

11. Highlight the Configuration field and press Enter. Specify the port to which this printer is attached, the printer type (parallel, serial, and so on), the location (manual load-workstation or network attached; or auto load-locally attached), the interrupt or polled mode (recommended). If interrupt is chosen it must match the configuration of the physical printer port. Specify an address restriction, if desired. When configuration is complete, press Esc.

12. If forms are being used, specify the starting form number.

13. Specify the banner type. This should be based on the type of printer you are using. PCL printers use text banners.

14. If multiple form types are being used, specify the forms service mode you desire.

15. Press Enter at "Print queues assigned" and use the Insert key to add a print queue to service this queue. Use the arrow keys to select the queue you created above and press Enter to select. When you have finished, press Esc.

16. Optional: Press Enter at Notification to add users or groups to be notified of printer problems. Use the Insert key to browse the NDS tree. Use the arrow keys to select the person to be notified, and press Enter to select. When you have finished, press Esc, then select Yes, then press Esc.

17. When you have completed the printer configuration, press Esc to save the changes, then press Esc to return to the Available options menu.

18. Select the Print Servers option from the Available options menu.

19. Use the Insert key to add a new print server. Enter a print server name that matches the naming conventions of your organization and press Enter.

20. Press Enter to select the print server you have just created.

21. Select Print Servers from the Print Server Information menu and press Enter.

22. Press the Insert key. Select the printer you created above, then press Enter.

23. Press Esc three times to return to the Available Options menu.

24. Press Esc, then select Yes and press Enter to exit the PCONSOLE utility.

EXERCISE 8-3: CUSTOMIZING INTRANETWARE PRINTING WITH PRINTCON

This exercise will walk you through the process of creating a print job configuration for the user you are currently logged in as.

1. From the DOS command line, run the PRINTCON utility by typing **PRINTCON** and then pressing Enter.

2. Select Edit Print Job Configurations from the Available Options menu and press Enter.

3. Press the Insert key to create a new print job configuration.

4. Enter a name for this new print job configuration and press Enter.

5. Press Enter to select the job configuration you just created.

6. Use the arrow keys to select Local printer.

7. Enter the printer port you want to capture (1=LPT1, 2=LPT2, and so on).

8. Use the arrow keys to select print queue and press Enter. Press Insert and browse the NDS tree to find the desired print queue, then press Enter to select it.

9. Specify other desired options such as form feed, banner, and form number.

10. When you have finished, press Esc, select Yes, and press Enter to save changes.

11. Press Esc twice, select Yes, and press Enter to exit.

EXERCISE 8-4: THE GREAT CHALLENGE

Circle the 20 printing terms hidden in this word search puzzle using the hints provided.

```
P  A  R  A  L  L  E  L  P  O  R  T  P  W  T  G  P  P  P
G  U  R  D  E  V  P  R  I  N  T  S  E  R  V  E  R  R  F
Y  T  L  F  Q  U  I  C  K  S  E  T  U  P  I  I  I  A  E
F  O  D  U  I  I  W  L  O  C  G  A  R  O  N  N  N  K  V
L  L  F  Y  I  W  F  F  K  N  M  X  R  T  T  N  T  C  T
O  O  L  I  H  L  T  J  L  M  S  O  J  Q  X  L  C  E  S
C  A  P  T  U  R  E  H  L  R  N  O  U  I  F  K  O  X  R
A  D  A  W  B  V  Q  Y  H  E  B  E  L  C  U  E  N  S  K
L  A  H  K  Z  K  T  G  U  A  Z  U  E  U  U  I  M  H
P  R  I  N  T  S  E  R  V  E  R  O  P  E  R  A  T  O  R
R  M  A  N  U  A  L  L  O  A  D  X  U  E  T  D  T  K  Y
I  B  U  D  M  P  P  P  D  L  R  Q  S  R  T  Z  X  M  D
N  A  V  C  Q  S  E  R  A  R  T  U  O  C  Y  X  U  S  F
T  J  L  B  O  R  L  C  I  N  W  X  Y  K  P  D  I  V  H
E  L  L  B  A  Y  P  R  I  N  T  D  R  I  V  E  R  X  U
R  X  Q  T  D  V  E  R  E  A  T  A  L  I  V  W  B  B  I
P  R  O  Z  D  L  P  O  L  L  E  D  M  O  D  E  P  G  P
R  R  X  H  S  W  D  P  S  E  R  V  E  R  N  L  M  L  D
E  A  G  X  T  P  E  Y  F  S  V  F  D  F  I  C  O  X  M
```

Hints:
1. Designation that indicates that a printer is directly connected to the print server.
2. Command line utility used to redirect DOS and OS/2 print jobs from applications designed to print to parallel ports.
3. Printer physically connected to the print server.
4. Designation that indicates that a printer is connected to a workstation, the network cable, or a server other than the print server.
5. Graphical utility running under MS Windows that can be used for printer redirection.

6. Type of port that typically provides better performance that a serial port.

7. Menu utility that can be used to set up the IntranetWare printing environment.

8. Default IntranetWare printer configuration option (where alternate choice is Interrupt mode).

9. Software that can be used to convert a print job into a format that can be used by a particular printer.

10. File stored in a print queue while waiting to be printed.

11. Network directory used for storing print jobs.

12. User or Group member who can edit the print jobs of other users, delete print jobs from the print queue, or modify the queue status.

13. Server used to direct print jobs from a print queue to a network printer.

14. User or Group member who has the rights needed to manage a print server.

15. Command line utility that can be used to create print job configurations for use with the CAPTURE, NETUSER, NPRINT, or PCONSOLE utilities.

16. Command line utility used to view, modify, import, or export print device definitions and create or modify printer forms.

17. A leaf object that represents a physical printing device on the network.

18. NLM used for loading print server software on a server.

19. Directory name extension used to indicate that a subdirectory is an IntranetWare print queue.

20. PCONSOLE option which provides a fast method for creating the initial printing environment.

See Appendix C for answers.

EXERCISE 8-5: THE GREATEST MYSTERY OF ALL

Across

2. Precedes print data to the printer
4. Print job has been placed on hold
6. Better than dot matrix
7. Used for printing multipart forms

11. Preferable application type
13. Connected directly to the print server
15. NetWare 3 print queue subdirectory
17. IntranetWare RPRINTER equivalent
18. Cause of printing problems
20. Not attached to the network
21. Used for Autoload printers
22. NPRINTER loaded by print server

Down

1. Print job is ready to print
2. Language used for H-P LaserJet printers
3. Print job is being printed
5. Only type of port that IntranetWare uses for printing
8. Transferring data from the computer to paper
9. Page Description Language for high quality printers
10. Computer containing print queues
11. Printing environment setup utility
12. IntranetWare parent directory for print queues
14. Not directly connected to the print server
16. Follows print data to the printer
19. Print output being received by the print queue
20. Typically is used as communications port

See Appendix C for answers.

PART III

Appendixes

Overview of Novell Education and the CNA Program

"I wanna be a CNA!"

In a world where people and businesses and organizations and governments and nations are being connected and sharing information at a dizzying rate, Novell's primary goal is to be the infrastructure that connects people and services together all over the world.

To help fulfill this goal, Novell Education is providing quality education programs and products to help create a strong support base of trained networking professionals. By itself, the Novell Education department isn't nearly large enough to provide high-quality training to the vast number of people who will require it. Therefore, Novell Education has developed authorized training partnerships throughout the world to provide authorized training. In addition, Novell Education created certification programs to help ensure that the standard for networking skills is maintained at a high level.

Today, Novell has more than 1,500 authorized education partners worldwide, including colleges, universities, professional training centers, and the like.

This appendix describes Novell Education and the CNA program. It also provides some practical tips, such as alternatives to formal classes, finding out how to take the test, and so on.

Certification Partners

Two types of education partners work with Novell worldwide: Novell Authorized Education Centers (NAECs) and Novell Education Academic Partners (NEAPs). These education partners provide top-quality training on Novell products. In fact, Novell guarantees complete customer satisfaction for all Novell courses when they are taught at Novell-authorized training partners.

NAECs are private, independent training organizations that meet Novell's strict quality standards. Some NAECs are also Novell product resellers, but many operate independent of Novell's reseller channels.

The advantage of attending an NAEC is that these organizations typically have a great deal of experience in technology training, and since their livelihood depends on enticing students to take their courses, they are driven to provide quality education.

ZEN

"Don't waste time learning the 'tricks of the trade.' Instead, learn the trade."

H. Jackson Brown, Jr., *Life's Little Instruction Book*

To become an NAEC, the training organization must meet the following strict education guidelines:

▸ The facility must use Novell-developed course materials.

▸ The course must be taught within a recommended time frame.

▸ The facility itself must be Novell-authorized. Authorization is based on a strict set of standards for equipment, instructional soundness, and student comfort.

▸ The course must be taught by a Certified Novell Instructor (CNI), who is certified to teach the specific course.

In addition, the prospective NAEC must submit an extensive application to Novell Education. The training center also pays an initiation fee and annual licensing fees. NAECs are required to offer various courses in a consistent, timely manner.

NEAPs are colleges or universities that provide Novell-authorized courses in a semester- or quarter-length curriculum. There are more than 100 such colleges and universities in the United States, as well as some in Canada, and the list is growing.

NEAPs must follow the same strict guidelines as NAECs and provide Novell courses as part of their standard curriculum.

Both NAECs and NEAPs offer the same courses, based on the same education materials, objectives, and information. They also offer a wide variety of classes (more than 40) on various Novell products and technologies. If you want to pursue Novell-authorized training in a classroom setting, with hands-on labs and knowledgeable instructors, either type of education partner will be beneficial.

Novell-authorized courses (through either NAECs or NEAPs) often offer the best way to get direct, hands-on training, using approved techniques, technologies, and training materials.

Certification Levels

Because Novell has so many different products, and because networking professionals have different reasons for getting trained on those products, Novell offers four different certification levels.

Depending on the level of certification you want to achieve, you take different exams (and, if you desire, the associated courses to prepare for the exams). While one or more certain core exams are required for all levels, you may also take exams for additional "electives" to achieve the certification and specialization you want.

ZEN

"Argue for your limitations, and sure enough, they're yours."

Richard Bach, *Illusions*

The following certification levels are available for Novell products:

- ► CNA (Certified Novell Administrator)

- ► CNE (Certified Novell "E")

- ► Master CNE

- ► CNI (Certified Novell Instructor)

Within each of these levels, there are areas of specialization. Let's look at these four programs in more detail.

CNA (CERTIFIED NOVELL ADMINISTRATOR)

The CNA certification is the entry-level certification for network administrators. It prepares you to manage your own IntranetWare network on a day-to-day basis.

The CNA level does not delve into the more complex and technical aspects of IntranetWare network design, troubleshooting, and implementation. Instead, it is designed for people who perform day-to-day general network administration tasks (such as adding and deleting users, setting up desktop environments, backing up network data, and maintaining network security).

TIP

As a prerequisite to taking the IntranetWare CNA exam, be sure you have a thorough knowledge of DOS, Windows, and general microcomputer concepts.

To prepare for the IntranetWare CNA exam, you can take the Novell-authorized course entitled IntranetWare Administration (course number 520). In addition to being the preparatory course for the CNA exam, this course is also a required course for the IntranetWare track of the CNE certification level (described in the next section). So, if you have plans to continue past the CNA level to get your CNE certification, too, you're killing two birds with one stone.

For a list of the course objectives for the IntranetWare Administration course, see Appendix B. That appendix cross-references all the course objectives with locations in this book that will help prepare you to meet those objectives.

TIP

CNAs qualify for associate membership in the Network Professional Association (NPA), which is explained in Appendix D.

You can pursue five different CNA specialization tracks. This book deals exclusively with the IntranetWare CNA track, of course, but you may be interested in knowing about the other tracks, too. Each CNA track involves a single exam that proves you have mastered the tasks associated with being a system administrator on that type of Novell product. You can achieve your CNA status in multiple tracks simply by passing the appropriate exam for each track.

Table A.1 shows the CNA tracks that are currently available.

CNE

The CNE certification ensures that you can adequately install and manage IntranetWare networks on a more advanced level than the CNA. The CNE starts with the basic CNA skills, then adds high-end skills that will allow you to support IntranetWare networks more fully.

	CNA TRACK	DESCRIPTION
TABLE A.1 *Current CNA Tracks*	IntranetWare	This track certifies that you understand and can administer LAN features of the WAN-based IntranetWare platform.
	NetWare 4	This track certifies that you understand and can administer features of your NetWare 4.1 network.
	NetWare 3	This track certifies that you understand and can administer features of your NetWare 3.12 network.
	GroupWise 4	This track certifies that you understand and can administer the GroupWise GroupWare product, including creating post offices and users, creating links between domains, installing GroupWise clients, and performing basic troubleshooting tasks.
	SoftSolutions 4	This track certifies that you understand and can administer the SoftSolutions product, including adding users, setting up basic applications, operating full-text indexers, and designing screens, reports, and workstation IDs.
	InForms 4	This track certifies that you understand and can administer the InForms product and its features, including creating forms, queries and reports; linking forms to the database; and creating simple macros.

While pursuing your CNE certification, you "declare a major," meaning that you choose to specialize in any of the following three particular Novell product families:

- IntranetWare

- NetWare 4

- NetWare 3

- GroupWare

Some skills you are expected to master as a CNE include managing multiple networks, performing network upgrades, improving network printing performance, and managing network databases.

CNEs are expected to provide support at the network operating system and network applications level.

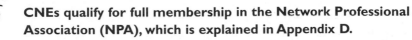

TIP

CNEs qualify for full membership in the Network Professional Association (NPA), which is explained in Appendix D.

MASTER CNE

The Master CNE certification level allows you to go beyond basic CNE certification. To get a Master CNE, you declare a "graduate major." These areas of specialization delve deeper into the integration- and solution-oriented aspects of running a network than the CNE level.

While CNEs provide support at the operating system and application level, Master CNEs are expected to manage advanced access, management, and workgroup integration for multiple environments. Master CNEs can support complex networks that span several different platforms, and can perform upgrades, migration, and integration for various systems.

There are three areas in which Master CNEs can specialize:

- ▶ Network management

- ▶ Infrastructure and advanced access

- ▶ GroupWare integration

TIP

Master CNEs qualify for membership in the Network Professional Association (NPA), which is explained in Appendix D.

The ECNE level is being phased out. The ECNE level's series of tests emphasized aspects of networking encountered in larger, enterprise-wide networks (such as routing, gateways, Novell Directory Services, and so on).

The Master CNE program is replacing the ECNE level because it adds more flexibility to the type of specialization the candidate can pursue. If you've already achieved ECNE status, you will retain the title, and Novell will still recognize it. However, Novell stopped certifying new ECNEs on September 30, 1995.

CNI (CERTIFIED NOVELL INSTRUCTOR)

The CNI certification level qualifies instructors to teach authorized IntranetWare courses through NAECs. The tests and classes specific to this level ensure that the individual taking them will be able to adequately teach others how to install and manage IntranetWare.

This CNI program is designed for people who want to make a career of teaching others how to install, configure, and use Novell networking products.

CNI candidates must attend the Novell courses they wish to be certified to teach, and they must pass proficiency tests at a higher level than other certification candidates. (The course they attend must be taught by an official NAEC or NEAP, and must be taught in the standard Novell format.)

In addition, CNIs must successfully complete a rigorous Instructor Performance Evaluation, as well as meet continuing certification requirements (which include additional training and testing as Novell updates courses and releases new products).

Alternatives to Taking the Novell Authorized Courses

If a typical course in a classroom or lab isn't your preferred method of learning, or if you are going through the course but like to have alternate study methods handy to reinforce your learning, you're in luck. You can use a variety of educational supplements to enhance your IntranetWare education.

Such supplements allow networking professionals to train at their own pace in a more convenient manner.

ZEN

"You are never given a wish without also being given the power to make it true. You may have to work for it, however."

Richard Bach, *Illusions*

Some of the educational alternatives you can use include:

▸ Video training

▸ Computer-Based Training (CBT)

▸ Student Kits

▸ Practice Tests

▸ Courses from other training centers or consultants

VIDEO TRAINING

If you would rather learn the fundamentals of IntranetWare administration in the comfort of your own testing lab (or in your home, for that matter), you're in luck. The IntranetWare Administrator's course has been put on both videotape and CD-ROM formats.

Novell contracts its video training to an organization named J3 Learning. Some NAECs sell these video- and CD-ROM-based courses. Additionally, you can order them directly from J3 Learning at 1-800-532-7672 (toll-free in Canada and the USA) or 1-612-930-0330.

COMPUTER-BASED TRAINING (CBT)

Many of the authorized Novell courses are available in Computer-Based Training (CBT) form. If you'd rather work through the material at your own pace, on your own workstation, you may want to obtain the CBT for the IntranetWare Administrator course.

Novell contracts their CBT coursework to a company named CBT Systems. Again, some NAECs sell these CBT courses, so you may want to contact your local NAEC to get a copy. You can also order the CBT course directly from CBT Systems by calling 1-800-929-9050 (toll free in Canada and the USA) or 1-415-737-9050.

STUDENT KITS

If you're interested in obtaining the materials that students of the authorized IntranetWare Administrator course use during their training, you can order the corresponding Student Kit. The Student Kit for course 520 (the IntranetWare Administration course) contains the following materials:

▶ The IntranetWare Administrator student manual, which is designed to be used with the instructor-led course. (What this means is that this manual doesn't contain exhaustive information—it's more sketchy in nature, meant to be used in conjunction with class discussions, lectures, and labs.)

▶ A two-user version of IntranetWare so that you can install it in your own testing lab and try things out on your own.

▶ A subset of the printed manuals (product documentation) that come with the IntranetWare product.

The Student Kit is only available from NAECs. Generally, NAECs sell them for approximately half of the cost of taking the course itself. (NAECs are at some liberty to set their own prices for the Student Kits, but the ballpark figure for the Student Kit is about $595.)

PRACTICE TESTS

Practice tests for the CNA and CNE exams are available, in case you want to see what you're in for before you tackle the exam itself. While they aren't exactly like the real exams, and don't substitute for study and experience, they can help you prepare for taking the exam.

Of course, we have also supplied you with the *Clarke Tests v3.0* on the CD-ROM that accompanies this book. The *Clarke Tests v3.0* is a next-generation, interactive learning system. It contains practice tests and study sessions that combine a variety of question types with interactive graphics, sounds, and clues. Each interactive answer includes a full page or more of explanation and study material, plus great references to other resources. See Appendix D for more information about the *Clarke Tests v3.0*, or call 1-800-684-8858.

INDEPENDENT COURSES

Numerous "unauthorized" organizations provide classes and seminars on IntranetWare products. Some of these unauthorized classes are quite good. Others are probably of lower quality, since Novell does not have any control over their course content or instructor qualifications.

If you are interested in using an unauthorized provider for your IntranetWare classes, be sure you do some homework beforehand, to try to determine if the course will be beneficial. Here are some hints:

1 • Try to talk to others who've taken a class from the provider, and get a feel for how good they thought the class was.

2 • Get a copy of the course's syllabus or objectives, and compare them to the Novell-authorized course. Are there any glaring gaps?

3 • Find out if there is any lab-time associated with the class. It's important to get the hands-on experience that goes along with the "book-larnin'," or your education will be only superficial at best.

4 • Ask about the instructor's experience, both in the classroom and in the industry.

5 • Find out if the course covers the material in about the same time frame as the Novell course (four days), or if it is "accelerated." If you have plenty of hands-on experience in IntranetWare already, and you're looking for a refresher course and some information to fill in a few of the missing pieces for you, an accelerated course may be just the ticket. If you are fairly new to the game, however, you'll want to find a course that will allow you the time to learn, practice, and digest the information. Don't shortchange yourself for the sake of a few hours of time.

If your homework reveals nothing worrisome about the course, then it may be a good investment. If you're hesitant about the course's quality, however, keep looking. There are plenty of courses and instructors out there that can do a good job of teaching you what you need to learn, so be picky. It's your life, after all.

Testing Your Mettle

Okay. You've finished the course, you've studied this book, you've spent hours in the lab or on your own network using the NetWare Administrator and other utilities to add users, change passwords, back up files, and the like. You're ready to show your stuff, and prove that you have the baseline of knowledge required to take on network administrator duties in the real world.

You're ready to take the test and become a CNA.

So, how do you sign up for the exam?

The IntranetWare Administrator exam is offered at NAECs and NEAPs all over the world. The first thing you must do is find one of these centers to administer the exam.

HOW DO YOU SIGN UP FOR AN EXAM?

All Novell exams are administered by a professional testing organization: Sylvan Prometric.

If you take the Novell-authorized course, you may be able to sign up to the take the test at the same location, because some (but not all) NAECs are also affiliated with Sylvan Prometric. In fact, the instructor most likely can give you information about where to take the exam locally.

Otherwise, to find a location that administers this exam, simply call one of the following numbers:

▶ The Novell Education phone number at 1-800-233-EDUC (toll-free in Canada and the USA) or 1-801-222-7800

▶ Sylvan Prometric, at 1-800-RED-TEST (toll-free), 1-800-RED-EXAM (toll-free), or 1-410-880-8700

Outside of the USA and Canada, contact your local Novell office, or a local Sylvan Prometric office.

> ### REAL WORLD
>
> In the past, there were two testing organizations that Novell used to administer its tests: Sylvan Learning Systems and Drake Prometric. However, Drake Prometric was recently bought by Sylvan Learning Systems. The merged organization changed its name to Sylvan Prometric, so now it's all just one big, happy family.

WHAT IS THE EXAM LIKE?

The IntranetWare Administrator exam, like all Novell exams, is computer-based. You take the exam by answering questions on the computer. However, unlike more traditional tests, the IntranetWare Administrator exam is performance-based. This means that instead of just asking you to regurgitate facts, the exam actually requires you to apply your knowledge to solve problems. For example, the exam may include simulations of network problems or tasks, such as adding a user. You must actually use IntranetWare utilities to complete the task or solve the problem.

The exam is also adaptive. This means that the exam offers easier or more difficult questions to you based on your last answer, in an effort to determine just how much you know. In other words, the exam starts off asking you a fairly easy question. If you answer it correctly, the next question will be slightly harder. If you answer that one correctly, too, it will offer you a slightly harder one again, and so on. If you answer a question incorrectly, on the other hand, the next question will be slightly easier. If you miss that one, too, the next will be easier yet, until you get one right. Then the questions will get more difficult again.

The number of questions you'll be asked will vary, depending on your level of knowledge. If you answer all of the questions correctly, you will continue to be offered questions until you have been tested on the full range of knowledge. If you answer incorrectly, you'll only answer questions until your level of knowledge is determined. Obviously, the higher the level of knowledge the computer determines you have, the better score you receive.

It will probably take you from 20 to 40 minutes to take this exam.

ZEN

"Be brave. Even if you're not, pretend to be. No one can tell the difference."

H. Jackson Brown, Jr.

The exam is closed-book and is graded on a pass/fail basis. The standard fee for the exam is $85. When you go to take the exam, remember to take two forms of identification with you (one must be a picture ID). You will not be allowed to take any notes into or out of the exam room.

If you fail the test, take heart. You can take it again. In fact, you can take it again as many times as you want—there are no limits to repeating it. You can repeat it as soon as you like, and as many times as it takes to pass (or until your checkbook runs dry, whichever comes first). Because of the way the exam is designed, questions are randomly pulled from a giant database. Therefore, chances are slim that you will ever get the same test questions twice, no matter how often you take the exam.

After the Test—Now What?

Congratulations! You passed the exam with flying colors, just like we knew you would! Now comes the easiest part—getting your official certification.

To receive your official certification status, you must sign a Novell Education Certification Agreement.

The certification agreement contains the usual legal jargon you might expect with such certification. Among other things, it grants you permission to use the trademarked name "CNA" on your resume or other advertising, as long as you use the name in connection with providing network administration services on a IntranetWare network. It also reminds you that if the network administration services you offer don't live up to Novell's high standards of quality, Novell can require you to meet those standards within "a commercially reasonable time."

After you've passed the exam, you can read the agreement, sign the "Signature Form," and mail it back to Novell. (Because Novell needs your legal signature on the form, they can't accept faxed copies of the form.) For your convenience, we've included a copy of the agreement, along with the signature form, at the end of this chapter. You can also receive additional copies of the form by calling your local NAEC, or by calling Novell's FaxBack phone line at 1-801-222-7800 or 1-800-233-EDUC and requesting a copy to be faxed to you. Novell Education, of course, reserves the right to change this form without notice.

For More Information . . .

You can get more information about Novell Education courses, exams, training supplements, programs, and so on, by using one of the following avenues:

- ► Call Novell Education at 1-801-222-7800 or 1-800-233-EDUC (toll free in the USA and Canada)

- ► Use Novell's FaxBack system to receive information by fax. The FaxBack system is available through the same numbers listed here. Select Option 3 for the FaxBack system, and follow the instructions to order the FaxBack master catalog of available documents. After you've received the FaxBack catalog of documents, you can call back and request the specific documents you want. You can order up to four documents per call.

- ► Call your local NAEC, NEAP, or Sylvan Prometric testing center.

- ► Go on-line to Novell Education's Internet site. You can get to the Novell Education information either through Novell's Internet site (GO NETWIRE on CompuServe, or *http://www.novell.com*), or by going directly to *http://education.novell.com*.

Novell Education Certification Agreement

1 **PURPOSE.** NOVELL is in the business of, among other things, manufacturing, distributing, selling, offering for sale, and promoting network computing products. Many of NOVELL's products are technically complex and require competent pre- and post-sales support. In order to provide adequate support, NOVELL has devised several programs under which individuals become certified to competently provide appropriate support. These are the Certified Novell Administrator (or "CNA"), the CNE, the Enterprise CNE (or "ECNE"), the Master CNE, and the Certified Novell Instructor (or "CNI") certification programs. Successful participants in these programs, through education, training, and/or testing become authorized to provide services and to use the NOVELL Marks pertaining to the particular certification program or programs that the participant has completed. Individuals may participate in one or more of these certification programs. Completion of one certification program does not entitle a participant to use the Marks or provide the services pertaining to any other certification program.

2 **DEFINITIONS.**

2.1 **Program** means one of the programs of certification that is offered by NOVELL, is available to participants, and may lead to certification under this Novell Education Certification Agreement ("Agreement"). The Programs include the CNA, CNE, Enterprise CNE, Master CNE, and CNI certification programs. As further provided in this Agreement, participants cannot administer Licensed Services under or otherwise use the Marks of a particular Program, claim any Program certification or status, or exercise any rights granted under this Agreement, except through the successful completion of NOVELL's requirements for that Program.

2.2 **MARKS** means, as the case may be, the Certified Novell Administrator and CNA marks and logos, the CNE marks and logos, Enterprise CNE and ECNE marks and logos, Master CNE marks and logos, and the Certified Novell Instructor and CNI marks and logos.

2.3 **LICENSED SERVICES** means the particular administration or pre- and post-sales service and support of NOVELL's network computing products that correspond with the Program or Programs successfully completed by the participant. The LICENSED SERVICES for each particular Program are described below. LICENSED SERVICES does not mean (I) any services provided with respect to non-NOVELL products or (ii) the teaching of courses relating to NOVELL products other than those courses permitted to be taught according to the CNI LICENSED SERVICES and described below.

2.3.1 **If YOU have successfully completed the CNA Program requirements, LICENSED SERVICES** means handling the day-to-day administration of the installed NOVELL networking product or products for which YOU have successfully completed a CNA Program. Successful completion of a particular CNA Program will allow YOU to administer the above services for one of several particular products, including (but not limited to) NetWare, GroupWare (GroupWise, InForms and SoftSolutions) and UnixWare.

2.3.2 **If YOU have successfully completed the CNE, Enterprise CNE and/or Master CNE Program requirements, LICENSED SERVICES** means the pre- and post-sales service and support of the NOVELL network computing product or products for which YOU have successfully completed a CNE, Enterprise CNE and/or Master CNE Program. Successful completion of a particular CNE Program will allow YOU to administer the above services in one of several particular products, including (but not limited to) NetWare, GroupWare (GroupWise, InForms and SoftSolutions) and UnixWare. Successful completion of a particular Master CNE Program will allow YOU to administer the above services in one of several particular service areas, including (but not limited to) Network Management, Infrastructure and Advanced Access, and GroupWare Integration.

2.3.3 **If YOU have successfully completed the CNI Program requirements, LICENSED SERVICES** means the teaching of NOVELL authorized courses under the auspices of a Novell Authorized Education Center. CNI Licensed Services does not mean the teaching of a course not authorized by NOVELL.

2.4 **NOVELL AUTHORIZED EDUCATION CENTER or NAEC** means any organization that has been approved by NOVELL as an authorized training facility and includes Novell Authorized Internal Training Organizations and Novell Education Academic Partners.

2.5 **NOVELL** means Novell Ireland Software Ltd. If YOU provide LICENSED SERVICES in Europe, the Middle East, or Africa (EMEA). If YOU do not provide LICENSED SERVICES in EMEA, Novell means Novell, Inc.

3 **CERTIFICATION.** YOUR Program certification is based on completing the required testing and complying with the requirements set forth in the brochure corresponding with the Program YOU have successfully completed. YOU acknowledge that NOVELL has the right to change the requirements for receiving Program certification, or

maintaining a Program certification, at any time. Once certification is granted, it will automatically renew if all continuing certification requirements are met. YOU are responsible for maintaining YOUR certification. To maintain certification, YOU must complete all Program continuing certification requirements, if any, corresponding with YOUR particular Program certification within the time frame specified by NOVELL. If YOU do not complete the continuing certification requirements within the time frame specified by NOVELL, YOUR certified Program status for that particular Program may expire, resulting in de-certification. NOTWITHSTANDING ANYTHING IN THIS AGREEMENT TO THE CONTRARY, NOVELL HAS THE RIGHT NOT TO GRANT OR RENEW YOUR CERTIFICATION IF NOVELL REASONABLY DETERMINES THAT YOUR CERTIFICATION OR USE OF THE MARKS WILL ADVERSELY AFFECT NOVELL. THIS AGREEMENT APPLIES TO ANY AND ALL PROGRAMS COMPLETED BY YOU.

4 **WHAT HAPPENS WHEN YOU LEAVE AN ORGANIZATION?** YOU retain YOUR Program certification if YOU move to a new organization

5 **GRANT AND CONSIDERATION.** NOVELL grants to YOU a non-exclusive and non-transferable license to use the MARKS solely in connection with providing the LICENSED SERVICES corresponding to the Program certification YOU have achieved. YOU or YOUR agents may use the MARKS on such promotional display and advertising materials as may, in YOUR judgment, promote the LICENSED SERVICES corresponding to YOUR Program certification. YOU may not use the MARKS for any purposes that are not directly related to the provision of the LICENSED SERVICES corresponding to YOUR particular Program certification. YOU may not use the MARKS of any Program unless YOU have completed the Program certification requirements and have been notified by NOVELL in writing that YOU have achieved certification status for that particular Program. YOUR CNI certification, if applicable, is subject to the restrictions of Section 5.1 of this Agreement.

5.1 **AFFILIATION WITH NAECS/CNI LICENSE GRANT**

5.1.1 **Affiliation with NAECs.** YOU are authorized, if YOU achieve the status of CNI, to teach authorized Novell courses only at NAECs. YOU may be employed by one NAEC or YOU may work independently, contracting with one or more NAECs on a case-by-case basis. If YOU are employed by an NAEC and move to another NAEC or obtain independent status, YOU retain the CNI certification status. It is YOUR responsibility to notify NOVELL of any address or NAEC change.

6 **TERM AND TERMINATION.**

6.1 **Term.** This Novell Education Certification Agreement will commence on the date YOU receive written notice from NOVELL that YOU have met all the requirements necessary to attain YOUR particular Program certification and will terminate in accordance with the terms and provisions of this Agreement. YOU understand that, for convenience of processing, YOU will indicate assent to this Agreement via the use of a computer as indicated electronically prior to YOUR completion of the Program requirements, or, in certain circumstances and when authorized by NOVELL, YOU will indicate assent by signing this Agreement. YOU acknowledge that this Agreement will not take effect until NOVELL has notified YOU in writing that all Program requirements have been met. YOU further acknowledge that this Agreement will remain in effect in the event YOU upgrade YOUR status to include any other Program certifications, and that those subparagraphs specific to those certification(s) will also apply to YOU.

6.2 **Termination by Either Party.** Either party may terminate this Agreement without cause by giving thirty (30) days or more prior written notice to the other party.

6.3 **Termination by NOVELL.** Without prejudice to any rights it may have under this Agreement or in law equity or otherwise, NOVELL may terminate this Agreement upon the occurrence of any one or more of the following events (called "Default"):

6.3.1 If YOU fail to perform any of YOUR obligations under this Agreement;

6.3.2 If YOU render the LICENSED SERVICES without complying with the testing required under this Agreement, or if YOU discontinue offering the LICENSED SERVICES;

6.3.3 If any government agency or court finds that LICENSED SERVICES as provided by YOU are defective in any way, manner or form; or

6.3.4 If actual or potential adverse publicity or other information, emanating from a third party or parties, about YOU, the LICENSED SERVICES, or the use of the MARKS by YOU causes NOVELL, in its sole judgment, to believe that NOVELL's reputation will be adversely affected.

Novell.

In the event any Default occurs, NOVELL will give YOU written notice of termination of this Agreement. In the event of a Default under Section 6.3.3 or 6.3.4, NOVELL may terminate this Agreement with no period for correction, and it will terminate automatically without further notice. In the event of a Default under Section 6.3.1 or 6.3.2, or at NOVELL's option under Section 6.3.3 or 6.3.4, YOU will be given thirty (30) days from receipt of notice in which to correct any Default. If YOU fail to correct the Default within the notice period, this Agreement will automatically terminate on the last day of the notice period.

6.4 **Return of Materials.** Upon termination of this Agreement, YOU agree to immediately cease to render the LICENSED SERVICES and to return all badges or other trademark collateral to NOVELL. Upon termination, all rights granted under this Novell Education Certification Agreement will immediately and automatically revert to NOVELL.

7 **CONDUCT OF BUSINESS.** YOU agree to (i) conduct business in a manner which reflects favorably at all times on the products, goodwill and reputation of NOVELL; (ii) avoid deceptive, misleading or unethical practices which are or might be detrimental to NOVELL or its products; and (iii) refrain from making any representations, warranties, or guarantees to customers that are inconsistent with the policies established by NOVELL. YOU further agree that YOU will not represent YOURSELF to possess the certification of any Program category until such time as YOU have completed all requirements for that Program and have been notified by NOVELL in writing that YOU have achieved the certification of that Program, including but not limited to the Program certifications of CNA, CNE, Enterprise CNE, Master CNE, and CNI.

8 **OWNERSHIP.** No title to or ownership of the MARKS or of any software or proprietary technology in hardware licensed to YOU pursuant to this Agreement is transferred to YOU. NOVELL, or the licensors through which NOVELL obtained the rights to distribute the products, owns and retains all title and ownership of all intellectual property rights in the products, including all software, firmware, software master diskettes, copies of software, documentation and related materials and, all modifications to and derivative works from software acquired as a Program certification holder which are made by YOU, NOVELL or any third party. NOVELL does not transfer any portion of such title and ownership, or any of the associated goodwill to YOU, and this Agreement should not be construed to grant YOU any right or license, whether by implication, estoppel or otherwise, except as expressly provided. YOU agree to be bound by and observe the proprietary nature of the products acquired as a CNA, CNE, Enterprise CNE, Master CNE, and/or CNI.

9 **QUALITY OF LICENSED SERVICES.** YOU agree that it is of fundamental importance to NOVELL that the LICENSED SERVICES be of the highest quality and integrity. Accordingly, YOU agree that NOVELL will have the right to determine in its absolute discretion whether the LICENSED SERVICES meet NOVELL's high standards of merchantability. In the event that NOVELL determines that YOU are no longer meeting accepted levels of quality and/or integrity, NOVELL agrees to so advise YOU and, except as otherwise provided in Section 6.3 of this Agreement, to provide YOU with a commercially reasonable time of no less than one (1) month to meet the above-referenced standards of quality and integrity.

10 **RESERVATION OF RIGHTS AND GOOD WILL IN NOVELL.** NOVELL retains all rights not expressly conveyed to YOU by this Agreement. YOU recognize the value of the publicity and goodwill associated with the MARKS and acknowledge that the goodwill will exclusively inure to the benefit of, and belong to, NOVELL. YOU have no rights of any kind whatsoever with respect to the MARKS licensed under this Agreement except to the extent of the license granted in this Agreement.

11 **NO REGISTRATION BY YOU.** YOU agree not to file any new trademark, collective mark, service mark, certification mark, and/or trade name application(s), in any class and in any country, for any trademark, collective mark, service mark, certification mark, and/or trade name that, in Novell's opinion, is the same as, similar to, or that contains, in whole or in part, any or all of Novell's trade names, trademarks, collective marks, service marks, and/or certification marks, including, without limitation, the MARKS licensed under this Agreement. This section will survive the expiration or other termination of this Agreement.

12 **PROTECTION OF RIGHTS.** YOU agree to assist NOVELL, to the extent reasonably necessary (and at NOVELL's expense), to protect or to obtain protection for any of NOVELL's rights to the MARKS. In addition, if at any time NOVELL requests that YOU discontinue using the MARKS and/or substitute using a new or different mark, YOU will immediately cease use of the MARKS and cooperate fully with NOVELL to ensure all legal obligations have been met with regards to use of the MARKS.

13 **INDEMNIFICATION BY YOU.** YOU agree to indemnify and hold NOVELL harmless against any loss, liability, damage, cost or expense (including reasonable legal fees) arising out of any claims or suits, whatever their nature and however arising, which may be brought or made against NOVELL (i) by reason of YOUR performance or non-performance of this Agreement; (ii) arising out of the use by YOU of the MARKS in any manner whatsoever except in the form expressly licensed under this Agreement; and/or (iii) for any personal injury, product liability, or other claim arising from the promotion

812

and/or provision of the LICENSED SERVICES. In the event NOVELL seeks indemnification under this Section, NOVELL will immediately notify YOU, in writing, of any claim or proceeding brought against it for which it seeks indemnification under this Agreement. In no event may YOU enter into any third party agreements which would in any manner whatsoever affect the rights of, or bind, NOVELL in any manner, without the prior written consent of NOVELL.

14 **REVISION OF TERMS.** NOVELL reserves the right to revise the terms of this Agreement from time to time. In the event of a revision, signing a new agreement may be a condition of continued certification.

15 **GENERAL PROVISIONS.**

15.1 **Governing Law and Venue.** This Agreement will in all respects be governed by the law of the country of Your residence, and venue of any actions will be proper either in the courts of the State of Utah of the United States of America or in those of the country of Your residence.

15.2 **Non-Waiver.** No waiver of any right or remedy on one occasion by either party will be deemed a waiver of such right or remedy on any other occasion.

15.3 **Course of Dealing.** This Agreement will not be supplemented or modified by any course of dealing or usage of trade.

15.4 **Assignment.** Neither this Agreement nor any of Your rights or obligations arising under this Agreement may be assigned without Novell's prior written consent. This Agreement is freely assignable by Novell, and will be for the benefit of Novell's successors and assigns.

15.5 **Independent Contractors.** YOU acknowledge that both parties are independent contractors and that YOU will not, except in accordance with this Agreement, represent YOURSELF as an agent or legal representative of NOVELL.

15.6 **Compliance with Laws.** YOU agree to comply, at YOUR own expense, with all statutes, regulations, rules, ordinances, and orders of any governmental body, department or agency which apply to or result from YOUR obligations under this Agreement. All holders of the CNE designation must not represent themselves as "engineers" or otherwise misrepresent the meaning of the CNE designation, which is an inventive and symbolic phrase only and not an acronym. Such holders must use only the "CNE" marks and logos, the "ECNE" or "Enterprise CNE" marks and logos, and/or the "Master CNE" marks and logos, as applicable and corresponding to your certification(s).

15.7 **Modifications.** Any modifications to the typewritten face of this Agreement will render it null and void. All modifications must be in writing and signed by both parties.

Signature Form

This Signature Form relates to and incorporates the terms and conditions of the Novell Education Certification Agreement ("Agreement") to which it is attached. YOU must either indicate assent electronically or sign this Agreement Signature Form and return it to the applicable address below:

**Novell Education
c/o Agreements
5001 W 80th St, Suite 401
Bloomington, MN 55437
USA**

**Novell Education
c/o Agreements
Level 6, Suite 602
25 Bligh Street
Sydney, NSW 2000
Australia**

**Novell Education
c/o Agreements
Pelmolenlaan 12-14
    3447 G W Woerden
The Netherlands**

Please note: If YOU are a minor under the laws of the state or country (whichever applies) where you sign this Signature Form, it needs to be countersigned below by YOUR parent, court-appointed curator, or legal guardian. The Agreement will automatically terminate when YOU reach the age of majority *unless* you affirm the Agreement by completing and signing the Novell Education Certification Agreement being used generally by Novell at that time and returning it to Novell. If YOU allow the Agreement to lapse, YOU will be decertified.

Certification Candidate:

By signing this form, YOU confirm that YOU have read and agree to be bound by the terms and conditions of the Novell Education Certification Agreement, including, but not limited to, the terms relating to YOUR limited right to use Novell's Marks (as that term is defined in the Agreement).

Signature _____

Print Name _____

Date _____

Test ID# _____

Daytime Phone # _____

[ ] Parent / [ ] Curator / [ ] Legal Guardian:
(Check appropriate box)

By signing this form, the candidate's parent / curator / legal guardian confirms that he / she has read the Novell Education Certification Agreement and accepts full responsibility for the candidate's compliance with its terms and conditions and will be liable for any breach of the candidate's obligations thereunder.

Signature _____

Print Name _____

Date _____

To receive a copy of the complete agreement from Certification Administration or by fax, call 1-800-233-EDUC or 1-801-222-7800.

Due to legal restrictions we cannot accept faxed copies of the signed form.

CNA Cross-Reference to Novell Course Objectives

Following is a list of the Novell-authorized course objectives for the IntranetWare/NetWare 4.11 CNA curriculum. Novell Education uses these objectives to write authorized courseware and to develop certification exams. In order to become a Certified Novell Administrator, you must be intimately familiar with every objective in the following course: *Novell Education Course 520-IntranetWare/NetWare 4.11 Administration*.

Novell's CNA Study Guide for IntranetWare/NetWare 4.11 enables you to learn these objectives (see page-numbered cross-references) in conjunction with Novell-authorized courseware. This appendix clarifies that relationship by pointing you in the right direction. Have fun and good luck!

Course 520—IntranetWare/NetWare 4.11 Administration

This is the foundation of the IntranetWare curriculum. In the *IntranetWare/NetWare 4.11 Administration* course, you are introduced to the fundamental technologies of IntranetWare, including Novell Directory Services, the File System, Security, Backup, Login Scripts, and, of course, Printing. It's a 5-day course covering almost 100 objectives.

It's time to learn, and this is a great place to start.

SECTION 1: INTRODUCTION TO NETWARE 4

1 • Describe a network, including its basic function and physical components. . . . **(92–96 + 563–565)**

2 • List several responsibilities of a network administrator. . . . **(35–52)**

3 • List the NetWare 4 network services you will learn to administer in this course. . . . **(96–111)**

4 • Describe Novell Directory Services (NDS) and explain its role on the network. . . . **(112–115)**

5 • Describe the Directory, including its function and basic components. . . . (115–122)

6 • Describe the Directory tree, including leaf and container objects. . . . (123–142)

7 • Browse the Directory tree. . . . (208–215)

8 • Demonstrate correct object-naming techniques. . . . (144–159 + 216–217)

SECTION 2: CONNECTING TO THE NETWORK AND LOGGING IN

1 • Describe how a workstation communicates with the network, and list the files required to connect a workstation to the network. . . . (466–469)

2 • Describe the function of the software and hardware, including local operating systems, Client 32, communications protocols, and network boards necessary to connect a workstation to the network. . . . (469–473)

3 • Connect a workstation to the network by executing the appropriate workstation files. . . . (471–472 + 542–547)

4 • Explain and perform the login procedure. . . . (473–475)

SECTION 3: ACCESSING DATA FILES AND APPLICATIONS ON THE NETWORK

1 • Explain the basic components of network file storage, including volumes, directory structures, network drives, and search drives. . . . (240–243 + 296–300)

2 • Display volume, directory, and file information. . . . (258–296)

3 • Define NetWare command line utilities, describe how they are used, and activate Help information for them. . . . (260 + 267–270 +276–280 + 289-296)

4 • Using a Volume object and a Directory Map object, map a network drive to a volume and navigate between the volumes. . . . **(300–315 + 319-322)**

5 • Using a Volume object and a Directory Map object, map a network drive to a directory and navigate the directories of a volume. . . . **(300–315 +319–322)**

6 • Using a Volume object and a Directory Map object, map a search drive to a directory containing an application. . . . **(300–315 +319–322)**

SECTION 4: PRINTING TO A NETWORK PRINTER

I • Describe the basic components of network printing and how they interrelate in processing a print job. . . . **(678–728)**

2 • View network printing information in Windows 95 and Windows 3.1 . . . . **(693–696)**

3 • Set up print job redirection, and print from Windows 95 and Windows 3.1. . . . **(693–696)**

4 • Set up print job redirection with CAPTURE and print a document from an application. . . . **(685–692 + 781–783)**

SECTION 5: SETTING UP USER ACCOUNTS AND LOGIN SECURITY

I • Describe the function of a User object and its property values. . . . **(132–133)**

2 • Create a User object and enter user identification property values. . . . **(225 + 229–230)**

3 • Create and modify User objects with the same property values using the Template object. . . . **(222–225 +434–445)**

4 • Create a user home directory automatically while creating a User object. Create user home directories. . . . **(225 + 230 +438)**

5 • Modify parameters for multiple users. . . . **(356 + 434–445)**

6 • Manage NDS objects by creating, deleting, and renaming objects, and by entering and modifying property values. . . . **(218–230 +434–445)**

7 • Create users with UIMPORT. . . . **(231–234)**

8 • Identify the levels and functions of network security. . . . **(330–341)**

9 • Describe and establish login security, including user account restrictions, time restrictions, station restrictions, and intruder detection. . . . **(344–371)**

SECTION 6: SETTING UP THE NETWORK FILE SYSTEM

1 • Explain guidelines for planning and creating custom volumes and directories in the network file system. . . . **(243–248)**

2 • List the system-created volumes and directories. Describe their contents and function. . . . **(248–253)**

3 • List suggested directories for organizing the file system. . . . **(253–256)**

4 • Identify the strengths and weaknesses of sample directory structures. . . . **(256–258)**

5 • Design and create a directory structure based on a given scenario. . . . **(317–318)**

SECTION 7: MANAGING THE FILE SYSTEM

1 • Manage the file system directory structure by creating, deleting, renaming, and moving directories. . . . **(270–280 + 323–326)**

2 • Manage files in the file system by copying, moving, deleting, salvaging, and purging files. . . . **(281–296 + 323–326)**

3 • Manage the use of volume space by viewing volume usage statistics; restricting space usage by user and directory; changing file ownership; locating files based on usage, owner, and size; setting compression attributes; and setting data migration attributes. . . . **(260–270)**

SECTION 8: SETTING UP FILE SYSTEM SECURITY

1 • Describe NetWare 4 file system security, including the concepts of directory and file rights, trustee assignments, inheritance, rights reassignment, Inherited Rights Filters (IRFs), security equivalence, and effective rights. . . . **(410–423)**

2 • Determine a user's effective rights. . . . **(421–423 + 450–455)**

3 • Perform basic security implementation tasks, such as assigning a trustee and granting rights, setting a directory IRF, creating a group object and assigning members, and making a user security equivalent to another user. . . . **(416–423 + 443–445)**

4 • Describe guidelines for planning a directory structure based on security considerations. . . . **(410–415 + 256–258 + 317–318)**

5 • Given a directory structure and the function of its directories, recommend the rights that should be granted and the trustee object that will make security implementation and management easiest. . . . **(413–414)**

6 • Describe and set the directory and file attributes that can be used to regulate access to files. . . . **(423–430)**

7 • Activate NetWare Administrator to navigate NDS and the NetWare file system. Use NetWare administrator Help. . . . **(323–326 + 434–445)**

8 • Based on a scenario, create and implement a file system security plan that appropriately grants directory and file rights to Container, Group, and User objects, and sets directory IRFs. . . . **(434–445)**

SECTION 9: ACCESSING AND PROTECTING THE NETWARE SERVER CONSOLE

1 • Describe the function of a NetWare 4 server and its interface. . . . **(583 + 595–597)**

2 • Define console command and NetWare Loadable Module (NLM). . . . **(584–607 +667–673)**

3 • Describe the function of the LOAD command. . . . **(591)**

4 • Describe remote console management. List the steps necessary to set up a server for both SPX and asynchronous remote connections. . . . **(650–654 + 667–673)**

5 • Use RCONSOLE to remotely access the server console, switch between console screens, and activate the RCONSOLE Available Options menu . . . . **(654–657 + 667–673)**

6 • Describe security strategies for a NetWare 4 server, such as setting a password on the monitor, setting a password for Remote Console, and placing the server in a secure location. . . . **(608–614)**

SECTION 10: SETTING UP NETWORK PRINTING

1 • Set up a network printing environment by creating and configuring related Print Queue, Printer, and Print Server objects. . . . (**704–716 + 776–780 + 787–788**)

2 • Set up network printing hardware by bringing up a print server on a NetWare 4 server and connecting a printer to the network through a NetWare server or DOS workstation. . . . (**716–719**)

3 • Regulate who can do any of the following: print to a print queue, manage print jobs in the print queue, be notified by a printer when a problem occurs, view the status of the print server, or manage the print server. . . . (**728–755**)

4 • Manage the flow of print jobs into and out of a print queue by managing the status of the print queue. . . . (**728–755 + 784–785**)

5 • Manage print jobs in a print queue by pausing, rushing, delaying, and deleting print jobs in the print queue. . . . (**728–755 + 784–785**)

6 • Describe how to customize print jobs by using print job configurations, printer definitions, and printer forms. . . . (**720–728 + 755–763 + 789**)

SECTION 11: INSTALLING AND CONFIGURING CLIENT 32 ON WORKSTATIONS

1 • Use the NetWare Client software to install Client 32 for Windows 95 . . . . (**619–622**)

2 • Use the Network Configuration Page to modify the network connection for Windows 95. . . . (**472–473**)

3 • Use the NetWare Client software to install Client 32 for Windows 3.1 . . . . (**622–626**)

4 • Modify the network connection for Windows 3.1 by modifying the NET.CFG file. . . . **(479–487 + 548–549)**

5 • Upgrade the client automatically to the most current version of Client 32. . . . **(621–622 + 624–626)**

SECTION 12: CREATING LOGIN SCRIPTS

1 • Describe the types of login scripts and how they coordinate at login . . . . **(487–495)**

2 • Recommend procedures that should be executed during login. . . . **(501)**

3 • Plan login scripts with correct login script command syntax. . . . **(495–510)**

4 • Create, execute, and debug a login script. . . . **(550–552)**

SECTION 13: CONFIGURING NETWORK APPLICATIONS FOR USERS

1 • Describe how to manage and launch network applications using Application objects and the NetWare Application Launcher (NAL). . . . **(527)**

2 • Configure NDS and the file system to access network applications with NAL. . . . **(528–529)**

3 • Use NAL to launch a network application from Windows. . . . **(529–531)**

SECTION 14: MANAGING NDS SECURITY

1 • Explain how access to the Directory is controlled by object trustees, object rights, and property rights. . . . **(371–400)**

2 • Given a Directory tree, determine effective rights for objects and properties and troubleshoot an NDS security scenario. . . . **(397–401 + 446–449)**

3 • Explain guidelines and considerations for managing NDS security. . . . **(401–409)**

4 • Implement NDS security by making trustee assignments; modifying Object, All Property, and Selected Property rights; and setting Inherited Rights Filters (IRFs). . . . **(434–445)**

SECTION 15: MANAGING RESOURCES IN A MULTICONTEXT ENVIRONMENT

1 • Describe how the Directory tree structure affects network use and management skills. . . . **(142–143)**

2 • Describe sample Directory structures and discuss basic guidelines for organizing resources. . . . **(188–207)**

3 • Demonstrate correct object-naming techniques. . . . **(144–159 + 216–217)**

4 • Change the current context and navigate the Directory tree. . . . **(146–150 + 213–215)**

5 • Log in, map network drives, and redirect print jobs to resources in other contexts. . . . **(144–149 + 305–315 + 542–547 + 781–783)**

6 •   Grant rights to file system and network printing resources in other
contexts. . . . **(405–408)**

7 •   Create shortcuts to objects in other contexts using Directory Map and
Alias objects. . . . **(140–141 + 304 + 311)**

8 •   Establish an initial context at login for a DOS workstation. . . .
(147–148 + 473 + 483)

9 •   Edit login scripts to access resources in other containers. . . . **(495–508)**

SECTION 16: BACKING UP SERVERS AND WORKSTATIONS

1 •   Compare and contrast backup strategies. . . . **(636–642 + 647–650)**

2 •   Describe the process of backing up a NetWare server and workstation's
file systems with SBACKUP. . . . **(643–646)**

3 •   Describe the process of restoring file system information with
SBACKUP. . . . **(646–647)**

SECTION 17: PERFORMING A SIMPLE NETWARE 4 INSTALLATION

1 •   Compare the requirements of the NetWare 4 Simple and Custom
Installation options. . . . **(560–570)**

2 •   Identify the major steps for installing NetWare 4. . . . **(570–582)**

3 •   Install a NetWare 4 server using the Simple Installation option. . . .
(659–673)

Solutions to Quizzes, Puzzles, Exercises, and Case Studies

"Scanner indicates no life forms, Captain . . . only the answers to CNA exercises"

Chapter 3: Understanding IntranetWare and NDS

ANSWERS TO QUIZZES

Q3-1

The only available matching color for the large present is red. Next, the only contrasting color available for the small wrapping is silver. Finally, that leaves green wrapping and a gold bow for the medium-sized gift. Happy birthday.

Q3-2

The only days the Lion can say "I lied yesterday" are Mondays and Thursdays. The only days the Unicorn can say "I lied yesterday" are Thursdays and Sundays. Therefore, the only day they can both say it is Thursday.

Q3-3

On no day of the week is this possible! Only on Mondays and Thursdays could he make the first statement; only on Wednesdays and Sundays could he make the second. So, there is no day he could say both. Poor Alice is stuck in the Land of Forgetfulness forever.

Q3-4

This is a very different situation! It illustrates well the difference between making two statements separately and making one statement that is the conjunction of the two. Indeed, given any two statements *X* and *Y*, if the single statement "*X and Y*" is true, then it follows that *X* and *Y* are true separately. But if the conjunction "*X and Y*" is false, then at least one of them is false.

Now, the only day of the week it could be true that the Lion lied yesterday and will lie again tomorrow is Tuesday (this is the only day that occurs between two of the Lion's lying days). So, the day the Lion said that couldn't be Tuesday, for on Tuesdays that statement is true, but the Lion doesn't make true statements on Tuesdays. Therefore, it is not Tuesday. Hence, the Lion's statement is false, so the Lion is lying. Therefore, the day must be either Monday or Wednesday. Tricky little Lion.

Q3-5

A-4
B-5,8
C-1
D-2, 6
E-3

Q3-6

The Hint (Synergy) means the whole is greater than the sum of its parts. This means we must be dealing with a whole number. Therefore, half of "What I'd be" must be a whole number. "What I'd be" must be an even number. "What I am" cannot end in 1. There are four possible arrangements of the three digits:

	(a)	(b)	(c)	(d)
What I am	1?3	13?	31?	?13
What I'd be	3?4	34?	43?	?34

"What I am" is "Nine less than half what I'd be." So ("What I am" + 9) • 2 = "What I'd be." Examination shows that only "A" fits the bill and "What I am" must be 183. No sweat.

EXERCISE 3-1: "TREE WALKING" FOR TODDLERS

1a. Answers will vary in terms of what objects are displayed when you activate the NetWare Administrator utility. Your current context is the topmost icon displayed on the screen. (You may need to use the scrollbar on the right side of the screen to get to the top of the screen.) When you first activate the NetWare Administrator utility, your *current context* is the one that was in effect the last time you used the utility on this workstation. This is because your current context in NetWare Administrator is utility-specific. In other words, it is independent of your current context as displayed at the command line.

1b. Answers will vary for all questions in this section.

EXERCISE 3-2: UNDERSTANDING NDS NAMING

1. .BMasterson.BLUE.CRIME.TOKYO.ACME

2. .CN=RHood.OU=WHITE.OU=CRIME.OU=TOKYO.O=ACME

3. CRIME.TOKYO.ACME

4. CN=BLUE-SRV1.OU=BLUE.OU=CRIME.OU=TOKYO.O=ACME (since the default current context is the [Root])

5. SHolmes

6. LJohn.WHITE.CRIME

7. CN=SirKay.OU=CHARITY.

8. Admin...

9. CN=BThomas.OU=PR..

10. CN=BLUE-SRV1_SYS.OU=BLUE.OU=CRIME.OU=TOKYO.O=ACME....

11. .BLUE.CRIME.TOKYO.ACME (since it's the context of the server)

    ▸ LOGIN .DHolliday.BLUE.CRIME.TOKYO.ACME

    ▸ LOGIN DHolliday (since NetWare 4 searches the server's context by default)

12. CX CHARITY..

13. Add the following statement to his NET.CFG file (if he has an MS Windows workstation):

    NAME CONTEXT="OU=CHARITY.OU=TOKYO.O=ACME"

Add the following to the Name Context field on the Client 32 page of the Novell NetWare Client 32 Properties dialog box:

OU=CHARITY.OU=TOKYO.O=ACME

14. LOGIN .CN=SHolmes.OU=CRIME.OU=TOKYO.O=ACME

LOGIN .SHolmes.CRIME.TOKYO.ACME

LOGIN SHolmes.

LOGIN CN=SHolmes.

LOGIN SHolmes.CRIME..

LOGIN CN=SHolmes.OU=CRIME..

LOGIN SHolmes.CRIME.TOKYO...

LOGIN CN=SHolmes.OU=CRIME.OU=TOKYO...

LOGIN SHolmes.CRIME.TOKYO.ACME....

LOGIN CN=SHolmes.OU=CRIME.OU=TOKYO.O=ACME....

15. CX /R

EXERCISE 3-3: PLANT A TREE IN A CLOUD

```
G L E A D I N G P E R I O D N X G X T Q W
Y C O U N T R Y R F T I O V S I H R R I Q
M U X C P S K V O O U N K N O W N E L M F
G R S W A K S K F B U D A L I A S K A X J
E R N H T L W Y I N J P V M M U U A I I N
R E G A J R I B L U Z E C E P C W B E Q H
Y N L S N H P T E H D W C E Y X Q X Q O
L T X P B F H R Y H H O R T A W V E S C T
I C B B F H I R X D N V G H R Q K E B Q E
B O R G A N I Z A T I O N A L R O L E T K
V N Y T L Y B X E S E R H F K F W G U Y K
J T D Y V R N X O T V G E E B T L Y E P X
K E T P S J T R W I L A N C S E J V B E U
R X F E H E S F G V H N A M T F B D Y L L
M T W F A S Q L H A Q I D K R O D Q I E R
T I N U L A N O I T A Z I N A G R O W S Z
M Y D L H S W N C X D A U Q I S N Y V S S
O D B N L R C G T J O T O O Y D A E M N M
R J P A A T J X N G F I T B V H J Y F A B
Q O H M H D I R E C T O R Y S C A N P M P
W U N E Z T R A I L I N G P E R I O D E V
```

1. ALIAS	11. OBJECT
2. COUNTRY	12. ORGANIZATION
3. CURRENT CONTEXT	13. ORGANIZATIONAL ROLE
4. CX	14. ORGANIZATIONAL UNIT
5. DIRECTORY MAP	15. PROFILE
6. DIRECTORY SCAN	16. SUPERVISOR
7. GROUP	17. TRAILING PERIOD
8. LEADING PERIOD	18. TYPEFUL NAME
9. LOCALITY	19. TYPELESS NAME
10. NAME CONTEXT	20. UNKNOWN

EXERCISE 3-4: INTRANETWARE CNA BASICS

The completed crossword puzzle solution:

Across:
1. BINDERY EMULATION
4. USER
7. SERVER CENTRIC
8. PARTITION
11. ORGANIZATION
13. DISTINGUISHED NAME
15. NDPS
19. REPLICA
20. CURRENT CONTEXT
21. NETWORK CENTRIC
22. CYBER ANGELS

Down:
1. BINDERY
2. NWADMIN
3. MAT
5. ALPHACEE
6. PROOF
9. UNLK
10. COME
12. NMANAGER
14. INTRANET
16. NA
17. NNAM
18. SAP

Chapter 4: IntranetWare File System

ANSWERS TO QUIZZES

Q4-1
28463

Q4-2
It doesn't matter what x is, because at some time during the calculation you will be multiplying by (x-x), which equals 0. Therefore, the product will be 0. Tricky!

Q4-3
69382

Q4-4
1, 4, 9, 6, 1, 5, 10, 4, 2

Now, change to Roman numerals:

I, IV, IX, VI, I, V, X, IV, II

Very tricky, and I like it for that reason, and because the Roman numeral IV appears in my name. Touché.

EXERCISE 4-1: MAPPING DRIVES WITH MAP

1. MAP /?

2. MAP

3. MAP F:=SYS:USERS

4. MAP G:=SYS:\SHARED\POL

5. MAP J:=F:

6. MAP S:=.WHITE-SRV1_SYS.WHITE.CRIME.TOKYO.ACME:SHARED

7. MAP INS S1:=SYS:\PUBLIC

8. MAP INS S2:=SYS:\PUBLIC\IBM_PC\MSDOS\V6.22

9. MAP S3:=SYS:\APPS\SS30

10. MAP ROOT S4:=SYS:\APPS\DB50

11. MAP

    In the map list, the false root has no space after the volume name, but does have a space followed by a backslash after the name of the directory it points to.

12. MAP S5:=W:=SYS:\APPS\WP70

    Yes.

13. The MAP command didn't work. To fix the problem, type CD \PUBLIC.

14. MAP DEL J:

15. MAP REM S3:

    The search drives with higher search drive numbers were renumbered accordingly.

    The network drive associated with the search drive was deleted.

16. MAP C S4:

    The search drive was deleted.

    The network drive associated with the search drive was moved to the top portion of the map list.

EXERCISE 4-4: INTRANETWARE FILE CABINET OF LIFE

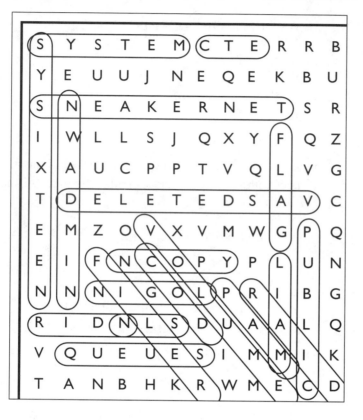

1. DELETED.SAV
2. DOC
3. ETC
4. FILER
5. FLAG
6. LOGIN
7. MAIL
8. MAP
9. NCOPY
10. NDIR
11. NLS
12. NWADMIN
13. PUBLIC
14. QUEUES
15. RAID
16. SIXTEEN
17. SNEAKERNET
18. SYS:
19. SYSTEM
20. VOLUME

Chapter 5: IntranetWare Security

ANSWERS TO QUIZZES

Q5-1

"A road map tells you everything except how to refold it." (Start at *A* in center.)

Q5-2

36421

Q5-3

He is abstemious. We discovered that he only likes words with all five vowels in them—an odd bird.

Q5-4

That's easy, man. It's "wrong."

Q5-5

ABORT: It is five letters long.
ACT: Last letter cannot be placed first to form another word
AGT: Not an actual word.
ALP: Does not end with a T.
OPT: Does not start with A.
APT: Not in alphabetical order with rest.

CASE STUDY: ACME SECURITY

F I G U R E   C5.1

*The .TOKYO.ACME NDS
Directory Tree*

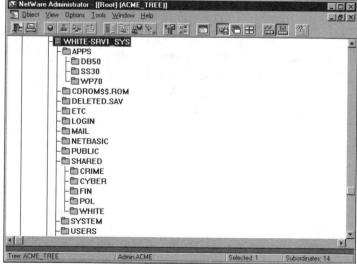

F I G U R E   C5.2

*The WHITE-SRV1_SYS File
System Directory Tree*

*Password Restrictions for
the User Template object in
.TOKYO.ACME*

NetWare Administrator - [[Root] [ACME_TREE]]

Template : TOKYO-UT

Password Restrictions

☑ Allow user to change password
☑ Require a password
   Minimum password length: 7
☑ Force periodic password changes
   Days between forced changes: 00
   Date password expires:
   09 /08 /98   3 :56 :21 PM
☑ Require unique passwords
☑ Limit grace logins
   Grace logins allowed: 6
☑ Set password after create

Identification
Environment
Login Restrictions
Password Restrictions
Login Time Restrictions
Network Address Restriction
Login Script
Group Membership
Security Equal To
Trustees Of New Object

OK   Cancel   Page Options...   Help

Tree: ACME_TREE   Admin.ACME   Selected: 1   Subordinates: 0

EXERCISE 5-1: CALCULATING NDS EFFECTIVE RIGHTS

CASE #1

See Figure C5.4 for answer to this case.

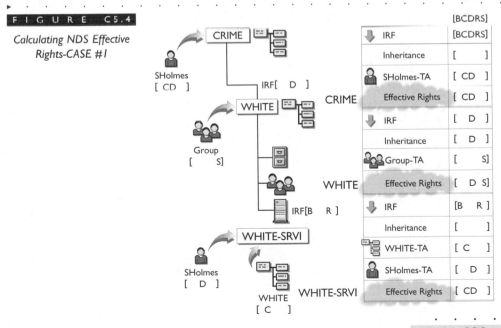

► F I G U R E   C5.4

*Calculating NDS Effective
Rights-CASE #1*

		[BCDRS]
⬇ IRF		[BCDRS]
Inheritance	[ ]	
👤 SHolmes-TA	[CD]	
Effective Rights	[CD]	
⬇ IRF	[D]	
Inheritance	[D]	
👥 Group-TA	[S]	
Effective Rights	[D S]	
⬇ IRF	[B R]	
Inheritance	[ ]	
🖳 WHITE-TA	[C]	
👤 SHolmes-TA	[D]	
Effective Rights	[CD]	

CRIME   IRF[D]   CRIME

SHolmes
[CD]

WHITE   WHITE

Group
[S]

IRF[B   R]

WHITE-SRVI

SHolmes
[D]

WHITE   WHITE-SRVI
[C]

CASE #1 *(continued)*

Explanation:

Sherlock Holmes is granted CD rights to the CRIME Organizational Unit. Since he has no rights from any other source, and explicit trustee assignments override the Inherited Rights Filter (IRF) for this container, his effective rights for the CRIME Organizational Unit are [CD].

These rights then flow down to the WHITE Organizational Unit as inherited rights, where they are partially blocked by an IRF of [D]—leaving inherited rights of [D]. Sherlock Holmes also gets the [S] right to the WHITE Organizational Unit as a member of the CRIME Group. If you add his inherited right of [D] to the [S] right granted to the CRIME-Group, you'll find that his effective rights for the WHITE container are [DS]. (Note: The fact that he has the [S] object right means that he implicitly has all object rights and all property rights for this object.)

Finally, his effective rights of [DS] in the WHITE container flow down and become inherited rights at the WHITE-SRV1 server, where they are blocked by an IRF of [BR]. (Even though he implicitly had all rights to the WHITE container, implied rights do not flow down-only explicit rights. Also, remember, that the [S] right *can* be blocked by an IRF in the NDS tree.) Sherlock Holmes does, however, receive an explicit trustee assignment of [D] to the WHITE-SRV1 server. His home container, the WHITE Organizational Unit, also receives a trustee assignment of [C]-meaning that his effective rights for the WHITE-SRV1 server are [CD].

CASE #2

See Figure C5.5 for answer to this case.

Explanation:

In Case #2, Sherlock Holmes receives an explicit trustee assignment of [BR] to the CRIME Organizational Unit. Because he has no rights from other sources, and an explicit assignment overrides the IRF, his effective rights in the CRIME Organizational Unit are [BR].

These rights then flow down and become inherited rights at the WHITE Organizational Unit, where they are partially blocked by an IRF of [CDRS]—leaving an inherited right of [R]. Sherlock Holmes also gets [BCD] rights through the CRIME-Admin Organizational Role, of which he is an occupant. If you add his inherited right of [R] to the [BCD] rights granted to the CRIME-Admin Organizational Role, you'll find that his effective rights for the WHITE container are [BCDR].

Finally, these rights flow down and become inherited rights at the WHITE-SRV1 server. These rights are partially blocked by the IRF of [BR]—leaving inherited rights of [BR]. The [R] inherited right is also blocked by a new trustee assignment made to the SHolmes User object (since explicit trustee assignments granted to the same object lower in the tree block inheritance to that same object from higher in the NDS tree). In other words, the [C] rights granted to the SHolmes User object for the WHITE-SRV1 server block the [R] inherited right that he originally received at the CRIME container. Sherlock Holmes also receives the [B] right that is granted to WHITE Organizational Unit, which is his home container. This means that Sherlock Holmes effective rights for the WHITE-SRV1 server are [BCD], which is a combination of his inherited right of [B], the [B] right he receives from the WHITE container, and the [CD] rights he receives from his User object.

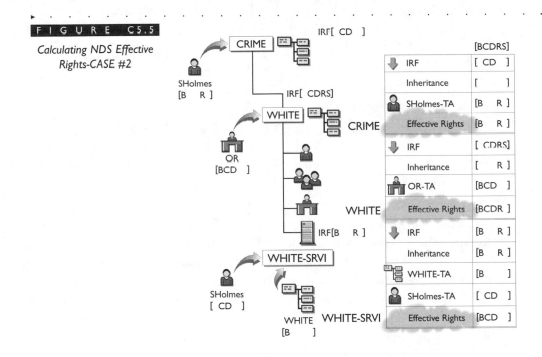

FIGURE C5.5

Calculating NDS Effective Rights-CASE #2

		[BCDRS]
⬇ IRF		[CD]
Inheritance		[ ]
👤 SHolmes-TA		[B R]
CRIME Effective Rights		[B R]
⬇ IRF		[CDRS]
Inheritance		[R]
🏢 OR-TA		[BCD]
WHITE Effective Rights		[BCDR]
⬇ IRF		[B R]
Inheritance		[B R]
WHITE-TA		[B]
👤 SHolmes-TA		[CD]
WHITE-SRVI Effective Rights		[BCD]

CASE #3

See Figure C5.6 for answer to this case.

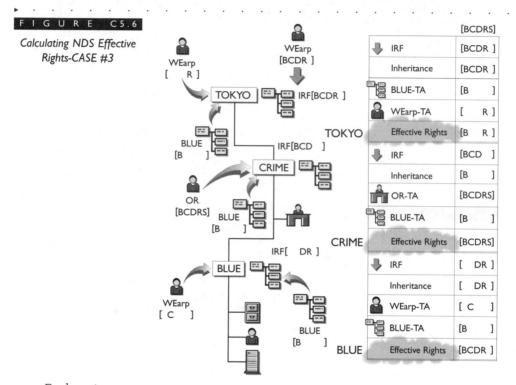

FIGURE C5.6

Calculating NDS Effective Rights-CASE #3

		[BCDRS]
⬇	IRF	[BCDR]
	Inheritance	[BCDR]
🖳	BLUE-TA	[B]
👤	WEarp-TA	[R]
TOKYO	Effective Rights	[B R]
⬇	IRF	[BCD]
	Inheritance	[B]
🖳	OR-TA	[BCDRS]
🖳	BLUE-TA	[B]
CRIME	Effective Rights	[BCDRS]
⬇	IRF	[DR]
	Inheritance	[DR]
👤	WEarp-TA	[C]
🖳	BLUE-TA	[B]
BLUE	Effective Rights	[BCDR]

Explanation:

In Case #3, Wyatt Earp inherits [BCDR] rights to the TOKYO Organizational Unit through a trustee assignment to his User object somewhere higher in the tree. These rights are then filtered by the Tokyo Organizational Unit's IRF of [BCDR]-which allows all four rights to flow through. He doesn't get to keep these rights, however, because his User object receives a new trustee assignment to the Tokyo Organizational Unit at this level—and such an assignment blocks inheritance from his User object from higher in the tree. Wyatt Earp does, however, receive the [B] trustee right for the TOKYO Organizational Unit from the Blue Organizational Unit, which is his home container, and the [R] right from his User object. This means that his inherited rights for the TOKYO container are [B] plus [R] or [BR].

These rights then flow down and become inherited rights at the CRIME Organizational Unit, where they are partially blocked by an IRF of [BCD]—leaving an inherited right of [B]. This right is also blocked, however, because the BLUE Organizational Unit receives a new trustee assignment to the CRIME Organizational Unit at this level-and such an assignment blocks inheritance for the BLUE Organizational Unit object from higher in the tree. Wyatt Earp does, however, receive [BCDRS] rights through the BLUE-Admin Organizational Role, of which he is an occupant and the [B] from the BLUE Organizational Unit, which is his home container. If you add the [BCDRS] rights that he receives from the BLUE-Admin Organizational Role to the [B] right he receives from the BLUE Organizational Unit, you'll find that his effective rights for the CRIME Organizational Unit are [BCDRS].

Finally, these rights flow down and become inherited rights at the BLUE Organizational Unit and are partially blocked by an IRF of [DR]—leaving inherited rights of [DR]. (Remember, the [S] right *can* be blocked by an IRF in the NDS tree.) Wyatt Earp also receives the [C] right to the BLUE Organizational Unit from his User object and the [B] right from the BLUE Organizational Unit, which is his parent container. This means that his effective rights to the BLUE Organizational Unit are the [DR] rights, which he received through inheritance, plus the [C] right which he received from his User object, plus the [B] right which he received from the BLUE Organizational Unit—or [BCDR].

EXERCISE 5-2: CALCULATING FILE SYSTEM EFFECTIVE RIGHTS

CASE #1

See Figure C5.7 for answer to this case.

FIGURE C5.7

*Calculating File System
Effective Rights-CASE #1*

SYS:SHARED	S	R	C	W	E	M	F	A
Inherited Rights Filter	S	R	C	W	E	M	F	A
Inherited Rights-User								
Inherited Rights-Group								
Trustee Assignment-User		R	C	W			F	
Trustee Assignment-Group								
Effective Rights		R	C	W			F	

SYS:SHARED\CYBER	S	R	C	W	E	M	F	A
Inherited Rights Filter	S	R					F	
Inherited Rights-User		R					F	
Inherited Rights-Group								
Trustee Assignment-User								
Trustee Assignment-Group								
Effective Rights		R					F	

CYBER.DOC	S	R	C	W	E	M	F	A
Inherited Rights Filter		R	C	W			F	
Inherited Rights-User		R					F	
Inherited Rights-Group								
Trustee Assignment-User								
Trustee Assignment-Group								
Effective Rights		R					F	

CASE #2

See Figure C5.8 for answer to this case.

FIGURE C5.8

Calculating File System Effective Rights-CASE #2

SYS:SHARED	S	R	C	W	E	M	F	A
Inherited Rights Filter	S	R	C	W	E	M	F	A
Inherited Rights-User								
Inherited Rights-Group								
Trustee Assignment-User								
Trustee Assignment-Group		R	C	W			F	
Effective Rights		R	C	W			F	

SYS:SHARED\FIN	S	R	C	W	E	M	F	A
Inherited Rights Filter	S							
Inherited Rights-User								
Inherited Rights-Group								
Trustee Assignment-User		R	C	W	E	M	F	
Trustee Assignment-Group								
Effective Rights		R	C	W	E	M	F	

99QTR4.RPT	S	R	C	W	E	M	F	A
Inherited Rights Filter	S	R		W			F	
Inherited Rights-User		R		W			F	
Inherited Rights-Group								
Trustee Assignment-User								
Trustee Assignment-Group		R						
Effective Rights		R		W			F	

CASE #3

See Figure C5.9 for answer to this case.

▶ · ◀

FIGURE   C5.9

*Calculating File System
Effective Rights-CASE #3*

SYS:SHARED	S	R	C	W	E	M	F	A
Inherited Rights Filter	S	R	C	W	E	M	F	A
Inherited Rights-User								
Inherited Rights-Group								
Trustee Assignment-User		R	C	W			F	
Trustee Assignment-Group								
Effective Rights		R	C	W			F	

SYS:SHARED\CRIME	S	R	C	W	E	M	F	A
Inherited Rights Filter	S							A
Inherited Rights-User								
Inherited Rights-Group								
Trustee Assignment-User								
Trustee Assignment-Group		R	C	W	E	M	F	
Effective Rights		R	C	W	E	M	F	

CRIME.DB	S	R	C	W	E	M	F	A
Inherited Rights Filter	S	R	C	W			F	
Inherited Rights-User								
Inherited Rights-Group		R	C	W			F	
Trustee Assignment-User								
Trustee Assignment-Group		R					F	
Effective Rights		R					F	

CASE #4

See Figure C5.10 for answer to this case.

FIGURE C5.10

*Calculating File System
Effective Rights-CASE #4*

SYS:SHARED	S	R	C	W	E	M	F	A
Inherited Rights Filter	S	R	C	W	E	M	F	A
Inherited Rights-User								
Inherited Rights-Group								
Trustee Assignment-User								
Trustee Assignment-Group		R	C	W	E		F	
Effective Rights		R	C	W	E		F	

SYS:SHARED\POL	S	R	C	W	E	M	F	A
Inherited Rights Filter	S							
Inherited Rights-User								
Inherited Rights-Group								
Trustee Assignment-User						M		A
Trustee Assignment-Group		R	C	W	E		F	
Effective Rights		R	C	W	E	M	F	A

CRIME.RPT	S	R	C	W	E	M	F	A
Inherited Rights Filter	S	R	C	W	E	M	F	A
Inherited Rights-User						M		A
Inherited Rights-Group		R	C	W	E		F	
Trustee Assignment-User								
Trustee Assignment-Group								
Effective Rights		R	C	W	E	M	F	A

CASE #5

See Figure C5.11 for answer to this case.

► ·◄

FIGURE C5.11

Calculating File System
Effective Rights-CASE #5

SYS:SHARED	S	R	C	W	E	M	F	A
Inherited Rights Filter	S	R	C	W	E	M	F	A
Inherited Rights-User								
Inherited Rights-Group								
Trustee Assignment-User	S	R	C	W	E	M	F	A
Trustee Assignment-Group								
Effective Rights	S	R	C	W	E	M	F	A

SYS:SHARED\CRIME	S	R	C	W	E	M	F	A
Inherited Rights Filter	S							
Inherited Rights-User	S							
Inherited Rights-Group								
Trustee Assignment-User								
Trustee Assignment-Group		R	C	W			F	
Effective Rights	S	R	C	W			F	

CRIME.DB	S	R	C	W	E	M	F	A
Inherited Rights Filter	S	R					F	
Inherited Rights-User	S							
Inherited Rights-Group								
Trustee Assignment-User								
Trustee Assignment-Group		R					F	
Effective Rights	S	R					F	

CASE #6

See Figure C5.12 for answer to this case.

See Figure C5.12 for answer to this case.

▶ . . . . ◀

FIGURE C5.12

*Calculating File System
Effective Rights-CASE #6*

SYS:SHARED	S	R	C	W	E	M	F	A
Inherited Rights Filter	S	R					F	A
Inherited Rights-User								
Inherited Rights-Group or [Public]								
Trustee Assignment-User								
Trustee Assignment-Group or [Public]		R					F	
Effective Rights		R					F	

SYS:SHARED\WHITE	S	R	C	W	E	M	F	A
Inherited Rights Filter	S	R					F	
Inherited Rights-User								
Inherited Rights-Group or [Public]		R					F	
Trustee Assignment-User	S	R	C	W	E	M	F	A
Trustee Assignment-Group or [Public]								
Effective Rights	S	R	C	W	E	M	F	A

SUMMARY.RPT	S	R	C	W	E	M	F	A
Inherited Rights Filter	S							
Inherited Rights-User	S							
Inherited Rights-Group or [Public]								
Trustee Assignment-User		R	C	W	E	M		
Trustee Assignment-Group or [Public]								
Effective Rights		R	C	W	E	M		

EXERCISE 5-3: HOW SECURE DO YOU FEEL?

```
S E C U R I T Y Z P K C G M G L S M Y
T J Z U N I Q U E P A S S W O R D S Y
A C M C K R S S Z P Z T V G O K B O W
T P R O O F S K P P W T T O M D R H P
I R U G R A C E L O G I N S N M X L Q
O I O B J E C T R I G H T S J U T H S
N V D Z L I T L T U T I Y A B T Z W R
R A J S G I N H E R I T A N C E C T V
E T E F F E C T I V E R I G H T S J Q
S E C U R I T Y E Q U I V A L E N C E
T K R P R Y B V D N F D G M L F D W R
R E S B Q P G W P X G F W T W B H P J
I Y Y O B G V X L G O T B B M C A V M
C L H F W T Y N B B T G Y P T Q Y E K
T I M E R E S T R I C T I O N S U F P
I N T R U D E R D E T E C T I O N X U
O R U S T H G I R Y T R E P O R P Q F
N C P P A C K E T S I G N A T U R E F
S N W P B Z S T H G I R E E T S U R T
```

1. ACL	11. PROPERTY RIGHTS
2. EFFECTIVE RIGHTS	12. PUBLIC
3. GRACE LOGINS	13. RISK
4. INHERITANCE	14. SECURITY
5. INTRUDER DETECTION	15. SECURITY EQUIVALENCE
6. IRF	16. STATION RESTRICTIONS
7. NCP PACKET SIGNATURE	17. TIME RESTRICTIONS
8. OBJECT RIGHTS	18. TRUSTEE RIGHTS
9. PRIVATE KEY	19. TTS
10. PROOF	20. UNIQUE PASSWORDS

EXERCISE 5-4: LET THE GOOD GUYS IN

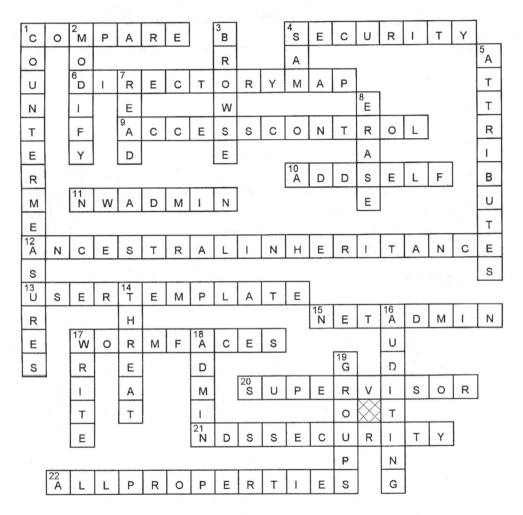

Chapter 6: IntranetWare Configuration

ANSWERS TO QUIZZES

Q6-1

The most common wrong answer is 25. If the problem had been, "What is the smallest number I must pick in order to be sure of getting at least two socks of *different* colors," then the correct answer would have been 25. But the problem calls for at least two socks of the *same* color, so the correct answer is three. If I pick three socks, then either they are all of the same color (in which case I certainly have at least two of the same color), or else two are of one color and the third is of the other color-so I have two of the same color.

Q6-2

J.

Q6-3

The bear must be white—it must be a polar bear. The usual answer is that the bear must have been standing at the North Pole. Well, this is indeed one possibility, but it's not the only one. From the North Pole, all directions are south, so if the bear is standing at the North Pole and the man is 100 yards south of him and walks 100 yards east, then when he faces north, he will be facing the North Pole again. I'll buy that.

But, there are many more alternative solutions. It could be, for example, that the man is very close to the South Pole on a spot where the Polar circle passing through that spot has a circumference of exactly 100 yards, and the bear is standing 100 yards north of him. Then if the man walks east 100 yards, he would walk right around that circle and be right back at the point he started from.

In addition, the man could be a little closer to the South Pole at a point where the polar circle has a circumference of exactly 50 yards, so if he walked east 100 yards, he would walk around that little circle twice and be back where he started. You get the idea.

Of course, in any of these solutions, the bear is sufficiently close to either the North Pole or the South Pole to qualify as a polar bear. There is, of course, the remote possibility that some mischievous human being deliberately transported a brown bear to the North Pole just to spite us—who's paranoid?

Q6-4

Cerebrum

Q6-5

1. The biologist is not Catherine and not from Canada. Therefore, she belongs to C house (she must have one C).

2. If Catherine were the doctor, then she would have to come from Brazil (we know she's not from Australia), and if she were the doctor, she couldn't be from Denmark. Therefore, the doctor is from Brazil—but we are told the doctor is not from Brazil. Therefore, Catherine is not the doctor. Therefore, she must be the author.

3. The biologist is not from Australia and not from Canada. Therefore, she must be from Denmark.

4. Since the biologist is from C house and from Denmark, she must be Alice.

5. Therefore, the doctor is not Alice, and the doctor is not Catherine. Therefore, the doctor is Brett, and Deirdre must be the cartoonist.

6. Since the doctor is Brett, she is not from B house. Therefore, the doctor is from A house (the only alternative left). Therefore, the doctor is from Canada.

7. Since the cartoonist is Deirdre, she cannot be from D house. Therefore, she is from B house. Therefore, the cartoonist is from Australia.

8. Therefore, Catherine, the author, is from Brazil and was in D house.

Complete solution:

Alice	Biologist	C	Denmark
Brett	Doctor	A	Canada
Catherine	Author	D	Brazil
Deirdre	Cartoonist	B	Australia

Q6-6

OK, here's what was going on inside the cerebrum of "C." If anyone were to see two red and two black, he would know that he was white. If anyone were to see two red, one black, and one white, he would know that he could not be black. If he were, the man with the white disc would see two red and two black and would know that he was white. Similarly, if anyone were to see one red, two black, and two white.

If anyone were to see one red, one black, and two white, he would know that he could not be black. If he were, either of the men wearing white would see one red, two black, and one white, and would argue as above. If anyone were to see two red and two white, he would argue that he could not be black. If he were, someone would see two red, one black, and one white and would argue as above.

If anyone were to see one red and three white, he would argue that he could not be black. If he were, someone would see one red, one black, and two white and would argue as above; similarly, he would know that he could not be red. Therefore, if anyone sees me wearing red or black, he can deduce his color. Therefore, I must be white.

C really needs to get a life.

Q6-7

Ensign Chekov

EXERCISE 6-1: WORKSTATION CONNECTIVITY WITH CLIENT 16

2b.   Look at Figure 6.16. You'll see that LSL.COM loads the Link Support Layer, provides version information, and activates the default NET.CFG file. From this, we can surmise that the Link Support Layer is in control of the client connection somehow. It's the traffic cop.

2d.   No. When IPXODI loads, it activates the internal NIC, but you still can't talk to the server without VLM.EXE.

2e.   IPXODI activates communications at the NIC level, whereas VLMs activate communications at the higher DOS level. Neither one is any good without the other.

3b.   Regardless of what you might think about the "logical" nature of IntranetWare NDS, you still have to attach to a server. In this case, LABS-SRV1 is our host server for all NDS resource access. Any other necessary server attachments will be made for you automatically in the background. You only need to attach to the initial host server.

EXERCISE 6-3: UNDERSTANDING NET.CFG

```
; Standard R&D Dept. NET.CFG file
; Created for LDaVinci on 10/28/99

SHOW DOTS = ON
LONG MACHINE TYPE = DELL

LINK DRIVER C35X9
  INT A
  PORT 320
  FRAME Ethernet_802.2
```

```
NETWARE DOS REQUESTER
        PREFERRED TREE=ACME_TREE
        PREFERRED SERVER=R&D-SRV1
  NAME CONTEXT="OU=R&D.OU=LABS.OU=NORAD.O=ACME"
  FIRST NETWORK DRIVE=F:
  PACKET BUFFERS = 10
  SIGNATURE LEVEL = 3
  LOAD CONN TABLE LOW = ON
  CONNECTIONS = 10
  NETWORK PRINTERS = 5
```

Note: Be sure you don't put a preceding period (.) in the NAME CONTEXT statement.

CASE STUDY: CONFIGURING ACME'S LOGIN SCRIPTS

1. Create the Container login script for the PR Organizational Unit. (If you already did this step, proceed to Step 2.)

    a. Log in as the Admin user and execute the NetWare Administrator utility.

        1) Click on the NORAD Organizational Unit using the right mouse button. A menu should be displayed. Click on the Details menu option. An Organizational Unit Identification page dialog box will be displayed.

        2) Use the scroll bar along the right edge of the screen to display the Login Script page button and click on it. Next, single-click in the upper-right corner of the window located in the center of the screen.

    b. Create the Container login script for the Public Relations department.

        1) Key in the appropriate statements for the Public Relations department Container login script using the clues in the Chapter 6 case study. (If you need help with what each script should look like, see Figure C6.1 and Figure C6.2.)

FIGURE C6.1

*PR Container Login Script
Part I*

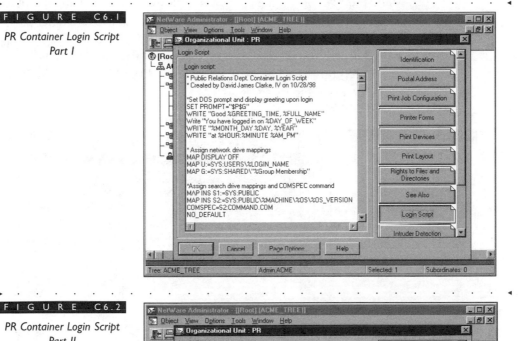

FIGURE C6.2

*PR Container Login Script
Part II*

2. Make the FDR user a member of the PRMGRS-Profile login script. (The PRMGRS-Profile login script is located in the ACME container.)

   a. Identify PRMGRS-Profile as the name of the Profile Login Script object in the Profile login script field of the FDR's user's login script screen (see Figure C6.3).

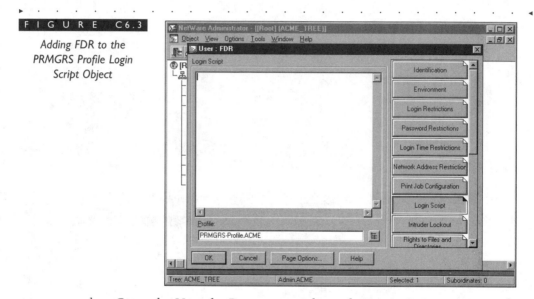

FIGURE C6.3

Adding FDR to the PRMGRS Profile Login Script Object

   b. Grant the User the R property right to the Login Script property of the Profile. Also, make sure that the B right to the Profile Login Script object that was granted by default to [Public] at the [Root] has not been blocked by an IRF.

3. Login as the FDR user by typing LOGIN .FDR.PR.RIO.ACME and pressing Enter. Watch as the Container and Profile login scripts are automatically executed. Fix any errors that occur.

CASE STUDY: CONFIGURING THE ACME MENU SYSTEM

1. Create a custom menu:

```
; PR Main Menu
; Created by David James Clarke, IV on 10/28/99

MENU 01,Public Relations Main Menu
   ITEM   ^AApplications
          SHOW 10
   ITEM   ^EE-Mail
          EXEC WIN WMAIL
   ITEM   ^NNetWare Commands
          SHOW 20
   ITEM   ^LLog off the network
          EXEC LOGOUT

MENU 10,Applications
   ITEM   Database
          EXEC DB
   ITEM   Spreadsheet
          EXEC SS
   ITEM   Word Processing
          EXEC WP

MENU 20,NetWare Utilities
   ITEM   File Management
          EXEC FILER
   ITEM   NCOPY
          GETP Enter Source File(s): { }80,,{}
          GETP Enter Destination File(s): { }80,,{}
          EXEC NCOPY %1 %2
   ITEM   NLIST
          GETO Enter Class Name and Option: { }25,USER/A,{}
          EXEC NLIST
   ITEM   User Tools
          EXEC WIN NWUSER
   ITEM   WHOAMI
          EXEC WHOAMI
```

2. Compile and execute the custom menu (and debug any problems):

```
MENUMAKE PRMAIN.SRC <Enter>
NMENU PRMAIN.DAT <Enter>
```

(See Figure C6.4 for a sample of what the PR Main Menu should look like.)

F I G U R E   C6.4

PR Main Menu

Novell Menu System 4.11	Friday June 12, 1998 12:40am

Public Relations Main Menu

```
A. Aplications
E. E-Mail
N. NetWare Commands
L. Log off the network
```

F2=Session Information   F1=Help

EXERCISE 6-4: INTRANETWARE CHILDHOOD

```
S  D  Y  P  J  G  I  D  F  N  G  R  H  M  U  M  G  N  S
F  I  L  E  A  T  T  R  I  B  U  T  E  S  F  F  X  N  H
I  S  L  T  N  E  I  L  C  W  N  M  E  N  U  M  A  K  E
R  T  X  W  M  G  E  T  O  Y  V  E  T  X  H  M  Z  J  L
S  R  H  V  Y  I  F  X  M  J  D  W  T  S  E  A  Y  Y  L
T  I  S  R  P  Q  K  W  S  W  M  Y  S  C  Y  C  H  K  C
M  B  T  Y  I  K  Y  E  P  U  C  E  O  T  F  Q  V  O  F
A  U  S  Q  O  T  I  L  E  K  R  N  P  V  F  G  Q  S  G
I  T  H  N  W  M  W  P  C  V  T  H  U  P  J  M  Y  Y  B
L  I  D  E  N  T  I  F  I  E  R  V  A  R  I  A  B  L  E
I  O  I  X  D  B  I  C  X  G  F  S  U  M  V  W  X  G  E
N  N  G  J  D  Q  E  T  A  B  T  E  N  T  R  A  T  S  Z
K  L  S  P  O  S  T  M  A  S  T  E  R  H  O  D  T  X  P
D  I  N  L  R  L  O  M  L  D  N  M  V  E  H  G  A  N  P
R  S  Y  Y  R  O  K  V  Q  A  Q  U  T  R  R  Q  R  Z  W
I  T  C  P  O  J  F  M  D  B  E  N  T  B  P  F  C  F  S
V  D  V  S  F  A  K  I  N  S  T  A  L  L  C  F  G  S  L
E  V  I  R  D  T  S  A  L  O  G  I  N  S  C  R  I  P  T
R  M  K  M  X  C  X  J  P  E  N  J  D  B  D  F  W  E  T
```

1. COMSPEC
2. DISTRIBUTION LIST
3. EXEC
4. FILE ATTRIBUTES
5. FIRST MAIL
6. GETO
7. IDENTIFIER VARIABLE
8. INSTALL.CFG
9. LAST DRIVE
10. LINK DRIVER

11. LOGIN SCRIPT
12. MENU MAKE
13. MHS SERVICES
14. NAME CONTEXT
15. NET.CFG
16. NWCLIENT
17. POST MASTER
18. PROFILE
19. SHELL.CFG
20. STARTNET.BAT

Chapter 7: IntranetWare Management

ANSWERS TO QUIZZES

Q7-1
Actually, the two trains will be at the *same* distance from Boston when they meet.

Q7-2
The answer is a quarter and a nickel. One of them (namely the quarter) is not a nickel.

Q7-3
Thanks — it's 3:31 P.M.

The only times that the hands of a watch are at right angles at an exact minute are 3:00 and 9:00. Since it was afternoon, we must be talking about 3:00 P.M. At 3:00 P.M., it was 30 minutes "before the half-hour." Also, at the next minute, it will be 60 seconds (twice as many seconds) after the same half-hour. Therefore, it's 3:31 P.M.

Q7-4
DAISY

Q7-5
Nice try. Roosters don't lay eggs.

Q7-6
Silence, Wedding Ring, Hole, Debt.

Q7-7
TYPEWRITER

Q7-8
Fools rush in where angels fear to tread. Which one are you?

CASE STUDY: SERVER MANAGEMENT AT ACME

1. VLM /U

   IPXODI /U

   NE2000 /U (or appropriate LAN driver)

   LSL /U

2. VLM /?

3. VLM /4

4. v1.20 (answers will vary)

5. Extended Memory (XMS)

6. CONN.VLM; NETX.VLM

7. The file server console prompt is displayed (that is, ACME-SRV1)

8. A message is displayed, indicating that a remote (RCONSOLE) connection has been granted. This is important to know in case unauthorized personnel (or, worse yet, a hacker) have gained access to your file server console through the RMF utility.

9. AUTOEXEC.NCF; STARTUP.NCF

10. Single Reference

11. 802.2

12. .2% (Answers will vary from .2 to 2%.)

13. No, this disk is not mirrored.

14. 64 KB. This default block size was assigned by the operating system during the installation of IntranetWare on the server due based on a hard disk size of 2+ GB. Your block size may vary. On the SYS: volume file compression and block suballocation are turned ON and data migration is turned OFF.

15. 25 (Answers will vary.)

16. If you wanted to create Client installation directories on the server or create client diskettes, you would choose Product options. Otherwise, you would load the IntranetWare /NetWare 4.11 CD-ROM and run INSTALL.BAT install.

17. 10 days, 2 hours, 6 minutes, and 34 seconds (answers will vary). The elapsed time since the server was last restarted is represented in the format DD:HH:MM:SS, where DD = number of days, HH = number of hours, MM = number of minutes, and SS = number of seconds. Current server utilization is at 8 percent (answers will vary). The total number of cache buffers currently being used would be the number of Original Cache Buffers (7,563) minus the Total Cache Buffers (6,131) (answers will vary). The number of current service processes in use is 5 (answers will vary). Twenty-three licensed connections are available at the moment (25 minus 2 in use).

18. Normal; no. (Answers may vary.)

19. IPX

20. DS.NLM; 677,208 bytes. (Size may vary.)

21. Idle loop (that is, polling)

22. Processor Uptime (called Server Up Time in MONITOR.NLM), Processor Utilization (called Utilization in MONITOR.NLM), Server Processes (called Current Service Processes in MONITOR.NLM), and Logged-in Users (called Current Licensed Connections in MONITOR.NLM).

23. SET command

24. Alt+F3; Alt+F1

25. The Transfer Files to Server option in SERVMAN performs a similar function to the Copy Files option in INSTALL.NLM. The difference between the two is that the RCONSOLE option copies the SYSTEM and PUBLIC files from the workstation's drive rather than the server's.

26. TRACK ON; ACME_TREE; answers will vary regarding the IPX internal network number of other server; AUTOEXEC.NCF in INSTALL.NLM, and CONFIG console command.

27. BROADCAST or SEND. You can acknowledge an incoming BROADCAST or SEND message displayed on the screen by pressing Ctrl+Enter. You can turn off receipt of incoming messages from other users by typing SEND /A=N at the workstation prompt after you exit RCONSOLE. (Note: You can also type SEND /A=C to receive SEND or BROADCAST messages from the server console only.)

28. HELP ALL

29. MODULES; SERVMAN.NLM

EXERCISE 7-1: INTRANETWARE ADULTHOOD

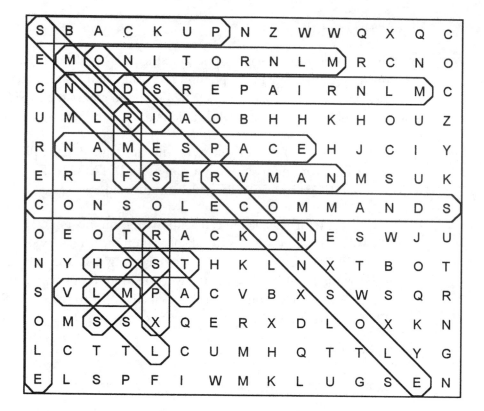

1. CONSOLE COMMANDS
2. DSREPAIR.NLM
3. HOST
4. LSL
5. MONITOR.NLM
6. NAME SPACE
4. INTERNATIONALIZATION
7. NLMS
9. RCONSOLE
10. RMF

11. RSPX
12. SAP
13. SBACKUP
14. SECURE CONSOLE
15. SERVMAN
16. SMDR
17. SMS
18. TRACK ON
19. TSA
20. VLM

Chapter 8: IntranetWare Printing

ANSWERS TO QUIZZES

Q8-1

There were 12 friends in the group.

Q8-2

QUEUE-pretty sneaky, huh?

Q8-3

V (vowel) 1 = A, and so on

C (consonant) 1 = B, and so on

"Well done! Message successfully decoded."

Q8-4

Like so many puzzles of its type, this looks much more complicated than it really is. In fact, it has a beautifully simple solution. The trick is first to work out how long it takes the man to walk home. You know that the dog has been running for all this time at its given constant speed, so it is then a simply matter to work out how many miles it has covered during this period.

In this case, the man walks for 7 miles at 3 m.p.h., which means he takes 2 1/3 hours, or 2 hours 20 minutes. The dog is, therefore, running for 2 1/3 hours at 8 m.p.h., which means it covers 18 2/3 miles.

Q8-5

This was a tough one. If you figured it out, you're definitely "IntranetWare Sleuth" material. As a matter of fact, printing is breeze compared to this brain puzzler.

7	13	4	10
2	12	5	15
9	3	14	8
16	6	11	1

CASE STUDY: BUILDING ACME'S PRINTING SYSTEM

Queue Creation

5. The user that created the queue (.Admin.ACME) and the container where the queue was created (.WHITE.CRIME.TOKYO.ACME)—because all users in the container usually need access.

6. There is a QUEUES directory off the root.

7. One or more.

Printer Creation

6. The print job owner disappears as the person to be notified.

7. The print job owner re-appears as the person to be notified.

Creating the Print Server

6. The context where the print server was created (.WHITE.CRIME.TOKYO.ACME)—because everyone in the container usually has access.

8. .Admin.ACME, because that is the user that created this print server.

10. Because the print server hasn't been loaded yet. It isn't yet running.

11. The print server is down.

Finding the Printer

9. The result of the search is CANONBJ-P1.WHITE.CRIME.TOKYO.ACME.

Loading the Print Server

4. It asks for a password.

5. Enter the password Secret.

7. The status is "waiting for a job; out of paper".

11. The CANONBJ-P1 printer is unloaded as well as the WHITE-SRV1 print server.

CASE STUDY: USING ACME'S PRINTING SYSTEM

3. Capturing is not currently active on LPT1, LPT2, or LPT3. In other words, they are all set to local ports.

4. An error will be displayed indicating that the default print job configuration cannot be found.

5. CX .WHITE.CRIME.TOKYO.ACME

6. CAPTURE Q=CANONBJ-PQ1

7. CAPTURE ENDCAP

13. Settings are: Form Feed, Auto Endcap, Enable Banner, First Banner Name=SHolmes, Second Banner Name=LPT1:, Copies 1.

17. Access not authorized. The only user authorized during print queue creation was the Admin.ACME user.

18. Use NetWare Administrator or PCONSOLE to assign SHolmes or his parent container as a print queue user.

19. Use CAPTURE (DOS), NetWare User Tools (Windows 3.1x) or the Printers icon in the Windows 95 Control Panel.

22. Double-click on the print queue and choose Job List to see the print job you just created when you did the print of the browser screen.

23. CAPTURE /SH

24. Use the DOS PRINT command. PRINT DOSFIL.TXT.

25. CAPTURE Endcap

26. Right-mouse click on the container WHITE.CRIME.TOKYO.ACME and choose Details. Next, choose Print Job Configuration, choose New, then choose the CANONBJ-PQ1 as the queue. Save the new configuration.

27. Choose the print queue by double-clicking. Choose Users. Add the context WHITE.CRIME.TOKYO.ACME to the list of allowed users.

29. CAPTURE still doesn't automatically set you up.

33. The workstation is captured with the settings of the default print job configuration for the .WHITE.CRIME.TOKYO.ACME container.

34. They match the settings in the "Main" print job configuration.

CASE STUDY: MANAGING ACME'S PRINTING SYSTEM

3. The value in the status field changes from "waiting for job" to "stopped".

4. Click on the Cancel button to return to the main NetWare Administrator browser screen. Use Ctrl+Esc to switch in the Windows Program Manager, then go ahead and execute the NetWare User Tools utility. In User Tools, use the "drag and drop" method to capture the LPT1: port to the CANONBJ-PQ1 print queue, then click on the Exit button to leave the utility. Finally, use the Ctrl+Esc method to return to the NetWare Administrator utility, then select the Print option from the Object menu twice to generate two print jobs.

5. Two jobs submitted.

7. Print job shows user hold.

9. The second job now prints on the printer—the first is still held.

11. Double-click on the CANONBJ-P1 printer and then click on the Printer Status page button. The status will be shown as "offline".

12. The status field shows the percentage of the print job completed as it prints.

14. Each shows a status that indicates that is operational, namely: WHITE-PS1 shows "Running on NetWare server WHITE-SRV1", CANONBJ-P1 shows "Waiting for Job", and CANONBJ-PQ1 shows "Currently Being Serviced."

15. The print server unloads automatically.

16. The print server has an exclamation point next to it. This means the server is not available.

17. The print server should show that it's down.

18. Return to the main NetWare Administrator browser screen, then select the Print option from the Object menu to submit a new print job.

20. The jobs have reordered themselves to place the job just modified at the top of the queue.

EXERCISE 8-4: THE GREAT CHALLENGE

```
P  A  R  A  L  L  E  L  P  O  R  T  P  W  T  G  P  P  P
G  U  R  D  E  V  P  R  I  N  T  S  E  R  V  E  R  R  F
Y  T  L  F  Q  U  I  C  K  S  E  T  U  P  I  I  I  A  E
F  O  D  U  I  I  W  L  O  C  G  A  R  O  N  N  N  K  V
L  L  F  Y  I  W  F  F  K  N  M  X  R  T  T  N  T  C  T
O  O  L  I  H  L  T  J  L  M  S  O  J  Q  X  L  C  E  S
C  A  P  T  U  R  E  H  L  R  N  O  U  I  F  K  O  X  R
A  D  A  W  B  V  Q  Y  H  E  B  E  L  C  U  E  N  S  K
L  A  H  K  Z  K  T  G  U  A  U  Z  U  E  U  U  I  M  H
P  R  I  N  T  S  E  R  V  E  R  O  P  E  R  A  T  O  R
R  M  A  N  U  A  L  L  O  A  D  X  U  E  T  D  T  K  Y
I  B  U  D  M  P  P  P  D  L  R  Q  S  R  T  Z  X  M  D
N  A  V  C  Q  S  E  R  A  R  T  U  O  C  Y  X  U  S  F
T  J  L  B  O  R  L  C  I  N  W  X  Y  K  P  D  I  V  H
E  L  L  B  A  Y  P  R  I  N  T  D  R  I  V  E  R  X  U
R  X  Q  T  D  V  E  R  E  A  T  A  L  I  V  W  B  B  I
P  R  O  Z  D  L  P  O  L  L  E  D  M  O  D  E  P  G  P
R  R  X  H  S  W  D  P  S  E  R  V  E  R  N  L  M  L  D
E  A  G  X  T  P  E  Y  F  S  V  F  D  F  I  C  O  X  M
```

1. AUTOLOAD	11. PRINT QUEUE
2. CAPTURE	12. PRINT QUEUE OPERATOR
3. MANUAL LOAD	13. PRINT SERVER
4. NDPS	14. PRINT SERVER OPERATOR
5. NWUSER	15. PRINTCON
6. PARALLEL PORT	16. PRINTDEF
7. PCONSOLE	17. PRINTER
8. POLLED MODE	18. PSERVER.NLM
9. PRINT DRIVER	19. QDR
10. PRINT JOB	20. QUICK SETUP

EXERCISE 8-5: THE GREATEST MYSTERY OF ALL

1 READY
2 PRINTHEADER
2 PCL
3 ACTIVE
4 HELD
5 LPT
6 LASERJET
7 DOTMATRIX
8 PRINTING
9 POSTSCRIPT
10 FILESERVER
11 NETWAREAWARE
11 NWADMIN
12 QUEUES
13 LOCALPRINTER
14 REMOTEPRINTER
15 SYSTEM
16 PRINTTAIL
17 NPRINTEREXE
18 PRINTERCABLES
19 ADDING
20 STANDALONE
20 SERIALPORT
21 NPRINTERNLM
22 AUTOLOAD

For More Information and Help

Whenever a product becomes as popular and as widely used as NetWare and IntranetWare, an entire support industry crops up around it. If you are looking for more information about IntranetWare, you're in luck. There is a wide variety of places you can go for help, advice, information, or even just camaraderie.

NetWare and IntranetWare information is as local as your bookstore or local user group, and as international as the Internet forums that focus on Novell products. It can be as informal as articles in a magazine, or as structured as a college course. Best of all, it's easy to tap into most of these resources, wherever you may happen to be on the planet.

There is no point in trudging along through problems by yourself, when there is such a vast array of helpful people and tools at your fingertips.

 ZEN

"Worrying is like standing in a mud hole; it gives you something to do, but it doesn't get you anywhere."

Texas Bix Bender, *Laughing Stock, A Cow's Guide to Life*

This chapter describes the following ways you can get more information or technical support for NetWare. With a little digging, you can probably turn up even more resources than these, but these will get you started.

- General Novell product information

- *The Novell Buyer's Guide*

- The IntranetWare manuals

- Novell information on the Internet

- Novell technical support

- The *Novell Support Encyclopedia*

- DeveloperNet (Novell's developer support)

> ▶ *Novell Application Notes*

> ▶ NetWare Users International (NUI)

> ▶ NetWork Professional Association (NPA)

> ▶ Novell Press books and other publications

> ▶ World Wire

> ▶ Cyber State University

General Novell Product Information

The main Novell information number, 1-800-NETWARE, can be your inroad to all types of information about Novell and its products. By calling this number, you can obtain information about Novell products, the locations of your nearest resellers, pricing information, and so on.

The Novell Buyer's Guide

If you are responsible for helping find networking solutions for your organization, you may want to get a copy of the *Novell Buyer's Guide*. This guide is a complete book on everything you could possibly want to buy from Novell.

The *Novell Buyer's Guide* explains all the products Novell is currently offering, complete with rundowns on the technical specifications, features, and benefits of those products.

The *Guide* is available in a variety of formats, too. It is available on-line through Novell's on-line service on the Internet (www.novell.com) and through CompuServe (Go Netwire).

The *Novell Buyer's Guide* also comes on CD-ROM with the Novell's Support Connection (formerly NSEPro) which is explained later in this chapter. If you prefer the written version, you can order the Novell Buyer's Guide by calling one of the following phone numbers (which are all toll-free in Canada and the USA):

- ▸ 1-800-NETWARE

- ▸ 1-800-544-4446

- ▸ 1-800-346-6855

There may be a small charge to purchase the printed version of the *Buyer's Guide*.

The NetWare 4.1 Manuals

The NetWare 4.1 manuals are the complete reference guides to the features and workings of NetWare 4.1. In your NetWare 4.1 package, you should have received a handful of printed manuals (just enough to get you started), plus a CD-ROM containing the full set of manuals on-line (see Figure D.1).

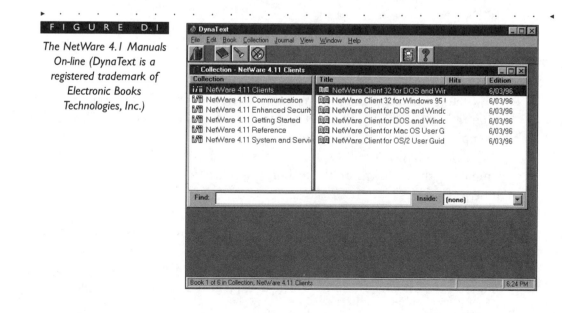

FIGURE D.1

The NetWare 4.1 Manuals On-line (DynaText is a registered trademark of Electronic Books Technologies, Inc.)

If you install the on-line documentation on your server, you'll be able to access the manuals from any workstation on the network that has the DynaText viewer installed. If you have a laptop computer, you may want to install the on-line documentation on it, so that you can carry the entire set around with you.

If you really like having printed documentation, you can order the full printed set of manuals from Novell.

> **TIP**
>
> **The only manual that is not included in the printed set is the System Messages manual. Believe me, you don't want to see how big that book would be if it were printed.**

To order the printed manuals for NetWare 4.1, you can use the order form that came in your NetWare 4.1 box, or call one of the following phone numbers:

- ► 1-800-336-3892 (toll-free in Canada and the USA)

- ► 1-512-834-6905

Novell on the Internet

A tremendous amount of information about Novell and NetWare products (both official and unofficial) is on the Internet. Officially, you can obtain the latest information about Novell from Novell's home page on the Internet, as well as from the Novell forums on CompuServe. Unofficially, there are several active user forums that deal specifically with Novell products, or generally with computers.

Novell's on-line forums offer you access to a wide variety of information and files dealing with IntranetWare and other Novell products (such as GroupWise, LAN Workplace, IntranetWare and ManageWise). You can receive information such as technical advice from sysops (system operators) and other users, updated files and drivers, and the latest patches and workarounds for known problems in Novell products.

ZEN

"Though a program be but three lines long, some day it will have to be maintained."

Geoffrey James, *The Zen of Programming*

Novell's on-line sites also provide a database of technical information from the Novell Technical Support division, as well as information about programs such as Novell Education classes and NetWare Users International (NUI). In addition, you can find marketing and sales information about the various products that Novell produces.

Novell's Internet and CompuServe sites are very dynamic, well-done, and packed with information. They are frequently updated with new information about products, education programs, promotions, and the like. In fact, the technical support features of NetWire on the Internet even garnered a place on the "What's Cool" list of Internet sites from Netscape.

Novell's Internet site is managed by Novell employees and by sysops who have extensive knowledge about NetWare and IntranetWare. Public forums can be quite active, with many knowledgeable users offering advice to those who experience problems.

TIP

To get technical help with a problem, post a message and address the message to the sysops. (But don't send the sysops a personal e-mail message asking for help-the public forums are the approved avenue for help.)

To access the Novell forums on CompuServe, you need a CompuServe account. There is no additional monthly fee for using the Novell forums, although you are charged the connection fee (on an hourly rate) for accessing the service. To get to the Novell forums, use GO NETWIRE. There, you will find information for new users, telling you how the forums are set up, how to get technical help, and so on.

If you have a connection to the Internet, you can access Novell's Internet site in one of the following ways:

- **World Wide Web:** http://www.novell.com

- **Gopher:** gopher.novell.com

- **File Transfer Protocol (FTP):** anonymous FTP to ftp.novell.com

(Users in Europe should replace .com with .de.)
To get to the Novell site on the Microsoft Network, use GO NETWIRE.

Novell Technical Support

If you encounter a problem with your network that you can't solve on your own, there are several places you can go for immediate technical help.

ZEN

"When you find yourself in over your head, don't open your mouth. Swim!"

Texas Bix Bender, *Laughing Stock, A Cow's Guide to Life*

Try some of the following resources:

- Try calling your reseller or consultant.

- Go on-line, and check out the Technical Support areas of Novell's Internet site. There, you will find postings and databases of problems and solutions. Someone else may have already found and solved your problem for you.

- While you're on-line, see if anyone in the on-line forums or Usenet forums knows about the problem or can offer a solution. The knowledge of people in those forums is broad and deep. Don't hesitate to take advantage of it, and don't forget to return the favor if you know some tidbit that might help others.

► Call Novell Technical Support. You may want to reserve this for a last resort, simply because Novell Technical Support charges a fee for each incident (an "incident" may involve more than one phone call, if necessary). The fee depends on the product for which you're requesting support.

When you call Technical Support, make sure you have all the necessary information ready (such as the versions of NetWare and any utility or application you're using, the type of hardware you're using, network or node addresses and hardware settings for any workstations or other machines being affected, and so on). You'll also need a major credit card.

To get to Novell's Technical Support, call 1-800-858-4000 (or 1-801-861-4000 outside of the U.S.).

Novell's Support Connection

A subscription to *Novell's Support Connection* formerly known as the *Novell Support Encyclopedia Professional Volume* (NSEPro), can update you every month with the latest technical information about Novell products. *Novell's Support Connection* is a CD-ROM containing technical information such as:

► Novell technical information documents

► Novell Labs hardware and software test bulletins

► On-line product manuals

► *Novell Application Notes*

► All available NetWare patches, fixes, and drivers

► The *Novell Buyer's Guide*

► Novell corporate information (such as event calendars and press releases)

Novell's Support Connection includes Folio information-retrieval software that allows you to access and search easily through the *Novell's Support Connection* information from your workstation using DOS, Macintosh, or Microsoft Windows.

ZEN

"If computers get too powerful, we can organize them into a committee— that will do them in."

from "Bradley's Bromide"

To subscribe to *Novell's Support Connection*, contact your Novell Authorized Reseller or Novell directly at 1-800-377-4136 (in the United States and Canada) or 1-303-297-2725.

DeveloperNet Novell's Developer Support

If you or others in your organization develop applications that must run on a NetWare 4.1 network, you can tap into a special information resource created just for developers.

DeveloperNet is a support program specifically for professional developers who create applications designed to run on NetWare. Subscription fees for joining DeveloperNet vary, depending on the subscription level and options you choose. If you are a developer, some of the benefits you can receive by joining DeveloperNet include:

▸ The Novell SDK (Software Development Kit) CD-ROM, which contains development tools you can use to create and test your application

▸ The *DeveloperNet Handbook*

▸ Special technical support geared specifically toward developers

▸ *Novell Developer Notes*, a bimonthly publication from the Novell Research department that covers software-development topics for NetWare products

▸ Discounts on various events, products, and Novell Press books

For more information, to apply for membership, or to order an SDK, call 1-800-REDWORD or 1-801-861-5281, or contact the program administrator via e-mail at devprog@novell.com.

TIP

More information about DeveloperNet is available on-line on CompuServe (GO NETWIRE) or on the World Wide Web. On the Web, you can connect to the DeveloperNet information through Novell's home site, at http://www.novell.com, or you can go directly to the DeveloperNet information at http://developer.novell.com. Both addresses get you to the same place.

Novell Application Notes

Novell's Research department produces a monthly publication called the *Novell Application Notes*. Each issue of *Novell Application Notes* contains research reports and articles on a wide range of topics. The articles delve into topics such as network design, implementation, administration, and integration.

A year's subscription costs $95 ($135 outside the United States), which includes access to the *Novell Application Notes* in their electronic form on CompuServe. An electronic-only subscription costs $35 (plus access charges).

To order a subscription, call 1-800-377-4136 or 1-303-297-2725. You can also fax an order to 1-303-294-0930.

NetWare Users International (NUI)

IntranetWare Users International (NUI) is a nonprofit association for networking professionals. With more than 250 affiliated groups worldwide, NUI provides a forum for networking professionals to meet face-to-face, to learn from each other, to trade recommendations, or just to share "war stories."

ZEN

"I believe in computer dating, but only if the computers are truly in love."

Groucho Marx

By joining the NetWare user group in your area, you can take advantage of the following benefits:

- Local user groups that hold regularly scheduled meetings.

- *IntranetWare Connection*, a bimonthly magazine that provides feature articles on new technologies, network management tips, product reviews, NUI news, and other helpful information.

- A discount on Novell Press books through the *IntranetWare Connection* magazine and also at NUI shows.

- NUInet, NUI's home page on the World Wide Web (available through Novell's home site, under "Programs," or directly at http://www.nuinet.com), which provides NetWare 3 and IntranetWare technical information, a calendar of NUI events, and links to local user group home pages.

- Regional NUI conferences, held in different major cities throughout the year (with a 15 percent discount for members).

The best news is, there's usually no fee or only a very low fee for joining an NUI user group.

For more information or to join an NUI user group, call 1-800-228-4NUI or send a fax to 1-801-228-4577.

For a free subscription to *IntranetWare Connection*, fax your name, address, and request for a subscription to 1-801-228-4576. You can also mail NUI a request at:

NetWare Connection
P.O. Box 1928
Orem, UT 84059-1928
USA

> **REAL WORLD**
>
> You don't even have to officially join NUI to get a subscription to *IntranetWare Connection*, but don't let that stop you from joining. "Networking" with other NetWare and IntranetWare administrators can help you in ways you probably can't even think of yet.

Network Professional Association (NPA)

If you've achieved (or are working toward) your CNA or CNE certification, you may want to join the Network Professional Association (NPA), formerly called CNEPA. The NPA is an organization for network computing professionals. Its goal is to keep its members current with the latest technology and information in the industry.

If you're a certified CNE, you can join the NPA as a full member. If you're a CNA, or if you've started the certification process, but aren't finished yet, you can join as an associate member. Associate members have all the benefits of full membership, except that they cannot vote or hold offices in the NPA.

ZEN

"The more I want to get something done, the less I call it work."

Richard Bach, *Illusions*

When you join the NPA you can enjoy the following benefits:

▶ Local NPA chapters (more than 100 worldwide) that hold regularly scheduled meetings that include presentations and hands-on demonstrations of the latest technology

▶ *Network News*, a monthly publication that offers technical tips for working with NetWare and IntranetWare networks, NPA news, classified ads for positions, and articles aimed at helping CNEs make the most of their careers

▶ Discounts on NPA Satellite Labs (satellite broadcasts of presentations)

▶ Product discounts from vendors

▶ Hands-On Technology Labs (educational forums at major trade shows and other locations as sponsored by local NPA chapters)

▶ Discount or free admission to major trade shows and conferences

Membership in NPA costs $150 per year. For more information or to join NPA, call 1-801-379-0330.

Novell Press Books and Other Publications

Every year, more and more books are being published about NetWare and IntranetWare and about networking in general. Whatever topic you can think up, someone's probably written a book about it.

Novell Press itself has an extensive selection of books written about NetWare and IntranetWare and other Novell products. For an up-to-date Novell Press catalog, you can send an e-mail to Novell Press at novellpress@novell.com.

You can also peruse the selection of books on-line. From Novell's main Internet site (http://www.novell.com), you can get to the Novell Press area (located under "Programs"). You can also get to the same location by going directly to http://corp.novell.com/programs/press.

In addition to books, there are a wide variety of magazines that are geared specifically toward networking and general computing professionals, such as *Network News*, *IntranetWare Connection* (from NUI), *LAN Times*, *PCWeek*, and so on.

World Wire

World Wire is an on-line service that gives you incredible new educational avenues for learning about NetWare. It provides you with technical support, technical information, Internet access, testing, and other benefits.

In addition, World Wire gives you access to actual, on-line IntranetWare and NetWare 4.1 LANs so that you can get some hands-on experience in the safety of a practice environment, rather than in your real, production environment.

For more information, call 1-510-253-TREK.

CyberState University

CyberState University is the world leader in on-line network certification training. They were the first organization in the world to develop and deliver complete certification training via the Internet. They offer complete CNA, CNE, MCSE, and other programs for a fraction of cost of traditional courses. All of this is made possible because of their proprietary *Synergy Learning System*. Let's take a closer look.

THE SYNERGY LEARNING SYSTEM

CyberState University has developed the Synergy Learning System (SLS) to reduce a student's total study time by accelerating retention and improving recall of course material. The SLS accomplishes these goals by combining multiple teaching mediums into a structured learning environment. These mediums incorporate visual, auditory, and kinesthetic sensory inputs into the educational process. Typically, a student will use one of these inputs as the primary method of learning, and then rely on the other two for reinforcement. The result is quicker absorption and easier recall of complex course material.

Here's a quick list of the many different mediums used at CyberState University:

▸ Study Guides from #1 best-selling authors (including this book).

▸ Video tapes which focus on "how to do it."

▸ On-line lectures to direct study efforts.

▸ On-line review sessions to reinforce key concepts.

▸ On-line assignments in a live, network Practice Lab. This anchors the course material with "hands-on" experience.

▸ Multimedia skills assessment to focus on critical study strengths and weaknesses.

▸ Multimedia testing to measure proficiency with the course material.

▸ On-line interaction with student from all over the world via "chat forums."

▸ On-line support from instructors via CyberState University's e-mail system.

▸ SmartLinks to related study material anywhere on the Internet.

It's the interactive combination of the complementary teaching mediums that makes up the SLS. By accelerating retention and improving recall, this innovative on-line curriculum reduces the total number of study hours you need to become a CNA, CNE, or MCSE.

THE CURRICULUM

CyberState University offers a variety of programs for Novell or Microsoft certification training. All of them use the SLS and cost 60 to 75 percent less than traditional courses. Here's a list of the most popular on-line programs and some benefits of CyberState's approach:

▸ *Novell CNE*—Choose from three programs: CNE-3, CNE-4, and IntranetWare CNE. Each program takes approximately 25 weeks and includes 6 required courses and 1 elective.

▶ *Novell CNE-3/CNE-4*—Combine the CNE-3 and CNE-4 tracks into a single, valuable dual certification. It only takes a few extra weeks.

▶ *Novell CNA*—Choose from three programs: CNA-3, CNA-4, and IntranetWare CNA. Each program takes approximately six weeks and provides a clear upgrade path to the CNE.

▶ *Microsoft MCSE*—Custom tailor your certification from a list of required and elective courses. Most programs last 30 weeks and cover a total of 6 courses.

▶ *Microsoft MCP*—Choose from several MCP-certification programs, each covering one Microsoft course. Combine MCP certificates to provide the most comprehensive coverage.

▶ *Novell CNE/Microsoft MCSE*—the ultimate certification. This combined Novell and Microsoft certification lasts approximately 50 weeks and covers 13 courses. It provides the greatest prize in the network arena. Students who complete this program will be head-and-shoulders above everybody else in the highly competitive networking job market.

▶ CyberState University has enjoyed a 100 percent certification rate for students who complete the curriculum. That means that every student who finishes becomes a CNE—hundreds of them.

▶ Study any time from anywhere with 24-hour Internet access. You also enjoy unlimited access to campus facilities, including a virtual student union, practice lab, classrooms, and more.

▶ Log in, with Supervisory access, to several servers in the CyberState University practice lab. This gives you the "hands-on" experience with Novell, Microsoft, and third-party products you need to pass Simulation-based and Performance-based certification exams.

▶ Completion of the certification exams is incorporated into the course schedule. Also, you have guaranteed support resources throughout the curriculum. A real person is always there to help you succeed.

► Study time is paced to three to four hours per week. In addition, your course length may be adjusted to meet individual needs. CyberState University is very flexible and understanding. Their goal is your goal: get certified!

FOR MORE INFORMATION ...

CyberState University is behind you every step of the way. Becoming a CNE or MCSE has never been easier, or more fun. If you need a little more help:

► Surf the Web at http://www.cyberstateu.com.

► Fax us at 1-510-254-9349.

► If you'd like to speak to a "real" person, call **1-888-GET-EDUC** or **1-510-253-8753** (*internationally*).

Good Luck, and thanks for learning with us.

► . . . . ◄

The Clarke Tests v3.0

Welcome to *The Clarke Tests v3.0*! It is unlike anything you have ever seen. It is more than just sample test questions-this is an Interactive Learning System for CNAs.

The CD-ROM included with this book contains the complete NetWare 4.11 CNA module of *The Clarke Tests v3.0*. Here's a more detailed look at this wonderful, multimedia learning system.

 ZEN

"The Teacher is like the candle which lights others in consuming itself!"

Giovanni Ruffini

FOUR STUDY MODULES TO CHOOSE FROM

Let us help you become a CNA or CNE! The entire *Clarke Tests* collection includes 12 courses, nearly 100 tests, and more than 4,000 study sessions on an interactive CD-ROM. Each test teaches you specific CNE objectives within a subsection of a required CNE course. *The Clarke Tests v3.0* offers four different study modules covering four major Novell certifications—NetWare 4.11 Certified Novell Engineer (CNE-4), NetWare 3.12 CNE (CNE-3), and both Certified Novell Administrators (CNA-4 and CNA-3). Here's a breakdown of the four *Clarke Tests* modules and their corresponding certifications:

- ▸ NetWare 4.11 CNE Target Courses—*part 1 of CNE-4*

- ▸ NetWare 3.12 CNE Target Courses—*part 1 of CNE-3*

- ▸ Core Technologies and Electives—*part 2 of CNE-4/CNE-3*

- ▸ NetWare 3.12 and 4.11 CNA—*covers CNA-4/CNA-3*

THE INTERACTIVE LEARNING SYSTEM

The Clarke Tests v3.0 uses a multimedia, Windows-based interface to maximize your learning potential. This interface closely resembles the software used by Sylvan Prometric and Drake Technologies for actual CNE certification. The goal is to prepare you for the entire testing experience, not just the test objectives. In addition, LearningWare has enhanced the interface to create a complete Interactive Learning System. Here's how it works.

The Tests

Each CNE course is divided into Study and Certification tests. *Study Tests* cover specific CNE objectives within a subsection of a required CNE course. They encompass 35 to 120 questions with the help of a proprietary Navigator. The Navigator allows you to answer questions in any order and return to previously answered questions for review. In addition, we've provided actual CNE *Certification Tests* for adaptive, form, simulation, and performance-based courses. Use the Study Tests to learn and the Certification Tests to prepare.

The Questions

Questions in *The Clarke Tests* are more than simple, one-dimensional brain teasers; they are complete interactive *Study Sessions*. They include a variety of learning tools to keep things interesting and make learning fun. Each of the following study session types presents the CNE study material in a slightly different way. This forces you to "truly" understand the testing objectives:

▶ *Hot Spots*—"Real life" graphical exhibits that test your hands-on knowledge.

▶ *Performance-based*—A *new* Novell testing strategy for Service and Support and NetWare 4.11 material. These questions test your ability to solve NetWare-related problems.

▶ *Traditional Multiple Choice*—One or more correct answers per question.

▶ *Matching,*—Combine many NetWare topics in one interactive study session.

▶ *Fill-In*—Require tough "open-ended" answers.

In addition, many study sessions include graphical exhibits. These exhibits enhance your learning experience by providing screen shots, 3-D graphics, and professional case studies. Finally, if your stuck along the way, *The Clarke Tests v3.0* offers interactive Clues in a separate window. These clues allow you to continue studying without divulging the complete answer. We are with you every step of the way!

Interactive Answers

These are the real stars of the show. Each study session includes a full page or more of explanation and CNE study material. Instead of just displaying the answer, we explain it in detail. In addition, each Interactive Answer includes page references to Novell Authorized courseware, the CyberState University on-line CNE program, *Novell's CNE Study Guide*, *Novell's CNE Study Guide for NetWare 4.1*, *Novell's CNE Study Guide for Core Technologies*, *Novell's CNA Study Guide for NetWare 4.1*, NetWare documentation, and the "So You Wanna Be A CNE?!" video series.

Tracker Scoring

The Clarke Tests v3.0 includes an exciting *new* interactive scoring system called *The Tracker*. The Tracker is a separate module that gathers detailed information about your performance on individual CNE tests. It classifies your results according to key testing objectives and presents them in a table format. Here's how it works:

▸ *Certification Scoring*—All actual CNE certification exams are scored on an 800 scale. In order to pass, you must exceed a specific threshold for each course. *The Clarke Tests v3.0* uses the same 800 scale and built-in thresholds as the actual exams. This allows you to accurately assess your chances of passing any given CNE exam.

▸ *Prescription Reports*—A series of detailed testing objectives are included with each exam. Your performance in each study area is tracked to help you identify your strengths and weaknesses. *The Clarke Tests v3.0* also includes comprehensive Prescription Reports to help you isolate specific areas of study and track testing improvement.

▸ *Database Analysis*—The Tracker data can be exported to numerous database and spreadsheet programs for further graphical analysis. This is a great way to chart your CNE progress.

Tracker scoring is a great way to build custom CNE study sessions. You can trust that when the Clarke Professor says your ready for the real CNE exam . . . . you're ready! Good Luck, and let us help you become a CNE!

ZEN

"I'll never take another CNE exam without first taking The Clarke Tests!"

Bill King

INSTALLING THE CLARKE TESTS V3.0

To install *The Clarke Tests v3.0*, insert the CD-ROM into your CD drive (drive D:, for example).

1 • If you are using Microsoft Windows 95, select Start and Run. Type **D:\CNA95\SETUP** in the input window and click OK. (Remember that drive D: is the CD-ROM drive.)

2 • If you are using Microsoft Windows 3.1, select File and Run. Type **D:\CNA31\SETUP** in the input window and click OK. (Remember that drive D: is the CD-ROM drive.)

3 • *The Clarke Tests v3.0* Setup will install the Delivery Module ("Clarke!!"), Tracker, and Administrator. By default, *all* tests will be highlighted. Click on any tests you do not want to install and the system will deselect them.

4 • As each test is installed, Setup will ask for a test directory. We recommend that you separate courses into different subdirectories and only install the tests on which you are currently working. In addition, *The Clarke Tests v3.0* includes a "Save" feature that allows you to exit a test without losing your place.

5 • Have Fun!

USING THE CLARKE TESTS V3.0

Once *The Clarke Tests v3.0* have been installed correctly, you will notice three icons in The Clarke Test program group. The "Clarke!" icon runs the interactive learning system, the "Admin Maker" is for test administration, and "Tracker" monitors your progress and prints Prescription Reports. Here are a few tips on using *The Clarke Tests v3.0*:

▸ *In the Beginning*—To begin *The Clarke Tests*, select "Clarke!" from the Start menu in Windows 95, or double click on the "Clarke!" icon within Windows 3.1. Next, choose a test and enter your name. Let the tests begin.

▶ *Navigation*—To navigate questions, simply click on the question number or use the arrows at the bottom right-hand corner of the screen. Indicate your desired response by clicking on the appropriate radio button, or by entering text into the fill-in or matching spaces provided. The radio button is the white circle or square to the left of a selection.

▶ *Clues*—The "Help" button provides clues to guide you in the right direction. Don't worry, they don't give away the answer. When you are finished viewing the Clue, click the Done button to return to the question.

▶ *Interactive Answers*—The Info button provides a detailed answer for each question, including page references to numerous study aids. This is the Interactive Answer. When you are finished viewing the study material, click the Done button to return to the question.

▶ *Scoring*—Once you have completed a question, move to the next one. The Professor will automatically score your response. Correct answers will appear in green, while incorrect responses turn red. Look for lots of green!

▶ *Custom Reports*—Each test includes a detailed Prescription Report. The report helps you identify your strengths and weaknesses by comparing your results against actual CNA and CNE testing objectives. Also, the Professor will allow you to generate sophisticated custom reports using the Tracker Module. With all this help, you are just moments away from an exciting new life as a NetWare or IntranetWare CNA or CNE.

TROUBLESHOOTING THE CLARKE TESTS V3.0

If you run into any problems with *The Clarke Tests v3.0*, we're with you every step of the way. First, try any of the tips listed here. If that doesn't work, gives us a call at 1-800-684-8858 or 1-801-423-2314 (*internationally*).

For Window 3.1 and Windows 95 Users

1 • The interactive test screen will fill your monitor if the Windows driver is set to 640x480. The 640x480 setting is best for "hotspot" test question graphics.

2 • If you are using a high-quality video driver (Viper VLB, for example), it may support a "large font" mode for high-quality text and graphics. This can cause the text of The Clarke Tests v3.0 to extend beyond designated areas. Avoid using "large fonts" mode.

3 • If you have installed a previous version of *The Clarke Tests*, uninstall or delete the program before you install version 3.0. If you receive an error indicating previously used files, select "IGNORE" and continue. If you receive "Runtime Error 31037," consult the appropriate troubleshooting section that follows.

For Windows 3.1 Users Only

1 • If you have a computer capable of playing .WAV files and you receive an error message indicating your computer is not capable of sound, copy the following file from the CD-ROM into the "TCS" directory on your hard drive:

D:\CNA31\TCS.SPT

2 • *Auto redraw*—"Runtime Error 480" and/or "Unable to create auto redraw image." Windows 3.1 does not have enough system/memory resources to display the screen. Over time the "memory leak" of Windows 3.1 will reduce system resources and available memory to draw the screen. Try this cure:

▶ Go to Program Manager and Help. View About Program Manager. You see that system resources are getting below 70 percent. A fresh install of Window 3.1 yields 85 to 90 percent resource availability.

▸ We must increase system resources to allow enough memory for the screen to redraw. If you have any other programs running at startup, remove them and reboot your system. You may have given yourself more available resources. If so, you're finished.

▸ If not, you may try using Memmaker (go to DOS and type **MEMMAKER**). By following the instructions, you may free up some conventional memory. This may have minimal affect on the resources that the screen needs (GDI resources) to re-draw the image. If it works for you, you're finished.

▸ If not, you may need to reinstall Windows 3.1. This may sound a bit drastic. However, it may be the fastest and easiest solution for many memory problems.

3 • *Share or Vshare*—SHARE.EXE or VSHARE.386 errors. These programs may not be loading properly. Try these simple cures:

▸ SHARE and VSHARE *cannot* both be loaded at the same time. And, SHARE.EXE needs certain parameters to run.

▸ SHARE.EXE is loaded in your AUTOEXEC.BAT file. AUTOEXEC.BAT is in the root directory (C:\). The parameters should look like this: C:\DOS\SHARE.EXE /L:500 /F:5100

▸ VSHARE.386 is loaded from the SYSTEM.INI file. SYSTEM.INI is in the C:\WINDOWS\SYSTEM subdirectory. It is in the 386ENH section ("device=vshare.386").

4 • Ensure that The Clarke Tests v3.0 files on your hard drive are *not read-only*. Ensure that TCSEMPTY.MDS exists on the hard drive in the directory that you installed TCS, and it, too, is *not read-only*.

5 • On some rare occasions, VESA local bus machines (typically 486's) using a VLB IDE controller with a special driver loading for higher performance (Dual Mode transfer, for example) may run into trouble. This driver may collide with VSHARE.EXE. In these instances, use SHARE.EXE.

For Windows 95 Users Only

1 • *Runtime Error 75*—"Path/file access error." After a certain percentage of *The Clarke Tests v3.0* loads, you may get this error. This error is caused by one of the following problems: media failure (CD-ROM or drive), dirty CD-ROM drive, corrupted file, bad CD-ROM disk, hard drive failure, bad sector on the hard drive, not enough hard drive space, and/or compressed drives giving error for "true" space available. Here are some quick cures:

▸ If the problem is caused by not enough drive space, delete the contents of the TCS directory. Next, free up enough hard drive space and re-install *The Clarke Tests v3.0* normally.

▸ If that doesn't work, copy the contents of *The Clarke Test v3.0* CD onto the hard drive in a TEMP directory. Use Explorer to make sure you do not have any 0 byte files (which means that it is not copying properly). Ensure that no file attributes of any file are set to *read-only*. Finally, run SETUP.EXE from TEMP and install *The Clarke Tests v3.0* normally.

2 • *Runtime Error 31037*—"Registry error." Your Registry thinks that *The Clarke Tests v3.0* can run from the CD ROM. It cannot, because, as you take the tests, the program keeps track of your scores. Therefore, the computer must write to the default media. The CD is *read-only*. The Registry has "misplaced" the THREED32.OCX file. Try these cures:

▸ Remove the TCS directory using "Add/remove programs" in the Control Panel. Go into Windows Explorer and check for any other directories containing *The Clarke Test v3.0* files. Remove them.

- Go to Start, Run.

- Type **REGEDIT** and then press Enter.

- In the Registry editor, search "My Computer" (using Edit, Find) for all references relating to *The Clarke Tests v3.0* that may have been installed. Manually delete them (being sure to delete the entire reference). Here are some examples of what to look for: your CD-ROM Drive D:\ (do not delete the Windows 95 CD references), \TCS\ directories (or other directory name you may have chosen), THREED32.OCX, DELIVERY.EXE, TCSADMIN.EXE, SETUP.EXE, and/or TRACKER.EXE.

- Copy REGCLN.EXE from the new Clarke Test CD into a temporary directory (it is D:\CNA95\REGCLN.EXE). This file is from Microsoft and is made to clean your Registry. It is a self-extracting file (which means that it may contain many files compressed into one, and that, when you execute it, it will decompress itself in the directory that it is in). Execute the command and let the files decompress.

- Run the Microsoft Registry Cleaner's SETUP.EXE program. This will clean your Registry.

- When you're finished, install *The Clarke Tests v3.0* normally.

- Finally, you may need to let the Registry "know" some critical information about THREED32.OCX. Bring up a DOS prompt, and change to the directory in which you installed *The Clarke Tests v3.0* (for example, C:\TCS). In this directory, type **REGOCX32 \WINDOWS\SYSTEM\THREED32.OCX**.

FOR MORE INFORMATION ...

The Clarke Tests Professor is behind you every step of the way. Becoming a CNA or CNE has never been easier, or more fun. If you need a little more help:

- ► Try *The Clarke Tests* Tutorial—It's a great start!

- ► Check out the "README.CLK" file on the CD-ROM for installation instructions and last-minute changes or suggestions.

- ► Surf the Web at http://www.world-wire.com/public/clarke.htm.

- ► Fax us at 1-801-423-2367.

- ► If you must speak to a "real" person call **1-800-684-8858** for orders and technical support.

Exploring the NetWare
Web Server

"We surfed here on the Web"

The NetWare Web Server 2.5 is an easy-to-install, high-performance World Wide Web (WWW) server that comes with IntranetWare. Installation and configuration is so easy that, if you already have TCP/IP configured on your server, you can view the sample NetWare Web Server home page in approximately 15 minutes. If you know how to create your own *HyperText Markup Language* (HTML) files, you can be viewing your own home page just a few minutes later.

This appendix introduces the NetWare Web Server 2.5 and explains how you can transform your NetWare Web Server into your own custom Internet or intranet Web site. Throughout this appendix, you will learn the basics of installing and using the NetWare Web Server, including how to:

- ▸ **Read the documentation**—To read the Web Server documentation, install a browser (such as Netscape Navigator, which is included with the Web Server) on a workstation and read the HTML-formatted documentation from the CD-ROM.

- ▸ **Install the Web Server**—To specify an IP address for the server and to bind TCP/IP to the network board, use INETCFG.NLM. To install the Web Server on the IntranetWare server, use INSTALL.NLM, select Product Options, and choose Install NetWare Web Server.

TIP

Creating Web pages (usually called "authoring") and administering a NetWare Web Server require different skills and are often performed by different people. This appendix focuses on NetWare Web Server administration, but it is undeniable that you can be a much better administrator if you also learn at least some of the basics of Web page authoring. Your first indication of this will come when Web page authors start linking pages to files all over the server and requesting write permissions. To learn more about Web page authoring, consider taking Novell Education Course 654, Web Authoring and Publishing.

▶ **Configure the Web Server**—To add a name service to your network, either create a hosts file on your server, or configure your server as a Domain Name Service (DNS) server or as a client of a DNS server.

To configure the Web Server, use the NetWare Web Manager utility.

What Is the NetWare Web Server?

A WWW server, such as the NetWare Web Server, is a file server that serves or publishes files in HTML format. You read these HTML files from workstations by using client applications called *browsers*. HTML files are text files with special tags (usually enclosed in less-than and greater-than symbols, < >) that tell the browser how to format the file on screen. The main differences between HTML files and standard word processing files are

▶ HTML files do not contain proprietary custom symbols or formatting characters. All formatting is specified with special combinations of ASCII text characters. For example, to indicate that text should be printed in bold, you might use the following command:

<B>**This will appear as bold text**.</B>

▶ HTML files can include text or graphic *links*, which users can click on to move to another location in the same file or to another file on any Web server in the world.

Many people get confused by the terms HTML and HTTP, and they are overwhelmed when WWW and Internet are also thrown into the same sentence. A WWW Web server publishes files in HTML format. A Web server communicates with browsers using the *HyperText Transfer Protocol* (HTTP), which runs over TCP/IP. The Internet is a global network of computers that provide many services, one of which is the WWW.

The NetWare Web Server provides the following features:

▶ Easy installation and configuration

- ▸ A Windows-based administration utility

- ▸ NDS Access control for Internet/intranet users and systems

- ▸ File security through NDS

- ▸ Internet/intranet access logging

- ▸ Browser access to NDS trees

- ▸ Support for dynamic Web pages

- ▸ NetBasic for creating Internet scripts

- ▸ Netscape Navigator (single-user license in IntranetWare, or multiuser license-up to your allowed NetWare user limit-in IntranetWare)

Dynamic Web page support allows Web page authors to add commands to HTML files that enhance the pages in ways that are not possible with HTML tags. For example, Web page authors can add commands that automatically insert variables (such as the date or time) into a page as it is sent to a browser. Other commands allow Web page authors to display animations or perform calculations on data entered by a browser user. The NetWare Web Server supports dynamic Web pages with the following features:

- ▸ Server Side Include (SSI) commands

- ▸ Local Common Gateway Interface (L-CGI)

- ▸ Remote Common Gateway Interface (R-CGI)

- ▸ BASIC script interpreters

- ▸ PERL script interpreters

- ▸ Support for Java applets

- ▸ Support for JavaScript

Installing the NetWare Web Server

Installing the Web Server consists of configuring the network to support TCP/IP and then running INSTALL.NLM to install the Web Server product.

To set up a NetWare Web Server site, you need the following hardware and software:

- ▸ A NetWare 4.11 (or IntranetWare) server with a CD-ROM drive.

- ▸ At least 2.5MB of hard disk space for the NetWare Web Server software, plus additional disk space for your new HTML files.

- ▸ A client workstation running Windows 3.1x, Windows 95, or Windows NT. The workstation must have a 386 processor, 4 MB of RAM, and 2.5 MB of hard disk space available for the Netscape Navigator browser installation. (You can use a different browser if you prefer.)

- ▸ Although you can use Windows word processing tools to create and edit HTML documents, you may want to add HTML authoring software, which would require additional disk space and memory. An HTML authoring tool is not included with the NetWare Web Server.

LOCATING THE WEB SERVER DOCUMENTATION

The Web Server documentation is in HTML format on the IntranetWare Operating System CD-ROM. To read or print this documentation, you must use a Web browser such as Netscape Navigator (included with the NetWare Web Server) on a workstation.

If you don't have a browser installed yet, complete the following steps to install the Netscape Navigator browser on a Windows 3.1x workstation:

1 • Insert the IntranetWare Operating System CD-ROM into a Windows 3.1x workstation's CD-ROM drive.

2 • From the workstation's Program Manager, choose Run from the File menu. Click Browse, and locate the SETUP.EXE file for the Web Server in the following directory: PRODUCTS\WEBSERV\BROWSER\N16E201. Select OK to begin the setup process.

To install the Netscape Navigator on a Windows 95 workstation, complete the following steps:

1 • Insert the IntranetWare Operating System CD-ROM into a Windows 3.1x workstation's CD-ROM drive.

2 • From Windows 95, click Start. Then choose Run and locate the SETUP.EXE file for the Web Server in the following directory: PRODUCTS\WEBSERV\BROWSER\N32E201. Select OK to begin the setup process.

After you've installed the viewer, launch it. From the Navigator's File menu, select Open File and select the drive and directory that contains the Web Server documentation (such as the CD-ROM drive, or a directory if you've copied the documentation files to the server or the client). Then double-click on the file you want to open.

CONFIGURING TCP/IP

To prepare for NetWare Web Server installation, install IntranetWare on the server and establish IPX and TCP/IP communications between the two. (TCP/IP software is provided with IntranetWare.) Use INETCFG.NLM to specify an IP address for the server and to bind TCP/IP to the network board. Then load the PING NLM on the server and use it to verify TCP/IP communications with the client.

BRINGING UP THE NETWARE WEB SERVER

NetWare Web Server installation is easier than most IntranetWare installations because the critical configuration is completed when you configure TCP/IP. Simply load INSTALL.NLM on the server, choose Product Options, and then choose Install NetWare Web Server. Follow the instructions that appear on the screen.

When the NetWare Web Server installation is complete, press Alt-Esc at the server console to switch between the following active services:

▸ Novell HTTP Server 2.5, which is the NetWare Web Server NLM

▸ Novell Basic language interpreter, for dynamic Web page support

▸ Novell Perl language interpreter, for dynamic Web page support

You have now created a Web site. Any network browser can now view the default home page if the user knows the TCP/IP address of your server.

To view the Web site you have just created, start the browser on your client workstation, select Open Location from the file menu, and enter the following *Universal Resource Locator* (URL):

```
http://server_ip_address
```

After you enter this command with your server IP address, you should see the Web page shown in Figure E.1.

The default Web site contains a number of sample pages and links. Browse through these pages to get an idea of what can be published on a NetWare Web Server. To see the HTML commands used to create any page, display the page and then select Document Source from the View menu.

FIGURE E.1

A Sample Web Page

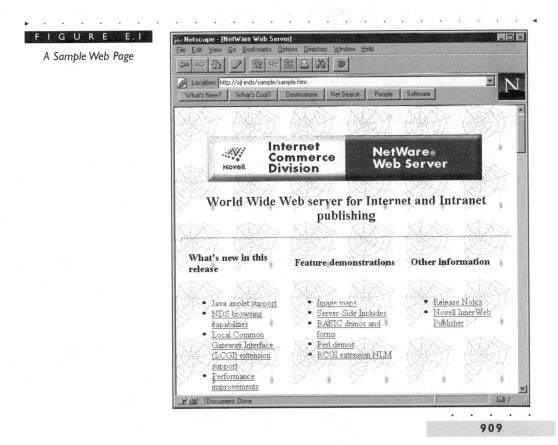

Exploring Your Web Site

You are now a Web site manager and, depending on your TCP/IP network connections, your site is available to your organization, and possibly the world. Let's take a closer look at what you have.

When you look at the default directory structure of the NetWare Web Server, you'll notice the INDEX.HTM file. This is the default HTML file that Web browsers see when they access your site using your IP address. We'll talk about changing the defaults and using names instead of IP addresses later. For now, what you need to know is that this is the entry point for your Web site. To create your own home page, start by editing this file or by replacing it with your own INDEX.HTM file.

By default, the INDEX.HTM file is in the SYS:\WEB\DOCS directory, which is the document root directory of your Web site. At least three root directories are on your NetWare Web Server. The one you are most familiar with is the SYS: root directory, which is the IntranetWare volume root directory.

The NetWare Web Server has two root directories of its own: the server root directory and the document root directory. The *server root directory* contains all the configuration and control files associated with your Web site. These are the files that you don't want your Web site visitors to see. The server root directory on any NetWare Web Server is SYS:\WEB and cannot be changed.

The *document root directory* is the default path to all the files you want to publish. To protect your server configuration files from undesired access, the document root directory should be a subdirectory of the server root directory, or it should be placed on another volume.

> **TIP**
>
> **When browsers access your site, they are restricted to files and directories that are contained in the document root directory—with one exception. You can configure the NetWare Web Server to allow browsers to access user home pages in the users' home directories.**

The document root directory can be changed to another directory or another volume, but it should be changed only after careful planning. Many links in the Web pages will use relative references that define the path from the document root directory to another file. Carelessly moving the document root can make all your internal Web site links invalid, rendering your Web site useless.

TIP

A NetWare Web Server is a live Web site. Users can connect to it at any time. To avoid user access errors, always edit published Web pages off-line in your home directory or on another computer. Otherwise your word processor or Web authoring tool may lock the file and prevent other users from accessing it. Also, test all links that you create in your Web pages. It's less embarrassing to find the mistakes yourself.

Configuring Name Services

Your Web server is up, but your customers (both internal and external) must remember your server's IP address to access it. Simplify your customers' access by creating a *name service*.

Name services use a table of IP addresses and names to establish names that can be used in place of IP addresses. Each IP address can be associated with one or more names or aliases.

There are two common ways to add a name service to your network. The easiest is to create a hosts file on your server. The second is to configure your server as a *Domain Name Service* (DNS) server or as a client of a DNS server. The hosts file approach provides name services only on your network or subnet. DNS provides name services over an entire network or the Internet.

CREATING AND USING A HOST'S FILE

To create a table of IP addresses and host names for your network or subnet, use a text editor to create a file named HOSTS.TXT in the SYS:ETC directory. Create a name table similar to Table E.1.

TABLE E.1	#IP ADDRESS	ALIASES	COMMENTS
Sample Name Table	ip_address	alias1 alias2	#NetWare Web Server
	ip_address	alias3	#jim's pc
	ip_address	alias4	#carol's pc

The # character indicates that all text to the right of it is a comment and is to be ignored. Each line starts with the IP address of a host, followed by one or more spaces. The second item on each line is the name you want to assign to the host. You can add several names, but be sure to separate each name with one or more spaces.

USING DOMAIN NAME SERVICES

DNS is an Internet protocol that allows administrators to associate internet addresses with names that people can remember. A DNS server stores the names and their corresponding IP addresses, and responds to clients that need names services. DNS is provided with NetWare/IP and FTP Services for IntranetWare. You can use these products to add DNS to your network, or you can use an existing DNS server.

To configure your NetWare Web Server to use the name services of a DNS server, use a text editor to create a file named RESOLV.CFG in the directory SYS:ETC. Enter the following text in this file:

```
domain domain_name
```

```
nameserver IP_address
```

The *domain_name* variable is the name of the domain in which your server is installed. The *IP_address* variable is the IP address of the DNS server. You should be able to get this information from the administrator of the DNS server.

TIP

To use the services of a DNS server, you must create the RESOLV.TXT file. Installing the DNS server on the same server as your NetWare Web Server does not remove this requirement.

Configuration Tools for Your Web Site

Although the NetWare Web Server does not require configuration, there are a number of configuration changes you may want to make. We describe the following changes in this appendix:

- ▶ Controlling access to your Web site

- ▶ Supporting dynamic Web pages

- ▶ Moving the document root directory

- ▶ Controlling directory indexing

- ▶ Checking site status

- ▶ Adjusting the Web server processing power

- ▶ For more information

Most of the configuration changes you will want to make can be performed using the NetWare Web Manager utility. Some configuration changes must be entered manually into the configuration files.

USING THE NETWARE WEB MANAGER UTILITY

The NetWare Web Manager utility (WEBMGR.EXE) is installed in the SYS:\ PUBLIC directory when the NetWare Web Server is installed. Because this is a Windows-based utility, you may want to create a program icon to launch this for you.

To start the NetWare Web Manager utility and select a NetWare Web Server to manage, complete the following steps:

1 • From your client computer, map a drive to the SYS: volume on your NetWare Web Server.

2 • Start the WEBMGR.EXE program in SYS:\PUBLIC using the Windows RUN command or a program icon that you have created.

3 • If the Web Server's IP address or domain name appears in the bottom section of the File menu, select the Web Server. If the NetWare Web Server does not appear in the File menu, choose Select Server from the File menu, select the Web server root directory, SYS:\WEB, and then click OK.

After you select the NetWare Web Server, the NetWare Web Server dialog box appears. This is the only dialog box that you can use to change the NetWare Web Server configuration.

4 • If the Full Server Name text box does not contain an IP address or a domain name for your server, you must enter it. This information is required. (Domain names are discussed later in this appendix.)

5 • Enter the e-mail address of the administrator for this server.

6 • After you complete your configuration changes, click OK to save the changes.

7 • If you have made changes to the Web Server configuration, the NetWare Web Manager utility prompts you to restart the server. To activate the changes, click Save & Restart, and then enter the password for the NetWare Web Server.

TIP

To restart the server using the NetWare Manager utility, you must know the password for the utility and your client must be configured for TCP/IP communications. If these conditions are not met, the utility saves your changes, but does not restart the server.

TIP

To restart the Web Server at the system console prompt, enter the following commands:

```
Unload HTTP

Load HTTP
```

EDITING THE NETWARE WEB SERVER CONFIGURATION FILES MANUALLY

The NetWare Web Server configuration settings are saved in the default configuration files shown in Table E.2.

T A B L E E . 2

Default Configuration Files

CONFIGURATION FILE	DESCRIPTION
SYS:\WEB\CONFIG\HTTPD.CFG	This is the principal NetWare Web Server configuration file. This file cannot be moved. It specifies the server name, the Web Server TCP/IP port, the administrator e-mail address, the administrator password, log file options, the location of the other configuration files, and the maximum number of threads to be allocated to the Web Server.
SYS:\WEB\CONFIG\SRM.CFG	This file specifies the resources available to the NetWare Web Server. It defines the locations of the document root directory, any script directories, and any image map directories. The default index filename (INDEX.HTM) is also defined here, as are the indexing options and other resource-related features. The location of this file is specified in HTTPD.CFG by the following directive: ResourceConfig config/srm.cfg
SYS:\WEB\CONFIG\ACCESS.CFG	This is the global Web access configuration file, which controls access and indexing options to the directories within your server root. This is also where SSI commands are enabled for a directory. The location of this file is specified in HTTPD.CFG by the following directive: AccessConfig config/access.cfg
path\ACCESS.WWW	This is the local Web access configuration file, which controls access to the files within the directory in which it is located. The name of this file is specified in SRM.CFG by the following directive: AccessFileName access.www
SYS:\WEB\CONFIG\MIME.TYP	This is the MIME type configuration file. Each line in this file specifies a *Multipurpose Internet Mail Extension* (MIME) type and one or more file extensions to be associated with that type. When the browser requests a file, the server refers to the MIME.TYP file to determine if a MIME type has been configured for that extension. If a MIME type is specified, that MIME type is sent to the browser to identify the type of file the server is forwarding. The location of this file is specified in HTTPD.CFG by the following directive: TypesConfig config/mime.typ

Many (but not all) of your configuration changes can be made with the NetWare Web Manager utility, which saves changes to these files. To edit any of these files manually, open a text editor program, make the changes, and save the file. To better understand how the NetWare Web Server uses these files, you may want to view them before and after you make changes with the NetWare Web Manager utility.

Controlling Access to Your Web Site

After you install the NetWare Web Server, everyone who has IP access to your network has the ability to read all the files in your Web site. Since you created the Web directory structure, you may be the only one who can make changes to Web pages. Most Web server administrators will need to make some changes to the Web Server access rights. These changes fall into two categories: Web Access Rights and NetWare File System Rights.

CHANGING WEB ACCESS RIGHTS

You can use the NetWare Web Manager utility to limit access to the site or to specific directories (and their subdirectories). You can limit access by restricting the following types of entities:

- ► Select NDS users

- ► All valid NDS users

- ► NDS user groups

- ► Hostnames

- ► IP addresses

- ► IP networks

- ► Domain names

TIP

You can also limit access to your site using filters provided in IntranetWare or the NetWare Multiprotocol Router.

Although the NetWare Web Server offers a variety of access control methods, they are not without cost. Using any of these methods restricts access to only those users that are explicitly defined to the Web Server, which means you must define and administer all the users and systems that can access your Web Server.

TIP

To administer access to NDS user groups, you must edit the ACCESS.CFG file manually. For instructions on this procedure, refer to the NetWare Web Server README file. The README.TXT file is in the server root directory (SYS:WEB) and on the CD-ROM under the directory WEBSERV\DISK1.

To restrict access to your Web Server, complete the following steps:

1 • Start the NetWare Web Server Manager program and select your NetWare Web Server, as described earlier in this appendix.

2 • Choose the User Access page (to restrict access by users) or the System Access page (to restrict access based on IP addresses, host names, or domain names) on the dialog box that appears.

3 • Select the directory to which you want the restrictions to apply.

TIP

Remember, you are disabling directory access to everyone who is not specified on this page. If your access list will be too large, you might want to reorganize your site so that you can create a smaller access list.

4 • Set the restrictions you want.

    a. If you're restricting access to specific NDS users, mark either the All Valid Users check box (to enable access to all valid NDS users) or select a user from the list that appears and click Add to Authorized Users List check box (to enable access for a specific user). If you do not enter a context for your users, each user will have to enter a fully distinguished name, starting with a period. To specify the NDS context of the users, enter a context in the NDS Context text box. If you must support users in multiple contexts, enter the context that is common to all the users. The users must then enter their usernames relative to this context.

    b. If you're restricting by system access, specify the IP address, full host name, or full domain name to which you want to give directory access. Then select a user from the list that appears and click Add to Authorized Systems List.

5 • Click OK to save your changes.

6 • If you have made changes to the Web Server configuration, the NetWare Web Manager utility prompts you to restart the server. To activate the changes, click Save & Restart, and then enter the password for the NetWare Web Server.

NETWARE RIGHTS ISSUES

NetWare rights control who can view the Web pages, who can edit and author Web pages, and who can change the NetWare Web Server configuration.

Unless you have changed Web access rights with the NetWare Web Manager, user Public (in the root container) should have read and file scan access rights to the site root directory and all subdirectories that contain pages, images, or page components that you want the public to view. When planning NetWare access rights for Web page authors, remember that the authors will need write, create, and modify access to all directories that contain the files they are publishing.

Table E.3 lists the default directories to which customers and Web authors need rights.

TABLE E.3	DIRECTORY	GUIDELINES
Directories That Customers and Web Authors Use	Document Root Directory	Default location: Sys:\WEB\DOCS
	Server Side Include directory	Default location: Sys:\WEB\DOCS\SSI
	Images/Graphics	Default location: Sys:WEB\DOCS\IMAGES

Table E.4 lists the directories that control NetWare Web Server configuration or enable program access to the server volumes. These directories should not be available to the public.

TABLE E.4	DIRECTORY	GUIDELINES
Directories That the Administrator Uses	\Config	Default location: SYS:\WEB\CONFIG Restrict rights to NetWare Web Server administrators. The files in this folder control NetWare Web Server operation and Web access rights.
	\Maps	Default location: SYS:\WEB\MAPS Restrict rights to the Web authors that create image maps. The files in this folder control how user mouse-clicks on a Web page graphic are interpreted. Most user mouse-clicks will activate a link to another Web page.
	Scripts directories	Default scripts directories: SYS:\WEB\SCRIPTS, SYS:\WEB\SCRIPTS\PERL Restrict rights to the people responsible for creating and maintaining scripts. Scripts enable the dynamic Web pages described later, and can write data to your server's hard disk.

Supporting Dynamic Web Pages

When creating dynamic Web pages, the first feature you will need to address is the Server Side Include (SSI) command set. Next, you'll need to administer the Common Gateway Interface (CGI) scripts.

ADMINISTERING SSI COMMAND USAGE

Server Side Include (SSI) commands allow Web authors to insert variables into their otherwise static Web pages. Using an SSI command, the author can dynamically insert text from another file or display the current date and time. The SSI commands supported by the NetWare Web Server are described in the default Web pages (INDEX.HTM) provided with the NetWare Web Server. This section describes what you need to know to support the Web page authors.

Three rules govern the use of SSI commands in Web pages:

▸ Any file that contains SSI commands must use the .SSI extension.

▸ An SSI file cannot include text from another SSI file.

▸ Before any SSI processing occurs, the NetWare Web Server administrator must enable SSI processing for the directory in which the SSI command is stored. (The SYS:WEB\DOCS\SSI directory is enabled when the NetWare Web Server is installed.)

SSI processing is not enabled for all directories because it requires additional processing power from the server and reduces response times for Web page viewers. This extra processing time is not excessive, but it is best to enable SSI processing only in those directories where it will be used.

To enable SSI command processing for a directory, complete the following steps:

1 • Start the NetWare Web Server Manager program and select your NetWare Web Server as described earlier in this appendix.

2 • Choose the Directories page in the dialog box that appears.

3 • If the directory for which you want to enable SSI commands appears in the Existing Directories box, select it.

4 • If the directory you want does not appear in the Existing Directories box, use the Browse button to locate the directory, click Add, and then select your directory in the Existing Directories box.

5 • After you have selected the directory, check the Enable Includes check box and click Change. (You must click Change. If you click OK instead of Change, it will not change the directory setting.)

6 • Click OK to save your changes.

7 • If you have made changes to the Web Server configuration, the NetWare Web Manager utility prompts you to restart the server. To activate the changes, click Save & Restart, and then enter the password for the NetWare Web Server.

SUPPORTING CGI SCRIPTS

The *Common Gateway Interface* (CGI) is the feature that allows the NetWare Web Server to modify Web pages before they are sent to a browser. First, the NetWare Web Server scans an HTML file for SSI commands or commands that reference other programs called *scripts*. If any SSI commands or scripts are located, the NetWare Web Server processes them, inserts the results in the HTML file, and sends it to the Web browser.

Because CGI scripts can write data to your server's hard drives, you should administer their use carefully. Store the script files in directories that the Web page users cannot access, and limit create, write, and modify rights to the script programmers. Table E.5 lists the default directories that store script files.

T A B L E E.5	SCRIPT TYPE	DEFAULT DIRECTORY/NOTES
Default Directories that Store Script Files	BASIC RCGI scripts	SYS:WEB\SCRIPTS These are BASIC computer programs. Remote CGI (RCGI) scripts are written to be platform-independent so that they can be easily adapted to other computer operating systems. This directory is defined in the SRM.CFG file with the following directive: RemoteScriptAlias /scripts/ localhost:8001/scripts

(continued)

T A B L E E.5	SCRIPT TYPE	DEFAULT DIRECTORY/NOTES
Default Directories that Store Script Files (continued)	Perl RCGI scripts	SYS:WEB\SCRIPTS\PERL These are Perl computer programs. This directory is defined in the SRM.CFG file with the following directive: RemoteScriptAlias /perl/ localhost:8002/sys:Web/scripts/perl
	LCGI NLM	SYS:WEB\CGI-BIN Local CGI (LCGI) scripts are written to take advantage of a specific computer operating system-in this case, IntranetWare. This directory is defined in the SRM.CFG file with the following directive: RemoteScriptAlias /cgiproc/ localhost:8003/sys:Web/samples/cgiapp

Moving the Web Server's Document Root Directory

The default location for the document root directory is on the SYS: volume under the server root (SYS:\WEB\DOCS). As your Web site grows, you may want to move the document root to another volume to avoid filling up the SYS: volume.

To move the document root to another volume or directory, complete the following steps:

1 • Copy the document root directory and all of its subdirectories to the new location.

 Be sure to copy the complete directory structure (using the /s option with NCOPY or XCOPY) so that relative links in the Web pages are not invalidated.

2 • Start the NetWare Web Server Manager program and select your NetWare Web Server as described earlier in this appendix.

3 • Change the Server Root Directory parameter on the Server page to specify the path to the Web server document root directory.

4 • Click OK to save your changes.

5 • If you have made changes to the Web Server configuration, the NetWare Web Manager utility prompts you to restart the server. To activate the changes, click Save & Restart, then enter the password for the NetWare Web Server.

6 • Test your Web site links to be sure that the directory move did not invalidate any links.

All relative links within the document root should work in the new location, as should all explicit references to other Web sites.

TIP

You can still view your old document root pages in your browser by entering the domain name and path to the index file in the old root (for example, file:///SYS:/ path_to_index_file/index_file). This may be useful while you are troubleshooting links that aren't working.

7 •. When you are satisfied that the Web site is working correctly with the new document root, delete the former document root.

Controlling Directory Indexing

Directory indexing is a feature that creates an index for a browser when the default directory is missing. If a browser user enters a URL for a file, the browser receives that file. If a browser enters a URL for a directory, one of the following occurs:

► If the default index file (INDEX.HTM) is present, that file is displayed. (The default name is defined in the SRM.CFG file with the DirectoryIndex directive.)

> ▶ If the default index file is missing and directory indexing is disabled, no files are found.

> ▶ If the default index file is missing and directory indexing is enabled, the server builds an index page that appears at the browser. This page lists all the files in the directory, along with links that can display or download the files.

You can use the NetWare Web Manager utility to manage directory indexing on a directory-by-directory basis. This utility stores your configuration in the ACCESS.CFG file. Table E.6 lists the index options.

T A B L E E.6 *Index Options*	INDEX OPTION	FUNCTION
	Fancy indexing	For each file in a directory, fancy indexing displays the filename listed by conventional indexing and adds an icon, the last modified date, the file size, and a file description.
	Icons are links	When fancy indexing is enabled, this option defines the file icons as links, so that the browser user can select the file by clicking on the icon.
	Scan titles	When fancy indexing is enabled, the "Scan titles" option causes the server to scan all HTML documents and include the HTML document title in the index as a file description. If this option is disabled, the file description is blank.

To set the directory indexing options for a directory, complete the following steps:

1 • Start the NetWare Web Server Manager program and select your NetWare Web Server as described earlier in this appendix.

2 • Choose the Directories page in the dialog box that appears.

3 • If the directory for which you want to set indexing options appears in the Existing Directories box, select it.

4 • If the directory you want does not appear in the Existing Directories box, use the Browse button to locate the directory, click Add, and then select your directory in the Existing Directories box.

5 • After you have selected the directory, check the Enable Indexing check box.

6 • If you want to enable any of the indexing options, check the corresponding check boxes.

7 • Click Change, and then click OK to save your changes.

8 • If you have made changes to the Web Server configuration, the NetWare Web Manager utility prompts you to restart the server. To activate the changes, click Save & Restart, and then enter the password for the NetWare Web Server.

Checking Site Status

You can check your site status by using the tools listed in Table E.7.

T A B L E E.7	TOOL	PURPOSE
Tools for Checking Site Status	NetWare Web Server console	The Web Server console displays the server and document roots, server statistics, and server status messages, which are recorded in the Web Server error log.
	Access log	The access log specifies the IP address or domain name of all users who access your server. It also lists the files that have been accessed. The default configuration of the server records IP addresses in the access log. If you set up the server as a DNS client as described earlier in this appendix, the access log records domain names whenever they are available.

(continued)

	TOOL	PURPOSE
TABLE E.7 *Tools for Checking Site* *Status (continued)*	Error log	The error log records the errors and messages that appear on the Web Server console.
	Debug log	The debug log records information that you can use to troubleshoot problems with the Web Server.

VIEWING THE NETWARE WEB SERVER CONSOLE

The NetWare Web Server console (see Figure E.2) is available whenever the Web Server is active, which is whenever the HTTP NLM is loaded. Just press Alt-Esc until the Novell HTTP Server console appears.

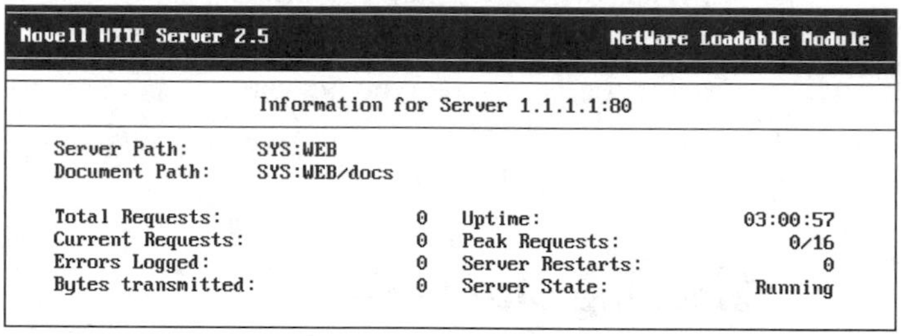

FIGURE E.2

The NetWare Web Server Console

```
Novell HTTP Server 2.5                              NetWare Loadable Module

                           Information for Server 1.1.1.1:80

      Server Path:      SYS:WEB
      Document Path:    SYS:WEB/docs

      Total Requests:               0    Uptime:                 03:00:57
      Current Requests:             0    Peak Requests:              0/16
      Errors Logged:                0    Server Restarts:               0
      Bytes transmitted:            0    Server State:            Running
```

Note the Peak Requests statistic on the Web Server console. This number, 0/16 in this example, lists the maximum number of server threads used (0) and the maximum number of server threads available (16). If the number of server threads used begins to approach the maximum number available, you can configure the NetWare Web Server to use more threads. If you are low on memory and the Web Server is not using many of the allocated threads, you can save memory by reducing the number of allocated threads. These procedures are provided later in this appendix.

VIEWING AND ADMINISTERING LOG FILES

You can use the NetWare Web Manager utility to view and administer log files. To view and administer any log file, complete the following steps:

1 • Start the NetWare Web Server Manager program and select your NetWare Web Server as described earlier in this appendix.

2 • Select the appropriate Open command from the Log menu.

3 • Choose the Logs page in the dialog box that appears.

4 • Set the log options using the information in Table E.8.

5 • Click OK to save your changes.

6 • If you have made changes to the Web Server configuration, the NetWare Web Manager utility prompts you to restart the server. To activate the changes, click Save & Restart, and then enter the password for the NetWare Web Server.

T A B L E E.8	
Log Options	

LOG OPTION	DESCRIPTION AND USAGE
Log file handling	This option determines whether there are one or more log files. If you select the "Do not roll logs" option, the NetWare Web Server creates one of each type of log file. When the log file is full, the oldest entries are deleted. If you select the "Roll logs as needed" option, the Web Server archives all the log file data when the log gets full, creating an empty log file in which to store new data.
Server debug log options	This option enables or disables the logging of server debug messages.
Maximum log size	This option defines the maximum size of each log file. Notice that the NetWare Web Manager utility calculates the maximum amount of disk space used by the log files and the old logs. This appears on the Logs page.
Maximum number of old logs	This option specifies how many old log files will be created. If you already have filled all the old logs and then you fill the current log, the data in the oldest log file is lost.
Default button	The default button returns all log options to the default options supplied with the NetWare Web Server

Adjusting the Web Server Processing Power

As mentioned earlier, the Web Server console displays the maximum number of threads used by the NetWare Web Server. To provide more performance capacity (at the expense of server memory), you can increase the number of threads available to the Web Server. To reduce the memory required by the Web Server (and decrease the performance capacity of the Web Server), you can decrease the number of threads available.

To adjust the maximum number of threads used by the Web Server, edit the MaxThreads directive in the HTTPD.CFG file. The valid entries are 1 through 255, but entries above 40 may decrease the server performance.

For More Information

This appendix introduced the concepts and administration tasks that will help you establish your Web site using the NetWare Web Server. For more information on the NetWare Web Server, refer to one of the following resources:

▶ The default Web pages (INDEX.HTM) provided with the NetWare Web Server.

▶ The *Dynamic Web Page Programmer's Guide*, which describes how to use BASIC and Perl CGI scripts to create dynamic Web pages. You can view this guide with your browser by specifying the following URL (replace x with the drive letter of the IntranetWare CD-ROM: File:///x:/PRODUCTS/WEBSERV/DISK1/WEB/DOCS/ONLINE/WPGUID E/INDEX.HTM

▶ The Novell Web site, at *www.novell.com*, for updated information about the NetWare Web Server.

Exploring the "Intranet" and Novell's Internet Access Server

Just when we were beginning to get comfortable with the Internet technology, the Intranet technology appeared. From a technical standpoint, an intranet is simply a Web server that is confined to a private internal network and publishes files to a private audience such as the employees of a corporation. A true WWW server is connected to the Internet and publishes files to the world.

The reason that intranet technology is so popular is that people can use their WWW browsers to view the private information. The intranet server publishes shared information in HTML files that can be created with almost any word processor or text editor and can be viewed with Internet browsers on almost every operating system.

Throughout this appendix, you will learn the basics of installing IntranetWare in this context, including how to

- ▶ **Install and Manage Novell Internet Access Server Components**

- ▶ To install the Novell Internet Access Server components on the server, use INSTALL.NLM, select Product Options, and choose Install a Product Not Listed. Then specify the path to the Novell Internet Access Server 4 CD-ROM.

- ▶ To configure the IPX/IP gateway on the server, use INETCFG.NLM.

- ▶ To install the client support for the IPX/IP gateway on workstations, install NetWare Client32 and choose Additional Options (on Windows 3.1x) or Customize (on Windows 95).

- ▶ To work with the IPX/IP gateway object in NDS and to configure access rights, add the IPX/IP gateway snap-in utility to the NetWare Administrator utility by editing the NWADMN3X.INI file.

- ▶ **Install and Manage FTP Services for IntranetWare**

- ▶ To install FTP Services for IntranetWare, use INSTALL.NLM, select Product Options, and choose Install a Product Not Listed. Then specify the path to the FTP Services for IntranetWare CD-ROM.

> ▶ To configure FTP Services for IntranetWare and to create an Anonymous FTP user account, use UNICON.NLM.

IntranetWare is Novell's comprehensive platform for a modern, full-service intranet. It starts with NetWare 4.11, then adds the following intranet and Internet features:

> ▶ IPX/IP Gateway. This gateway enables administrators to allow IPX-based workstations to access TCP/IP-based resources, such as FTP and the World Wide Web, without having to install or configure TCP/IP on those workstations. The gateway also lets you implement access control—you can limit users by TCP port number, IP address or the target host, and the time of day.

> ▶ MultiProtocol Router 3.1. This feature provides WAN (Wide Area Network) connectivity, routing multiple protocols over leased lines, frame relay, or ISDN lines. This capability allows you to connect network users to an Internet Service Provider (ISP).

> ▶ Netscape Navigator. This is the Web browser that lets you locate and read information stored on the Internet or intranet.

> ▶ FTP Services for IntranetWare. FTP services let you configure FTP access for your intranet.

In your IntranetWare package, you'll find the following CD-ROMs:

> ▶ The NetWare 4.11 Operating System CD-ROM, which contains the regular NetWare 4.11 product software and the NetWare Web Server. The NetWare Web Server also contains the Netscape Navigator Web browser (and a single-user license for the browser).

> ▶ The NetWare 4.11 Online Documentation CD-ROM, which contains the DynaText documentation for NetWare 4.11.

▸ The Novell Internet Access Server 4 CD-ROM, which contains most of the IntranetWare features: the IPX/IP gateway, MultiProtocol Router 3.1 for WAN connectivity, and the Netscape Navigator Web browser (multi-user license). This CD-ROM also contains HTML-formatted documentation for the IPX/IP gateway.

▸ The FTP Services for IntranetWare CD-ROM, which contains the FTP services and configuration utilities.

TIP

To read the HTML-formatted documentation for the Novell Internet Access Server product, use a Web browser from a workstation.

For instructions on installing the Netscape Navigator browser that comes with the NetWare Web Server on the NetWare 4.11 Operating System CD-ROM, see Appendix E. For instructions on installing the browser from the Novell Internet Access Server CD-ROM, see the Internet Access Server 4 Quick Reference Guide, which comes with your IntranetWare kit. The two browsers are identical, and they are placed on both CD-ROMs primarily for convenience.

TIP

If you have IntranetWare, you are allowed to use as many copies of the Web browser as your IntranetWare user license permits. In other words, if you bought a 50-user version of IntranetWare, you can let 50 users use the browser. If you have NetWare 4.11 alone, you have only a single-user license to the browser.

Installing the Novell Internet Access Server Software

Before installing the Novell Internet Access Server software, which will provide the software necessary to run the routing, wan connectivity, and IPX/IP gateway, you must first install a NetWare 4.11 server as usual. Then you can install the Novell Internet Access Server software. During the installation, the Netscape

Navigator browser will be copied to the SYS:NETSCAPE so that you can later install it on workstations.

To install Novell Internet Access Server components on the NetWare 4.11 server, complete the following steps:

1 • Insert the Novell Internet Access Server 4 CD-ROM in a drive on the server and mount the CD-ROM as a NetWare volume.

2 • At the server console, load INSTALL.NLM.

3 • From the Installation Options menu, choose Product Options, then choose Install a Product Not Listed.

4 • To specify a path to the installation software, press <F3> and type

```
NIAS4:\NIAS\INSTALL
```

5 • Choose Install Product. The Install To Servers list displays the local server name. The value in the title reflects the number of servers to be installed. If you want to install Novell Internet Access Server software on a remote server, press Insert to add the server to the list. If an expected server is not displayed, ensure that the latest version of RSPAWN.NLM is loaded on that server. To remove a server from the Install To Servers list, select the server, press Delete, and select Yes at the prompt.

6 • From the Install To Servers menu, press Enter and select Yes to begin the installation. Servers are installed in alphabetical order. If you are installing to a remote server, you will be prompted to log in as an administrator. Enter the administrator's full login name and password.

7 • When the prompt "Install previously created configuration files?" appears, select No.

8 • When prompted for the Novell Internet Access Server license diskette, insert the NetWare 4.11/IntranetWare license diskette in the specified drive and press Enter. Once the login, license, and configuration file information for each server are provided, the installation begins copying files to the destinations.

9 • When the installation is completed, you can read the installation log file if you desire. Choose Display Log File. When you're finished reviewing the log, press Esc to return to the Installation Options menu.

10 • To verify that the Novell Internet Access Server software installed correctly, choose Product Options from the Installation Options menu, then select Configure/View/Remove Installed Products. The Currently Installed Products list appears, showing entries for the NetWare MultiProtocol Router 3.1 software, WAN Extensions 3.1, and Novell Internet Access Server 4. Press Esc to return to the Installation Options menu.

11 • From the Installation Options menu, select NCF Files Options, then choose the Edit STARTUP.NCF file. Modify the STARTUP.NCF file for each installed server to include the following line at the end of the file if you are using the IntranetWare server to make a WAN connection:

```
SET MINIMUM PACKET RECEIVE BUFFERS=400

SET MAXIMUM PACKET RECEIVE BUFFERS=1000
```

The value of the second parameter can be increased as needed.

12 • To exit the installation screen, press Esc and then select Yes to save the changes.

13 • Bring down and restart the server to make sure all the correct NLMs are loaded. At the server's console, type:

```
DOWN

RESTART SERVER
```

In addition to updating server NLM files stored in SYS:\SYSTEM, the installation process installs the client files in the SYS:\PUBLIC\CLIENT\WIN95 and SYS:\PUBLIC\CLIENT\WIN31 directories. The Netscape Navigator files are installed in the SYS:\NETSCAPE\32 and SYS:\NETSCAPE\16 directories.

The IPX/IP Gateway

The IPX/IP gateway is an important part of the Novell Internet Access Server components of IntranetWare. With this gateway, IPX-based clients can access the Internet and other IP-based resources without having to install TCP/IP on the workstations themselves. The IPX/IP gateway gets installed on the server as part of the Novell Internet Access Server installation. To take advantage of the gateway, you must install IPX/IP Gateway support on each workstation. Client gateway support is included as an option in the NetWare Client32 installation.

Not having to use TCP/IP on each workstation is a benefit in many cases because there are significant management tasks associated with maintaining TCP/IP workstations. With TCP/IP, you have to manually keep track of and configure many items for each individual workstation, such as the unique IP address, subnet mask, IP addresses of the default router and the domain name servers, and the domain name.

An IPX/IP gateway removes much of the individual management hassles that occur with maintaining TCP/IP workstations by letting you retain IPX on those workstations.

When the IPX/IP gateway is installed on the IntranetWare server, the server runs IPX to communicate with the IPX workstations on the network and TCP/IP so that it can communicate with the Internet. From the viewpoint of a remote host on the Internet, all traffic through the gateway seems to originate from the IP address assigned to the gateway server. Because the IPX/IP gateway uses only a single IP address, regardless of the number of users it supports, the private network is safe from outside interference. Using the Novell IPX/IP Gateway alleviates the difficulties of administering a TCP/IP environment by providing ease of management and centralized control over Internet access.

By using Novell's IPX/IP gateway, you can run only IPX on the network workstations. Compared to IP, IPX is simple to manage. It assigns user connections dynamically, eliminating the need for a registered address to be configured at each desktop. Since IPX addresses are assigned dynamically, workstation IPX address conflicts do not occur. Users can move transparently between IPX networks, and traveling IPX users can roam between multiple networks within an enterprise.

The Novell IPX/IP Gateway allows you to limit access to Internet services by the type of traffic (for example, Web browsing or FTP) and by remote host. Either type of restriction can be limited to specific times during the day to reduce "rush hour" traffic on an Internet connection.

CONFIGURING THE IPX/IP GATEWAY

After you've installed Novell Internet Access Server on the server, you can configure the IPX/IP gateway. To do this, complete the following steps:

1 • At the server console, load INETCFG.NLM. If you are asked if you want to transfer your LAN driver, protocol, and remote access commands, choose Yes. What this really means is that you will move the LOAD and BIND commands from the AUTOEXEC.NCF file to INETCFG's startup files.

2 • From the main menu, select Protocols, then choose TCP/IP, then choose IPX/IP Gateway Configuration.

3 • Specify "enabled" in the Enabled for the IPX/IP Gateway field so that the gateway will become operational.

4 • If you want to record when clients access a service over the gateway, enable the Client Logging field. The log is stored in a field called GW_AUDIT.LOG in the SYS: volume.

5 • In the Console Messages field, specify the type of messages you want to display on the gateway logging screen and the gateway status log file (GW_INFO.LOG in the SYS: volume). You can choose "Informational, warning, and errors" (the default), "Warnings and errors only," or "Errors only."

6 • To enforce access restrictions (which you set using the NetWare Administrator utility), enable the Access Control field.

7 • In the Domain Name field, specify the name of the domain in which the gateway is installed. Your Internet Service Provider may provide you with this name.

8 • In the Name Server fields, specify the IP addresses of any active domain name servers. Your Internet Service Provider may provide these addresses.

9 • Press Esc twice, then log in as user Admin when prompted.

10 • If you want to configure the gateway to use leased lines, frame relay, or ISDN lines, complete the following steps (see the documentation that came with Novell Internet Access Server for more specific details about parameters):

   a. Choose Boards from the INETCFG.NLM main menu. Then specify the appropriate WAN driver and configure any necessary parameters.

   b. Choose Network Interfaces from the INETCFG.NLM main menu. Then configure the appropriate WAN interfaces.

   c. Choose WAN Call Directory from INETCFG's main menu and press Ins to configure a new WAN call destination, then configure any necessary parameters.

   d. Choose Bindings from INETCFG's main menu, press Ins, and bind TCP/IP to the appropriate board or driver.

11 • Exit INETCFG.NLM and save the changes you made.

12 • Reboot the server to make the changes take effect.

After you've enabled and configured the gateway, a gateway server NDS object appears in the NDS tree in the same context as the server on which it is installed. The gateway object's name is the same as the server's name, with -GW added to the end of the name. This gateway object assists gateway clients in locating active IPX/IP gateway servers.

ADDING IPX/IP GATEWAY TOOLS TO THE NETWARE ADMINISTRATOR UTILITY

To work with the IPX/IP gateway object, you'll need to add the gateway's snap-in utility to the NetWare Administrator utility. This will allow NetWare Administrator to recognize the new gateway object and the new access control property that was added to certain objects. (This property is explained later in this appendix.)

The IPX/IP gateway snap-in utility works only with the 16-bit version of NetWare Administrator (which runs on Windows 3.1x).

To add the IPX/IP gateway support to the NetWare Administrator utility on a Windows 3.1 workstation, complete the following steps:

1 • If you haven't yet opened the NetWare Administrator utility, open it and close it.

2 • From the Windows File Manager on your workstation, double-click on the NWADMN3X.INI file (located in the WINDOWS directory) to open it for editing.

3 • Under the heading [Snapin Object DLLs WIN3X], add the following line:

   IPXGW3X=IPXGW3X.DLL

4 • Save and close the file. Now the NetWare Administrator utility will recognize the IPX/IP gateway object.

CONTROLLING ACCESS TO THE IPX/IP GATEWAY

After the IPX/IP Gateway server is fully installed and configured, you can use the NetWare Administrator utility to give the IPX/IP gateway server access control information for the various objects in the NDS tree. Then you can use NetWare Administrator to set restrictions for users, groups, or containers.

To give the gateway server access control information, use the NetWare Administrator utility to make the following changes to the NDS tree:

▸ Make the Public object a trustee of the Gateway object, with browse object rights and read and compare property rights (for all properties).

▶ Make the Public object a trustee of the File Server Object that is running the IPX/IP Gateway, with browse object rights and read and compare property rights for the Network Address property only (under selected properties).

▶ Make the Gateway object a trustee in the Root object, with browse object rights and read and compare property rights (for all properties).

You control user access through the IPX/IP Gateway by using the NetWare Administrator utility. As the point of connection between a NetWare network and a TCP/IP network, an IPX/IP gateway is in an ideal position to enforce restrictions on traffic between the two networks.

These access restrictions can be stored in two properties that are added to the User, Group, Organization, or Organizational Unit objects when the gateway is enabled:

▶ The first property, service restrictions, tells the gateway object which applications may be used by the object and which are restricted. These restrictions are based on the port number.

▶ The second property, host restrictions, tells the gateway which remote hosts are restricted from the object. These restrictions are based on the IP address.

Storing access restrictions in the NDS objects provides a single database of restrictions that all gateway servers share. You do not need to configure access control separately on each gateway. Restrictions are active on all gateways regardless of whether they are applied to an entire organization or created individually for each user.

To place access restrictions on a User, Group, Organization, or Organizational Unit object, use the NetWare Administrator utility and select the object in question. Then choose Details under the Object menu and open the IPX/IP Gateway Service Restrictions page. On this page, you can enter restrictions for this object.

To restrict access to a specific Internet site, place a host restriction on the IP address of that site. To prevent certain types of traffic from being forwarded by the server, create a service restriction for the appropriate port number. For example, you might restrict

Web browser access to certain hours during the day, but allow FTP or TELNET access during those same hours. You could also place the remote host "www.games.com" off-limits. To prevent news readers from operating across the gateway, you might place a restriction on traffic to port number 119 (News) at any site.

INSTALLING THE IPX/IP GATEWAY CLIENT

The IPX/IP gateway support is installed as an option in the NetWare Client32 workstation software. The following instructions explain how to install this support on Windows 3.1x workstations and Windows 95 workstations.

The Windows 3.1x Client

To configure the IPX/IP gateway support on a Windows 3.1x workstation, you install NetWare Client32. During the installation process when the Additional Options screen appears, complete the following steps:

1 • Select the NetWare IPX/IP Gateway check box, then select Next to continue.

2 • When the Configuration menu for these options appears, enter the appropriate information and select Next to continue.

3 • When you've finished, choose OK to restart your computer. When the workstation comes back up, the Novell IPX/IP Gateway Switcher icon appears in the NetWare Tools program group. The gateway switcher program switches the client from gateway operation to native TCP/IP operation (if TCP/IP is available on the client).

4 • Double-click the Gateway Switcher icon, then click Enable Gateway to enable the gateway. You can also enter the name of a preferred gateway server if you have more than one gateway installed in the network. If a preferred gateway server is configured, the gateway task will attempt to locate that gateway server through NDS and connect to it. If the preferred gateway server is not available, the gateway client will search for other gateway servers, first in the user's NDS context, then in the bindery of the attached server, then finally it will query for a SAP broadcast of any gateway server.

Note: There is no linkage between the preferred file server and the preferred gateway server. A user may be attached to file server A while using a gateway server that resides on file server B.

The Windows 95 Client

To configure the IPX/IP gateway support on a Windows 95 workstation, you install NetWare Client 32. When the installation is finished, complete the following steps:

1 • Click on Customize to customize the client.

2 • Choose Add.

3 • In the Type of Network Component You Want to Install box, double-click on Protocol.

4 • In the Manufacturers box, choose Novell, then double-click on Novell NetWare IPX/IP Gateway.

5 • Choose OK to exit the Network configuration screen.

6 • If you receive a prompt to select a preferred gateway server, click Yes, enter the name of your preferred IPX/IP Gateway server, and select OK. If a preferred gateway server is configured, the gateway task will attempt to locate that gateway server through NDS and connect to it. If the preferred gateway server is not available, the gateway client will search for other gateway servers, first in the user's NDS context, then in the bindery of the attached server, then finally it will query for a SAP broadcast of any gateway server.

7 • If you asked for additional files, type the location of those files in the Copy Files From box. If you are asked for Client32 files, type in the path to the directory from which you ran SETUP.EXE.

8 • Click Yes to restart the computer. The IPX/IP Gateway Switcher program runs automatically during the first restart after installation. This switcher program switches the client from gateway operation to native TCP/IP operation (if TCP/IP is available on the client).

9 • To enable the gateway, click the Enable IPX/IP Gateway button, then click OK.

FTP Services for IntranetWare

In addition to the Novell Internet Access Server components, IntranetWare also includes FTP Services for IntranetWare. This feature, which is a subset of the NetWare UNIX Print Services 2.11 product, allows NetWare clients to use FTP to work with files on the Internet or intranet.

INSTALLING FTP SERVICES

To install FTP Services for IntranetWare on your server, complete the following steps:

1 • Mount the FTP Services CD-ROM as a volume on the NetWare 4.11 server.

2 • Load INSTALL.NLM on the server.

3 • Choose Product Options, then choose Install a Product Not Listed.

4 • Press F3, then type in the following path to the FTP Services files on the CD-ROM:

NWUXPS:\NWUXPS

5 • If you are asked to specify a host name, either press Enter to accept the default name displayed or enter the correct host name.

6 • Accept the default boot drive (or specify the correct drive from which the server boots).

7 • To install the online documentation for FTP Services, choose Yes. This documentation is separate from the regular NetWare online documentation and describes how to install and use FTP Services.

8 • If you have already installed the NetWare 4.11 DynaText viewer, choose No when asked if you want to install a new one.

   Note: If you receive the message "hosts.db does not exist," ignore it.

9 • When prompted for a user name, enter the ADMIN name and password.

10 • Choose the name service option you want to use on this server and answer any prompts necessary for the name service you choose. If you choose to use a local name service, the database that holds the name service information will be stored on this server and will be the master database. You can use the UNICON.NLM utility to work with the master database on a local server. If you choose to use a remote name service, that database will reside on another server. You can use UNICON.NLM only to view the database information but not modify it. You can choose one of the following options:

   ▸ Local DNS and Local NIS. This option stores both master databases on this server.

   ▸ Remote DNS and Remote NIS. This option uses the master databases stored on another server.

   ▸ Remote DNS and Local NIS. This option stores the master NIS database on this server and the DNS database on another server.

   ▸ No DNS and Remote NIS. This option stores the master NIS database on another server and does not provide DNS service at all.

11 • Follow any prompts necessary to initialize the name service and the product.

12 • To start FTP Services, press Ins and choose FTP Server. FTP Services will start running and will appear in the Running Services menu.

13 • To exit the installation program, press Esc as many times as necessary.

14 • Restart the server to make the new settings take effect, by typing:

```
DOWN
RESTART SERVER
CONFIGURING FTP SERVICES
```

With FTP Services, users can use FTP to access and transfer files from the intranet or Internet. If you desire, you can create an Anonymous FTP account for users to use. With an Anonymous account, any user can access the FTP service by typing in any password. (Any password will work; the FTP service doesn't actually authenticate the password.)

To configure an Anonymous FTP account, complete the following steps:

1 • At the server console, load UNICON.NLM.

2 • When prompted, enter the ADMIN user name and password.

3 • Choose Manage Services, then choose FTP Server, then choose Set Parameters.

4 • Choose Default Name Space and enter NFS. This will install the NFS name space on the server, which will allow the server to store UNIX files.

5 • Change the Anonymous User Access field to Yes so that the Anonymous account will be enabled.

6 • Choose Anonymous User's Home Directory and change the path from the volume SYS: (displayed as /sys) to a directory you prefer to use as the login directory for Anonymous FTP users.

7 • When finished, press Esc to exit the installation program and save the changes you've made.

8 • Return to the main menu by pressing Esc twice, then choose Perform File Operations, then choose View/Set File Permissions.

9 • Enter the path to the Anonymous user's home directory (specified in Step 6) and press F9 to see the permissions (the UNIX equivalent of trustee rights) that have been set for this directory. If the permissions are not correct, modify them on this screen. The permissions should be:

```
[U = rwx] [G = ---] [o = ---]
```

10 • Press Esc multiple times to exit UNICON and save the changes you've made.

11 • Even though you specified the NFS name space in Step 4, you still need to add it to the volume. (You only need to add the name space to the volume once. To see if you've already added NFS name space to a volume, type VOLUMES at the server console-the display will show which name spaces are supported on each volume.) If you need to add the name space, type the following command, replacing volume with the name of the volume:

```
ADD NAME SPACE NFS TO volume
```

Index

A

Access Control List. *See* ACL
access rights
  assigning to network applications, 526–527
  displaying for root directory, 365
  for NDS security, 113, 373–383
  printing, 731
  to SYSTEM directory, 250
  for traveling users, 406–407
  See also ACL; file system access rights; NDS
    security; *and specific rights listed by name*
account restrictions, 355, 357–359
  disabling accounts, 358
  expired accounts, 359
  Intruder Detection/Lockout, 369–371
  limiting concurrent connections, 359
  parameters for last login, 359
accounts
  group, 44
  user, 43–44
ACE (American Council on Education), 8
ACL (Access Control List), 412
  assigning rights to NDS objects, 372
  types of rights for, 337–338
ACME (A Cure for Mother Earth)
  building the NDS tree for, 218–234
  case study of security, 434–445
  divisions
    Administration, 200–203
    Crime Fighting, 198–199, 201
    Human Rights, 193–195
    Labs, 195–197
    Operations, 197–198, 199
  heroes of, 192
  mission of, 188–193
  organizational chart for, 192
  workflow, 204–207
    Administration, 207
    calculating the WHI, 206
    Crime Fighting division, 207
    for Distribution department, 205
    for Financial department, 204–205
    for Labs division, 205–206
    Public Relations department, 206
Add Self rights, 375
Admin user rights, 378, 401–402
Administration division (ACME), 200–203, 207
advantages
  of certification, 4–11, 24–29
  CNA education, 18–19
  of e-mail, 531–532
  of NLMs, 597
  of replication, 167–168
advertising Help Desks, 54–55

AFO (Auditing File objects), 138, 139
AFP Server objects, 139
Alias objects, 125, 140
  rights for, 407
American Council on Education (ACE), 8
ancestral inheritance, 391, 420
Application objects, 139
  NAL and, 529
  NDS resource access rights for, 407
  network applications, 528–529
application services, 105–106, 110
applications
  checking for multiuser capabilities, 525
  directories for, 249, 255
  drive mappings and DOS, 302
  MHS, 535–536
  network
    installing on workstations, 529–531
    managing, 525–526
  See also installation
architecture
  device drivers and SMS, 637, 638
  IntranetWare server, 596
  managing Client 16, 626–634
  managing Client 32, 616–618
  for NDS database, 120
  Novell Peripheral Architecture, 598
  RMF, 651–654
  SMS, 637–639
Archive Needed feature attribute, 426
assigning property rights, 376–377
Assignments page (NWADMIN), 708
asynchronous connections, 653–654
Attached Print Servers option (PCONSOLE), 736
attributes
  abbreviations for containers and objects, 155–156
  disk management, 340, 427–430
  displaying for root directory, 265
  feature, 340, 426–427
  on-line information for file system, 430
  security, 340, 424–426
  See also directory/file attributes
Attributes page button (NWADMIN), 265
Auditing File objects (AFO), 138, 139
auditing print servers, 714, 747–748
authentication. *See* login/password authentication
authenticators, 349, 350
AutoEndCap (/AU) line option (CAPTURE), 688
AUTOEXEC.BAT, 477
AUTOEXEC.NCF file, 581
automatic call distribution, 60–61
automatic client upgrades for Client 32, 621–622
automatic driver download (NDPS), 767
automatic hardware detection, 599
Available options menu (FILER utility), 262, 271

B

background authentication, 335–336, 351–353
   NCP packet signing, 352–353
   system performance, 352
   unique proof, 351, 352
   See also login/password authentication
Backing Up and Restoring Netware Directory Services in
   NetWare 4, 647
backing up files
   disaster planning and recovery, 83–85
   network management, 46–47
   on-line information about, 647
   responsibility for, 648
   SBACKUP session files and backup logs, 649
   steps for, 644–646
   Storage Management Services, 636–637
   strategies for, 641–642
   workstation backups, 648–649
   See also SBACKUP command (SMS)
bad block tables, 78
bad block tracking, 78–80
Banner (/B) line option (CAPTURE), 689
Banner type parameter (PCONSOLE), 742
batch files, documenting, 81
before you begin, installing the server, 562–564
bidirectional communication (NDPS), 766
BIND console command, 585
bindery
   distributing replicas and bindery context, 175
   flat server-centric, 115
   NDS and, 117–120
   partitioning, 163
   supervisor bindery password, 610
bindery mode (PCONSOLE), 733
Bindery Queue objects, 141
Bindery Reference Queue, 707
BLOCK.NDS file, 118
block suballocation, 263
blocking Supervisor rights, 394
boot files
   copying to DOS partition, 574
   documenting, 81, 82
BREAK command, 507
BROADCAST console command, 585–586
Browse rights, 374
Buffer size parameter (PCONSOLE), 742
building
   forms for printing, 720–721
   a log book, 559–560
   an NDS tree, 218–234
   print devices, 721–723
   a printing system (case study), 776–780

C

cabling
   maintenance of, 38
   troubleshooting, 87
cache size
   allocating, 566
   monitoring, 41, 42
calculating
   effective rights
      for file system, 421–423, 450–455
      for NDS, 397–401, 446–449
   server memory, 565
   the World Health Index, 206
Can't Compress disk management attribute, 427
CAPTURE command line utility, 682–683
   line options, 686–692
      AutoEndCap (/AU), 688
      Banner (/B), 689
      Copies (/C), 689
      Create (/CR), 691
      EndCapture (/EC), 691
      Form (/F), 690
      FormFeed (/FF), 690
      help (/?), 686
      Keep/No Keep (/K), 689
      Local Port Number (/L=n), 690
      No Banner (/NB), 689
      NoFormFeed (/NFF), 690
      Notify (/NOTI), 691
      Queue (/Q), 687
      Server (/S), 687
      Show (/SH), 687
      Tabs (/T), 689
      TimeOut (/TI), 688
   on-line information for, 692
   parallel and serial ports, 638
   PRINTCON, 755–756
   sample command, 691–692
career advantages for CNAs, 8–10, 24–29
case studies
   building an NDS tree, 218–234
   configuring
      login scripts, 550–552
      menu systems, 553–554
   creating directory structures, 317–318
   managing servers, 667–673
   printing systems
      building, 776–780
      managing, 784–785
      using, 781–783
   of security, 434–445
   simple installation, 659–666
CD command, 297–299
CD-ROM
   configuring as DOS device, 572

installing NetWare 4.11 using, 566
certification, 4–11
  for CNEs, 27–29
  college credit, 7–8
  credentials vs. experience, 13–15
  as educational intensive, 6–7
  employment advantages of, 8–10
  professional organizations, 11
  as proof of competence, 5
  salary and, 11
Certified Novell Administrator. *See* CNA (Certified Novell Administrator)
changing context, 209–212, 228–229
changing passwords, 360–361, 362
chaos theory, 203
choosing an installation method, 573
choosing printers, 696
Clarke, David J., 774
Class C-2 network systems, 342–343
CLEAR STATION console command, 586
CLIENT32.NLM file, 617
client support features, 100
Client 16 software, 286, 475–487
  AUTOEXEC.BAT, 477
  CONFIG.SYS file, 476–477
  NET.CFG, 479–487
  STARTNET.BAT, 477–479
  start-up files for, 475–476
  workstation management
    Netware DOS Requester, 630–634
    ODI and, 627–630
Client 32 software, 286–287, 466–475
  allocating cache size, 566
  connectivity
    downloading connectivity files, 465
    understanding network connections, 467–469
    with Windows 95, 469–471
    with Windows 3.1, 471–473
  installing for Windows 95, 619–622
    automatic client upgrades, 621–622
    installation steps, 620–621
    options, 619
  installing for Windows 3.1, 622–626
    Automatic Client Upgrade, 624–626
    configuration files modified while, 622
  logging in, 473–475
  security, 336, 346
  workstation architecture, 616–618
  workstation NLMs, 597
Cloud, the, 113–116
CLS command, 507
CNA (Certified Novell Administrator)
  applying education on the job, 15–17
  benefits to managers, 12–13
  career advantages for, 4–11, 24–29
  costs of certification, 19–24

credentials vs. experience, 13–15
  printing tasks (NWADMIN), 749–750
  role in network management, 32–33
  training and job security, 18–19
CNEs
  certification for, 27–29
  responsibilities of, 143
college credit, 7–8
commands
  additional login script, 507–508
  BREAK, 507
  CD, 297–299
  CLS, 507
  comparison of copy, 279
  console, 585–595
  CONTEXT, 507
  DOS CD, 305
  EXEC, 516–517
  FDISPLAY, 507
  FIRE PHASERS, 507
  GETO, 518–519
  GETP, 520
  GETR, 519
  GOTO, 508
  INCLUDE, 508
  ITEM, 515
  LASTLOGINTIME, 508
  LOAD, 517
  for login scripts, 495–498
  MAX CACHE SIZE, 566
  MENU, 513–514
  NCOPY, 279, 293–294
  NDIR, 278, 292
  Print Queue menu options (PCONSOLE), 736–737
  RENDIR, 280–281
  SHOW, 517
  summary of file management utility, 294–296
  summary of MAP, 312–313
  SWAP, 508
communications protocol
  for Client 32, 617
  networking, 469
Compare rights, 375
compatibility, 524–525
complex effective rights, 399–400
components
  of ODI, 627–628
  printing, 729–730
components of MHS, 533–536
Compressed disk management attribute, 427
CompuServe forums about Novell, 89
Computer objects, 140
COMSPEC
  on-line information about, 504
  using with login scripts, 503–504
concurrent connections, limiting, 359

Configuration parameter (PCONSOLE), 741
Configuring ACME's Login Scripts (exercise), 550–552
configuring IntranetWare, 463–556
   application objects, 528–529
   CD-ROM as DOS device, 572
   Client 32
      files modified installing, 622
      network board configuration for, 618
   configuration files
      CONFIG console command, 587–588
      CONFIG.SYS file, 476–477
      directories for, 249, 255
      NET.CFG file, 479–487
      renaming directories, 280
   creating menu systems, 511–522
      about menus, 511–513
      case study for, 553–554
      control commands, 516–520
      menu execution, 520–522
      organizational commands, 513–515
   documenting
      settings for servers, 73–75, 76, 77,
         81–83
      worksheets for, 75–77, 177
   e-mail, 531–541
      advantages of, 531–532
      components of MHS Services, 533–536
      managing MHS Services, 536–539
      using FirstMail, 539–541
   exercises, 542–556
      IntranetWare 4 Childhood, 555–556
      Understanding NET.CFG, 548–549
      Workstation Connectivity with Client 16,
         542–544
      Workstation Connectivity with Client 32,
         545–548
   installing network applications, 523–531
      assigning file attributes and access rights,
         526–527
      configuring workstations, 529–531
      creating and configuring application
         objects, 528–529
      customization, 527
      ensuring compatibility, 524–525
      managing the installation, 525–526
   login scripts, 487–511, 550–552
      commands and identifiers for, 495–498,
         504–508
      COMSPEC command with, 503–504
      Container, 488, 489–491
      Default, 488, 494–495
      GUI login script management, 508–511
      guidelines for, 499
      network drive mapping, 500–502
      Profile, 488, 491–493
      search drive mapping, 502–503

      types of, 487–488, 489
      User, 488, 493–494
   for offset threshold, 182
   overview of steps in, 462–465
   for printing
      configuring third-party support, 713
      default print job configuration, 720,
         726–728
      modifying defaults in PCONSOLE, 739–742
      NDPS, 769
      plug-and-print feature (NDPS), 769–770
      with PRINTCON, 755–756
      in PSC, 755
      remote printers, 711
   for time
      custom, 181, 185–186
      default, 179, 183–185
      parameters worksheet, 177
   workstation connectivity, 466–487
      with Client 16, 475–487
      with Client 32, 466–475
      for workstations, 529–531
      See also NET.CFG configuration file
Configuring the ACME Menu System (exercise), 553–554
connectivity
   choices with RCONSOLE command, 654–655
   Client 16 software, 475–487
   Client 32, 465, 467–475
   improvements in, 104–105, 109
   SPX and asynchronous, 651–654
   See also Client 16 software; Client 32 software;
      workstation connectivity
considerations for SMS (Storage Management Services),
      647–650
CONSOLE commands
   BIND, 585
   BROADCAST, 585–586
   CLEAR STATION, 586
   CONFIG, 587–588
   DOWN, 588
   DSTRACE, 589–590
   ENABLE/DISABLE LOGIN, 590
   EXIT, 590
   HELP, 591
   LOAD/UNLOAD, 591
   MODULES, 591
   MOUNT, 591
   REMOVE DOS, 592
   RESTART SERVER, 592
   for server management, 584–595
   TRACK ON, 592–595
   See also PCONSOLE command
CONSOLE.LOG error log, 50, 51
consultants, 57
Container login scripts, 488, 489–491
Container objects, 126–131

abbreviations for attributes, 155–156
choosing for printing devices, 722
Country objects, 128, 158, 159
creating print jobs for, 727
default NDS rights for, 381–382
defined, 113–114
defining printer forms, 761
Locality objects, 128–129
locating printer, print server, and queue in, 710
moving, 176
opening and viewing, 210–211
Organization objects, 129–130
Organizational Unit objects, 130–131
typeless naming, 158
Container trustee type, 384
context
    bindery, 175
    changing
        with NETADMIN utility, 211–212, 228–229
        with NWADMIN utility, 209–210
    current, 147–148, 159
    CX utility and, 148–150, 213–215
    defining for printing system, 720, 732–733
    distinguished names, 151–152
    logging in, 484
    object, 148
    restrictions on, 344–345
    typeless naming, 158
CONTEXT command, 507
control commands, 516–520
    EXEC, 516–517
    GETO, 518–519
    GETP, 520
    GETR, 519
    LOAD, 517
    SHOW, 517
Copies (/C) line option (CAPTURE), 689
copy commands, 279
Copy Inhibit security attribute, 425
core operating system, 93–94, 595–596
costs of certification, 19–24
countermeasures, 331–333
Country objects, 128, 158, 159
CPUs. See processors
Create (/CR) line option (CAPTURE), 691
Create rights, 374, 412
creating
    directory structures (case study), 317–318
    organizational units with NWADMIN utility, 220–227
    the print queue, 706–709
    the print server, 713–716
    the printer, 710–713
Creator rights, 379
Crime Fighting division (ACME), 198–199, 201, 207
Cure for Mother Earth, A. See ACME
current context, 147–148, 159

custom backups, 642, 643
custom forms. See forms
Custom installation
    installing network applications and, 527
    on-line information about, 582
    overview of, 568
custom time configuration, 181, 185–186
customizing printing, 720–728
    with PRINTCON, 789
    using custom forms, 757–762
CX utility
    context, 148–150
    exercises for, 213–215

D

data migration, 263
dataflow, 204
dates and times, 265
Dates and Times page button (NWADMIN), 265
default configurations
    for print jobs, 720, 726–728
    for printers, 739–742
    for time, 179, 183–185
Default login scripts, 488, 494–495
default NDS rights, 378
    for Container objects, 381–382
    file server installation, 379–380
    on initial installation, 378–379
    for security, 373–383
    summary of, 382
    for users, 380–381
Delete Inhibit security attribute, 425
Delete rights, 374
DELETED.SAV directory, 252
deleting print jobs, 750, 752
*Department of Defense Trusted Computer System Evaluation
    Criteria, The* (TCSEC), 341–343
Designing NetWare 4.x Security, 400
device drivers, 637, 638
differential backups, 641, 642, 643
directories, 245–246
    application, 255
    configuration file, 249, 255
    designing structure of, 256–258
    directory trees, 240–241
    DOS, 249, 254–255
    drive letters, 297
    home, 249, 255
    local, 297, 298
    managing, 270–281
        with FILER, 271–273
        with NCOPY utility, 278–279
        with NDIR, 276–278
        with NWADMIN, 274–276, 277
    naming rules for, 245, 246–247, 280

directories (continued)
  renaming with wildcards, 280
  shared data, 249, 255–256
  structuring, 65, 257, 525
  summary of file management utilities, 295
  syntax and naming rules for, 245
  system-created, 248–253
    DELETED.SAV, 252
    DOC, 252
    DOCVIEW, 252
    ETC, 252
    LOGIN, 250
    MAIL, 251
    NLS, 251
    PUBLIC, 251
    QUEUES, 252
    SYSTEM, 250
  in volumes, 245–247
  See also directory/file attributes; drive mapping
Directory Map objects, 135
  MAP command, 311
  mapping drives, 304–305
  NDS resource access rights for, 406, 408
  security equivalence, 392–393, 420
Directory objects, 408
Directory Services Queue, 707
directory structure
  for network applications, 525
  options for, 257
  training about, 65
directory/file attributes, 335, 339–340, 423–430
  assigning file attributes with network applications, 526
  disk management attributes, 427–430
  feature attributes, 426–427
  security attributes, 424–426
disabling accounts, 358
disaster planning and recovery, 66–89
  backups and mirrored servers, 83–85
  developing disaster plans, 62, 68–71
  network documentation, 71–83
  rationale for, 66–67
  troubleshooting tips, 85–89
disaster plans, 62, 68–71
disk driver NLM, 598
disk management attributes, 340, 427–430
disk redirection area, 78–80
disk space
  checking, 40
  displaying user space limits, 265
  freeing up, 48–49
  miniumum hardware requirements, 564–565
  restrictions on, 65
  volumes, 244
distinguished names, 151–155, 156
distributed administration, 401, 402–405

Distribution department (ACME), 205
Distribution List objects, 536, 538
distributions list, 138
DOC directory, 252
documentation
  building a log book, 559–560
  Help Desk handbooks, 61–63
  IntranetWare reference materials, 560
  network, 71–83
  reading the manual, 87–88, 89
  for solutions, 89
  for time servers, 81, 82
  training users about on-line, 65
  for volumes, 77–78, 79
  See also network documentation; on-line information
DOCVIEW directory, 252
DOD (Department of Defense), security requirements, 341–343
Don't Compress disk management attribute, 427–428
Don't Migrate disk management attribute, 428
Don't Suballocate disk management attribute, 428
do's and don'ts of security, 431–433
DOS applications, 302
DOS CD command, 305
DOS directories, 249, 254–255
DOS executable # command, 505
DOS partition, 574
dots, 272
double dots, 272
DOWN console commands, 588
downloading
  connectivity files for Client 32, 465
  MHS Service for NetWare 4.11, 533
  NDPS drivers, 767
drive letters
  directories, 297
  network drive mapping and, 300, 308
  specifying network, 308
  using with MAP command, 306–307
drive mapping, 296–316
  confusing local and network drive mapping, 296–299
  Directory Map objects, 304–305
  DOS applications, 302
  exercises for mapping drives, 319–322
  MAP command, 305–313
  network, 300–301, 500–502
  search drive, 301–304, 502–503
  in Windows environments, 313–316
drivers
  automatic driver download (NDPS), 767
  disk driver NLM, 598
  LAN drivers NLM, 598–599
  loading LAN, 576–577
  ODI command line switches for, 630
  SMS architecture and device, 637, 638
DS Migrate, 103–104
DSREPAIR.NLM, 607–608

DSTRACE console command, 589–590
DynaText viewer, 95

E

EDIT.NLM, 50–51
education
    advantage of CNA, 18–19
    applying on the job, 15–17
    certification and college credit, 6–8
    costs of CNA, 19
    financial assistance for, 20–24
effective rights, 397–401
    defined, 338
    for file system, 421–423, 450–455
    NDS security, 397–401, 446–449
        complex, 399–400
        exercises for calculating, 446–449
        simple, 397–398
    on-line information for, 400
e-mail, 531–541
    advantages of, 531–532
    components of MHS Services, 533–536
        messaging server, 534–535, 536
        MHS applications, 535–536
        user mailboxes, 535, 536
    managing MHS Services, 536–539
        Distribution List object, 538
        External Entity object, 538
        Mailbox objects, 539
        message routing group, 537
        messaging server, 537–538
    using FirstMail, 539–541
employment advantages of certification, 8–10
ENABLE/DISABLE console command, 590
encrypted private keys, 349, 350
encryption algorithms, 348
EndCapture (/EC) line option (CAPTURE), 691
ENTRY.NDS file, 118
Erase rights, 412
error logs
    limiting size of files, 51, 52
    login error codes, 346
    monitoring, 49–52
    viewing with EDIT.NLM, 50–51
error messages, 344–346
ETC directory, 252
event notification (NDPS), 770
evolution of IntranetWare, 96–100
exceptions to typeless naming, 158–159
EXEC command, 516–517
Execute Only security attribute, 425
exercises
    Calculating File System Effective Rights, 450–455
    Calculating NDS Effective Rights, 446–449
    How Secure Do You Feel?, 456–457

IntranetWare Adulthood, 674
IntranetWare CNA Basics, 237–238
IntranetWare File Cabinet, 327–328
IntranetWare File Management with NetWare
        Administrator, 323–326
IntranetWare 4 Childhood, 555–556
Let the Good Guys In, 458–459
Mapping Drives with MAP, 319–320
Mapping Drives with MS Windows, 321–322
Plant a Tree in a Cloud, 235–236
Server Management at ACME, 667–673
Simple Installation for ACME, 659–666
"Tree Walking" for Toddlers, 208–215
Understanding NDS Naming, 216–234
Understanding NET.CFG, 548–549
Workstation Connectivity with Client 16, 542–544
Workstation Connectivity with Client 32, 545–548
    See also case studies; puzzles; quizzes
EXIT console command, 590
EXIT login script command, 506–507
expired accounts, 359
External Entity object, 138, 538

F

Facts page for directories (NWADMIN), 275
fault tolerance, 174, 247–248
FDISPLAY command, 507
feature attributes, 340, 426–427
features
    of NDPS, 765, 768–770
    of NDS, 96–97
    of NDS partitioning, 163–166
    of NLM, 596–597
Federal Student Aid Information Line, 21
file attributes. See directory/file attributes
File Cabinet of Life, The, 242, 243
File Information Screen (FILER), 283
File Manager (Windows 3.1), 288–289
File Scan rights, 412
file servers
    assigning NDS default rights, 379–380
    naming rules for, 245, 246–247
file system. See IntranetWare file system
file system access rights, 410–423
    assigning trustee rights, 416–420, 450–455
    calculating effective rights, 421–423, 450–455
    defined, 335, 338–339
    filtering IRF rights, 420–421
    functional planes of security, 410
    on-line information for, 413, 420
    requirements for common tasks, 414
    RIGHTS utility, 416
    understanding, 411–415
    WoRMFACES, 338–339, 411–413
    See also NDS security

FILER menu utility, 261–263
  assigning file system access rights with, 416
  managing directories with, 271–273
  managing files with, 282–284
  options for, 262
  volume features for, 261–263
files, 245, 247
  backing up, 46–47
  compressing, 263
  conventions for NET.CFG, 479–480
  managing, 281–296
    file systems and, 97, 99
    with FILER menu utility, 282–284
    improvements in file services, 105, 109
    with NCOPY utility, 293–294
    with NDIR utility, 289–292
    with NWADMIN utility, 284–289
    summary of utilities for, 295–296
  naming rules for, 245, 246–247
  purging, 48–49, 284
  salvaging, 284
  in volumes, 245–247
  See also file system access rights; IntranetWare file
    system; *and specific types of files*
filtering IRF rights, 394–397, 420–421
Financial department (ACME), workflow for, 204–205
FIRE PHASERS command, 507
FirstMail, 535, 539–541
FLAG command line utility, disk management attributes and,
  428
Form (/F) line option (CAPTURE), 690
formatting options, for NDIR displays, 290
FormFeed (/FF) line option (CAPTURE), 690
forms
  consolidating multiple forms to single printer, 758
  custom, 757–762
    changing, 743–744, 760–762
    defining, 758–759
    selecting, 759–760
  defining, 761
  mounting new printer, 749
  servicing print, 700, 759–760
full backups, 641, 643
function keys for RCONSOLE command, 657
functional planes of security, 410

G

Get Status of All Printers option (PSC), 753–754
GETO command, 518–519
GETP command, 519, 520
GETR command, 519
GMT (Greenwich Mean Time), 177
GOTO command, 508
grace logins, 362, 363
Greenwich Mean Time (GMT), 177

group accounts, 44
Group objects, 133
  NDS resource access rights for, 408
Group trustee type, 384
groups
  security equivalence, 392, 420
  time provider, 185
GUI login script management, 508–511
  enhancements to, 97, 99
  entering passwords on GUI login page, 474
  GUI login utility, 473–474
  script page, 509
  variables page, 509–510
guidelines
  do's and don'ts of security, 431–433
  for login scripts, 499
  for using SBACKUP command, 643–644

H

hard disks
  preparing for server installation, 571–575
  volumes and, 244
hardware
  automatic detection of, 599
  inventories of, 72–73, 74
  maintenance tasks for, 37–39
  network board configuration for Client 32, 618
  and software compatibility, 525
  troubleshooting tips for, 87
Help Desks
  advertising, 54–55
  asking for outside help, 57
  assigning and prioritizing problem reports, 56
  problem solving sequence for, 53–54
  recording and reporting solutions, 58–59
  resolving problems, 57–58
  tools, 59–62
  tracking problems and solutions, 56–57
help options
  for command line utilities, 260
  help (/?) line options, 686
  HELP console command, 591
Hidden security attribute, 425
home directories, 249, 255
Hot Fix bad block tracking, 78–80
How Secure Do You Feel? (puzzle), 456–457
HP JetDirect card, 703–704
Human Rights division (ACME), 193–195

I

Identification page for directories (NWADMIN), 275
Identification page for volumes (NWADMIN), 264
IF...THEN...ELSE command, 504–505
Immediate Compress disk management attribute, 428

improvements
    to menu system, 96
    to security, 107, 110
    to SMS, 106, 110
INCLUDE command, 508
incremental backups, 641, 642, 643
Information for directory option (FILER), 273
Information option (PCONSOLE), 736
Information Services departments, 33–34
informational objects, 139–140
inherited rights
    concept for, 377
    defined, 338
    trustee rights, 388–390
    See also trustee rights
Inherited Rights Filter. See IRF rights
initial authentication, 347–351
    key concepts of, 350–351
    steps in, 348–349
    See also login/password authentication
installation
    checklist for, 569–570
    Client 32
        for Windows 95, 619–622
        for Windows 3.1, 622
    documenting settings for, 73–75, 76, 77
    improvements to, 103–104, 109
    initial, 378–379
    of NDS, 578–580
    network applications, 523–531
        configuring workstations, 529–531
        creating and configuring application
            objects, 528–529
        customization, 527
        ensuring compatibility, 524–525
        managing the installation, 525–526
        as network management, 47
    server, 560–583
        before you begin, 562–564
        building a log book, 559–560
        Custom installation, 568
        installing NDS, 578–580
        loading NetWare drivers, 576–577
        miniumum hardware requirements, 564–565
        preparing the hard disk, 571–575
        running INSTALL.NLM, 577–578, 599–601
        running SERVER.EXE, 575
        Simple installation, 567–568
        summary of steps, 571–572
    worksheets for, 75, 76, 77
    See also INSTALL.NLM command
INSTALLBAT, 573, 574
INSTALL.NLM command
    installing the server, 577–578
    loading disk drivers in, 576
    options for, 599–601

Integrating MHS Services with Other Novell Products, 540
Intel NetPort, 704
international language support, 94, 95
    NLS directory, 251
    selecting a language, 572
IntranetWare
    evolution of, 96–100
    improvements, 93–96, 100–112
        for application services, 105–106, 110
        in connectivity, 104–105, 109
        for file services, 105, 109
        to installation procedures, 103–104, 109
        NDS, 101, 108–109
        NetWare Licensing Services (NLS), 104, 109
        print services, 107–108, 110
        security, 107, 110
        server operating system, 101–103, 109
        Storage Management Services (SMS), 106, 110
    NDS and, 92–93, 101, 108–109
    NetWare 3.12, 93–96, 99–100
    NetWare versions, 93
    network-centric NDS cloud, 115–116
    security model for, 334–343
    See also IntranetWare file management
IntranetWare Adulthood (exercise), 674
IntranetWare CNA Basics (puzzle), 237–238
IntranetWare File Cabinet (puzzle), 327–328
IntranetWare File Management with NetWare Administrator
    (exercise), 323–326
IntranetWare File Migration Utility, 104
IntranetWare file system, 240–328
    access rights for common tasks, 414
    case studies for, 317–318
    directories
        application, 255
        configuration file, 249, 255
        designing structure of, 256–258
        DOS, 249, 254–255
        home, 249, 255
        managing, 270–281
        shared data, 249, 255–256
        system-created, 248–253
    directory trees, 240–241
    drive mapping, 296–316
    file management, 281–296, 323–326
    naming rules for, 245, 246–247
    NetWare 3.12 features, 99
    on-line information about attributes, 430
    overview of, 241–243
    volumes, 243–248
        directories and files, 245–247
        managing, 260–270
    See also directories; file system access rights;
        files; volumes
IntranetWare 4 Childhood (puzzle), 555–556
IntranetWare Printing Setup. See printing

IntranetWare reference materials, 560
Intruder Detection/Lockout, 356, 368–371
    intruder detection limits, 368–369
    locking accounts after detection, 369–370
    at login, 345–346
    unlocking accounts, 370–371
IPX RETRY COUNT parameter (NET.CFG configuration file),
    485
IRF rights, 389
    filtering, 394–397, 420–421
    Selected Properties option, 395, 396
ITEM command, 515

J

Job List page (NWADMIN utility), 709
job security, 18–19
Job Training Partnership Act (JTPA), 22
job-to-printer matching (NDPS), 767

K

Keep/No Keep (/K) line option (CAPTURE), 689

L

Labs division (ACME), 195–197, 205–206
LAN drivers, 576–577, 598–599
last login parameters, 359
LASTDRIVE statement, 476–477
LASTLOGINTIME command, 508
Leaf objects, 131–142
    informational, 139–140
    messaging, 137–138
    miscellaneous, 140–142
    network services, 138–139
    printer, 136–137
    server, 134–136
    typeless naming, 158
    user, 132–134
Let the Good Guys In (puzzle), 458–459
letters for menu items, 515
licensing, 104, 109, 580
LINK DRIVER (NET.CFG configuration file), 480–481
Link Support Layer. See LSL
LOAD command, 517
LOAD REMOTE command, 612–613
LOAD/UNLOAD console command, 591
loading print servers, 716–717
local drive mapping, network, 296–299
Local Port Number (/L=n) line option (CAPTURE), 690
local printers, 701–702, 711
Locality objects, 128–129
locations for print servers, 701, 706
logging in
    automatic input of passwords on, 479
    with Client 32, 473–475

context, 484
    login utilities for, 475
    NDS naming, 144
    partitions and replicas for, 175
    security measures, 344–347
    training about, 64
    See also login restrictions; login scripts;
        login/password authentication
logging out, 365
logical directories, 297, 298
LOGIN directory, 250
login restrictions, 335, 336, 354–371
    account restrictions, 357–359
    categories of, 354–357
    context restrictions, 344–345
    intruder detection/lockout, 368–371
    on-line information for, 356
    password restrictions, 359–364
    station restrictions, 366–368
    time restrictions, 345, 364–366
    See also logging in; login scripts; login/password
        authentication
login scripts, 487–511
    commands and identifiers, 495–498, 507–508
        DOS executable # command, 505
        EXIT command, 506–507
        IF...THEN...ELSE command, 504–505
        NO_DEFAULT command, 506
        REMARK command, 499–500, 501
        SET command, 504
        WRITE command, 495, 499–500, 501
    Container, 488, 489–491
    Default, 488, 494–495
    GUI login script management, 508–511
    guidelines for, 499
    identifier variables for, 496–498
    network drive mapping, 500–502
    Profile, 488, 491–493
    search drive mapping, 502–503
    types of, 487–488, 489
    User, 488, 493–494
    using COMSPEC with, 503–504
    See also logging in; login restrictions;
        login/password authentication
login/password authentication, 335–336, 344–353
    background authentication, 335–336, 351–353
    decisions in, 346
    getting in, 344–347
    initial authentication, 347–351
    initialization, 335
    See also logging in; login restrictions; login scripts
LONG MACHINE TYPE parameter (NET.CFG configuration
    file), 485
LPT ports
    CAPTURE utility, 683
    output from, 680–681

LSL (Link Support Layer), 468, 469
  for Client 32 software, 617
  as ODI component, 628
LSP (License Service Provider), 138, 139

M

mail. *See* e-mail; MHS (Message Handling Services)
MAIL directory, 251
Mailbox objects, managing, 539
mailboxes, 535, 536
mailing list administrators, 406
main menu (PCONSOLE), 733
maintenance histories, 75–76, 78
maintenance messages for printers (NDPS), 770
maintenance tasks, 36–37
managers, 12–13
Managing ACME's Printing System (case study), 784–785
managing IntranetWare, 558–675
  case studies
    Server Management at ACME, 667–673
    Simple Installation for ACME, 659–666
  daily activities, 35–36
  directories, 270–281
  exercise, IntranetWare Adulthood, 674
  files, 281–296
  message routing group, 537
  messaging server, 537–538
  objects
    External Entity, 538
    List, 538
    Mailbox, 539
    with NETADMIN utility, 212–213, 227–228
  print queues, 735–739
  print servers, 744–747
  printers
    modifying default printer configurations,
      739–742
    with PCONSOLE command, 739–744
  printing, 728–763
    access rights, 731
    components, 729–730
    with NWADMIN, 748–753
    PCONSOLE and, 732–748
    with PRINTCON, 755–756
    with PSC, 753–755
    utilities for, 730
  Remote Management Facility (RMF), 650–658
    RMF architecture, 651–654
    using RCONSOLE, 654–659
  replication, 174–176
  server installation, 560–583
    before you begin, 562–564
    building a log book, 559–560
    creating server startup files, 581–583
    installing NDS, 578–580

loading NetWare drivers, 576–577
    miniumum hardware requirements, 564–565
    overview of installation methods, 566–571
    preparing the hard disk, 571–575
    running INSTALL.NLM, 577–578
    running SERVER.EXE, 575
  server management, 583–614
    console commands, 584–595
    NetWare Loadable Modules (NLM), 595–608
    server protection, 608–614
      locking up the physical server,
        609
      MONITOR.NLM locking, 610
      with REMOTE.NLM, 611–613
      SECURE CONSOLE command, 611
  Storage Management Services (SMS), 636–650
    considerations for, 647–650
    SMS architecture, 637–639
    using SBACKUP, 640–647
  volumes, 260–270
  workstation management, 614–635
    for Client 16 architecture, 626–634
    for Client 32 architecture, 616–618
    installing Client 32, 619–626
    non-DOS workstation support, 634–635
    overview of, 614–616
MAP command, 305–313
  Directory Map objects, 311
  with drive letters, 306–307
  exercise for mapping drives, 319–320
  login scripts and, 501
  with NP parameter, 307
  options
    MAP /?, 311
    MAP /VER, 311
    MAP CHANGE, 310
    MAP DEL, 309
    MAP INSERT, 308–309, 503
    MAP NEXT, 310, 311
    MAP ROOT, 309–310
    MAP SEARCH, 307
  searching specific drives with, 307–308
  summary of, 312–313
mapping drives. *See* drive mapping
Mapping Drives with MAP (exercise), 319–320
Mapping Drives with MS Windows (exercise), 321–322
Master CNE certification, 27–28
Master replicas, 169–170
MAX CACHE SIZE command, settings for, 566
memory
  calculating for server, 565
  managing, 98
  minimum hardware requirements for, 564
  registering for PCI bus, 40
MENU command, 513–514
menu execution, 520–522

menu numbers, 514
menu system, 511–522
menu system (continued)
    about menus, 511–513
    assigning letters to options, 515
    control commands, 516–520
      EXEC command, 516–517
      GETO command, 518–519
      GETP command, 520
      GETR command, 519
      LOAD command, 517
      SHOW command, 517
    improvements to, 96
    menu execution, 520–522
    menu numbers, 514
    organizational commands, 513–515
      ITEM command, 515
      MENU command, 513–514
    See also FILER menu utility
Message Handling Services. *See* MHS
message routing group, 138
    as component of MHS Services, 536
    managing, 537
Messaging objects, 137–138
Messaging Server objects, 138
Messaging Servers, 380, 534–538
MHS (Message Handling Services), 95
    components of, 533–536
    managing, 536–539
      Distribution List object, 536, 538
      External Entity object, 538
      Mailbox objects, 539
      message routing group, 536, 537
      Messaging Servers, 380, 534–535, 536,
        537–538
    MHS applications, 535–536
    on-line information
      Integrating MHS Services with Other Novell
        Products, 540
      MHS Service for NetWare 4.11, 533
MHS Service for NetWare 4.11, 533
Migrated disk management attribute, 428
migration procedures, 103–104
minimizing form changes (PRINTDEF), 760–761
miniumum hardware requirements, 564–565
mirrored servers, 83–85
miscellaneous objects, 140–142
mission statement for ACME, 188–193
MLID component (ODI), 628
modes for printing devices, 721–723
Modify rights, 412, 413
MODULES console command, 591
MONITOR.NLM command, 42, 601–604
Monitoring Print Server Status page (NWADMIN), 716
monitoring security, 44–46
monitoring servers, 40–43

    cache buffers, 41, 42
    packet receive buffers, 41, 42–43
    processor utilization, 42
Mount a New Form in a Printer option (PSC), 754
MOUNT console command, 591
mounting new printer forms, 749
multifunction printer and device support (NDPS), 767–768
multiuser capabilities, 525
multivalued properties, 124

N

NAL (NetWare Application Launcher), 105
    NAM and, 529–530
    replacing Windows interface with, 530
NAM (NetWare Application Manager), 105, 527–531
    configuring NDS and file system for, 528–529
    drives and port option in, 529
    NAL and, 529–530
NAME CONTEXT parameter, 484
name space NLM, 245, 599
naming
    directories, 245, 246–247, 280
    file system rules for, 245, 246–247
    NDS, 142–161
    print queues, 707, 735
    print servers in PCONSOLE, 744–745
    servers in INSTALLBAT, 574
    typeful, 158
    typeless, 156–160
    See also NDS naming
NCCP (Novell College Credit Program), p., 8
NCOPY utility, 278–279
    managing directories with, 278–279
    managing files with, 293–294
NCP packet signing, 351–353
    background authentication, 352–353
    options for, 353
NDIR utility
    managing directories with, 276–278
    managing files with, 289–292
    managing volumes with, 268–270
    NDIR /DO command, 278
    NDIR /FO command, 291
    NDIR /VOL command, 269
NDPS (Novell Distributed Print Services), 764–774
    automatic driver download, 767
    bidirectional communication, 766
    event notification, 770
    job-to-printer matching, 767
    multifunction printer and device support, 767–768
    on-line information about, 765
    plug-and-print feature, 769–770
    print job move/copy options, 766
    reduced network traffic, 770
    streamlined configuration of, 769

NDS (Novell Directory Services), 112–238
  the "Cloud," 113–116
  database
    architecture for, 120
    as central company database, 133
    files for, 118, 120, 133
  directory tree, 240
  features of, 96–97
  installing, 578–580
  IntranetWare, 92–93, 101, 108–109
  naming, 142–143, 144–161
  NDS tree, 120–122
  NetWare bindery, 117–120
  objects, 123–125
    Application objects, 407
    assigning ACL rights for, 372
    Container objects, 126–131, 381–382
    Leaf objects, 131–142
    naming types for, 146–147
    [Root] object, 125–126
  overview of, 113–115
  partitioning, 142 143, 161 176
    characteristics of, 163–166
    moving containers, 176
    of NDS trees, 161–163
    replication, 170 172
  server-centric vs. network-centric systems, 115–116
  switching to bindery mode, 733
  time synchronization, 142–143, 176–188
  tree, 120–122
    building for ACME, 218–234
    exploring with NWADMIN utility, 208–215
    partitioning, 161–163
    See also replication
NDS naming, 142–143, 144–161
  context, 144–145, 146–150
    current, 147–148
    CX utility, 148–150, 213–215
    object, 148
  distinguished and relative distinguished names, 151–155, 156
  exercise for, 216–234
  mixed naming schemes, 158–159
  naming types, 146–147
  rules, 150–151
    for volumes, directories, and files, 245–247
  setting naming standards, 145
  syntax for filenames, 245
  typeful names, 155–156
  typeless naming, 156–160
  See also naming
NDS security, 98, 99, 335, 336–338
  access rights, 373–383
    assigning trustee rights, 338, 383–393
    calculating effective rights, 397–401,

446–449
    default NDS rights, 378, 382
    filtering IRF rights, 394–397
    for objects, 373–378
    for print queue operator, 408
  administration, 401–410
    Admin user, 401–402
    distributed, 401, 402–405
  functional planes of security, 410
  on-line information for, 377
  overview of, 371–372
  special circumstances and, 405–407
NDS Server object, 134, 135
NEAPs (Novell Education Academic Partners), 7
need for security, 330
NET.CFG configuration file, 479–487
  additional parameters for, 485–487
  Client 16 and, 479–487
  conventions for creating, 479–480
  LINK DRIVER section of, 480–481
  NETWARE DOS REQUESTER section of, 482–484
  on-line information for, 482
  using with ODI and VLMs, 633–634
NETADMIN utility, 211–213
  changing context with, 211–212, 228–229
  creating objects with, 229–230
  disk management attributes, 428
  managing objects with, 212–213, 227–228
  managing volumes with, 266–267
NetWare 3.12
  features of IntranetWare, 99–100
  flat server-centric bindery, 115
  as foundation for IntranetWare, 93–96
NetWare 4.11
  license diskette, 580
  as primary operating system, 94, 563
  running 80386 processors with, 575
  Server Installation screen, 573
  See also installation
NETUSER (NetWare User Tools for DOS), 692–693
NetWare Administrator utility. See NWADMIN utility
Netware Application Launcher. See NAL
NetWare Application Manager. See NAM
Netware DOS Requester, 482–484, 630–634
  functions of, 630
  VLM load order, 631–632
NetWare Licensing Services (NLS), 104, 109
NetWare Loadable Modules. See NLM
NetWare User Tools for DOS (NETUSER), 692–693
NetWare User Tools for Windows. See NWUSER
NetWare Users International (NUI), 11
network address restrictions, 355, 366–367
network administration, 24–29
network board configuration, 618
network documentation, 71–83
  bad block tracking, 78–80

network documentation (*continued*)
  for hardware and software inventories, 72–73, 74
  for installation and configuration settings, 73–75,
    76, 77
  for maintenance histories, 75–76, 78
  for network layout, 81
  recording volume information, 77–78, 79
  recording workstation batch files and boot files, 81
  for server configuration settings, 81–83
  for time synchronization servers, 81, 82
  See also documentation
network drive letters, 308
network drive mappings, 300–301
  assigning first, 302
  drive letters, 300, 308
  local, 296–299
  login scripts, 500–502
  search drive mappings, 303
network interface card. *See* NIC
network layout, 81
network management
  backing up files, 46–47
  comparison of IntranetWare and NetWare 3.12 features,
    99–100
  daily activities, 35–36
  disaster planning and recovery, 66–89
    backups and mirrored servers, 83–85
    developing disaster plans, 62, 68–71
    network documentation, 71–83
    rationale for, 66–67
    troubleshooting tips, 85–89
  exercises for special cases, 233–234
  Information Services departments, 33–34
  installing applications, 47
  maintenance tasks, 36–37
    adding to server capacity, 39–40
    hardware, 37–39
  managing user accounts, 43–44
  monitoring error logs, 49–52
  monitoring security, 44–46
  purging files, 48–49, 284
  role of CNA in, 32–33
  tracking server performance, 40–43
  user support, 52–66
    Help Desks, 53–62
    user training, 62–66
network printers, 684
network printing, 682–684
  print queues, 683
  print servers, 683–684
  standalone printing vs., 679–682
Network Professional Association (NPA), 11
Network Services objects, 138–139
Network Trusted Computing Base (NTCB) partition, 342
network-centric systems, 115–116
NIC (network interface card), 468

  hardware requirements for, 564
  as workstation component, 615
NLIST utility, 267–268
NLM (NetWare Loadable Modules), 595–608
  advantages of, 597
  disk driver, 598
  DSREPAIR.NLM, 607–608
  features offered by, 596–597
  INSTALL.NLM, 599–601
  LAN drivers, 598–599
  MONITOR.NLM, 601–604
  name space, 599
  SERVMAN.NLM, 604–607
NLS directory, 251
No Banner (/NB) line option (CAPTURE), 689
node restrictions, 355, 366–367
NO_DEFAULT command, for login scripts, 506
NoFormFeed (/NFF) line option (CAPTURE), 690
Nomadic User Syndrome (NUS), 366
nonchaotic attractor, 247
non-DOS workstations, 634–635
Normal security attribute, 425
Notification parameter (PCONSOLE), 742
Notify (/NOTI) line option (CAPTURE), 691
Novell College Credit Program (NCCP), 8
Novell Directory Services. *See* NDS
Novell Distributed Print Services. *See* NDPS
Novell Education Academic Partners (NEAPs), 7
Novell forums on CompuServe, 89
Novell NetWare 4.11 Installation Manual, 566
Novell Peripheral Architecture, 598
NP parameter (MAP command), 307
NPA (Network Professional Association), 11
NPRINTER.EXE module, 702
NTCB (Network Trusted Computing Base) partition, 342
NUI (NetWare Users International), 11
null characters, 361
NUS (Nomadic User Syndrome), 366
NWADMIN utility
  assigning trustee rights in, 386
  creating organizational units, 220–227
  creating QUEUES directory, 706
  disk management attributes, 428
  exploring NDS tree with, 208–215
  importing devices with, 725
  managing directories with, 274–276, 277
  managing files with, 284–289
  managing printing, 748–753
    CNA tasks, 749–750
    summary of tasks handled, 729–730
    user tasks, 751–753
  managing volumes with, 263–266
  Print Queue Job List screen, 751
  print queue pages, 708–709
  print server pages, 713–716
  printer pages, 710–713

printer queue job list screen, 751
printer status screen, 750
NWUSER (NetWare User Tools for Windows), 290
    capturing printers with, 694–696
    exercise for mapping drives, 322
    mapping drives, 314–316

O

object dialog, 210–211
object rights, 374–375
objects
    assigning rights
        description of, 374–375
        on-line information about, 377
        trustee rights, 387
        vs. property rights, 373
    context, 148
    creating, 229–230
    managing, 212–213, 227–228
ODI (Open Datalink Interface)
    command line switches for drivers, 630
    components of, 627–628
    Link Support Layer, 628
    MLID component, 628
    protocol stack, 629
offset threshold, configuring, 182
on-line information
    for backing up files, 647
    for CAPTURE parameters, 692
    for COMSPEC strategy, 504
    for file system access rights, 413, 420
    for file system attributes, 430
    for identification and authentication, 351
    for integrating MHS Services, 533, 540
    for IntranetWare security, 341
    for login error codes, 346
    for login restrictions, 356
    for multiple language support, 251
    for NDPS, 765
    for NDS effective rights, 93, 400
    for NET.CFG configuration file, 482
    for object and property rights, 377
    for passwords, 364
    for PCONSOLE command, 748
    for PRINTDEF utility, 763
    for printing utilities, 729
    for third-party printing solutions, 704
    training users to access, 65
    for utilities, 291
    for volumes, 248
    See also documentation
Open Datalink Interface. *See* ODI
opening Container objects, 210–211
Operations division (ACME), 197–198, 199
Operator page (NWADMIN utility), 708–709

Operators option (PCONSOLE), 737
operators security for print server, 700
options
    for CAPTURE command, 686–692
    for FILER menu utility, 262
    for formatting NDIR displays, 290
    for ITEM command, 515
    for NCP packet signing, 353
    for NLIST, 268
    with RCONSOLE command, 655, 656–657
    squiggly, 515, 517
    for structuring directories, 257
Orange Book, The, 332, 341–343
Organization objects, 129–130
organizational chart for ACME, 192
organizational commands, 513–515
    ITEM command, 515
    MENU command, 513–514
Organizational Roles, 133–134
    NDS resource access rights for, 408
    security equivalence, 391–392, 420
    trustee assignments, 384
Organizational Unit objects, 130–131
    creating with NWADMIN utility, 220–227
overview
    of configuring IntranetWare, 462–465
    of file system access rights, 411–415
    of installation methods, 566–571
    of IntranetWare file system, 241–243
    of managing workstations, 614–616
    of menus, 511–513
    of NDPS, 764–765
    of NDS, 100, 113–115

P

packet receive buffers, 41, 42–43
paper CNAs, 13–15
parallel ports
    CAPTURE utility, 683
    redirecting parallel output from, 680, 681
parameters
    for CONFIG console command, 587–588
    for LINK DRIVER (NET.CFG), 481
    for modifying printer configurations (PCONSOLE),
        741–742
    for NET.CFG configuration file, 485–487
    Netware DOS Requester (NET.CFG), 482–484
    for Printer Server information screen (PCONSOLE), 745, 746
    for TRACK ON console command, 593–595
PARTITIO.NDS file, 118
Partition Root objects, 164
partitions. *See* NDS
passive network cabling, 342–343
passwords, 44
    authentication, 349, 350, 360

passwords (continued)
   automatic input of, 479
   entering on GUI login page, 474
   on-line information about, 364
   restrictions, 355, 359–364
     authentication, 360
     for changing passwords, 360–361, 362
     limiting grace logins, 363
     requiring passwords, 361
     unique passwords, 362–363
   supervisor bindery, 610
   training about, 64
   See also login/password authentication; security
patches and workarounds, 88
PCONSOLE command, 732–748
   auditing print servers, 747–748
   context, 732–733
   main menu, 733
   managing print queues, 735–739
     assigning print queue users and operators, 738–739
     Print Queue menu options, 736–737
     putting print queues on hold, 738
     viewing jobs in queue, 737–738
   managing print servers, 744–747
     assigning printers to be serviced, 745–746
     naming print servers, 744–745
   managing printers, 739–744
     modifying printer configurations, 739–742
   on-line information for, 748
   Print Job Information screen, 737
   summary of printing tasks managed with, 729–730
   using forms, 743–744
   using Quick Setup, 733–735
   See also CONSOLE commands
performance. See system performance
periods
   distinguished names, 152, 155
   trailing, 154, 155
PICs (Private Industry Councils), 23–24
planning user training programs, 62–63
planning volumes, 247–248
Plant a Tree in a Cloud (puzzle), 235–236
plug-and-print feature (NDPS), 769–770
point of view, assigning rights, 417–419
polling intervals, 181
Postmasters and Postmaster Generals, 535, 536
Primary time servers, 178, 181–182, 183
   Reference servers, 180
print capturing, 685–697
   with DOS, 685–693
   with Windows, 693–696
print devices
   building, 721–723
   exporting, 725–726
   importing, 724–725

Print Devices option (PRINTDEF), 762–763
print forms. See forms
print header, 697
Print Job Detail screen (NWADMIN), 699
Print Job Information screen (PCONSOLE), 737
print jobs
   administrative access to, 731
   configurations for, 720, 726–728, 755–756
   creating, 727
   holds on, 750, 752
   job-to-printer matching (NDPS), 767
   move and copy options in NDPS, 766
   viewing
     percent complete, 752
     in queue, 737–738
     status of, 751
Print Jobs options (PCONSOLE), 736
Print Queue identification page (NWADMIN), 708
Print Queue Information screen (PCONSOLE), 736
Print Queue Job List screen (NWADMIN), 751
Print Queue menu options (PCONSOLE), 736–737
print queue operators
   administrative access to print jobs, 731
   assigning with PCONSOLE command, 738–739
   as distributed administrator, 405
   NDS resource access rights for, 408
   unloading print servers after changes to, 718–719
print queue users
   administrative access to print jobs, 731
   assigning with PCONSOLE command, 738–739
   unloading print servers after changes to, 718–719
Print Queue Users page (NWADMIN utility), 709
print queues
   assigning, 742–743
   attaching print servers to a, 739
   automatic capturing in, 696
   creating, 706–709
   factors affecting service to, 699–700
   function of in print stream, 697, 698
   locations for, 706
   managing, 729, 735–739
   minimizing form changes, 760–761
   moving data to, 697–699
   for network printing, 683–684
   properties of, 707
   putting on hold, 738
   searching with NWADMIN utility, 708–709
   viewing jobs in, 737–738
   volume, 707
   See also print queue operators; print queue users
Print queues assigned parameter (PCONSOLE), 742
Print Server Assignments page (NWADMIN), 714, 715
Print Server Auditing Log page (NWADMIN), 714
Print Server Control. See PSC
Print Server Identification page (NWADMIN), 713
Print Server Operator page (NWADMIN), 714

print server operators
  administrative access to print jobs, 731
  assigning, 746–747
  as distributed administrator, 405
  unloading print servers after changes to, 718–719
Print server parameter (PCONSOLE), 741
Print Server Print Layout page (NWADMIN), 714–715
print server users
  administrative access to print jobs, 731
  assigning, 746–747
  unloading print servers after changes to, 718–719
Print Server Users page (NWADMIN), 714
print servers
  attaching to a queue, 739
  auditing with PCONSOLE, 747–748
  creating, 713–716
  locations for, 701, 706
  managing, 729, 744–747
  network printing, 683–684
  queue priorities, 699–700, 701
  security for, 700
  servicing print forms, 700, 759–760
  software for, 701–703
  starting, 716–717
  unloading, 749
  unloading from printers, 718–719
  See also print server operators; print server users
Print Servers option (PCONSOLE), 737
print tail, 697
PRINTCON utility, configuring print jobs with, 755–756
PRINTDEF utility, 756–763
  custom forms, 757–762
    changing print forms, 760–762
    defining, 758–759
    selecting print forms, 759–760
  on-line information for, 763
  using print devices, 762–763
Printer Assignments page (NWADMIN), 711, 712
Printer Configuration page (NWADMIN), 711, 713
Printer Configuration screen (PCONSOLE), 740–742
Printer Features page (NWADMIN), 711
Printer Identification Page (NWADMIN), 710
printer installation and configuration settings, 77
Printer Notification page (NWADMIN), 711
Printer number parameter (PCONSOLE), 741
Printer objects, 136–137
Printer Queue objects, 136
Printer Server information screen (PCONSOLE), 745, 746
Printer Server objects, 137
Printer status parameter (PCONSOLE), 741
Printer Status screen (NWADMIN), 750
Printer type parameter (PCONSOLE), 741
printers, 701–703
  assigning to be serviced (PCONSOLE), 745
  assigning to queues, 711, 742–743
  choosing by name, 696

configurations
  modifying default, 739–742
  for remote printers, 702–703, 711
  streamlined in NDPS, 769
  worksheet for, 77
  creating the, 710–713
  HP JetDirect card, 703–704
  Intel NetPort, 704
  job-to-printer matching (NDPS), 767
  local, 701–702, 711
  maintenance messages in NDPS, 770
  managing, 730, 739–744
  multifunction printer and device support (NDPS),
    767–768
  providing information for NDS searches, 710–712
  shutting down print servers, 718–719
  standalone printing, 679–682
  starting and stopping, 749
  understanding network, 684
  viewing job status, 751
  See also forms; PCONSOLE command; printing; PSC;
    PSERVER NLM
printing, 679–793
  to a file, 696
  activating the printing system, 716–719
  case studies
    Building ACME's Printing System, 776–780
    Managing ACME's Printing System, 784–785
    Using ACME's Printing System, 781–783
  components to manage, 729–730
  creating
    the print queue, 706–709
    the print server, 713–716
    the printer, 710–713
  customizing printing, 720–728, 756–763
  exercises
    Customizing IntranetWare printing with
      PRINTCON, 789
    Manual Printing Setup in PCONSOLE, 787–788
    The Great Challenge, 790–791
    The Greatest Mystery of All, 792–793
    Using Quick Setup in PCONSOLE, 786
  improvements to, 107–108, 110
  managing, 728–763
    access rights, 731
    with NWADMIN, 748–753
    PCONSOLE, 732–748
    with PRINTCON, 755–756
    with PSC, 753–755
    utilities for, 730
  moving print data to the queue, 697–699
  NDPS, 764–771
    features of, 765, 768–770
    overview of, 764–765
  network, 682–684
  print capturing, 685–697

printers (continued)
    print server, 699–701
    printers and, 701–703
        HP JetDirect card, 703–704
        Intel NetPort, 704
        local printers, 701–702, 711
        remote printers, 702–703, 711
    reducing network traffic with NDPS, 770
    standalone, 679–682
    third-party solutions for, 704
    See also printers
Private Industry Councils (PICs), 23–24
private keys. See initial authentication
problem solving
    isolating problems, 85–86
    problem reports, 55, 56
    resolving problems, 57–58
    sequence for Help Desks, 53–54
    tracking problems and solutions, 56–57
processors
    monitoring utilization of, 42
    running 80386 with NetWare 4.11, 575
    speed ratings for, 606
professional organizations, 11
Profile login scripts, 488, 491–493
    special rights for, 405–406
Profile objects, 134, 408
proof, 349, 351, 352
properties
    NDS objects, 123–125
    of print queues, 707
property rights
    assigning, 376–377
    on-line information about, 377
    types of, 375–376
    vs. object rights, 373
protocol
    networking and communications, 469
    restrictions for, 366–367
protocol stack (ODI), 629
PSC (Print Server Control), 753–755
    Get Status of All Printers option, 753–754
    Mount a New Form in a Printer option, 754
    Show Printer Server Configuration option, 755
    Start/Stop a Printer from Servicing Jobs options, 754
    summary of printing management tasks, 730
PSERVER.NLM
    loading the utility, 716
    local printers, 701–702
    remote printers, 702
    shutting down printers, 718–719
    viewing the printer status, 717–718
PUBLIC directory, 251
Public Relations department (ACME), workflow for, 206
[Public] rights, 127
    default rights for users, 381

Messaging Servers, 380
[Public] trustee object, 378–379
Purge feature attribute, 426
purging files, 48–49, 284
puzzles, 555–556
    How Secure Do You Feel?, 456–457
    IntranetWare CNA Basics, 237–238
    IntranetWare File Cabinet, 327–328
    IntranetWare 4 Childhood, 555–556
    Let the Good Guys In, 458–459
    Plant a Tree in a Cloud, 235–236

Q

Queue (/Q) line option (CAPTURE), 687
queues. See print queues
QUEUES directory, 252, 706
Quick Setup utility (PCONSOLE), 733–735
quizzes
    Chapter 3, 111, 131, 157, 172–174, 188
    Chapter 4, 256, 273, 284, 309
    Chapter 5, 340, 363, 373, 401, 409
    Chapter 6, 478, 482, 494, 502, 511, 532, 539
    Chapter 7, 571, 584, 608, 622, 634, 644, 650, 658
    Chapter 8, 684–685, 726, 748, 763, 771

R

RAID (Redundant Array of Inexpensive Disks), 244, 245
RAM
    adding to server, 39
    miniumum hardware requirements, 564–565
rationale for disaster planning and recovery, 66–67
RCONSOLE command (RMF), 654–659
    connection choices with, 654–655
    deactivating SPX, 653
    function keys for, 657
    options with, 655, 656–657
reactivating server console, 588
Read rights, 375, 411
Read/Write replicas, 169–170
Read/Write security attribute, 425
read-after-write verification, 78
Read-Only replicas, 169–170
Read-Only security attribute, 425
recovery. See disaster planning and recovery
reduced network traffic (NDPS), 770
Redundant Array of Inexpensive Disks (RAID), 244, 245
Reference time servers, 178, 180–181, 182
REGISTER MEMORY console utility, 40
relative distinguished names, 151–155, 156
REMARK commands, 499–500, 501
Remote Management Facility. See RMF
remote printers, 702–703, 711
REMOVE DOS console command, 592
Rename Inhibit security attribute, 426

Rename rights, 374
RENDIR utility, managing directories and, 280–281
replica rings, 174
replica types, 169–170
replicas, 589–590
replication, 161, 163, 167–172, 174–176
    advantages of, 167–168
    guidelines for managing, 174–176
    managing partitions and, 170–172
    replica types, 169–170
    timing updates for, 174–175
required properties, 124
requiring passwords, 361
resource access
    NDS naming, 144
    replication, 167
RESTART SERVER console command, 592
restoring files, 643, 646–647
rights. See access rights; and specific rights listed by name
risk analysis, 331–333
RMF (Remote Management Facility), 464, 650–658
    restricting access with REMOTE.NLM, 611–613
    RMF architecture, 651–654
        asynchronous connections, 653–654
        SPX connections, 652–653
    using RCONSOLE, 654–659
root directory, 365
[Root] object, 125–126
    creation of, 378
    default rights for users, 381
    square brackets, 127
[Root] partition, 164
    replicating the, 175
RSA public key, 348, 350
RSPX.NLM command, 652–653

S

Saber Menu System, 512, 520
salaries, 11
Salvage menu (NWADMIN), 286
salvaging files, 284, 285–286
Sampling interval parameter (PCONSOLE), 742
saturated replication, 170–172
SBACKUP command (SMS), 640–647
    backup steps for, 644–646
    as component of SMS architecture, 637, 638
    guidelines for using, 643–644
    responsibility for backups, 648
    restore steps, 646–647
    session files and backup logs, 649
    strategies for backups, 641–642, 643
SCRAWling, 375
script page, 509
search drive mappings, 301–304
    login scripts, 502–503

network drive mappings, 303
    remapping existing search drive numbers, 308
search lists, 303
Search Pattern and Filter menu (FILER), 272
searching drives, 307–308
Secondary time servers, 178, 181–183, 185
security, 330–459
    case study of ACME, 434–445
    Client 32 and, 336, 346
    countermeasures, 331–333
    Department of Defense criteria for, 341–343
    directory/file attributes, 339–340, 423–430
        disk management attributes, 427–430
        feature attributes, 426–427
        security attributes, 424–426
    displaying root directory access rights, 365
    do's and don'ts of, 431–433
    exercises
        How Secure Do You Feel?, 456–457
        Let the Good Guys In, 458–459
    file system access rights, 335, 338–339, 410–423
        assigning trustee rights, 338, 416–420,
            450–455
        calculating effective rights, 421–423,
            450–455
        filtering IRF rights, 420–421
        understanding, 411–415
    functional planes of, 410
    improvements to, 107, 110
    IntranetWare and NetWare 3.12, 99
    IntranetWare model, 334–343
    login error codes, 346
    login restrictions, 336, 351–371
        account restrictions, 357–359
        categories of, 354–357
        intruder detection/lockout, 368–371
        password restrictions, 355, 359–364
        station restrictions, 366–368
        time restrictions, 364–366
    login/password authentication, 335–336, 344–353
        background authentication, 335–336,
            351–353
        getting in, 344–347
        initial authentication, 347–351
    monitoring, 44–46
    NDS, 98, 99, 336–338
        administration, 401–410
        assigning trustee rights for, 338, 383–393
        calculating effective rights, 397–401,
            446–449
        default access rights for, 373–383
        filtering IRF rights, 394–397
    need for, 330
    NetWare features for, 45
    for print servers, 700
    for queues, 698

security (*continued*
    for remote printers, 711
    training about, 65
security attributes, 340, 424–426
security equivalence, 390–393
security equivalence (continued)
    ancestral inheritance, 391, 420
    Directory Map objects, 392–393, 420
    distributed administration, 403
    groups, 392, 420
    Organizational Roles, 391–392, 420
    rights and, 338
Security Information window, trustee assignments and, 417
        See Also page button (NWADMIN), 266
Selected Properties option, IRF rights, 395, 396
selecting a language, 572
serial ports
    CAPTURE utility, 683
    redirecting output to, 680, 681
Server (/S) line option (CAPTURE), 687
server console, 588
SERVER.EXE command, installing the server, 575
Server Management at ACME (case study), 667–673
Server Memory (*Novell Application Notes*), 565
server NLM. *See* SERVMAN.NLM command
server objects, 134–136
Server rights, 379
server-centric systems, 115–116
servers
    adding to capacity, 39–40
    creating server startup files, 581–583
    documenting installation and configuration settings,
        73–75, 76, 77, 81–83
    documenting time synchronization, 81, 82
    improvements to operating system, 101–103, 109
    increasing protection for, 612–613
    managing, 583–614
        console commands, 584–595
        NetWare Loadable Modules (NLM), 595–608
        server protection, 608–614
    messaging, 534–535, 536, 537–538
    monitoring, 40–43
    naming in INSTALLBAT, 574
    NetWare Enhanced Security, 342–343
    parameters for, 41
    protecting, 608–614
    tracking performance of, 40–43
    See also print servers
Service mode parameter (PCONSOLE), 742
Service Modes for Custom Forms screen (PCONSOLE), 744
SERVMAN.NLM command, 39, 41
    options for, 604–607
    setting maximum sizes for error logs, 51, 52
SET command
    customizing NCP packet signing with, 352

using with login scripts, 504
SET parameters, 41, 81–83
Seuss, Dr., 112, 207
Sharable security attribute, 426
shared data directories, 249, 255–256
Show (/SH) line option (CAPTURE), 687
SHOW command, 517
SHOW DOTS parameter (NET.CFG configuration file), 485
Show Printer Server Configuration option (PSC), 755
signature, 349, 351
simple effective rights, 397–398
Simple installation, 567–568, 659–666
Single-Reference time servers, 178, 179–180, 182
SMS (Storage Management Services), 95–96, 464, 636–650
    improvements to, 106, 110
    SMS architecture, 637–639
    using SBACKUP, 637, 638, 640–650
        backup steps, 644–646
        responsibility for backups, 648
        restore steps, 646–647
        SBACKUP session files and backup logs, 649
        strategies for, 641–642, 643
        workstation backups, 648–649
software
    inventories of, 72–73, 74
    for print servers, 701–703
solutions
    documenting, 89
    implementing, 88
    recording and reporting, 58–59
    resolving problems, 57–58
    tracking problems and solutions, 56–57
spaces in passwords, 361
spare parts, 38–39
SPX
    connecting from direct workstations, 652–653
    SPX ABORT TIMEOUT parameter (NET.CFG configuration
        file), 485
squiggly options for ITEM command, 515, 517
standalone printing, 679–682
Start/Stop a Printer from Servicing Jobs options (PSC), 754
starting and stopping printers, 749, 754
Starting form parameter (PCONSOLE), 742
STARTNET.BAT, 477–479
start-up files, 475–476
STARTUP.NCF file, 581
station restrictions, 355, 366–368
statistics for servers, 601–604
Statistics page for volumes (NWADMIN), 265
status messages, 50
Status option (PCONSOLE), 736
Storage Management Services. *See* SMS
Student Guide, The, 21
subdirectory names, 245, 246–247
Subdirectory options (FILER), 274

Subordinate Reference replicas, 169–170
supervisor bindery password, 610
Supervisor rights
    blocking, 394
    file system access rights, 412, 413
    to objects, 374
    to properties, 375
    Supervisor [S] object rights, 375
        Admin rights, 378
        Creator rights, 379
        IRF filtering, 394
        Server rights, 379
        [Supervisor], 127
SWAP command, 508
switches
    ODI command line, 630
    for VLM.EXE, 633
synchronization flags, 179
    time servers, 179
synchronization radius, 179
SYS$LOG.ERR error log, 50, 51
SYS: volume, 578
SYSTEM directory, 250
system performance
    background authentication and, 352
    tracking for servers, 40–43
System security attribute, 426
system-created directories, 248–253

T

TAA (Trade Adjustment Assistance), 23
Tabs (/T) line option (CAPTURE), 689
Target Service Agents (TSA), 637
tax deductions, 20
technical support resources, 88–89
telephony systems, 60–61
third-party printing support, 704, 713
Time Configuration Parameters Worksheet, 177
time consumer servers, 178
time provider groups, 185
time provider servers, 178
time restrictions, 355, 364–366
    as connection restrictions, 355
    strategies for, 365
time servers
    documenting, 81, 82
    polling intervals, 181
    synchronization flags and, 179
    types of, 178–183
    See also time synchronization
time synchronization, 142–143, 176–188
    methods of configuring, 183–188
    time stamps and, 176–177
    types of time servers, 178–183

time zones, 579
TimeOut (/TI) line option (CAPTURE), 688
timing updates for replication, 174–175
tools, 59–62
    disaster plan, 62
    Help Desk handbooks, 61–63
    IntranetWare volume management, 269
    NetWare User Tools for Windows, 290, 314–316, 322
    overview of printing management, 730
    telephony systems, 60–61
    tracking software, 60
    for training users, 66
    See also utilities
TRACK ON console command, 592–595
tracking software, 60
Trade Adjustment Assistance (TAA), 23
trailing periods, 154, 155
training
    about passwords, 64
    about security, 65
Transaction Tracking System (TTS), 84, 426–427
traveling users, 406–407
"Tree Walking" for Toddlers (exercise), 208–215
troubleshooting tips, 85–89
trustee rights
    assigning, 338, 383–393, 416–420
        exercises for, 450–455
        file system access rights, 416–420
        at high levels on tree, 392
        IRF filtering, 396–397
        NDS access rights, 383–393
        point of view, 386–388
        Security Information window and, 117
        types of, 384–385
    defined, 338
    inheritance and, 377, 388–390
    security equivalence, 390–393
        ancestral inheritance, 391
        Directory Map objects, 392–393
        groups, 392
        organizational role, 391–392
        See also inherited rights
Trustees of the Root Directory page button (NWADMIN), 265
Trustees of This Directory page (NWADMIN), 276
TSA (Target Service Agents), 637
TTS$LOG.ERR error log, 50, 51
TTS (Transaction Tracking System), 84, 426–427
typeful naming, 158
typeless naming, 156–160
    exceptions to, 158–159
    typeful naming, 158
types
    of ACL rights, 337–338
    of login scripts, 487–488, 489
    of property rights, 375–376

U

UIMPORT utility, adding users with, 231–232
Understanding NDS Naming (exercise), 216–234
Understanding NET.CFG (exercise), 548–549
Understanding the Role of Identification and Authentication in NetWare 4, 351
unique passwords, 362–363
unique proof, 351, 352
Universal Time Coordinated (UTC), 177
Unknown objects, 141
unloading print servers, 749
user accounts, 43–44
User login scripts, 488, 493–494
user mailboxes, 535, 536
User objects, 132–134, 474
User Space Limits page button (NWADMIN), 265
User Template object, 132, 356, 357
user training programs
    planning, 62–63
    topics for, 64–65
    training tools for, 66
    See also Help Desks
User trustee type, 384
users
    adding with UIMPORT utility, 231–232
    assigning trustee rights, 387
    creating print jobs for, 727
    default NDS rights for, 380–381
    deleting and placing holds on print jobs, 752
    printing tasks in NWADMIN, 751–752
    restricting specific, 365
    security for print server, 700
    special rights for traveling, 406–407
Users option (PCONSOLE), 737
Using ACME's Printing System (case study), 781–783
Using the DOS Requester with NetWare 4.0, 486
UTC (Univeral Time Coordinated), 177
utilities
    GUI, 97, 99, 473–474
    help for command line, 260
    login, 475
    NCOPY
        managing directories with, 278–279
        managing files with, 293–294
    NDIR
        managing directories with, 276–278
        managing files with, 289–292
        managing volumes with, 268–270
    NLIST, 267–268
    on-line information about printing, 729
    on-line references for, 291
    for print management, 730
    Quick Setup (PCONSOLE), 733–735
    RENDIR, 280–281
    summary of file management, 294–296

UIMPORT, 231–232
    See also FILER menu utility; NETADMIN utility; NWADMIN utility; tools

V

VALUE.NDS file, 118
variables, 496–498
variables page, 509–510
Veterans' Administration, 24
viewing
    Container objects, 210–211
    percent complete of print jobs, 752
    print job status, 751
    View or edit volume menu (NETADMIN), 266
VLMs (Virtual Loadable Modules), 95
    load order for Netware DOS Requester, 631–632
VOL$LOG.ERR error log, 50, 51
VOLUME ID command (NLIST), 268
Volume objects, 134–135
    NDS resource access rights for, 408
Volume statistics option (FILER), 262, 263
Volume statistics option (NETADMIN), 266
volumes, 243–248
    creating SYS:, 578
    directories and files in, 245–247
    disk space, 244
    displaying dates and times of creation, 265
    documenting, 77–78, 79
    managing, 260–270
        with FILER, 261–263
        with NDIR, 268–270
        with NETADMIN, 266–267
        with NLIST, 267–268
        with NWADMIN, 263–266
    managing with NETADMIN utility, 266–267
    naming rules for, 245, 246–247
    on-line information about, 248
    planning, 247–248
    print queue, 707
    reviewing statistics for, 262–263, 266
    summary of file management utilities, 294–295
    worksheets for, 79

W

weekend computer access, 365
WHI (World Health Index), 189, 206
wildcards, 280
Windows 95
    drive mappings, 313–314
    exercise for mapping drives with, 321
    file management support, 287–288
    installing Client 32 for, 619–622
    replacing interface with NAL, 530
    using Client 32 with, 469–471

Windows 95 Print Manager, 693–694
Windows 3.1
    connectivity with Client 32, 471–473
    File Manager, 288–289
    installing Client 32 for, 622–626
    replacing interface with NAL, 530
    using with Client 32, 471–473
workarounds, 88
workflow, 204
workgroups, 175
worksheets
    for backup schedules, 84
    for hardware and software purchases, 74
    maintenance history, 78
    printer installation and configuration, 77
    for server installation and configuration, 75
    for time synchronization servers, 82
    for volumes, 79
    workstation installation and configuration, 76
workstation connectivity, 166–187
    with Client 16, 475–487
        AUTOEXEC.BAT, 477
        CONFIG.SYS file, 476–477
        NET.CFG, 479–487
        STARTNET.BAT, 477–479
        start-up files for, 475–476
    with Client 32, 466–475
        logging in, 473–475
        understanding network connections, 167–169

    with Windows 95, 469–471
    with Windows 3.1, 471–473
exercises
    Workstation Connectivity with Client 16,
        542–544
    Workstation Connectivity with Client 32,
        545–548
See also connectivity
workstations
    backing up, 648–649
    documenting batch and boot files, 81
    installing
        Client 32 (Windows 95), 619–622
        Client 32 (Windows 3.1), 622–626
        configuration settings for, 76
        network applications on, 529–531
    managing, 614–635
        Client 16 architecture, 626–634
        Client 32 architecture, 616–618
        non-DOS workstation support, 634 635
        overview of, 614–616
    NetWare Enhanced Security, 342–343
    workstation operating system (WOS), 615
    See also workstation connectivity
World Health Index (WHI), 189, 206
WoRMFACES, 338–339, 411–413
WOS (workstation operating system), 615
WRITE command, 495, 499–500, 501
Write rights, 375, 411

IDG BOOKS WORLDWIDE, INC.—END-USER LICENSE AGREEMENT

4. Restrictions on Use of Individual Programs. You must follow the individual requirements and restrictions detailed for each individual program in Appendix D of this Book. These limitations are contained in the individual license agreements recorded on the disk(s)/CD-ROM. These restrictions may include a requirement that after using the program for the period of time specified in its text, the user must pay a registration fee or discontinue use. By opening the Software packet(s), you will be agreeing to abide by the licenses and restrictions for these individual programs. None of the material on this disk(s) or listed in this Book may ever be distributed, in original or modified form, for commercial purposes.

5. Limited Warranty.

(a)   IDGB warrants that the Software and disk(s)/CD-ROM are free from defects in materials and workmanship under normal use for a period of sixty (60) days from the date of purchase of this Book. If IDGB receives notification within the warranty period of defects in materials or workmanship, IDGB will replace the defective disk(s)/CD-ROM.

(b)   **IDGB AND THE AUTHOR OF THE BOOK DISCLAIM ALL OTHER WARRANTIES, EXPRESS OR IMPLIED, INCLUDING WITHOUT LIMITATION IMPLIED WARRANTIES OF MERCHANTABILITY AND FITNESS FOR A PARTICULAR PURPOSE, WITH RESPECT TO THE SOFTWARE, THE PROGRAMS, THE SOURCE CODE CONTAINED THEREIN, AND/OR THE TECHNIQUES DESCRIBED IN THIS BOOK IDGB DOES NOT WARRANT THAT THE FUNCTIONS CONTAINED IN THE SOFTWARE WILL MEET YOUR REQUIREMENTS OR THAT THE OPERATION OF THE SOFTWARE WILL BE ERROR FREE.**

(c)   This limited warranty gives you specific legal rights, and you may have other rights which vary from jurisdiction to jurisdiction.

6. Remedies.

(a)   IDGB's entire liability and your exclusive remedy for defects in materials and workmanship shall be limited to replacement of the Software, which may be returned to IDGB with a copy of your receipt at the following address: Disk Fulfillment Department, Attn: CNA Study Guide-IntranetWare/NetWare 4.11, IDG Books Worldwide, Inc., 7260 Shadeland Station, Ste. 100, Indianapolis, IN 46256, or call 1-800-762-2974. Please allow 3-4 weeks for delivery. This Limited Warranty is void if failure of the Software has resulted from accident, abuse, or misapplication. Any replacement Software will be warranted for the remainder of the original warranty period or thirty (30) days, whichever is longer.

(b)   In no event shall IDGB or the author be liable for any damages whatsoever (including without limitation damages for loss of business profits, business interruption, loss of business information, or any other pecuniary loss) arising from the use of or inability to use the Book or the Software, even if IDGB has been advised of the possibility of such damages.

(c)   Because some jurisdictions do not allow the exclusion or limitation of liability for consequential or incidental damages, the above limitation or exclusion may not apply to you.

7. <u>U.S. Government Restricted Rights</u>. Use, duplication, or disclosure of the Software by the U.S. Government is subject to restrictions stated in paragraph (c) (1) (ii) of the Rights in Technical Data and Computer Software clause of DFARS 252.227-7013, and in subparagraphs (a) through (d) of the Commercial Computer—Restricted Rights clause at FAR 52.227-19, and in similar clauses in the NASA FAR supplement, when applicable.

8. <u>General</u>. This Agreement constitutes the entire understanding of the parties and revokes and supersedes all prior agreements, oral or written, between them and may not be modified or amended except in a writing signed by both parties hereto which specifically refers to this Agreement. This Agreement shall take precedence over any other documents that may be in conflict herewith. If any one or more provisions contained in this Agreement are held by any court or tribunal to be invalid, illegal, or otherwise unenforceable, each and every other provision shall remain in full force and effect.

Novell's CNE® Study Guide for Core Technologies

by David James. Clarke, IV

The ideal preparation guide for the two non-NetWare specific exams required for CNE® certification: Service and Support (801) and Networking Technologies (200). This study guide contains real-world case studies, sample test questions and other valuable information. You'll also receive the exclusive Novell NetWire Starter Kit, the ClarkTests v.2 and MICROHOUSE I/O Card Encyclopedia demo.

932 pp plus CD-ROM
$74.99 USA
$104.99 Canada
0-7645-4501-9

Novell's CNA℠ Study Guide for IntranetWare™

by David James Clarke, IV and Kelley J.P. Lindberg

A must for system managers studying for their CNA℠ credential. Organized and easy-to-read, this resource covers all CNA course material including NetWare 2.2 and NetWare 3.1x with real-world scenarios, sample tests and a live on-line NetWare lab. The accompanying Novell Advantage CD contains Novell exclusive software.

700 pp plus CD-ROM
$69.99 USA
$96.99 Canada
0-7645-4513-2

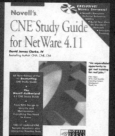

Novell's CNE® Study Guide for IntranetWare™

by David James Clarke, IV

Learn all aspects of Novell's IntranetWare CNE program as well as NDS design and implementation. Covers certification courses 520, 525, 526, 532 and 804. Includes a free Novell Support Connection CD plus hundreds of CNE test questions.

1600 pp plus CD-ROM
$89.99 USA
$124.99 Canada
0-7645-4512-4

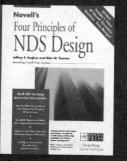

Novell's Four Principles of NDS™ Design

by Jeffrey F. Hughes and Blair W. Thomas

Take full advantage of the powerful new features of the NetWare 4 operating system with this clearly illustrated reference guide zeroing in on four essential Novell Directory Services (NDS) design principles: physical infrastructure, organizational structure, optimal partition size and minimum replicas placements, and time synchronization.

343 pp
$39.99 USA
$54.99 Canada
0-7645-4522-1

SMART BOOKS™
from the Novell Experts

WE WROTE THE BOOK ON NETWORKING

Novell Press® and IDG Books Worldwide

Novell's Guide to IntranetWare™ Networks

by Jeffrey F. Hughes and Blair W. Thomas

The ideal reference tool for integrating the latest intranet and Internet technologies from Novell®. Focusing on design techniques, master CNEs Hughes and Thomas guide you through the crux of the IntranetWare™ network -- Novell Directory Services™ - providing never-before-published tips, tricks and techniques for managing IntranetWare. Includes a two-user version of NetWare® 4.11 on CD.

1200 pp plus CD-ROM
$59.99 USA
$84.99 Canada
0-7645-4516-7

Novell's IntranetWare™ Administrator's Handbook

by Kelley J.P. Lindberg

The only book you will ever need to implement and troubleshoot IntranetWare. Kelley Lindberg has created a compact, easy-to-read guide for running a network effectively with step-by-step directions for complex configurations, coverage of each IntranetWare feature, troubleshooting tips and a resource directory.

576 pp plus disk
$39.99 USA
$54.99 Canada
0-7645-4517-5

Novell's Guide to Integrating NetWare® and TCP/IP

by Drew Heywood

The perfect resource for all internetworking professionals. Learn to link TCP/IP, the most widely implemented set of network protocols, with key Novell products through an approach tailored to meet your exact software requirements.

556 pp plus CD-ROM
$44.99 USA
$62.99 Canada
1-56884-818-8

Novell's Guide to NetWare® Printing

by J.D. Marymee and Sandy Stevens

Everything a NetWare® manager needs to know to predict, resolve and prevent printing problems. Learn both "how to" and theory for proper configurations and naming conventions, design and implementation off-line, network management techniques and more. Covers both NetWare 3 and NetWare 4 systems.

512 pp plus disk
$44.99 USA
$62.99 Canada
0-7645-4514-0